Collins
World Atlas

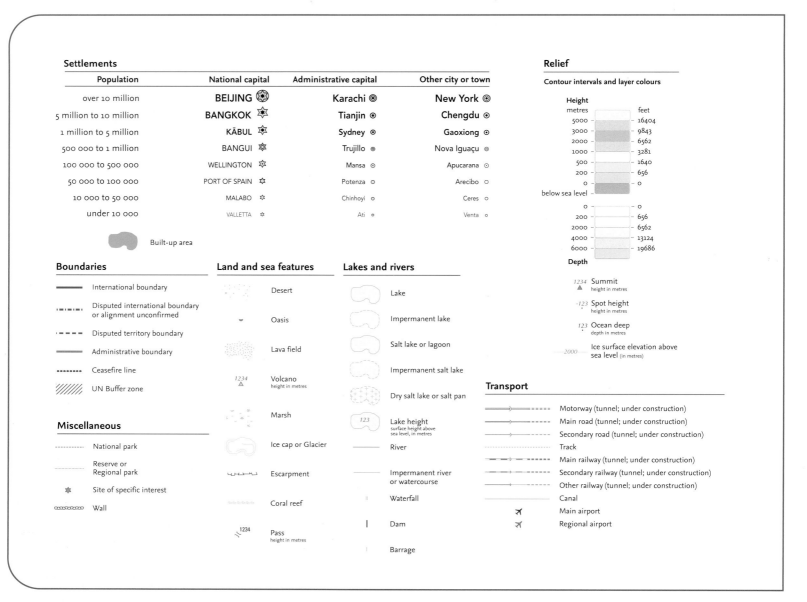

Settlements

Population	National capital	Administrative capital	Other city or town
over 10 million	BEIJING ◉	Karachi ◎	New York ◎
5 million to 10 million	BANGKOK ✡	Tianjin ◎	Chengdu ◎
1 million to 5 million	KĀBUL ✡	Sydney ◉	Gaoxiong ◉
500 000 to 1 million	BANGUI ✡	Trujillo ◎	Nova Iguaçu ◎
100 000 to 500 000	WELLINGTON ✿	Mansa ◎	Apucarana ◉
50 000 to 100 000	PORT OF SPAIN ✿	Potenza ◯	Arecibo ◯
10 000 to 50 000	MALABO ✿	Chinhoyi ◯	Ceres ◯
under 10 000	VALLETTA ✿	Ati ◦	Venta ◦

▨ Built-up area

Boundaries

▬▬▬	International boundary
▬▪▬▪▬	Disputed international boundary or alignment unconfirmed
▬ ▬ ▬	Disputed territory boundary
▬▬▬	Administrative boundary
••••••	Ceasefire line
▨▨▨	UN Buffer zone

Miscellaneous

----------	National park
··········	Reserve or Regional park
✸	Site of specific interest
◌◌◌◌	Wall

Land and sea features

░░░	Desert
◡	Oasis
∴	Lava field
1234 ▲	Volcano height in metres
✽	Marsh
◖◗	Ice cap or Glacier
◡◡◡	Escarpment
◡◡	Coral reef
╱ 1234	Pass height in metres

Lakes and rivers

◯	Lake
◯	Impermanent lake
◯	Salt lake or lagoon
◯	Impermanent salt lake
◯	Dry salt lake or salt pan
123	Lake height surface height above sea level, in metres
▬▬	River
▬▬	Impermanent river or watercourse
‖	Waterfall
		Dam
		Barrage

Relief

Contour intervals and layer colours

Height

metres		feet
5000		16404
3000		9843
2000		6562
1000		3281
500		1640
200		656
0		0
below sea level		
0		0
200		656
2000		6562
4000		13124
6000		19686

Depth

1234 ▲	Summit height in metres
-123	Spot height height in metres
123	Ocean deep depth in metres
2000	Ice surface elevation above sea level (in metres)

Transport

▬▬►┄┄	Motorway (tunnel; under construction)
▬▬►┄┄	Main road (tunnel; under construction)
▬▬►┄┄	Secondary road (tunnel; under construction)
··········	Track
▬▬┄┄	Main railway (tunnel; under construction)
▬▬┄┄	Secondary railway (tunnel; under construction)
▬▬┄┄	Other railway (tunnel; under construction)
▬▬▬	Canal
✈	Main airport
✈	Regional airport

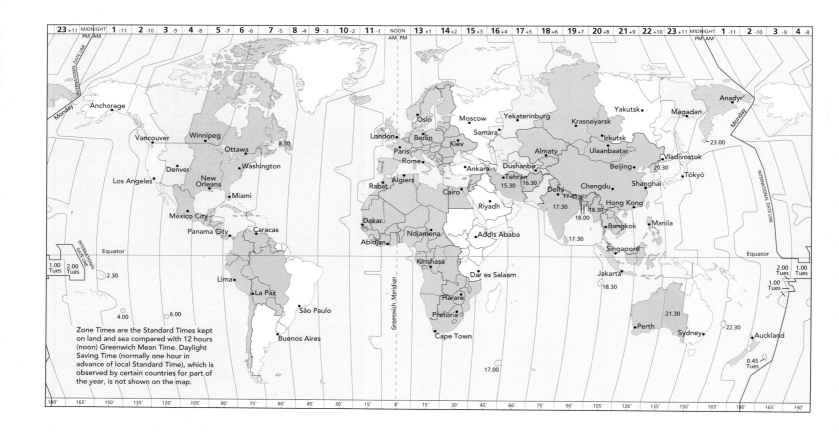

Zone Times are the Standard Times kept on land and sea compared with 12 hours (noon) Greenwich Mean Time. Daylight Saving Time (normally one hour in advance of local Standard Time), which is observed by certain countries for part of the year, is not shown on the map.

Map Symbols and Time Zones

Europe

Europe		Area sq km	Area sq miles	Population	Capital	Languages	Religions	Currency	Internet Link
ALBANIA		28 748	11 100	3 173 000	Tirana	Albanian, Greek	Sunni Muslim, Albanian Orthodox, Roman Catholic	Lek	www.km.gov.al
ANDORRA		465	180	79 000	Andorra la Vella	Catalan, Spanish, French	Roman Catholic	Euro	www.govern.ad
AUSTRIA		83 855	32 377	8 495 000	Vienna	German, Croatian, Turkish	Roman Catholic, Protestant	Euro	www.bundeskanzleramt.at
BELARUS		207 600	80 155	9 357 000	Minsk	Belarusian, Russian	Belarusian Orthodox, Roman Catholic	Belarusian rouble	www.belarus.by
BELGIUM		30 520	11 784	11 104 000	Brussels	Dutch (Flemish), French (Walloon), German	Roman Catholic, Protestant	Euro	www.belgium.be
BOSNIA AND HERZEGOVINA		51 130	19 741	3 829 000	Sarajevo	Bosnian, Serbian, Croatian	Sunni Muslim, Serbian Orthodox, Roman Catholic, Protestant	Marka	www.fbihvlada.gov.ba
BULGARIA		110 994	42 855	7 223 000	Sofia	Bulgarian, Turkish, Romany, Macedonian	Bulgarian Orthodox, Sunni Muslim	Lev	www.government.bg
CROATIA		56 538	21 829	4 290 000	Zagreb	Croatian, Serbian	Roman Catholic, Serbian Orthodox, Sunni Muslim	Kuna	www.vlada.hr
CZECH REPUBLIC		78 864	30 450	10 702 000	Prague	Czech, Moravian, Slovak	Roman Catholic, Protestant	Koruna	www.czech.cz
DENMARK		43 075	16 631	5 619 000	Copenhagen	Danish	Protestant	Danish krone	www.denmark.dk
ESTONIA		45 200	17 452	1 287 000	Tallinn	Estonian, Russian	Protestant, Estonian and Russian Orthodox	Euro	www.valitsus.ee
FINLAND		338 145	130 559	5 426 000	Helsinki	Finnish, Swedish, Sami languages	Protestant, Greek Orthodox	Euro	www.valtioneuvosto.fi
FRANCE		543 965	210 026	64 291 000	Paris	French, German dialects, Italian, Arabic, Breton	Roman Catholic, Protestant, Sunni Muslim	Euro	www.premier-ministre.gouv.fr
GERMANY		357 022	137 849	82 727 000	Berlin	German, Turkish	Protestant, Roman Catholic	Euro	www.bundesregierung.de
GREECE		131 957	50 949	11 128 000	Athens	Greek	Greek Orthodox, Sunni Muslim	Euro	www.primeminister.gr
HUNGARY		93 030	35 919	9 955 000	Budapest	Hungarian	Roman Catholic, Protestant	Forint	www.magyarorszag.hu
ICELAND		102 820	39 699	330 000	Reykjavík	Icelandic	Protestant	Icelandic króna	www.iceland.is
IRELAND		70 282	27 136	4 627 000	Dublin	English, Irish	Roman Catholic, Protestant	Euro	www.gov.ie
ITALY		301 245	116 311	60 990 000	Rome	Italian	Roman Catholic	Euro	www.governo.it
KOSOVO		10 908	4 212	1 815 606	Prishtinë	Albanian, Serbian	Sunni Muslim, Serbian Orthodox	Euro	www.rks-gov.net/en-US
LATVIA		64 589	24 938	2 050 000	Rīga	Latvian, Russian	Protestant, Roman Catholic, Russian Orthodox	Euro	www.saeima.lv
LIECHTENSTEIN		160	62	37 000	Vaduz	German	Roman Catholic, Protestant	Swiss franc	www.liechtenstein.li
LITHUANIA		65 200	25 174	3 017 000	Vilnius	Lithuanian, Russian, Polish	Roman Catholic, Russian Orthodox	Litas	www.lrv.lt
LUXEMBOURG		2 586	998	530 000	Luxembourg	Letzeburgish, German, French	Roman Catholic	Euro	www.gouvernement.lu
MACEDONIA (F.Y.R.O.M.)		25 713	9 928	2 107 000	Skopje	Macedonian, Albanian, Turkish	Macedonian Orthodox, Sunni Muslim	Macedonian denar	www.vlada.mk
MALTA		316	122	429 000	Valletta	Maltese, English	Roman Catholic	Euro	www.gov.mt
MOLDOVA		33 700	13 012	3 487 000	Chişinău	Romanian, Ukrainian, Gagauz, Russian	Romanian Orthodox, Russian Orthodox	Moldovan leu	www.moldova.md
MONACO		2	1	38 000	Monaco-Ville	French, Monegasque, Italian	Roman Catholic	Euro	www.monaco.gouv.mc
MONTENEGRO		13 812	5 333	621 000	Podgorica	Serbian (Montenegrin), Albanian	Montenegrin Orthodox, Sunni Muslim	Euro	www.gov.me
NETHERLANDS		41 526	16 033	16 759 000	Amsterdam/The Hague	Dutch, Frisian	Roman Catholic, Protestant, Sunni Muslim	Euro	www.overheid.nl
NORWAY		323 878	125 050	5 043 000	Oslo	Norwegian, Sami languages	Protestant, Roman Catholic	Norwegian krone	www.norway.no
POLAND		312 683	120 728	38 217 000	Warsaw	Polish, German	Roman Catholic, Polish Orthodox	Złoty	www.poland.gov.pl
PORTUGAL		88 940	34 340	10 608 000	Lisbon	Portuguese	Roman Catholic, Protestant	Euro	www.portugal.gov.pt
ROMANIA		237 500	91 699	21 699 000	Bucharest	Romanian, Hungarian	Romanian Orthodox, Protestant, Roman Catholic	Romanian leu	www.guv.ro
RUSSIA		17 075 400	6 592 849	142 834 000	Moscow	Russian, Tatar, Ukrainian, other local languages	Russian Orthodox, Sunni Muslim, Protestant	Russian rouble	www.gov.ru
SAN MARINO		61	24	31 000	San Marino	Italian	Roman Catholic	Euro	www.consigliograndeegenerale.sm
SERBIA		77 453	29 904	7 181 505	Belgrade	Serbian, Hungarian	Serbian Orthodox, Roman Catholic, Sunni Muslim	Serbian dinar,	www.srbija.gov.rs
SLOVAKIA		49 035	18 933	5 450 000	Bratislava	Slovak, Hungarian, Czech	Roman Catholic, Protestant, Orthodox	Euro	www.government.gov.sk
SLOVENIA		20 251	7 819	2 072 000	Ljubljana	Slovene, Croatian, Serbian	Roman Catholic, Protestant	Euro	www.gov.si
SPAIN		504 782	194 897	46 927 000	Madrid	Spanish (Castilian), Catalan, Galician, Basque	Roman Catholic	Euro	www.la-moncloa.es
SWEDEN		449 964	173 732	9 571 000	Stockholm	Swedish, Sami languages	Protestant, Roman Catholic	Swedish krona	www.sweden.se
SWITZERLAND		41 293	15 943	8 078 000	Bern	German, French, Italian, Romansch	Roman Catholic, Protestant	Swiss franc	www.swissworld.org
UKRAINE		603 700	233 090	45 239 000	Kiev	Ukrainian, Russian	Ukrainian Orthodox, Ukrainian Catholic, Roman Catholic	Hryvnia	www.kmu.gov.ua
UNITED KINGDOM		243 609	94 058	63 136 000	London	English, Welsh, Gaelic	Protestant, Roman Catholic, Muslim	Pound sterling	www.direct.gov.uk
VATICAN CITY		0.5	0.2	800	Vatican City	Italian	Roman Catholic	Euro	www.vaticanstate.va

Asia

Asia		Area sq km	Area sq miles	Population	Capital	Languages	Religions	Currency	Internet Link
AFGHANISTAN		652 225	251 825	30 552 000	Kābul	Dari, Pashto (Pashtu), Uzbek, Turkmen	Sunni Muslim, Shi'a Muslim	Afghani	www.president.gov.af
ARMENIA		29 800	11 506	2 977 000	Yerevan	Armenian, Kurdish	Armenian Orthodox	Dram	www.gov.am
AZERBAIJAN		86 600	33 436	9 413 000	Baku	Azeri, Armenian, Russian, Lezgian	Shi'a Muslim, Sunni Muslim, Russian and Armenian Orthodox	Azerbaijani manat	www.president.az
BAHRAIN		691	267	1 332 000	Manama	Arabic, English	Shi'a Muslim, Sunni Muslim, Christian	Bahrain dinar	www.bahrain.bh
BANGLADESH		143 998	55 598	156 595 000	Dhaka	Bengali, English	Sunni Muslim, Hindu	Taka	www.bangladesh.gov.bd
BHUTAN		46 620	18 000	754 000	Thimphu	Dzongkha, Nepali, Assamese	Buddhist, Hindu	Ngultrum, Indian rupee	www.bhutan.gov.bt
BRUNEI		5 765	2 226	418 000	Bandar Seri Begawan	Malay, English, Chinese	Sunni Muslim, Buddhist, Christian	Brunei dollar	www.pmo.gov.bn
CAMBODIA		181 035	69 884	15 135 000	Phnom Penh	Khmer, Vietnamese	Buddhist, Roman Catholic, Sunni Muslim	Riel	www.cambodia.gov.kh
CHINA		9 606 802	3 709 186	1 369 993 000	Beijing	Mandarin (Putonghua), Wu, Cantonese, Hsiang, regional languages	Confucian, Taoist, Buddhist, Christian, Sunni Muslim	Yuan, HK dollar*, Macau pataca	www.gov.cn
CYPRUS		9 251	3 572	1 141 000	Nicosia	Greek, Turkish, English	Greek Orthodox, Sunni Muslim	Euro	www.cyprus.gov.cy
EAST TIMOR (TIMOR-LESTE)		14 874	5 743	1 133 000	Dili	Portuguese, Tetun, English	Roman Catholic	United States dollar	www.gov.east-timor.org
GEORGIA		69 700	26 911	4 341 000	Tbilisi	Georgian, Russian, Armenian, Azeri, Ossetian, Abkhaz	Georgian Orthodox, Russian Orthodox, Sunni Muslim	Lari	www.parliament.ge
INDIA		3 166 620	1 222 632	1 252 140 000	New Delhi	Hindi, English, many regional languages	Hindu, Sunni Muslim, Shi'a Muslim, Sikh, Christian	Indian rupee	www.india.gov.in
INDONESIA		1 919 445	741 102	249 866 000	Jakarta	Indonesian, other local languages	Sunni Muslim, Protestant, Roman Catholic, Hindu, Buddhist	Rupiah	www.indonesia.go.id
IRAN		1 648 000	636 296	77 447 000	Tehrān	Farsi, Azeri, Kurdish, regional languages	Shi'a Muslim, Sunni Muslim	Iranian rial	www.president.ir
IRAQ		438 317	169 235	33 765 000	Baghdād	Arabic, Kurdish, Turkmen	Shi'a Muslim, Sunni Muslim, Christian	Iraqi dinar	www.cabinet.iq
ISRAEL		22 072	8 522	7 733 000	Jerusalem (Yerushalayim) (El Quds)**	Hebrew, Arabic	Jewish, Sunni Muslim, Christian, Druze	Shekel	www.gov.il
JAPAN		377 727	145 841	127 144 000	Tōkyō	Japanese	Shintoist, Buddhist, Christian	Yen	www.kantei.go.jp
JORDAN		89 206	34 443	7 274 000	'Ammān	Arabic	Sunni Muslim, Christian	Jordanian dinar	www.jordan.gov.jo
KAZAKHSTAN		2 717 300	1 049 155	16 441 000	Astana	Kazakh, Russian, Ukrainian, German, Uzbek, Tatar	Sunni Muslim, Russian Orthodox, Protestant	Tenge	www.government.kz
KUWAIT		17 818	6 880	3 369 000	Kuwait	Arabic	Sunni Muslim, Shi'a Muslim, Christian, Hindu	Kuwaiti dinar	www.e.gov.kw
KYRGYZSTAN		198 500	76 641	5 548 000	Bishkek	Kyrgyz, Russian, Uzbek	Sunni Muslim, Russian Orthodox	Kyrgyz som	www.gov.kg
LAOS		236 800	91 429	6 770 000	Vientiane	Lao, other local languages	Buddhist, traditional beliefs	Kip	www.na.gov.la
LEBANON		10 452	4 036	4 822 000	Beirut	Arabic, Armenian, French	Shi'a Muslim, Sunni Muslim, Christian	Lebanese pound	www.presidency.gov.lb
MALAYSIA		332 965	128 559	29 717 000	Kuala Lumpur/Putrajaya	Malay, English, Chinese, Tamil, other local languages	Sunni Muslim, Buddhist, Hindu, Christian, traditional beliefs	Ringgit	www.malaysia.gov.my

**De facto capital. Disputed   *Hong Kong dollar

Asia continued		Area sq km	Area sq miles	Population	Capital	Languages	Religions	Currency	Internet Link
MALDIVES		298	115	345 000	Male	Divehi (Maldivian)	Sunni Muslim	Rufiyaa	www.presidencymaldives.gov.mv
MONGOLIA		1 565 000	604 250	2 839 000	Ulan Bator	Khalka (Mongolian), Kazakh, other local languages	Buddhist, Sunni Muslim	Tugrik (tögrög)	www.pmis.gov.mn
MYANMAR (BURMA)		676 577	261 228	53 259 000	Nay Pyi Taw	Burmese, Shan, Karen, other local languages	Buddhist, Christian, Sunni Muslim	Kyat	www.mofa.gov.mm
NEPAL		147 181	56 827	27 797 000	Kathmandu	Nepali, Maithili, Bhojpuri, English, other local languages	Hindu, Buddhist, Sunni Muslim	Nepalese rupee	www.nepalgov.gov.np
NORTH KOREA		120 538	46 540	24 895 000	P'yŏngyang	Korean	Traditional beliefs, Chondoist, Buddhist	North Korean won	www.korea-dpr.com
OMAN		309 500	119 499	3 632 000	Muscat	Arabic, Baluchi, Indian languages	Ibadhi Muslim, Sunni Muslim	Omani riyal	www.oman.om
PAKISTAN		881 888	340 497	182 143 000	Islamabad	Urdu, Punjabi, Sindhi, Pashto (Pashtu), English, Balochi	Sunni Muslim, Shi'a Muslim, Christian, Hindu	Pakistani rupee	www.pakistan.gov.pk
PALAU		497	192	21 000	Melekeok (Ngerulmud)	Palauan, English	Roman Catholic, Protestant, traditional beliefs	United States dollar	www.palaugov.net
PHILIPPINES		300 000	115 831	98 394 000	Manila	English, Filipino, Tagalog, Cebuano, other local languages	Roman Catholic, Protestant, Sunni Muslim, Aglipayan	Philippine peso	http://president.gov.ph/
QATAR		11 437	4 416	2 169 000	Doha	Arabic	Sunni Muslim	Qatari riyal	www.gov.qa
RUSSIA		17 075 400	6 592 849	142 834 000	Moscow	Russian, Tatar, Ukrainian, other local languages	Russian Orthodox, Sunni Muslim, Protestant	Russian rouble	www.gov.ru
SAUDI ARABIA		2 200 000	849 425	28 829 000	Riyadh	Arabic	Sunni Muslim, Shi'a Muslim	Saudi Arabian riyal	www.saudi.gov.sa
SINGAPORE		639	247	5 412 000	Singapore	Chinese, English, Malay, Tamil	Buddhist, Taoist, Sunni Muslim, Christian, Hindu	Singapore dollar	www.gov.sg
SOUTH KOREA		99 274	38 330	49 263 000	Seoul	Korean	Buddhist, Protestant, Roman Catholic	South Korean won	www.korea.net
SRI LANKA		65 610	25 332	21 273 000	Sri Jayewardenepura Kotte	Sinhalese, Tamil, English	Buddhist, Hindu, Sunni Muslim, Roman Catholic	Sri Lankan rupee	www.priu.gov.lk
SYRIA		184 026	71 052	21 898 000	Damascus	Arabic, Kurdish, Armenian	Sunni Muslim, Shi'a Muslim, Christian	Syrian pound	www.parliament.gov.sy
TAIWAN		36 179	13 969	23 344 000	Taibei (T'aipei)	Mandarin (Putonghua), Min, Hakka, other local languages	Buddhist, Taoist, Confucian, Christian	Taiwan dollar	www.gov.tw
TAJIKISTAN		143 100	55 251	8 208 000	Dushanbe	Tajik, Uzbek, Russian	Sunni Muslim	Somoni	www.prezident.tj
THAILAND		513 115	198 115	67 011 000	Bangkok	Thai, Lao, Chinese, Malay, Mon-Khmer languages	Buddhist, Sunni Muslim	Baht	www.thaigov.go.th
TURKEY		779 452	300 948	74 933 000	Ankara	Turkish, Kurdish	Sunni Muslim, Shi'a Muslim	Lira	www.tccb.gov.tr
TURKMENISTAN		488 100	188 456	5 240 000	Ashgabat (Aşgabat)	Turkmen, Uzbek, Russian	Sunni Muslim, Russian Orthodox	Turkmen manat	www.turkmenistan.gov.tm
UNITED ARAB EMIRATES		77 700	30 000	9 346 000	Abu Dhabi	Arabic, English	Sunni Muslim, Shi'a Muslim	United Arab Emirates dirham	www.government.ae
UZBEKISTAN		447 400	172 742	28 934 000	Toshkent (Tashkent)	Uzbek, Russian, Tajik, Kazakh	Sunni Muslim, Russian Orthodox	Uzbek som	www.gov.uz
VIETNAM		329 565	127 246	91 680 000	Ha Nôi	Vietnamese, Thai, Khmer, Chinese, other local languages	Buddhist, Taoist, Roman Catholic, Cao Dai, Hoa Hao	Dong	www.na.gov.vn
YEMEN		527 968	203 850	24 407 000	Şan'ä'	Arabic	Sunni Muslim, Shi'a Muslim	Yemeni rial	www.yemen-nic.info

Africa		Area sq km	Area sq miles	Population	Capital	Languages	Religions	Currency	Internet Link
ALGERIA		2 381 741	919 595	39 208 000	Algiers	Arabic, French, Berber	Sunni Muslim	Algerian dinar	www.el-mouradia.dz
ANGOLA		1 246 700	481 354	21 472 000	Luanda	Portuguese, Bantu, other local languages	Roman Catholic, Protestant, traditional beliefs	Kwanza	www.governo.gov.ao
BENIN		112 620	43 483	10 323 000	Porto-Novo	French, Fon, Yoruba, Adja, other local languages	Traditional beliefs, Roman Catholic, Sunni Muslim	CFA franc*	www.gouv.bj
BOTSWANA		581 370	224 468	2 021 000	Gaborone	English, Setswana, Shona, other local languages	Traditional beliefs, Protestant, Roman Catholic	Pula	www.gov.bw
BURKINA FASO		274 200	105 869	16 935 000	Ouagadougou	French, Moore (Mossi), Fulani, other local languages	Sunni Muslim, traditional beliefs, Roman Catholic	CFA franc*	www.gouvernement.gov.bf
BURUNDI		27 835	10 747	10 163 000	Bujumbura	Kirundi (Hutu, Tutsi), French	Roman Catholic, traditional beliefs, Protestant	Burundian franc	
CAMEROON		475 442	183 569	22 254 000	Yaoundé	French, English, Fang, Bamileke, other local languages	Roman Catholic, traditional beliefs, Sunni Muslim, Protestant	CFA franc*	www.spm.gov.cm
CAPE VERDE (CABO VERDE)		4 033	1 557	499 000	Praia	Portuguese, creole	Roman Catholic, Protestant	Cape Verde escudo	www.governo.cv
CENTRAL AFRICAN REPUBLIC		622 436	240 324	4 616 000	Bangui	French, Sango, Banda, Baya, other local languages	Protestant, Roman Catholic, traditional beliefs, Sunni Muslim	CFA franc*	www.centrafricaine.info
CHAD		1 284 000	495 755	12 825 000	Ndjamena	Arabic, French, Sara, other local languages	Sunni Muslim, Roman Catholic, Protestant, traditional beliefs	CFA franc*	www.presidence-tchad.org
COMOROS		1 862	719	735 000	Moroni	Shikomor (Comorian), French, Arabic	Sunni Muslim, Roman Catholic	Comoros franc	www.beit-salam.km
CONGO		342 000	132 047	4 448 000	Brazzaville	French, Kongo, Monokutuba, other local languages	Roman Catholic, Protestant, traditional beliefs, Sunni Muslim	CFA franc*	www.presidence.cg
CONGO, DEM. REP. OF THE		2 345 410	905 568	67 514 000	Kinshasa	French, Lingala, Swahili, Kongo, other local languages	Christian, Sunni Muslim	Congolese franc	www.un.int/drcongo
CÔTE D'IVOIRE (IVORY COAST)		322 463	124 504	20 316 000	Yamoussoukro	French, creole, Akan, other local languages	Sunni Muslim, Roman Catholic, traditional beliefs, Protestant	CFA franc*	www.gouv.ci
DJIBOUTI		23 200	8 958	873 000	Djibouti	Somali, Afar, French, Arabic	Sunni Muslim, Christian	Djibouti franc	www.presidence.dj
EGYPT		1 001 450	386 660	82 056 000	Cairo	Arabic	Sunni Muslim, Coptic Christian	Egyptian pound	www.egypt.gov.eg
EQUATORIAL GUINEA		28 051	10 831	757 000	Malabo	Spanish, French, Fang	Roman Catholic, traditional beliefs	CFA franc*	www.guineaecuatorialpress.com
ERITREA		117 400	45 328	6 333 000	Asmara	Tigrinya, Tigre	Sunni Muslim, Coptic Christian	Nakfa	www.shabait.com
ETHIOPIA		1 133 880	437 794	94 101 000	Addis Ababa	Oromo, Amharic, Tigrinya, other local languages	Ethiopian Orthodox, Sunni Muslim, traditional beliefs	Birr	www.ethiopia.gov.et
GABON		267 667	103 347	1 672 000	Libreville	French, Fang, other local languages	Roman Catholic, Protestant, traditional beliefs	CFA franc*	www.legabon.org
THE GAMBIA		11 295	4 361	1 849 000	Banjul	English, Malinke, Fulani, Wolof	Sunni Muslim, Protestant	Dalasi	www.visitthegambia.gm
GHANA		238 537	92 100	25 905 000	Accra	English, Hausa, Akan, other local languages	Christian, Sunni Muslim, traditional beliefs	Cedi	www.ghana.gov.gh
GUINEA		245 857	94 926	11 745 000	Conakry	French, Fulani, Malinke, other local languages	Sunni Muslim, traditional beliefs, Christian	Guinea franc	www.guinee.gov.gn
GUINEA-BISSAU		36 125	13 948	1 704 000	Bissau	Portuguese, crioulo, other local languages	Traditional beliefs, Sunni Muslim, Christian	CFA franc*	www.gov.gw
KENYA		582 646	224 961	44 354 000	Nairobi	Swahili, English, other local languages	Christian, traditional beliefs	Kenyan shilling	www.information.go.ke
LESOTHO		30 355	11 720	2 074 000	Maseru	Sesotho, English, Zulu	Christian, traditional beliefs	Loti, S. African rand	www.gov.ls
LIBERIA		111 369	43 000	4 294 000	Monrovia	English, creole, other local languages	Traditional beliefs, Christian, Sunni Muslim	Liberian dollar	www.emansion.gov.lr
LIBYA		1 759 540	679 362	6 202 000	Tripoli	Arabic, Berber	Sunni Muslim	Libyan dinar	www.libyanmission-un.org
MADAGASCAR		587 041	226 658	22 925 000	Antananarivo	Malagasy, French	Traditional beliefs, Christian, Sunni Muslim	Malagasy Ariary, Malagasy franc	www.madagascar.gov.mg
MALAWI		118 484	45 747	16 363 000	Lilongwe	Chichewa, English, other local languages	Christian, traditional beliefs, Sunni Muslim	Malawian kwacha	www.malawi.gov.mw
MALI		1 240 140	478 821	15 302 000	Bamako	French, Bambara, other local languages	Sunni Muslim, traditional beliefs, Christian	CFA franc*	www.primature.gov.ml
MAURITANIA		1 030 700	397 955	3 890 000	Nouakchott	Arabic, French, other local languages	Sunni Muslim	Ouguiya	www.mauritania.mr
MAURITIUS		2 040	788	1 244 000	Port Louis	English, creole, Hindi, Bhojpurī, French	Hindu, Roman Catholic, Sunni Muslim	Mauritius rupee	www.gov.mu
MOROCCO		446 550	172 414	33 008 000	Rabat	Arabic, Berber, French	Sunni Muslim	Moroccan dirham	www.maroc.ma
MOZAMBIQUE		799 380	308 642	25 834 000	Maputo	Portuguese, Makua, Tsonga, other local languages	Traditional beliefs, Roman Catholic, Sunni Muslim	Metical	www.portaldogoverno.gov.mz
NAMIBIA		824 292	318 261	2 303 000	Windhoek	English, Afrikaans, German, Ovambo, other local languages	Protestant, Roman Catholic	Namibian dollar	www.grnnet.gov.na
NIGER		1 267 000	489 191	17 831 000	Niamey	French, Hausa, Fulani, other local languages	Sunni Muslim, traditional beliefs	CFA franc*	www.presidence.ne
NIGERIA		923 768	356 669	173 615 000	Abuja	English, Hausa, Yoruba, Ibo, Fulani, other local languages	Sunni Muslim, Christian, traditional beliefs	Naira	www.nigeria.gov.ng
RWANDA		26 338	10 169	11 777 000	Kigali	Kinyarwanda, French, English	Roman Catholic, traditional beliefs, Protestant	Rwandan franc	www.gov.rw
SÃO TOMÉ AND PRÍNCIPE		964	372	193 000	São Tomé	Portuguese, creole	Roman Catholic, Protestant	Dobra	www.gov.st
SENEGAL		196 720	75 954	14 133 000	Dakar	French, Wolof, Fulani, other local languages	Sunni Muslim, Roman Catholic, traditional beliefs	CFA franc*	www.gouv.sn

*Communauté Financière Africaine franc

Africa continued

		Area sq km	Area sq miles	Population	Capital	Languages	Religions	Currency	Internet Link
SEYCHELLES		455	176	93 000	Victoria	English, French, creole	Roman Catholic, Protestant	Seychelles rupee	www.virtualseychelles.sc
SIERRA LEONE		71 740	27 699	6 092 000	Freetown	English, creole, Mende, Temne, other local languages	Sunni Muslim, traditional beliefs	Leone	www.statehouse-sl.org
SOMALIA		637 657	246 201	10 496 000	Mogadishu	Somali, Arabic	Sunni Muslim	Somali shilling	www.somaligov.net
SOUTH AFRICA		1 219 090	470 693	52 776 000	Pretoria/Cape Town/Bloemfontein	Afrikaans, English, nine official other local languages	Protestant, Roman Catholic, Sunni Muslim, Hindu	Rand	www.gov.za
SOUTH SUDAN		644 329	248 775	11 296 000	Juba	Arabic, Dinka, Nubian, Beja, English, other local languages	Christian, Sunni Muslim, traditional beliefs	South Sudanese pound	www.goss.org
SUDAN		1 861 484	718 725	37 964 000	Khartoum	Arabic, English, Nubian, Beja, Fur, other local languages	Sunni Muslim, traditional beliefs, Christian	Sudanese pound (Sudani)	www.presidency.gov.sd
SWAZILAND		17 364	6 704	1 250 000	Mbabane	Swazi, English	Christian, traditional beliefs	Emalangeni, South African rand	www.gov.sz
TANZANIA		945 087	364 900	49 253 000	Dodoma	Swahili, English, Nyamwezi, other local languages	Shi'a Muslim, Sunni Muslim, traditional beliefs, Christian	Tanzanian shilling	www.tanzania.go.tz
TOGO		56 785	21 925	6 817 000	Lomé	French, Ewe, Kabre, other local languages	Traditional beliefs, Christian, Sunni Muslim	CFA franc*	www.republicoftogo.com
TUNISIA		164 150	63 379	10 997 000	Tunis	Arabic, French	Sunni Muslim	Tunisian dinar	www.ministeres.tn
UGANDA		241 038	93 065	37 579 000	Kampala	English, Swahili, Luganda, other local languages	Roman Catholic, Protestant, Sunni Muslim, traditional beliefs	Ugandan shilling	www.statehouse.go.ug
ZAMBIA		752 614	290 586	14 539 000	Lusaka	English, Bemba, Nyanja, Tonga, other local languages	Christian, traditional beliefs	Zambian kwacha	www.statehouse.gov.zm
ZIMBABWE		390 759	150 873	14 150 000	Harare	English, Shona, Ndebele	Christian, traditional beliefs	US dollar and other currencies	www.gta.gov.zw

*Communauté Financière Africaine franc

Oceania

		Area sq km	Area sq miles	Population	Capital	Languages	Religions	Currency	Internet Link
AUSTRALIA		7 692 024	2 969 907	23 343 000	Canberra	English, Italian, Greek	Protestant, Roman Catholic, Orthodox	Australian dollar	www.australia.gov.au
FIJI		18 330	7 077	881 000	Suva	English, Fijian, Hindi	Christian, Hindu, Sunni Muslim	Fiji dollar	www.fiji.gov.fj
KIRIBATI		717	277	102 000	Bairiki	Gilbertese, English	Roman Catholic, Protestant	Australian dollar	www.parliament.gov.ki
MARSHALL ISLANDS		181	70	53 000	Delap-Uliga-Djarrit	English, Marshallese	Protestant, Roman Catholic	United States dollar	www.rmigovernment.org
MICRONESIA, FEDERATED STATES OF		701	271	104 000	Palikir	English, Chuukese, Pohnpeian, other local languages	Roman Catholic, Protestant	United States dollar	www.fsmgov.org
NAURU		21	8	10 000	Yaren	Nauruan, English	Protestant, Roman Catholic	Australian dollar	www.naurugov.nr
NEW ZEALAND		270 534	104 454	4 506 000	Wellington	English, Maori	Protestant, Roman Catholic	New Zealand dollar	http://newzealand.govt.nz
PAPUA NEW GUINEA		462 840	178 704	7 321 000	Port Moresby	English, Tok Pisin (creole), other local languages	Protestant, Roman Catholic, traditional beliefs	Kina	www.pm.gov.pg
SAMOA		2 831	1 093	190 000	Apia	Samoan, English	Protestant, Roman Catholic	Tala	www.govt.ws
SOLOMON ISLANDS		28 370	10 954	561 000	Honiara	English, creole, other local languages	Protestant, Roman Catholic	Solomon Islands dollar	www.pmc.gov.sb
TONGA		748	289	105 000	Nuku'alofa	Tongan, English	Protestant, Roman Catholic	Pa'anga	www.pmo.gov.to
TUVALU		25	10	10 000	Vaiaku	Tuvaluan, English	Protestant	Australian dollar	
VANUATU		12 190	4 707	253 000	Port Vila	English, Bislama (creole), French	Protestant, Roman Catholic, traditional beliefs	Vatu	www.vanuatugovernment.gov.vu

North America

		Area sq km	Area sq miles	Population	Capital	Languages	Religions	Currency	Internet Link
ANTIGUA AND BARBUDA		442	171	90 000	St John's	English, creole	Protestant, Roman Catholic	East Caribbean dollar	www.ab.gov.ag
THE BAHAMAS		13 939	5 382	377 000	Nassau	English, creole	Protestant, Roman Catholic	Bahamian dollar	www.bahamas.gov.bs
BARBADOS		430	166	285 000	Bridgetown	English, creole	Protestant, Roman Catholic	Barbados dollar	www.barbados.gov.bb
BELIZE		22 965	8 867	332 000	Belmopan	English, Spanish, Mayan, creole	Roman Catholic, Protestant	Belize dollar	www.belize.gov.bz
CANADA		9 984 670	3 855 103	35 182 000	Ottawa	English, French, other local languages	Roman Catholic, Protestant, Eastern Orthodox, Jewish	Canadian dollar	www.canada.gc.ca
COSTA RICA		51 100	19 730	4 872 000	San José	Spanish	Roman Catholic, Protestant	Costa Rican colón	www.presidencia.go.cr
CUBA		110 860	42 803	11 266 000	Havana	Spanish	Roman Catholic, Protestant	Cuban peso	www.cubagob.gov.cu
DOMINICA		750	290	72 000	Roseau	English, creole	Roman Catholic, Protestant	East Caribbean dollar	www.dominica.gov.dm
DOMINICAN REPUBLIC		48 442	18 704	10 404 000	Santo Domingo	Spanish, creole	Roman Catholic, Protestant	Dominican peso	www.cig.gov.do
EL SALVADOR		21 041	8 124	6 340 000	San Salvador	Spanish	Roman Catholic, Protestant	El Salvador colón, United States dollar	www.presidencia.gob.sv
GRENADA		378	146	106 000	St George's	English, creole	Roman Catholic, Protestant	East Caribbean dollar	www.gov.gd
GUATEMALA		108 890	42 043	15 468 000	Guatemala City	Spanish, Mayan languages	Roman Catholic, Protestant	Quetzal, United States dollar	www.guatemala.gob.gt
HAITI		27 750	10 714	10 317 000	Port-au-Prince	French, creole	Roman Catholic, Protestant, Voodoo	Gourde	www.haiti.org
HONDURAS		112 088	43 277	8 098 000	Tegucigalpa	Spanish, Amerindian languages	Roman Catholic, Protestant	Lempira	http://congresonacional.hn/
JAMAICA		10 991	4 244	2 784 000	Kingston	English, creole	Protestant, Roman Catholic	Jamaican dollar	www.jamaica.gov.jm
MEXICO		1 972 545	761 604	122 332 000	Mexico City	Spanish, Amerindian languages	Roman Catholic, Protestant	Mexican peso	www.gob.mx
NICARAGUA		130 000	50 193	6 080 000	Managua	Spanish, Amerindian languages	Roman Catholic, Protestant	Córdoba	www.presidencia.gob.ni
PANAMA		77 082	29 762	3 864 000	Panama City	Spanish, English, Amerindian languages	Roman Catholic, Protestant, Sunni Muslim	Balboa	www.presidencia.gob.pa
ST KITTS AND NEVIS		261	101	54 000	Basseterre	English, creole	Protestant, Roman Catholic	East Caribbean dollar	www.gov.kn
ST LUCIA		616	238	182 000	Castries	English, creole	Roman Catholic, Protestant	East Caribbean dollar	www.stlucia.gov.lc
ST VINCENT AND THE GRENADINES		389	150	109 000	Kingstown	English, creole	Protestant, Roman Catholic	East Caribbean dollar	www.gov.vc
TRINIDAD AND TOBAGO		5 130	1 981	1 341 000	Port of Spain	English, creole, Hindi	Roman Catholic, Hindu, Protestant, Sunni Muslim	Trinidad and Tobago dollar	www.ttconnect.gov.tt
UNITED STATES OF AMERICA		9 826 635	3 794 085	320 051 000	Washington D.C.	English, Spanish	Protestant, Roman Catholic, Sunni Muslim, Jewish	United States dollar	www.usa.gov

South America

		Area sq km	Area sq miles	Population	Capital	Languages	Religions	Currency	Internet Link
ARGENTINA		2 766 889	1 068 302	41 446 000	Buenos Aires	Spanish, Italian, Amerindian languages	Roman Catholic, Protestant	Argentinian peso	www.argentina.gov.ar
BOLIVIA		1 098 581	424 164	10 671 000	La Paz/Sucre	Spanish, Quechua, Aymara	Roman Catholic, Protestant, Baha'i	Boliviano	www.bolivia.gob.bo
BRAZIL		8 514 879	3 287 613	200 362 000	Brasília	Portuguese	Roman Catholic, Protestant	Real	www.brazil.gov.br
CHILE		756 945	292 258	17 620 000	Santiago	Spanish, Amerindian languages	Roman Catholic, Protestant	Chilean peso	www.gobiernodechile.cl
COLOMBIA		1 141 748	440 831	48 321 000	Bogotá	Spanish, Amerindian languages	Roman Catholic, Protestant	Colombian peso	www.gobiernoenlinea.gov.co
ECUADOR		272 045	105 037	15 738 000	Quito	Spanish, Quechua, other Amerindian languages	Roman Catholic	US dollar	www.presidencia.gob.ec
GUYANA		214 969	83 000	800 000	Georgetown	English, creole, Amerindian languages	Protestant, Hindu, Roman Catholic, Sunni Muslim	Guyana dollar	www.gina.gov.gy
PARAGUAY		406 752	157 048	6 802 000	Asunción	Spanish, Guaraní	Roman Catholic, Protestant	Guaraní	www.presidencia.gov.py
PERU		1 285 216	496 225	30 376 000	Lima	Spanish, Quechua, Aymara	Roman Catholic, Protestant	Nuevo sol	www.peru.gob.pe
SURINAME		163 820	63 251	539 000	Paramaribo	Dutch, Surinamese, English, Hindi	Hindu, Roman Catholic, Protestant, Sunni Muslim	Suriname guilder	www.president.gov.sr
URUGUAY		176 215	68 037	3 407 000	Montevideo	Spanish	Roman Catholic, Protestant, Jewish	Uruguayan peso	www.presidencia.gub.uy
VENEZUELA		912 050	352 144	30 405 000	Caracas	Spanish, Amerindian languages	Roman Catholic, Protestant	Bolívar fuerte	www.presidencia.gob.ve

World
Countries

The current pattern of the world's countries and territories is a result of a long history of exploration, colonialism, conflict and politics. The fact that there are currently 196 independent countries in the world – the most recent, South Sudan, only being created in July 2011 – illustrates the significant political changes which have occurred since 1950 when there were only eighty-two. There has been a steady progression away from colonial influences over the last fifty years, although many dependent overseas territories remain.

The shapes of countries and the pattern of international boundaries reflect both physical and political processes. Some borders follow natural features – rivers, mountain ranges, etc – others are defined according to political agreement or as a result of war. Some are still subject to dispute between two or more countries, and many remain undefined on the ground.

Facts

- The longest single continuous land border stretches for 6 416 kilometres between Canada and the USA
- Both China and Russia have land borders with 14 different countries
- Vatican City, the smallest independent country, was created in 1929 as an enclave within Rome, the capital of Italy
- All countries of the world are members of the United Nations except Kosovo, Taiwan and Vatican City

Internet Links

United Nations	**www.un.org**
Foreign and Commonwealth Office	**www.fco.gov.uk**
International Boundaries Research Unit	**www.dur.ac.uk/ibru**
Permanent Committee on Geographical Names	**www.pcgn.org.uk**
U.S. Board on Geographic Names	**geonames.usgs.gov**

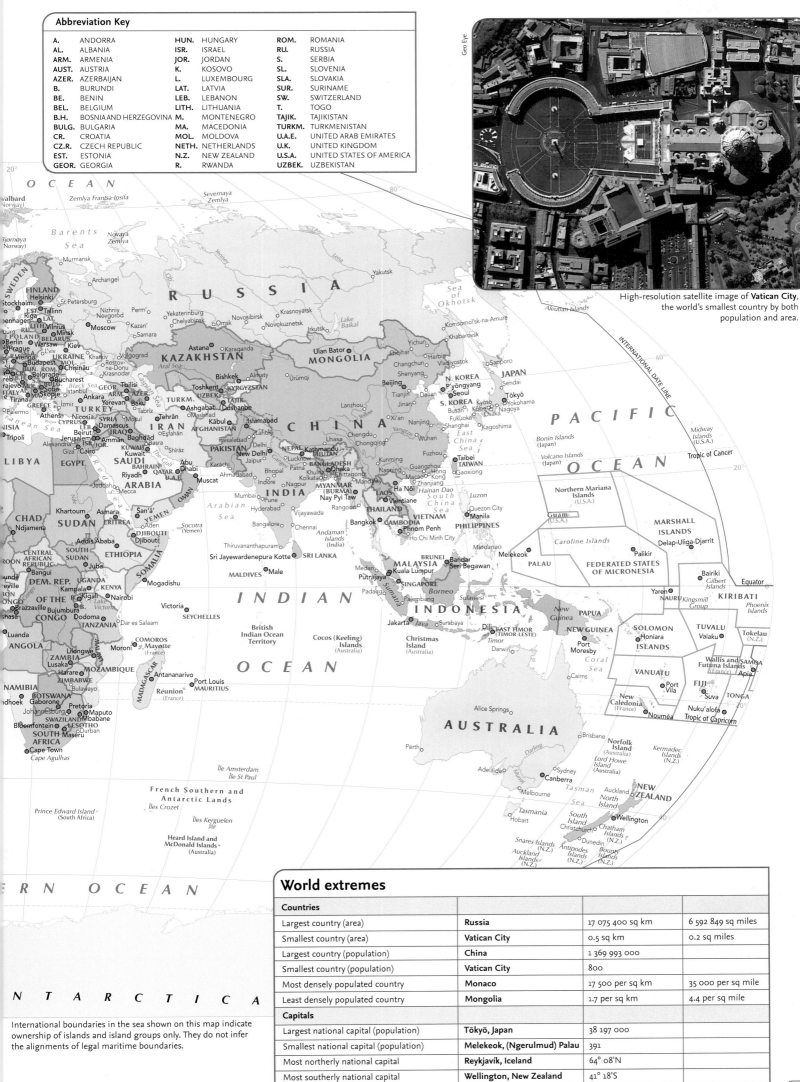

Abbreviation Key

A.	ANDORRA	HUN.	HUNGARY	ROM.	ROMANIA
AL.	ALBANIA	ISR.	ISRAEL	RU.	RUSSIA
ARM.	ARMENIA	JOR.	JORDAN	S.	SERBIA
AUST.	AUSTRIA	K.	KOSOVO	SL.	SLOVENIA
AZER.	AZERBAIJAN	L.	LUXEMBOURG	SLA.	SLOVAKIA
B.	BURUNDI	LAT.	LATVIA	SUR.	SURINAME
BE.	BENIN	LEB.	LEBANON	SW.	SWITZERLAND
BEL.	BELGIUM	LITH.	LITHUANIA	T.	TOGO
B.H.	BOSNIA AND HERZEGOVINA	M.	MONTENEGRO	TAJIK.	TAJIKISTAN
BULG.	BULGARIA	MA.	MACEDONIA	TURKM.	TURKMENISTAN
CR.	CROATIA	MOL.	MOLDOVA	U.A.E.	UNITED ARAB EMIRATES
CZ.R.	CZECH REPUBLIC	NETH.	NETHERLANDS	U.K.	UNITED KINGDOM
EST.	ESTONIA	N.Z.	NEW ZEALAND	U.S.A.	UNITED STATES OF AMERICA
GEOR.	GEORGIA	R.	RWANDA	UZBEK.	UZBEKISTAN

High-resolution satellite image of **Vatican City**, the world's smallest country by both population and area.

International boundaries in the sea shown on this map indicate ownership of islands and island groups only. They do not infer the alignments of legal maritime boundaries.

World extremes

Countries			
Largest country (area)	**Russia**	17 075 400 sq km	6 592 849 sq miles
Smallest country (area)	**Vatican City**	0.5 sq km	0.2 sq miles
Largest country (population)	**China**	1 369 993 000	
Smallest country (population)	**Vatican City**	800	
Most densely populated country	**Monaco**	17 500 per sq km	35 000 per sq mile
Least densely populated country	**Mongolia**	1.7 per sq km	4.4 per sq mile
Capitals			
Largest national capital (population)	**Tōkyō, Japan**	38 197 000	
Smallest national capital (population)	**Melekeok, (Ngerulmud) Palau**	391	
Most northerly national capital	**Reykjavík, Iceland**	64° 08'N	
Most southerly national capital	**Wellington, New Zealand**	41° 18'S	
Highest national capital	**La Paz, Bolivia**	3 636 m	11 910 ft

The earth's physical features, both on land and on the sea bed, closely reflect its geological structure. The current shapes of the continents and oceans have evolved over millions of years. Movements of the tectonic plates which make up the earth's crust have created some of the best-known and most spectacular features. The processes which have shaped the earth continue today with earthquakes, volcanoes, erosion, climatic variations and man's activities all affecting the earth's landscapes.

The total topographic range of the earth's surface is nearly 20 000 metres, from the highest point Mount Everest, to the lowest point in the Mariana Trench. Major mountain ranges include the Himalaya, the Andes and the Rocky Mountains, each of which give rise to some of the world's greatest rivers. In contrast, the deserts of the Sahara, Australia, the Arabian Peninsula and the Gobi cover vast areas and each provide unique landscapes.

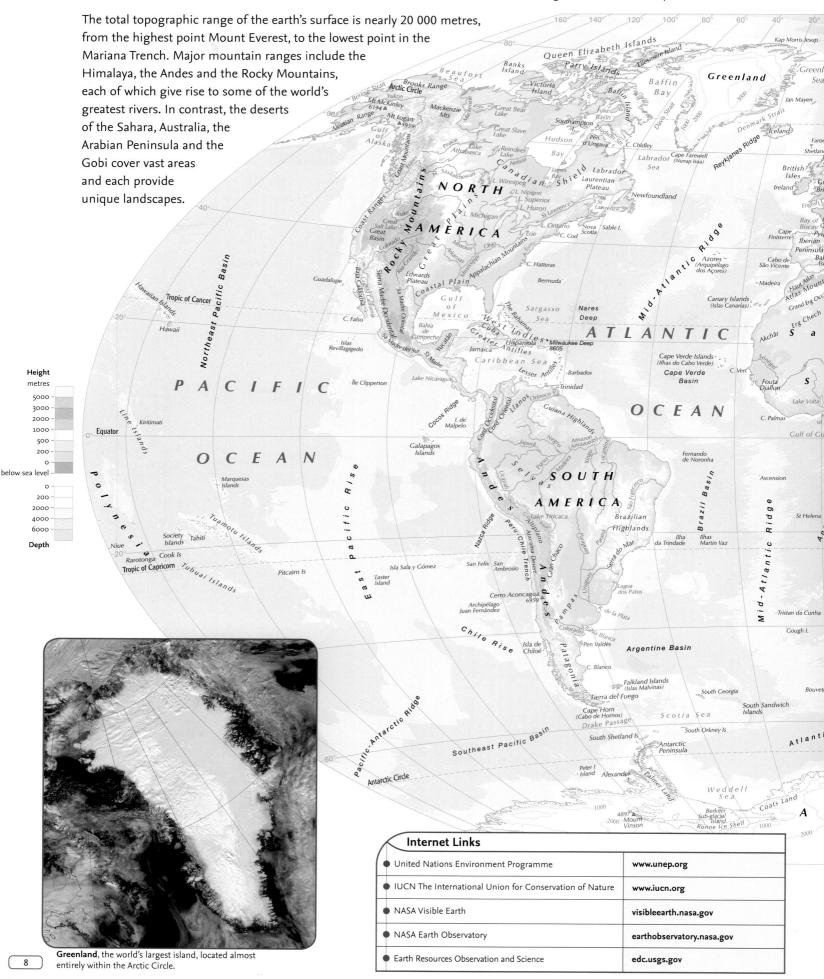

Height

metres

5000
3000
2000
1000
500
200
0

below sea level

0
200
2000
4000
6000

Depth

Greenland, the world's largest island, located almost entirely within the Arctic Circle.

Internet Links	
● United Nations Environment Programme	**www.unep.org**
● IUCN The International Union for Conservation of Nature	**www.iucn.org**
● NASA Visible Earth	**visibleearth.nasa.gov**
● NASA Earth Observatory	**earthobservatory.nasa.gov**
● Earth Resources Observation and Science	**edc.usgs.gov**

Earth's dimensions

Mass	5.974×10^{21} tonnes
Total area	509 450 000 sq km / 196 698 645 sq miles
Land area	149 450 000 sq km / 57 702 645 sq miles
Water area	360 000 000 sq km / 138 996 000 sq miles
Volume	$1\ 083\ 207 \times 10^{6}$ cubic km / $259\ 911 \times 10^{6}$ cubic miles
Equatorial diameter	12 756 km / 7 927 miles
Polar diameter	12 714 km / 7 900 miles
Equatorial circumference	40 075 km / 24 903 miles
Meridional circumference	40 008 km / 24 861 miles

Facts

- Approximately 10% of the Earth's land surface is permanently covered by ice
- The Pacific Ocean is larger than all the continents' land areas combined
- The world's highest waterfall, 979 metres high, is Angel Falls, Venezuela
- 52% of the Earth's land surface is below 500 metres
- The mean elevation of the Earth's land surface is 840 metres
- Lake Baikal is the world's deepest lake with a maximum depth of 1 741 metres

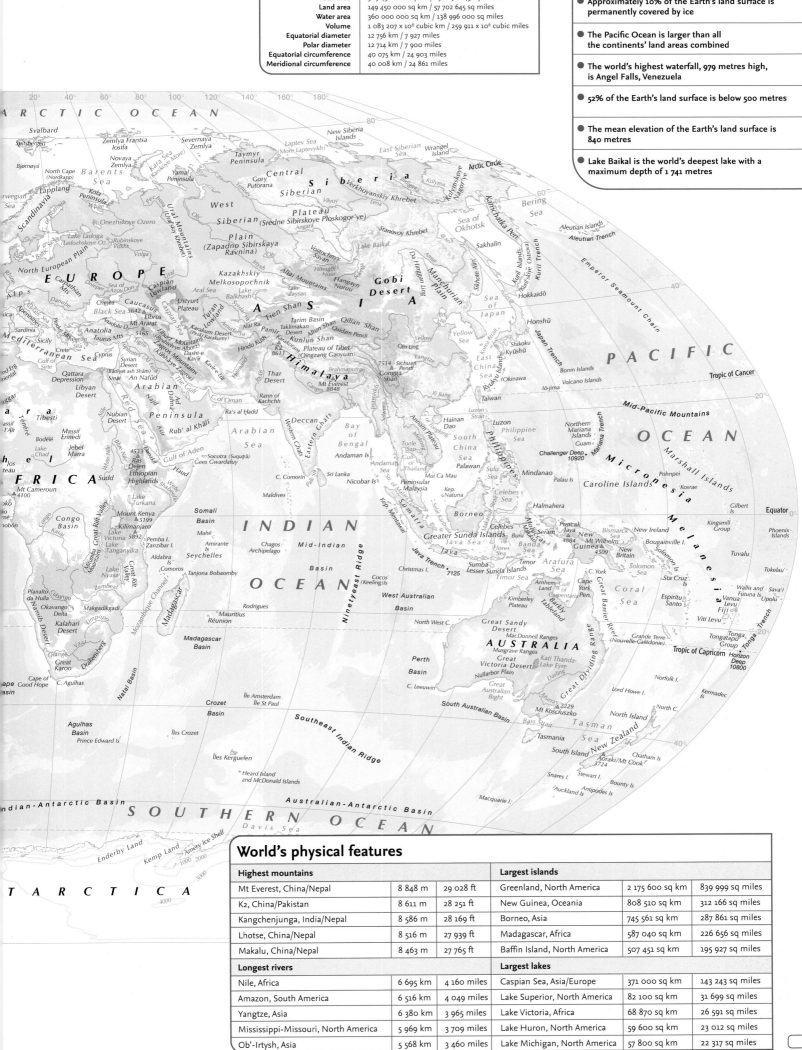

World's physical features

Highest mountains

Highest mountains			Largest islands		
Mt Everest, China/Nepal	8 848 m	29 028 ft	Greenland, North America	2 175 600 sq km	839 999 sq miles
K2, China/Pakistan	8 611 m	28 251 ft	New Guinea, Oceania	808 510 sq km	312 166 sq miles
Kangchenjunga, India/Nepal	8 586 m	28 169 ft	Borneo, Asia	745 561 sq km	287 861 sq miles
Lhotse, China/Nepal	8 516 m	27 939 ft	Madagascar, Africa	587 040 sq km	226 656 sq miles
Makalu, China/Nepal	8 463 m	27 765 ft	Baffin Island, North America	507 451 sq km	195 927 sq miles

Longest rivers			Largest lakes		
Nile, Africa	6 695 km	4 160 miles	Caspian Sea, Asia/Europe	371 000 sq km	143 243 sq miles
Amazon, South America	6 516 km	4 049 miles	Lake Superior, North America	82 100 sq km	31 699 sq miles
Yangtze, Asia	6 380 km	3 965 miles	Lake Victoria, Africa	68 870 sq km	26 591 sq miles
Mississippi-Missouri, North America	5 969 km	3 709 miles	Lake Huron, North America	59 600 sq km	23 012 sq miles
Ob'-Irtysh, Asia	5 568 km	3 460 miles	Lake Michigan, North America	57 800 sq km	22 317 sq miles

Conic Equidistant Projection

1:10 000 000

Europe
Western Russia

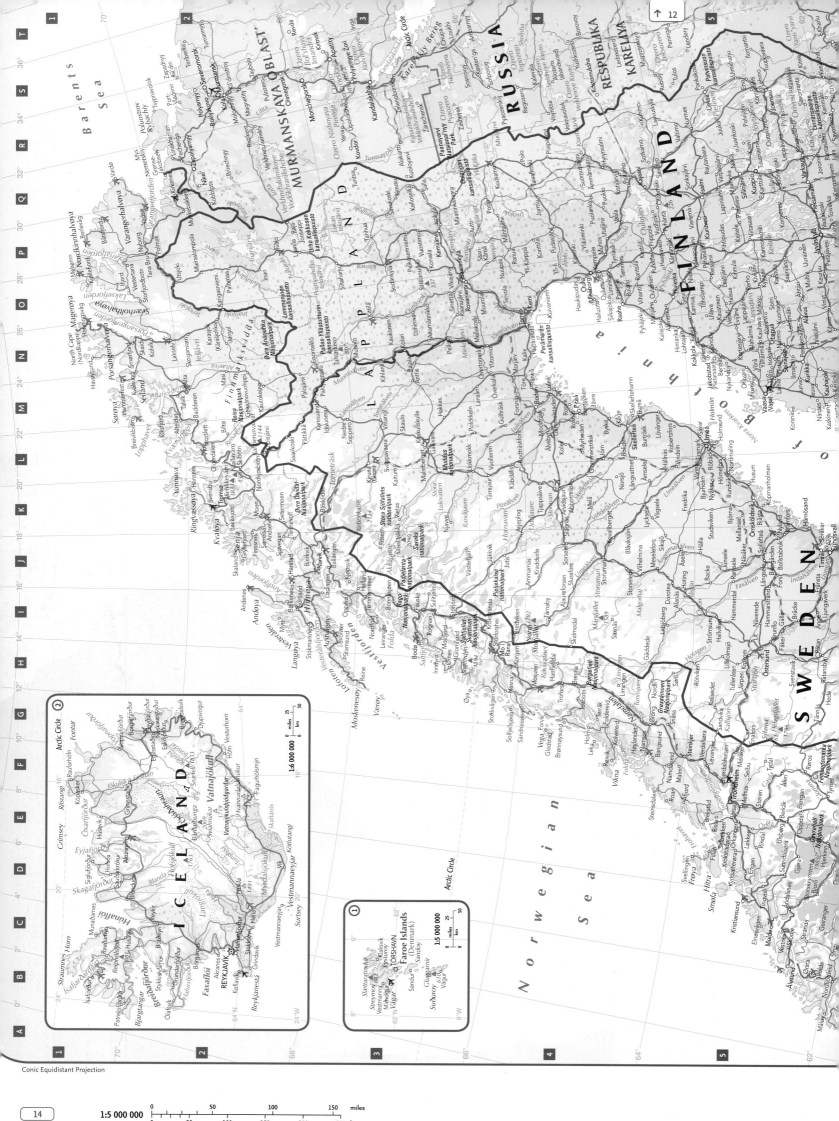

Conic Equidistant Projection

1:5 000 000

| 0 | 50 | 100 | 150 | miles |

| 0 | 50 | 100 | 150 | 200 | 250 | km |

Europe
Scandinavia and the Baltic States

Europe
Northwest Europe

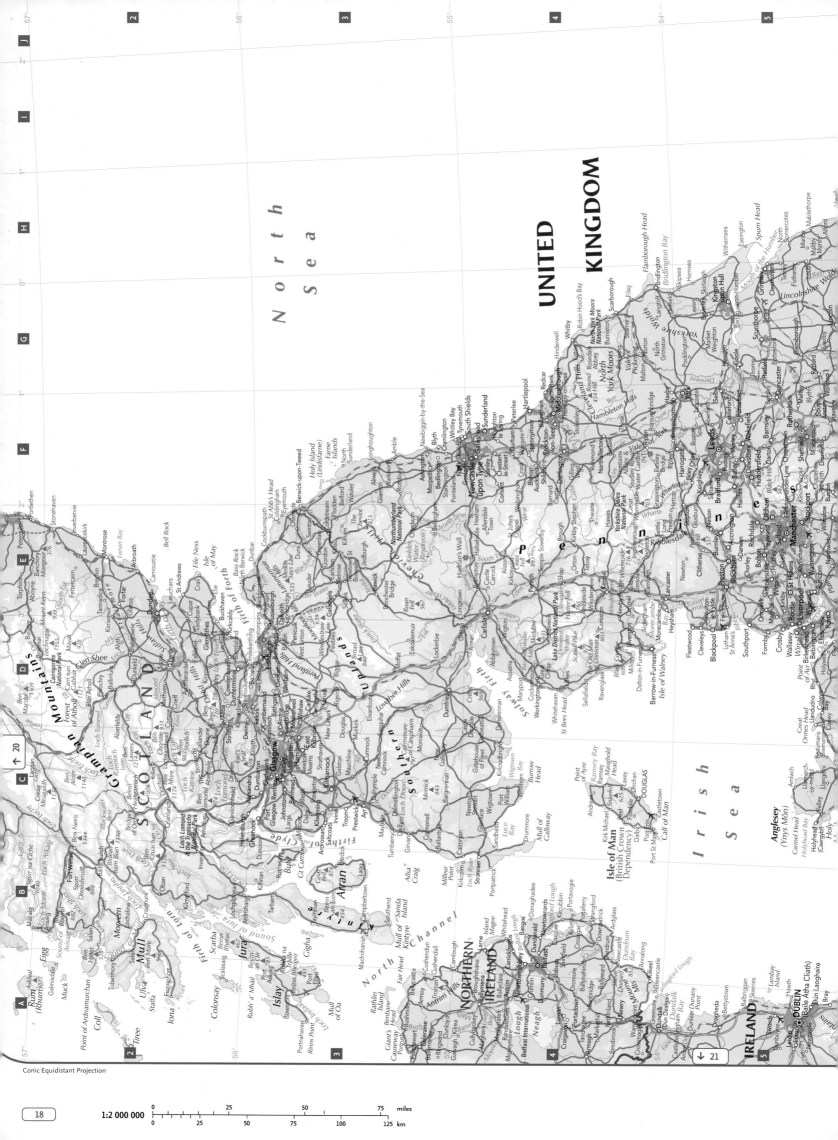

Conic Equidistant Projection

1:2 000 000

miles
0   25   50   75

km
0   25   50   75   100   125

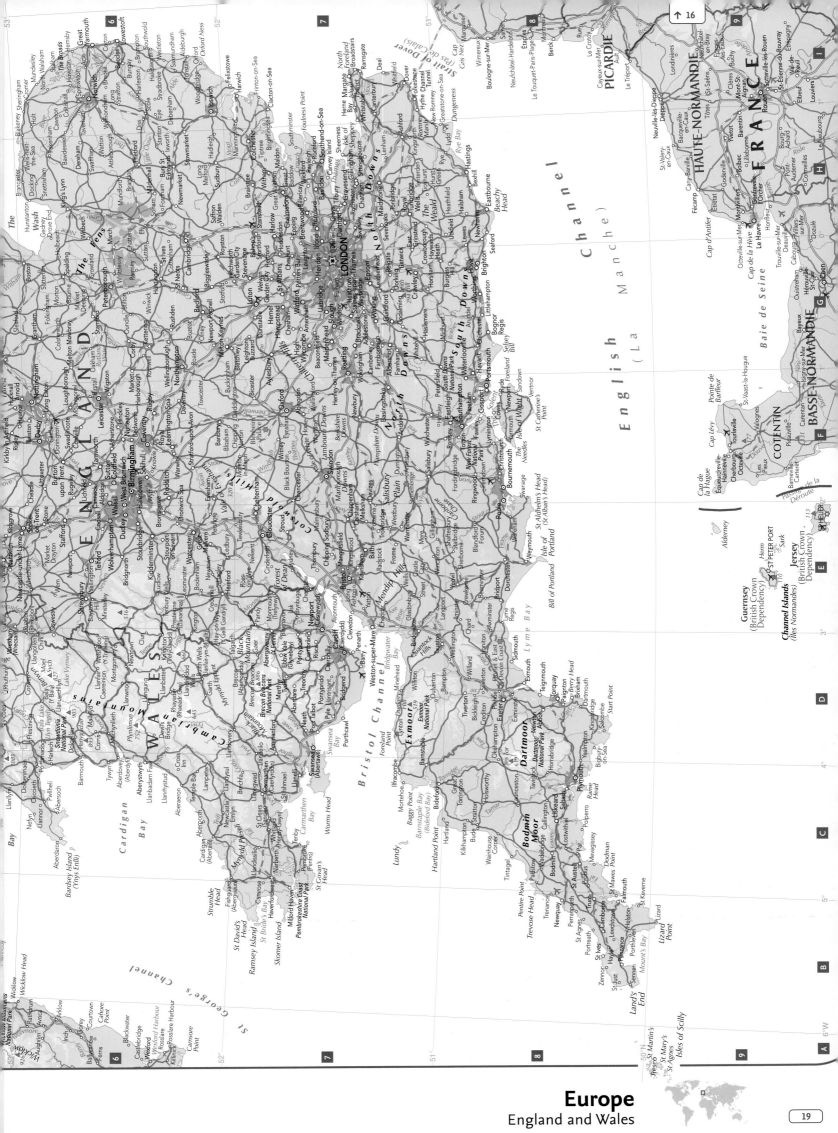

Europe

England and Wales

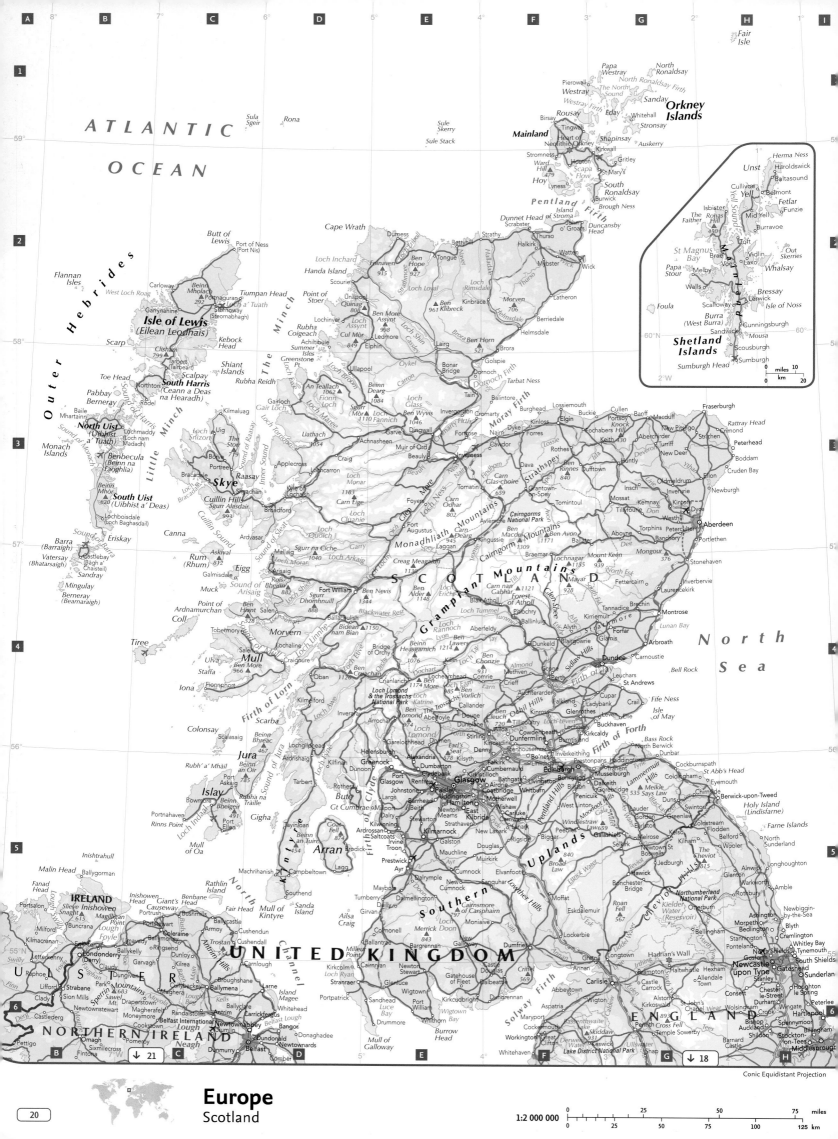

Europe
Scotland

1:2 000 000

Conic Equidistant Projection

Conic Equidistant Projection

1:2 000 000

Europe
Ireland

Europe

Southern Europe and the Mediterranean

Europe
France

Conic Equidistant Projection

1:5 000 000

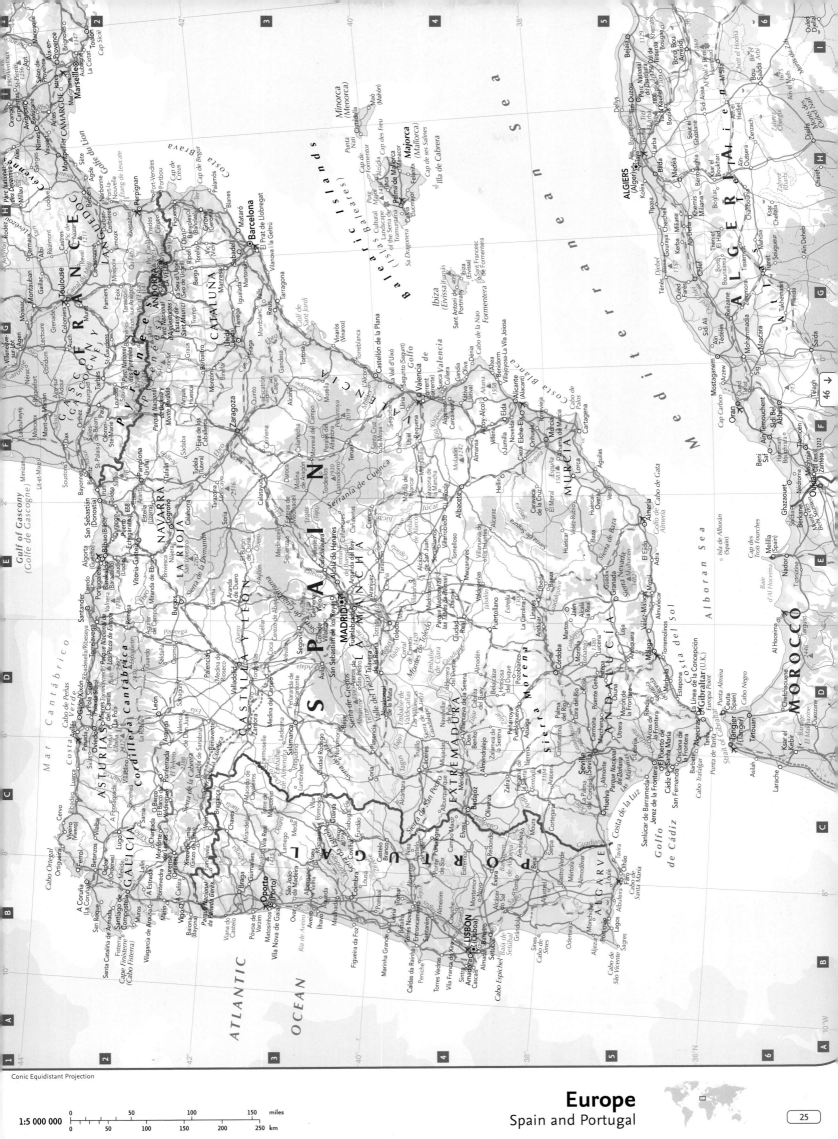

Europe
Spain and Portugal

Conic Equidistant Projection

1:5 000 000

Conic Equidistant Projection

1:5 000 000

Conic Equidistant Projection

1:20 000 000

Asia
Northern Asia

Albers Conic Equal Area Projection

1:20 000 000

| 0 | 200 | 400 | 600 miles |

| 0 | 200 | 400 | 600 | 800 | 1000 km |

↓ 48

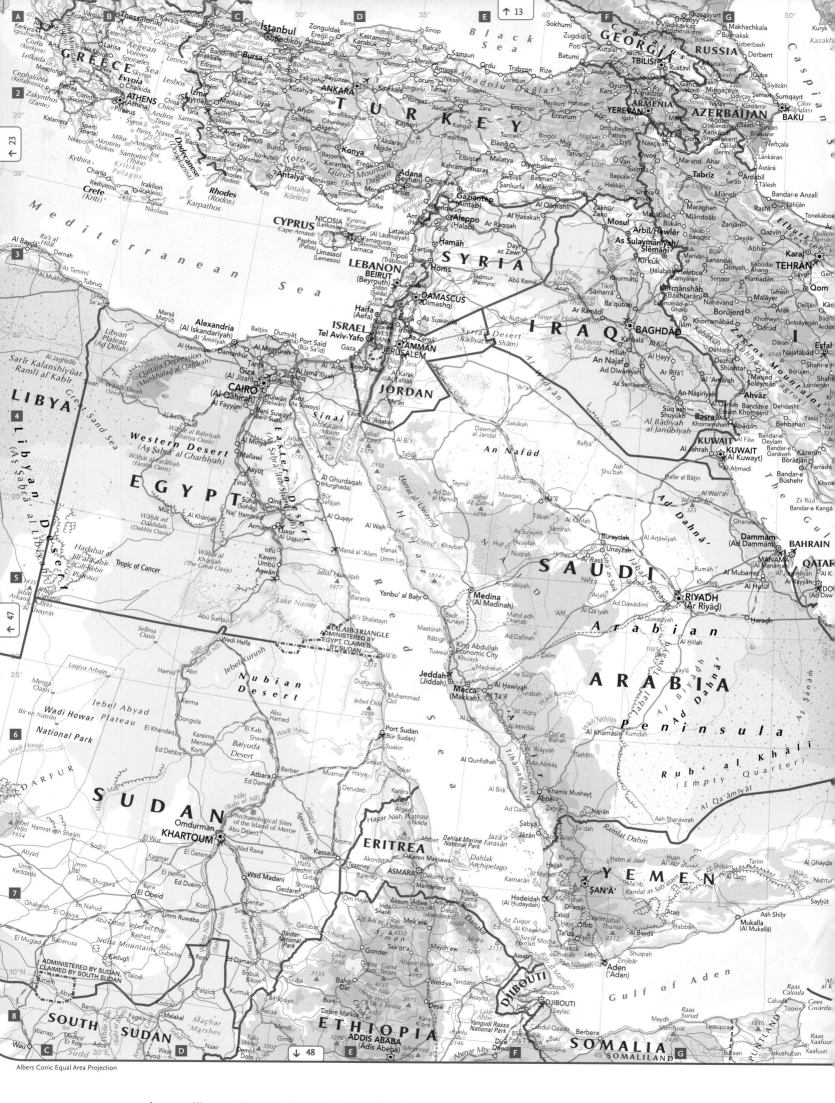

Albers Conic Equal Area Projection

1:13 000 000

0 100 200 300 400 500 miles

0 100 200 300 400 500 600 700 800 km

Asia
Southwest Asia

Administrative divisions in Russia
numbered on the map:

1. RESPUBLIKA KALMYKIYA-KHALM'G-TANGCH (G1)
2. RESPUBLIKA DAGESTAN (G2)
3. CHECHENSKAYA RESPUBLIKA (G2)
4. RESPUBLIKA INGUSHETIYA (G2)
5. RESPUBLIKA SEVERNAYA OSETIYA-ALANIYA (G2)
6. KABARDINO-BALKARSKAYA RESPUBLIKA (F2)
7. KARACHAYEVO-CHERKESSKAYA RESPUBLIKA (F2)
8. RESPUBLIKA ADYGEYA (F1)

Conic Equidistant Projection

1:7 000 000

0 ... 100 ... 200 miles

0 100 200 300 400 km

Conic Equidistant Projection

1:7 000 000

Administrative divisions in India
numbered on the map:

1. DADRA AND NAGAR HAVELI (C5)
2. DAMAN AND DIU (B5, C5)

→ 31

→ 42

Asia

Northern India, Nepal, Bhutan and Bangladesh

Asia
Southern India and Sri Lanka

Administrative divisions in India numbered on the map:

1. DADRA AND NAGAR HAVELI (B1)
2. DAMAN AND DIU (A1, B1)
3. PUDUCHERRY (C4)

Conic Equidistant Projection

1:7 000 000

TURKEY

MERSIN
KARAMAN

CYPRUS

ADMINISTERED AS
NORTHERN CYPRUS

GREEN LINE
(Güzelyurt)
NICOSIA
(Lefkoşía)
(Lefkoşa)

HATAY

Aleppo
(Halab)

SYRIA

GAZIANTEP
KILIS
ŞANLIURFA

Ar Raqqah

Hamāh

Homs

LEBANON

BEIRUT
(Beyrouth)

Tripoli
(Tráblous)

Mediterranean

Sea

DAMASCUS
(Dimashq)

IRAQ

CEASE
FIRE
LINES
1974

Haifa
(Hefa)

Syrian Desert
(Bādiyat ash Shām)

WEST
BANK

Tel Aviv-Yafo

JERUSALEM
(Yerushalayim)
(El Quds)

Amman

JORDAN

GAZA
Gaza

ISRAEL

Negev

**SAUDI
ARABIA**

PORT SAÏD

SUWAYS

EGYPT

Sinai
(Shibh Jazīrat Sīnā')

SHAMAL SĪNĀ'

JANŪB SĪNĀ'

Gulf of Suez

Conic Equidistant Projection

0   25   50   75   100   miles

1:3 000 000

0   25   50   75   100   125   150   175   km

Asia
Middle East

Tropic of Cancer

H

G

F

↑ 29

E

D

C

B

A

Albers Conic Equal Area Projection

1:20 000 000

0   200   400   600   miles
0   200   400   600   800   1000 km

↓ 31

RUSSIA

MONGOLIA

ULAN BATOR
(Ulaanbaatar)

CHINA

KAZAKHSTAN

Gobi Desert

Altay Mountains

INNER MONGOLIA

MANCHURIA

NORTH KOREA
PYONGYANG

SOUTH KOREA
SEOUL

JAPAN
TŌKYŌ

TAIWAN
TAIBEI (Taipei)

The People's Republic of China claims Taiwan as its 23rd province

MYANMAR (BURMA)
NAY PYI TAW

INDIA

BHUTAN

Sea of Okhotsk
(Okhotskoye More)

Sea of Japan
(East Sea)

Yellow Sea
(Huang Hai)

East China Sea
(Dong Hai)

Kamchatka Peninsula
(Poluostrov Kamchatka)

Sakhalin

Hokkaidō

BEIJING (Peking)

Shanghai

Guangzhou

Hong Kong

Macao

DHAKA (Dacca)

Asia
Eastern and Southeast Asia

Albers Conic Equal Area Projection

1:15 000 000

Asia
Eastern Asia

↓ 41

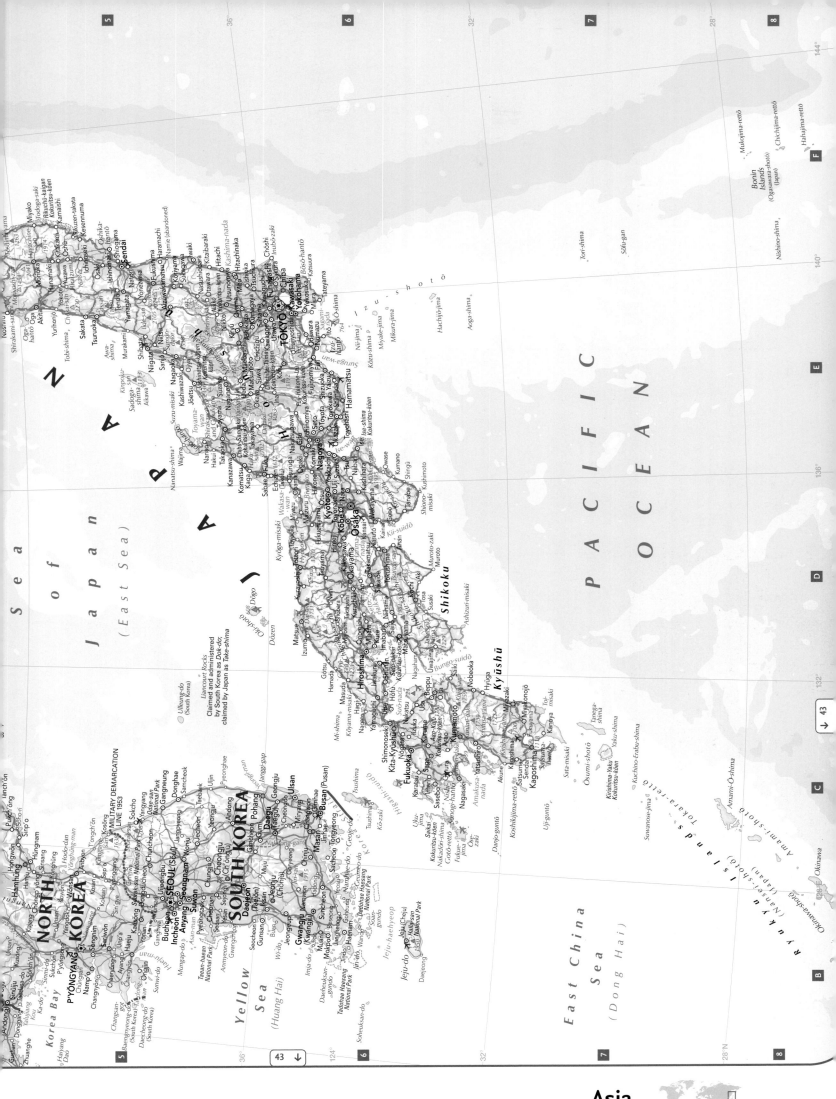

Asia

Japan, North Korea and South Korea

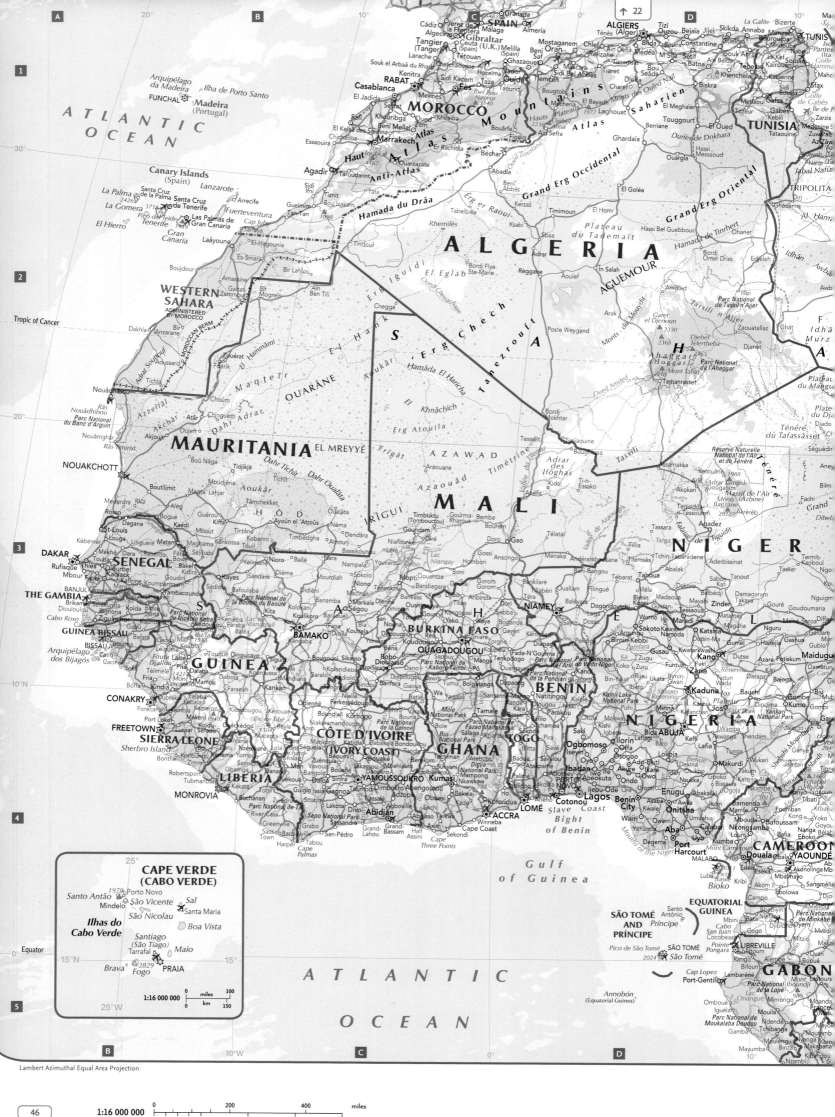

ATLANTIC OCEAN

A **B** **C** **D**

1

Arquipélago da Madeira

FUNCHAL Madeira (Portugal) Ilha de Porto Santo

30°

Canary Islands (Spain)

La Palma Lanzarote
Santa Cruz de la Palma Arrecife
La Gomera Santa Cruz de Tenerife Fuerteventura
El Hierro Pico de Teide Las Palmas de Gran Canaria
Gran Canaria Cap Juby

2

WESTERN SAHARA
ADMINISTERED BY MOROCCO

Tropic of Cancer

Dakhla Anzarane

Nouâdhibou
Râs Nouâdhibou
Parc National du Banc d'Arguin
Nouâmghâr
Râs Timirist

MAURITANIA EL MREYYÉ

NOUAKCHOTT

3

DAKAR
Rufisque Mbour Thiès
SENEGAL Kaolack Diourbel
THE GAMBIA
BANJUL Brikama Serekunda
Cabo Roxo Ziguinchor
GUINEA-BISSAU
BISSAU
Arquipélago dos Bijagós

CONAKRY

FREETOWN
SIERRA LEONE
Sherbro Island

GUINEA

LIBERIA
MONROVIA

CÔTE D'IVOIRE
(IVORY COAST)
YAMOUSSOUKRO
Abidjan

MOROCCO
RABAT
Casablanca
Marrakech
Agadir

Atlas

Anti-Atlas

Hamada du Drâa

Es-Smara

BAMAKO

GUINEA

10°N

GHANA
ACCRA

SPAIN
ALGIERS (Alger)
TUNIS
TUNISIA

Atlas Mountains Saharien Atlas

ALGERIA

Grand Erg Occidental Grand Erg Oriental

Plateau du Tademaït

AGUEMOUR

S A H A R A

Tanezrouft AZAWAD

AHAGGAR Hoggar
Tamanrasset

MALI

Timbuktu (Tombouctou) Gao

OUAGADOUGOU
BURKINA FASO

Parc National de la Comoé

Kumasi

Bight of Benin

NIGER

NIAMEY

Kano

NIGERIA
ABUJA

Kaduna

BENIN
PORTO-
NOVO
Lagos
Ibadan

TOGO
LOMÉ Cotonou

Gulf of Guinea

4

CAPE VERDE (CABO VERDE)

Santo Antão Porto Novo
Mindelo São Vicente Sal
São Nicolau Santa Maria
Ilhas do Cabo Verde
Boa Vista

Santiago (São Tiago) Maio
Tarrafal PRAIA
Brava Fogo

1:16 000 000

15°N

Equator

25°W

CAMEROON
YAOUNDÉ

Douala

EQUATORIAL GUINEA

SÃO TOMÉ AND PRÍNCIPE

Pico de São Tomé SÃO TOMÉ
São Tomé

LIBREVILLE

GABON

ATLANTIC OCEAN

Gulf of Guinea

5

B **C** **D**

Lambert Azimuthal Equal Area Projection

1:16 000 000

miles 200 400

km 200 400 600 800

Africa
Northern Africa

Africa
Central and Southern Africa

ATLANTIC

OCEAN

GHANZI

BOTSWANA

KWENEN

SOUTHER

NAMIBIA

ERONGO

KHOMAS

OTJOZONDJUPA

OMAHEKE

HARDAP

KGALAGADI

Kalahari

Desert

GREAT NAMAQUALAND

!KARAS

NORTHERN

CAPE

AFRIC

NAMAQUALAND

SOUT

GRIQUALAND WEST

NORTH

Great Karoo

Little Karoo

WESTERN CAPE

CAPE TOWN

Lambert Azimuthal Equal Area Projection

1:5 000 000

0   50   100   150   miles
0   50   100   150   200   250   km

Africa
South Africa

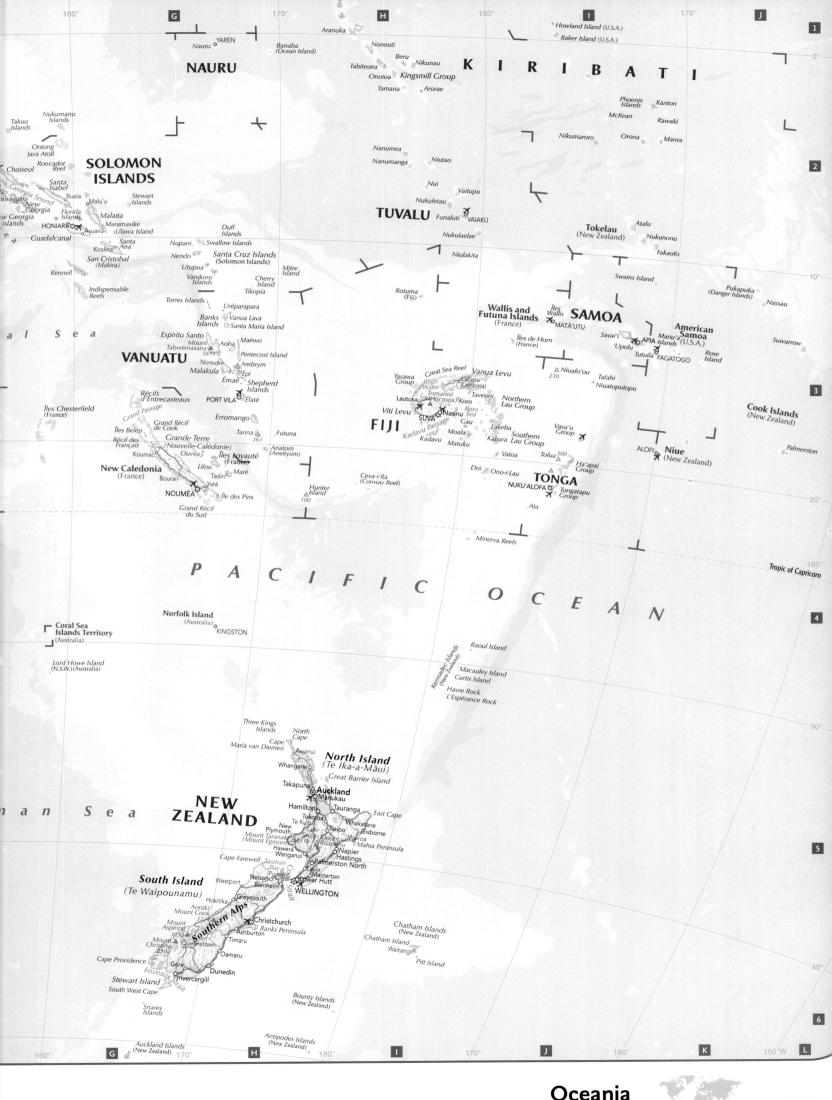

G · 160° · H · 170° · 180° · I · 170° · J

1

Aranuka
Howland Island (U.S.A.)
Baker Island (U.S.A.)
0°

YAREN · Nauru
Nauru
Banaba
(Ocean Island)
Nonouti
Beru · Nikunau
Tabiteuea
Onotoa · Kingsmill Group
Tamana · Arorae

NAURU

K I R I B A T I

Phoenix
Islands · Kanton
McKean · Rawaki
Nikumaroro · Orona · Manra

Takuu
Islands · Nukumanu
Islands

Ontong
Java Atoll · Roncador
Reef

**SOLOMON
ISLANDS**

Choiseul
Santa
Isabel

2
2°

w Georgia Sound
Bangara
New
Georgia
Islands

Buala
Malu'u
Florida
Islands
HONIARA · Auvavu

Stewart
Islands

Nanumea
Nanumanga

Niutao

Nui
Vaitupu

TUVALU · Funafuti · VAIAKU
Nukufetau

Tokelau
(New Zealand)
Atafu
Nukunonu
Fakaofo

Guadalcanal
Kiralora
Santa
Ana
San Cristobal
(Makira)

Malaita
Maramasike
Ulawa Island

Duff
Islands
Nupani · Swallow Islands
Nendo · Santa Cruz Islands
(Solomon Islands)
Utupua
Vanikoro
Islands
Tikopia

Mitre
Island

Nukulaelae
Niulakita

Swains Island

Pukapuka
(Danger Islands) · Nassau

Rennell
Indispensable
Reefs

Torres Islands

Uréparapara
Banks
Islands · Vanua Lava
Santa Maria Island

Rotuma
(Fiji)

Wallis and
Futuna Islands
(France)
Îles
Wallis
MATĀ'UTU

SAMOA
American
Samoa
(U.S.A.)

Suwarrow
10°

al Sea

Îles Chesterfield
(France)

Espiritu Santo
Mount
Tabwémasana
1879

VANUATU

Maéwo
Aoba
Pentecost Island
Norsup · Ambrym
Malakula
1270 Épi
Émaé · Shepherd
Islands

Îles de Horn
(France)

Great Sea Reef
Yasawa
Group
Bligh
Water · Vanua Levu
Labasa
(Lambasa)
Tomanivi · Taveuni
Lautoka Mt Victoria · Koro
Viti Levu · Koro
Sea
SUVA · Nasinu
Gau

Savai'i
'Upolu · APIA · Manu'a
Tutuila · Islands
FAGATOGO
Rose
Island

Niuafo'ou
210
Tafahi
Niuatoputapu

Northern
Lau Group

Vava'u
Group

Cook Islands
(New Zealand)
3°

Récifs
d'Entrecasteaux
Grand Passage
Grand Récif
de Cook
Îles Belep
Récif des
Français
Koumac

PORT VILA · Éfaté
Erromango

Tanna · 361
Futuna

Anatom
(Aneityum)

Kadavu Passage
Viti Levu
Nasinu

Kadavu
Moala
Matuku

Lakeba
Southern
Kabara Lau Group

Vatoa

Tofua 500

Doi · Ono-i-Lau

Vava'u
Group

ALOFI · **Niue**
(New Zealand)

Palmerston

FIJI

Ha'apai
Group

Grande Terre
(Nouvelle-Calédonie)
Ouvéa
Lifou

New Caledonia
(France)
Bourail
NOUMÉA · Yaté
Îles des Pins

Tadin · Maré

Hunter
Island
100

Ceva-i-Ra
(Conway Reef)

TONGA
NUKU'ALOFA · Tongatapu
Group
Ata

20°

Grand Récif
du Sud

Minerva Reefs

160°
Tropic of Capricorn

4

P A C I F I C   O C E A N

Coral Sea
Islands Territory
(Australia)

Norfolk Island
(Australia)
KINGSTON

Lord Howe Island
(N.S.W.)(Australia)

Raoul Island

Kermadec Islands
(New Zealand)
Macauley Island
Curtis Island

Havre Rock
L'Espérance Rock

30°

man Sea

Three Kings
Islands
North
Cape
Cape
Maria van Diemen · Awanui
Whangarei

North Island
(Te Ika-a-Māui)
Great Barrier Island

Takapuna · Auckland
Manukau
Hamilton · Tauranga
Te Kuiti
Tokoroa
Taupo · Whakatane
Te Kuiti · Gisborne
Rotorua
New
Plymouth · Mount
Mount Taranaki 2518 · Ruapehu
(Mount Egmont) 1751
Hawera · Napier
Wanganui · Hastings
Palmerston North
Levin
Masterton
Nelson · Lower Hutt
Blenheim · WELLINGTON
WELLINGTON

East Cape

Wairoa
Mahia Peninsula

Chatham Islands
(New Zealand)

Chatham Island

5

**NEW
ZEALAND**

South Island
(Te Waipounamu)

Westport
Hokitika
Greymouth

Picton
Tasman
Bay
Cook
Strait

Waitangi
Pitt Island

40°

Mount
Aspiring
3030
Mount
Christina
2502
Cape Providence

Aoraki/
Mount Cook
3724
Southern Alps
Queenstown
Timaru
Oamaru

Christchurch
Banks Peninsula
Ashburton

Gore
Invercargill · Dunedin
Stewart Island
South West Cape
Foveaux Strait
Snares
Islands

Bounty Islands
(New Zealand)

6

Auckland Islands
(New Zealand)

Antipodes Islands
(New Zealand)

G · 160° · H · 170° · 180° · I · 170° · J · 160° · K · 150° W · L

Oceania
Australia, New Zealand and Southwest Pacific

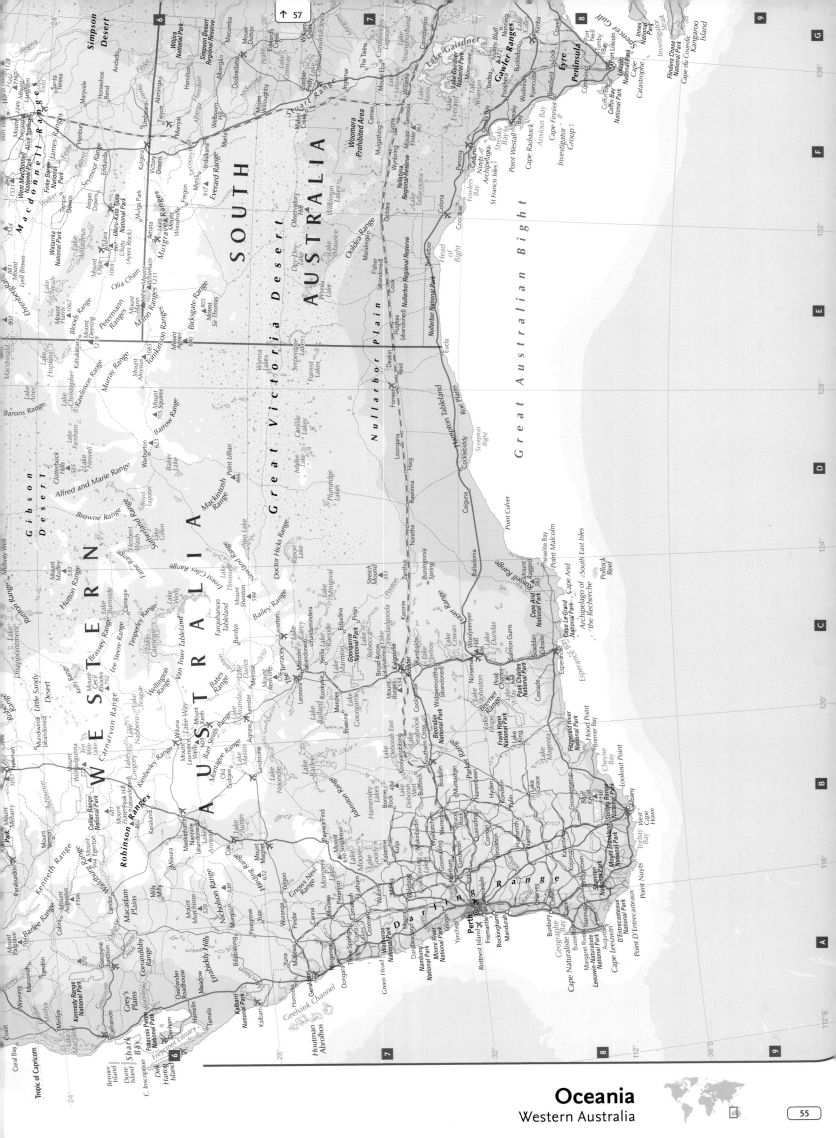

Oceania
Western Australia

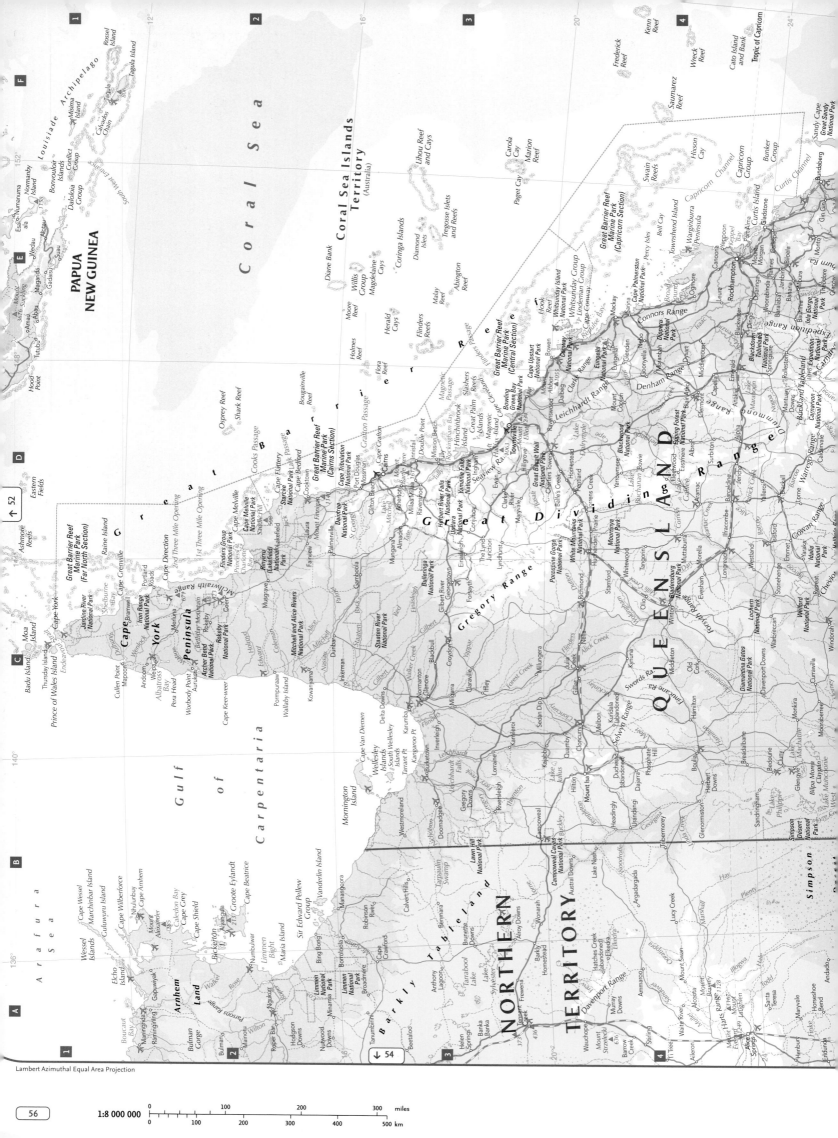

Oceania

Eastern Australia

Oceania
Southeast Australia

Lambert Azimuthal Equal Area Projection

1:5 000 000

Conic Equidistant Projection

1:5 250 000

Oceania
New Zealand

Lambert Conformal Conic Projection

1:16 000 000

States in the U.S.A.
numbered on the map:

1. CONNECTICUT (K5)
2. MASSACHUSETTS (K5)
3. NEW HAMPSHIRE (K5)
4. RHODE ISLAND (K5)
5. VERMONT (K5)

North America
Canada

Lambert Conformal Conic Projection

1:12 000 000

North America
United States of America

North America
Northeast United States

Lambert Conformal Conic Projection

1:3 500 000

North America

Southwest United States

Lambert Conformal Conic Projection

1:3 500 000

Lambert Conformal Conic Projection

1:14 000 000

North America
Central America and the Caribbean

PACIFIC

OCEAN

Galapagos Islands
(Islas Galápagos)
(Ecuador)

Parque Nacional
Galápagos

Equator

Isla Fernandina

Isla Isabela

Isla
Santiago

Isla
Santa Cruz

Isla
San Cristóbal

Isla
Floreana

Baquerizo Moreno

1:14 000 000

miles 100

km 150

NICARAGUA

MANAGUA

COSTA RICA

SAN JOSÉ

PANAMA

PANAMA CITY

COLOMBIA

BOGOTÁ

ECUADOR

QUITO

Guayaquil

PERU

LIMA

Callao

BOLIVIA

LA PAZ

SUCRE

CHILE

VENEZUELA

CARACAS

TRINIDAD
AND
TOBAGO

GRENADA

ARGENTINA

Equator

Tropic of Capricorn

Lambert Azimuthal Equal Area Projection

1:14 000 000

miles
0   200   400

0   200   400   600   800 km

South America
Northern South America

South America
Southern South America

1:14 000 000

Lambert Azimuthal Equal Area Projection

South America
Southeast Brazil

1:7 000 000

Lambert Azimuthal Equal Area Projection

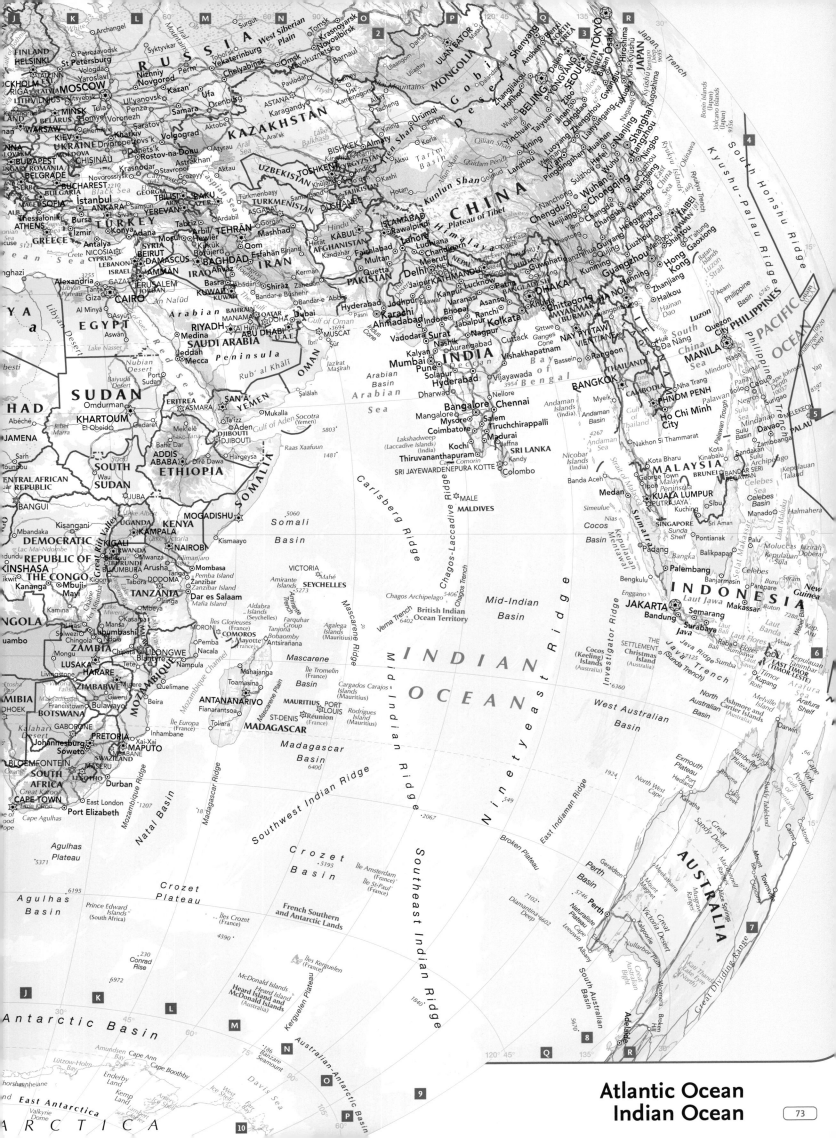

Atlantic Ocean
Indian Ocean

73

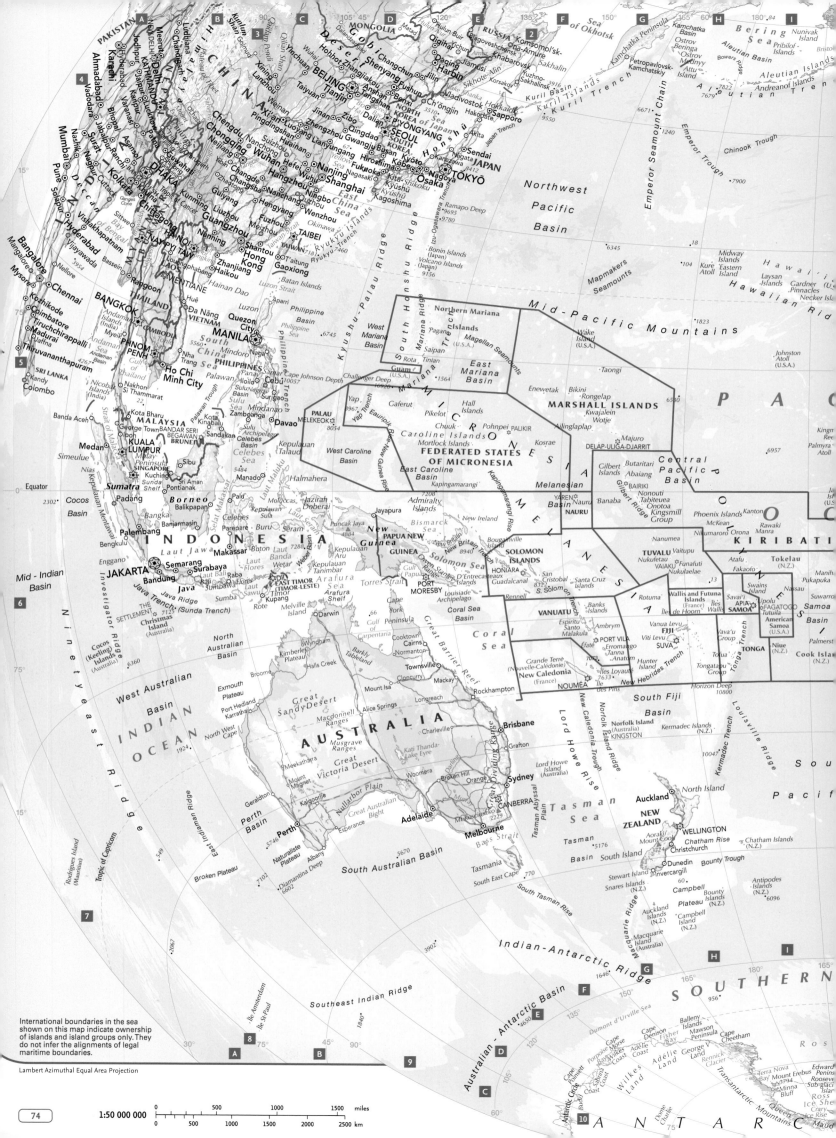

International boundaries in the sea shown on this map indicate ownership of islands and island groups only. They do not infer the alignments of legal maritime boundaries.

Lambert Azimuthal Equal Area Projection

1:50 000 000

| 0 | 500 | 1000 | 1500 miles |

| 0 | 500 | 1000 | 1500 | 2000 | 2500 km |

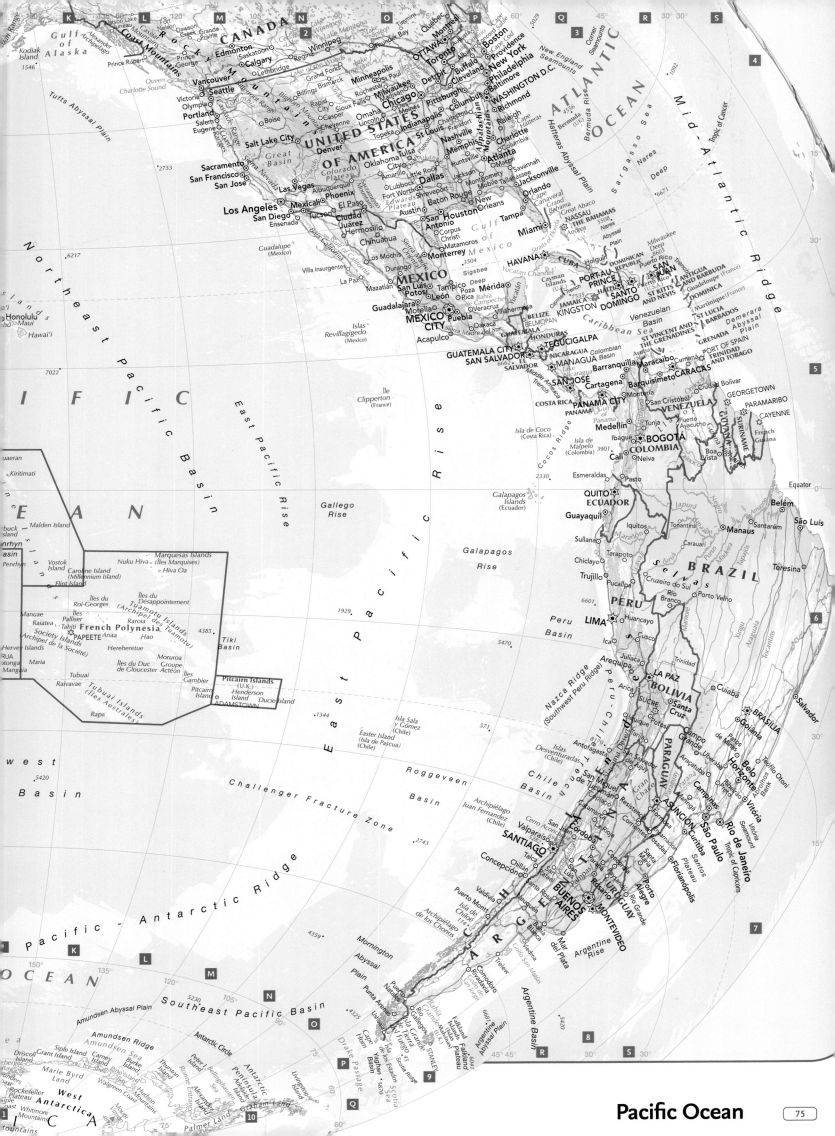

Pacific Ocean

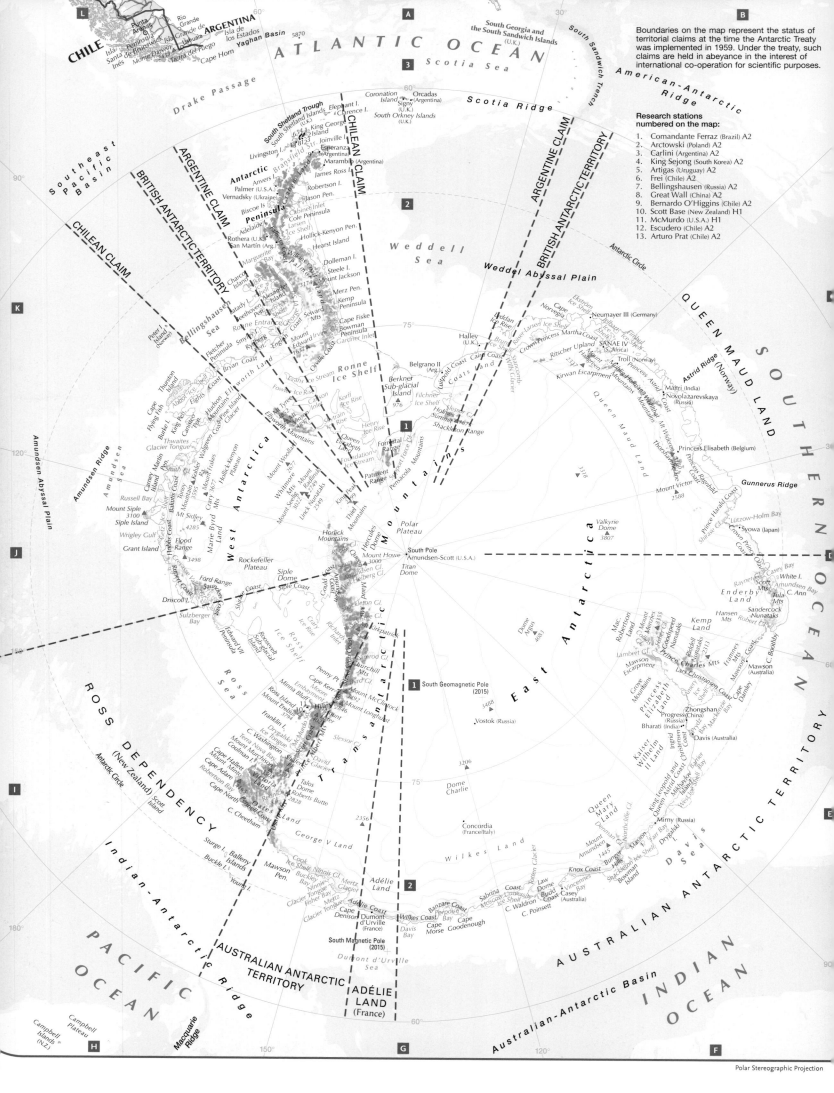

Boundaries on the map represent the status of territorial claims at the time the Antarctic Treaty was implemented in 1959. Under the treaty, such claims are held in abeyance in the interest of international co-operation for scientific purposes.

Research stations numbered on the map:

1. Comandante Ferraz (Brazil) A2
2. Arctowski (Poland) A2
3. Carlini (Argentina) A2
4. King Sejong (South Korea) A2
5. Artigas (Uruguay) A2
6. Frei (Chile) A2
7. Bellingshausen (Russia) A2
8. Great Wall (China) A2
9. Bernardo O'Higgins (Chile) A2
10. Scott Base (New Zealand) H1
11. McMurdo (U.S.A.) H1
12. Escudero (Chile) A2
13. Arturo Prat (Chile) A2

1:26 000 000

Polar Stereographic Projection

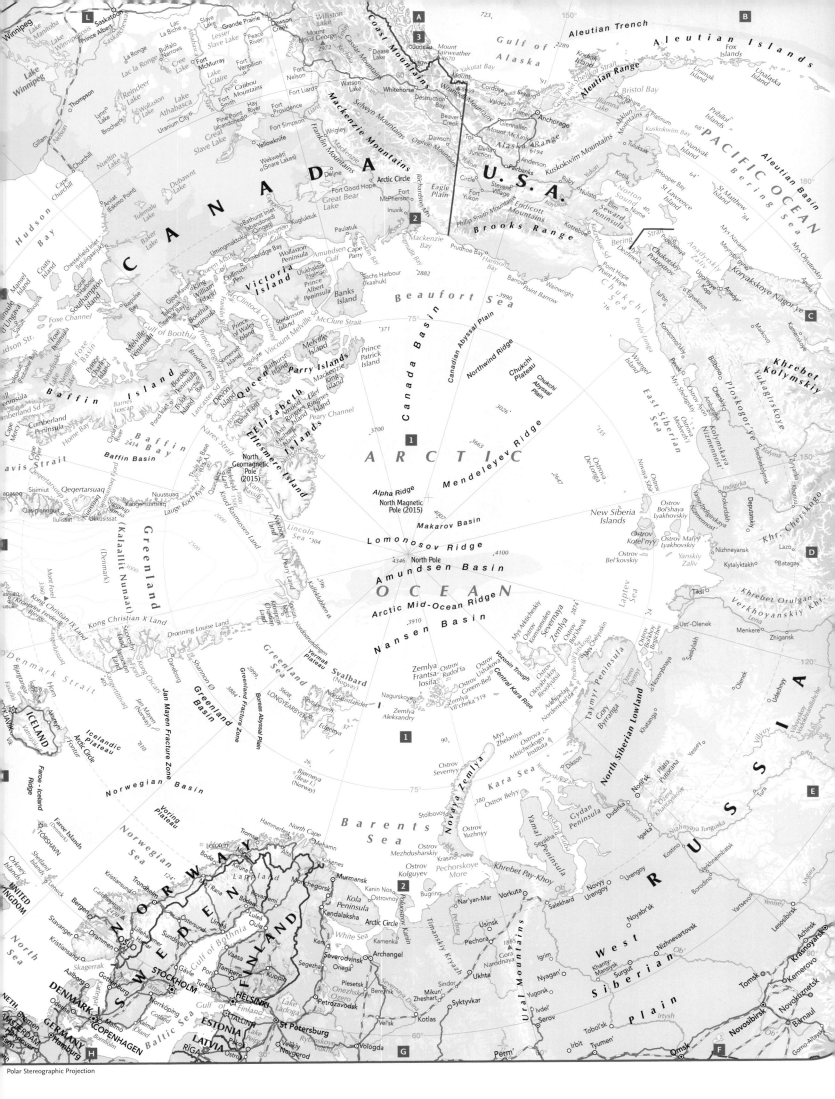

The Arctic

Polar Stereographic Projection

1:26 000 000

| 0 | 200 | 400 | 600 | 800 | 1000 miles |
| 0 | 200 | 400 | 600 | 800 | 1000 | 1200 | 1400 | 1600 km |

Index

Introduction to the index

The index includes all names shown on the reference maps in the atlas. Each entry includes the country or geographical area in which the feature is located, a page number and an alphanumeric reference. Additional entry details and aspects of the index are explained below.

Name forms

The names policy in this atlas is generally to use local name forms which are officially recognized by the governments of the countries concerned. Rules established by the Permanent Committee on Geographical Names for British Official Use (PCGN) are applied to the conversion of non-roman alphabet names, for example in the Russian Federation, into the roman alphabet used in English.

However, English conventional name forms are used for the most well-known places for which such a form is in common use. In these cases, the local form is included in brackets on the map and appears as a cross-reference in the index. Other alternative names, such as well-known historical names or those in other languages, may also be included in brackets on the map and as cross-references in the index. All country names and those for international physical features appear in their English forms. Names appear in full in the index, although they may appear in abbreviated form on the maps.

Referencing

Names are referenced by page number and by grid reference. The grid reference relates to the alphanumeric values which appear on the edges of each map. These reflect the graticule on the map – the letter relates to longitude divisions, the number to latitude divisions.

Names are generally referenced to the largest scale map page on which they appear. For large geographical features, including countries, the reference is to the largest scale map on which the feature appears in its entirety, or on which the majority of it appears.

Rivers are referenced to their lowest downstream point – either their mouth or their confluence with another river. The river name will generally be positioned as close to this point as possible.

Alternative names

Alternative names appear as cross-references and refer the user to the index entry for the form of the name used on the map.

For rivers with multiple names - for example those which flow through several countries - all alternative name forms are included within the main index entries, with details of the countries in which each form applies.

Administrative qualifiers

Administrative divisions are included in entries to differentiate duplicate names - entries of exactly the same name and feature type within the one country - where these division names are shown on the maps. In such cases, duplicate names are alphabetized in the order of the administrative division names.

Additional qualifiers are included for names within selected geographical areas, to indicate more clearly their location.

Descriptors

Entries, other than those for towns and cities, include a descriptor indicating the type of geographical feature. Descriptors are not

included where the type of feature is implicit in the name itself, unless there is a town or city of exactly the same name.

Insets

Where relevant, the index clearly indicates [inset] if a feature appears on an inset map.

Alphabetical order

The Icelandic characters Þ and þ are transliterated and alphabetized as 'Th' and 'th'. The German character ß is alphabetized as 'ss'. Names beginning with Mac or Mc are alphabetized exactly as they appear. The terms Saint, Sainte, etc, are abbreviated to St, Ste, etc, but alphabetized as if in the full form.

Numerical entries

Entries beginning with numerals appear at the beginning of the index, in numerical order. Elsewhere, numerals are alphabetized before 'a'.

Permuted terms

Names beginning with generic geographical terms are permuted - the descriptive term is placed after, and the index alphabetized by, the main part of the name. For example, Mount Everest is indexed as Everest, Mount; Lake Superior as Superior, Lake. This policy is applied to all languages. Permuting has not been applied to names of towns, cities or administrative divisions beginning with such geographical terms. These remain in their full form, for example, Lake Isabella, USA.

Abbreviations

admin. dist.	administrative district	ID	Idaho	pen.	peninsula
admin. div.	administrative division	IL	Illinois	Phil.	Philippines
admin. reg.	administrative region	imp. l.	impermanent lake	plat.	plateau
Afgh.	Afghanistan	IN	Indiana	P.N.G.	Papua New Guinea
AK	Alaska	Indon.	Indonesia	Port.	Portugal
AL	Alabama	Kazakh.	Kazakhstan	pref.	prefecture
Alg.	Algeria	KS	Kansas	prov.	province
AR	Arkansas	KY	Kentucky	pt	point
Arg.	Argentina	Kyrg.	Kyrgyzstan	Qld	Queensland
aut. comm.	autonomous community	l.	lake	Que.	Québec
aut. reg.	autonomous region	LA	Louisiana	r.	river
aut. rep.	autonomous republic	lag.	lagoon	reg.	region
AZ	Arizona	Lith.	Lithuania	res.	reserve
Azer.	Azerbaijan	Lux.	Luxembourg	resr	reservoir
b.	bay	MA	Massachusetts	RI	Rhode Island
Bangl.	Bangladesh	Madag.	Madagascar	S.	South, Southern
B.C.	British Columbia	Man.	Manitoba	S.A.	South Australia
Bol.	Bolivia	MD	Maryland	salt l.	salt lake
Bos. & Herz.	Bosnia and Herzegovina	ME	Maine	Sask.	Saskatchewan
Bulg.	Bulgaria	Mex.	Mexico	SC	South Carolina
c.	cape	MI	Michigan	SD	South Dakota
CA	California	MN	Minnesota	sea chan.	sea channel
Cent. Afr. Rep.	Central African Republic	MO	Missouri	Sing.	Singapore
CO	Colorado	Mont.	Montenegro	Switz.	Switzerland
Col.	Colombia	Moz.	Mozambique	Tajik.	Tajikistan
CT	Connecticut	MS	Mississippi	Tanz.	Tanzania
Czech Rep.	Czech Republic	MT	Montana	Tas.	Tasmania
DC	District of Columbia	mt.	mountain	terr.	territory
DE	Delaware	mts	mountains	Thai.	Thailand
Dem. Rep. Congo	Democratic Republic of the Congo	N.	North, Northern	TN	Tennessee
depr.	depression	nat. park	national park	Trin. and Tob.	Trinidad and Tobago
des.	desert	N.B.	New Brunswick	Turkm.	Turkmenistan
disp. terr.	disputed territory	NC	North Carolina	TX	Texas
Dom. Rep.	Dominican Republic	ND	North Dakota	U.A.E.	United Arab Emirates
E.	East, Eastern	NE	Nebraska	U.K.	United Kingdom
Equat. Guinea	Equatorial Guinea	Neth.	Netherlands	Ukr.	Ukraine
esc.	escarpment	NH	New Hampshire	U.S.A.	United States of America
est.	estuary	NJ	New Jersey	UT	Utah
Eth.	Ethiopia	NM	New Mexico	Uzbek.	Uzbekistan
Fin.	Finland	N.S.	Nova Scotia	VA	Virginia
FL	Florida	N.S.W.	New South Wales	Venez.	Venezuela
for.	forest	N.T.	Northern Territory	Vic.	Victoria
Fr. Guiana	French Guiana	NV	Nevada	vol.	volcano
F.Y.R.O.M.	Former Yugoslav Republic of Macedonia	N.W.T.	Northwest Territories	vol. crater	volcanic crater
g.	gulf	NY	New York	VT	Vermont
GA	Georgia	N.Z.	New Zealand	W.	West, Western
Guat.	Guatemala	OH	Ohio	WA	Washington
HI	Hawaii	OK	Oklahoma	W.A.	Western Australia
H.K.	Hong Kong	OR	Oregon	WI	Wisconsin
Hond.	Honduras	PA	Pennsylvania	WV	West Virginia
i.	island	Para.	Paraguay	WY	Wyoming
IA	Iowa	P.E.I.	Prince Edward Island	Y.T.	Yukon

1

1st Three Mile Opening *sea chan.* Australia **56** D2
2nd Three Mile Opening *sea chan.* Australia **56** C2
5 de Outubro Angola *see* **Xá-Muteba**
9 de Julio Arg. **70** D5
25 de Mayo *Buenos Aires* Arg. **70** D5
25 de Mayo *La Pampa* Arg. **70** C5
100 Mile House *B.C.* Canada **62** C1

A

Aabenraa Denmark **15** F9
Aachen Germany **17** K5
Aalborg Denmark **15** F8
Aalborg Bugt *b.* Denmark **15** G8
Aalen Germany **17** M6
Aalesund Norway *see* **Ålesund**
Aaley Lebanon *see* **Aley**
Aalo India **37** H3
Aalst Belgium **16** J5
Aanaar Fin. *see* **Inari**
Aarhus Denmark **15** G8
Aarlen Belgium *see* **Arlon**
Aars Denmark **15** F8
Aasiaat Greenland **61** M3
Aba China **42** I6
Aba Dem. Rep. Congo **48** D3
Aba Nigeria **46** D4
Abacaxis *r.* Brazil **69** G4
Ābādān Iran **35** H5
Abadan Turkm. **33** I2
Ābādeh Iran **35** I5
Ābādeh Ţashk Iran **35** I5
Abadla Alg. **22** D5
Abaeté Brazil **71** B2
Abaetetuba Brazil **69** I4
Abagnar Qi China *see* **Xilinhot**
Abaiang *atoll* Kiribati **74** H5
Abakaliki Nigeria **46** D4
Abakan Russia **42** G2
Abakanskiy Khrebet *mts* Russia **42** F2
Abalak Niger **46** D3
Abana Turkey **34** D2
Abancay Peru **68** D6
Abariringa *atoll* Kiribati *see* **Kanton**
Abarkūh Iran **35** I5
Abarkūh, Kavīr-e *des.* Iran **35** I5
Abarshahr Iran *see* **Neyshābūr**
Abashiri Japan **44** G3
Abashiri-wan *b.* Japan **44** G3
Abau P.N.G. **56** E1
Abaya, Lake Eth. **48** D3
Ābaya Hāyk' *l.* Eth. *see* **Abaya, Lake**
Ābay Wenz *r.* Eth./Sudan *see* **Blue Nile**
Abaza Russia **42** G2
Abba Cent. Afr. Rep. **48** B3
'Abbāsābād Iran **35** I4
Abbasanta *Sardinia* Italy **26** C4
Abbatis Villa France *see* **Abbeville**
Abbe, Lake Djibouti/Eth. **32** F7
Abbeville France **24** E1
Abbeville *LA* U.S.A. **63** I6
Abbeyfeale Ireland **21** C5
Abbeytown U.K. **18** D4
Abborrträsk Sweden **14** K4
Abbot, Mount Australia **56** D4
Abbot Ice Shelf Antarctica **76** K2
Abbott *VA* U.S.A. **64** A4
Abbottabad Pak. **33** L3
'Abd al 'Azīz, Jabal *h.* Syria **35** F3
'Abd al Kūrī *i.* Yemen **32** H7
'Abd Allah, Khawr *sea chan.* Iraq/Kuwait **35** H5
Abd al Ma'asīr *well* Saudi Arabia **39** D4
Ābdānān Iran **35** G4
'Abdollāhābād Iran **35** I4
Abdulino Russia **11** Q5
Abéché Chad **47** F3
Abellinum Italy *see* **Avellino**
Abel Tasman National Park N.Z. **59** D5
Abengourou Côte d'Ivoire **46** C4
Åbenrå Denmark *see* **Aabenraa**
Abeokuta Nigeria **46** D4
Aberaeron U.K. **19** C6
Aberchirder U.K. **20** G3
Abercorn Zambia *see* **Mbala**
Abercrombie *r.* Australia **58** D4
Aberdare U.K. **19** D7
Aberdaron U.K. **19** C6
Aberdaugleddau U.K. *see* **Milford Haven**
Aberdeen Australia **58** E4
Aberdeen S. Africa **50** G7
Aberdeen U.K. **20** G3
Aberdeen *SD* U.S.A. **62** H2
Aberdeen Lake *Nunavut* Canada **61** I3
Aberdovey U.K. **19** C6
Aberfeldy U.K. **20** F4
Aberford U.K. **18** F5
Aberfoyle U.K. **20** E4
Abergavenny U.K. **19** D7
Abergwaun U.K. *see* **Fishguard**
Aberhonddu U.K. *see* **Brecon**
Abermaw U.K. *see* **Barmouth**
Aberporth U.K. **19** C6
Abersoch U.K. **19** C6
Abertawe U.K. *see* **Swansea**
Aberteifi U.K. *see* **Cardigan**
Aberystwyth U.K. **19** C6
Abeshr Chad *see* **Abéché**
Abez' Russia **11** S2
Abhā Saudi Arabia **32** F6
Abhar Iran **35** H3
Abiad, Bahr el *r.* Africa *see* **White Nile**
Abidjan Côte d'Ivoire **46** C4
Abijatta-Shalla National Park Eth. **48** D3
Abilene *TX* U.S.A. **62** H5
Abingdon U.K. **19** F7
Abington Reef Australia **56** E3
Abinsk Russia **34** E1
Abitibi, Lake *Ont./Que.* Canada **63** K2
Abkhazia *disp. terr.* Georgia **35** F2
Abminga Australia **55** F6
Abnūb Egypt **34** C6
Åbo Fin. *see* **Turku**
Abohar India **36** C3
Aboisso Côte d'Ivoire **46** C4
Abomey Benin **46** D4
Abong Mbang Cameroon **46** E4
Abou Déia Chad **47** E3
Abovyan Armenia **35** G2
Aboyne U.K. **20** G3
Abqaiq Saudi Arabia **48** E1
Abramovskiy, Mys *pt* Russia **12** I2
Abrantes Port. **25** B4
Abra Pampa Arg. **70** C2
'Abri Sudan **32** D5
Abrolhos Bank *sea feature* S. Atlantic Ocean **72** F7
Abruzzo, Lazio e Molise, Parco Nazionale d' *nat. park* Italy **26** E4
Absaroka Range *mts WY* U.S.A. **62** E3
Abtar, Jabal al *hills* Syria **39** C2
Abū aḑ Ḑuhūr Syria **39** C2
Abū al Ḩusayn, Qā' *imp. l.* Jordan **39** D3
Abū 'Alī *i.* Saudi Arabia **35** H6
Abū 'Āmūd, Wādī *watercourse* Jordan **39** C4
Abū 'Arīsh Saudi Arabia **32** F6
Abu 'Aweigîla *well* Egypt *see* **Abū 'Uwayqīlah**
Abu Deleiq Sudan **32** D6
Abu Dhabi U.A.E. **33** H5
Abū Du'ān Syria **39** D1
Abu Gubeiha Sudan **32** D7
Abū Ḩafnah, Wādī *watercourse* Jordan **39** D3
Abu Haggag Egypt *see* **Ra's al Ḩikmah**
Abū Ḩallūfah, Jabal *h.* Jordan **39** C4
Abu Hamed Sudan **32** D6
Abuja Nigeria **46** D4
Abū Jurdhān Jordan **39** B4
Abū Kamāl Syria **35** F4
Abu Matariq Sudan **47** F3
Abumombazi Dem. Rep. Congo **48** C3
Abunã *r.* Bol. **68** E5
Abunã Brazil **68** E5
Ābune Yosēf *mt.* Eth. **32** E7
Abū Nujaym Libya **47** E1
Abū Qa'ţūr Syria **39** C2
Abū Rawthah, Jabal *mt.* Egypt **39** B5
Aburo *mt.* Dem. Rep. Congo **48** D3
Abu Road India **31** G4
Abū Rujmayn, Jabal *mts* Syria **39** D2
Abu Rûtha, Gebel *mt.* Egypt *see* **Abū Rawthah, Jabal**
Abu Simbil Egypt *see* **Abū Sunbul**
Abū Sunbul Egypt **32** D5
Abū Ţarfā', Wādī *watercourse* Egypt **39** A5
Abut Head *hd* N.Z. **59** C6
Abū 'Uwayqīlah *well* Egypt **39** B4
Abu Zabad Sudan **32** C7
Abū Ẓabī U.A.E. *see* **Abu Dhabi**
Abū Zanīmah Egypt **34** D5
Abu Zenîma Egypt *see* **Abū Zanīmah**
Abyad Sudan **32** C7
Abyaḑ, Jabal al *mts* Syria **39** C2
Abyār al Ḩakīm *well* Libya **34** A5
Abydos Australia **54** B5
Abyei Sudan **32** C8
Abyssinia *country* Africa *see* **Ethiopia**
Academician Vernadskiy *research stn* Antarctica *see* **Vernadsky**
Academy Bay Russia *see* **Akademii, Zaliv**
Acadia *prov.* Canada *see* **Nova Scotia**
Açailândia Brazil **69** I5
Acamarachi *mt.* Chile *see* **Pili, Cerro**
Acampamento de Caça do Mucusso Angola **49** C5
Acandí Col. **68** C2
A Cañiza Spain **25** B2
Acaponeta Mex. **66** C4
Acapulco Mex. **66** E5
Acapulco de Juárez Mex. *see* **Acapulco**
Acará Brazil **69** I4
Acarai Mountains *hills* Brazil/Guyana **69** G3
Acaraú Brazil **69** J4
Acaray, Represa de *resr* Para. **70** E3
Acarigua Venez. **68** E2
Acatlán Mex. **66** E5
Accho Israel *see* **'Akko**
Accomac *VA* U.S.A. **64** D4
Accra Ghana **46** C4
Accrington U.K. **18** E5
Achacachi Bol. **68** E7
Achaguas Venez. **68** E2
Achalpur India **36** D5
Achampet India **38** C2
Achan Russia *see* **Bolon'**
Achayvayam Russia **29** S3
Acheng China **44** B3
Achhota India **38** D1
Achill Ireland **21** C4
Achillbeg Island Ireland **21** C4
Achill Island Ireland **21** B4
Achiltibuie U.K. **20** D2
Achinsk Russia **28** K4
Achit Russia **11** R4
Achit Nuur *l.* Mongolia **42** G3
Achkhoy-Martan Russia **35** G2
Achna Cyprus **39** A2
Achnasheen U.K. **20** D3
Acıgöl *l.* Turkey **27** M6
Acıpayam Turkey **27** M6
Acireale *Sicily* Italy **26** F6
Acklins Island Bahamas **67** J4
Acle U.K. **19** I6
Aconcagua, Cerro *mt.* Arg. **70** B4
Acopiara Brazil **69** K5
Açores *terr.* N. Atlantic Ocean *see* **Azores**
Açores, Arquipélago dos *terr.* N. Atlantic Ocean *see* **Azores**
A Coruña Spain **25** B2
Acquaviva delle Fonti Italy **26** G4
Acqui Terme Italy **26** C2
Acra *NY* U.S.A. **64** D1
Acragas *Sicily* Italy *see* **Agrigento**
Acraman, Lake *imp. l.* Australia **57** A7
Acre *r.* Brazil **68** E6
Acre Israel *see* **'Akko**
Acre, Bay of Israel *see* **Haifa, Bay of**
Acri Italy **26** G5
Ács Hungary **17** Q7
Actaeon Group *is* Fr. Polynesia *see* **Actéon, Groupe**
Actéon, Groupe *is* Fr. Polynesia **75** K7
Acton *Ont.* Canada **64** A1
Acton *CA* U.S.A. **65** C3
Açungui Brazil **71** A4
Acunum Acusio France *see* **Montélimar**
Ada *OK* U.S.A. **63** H5
Adaja *r.* Spain **25** D3
Adalia Turkey *see* **Antalya**
Adam Oman **33** I5
Adam, Mount *h.* Falkland Is **70** E8
Adamantina Brazil **71** A3
Adams *MA* U.S.A. **64** E1
Adam's Peak Sri Lanka **38** D5
Adamstown Pitcairn Is **75** L7
'Adan Yemen *see* **Aden**
Adana Turkey **39** B1
Adana *prov.* Turkey **39** B1
Adana Yemen *see* **Aden**
Adapazarı Turkey **27** N4
Adare Ireland **21** D5
Adare, Cape Antarctica **76** H2
Adavale Australia **57** D5
Ad Dabbah Sudan *see* **Ed Debba**
Ad Dafīnah Saudi Arabia **32** F5
Ad Dahnā' *des.* Saudi Arabia **32** G5
Ad Damir Sudan *see* **Ed Damer**
Ad Dammām Saudi Arabia *see* **Dammam**
Addanki India **38** C3
Ad Dār al Ḩamrā' Saudi Arabia **32** E4
Ad Darb Saudi Arabia **32** F6
Ad Dawādimī Saudi Arabia **32** F5
Ad Dawḩah Qatar *see* **Doha**
Ad Dawr Iraq **35** F4
Ad Daww *plain* Syria **39** C2
Ad Dayr Iraq **35** G5
Ad Dibdibah *plain* Saudi Arabia **35** G6
Ad Ḑiffah *plat.* Egypt *see* **Libyan Plateau**
Addis Ababa Eth. **48** D3
Addison *NY* U.S.A. **64** C1
Ad Dīwānīyah Iraq **35** G5
Addlestone U.K. **19** G7
Addo Elephant National Park S. Africa **51** G7
Ad Duqm Oman **33** I6
Ad Duwayd *well* Saudi Arabia **35** F5
Ad Duwaym Sudan *see* **Ed Dueim**
Adegaon India **36** D5
Adelaide Australia **57** B7
Adelaide *r.* Australia **54** E3
Adelaide Island Antarctica **76** L2
Adelaide River Australia **54** E3
Adele Island Australia **54** C3
Adélie Coast Antarctica **76** G2
Adélie Land Antarctica **76** G2
Adelong Australia **58** D5
Aden Yemen **32** F7
Aden, Gulf of Somalia/Yemen **32** G7
Adena *OH* U.S.A. **64** A2
Aderbissinat Niger **46** D3
Aderno *Sicily* Italy *see* **Adrano**
Adesar India **36** B5
Adh Dhāyūf *well* Saudi Arabia **35** G6
'Adhfā' *well* Saudi Arabia **35** F5
'Adhirīyāt, Jibāl al *mts* Jordan **39** C4
Adi *i.* Indon. **41** F8
Ādī Ārk'ay Eth. **32** E7
Adige *r.* Italy **26** E2
Ādīgrat Eth. **48** D2
Adilabad India **38** C2
Adilcevaz Turkey **35** F3
Adīrī Libya **47** E2
Adirondack Mountains *NY* U.S.A. **64** D1
Ādīs Ābeba Eth. *see* **Addis Ababa**
Adi Ugri Eritrea *see* **Mendefera**
Adıyaman Turkey **34** E3
Adjud Romania **27** L1
Admiralty Island *Nunavut* Canada **61** H3
Admiralty Island National Monument-Kootznoowoo Wilderness *nat. park AK* U.S.A. **60** E4
Admiralty Islands P.N.G. **52** E2
Ado-Ekiti Nigeria **46** D4
Adok South Sudan **32** D8
Adonara *i.* Indon. **54** C2
Adoni India **38** C3
Ado-Tymovo Russia **44** F2
Adour *r.* France **24** D5
Adra Spain **25** E5
Adramyttium Turkey *see* **Edremit**
Adramyttium, Gulf of Turkey *see* **Edremit Körfezi**
Adrano *Sicily* Italy **26** F6
Adrar Alg. **46** C2
Adrar *hills* Mali *see* **Ifôghas, Adrar des**
Adrar, Ḑahr *hills* Mauritania **46** B3
Adré Chad **47** F3
Adrian *TX* U.S.A. **62** G4
Adrianople Turkey *see* **Edirne**
Adrianopolis Turkey *see* **Edirne**
Adriatic Sea Europe **26** E2
Adua Eth. *see* **Ādwa**
Adunara *i.* Indon. *see* **Adonara**
Adusa Dem. Rep. Congo **48** C3
Aduwa Eth. *see* **Ādwa**
Adverse Well Australia **54** C5
Ādwa Eth. **48** D2
Adycha *r.* Russia **29** O3
Adyk Russia **13** J7
Adzopé Côte d'Ivoire **46** C4
Aegean Sea Greece/Turkey **27** K5
Aegina *i.* Greece *see* **Aigina**
Aegyptus *country* Africa *see* **Egypt**
Aela Jordan *see* **Al 'Aqabah**
Aelana Jordan *see* **Al 'Aqabah**
Aelia Capitolina Israel/West Bank *see* **Jerusalem**
Aelönlaplap *atoll* Marshall Is *see* **Ailinglaplap**
Aenus Turkey *see* **Enez**
Aesernia Italy *see* **Isernia**
A Estrada Spain **25** B2
Afabet Eritrea **32** E6
Afanas'yevo Russia **12** L4
Affreville Alg. *see* **Khemis Miliana**
Afghānestān *country* Asia *see* **Afghanistan**
Afghanistan *country* Asia **33** K3
Afgooye Somalia **48** E3
'Afīf Saudi Arabia **32** F5
Afiun Karahissar Turkey *see* **Afyon**
Åfjord Norway **14** G5
Aflou Alg. **22** E5
Afmadow Somalia **48** E3
Afogados da Ingazeira Brazil **69** K5
A Fonsagrada Spain **25** C2
Afonso Cláudio Brazil **71** C3
Āfrēra *vol.* Eth. **32** F7
Africa Nova *country* Africa *see* **Tunisia**
'Afrīn Syria **39** C1
'Afrīn, Nahr *r.* Syria/Turkey **39** C1
Afşin Turkey **34** E3
Afuá Brazil **69** H4
'Afula Israel **39** B3
Afyon Turkey **27** N5
Afyonkarahisar Turkey *see* **Afyon**
Agadès Niger *see* **Agadez**
Agadez Niger **46** D3
Agadir Morocco **46** C1
Agalega Islands Mauritius **73** L6
Agara Georgia **35** F2
Agartala India **37** G5
Agashi India **38** B2
Agathe France *see* **Agde**
Agathonisi *i.* Greece **27** L6
Agatti *i.* India **38** B4
Agboville Côte d'Ivoire **46** C4
Ağcabädi Azer. **35** G2
Ağdam (abandoned) Azer. **35** G3
Ağdaş Azer. **35** G2
Agdash Azer. *see* **Ağdaş**
Agde France **24** F5
Agdzhabedi Azer. *see* **Ağcabädi**
Agedabia Libya *see* **Ajdābiyā**
Agen France **24** E4
Aggeneys S. Africa **50** D5
Aggteleki *nat. park* Hungary **17** R6
Aghil Dawan China **36** D1
Ağın Turkey **34** E3
Aginskoye Russia **42** G1
Aginum France *see* **Agen**
Agios Dimitrios Greece **27** J6
Agios Efstratios *i.* Greece **27** K5
Agios Georgios *i.* Greece **27** J6
Agios Nikolaos Greece **27** K7
Agios Theodoros Cyprus **39** B2
Agiou Orous, Kolpos *b.* Greece **27** J4
Agirwat Hills Sudan **32** E6
Agisanang S. Africa **51** G4
Agnes, Mount *h.* Australia **55** E6
Agnew Australia **55** C6
Agnibilékrou Côte d'Ivoire **46** C4
Agnita Romania **27** K2
Agniye-Afanas'yevsk Russia **44** E2
Agra India **36** D4
Agrakhanskiy Poluostrov *pen.* Russia **35** G2
Agram Croatia *see* **Zagreb**
Ağrı Turkey **35** F3
Agria Gramvousa *i.* Greece **27** J7
Ağrı Dağı Turkey *see* **Ararat, Mount**
Agrigento *Sicily* Italy **26** E6
Agrigentum *Sicily* Italy *see* **Agrigento**
Agrinio Greece **27** I5
Agropoli Italy **26** F4
Agryz Russia **11** Q4
Ağsu Azer. **35** H2
Agua, Volcán de *vol.* Guat. **66** F6
Água Clara Brazil **70** F2
Aguadilla Puerto Rico **67** K5
Agua Escondida Arg. **70** C5
Aguanga *CA* U.S.A. **65** D4
Aguapeí *r.* Brazil **71** A3
Agua Prieta Mex. **66** C2
Aguaro-Guariquito, Parque Nacional *nat. park* Venez. **68** E2
Aguascalientes Mex. **66** D4
Agudos Brazil **71** A3
Águeda Port. **25** B3
Aguemour *reg.* Alg. **46** D2
Aguié Niger **46** D3
Aguilar de Campoo Spain **25** D2
Águilas Spain **25** F5
Agulhas, Cape S. Africa **50** E8
Agulhas Basin *sea feature* Southern Ocean **73** J9
Agulhas Negras *mt.* Brazil **71** B3
Agulhas Plateau *sea feature* Southern Ocean **73** J8
Agulhas Ridge *sea feature* S. Atlantic Ocean **72** I8
Ağva Turkey **27** M4
Agvali Russia **35** G2
Ahaggar *plat.* Alg. **46** D2
Ahaggar, Tassili oua-n- *plat.* Alg. **46** D2
Ahar Iran **35** G3
Ahaura N.Z. **59** C6
Ahipara Bay N.Z. **59** D2
Ahiri India **38** D2
Ahklun Mountains *AK* U.S.A. **60** B4
Ahmadabad India **36** C5
Aḩmad al Bāqir, Jabal *mt.* Jordan **39** B5
Ahmadnagar India **38** B2
Ahmadpur East Pak. **33** L4
Ahmar *mts* Eth. **48** E3
Ahmar Mountains Eth. *see* **Ahmar**
Ahmedabad India *see* **Ahmadabad**
Ahmednagar India *see* **Ahmadnagar**
Ahram Iran **35** H5
Ähtäri Fin. **14** N5
Ahtme Estonia **15** O7
Āhū Iran **35** H5
Ahun France **24** F3
Ahvāz Iran **35** H5
Ahwa India **38** B1
Ahwāz Iran *see* **Ahvāz**
Ai-Ais Namibia **50** C4
Ai-Ais Hot Springs and Fish River Canyon Park *nature res.* Namibia **50** C4
Aībak Afgh. **36** B1
Aicheng China *see* **Yuanling**
Aichwara India **36** D4
Aigialousa Cyprus **39** B2
Aigina *i.* Greece **27** J6
Aigio Greece **27** J5
Aigle de Chambeyron *mt.* France **24** H4
Aigüestortes i Estany de Sant Maurici, Parc Nacional d' *nat. park* Spain **25** G2
Ai He *r.* China **44** B4
Aihui China *see* **Heihe**
Aijal India *see* **Aizawl**
Aikawa Japan **45** E5
Aiken *SC* U.S.A. **63** K5
Aileron Australia **54** F5
Ailinglabelab *atoll* Marshall Is *see* **Ailinglaplap**
Ailinglaplap *atoll* Marshall Is **74** H5
Ailsa Craig *Ont.* Canada **64** A1
Ailsa Craig *i.* U.K. **20** D5
Ailt an Chorráin Ireland **21** D3
Aimorés, Serra dos *hills* Brazil **71** C2
Aïn Beïda Alg. **26** B7
'Aïn Ben Tili Mauritania **46** C2
'Ain Dâlla *spring* Egypt *see* **'Ayn Dāllah**
Aïn Defla Alg. **25** H5
Aïn Deheb Alg. **25** G6
Aïn el Hadjel Alg. **25** H6
'Ain el Maqfi *spring* Egypt *see* **'Ayn al Maqfī**
Aïn el Melh Alg. **25** I6
Aïn Mdila *well* Alg. **26** B7
Aïn-M'Lila Alg. **22** F4
Aïn Oussera Alg. **25** H6
Aïn Salah Alg. *see* **In Salah**
Aïn Sefra Alg. **22** D5
Ainsworth *NE* U.S.A. **62** H3
Aintab Turkey *see* **Gaziantep**
Aïn Taya Alg. **25** H5
Aïn Tédélès Alg. **25** G6
Aïn Temouchent Alg. **25** F6
'Ain Tibaghbagh *spring* Egypt *see* **'Ayn Tabaghbugh**
'Ain Timeira *spring* Egypt *see* **'Ayn Tumayrah**
'Ain Zeitûn Egypt *see* **'Ayn az Zaytūn**
Aiquile Bol. **68** E7
Aïr, Massif de l' *mts* Niger **46** D3
Airdrie *Alta* Canada **62** E1
Airdrie U.K. **20** F5
Aire-sur-l'Adour France **24** D5
Air Force Island *Nunavut* Canada **61** K3
Airpanas Indon. **54** D1
Aisatung Mountain Myanmar **37** H5
Aisne *r.* France **24** F2
Aïssa, Djebel *mt.* Alg. **22** D5
Aitamännikkö Fin. **14** N3
Aitana *mt.* Spain **25** F4
Aït Benhaddou *tourist site* Morocco **22** C5
Aiud Romania **27** J1
Aix France *see* **Aix-en-Provence**
Aix-en-Provence France **24** G5
Aix-la-Chapelle Germany *see* **Aachen**
Aix-les-Bains France **24** G4
Aiyina *i.* Greece *see* **Aigina**
Aíyion Greece *see* **Aigio**
Aizawl India **37** H5
Aizkraukle Latvia **15** N8
Aizpute Latvia **15** L8
Aizuwakamatsu Japan **45** E5
Ajaccio *Corsica* France **24** I6
Ajanta India **38** B1
Ajanta Range *hills* India *see* **Sahyadriparvat Range**
Ajaureforsen Sweden **14** I4
Ajayameru India *see* **Ajmer**
Ajdābiyā Libya **47** F1
a-Jiddét *des.* Oman *see* **Ḩarāsīs, Jiddat al**
Ajjer, Tassili n' Alg. **46** D2
Ajjer, Tassili n' *plat.* Alg. **46** D2
'Ajlūn Jordan **39** B3
Ajmer India **36** C4
Ajmer-Merwara India *see* **Ajmer**
Ajnala India **36** C3
Ajo *AZ* U.S.A. **65** F4
Ajrestān Afgh. **36** A2
Ajyyap Turkm. **35** I3
Akademii, Zaliv *b.* Russia **44** E1
Akadyr Kazakh. **42** C3
Akagera National Park Rwanda **48** D4
Akalkot India **38** C2
Akama, Akra *c.* Cyprus *see* **Arnauti, Cape**
Akamagaseki Japan *see* **Shimonoseki**
Akan Kokuritsu-kōen Japan **44** G4
Akaroa N.Z. **59** D6
Akāshat Iraq **35** E4
Akbarābād Iran **35** I5
Akbarpur *Uttar Prad.* India **36** E4
Akbarpur *Uttar Prad.* India **37** E4
Akbez Turkey **39** C1
Akçadağ Turkey **34** E3
Akçakale Turkey **39** D1
Akçakoca Turkey **27** N4
Akçakoca Dağları *mts* Turkey **27** N4
Akçakoyunlu Turkey **39** C1
Akçalı Dağları *mts* Turkey **39** A1
Akchâr *reg.* Mauritania **46** B3
Akdağlar *mts* Turkey **27** M6
Akdağmadeni Turkey **34** D3
Akdere Turkey **39** A1
Åkersberga Sweden **15** K7
Aketi Dem. Rep. Congo **48** C3
Akgyr Erezi *hills* Turkm. **35** I2
Akhali-Afoni Georgia *see* **Akhali Atoni**
Akhali Atoni Georgia **35** F2
Akhḑar, Al Jabal al *mts* Libya **47** F1
Akhḑar, Jabal *mts* Oman **33** I5
Akhisar Turkey **27** L5
Akhnoor India **36** C2
Akhsu Azer. *see* **Ağsu**
Akhta Armenia *see* **Hrazdan**
Akhtarīn Syria **39** C1
Akhtubinsk Russia **13** J6
Akhty Russia **35** G2
Akhtyrka Ukr. *see* **Okhtyrka**
Aki Japan **45** D6
Akiéni Gabon **48** B4
Akimiski Island *Nunavut* Canada **63** K1
Akishma *r.* Russia **44** D1
Akita Japan **45** F5
Akjoujt Mauritania **46** B3
Akkajaure *l.* Sweden **14** J3
Akkerman Ukr. *see* **Bilhorod-Dnistrovs'kyy**
Akkeshi Japan **44** G4
'Akko Israel **39** B3
Akkol' *Akmolinskaya Oblast'* Kazakh. **28** I4
Akkol' *Atyrauskaya Oblast'* Kazakh. **13** K7
Akku Kazakh. **42** D2
Akkul' Kazakh. *see* **Akkol'**
Akkuş Turkey **34** E2
Akkyr, Gory *hills* Turkm. *see* **Akgyr Erezi**
Aklavik *N.W.T.* Canada **60** E3
Aklera India **36** D4
Ak-Mechet Kazakh. *see* **Kyzylorda**
Akmeņrags *pt* Latvia **15** L8
Akmeqit China **36** D1
Akmola Kazakh. *see* **Astana**
Akmolinsk Kazakh. *see* **Astana**
Akobo South Sudan **47** G4
Akobo Wenz *r.* Eth./South Sudan **48** D3
Akokan Niger **46** D3
Akola India **38** C1
Akom II Cameroon **46** E4
Akonolinga Cameroon **46** E4
Akordat Eritrea **32** E6
Akören Turkey **34** D3
Akot India **36** D5
Akpatok Island *Nunavut* Canada **61** L3
Akqi China **42** D4
Akra, Jabal *mt.* Syria/Turkey *see* **Aqra', Jabal al**
Akranes Iceland **14** [inset 2]
Åkrehamn Norway **15** D7
Akrérèb Niger **46** D3
Akron *CO* U.S.A. **62** G3
Akron *OH* U.S.A. **64** A2
Akrotiri Bay Cyprus **39** A2
Akrotirion Bay Cyprus *see* **Akrotiri Bay**
Akrotiriou, Kolpos *b.* Cyprus *see* **Akrotiri Bay**
Akrotiri Sovereign Base Area *military base* Cyprus **39** A2
Aksai Chin *disp. terr.* Asia **36** D2
Aksaray Turkey **34** D3
Aksay China **42** G5
Aksay Kazakh. **11** Q5
Ak-Say *r.* Kyrg. **33** M1
Aksay Russia **13** H7
Akşehir Turkey **27** N5
Akşehir Gölü *l.* Turkey **27** N5
Akseki Turkey **34** C3
Aksha Russia **43** K2
Akshiganak Kazakh. **42** A3
Akshukyr Kazakh. **35** H2
Aksu China **42** E4
Aksu Kazakh. **42** D2
Aksu *r.* Turkey **27** N6
Aksuat Kazakh. **42** E3
Aksu-Ayuly Kazakh. **42** C3
Aksubayevo Russia **13** K5
Āksum Eth. **32** E7
Aktag *mt.* China **37** F1
Aktas Dağı *mt.* Turkey **35** G3
Aktau Kazakh. **30** E2
Aktobe Kazakh. **30** E1
Aktogay *Karagandinskaya Oblast'* Kazakh. **42** D3
Aktogay *Vostochnyy Kazakhstan* Kazakh. **42** D3
Aktsyabrski Belarus **13** F5
Aktyubinsk Kazakh. *see* **Aktobe**
Akulivik *Que.* Canada **61** K3
Akune Japan **45** C6
Akure Nigeria **46** D4
Akuressa Sri Lanka **38** D5
Akureyri Iceland **14** [inset 2]
Akusha Russia **13** J8
Akwanga Nigeria **46** D4
Akxokesay China **37** G1
Akyab Myanmar *see* **Sittwe**
Akyatan Gölü *salt l.* Turkey **39** B1
Akyazı Turkey **27** N4
Akzhaykyn, Ozero *salt l.* Kazakh. **42** B4
Ål Norway **15** F6
'Alā, Jabal al *hills* Syria **39** C2
Alabama *r. AL* U.S.A. **63** J5
Alabama *state* U.S.A. **63** J5
Al 'Abţīyah *well* Iraq **35** G5
Alaca Turkey **34** D2
Alacahan Turkey **34** E3
Alaçam Turkey **34** D2
Alaçam Dağları *mts* Turkey **27** M5
Alacant Spain *see* **Alicante**
Alaçatı Turkey **27** L5
Aladağ Turkey **34** D3
Ala Dağlar *mts* Turkey **35** F3
Ala Dağları *mts* Turkey **34** D3
Al 'Adam Libya **34** A5
Alag Hu *l.* China **37** I2
Alagir Russia **35** G2
Alagoinhas Brazil **71** D1
Alahärmä Fin. **14** M5
Al Aḩmadī Kuwait **35** H5
Alai Range *mts* Asia **33** L2
Ālājah Syria **39** B2
Alajärvi Fin. **14** M5
Al 'Ajrūd *well* Egypt **39** B4
Alakanuk *AK* U.S.A. **60** B3
Al Akhḑar Saudi Arabia **34** E5
Alakol', Ozero *salt l.* Kazakh. **28** J5
Ala Kul *salt l.* Kazakh. *see* **Alakol', Ozero**
Alakurtti Russia **12** F2
Al 'Alamayn Egypt **34** C5
Al 'Alayyah Saudi Arabia **32** F6
Alama Somalia **48** E3
Al 'Amārah Iraq **35** G5
'Alam ar Rūm, Ra's *pt* Egypt **34** B5
'Alāmarvdasht *watercourse* Iran **35** I5
Alameda *CA* U.S.A. **65** A2
'Alam el Rûm, Râs *pt* Egypt *see* **'Alam ar Rūm, Ra's**
Al Amghar *waterhole* Iraq **35** G5
Al 'Āmirīyah Egypt **34** C5
Alamo *NV* U.S.A. **65** E2
Alamo Dam *AZ* U.S.A. **65** F3
Alamogordo *NM* U.S.A. **62** F5
Alamos *Sonora* Mex. **66** B3
Alamos *Sonora* Mex. **66** C3
Alamos *r.* Mex. **62** G6
Alamosa *CO* U.S.A. **62** F4
Alampur India **38** C3
Alan Myanmar *see* **Aunglan**
Alanäs Sweden **14** I4
Åland *is* Fin. *see* **Åland Islands**
Aland India **38** C2
Al Andarīn Syria **39** C2
Åland Islands Fin. **15** K6
Alando China **37** H3
Alandur India **38** D3
Alanya Turkey **34** D3
Alaplı Turkey **27** N4
Alappuzha India **38** C4
Alapuzha India *see* **Alappuzha**
Al 'Aqabah Jordan **39** B5
'Alāqahdārī Gēlān Afgh. **36** A2
'Alāqahdārī Shāh Jōy Afgh. **36** A2
'Alāqahdārī Shumūlzaī Afgh. **36** A3
'Alāqahdārī-ye Kirān wa Munjān Afgh. **36** B1
Al 'Aqīq Saudi Arabia **32** F5
Al 'Arabīyah as Sa'ūdīyah *country* Asia *see* **Saudi Arabia**
Alarcón, Embalse de *resr* Spain **25** E4
Al 'Arīsh Egypt **39** A4
Al Arţāwīyah Saudi Arabia **32** G4
Alas, Selat *sea chan.* Indon. **54** B2
Alaşehir Turkey **27** M5
Alashiya *country* Asia *see* **Cyprus**
Al Ashmūnayn Egypt **34** C6
Alaska *state* U.S.A. **60** D3
Alaska, Gulf of *AK* U.S.A. **60** D4
Alaska Peninsula *AK* U.S.A. **60** B4
Alaska Range *mts AK* U.S.A. **60** D3
Ālāt Azer. **35** H3
Al Atwā' *well* Saudi Arabia **35** F5
Alatyr' Russia **13** J5
Alatyr' *r.* Russia **13** J5
Alausí Ecuador **68** C4
Alaverdi Armenia **35** G2
Alavieska Fin. **14** N4
'Alavījeh Iran **35** H4
Alavus Fin. **14** M5
Alawoona Australia **57** C7
Alay Kyrka Toosu *mts* Asia *see* **Alai Range**
Alayskiy Khrebet *mts* Asia *see* **Alai Range**
Al 'Azīzīyah Iraq **35** G4
Al 'Azīzīyah Libya **23** G5
Al Azraq al Janūbī Jordan **39** C4
Alba Italy **26** C2
Al Bāb Syria **39** C1
Albacete Spain **25** F4
Al Bādiyah al Janūbīyah *des.* Iraq **35** G5
Al Baḩrayn *country* Asia *see* **Bahrain**
Alba Iulia Romania **27** J1
Albājī Iran **35** H5
Albania *country* Europe **27** H4
Albany Australia **55** B8
Albany *r. Ont.* Canada **63** K1
Albany *GA* U.S.A. **63** K5
Albany *NY* U.S.A. **64** E1
Albany *OR* U.S.A. **62** C3
Albany Downs Australia **58** D1
Al Bārdah *hills* Saudi Arabia **39** D5
Al Başrah Iraq *see* **Basra**
Al Baţḩa' *marsh* Iraq **35** G5
Albatross Bay Australia **56** C2
Albatross Island Australia **57** [inset]
Al Bawīţī Egypt **34** C5
Al Bayḑā' Libya **32** B3
Al Bayḑā' Yemen **32** G7
Albemarle Island *Galápagos* Ecuador *see* **Isabela, Isla**
Albenga Italy **26** C2
Alberche *r.* Spain **25** D4
Alberga Australia **57** A5
Alberga *watercourse* Australia **57** A5
Albergaria-a-Velha Port. **25** B3
Albert Australia **58** C4
Albert France **24** F2
Albert, Lake Dem. Rep. Congo/Uganda **48** D3
Albert, Parc National *nat. park* Dem. Rep. Congo *see* **Virunga, Parc National des**
Alberta *prov.* Canada **62** E1
Alberta *VA* U.S.A. **64** C4
Albert Lea *MN* U.S.A. **63** I3
Albert Nile *r.* South Sudan/Uganda **47** G4
Alberto de Agostini, Parque Nacional *nat. park* Chile **70** B8
Alberton S. Africa **51** I4
Albertville Dem. Rep. Congo *see* **Kalemie**
Albertville France **24** H4
Albi France **24** F5
Albina Suriname **69** H2
Albino Italy **26** C2
Albion *NY* U.S.A. **64** B1
Albion *PA* U.S.A. **64** A2
Al Biqā' *val.* Lebanon *see* **El Béqaa**
Al Bi'r Saudi Arabia **34** E5
Al Birk Saudi Arabia **32** F6
Al Biyāḑh *reg.* Saudi Arabia **32** G5
Alborán, Isla de *i.* Spain **25** E6
Alboran Sea Europe **25**
Ålborg Denmark *see* **Aalborg**
Ålborg Bugt *b.* Denmark *see* **Aalborg Bugt**
Albro Australia **56** D4
Albufeira Port. **25** B5
Al Buḩayrāt al Murrah *lakes* Egypt *see* **Bitter Lakes**
Albuquerque *NM* U.S.A. **62** F4
Al Burayj Syria **39** C2
Al Buraymī Oman **33** I5
Al Burdī Libya **34** B5
Al Burj Jordan **39** B5
Alburquerque Spain **25** C4
Albury Australia **58** C6
Al Buşayrah Syria **35** F4
Al Busayţā' *plain* Saudi Arabia **39** D4
Al Bushūk *well* Saudi Arabia **35** G5
Alcácer do Sal Port. **25** B4
Alcalá de Henares Spain **25** E3
Alcalá la Real Spain **25** E5
Alcamo *Sicily* Italy **26** E6
Alcañiz Spain **25** F3
Alcántara Spain **25** C4
Alcaraz Spain **25** E4
Alcázar de San Juan Spain **25** E4
Alcazarquivir Morocco *see* **Ksar el Kebir**
Alchevs'k Ukr. **13** H6
Alcobaça Brazil **71** D2
Alcoi Spain *see* **Alcoy-Alcoi**
Alcoota Australia **54** F5
Alcoy Spain *see* **Alcoy-Alcoi**
Alcoy-Alcoi Spain **25** F4
Alcúdia Spain **25** H4
Aldabra Islands Seychelles **49** E4
Aldan Russia **29** N4
Aldan *r.* Russia **29** N3
Alde *r.* U.K. **19** I6
Aldeburgh U.K. **19** I6
Alder Creek *NY* U.S.A. **64** D1
Alderney *i.* Channel Is **19** E9
Alder Peak *CA* U.S.A. **65** B3
Aldershot U.K. **19** G7
Aldingham U.K. **18** D4
Aldridge U.K. **19** F6
Aleg Mauritania **46** B3
Alegre *Espírito Santo* Brazil **71** C3
Alegre *Minas Gerais* Brazil **71** B2

Anhwei prov. China see Anhui
Aniak AK U.S.A. 60 C3
Aniakchak National Monument and Preserve nat. park AK U.S.A. 60 C4
Anitápolis Brazil 71 A4
Anıtlı Turkey 39 A1
Aniva Russia 44 F3
Aniva, Mys c. Russia 44 F3
Aniva, Zaliv b. Russia 44 F3
Anjadip i. India 38 B3
Anjengo India see Anchuthengu
Anjīr Āvand Iran 35 I4
Anjou reg. France 24 D3
Anjouan i. Comoros see Ndzuani
Anjozorobe Madag. 49 E5
Anjuthengu India see Anchuthengu
Ankang China 43 J6
Ankara Turkey 34 D3
Ankaratra mt. Madag. 49 E5
Ankazoabo Madag. 49 E6
Ankleshwar India 36 C5
Anklesvar India see Ankleshwar
Ankola India 38 B3
Anlu China 43 K6
Anmoore WV U.S.A. 64 A3
An Muileann gCearr Ireland see Mullingar
Anmyeon-do i. S. Korea 45 B5
Ann, Cape Antarctica 76 D2
Ann, Cape MA U.S.A. 64 F1
Anna Russia 13 I6
Anna, Lake VA U.S.A. 64 C3
Annaba Alg. 26 B6
An Nābiyah Yemen 32 F7
An Nabk Saudi Arabia 39 C4
An Nabk Syria 39 C2
An Nafūd des. Saudi Arabia 35 F5
An Najaf Iraq 35 G5
Annalee r. Ireland 21 E3
Annalong U.K. 21 G3
Annan U.K. 20 F6
Annan r. U.K. 20 F6
'Annān, Wādī al watercourse Syria 39 D2
Annandale VA U.S.A. 64 C3
Anna Plains Australia 54 C4
Annapolis MD U.S.A. 64 C3
Annapurna Conservation Area nature res. Nepal 37 F3
Annapurna I mt. Nepal 37 E3
Ann Arbor MI U.S.A. 63 K3
Anna Regina Guyana 69 G2
An Nás Ireland see Naas
An Nāşirīyah Iraq 35 G5
Annean, Lake imp. l. Australia 55 B6
Annecy France 24 H4
An Nimārah Syria 39 C3
An Nimāş Saudi Arabia 32 F6
Anniston AL U.S.A. 63 J5
Annobón i. Equat. Guinea 46 D5
Annonay France 24 G4
An Nu'mānīyah Iraq 35 G4
Anorontany, Tanjona hd Madag. 49 E5
Anqing China 43 L6
Ansbach Germany 17 M6
Anser Group is Australia 58 C7
Anshan China 44 A4
Anshun Guizhou China 42 J7
Anshun Sichuan China 42 I7
Anson Bay Australia 54 E3
Ansongo Mali 46 D3
Ansted WV U.S.A. 64 A3
Antabamba Peru 68 D6
Antakya Turkey 39 C1
Antalaha Madag. 49 F5
Antalya Turkey 27 N6
Antalya prov. Turkey 39 A1
Antalya Körfezi g. Turkey 27 N6
Antananarivo Madag. 49 E5
An tAonach Ireland see Nenagh
Antarctica 76
Antarctic Peninsula Antarctica 76 L2
Antas r. Brazil 71 A5
An Teallach mt. U.K. 20 D3
Antelope Range mts NV U.S.A. 65 D1
Antequera Spain 25 D5
Anthony Lagoon Australia 56 A3
Anti-Atlas mts Morocco 22 C6
Antibes France 24 H5
Anticosti, Île d' i. Que. Canada 61 L5
Anticosti Island Que. Canada see Anticosti, Île d'
Antifer, Cap d' c. France 19 H9
Antigua i. Antigua and Barbuda 67 L5
Antigua country West Indies see Antigua and Barbuda
Antigua and Barbuda country West Indies 67 L5
Antikythira i. Greece 27 J7
Antikythiro, Steno sea chan. Greece 27 J7
Anti Lebanon mts Lebanon/Syria see Sharqī, Jabal ash
Antimilos i. Greece 27 K6
An tInbhear Mór Ireland see Arklow
Antioch Turkey see Antakya
Antioch CA U.S.A. 65 B1
Antiocheia ad Cragum tourist site Turkey 39 A1
Antiochia Turkey see Antakya
Antiparos i. Greece 27 K6
Antipodes Islands N.Z. 53 H6
Antipsara i. Greece 27 K5
Antium Italy see Anzio
Antofagasta Chile 70 B2
Antofagasta de la Sierra Arg. 70 C3
Antofalla, Volcán vol. Arg. 70 C3
António Enes Moz. see Angoche
Antri India 36 D4
Antrim U.K. 21 F3
Antrim Hills U.K. 21 F2
Antrim Plateau Australia 54 E4
Antropovo Russia 12 I4
Antsalova Madag. 49 E5
Antseranana Madag. see Antsirañana
Antsirabe Madag. 49 E5
Antsirañana Madag. 49 E5
Antsla Estonia 15 O8
Antsohihy Madag. 49 E5
Anttis Sweden 14 M3
Anttola Fin. 15 O6
Antwerp Belgium 16 J5
Antwerpen Belgium see Antwerp
An Uaimh Ireland see Navan
Anuchino Russia 44 D4
Anugul India see Angul
Anupgarh India 36 C3
Anuradhapura Sri Lanka 38 D4
Anveh Iran 35 I6
Anvers Island Antarctica 76 L2
Anvik AK U.S.A. 60 B3
Anxious Bay Australia 55 F8
Anyang China 43 K5
Anyang S. Korea 45 B5
A'nyêmaqên Shan mts China 42 H6
Anyuy r. Russia 44 E2
Anyuysk Russia 29 R3
Anzhero-Sudzhensk Russia 28 J4
Anzi Dem. Rep. Congo 48 C4
Anzio Italy 26 E4
Aoba i. Vanuatu 53 G3
Aoga-shima i. Japan 45 E6
Aomen China see Macao
Aomori Japan 44 F4
Aoraki/Mount Cook mt. N.Z. 59 C6
Aoraki/Mount Cook National Park N.Z. 59 C6
Aorangi mt. N.Z. see Aoraki/Mount Cook
Aosta Italy 26 B2
Aotearoa country Oceania see New Zealand
Aouk, Bahr r. Cent. Afr. Rep./Chad 47 E4
Aoukâr reg. Mali/Mauritania 46 C2
Aoulef Alg. 46 D2
Aoussard W. Sahara 46 B2
Aozou Chad 47 E2
Apa r. Brazil 70 E2
Apaiang atoll Kiribati see Abaiang
Apalachee Bay FL U.S.A. 63 K6
Apalachin NY U.S.A. 64 C1
Apamea Turkey see Dinar
Apaporis r. Col. 68 E4
Aparecida do Tabuado Brazil 71 A3
Aparima N.Z. see Riverton
Aparri Phil. 74 E4
Apatity Russia 14 R3
Apatzingán Mex. 66 D5
Ape Latvia 15 O8
Apeldoorn Neth. 17 J4
Apennines mts Italy 26 C2
Api mt. Nepal 36 E3
Api i. Vanuatu see Épi
Apia atoll Kiribati see Abaiang
Apia Samoa 53 I3
Apiacas, Serra dos hills Brazil 69 G6
Apiaí Brazil 71 A4
Apiti N.Z. 59 E4
Aplao Peru 68 D7
Apoera Suriname 69 G2
Apollo Bay Australia 58 A7
Apollonia Bulg. see Sozopol
Apolo Bol. 68 E6
Aporé Brazil 71 A2
Aporé r. Brazil 71 A2
Apostelens Tommelfinger mt. Greenland 61 N3
Apostolos Andreas, Cape Cyprus 39 B2
Apoteri Guyana 69 G3
Apozai Pak. 36 B3
Appalachian Mountains U.S.A. 63 K4
Appalla i. Fiji see Kabara
Appennino mts Italy see Apennines
Appennino Abruzzese mts Italy 26 E3
Appennino Tosco-Emiliano mts Italy 26 D3
Appennino Umbro-Marchigiano mts Italy 26 E3
Applecross U.K. 20 D3
Appleton WI U.S.A. 63 J3
Apple Valley CA U.S.A. 65 D3
Appomattox VA U.S.A. 64 B4
Aprilia Italy 26 E4
Apsheronsk Russia 13 H7
Apsheronskaya Russia see Apsheronsk
Apt France 24 G5
Apucarana Brazil 71 A3
Apucarana, Serra da hills Brazil 71 A3
Apuka Russia 29 R3
Apulum Romania see Alba Iulia
Aq"a Georgia see Sokhumi
'Aqaba Jordan see Al 'Aqabah
Aqaba, Gulf of Asia 34 D5
'Aqaba, Wâdi el watercourse Egypt see 'Aqabah, Wādī al
'Aqabah, Wādī al watercourse Egypt 39 A4
Aqadyr Kazakh. see Akadyr
Aqdoghmish r. Iran 35 G3
Aqköl Akmolinskaya Oblast' Kazakh. see Akkol'
Aqköl Atyrauskaya Oblast' Kazakh. see Akkol'
Aqmola Kazakh. see Astana
Aqqan China 37 F1
Aqqikkol Hu salt l. China 37 G1
Aqra', Jabal al mt. Syria/Turkey 39 B2
'Aqran h. Saudi Arabia 39 D4
Aqsay Kazakh. see Aksay
Aqsayqin Hit disp. terr. Asia see Aksai Chin
Aqshuqyr Kazakh. see Akshukyr
Aqsū Kazakh. see Aksu
Aqsūat Kazakh. see Aksuat
Aqsū-Ayuly Kazakh. see Aksu-Ayuly
Aqtaū Kazakh. see Aktau
Aqtöbe Kazakh. see Aktobe
Aqtoghay Kazakh. see Aktogay
Aquae Grani Germany see Aachen
Aquae Gratianae France see Aix-les-Bains
Aquae Sextiae France see Aix-en-Provence
Aquae Statiellae Italy see Acqui Terme
Aquarius Mountains AZ U.S.A. 65 F3
Aquidauana Brazil 70 E2
Aquincum Hungary see Budapest
Aquiry r. Brazil see Acre
Aquisgranum Germany see Aachen
Aquitaine reg. France 24 D5
Aquitania reg. France see Aquitaine
Aqzhayqyn Köli salt l. Kazakh. see Akzhaykyn, Ozero
Ara India see Arrah
Āra Ārba Eth. 48 E3
Arab, Bahr el watercourse Sudan 47 F4
'Arab, Khalîg el b. Egypt see 'Arab, Khalīj al
'Arab, Khalīj al b. Egypt 34 C5
'Arabah, Wādī al watercourse Israel/Jordan 39 B5
Arabian Basin sea feature Indian Ocean 73 M5
Arabian Gulf Asia see The Gulf
Arabian Peninsula Asia 32 G5
Arabian Sea Indian Ocean 33 K6
Araç Turkey 34 D2
Araça r. Brazil 68 F4
Aracaju Brazil 69 K6
Aracati Brazil 69 K4
Aracatu Brazil 71 C1
Araçatuba Brazil 71 A3
Aracena Spain 25 C5
Aracruz Brazil 71 C2
Araçuaí Brazil 71 C2
Araçuaí r. Brazil 71 C2
'Arad Israel 39 B4
Arad Romania 27 I1
Arafura Sea Australia/Indon. 52 D2
Arafura Shelf sea feature Australia/Indon. 74 E6
Aragarças Brazil 69 H7
Aragón r. Spain 25 F2
Araguaçu Brazil 71 A1
Araguaia r. Brazil 71 A1
Araguaia, Parque Nacional do nat. park Brazil 69 H6
Araguaiana Brazil 71 A1
Araguaína Brazil 69 I5
Araguari Brazil 71 A2
Araguari r. Brazil 69 H3
Araguatins Brazil 69 I5
Araí Brazil 71 B1
'Arâif el Naga, Gebel h. Egypt see 'Urayf an Nāqah, Jabal
Araioses Brazil 69 J4
Arak Alg. 46 D2
Ārāk Iran 35 H4
Arak Syria 39 D2
Arakan Yoma mts Myanmar 37 H5
Arakkonam India 38 C3
Araks r. Azer. see Araz
Araku India 38 D2
Aral China 42 E4
Aral Kazakh. see Aral'sk
Aral Tajik. see Vose'
Aral Sea salt l. Kazakh./Uzbek. 30 F2
Aral'sk Kazakh. 28 H5
Aral'skoye More salt l. Kazakh./Uzbek. see Aral Sea
Aralsor, Ozero l. Kazakh. 13 K6
Aral Tengizi salt l. Kazakh./Uzbek. see Aral Sea
Aramac Australia 56 D4
Aramac Creek watercourse Australia 56 D4
Aran r. India 38 C2
Aranda de Duero Spain 25 E3
Aranđelovac Serbia 27 I2
Arandis Namibia 50 B2
Arang India 37 E5
Arani India 38 C3
Aran Islands Ireland 21 C4
Aranjuez Spain 25 E3
Aranos Namibia 50 D3
Aransas Pass TX U.S.A. 63 H6
Arantangi India 38 C4
Aranuka atoll Kiribati 53 H1
Arao Japan 45 C6
Araouane Mali 46 C3
Arapgir Turkey 34 E3
Arapiraca Brazil 69 K5
Arapis, Akrotirio pt Greece 27 K4
Arapkir Turkey see Arapgir
Arapongas Brazil 71 A3
Araquari Brazil 71 A4
'Ar'ar Saudi Arabia 35 F5
Araracuara Col. 68 D4
Araranguá Brazil 71 A5
Araraquara Brazil 71 A3
Araras Brazil 69 H5
Ararat Armenia 35 G3
Ararat Australia 58 A6
Ararat, Mount Turkey 35 G3
Araria India 37 F4
Araripina Brazil 69 J5
Aras r. Azer. see Araz
Aras Turkey 35 F3
Arataca Brazil 71 D1
Arauca Col. 68 D2
Arauca r. Venez. 68 E2
Aravalli Range mts India 36 C4
Aravete Estonia 15 N7
Arawa P.N.G. 52 F2
Araxá Brazil 71 B2
Araxes r. Azer. see Araz
Arayıt Dağı mt. Turkey 27 N5
Arbailu Iraq see Arbīl/Hewlêr
Arbela Iraq see Arbīl/Hewlêr
Arberth U.K. see Narberth
Arbīl/Hewlêr Iraq 35 G3
Arboga Sweden 15 I7
Arbroath U.K. 20 G4
Arbuckle CA U.S.A. 65 A1
Arbū-ye Shamālī, Dasht-e des. Afgh. 33 J4
Arcachon France 24 D4
Arcade NY U.S.A. 64 B1
Arcadia FL U.S.A. 63 K6
Arc Dome mt. NV U.S.A. 65 D1
Arcelia Mex. 66 D5
Archaeological Sites of the Island of Meroe tourist site Sudan 47 G3
Archangel Russia 12 I2
Archer r. Australia 41 G9
Archer Bend National Park Australia 56 C2
Archipiélago Los Roques, Parque Nacional nat. park Venez. 68 E1
Ärçivan Azer. 35 H3
Arckaringa watercourse Australia 57 A6
Arco ID U.S.A. 62 E3
Arcos Brazil 71 B3
Arcos de la Frontera Spain 25 D5
Arctic Bay Nunavut Canada 61 J2
Arctic Institute Islands Russia see Arkticheskogo Instituta, Ostrova
Arctic Mid-Ocean Ridge sea feature Arctic Ocean 77 H1
Arctic Ocean 77 B1
Arctic Red r. N.W.T. Canada 60 E3
Arctowski (Poland) research stn Antarctica 76 A2
Ardabīl Iran 35 H3
Ardahan Turkey 35 F2
Ardakān Iran 35 I4
Ardalstangen Norway 15 E6
Ardara Ireland 21 D3
Ardas r. Greece see Arda
Ard aş Şawwān plain Jordan 39 C4
Ardatov Nizhegorodskaya Oblast' Russia 13 I5
Ardatov Respublika Mordoviya Russia 13 J5
Ardee Ireland 21 F4
Ardennes plat. Belgium 16 J6
Arden Town CA U.S.A. 65 B1
Arderin h. Ireland 21 E4
Ardestān Iran 35 I4
Ardglass U.K. 21 G3
Ardila r. Port. 25 C4
Ardlethan Australia 58 C5
Ardmore OK U.S.A. 63 H5
Ardnamurchan, Point of U.K. 20 C4
Ardon Russia 35 G2
Ardrishaig U.K. 20 D4
Ardrossan U.K. 20 E5
Ardvasar U.K. 20 D3
Areia Branca Brazil 69 K4
Arel Belgium see Arlon
Arelas France see Arles
Arelate France see Arles
Arena, Point CA U.S.A. 62 C4
Arenas de San Pedro Spain 25 D3
Arendal Norway 15 F7
Areopoli Greece 27 J6
Arequipa Peru 68 D7
Arere Brazil 69 H4
Arévalo Spain 25 D3
Arezzo Italy 26 D3
'Arfajah well Saudi Arabia 39 D4
Argadargada Australia 56 B4
Arganda del Rey Spain 25 E3
Argel Alg. see Algiers
Argentan France 24 D2
Argentario, Monte h. Italy 26 D3
Argentera, Cima dell' mt. Italy 26 B2
Argentina country S. America 70 C5
Argentine Abyssal Plain sea feature S. Atlantic Ocean 72 E9
Argentine Basin sea feature S. Atlantic Ocean 72 F8
Argentine Republic country S. America see Argentina
Argentine Rise sea feature S. Atlantic Ocean 72 E8
Argentino, Lago l. Arg. 70 B8
Argenton-sur-Creuse France 24 E3
Argentoratum France see Strasbourg
Argeş r. Romania 27 L2
Arg-e Zārī Afgh. 36 A2
Arghandāb Rōd r. Afgh. 36 A3
Argi r. Russia 44 C1
Argolikos Kolpos b. Greece 27 J6
Argos Greece 27 J6
Argostoli Greece 27 I5
Arguis Spain 25 F2
Argun' r. China/Russia 43 M2
Argun Russia 35 G2
Argungu Nigeria 46 D3
Argus, Dome Antarctica 76 E1
Argus Range mts CA U.S.A. 65 D3
Argyle, Lake Australia 54 E4
Argyrokastron Albania see Gjirokastër
Ar Horqin Qi China see Tianshan
Århus Denmark see Aarhus
Ariah Park Australia 58 C5
Ariamsvlei Namibia 50 D5
Ariana Tunisia see L'Ariana
Ariano Irpino Italy 26 F4
Aribinda Burkina Faso 46 C3
Arica Chile 68 D7
Arid, Cape Australia 55 C8
Arīḩā Syria 39 C2
Arīḩā West Bank see Jericho
Arima Trin. and Tob. 67 L6
Ariminum Italy see Rimini
Arinos Brazil 71 B1
Aripuanã Brazil 69 G6
Aripuanã r. Brazil 68 F5
Ariquemes Brazil 68 F5
Aris Namibia 50 C2
Arisaig U.K. 20 D4
Arisaig, Sound of sea chan. U.K. 20 D4
'Arīsh, Wādī al watercourse Egypt 39 A4
Arixang China see Wenquan
Ariyalur India 38 C4
Arizaro, Salar de salt flat Arg. 70 C2
Arizona Arg. 70 C5
Arizona state U.S.A. 62 E5
Arizpe Mex. 62 E5
'Arjah Saudi Arabia 32 F5
Arjeplog Sweden 14 J3
Arjuni Chhattisgarh India 38 D1
Arjuni Mahar. India 36 E5
Arkadak Russia 13 I6
Arkadelphia AR U.S.A. 63 I5
Arkaig, Loch l. U.K. 20 D4
Arkalyk Kazakh. 42 B2
Arkansas r. AR U.S.A. 63 I5
Arkansas state U.S.A. 63 I4
Arkansas City KS U.S.A. 63 H4
Arkanū, Jabal mt. Libya 32 B5
Arka Tag mts China 37 G1
Arkhangel'sk Russia see Archangel
Arkhara Russia 44 C2
Arkhipovka Russia 44 D4
Arki i. Greece see Arkoi
Arklow Ireland 21 F5
Arkoi i. Greece 27 L6
Arkona Ont. Canada 64 A1
Arkona, Kap c. Germany 17 N3
Arkonam India see Arakkonam
Arkport NY U.S.A. 64 C1
Arkticheskogo Instituta, Ostrova is Russia 28 J2
Arkul' Russia 12 K4
Arlandag mt. Turkm. 35 I3
Arles France 24 G5
Arli, Parc National de l' nat. park Burkina Faso 46 D3
Arlington S. Africa 51 H5
Arlington NY U.S.A. 64 E2
Arlington VA U.S.A. 64 C3
Arlit Niger 46 D3
Arlon Belgium 17 J6
Armadale Australia 55 A8
Armagh U.K. 21 F3
Armant Egypt 32 D4
Armavir Armenia 35 G2
Armavir Russia 13 I7
Armenia country Asia 35 G2
Armenia Col. 68 C3
Armenopolis Romania see Gherla
Armeria Mex. 66 D5
Armidale Australia 58 E3
Armori India 38 D1
Armoy U.K. 21 F2
Armstrong r. Australia 54 E4
Armstrong Island Cook Is see Rarotonga
Armu r. Russia 44 E3
Armur India 38 C2
Armutçuk Dağı mts Turkey 27 L5
Armyanskaya S.S.R. country Asia see Armenia
Arnaoutis, Cape Cyprus see Arnauti, Cape
Arnauti, Cape Cyprus 39 A2
Årnes Norway 15 G6
Arnhem Neth. 17 J5
Arnhem, Cape Australia 56 B2
Arnhem Land reg. Australia 54 F3
Arniston S. Africa 50 E8
Arno r. Italy 26 D3
Arno Bay Australia 57 B7
Arnold U.K. 19 F5
Arnon r. Jordan see Mawjib, Wādī al
Arnprior Ont. Canada 63 L2
Arnsberg Germany 17 L5
Aroab Namibia 50 D4
Aroma Sudan 32 E6
Arona Italy 26 C2
Arorae i. Kiribati 53 H2
Arore i. Kiribati see Arorae
Aros r. Mex. 62 F6
Arossi i. Solomon Is see San Cristobal
Arqalyq Kazakh. see Arkalyk
Arquipélago da Madeira aut. reg. Port. 46 B1
Arrabury Australia 57 C5
Arrah India 37 F4
Arraias Brazil 71 B1
Arraias, Serra de hills Brazil 71 B1
Ar Ramādī Iraq 35 F4
Ar Ramlah Jordan 39 B5
Ar Ramthā Jordan 39 C3
Arran i. U.K. 20 D5
Arranmore Island Ireland 21 D3
Ar Raqqah Syria 39 D2
Arras France 24 F1
Ar Rass Saudi Arabia 32 F4
Ar Rastān Syria 39 C2
Ar Rayyān Qatar 32 H4
Arrecife Canary Is 46 B2
Arretium Italy see Arezzo
Arriagá Mex. 66 F5
Ar Rifā'ī Iraq 35 G5
Ar Rihāb salt flat Iraq 35 G5
Ar Rimāl reg. Saudi Arabia 48 F1
Arrington VA U.S.A. 64 B4
Ar Riyāḑ Saudi Arabia see Riyadh
Arrochar U.K. 20 E4
Arrojado r. Brazil 71 B1
Arrow, Lough l. Ireland 21 D3
Arrowsmith, Mount N.Z. 59 C6
Arroyo Grande CA U.S.A. 65 B3
Ar Rummān Jordan 39 B3
Ar Ruq'ī well Saudi Arabia 35 G5
Ar Ruşāfah Syria 39 D2
Ar Ruşayfah Jordan 39 C3
Ar Rustāq Oman 33 I5
Ar Ruţbah Iraq 35 F4
Ar Ruwaydah Syria 39 C2
Års Denmark see Aars
Ars Iran 35 G3
Arsen'yev Russia 44 D3
Arsk Russia 12 K4
Arta Greece 27 I5
Artem Russia 44 D4
Artemivs'k Ukr. 13 H6
Artemovsk Ukr. see Artemivs'k
Artenay France 24 E2
Artesia NM U.S.A. 62 G5
Arthur, Lake PA U.S.A. 64 A2
Arthur's Pass National Park N.Z. 59 C6
Arti Russia 11 R4
Artigas Uruguay 70 E4
Artigas (Uruguay) research stn Antarctica 76 A2
Art'ik Armenia 35 F2
Artillery Lake N.W.T. Canada 60 H3
Artisia Botswana 51 H3
Artois reg. France 24 E1
Artos Dağı mt. Turkey 35 F3
Artova Turkey 34 E2
Artsakh disp. terr. Azer. see Nagorno-Karabakh
Artsiz Ukr. see Artsyz
Artsyz Ukr. 27 M2
Artur de Paiva Angola see Kuvango
Arturo Prat (Chile) research stn Antarctica 76 A2
Artux China 42 D5
Artvin Turkey 35 F2
Aru, Kepulauan is Indon. 41 F8
Arua Uganda 48 D3
Aruanã Brazil 71 A1
Aruba terr. West Indies 67 K6
Arumã Brazil 68 F4
Arunachal Pradesh state India 37 H4
Arundel U.K. 19 G8
Arun Gol r. China see Arun He
Arun He r. China 44 B3
Arun Qi China see Naji
Aruppukkottai India 38 C4
Arusha Tanz. 48 D4
Aruwimi r. Dem. Rep. Congo 48 C3
Arvagh Ireland 21 E4
Arvayheer Mongolia 42 I3
Arviat Nunavut Canada 61 I3
Arvidsjaur Sweden 14 K4
Arvika Sweden 15 H7
Arvonia VA U.S.A. 64 B4
Arwād i. Syria 39 B2
Arwala Indon. 54 D1
Arxan China 43 L3
Aryanah Tunisia see L'Ariana
Āryanshahr Iran 33 I3
Arys Kazakh. 42 B4
Arzamas Russia 13 I5
Arzew Alg. 25 F6
Arzgir Russia 35 G1
Arzila Morocco see Asilah
Asaba Nigeria 46 D4
Asad, Buḩayrat al resr Syria 39 D1
Asadābād Afgh. 36 B2
Asadābād Iran 35 H4
Asahi-dake vol. Japan 44 F4
Asahikawa Japan 44 F4
'Asal Egypt 39 A5
Āsalē l. Eth. 48 E2
Asālem Iran 35 H3
'Asalūyeh Iran 35 I6
Asan-man b. S. Korea 45 B5
Asansol India 37 F5
Āsayita Eth. 48 E2
Asbestos Mountains S. Africa 50 F5
Asbury Park NJ U.S.A. 64 D2
Ascalon Israel see Ashqelon
Ascea Italy 26 F4
Ascensión Bol. 68 F7
Ascension atoll Micronesia see Pohnpei
Ascension i. S. Atlantic Ocean 72 H6
Ascensión, Bahía de la b. Mex. 67 G5
Aschaffenburg Germany 17 L6
Ascoli Piceno Italy 26 E3
Asculum Italy see Ascoli Piceno
Asculum Picenum Italy see Ascoli Piceno
Ascutney VT U.S.A. 64 E1
Āseb Eritrea see Assab
Åseda Sweden 15 I8
Åsele Sweden 14 J4
Asenovgrad Bulg. 27 K3
Aşfar, Jabal al mt. Jordan 39 C3
Aşfar, Tall al h. Syria 39 C3
Aşgabat Turkm. see Ashgabat
Aşgabat Turkm. see Ashgabat
Asha Russia 11 R5
Ashburton watercourse Australia 54 A5
Ashburton N.Z. 59 C6
Ashburton Range hills Australia 54 F4
Ashdod Israel 39 B4
Asheville NC U.S.A. 63 K4
Ashford Australia 58 E2
Ashford U.K. 19 H7
Ashgabat Turkm. 30 E3
Ashibetsu Japan 44 F4
Ashikaga Japan 45 E5
Ashington U.K. 18 F3
Ashizuri-misaki pt Japan 45 D6
Ashkelon Israel see Ashqelon
Ashland OR U.S.A. 62 C3
Ashland VA U.S.A. 64 C4
Ashland WI U.S.A. 63 I2
Ashley Australia 58 D2
Ashmore and Cartier Islands terr. Australia 54 C3
Ashmore Reef Australia 54 C3
Ashmore Reefs Australia 56 D1
Ashmyany Belarus 15 N9
Ashqelon Israel 39 B4
Ash Shabakah Iraq 35 F5
Ash Shaddādah Syria 35 F3
Ash Shallūfah Egypt 39 A4
Ash Sham Syria see Damascus
Ash Shanāfīyah Iraq 35 G5
Ash Shaqīq well Saudi Arabia 35 F5
Ash Sharāh reg. Jordan 39 B4
Ash Sharawrah Saudi Arabia 32 G6
Ash Shāriqah U.A.E. see Sharjah
Ash Sharqāţ Iraq 35 F4
Ash Shaţrah Iraq 35 G5
Ash Shaţţ Egypt 39 A5
Ash Shawbak Jordan 39 B4
Ash Shaybānī well Saudi Arabia 35 F5
Ash Shaykh Ibrāhīm Syria 39 D2
Ash Shiblīyāt h. Saudi Arabia 39 C5
Ash Shiḩr Yemen 32 G7
Ash Shu'aybah Saudi Arabia 35 F6
Ash Shu'bah Saudi Arabia 32 F4
Ash Shurayf Saudi Arabia see Khaybar
Ashta India 36 D5
Ashtabula OH U.S.A. 64 A2
Ashtarak Armenia 35 G2
Ashti Mahar. India 36 D5
Ashti Mahar. India 38 B2
Ashti Mahar. India 38 C2
Āshtīān Iran 35 H3
Ashton S. Africa 50 E7
Ashton-under-Lyne U.K. 18 E5
Ashuanipi Lake Nfld. and Lab. Canada 61 L4
Ashur Iraq see Ash Sharqāţ
Asi r. Asia see 'Āşī, Nahr al
'Āşī r. Lebanon/Syria see Orontes
Āsīā Bak Iran 35 H4
Asifabad India 38 C2
Asika India 38 E2
Asilah Morocco 25 C6
Asinara, Golfo dell' b. Sardinia Italy 26 C4
Asino Russia 28 J4
Asipovichy Belarus 13 F5
Asīr Iran 35 I6
'Asīr reg. Saudi Arabia 32 F5
Asisium Italy see Assisi
Askale Pak. 36 C2
Aşkale Turkey 35 F3
Asker Norway 15 G7
Askersund Sweden 15 I7
Askim Norway 15 G7
Askī Mawşil Iraq 35 F3
Askino Russia 11 R4
Askival h. U.K. 20 C4
Asl Egypt see 'Asal
Aslanköy r. Turkey 39 B1
Asmara Eritrea 32 E6
Āsmera Eritrea see Asmara
Åsnen l. Sweden 15 I8
Aso-Kuju Kokuritsu-kōen Japan 45 C6
Asop India 36 C4
Āsosa Eth. 48 D2
Aspang-Markt Austria 17 P7
Aspatria U.K. 18 D4
Aspen CO U.S.A. 62 F4
Aspiring, Mount N.Z. 59 B7
Aspro, Cape Cyprus 39 A2
Aspromonte, Parco Nazionale dell' nat. park Italy 26 F5
Aspron, Cape Cyprus see Aspro, Cape
As Sa'an Syria 39 C2
Assab Eritrea 32 F7
Assad, Lake resr Syria see Asad, Buḩayrat al
Aş Şafā lava field Syria 39 C3
Aş Şafāqis Tunisia see Sfax
Aş Şaff Egypt 34 C5
As Safīrah Syria 39 C1
Aş Şaḩrā' al Gharbīyah des. Egypt see Western Desert
Aş Şaḩrā' ash Sharqīyah des. Egypt see Eastern Desert
Assake-Audan, Vpadina depr. Kazakh./Uzbek. 35 J2
'Assal, Lac l. Djibouti see Assal, Lake
Assal, Lake Djibouti 32 F7
Aş Şāliḩīyah Syria 35 F4
As Sallūm Egypt 34 B5
As Salmān Iraq 35 G5
As Salţ Jordan 39 B3
Assam state India 37 G4
Assamakka Niger 46 D3
As Samāwah Iraq 35 G5
As Samrā' Jordan 39 C3
Aş Şanām reg. Saudi Arabia 32 H5
As Sarīr reg. Libya 47 F2
Assateague Island MD U.S.A. 64 D3
Assayeta Eth. see Āsayita
Assen Neth. 17 K4
As Sidrah Libya 47 E1
Assiniboia Sask. Canada 62 F2
Assiniboine r. Man./Sask. Canada 62 H2
Assiniboine, Mount Alta/B.C. Canada 60 G4
Assis Brazil 71 A3
Assisi Italy 26 E3
Aş Şubayḩīyah Kuwait 35 G5
Aş Şufayrī well Saudi Arabia 35 G5
As Sukhnah Syria 39 D2
As Sulaymānīyah/Slêmānî Iraq 35 G4
As Sulaymī Saudi Arabia 32 F4
As Sūq Saudi Arabia 32 F5
As Sūrīyah country Asia see Syria
Aş Şuwar Syria 35 F4
As Suwaydā' Syria 39 C3
As Suways Egypt see Suez
As Suways governorate Egypt 39 A4
Assynt, Loch l. U.K. 20 D2
Astacus Turkey see İzmit
Astakida i. Greece 27 L7
Astakos Greece 27 I5
Astana Kazakh. 42 C2
Āstāneh-ye Ashrafīyeh Iran 35 H3
Astara Azer. 35 H3
Āstārā Iran 32 G2
Asterabad Iran see Gorgān
Asti Italy 26 C2
Astillero Peru 68 E6
Astin Tag mts China see Altun Shan
Astipálaia i. Greece see Astypalaia
Astor r. Pak. 36 C2
Astorga Spain 25 C2
Astoria OR U.S.A. 62 C2
Åstorp Sweden 15 H8
Astrabad Iran see Gorgān
Astrakhan' Russia 13 K7
Astrakhan' Bazar Azer. see Cälilabad
Astravyets Belarus 15 N9
Astrida Rwanda see Butare
Asturias aut. comm. Spain 25 C2
Asturias, Principado de aut. comm. Spain see Asturias
Asturica Augusta Spain see Astorga
Astypalaia i. Greece 27 L6
Asunción Para. 70 E3
'Aşūr, Tall mt. West Bank 39 B4
Aswân Egypt see Aswān
Aswān Egypt 32 D5
Asyūţ Egypt 34 C6
Asyût Egypt see Asyūţ
Ata i. Tonga 53 I4
Atacama, Desierto de des. Chile see Atacama Desert
Atacama, Salar de salt flat Chile 70 C2
Atacama Desert Chile 70 C3
Atafu atoll Tokelau 53 I2
Atafu i. Tokelau 74 I6
'Aţā'iţah, Jabal al mt. Jordan 39 B4
Atakent Turkey 39 B1
Atakpamé Togo 46 D4
Atalándi Greece see Atalanti
Atalanti Greece 27 J5
Atalaya Peru 68 D6
Ataléia Brazil 71 C2
Atambua Indon. 54 D2
Atamyrat Turkm. 30 F3
Ataniya Turkey see Adana
Atanur India 38 C2
'Ataq Yemen 32 G7
Atâr Mauritania 46 B2
Atari Pak. 36 C3
Atascadero CA U.S.A. 65 B3
Ātashān Iran 35 I4
Atasu Kazakh. 42 C3
Ataúro, Ilha de i. East Timor 54 D2
Atáviros mt. Greece see Atavyros
Atavyros mt. Greece 27 L6
Atayurt Turkey 39 A1
Atbara Sudan 32 D6
Atbara r. Sudan 32 D6
Atbasar Kazakh. 28 H4
Atchison KS U.S.A. 63 H4
Atebubu Ghana 46 C4
Ateransk Kazakh. see Atyrau
Atessa Italy 26 F3
Athabasca r. Alta Canada 60 G4
Athabasca, Lake Alta/Sask. Canada 60 H4
Atharan Hazari Pak. 36 C3
Athboy Ireland 21 F4
Athenae Greece see Athens
Athenry Ireland 21 D4
Athens Greece 27 J6
Athens GA U.S.A. 63 K5
Athens OH U.S.A. 63 K4
Athens PA U.S.A. 64 C2
Athens TN U.S.A. 63 K4
Atherstone U.K. 19 F6
Atherton Australia 56 D3
Athina Greece see Athens
Athínai Greece see Athens
Athleague Ireland 21 D4

Athlone Ireland 21 E4
Athnā', Wādī an watercourse Jordan 39 D3
Athni India 38 B2
Athol MA U.S.A. 64 E1
Athol, Forest of reg. U.K. 20 E4
Athol N.Z. 59 B7
Athos mt. Greece 27 K4
Ath Thamad Egypt 39 B5
Ath Thayat m. Saudi Arabia 39 C5
Ath Thumāmī well Saudi Arabia 35 G6
Athy Ireland 21 E5
Ati Chad 47 E3
Atico Peru 68 D7
Atikokan Ont. Canada 61 I5
Atka Russia 29 Q3
Atka AK U.S.A. 60 A4
Atkarsk Russia 13 J6
Atlanta GA U.S.A. 63 K5
Atlantic IA U.S.A. 63 H3
Atlantic City NJ U.S.A. 64 D3
Atlantic-Indian-Antarctic Basin sea feature
  S. Atlantic Ocean 72 H10
Atlantic-Indian Ridge sea feature
  Southern Ocean 72 H9
Atlantic Ocean 72
Atlantis S. Africa 50 D7
Atlas Méditerranéen mts Alg. see
  Atlas Tellien
Atlas Mountains Africa 22 C5
Atlas Saharien mts Alg. 22 E5
Atlas Tellien mts Alg. 25 H6
Atmakur India 38 C3
Atmore AL U.S.A. 63 J5
Atocha Bol. 68 E8
Atouila, Erg des. Mali 46 C2
Atqan China see Aqqan
Atrak r. Iran/Turkm. see Atrek
Atrato r. Col. 68 C2
Atrek r. Iran/Turkm. 33 H2
Atrek r. Iran/Turkm. 35 I2
Atropatene country Asia see Azerbaijan
Atsonupuri vol. Russia 44 G3
Aţ Ţafilah Jordan 39 B4
Aţ Ţā'if Saudi Arabia 32 E5
Attalea Turkey see Antalya
Attalia Turkey see Antalya
At Tamīmī Libya 34 A4
Attawapiskat Ont. Canada 63 K1
Attawapiskat r. Ont. Canada 63 K1
Attawapiskat Lake Ont. Canada 63 J1
Aţ Ţawil mts Saudi Arabia 35 F5
Aţ Taysīyah plat. Saudi Arabia 35 F5
Attersee l. Austria 17 N7
Attleborough U.K. 19 I6
Attu Greenland 61 M3
Attu Island AK U.S.A. 29 S4
Aţ Tūnisīyah country Africa see Tunisia
Aţ Ţūr Egypt 34 D5
Attur India 38 C4
Aţ Ţuwayyah well Saudi Arabia 35 F6
Atuk Mountain h. AK U.S.A. 60 A3
Åtvidaberg Sweden 15 I7
Atwater CA U.S.A. 65 B3
Atyashevo Russia 13 J5
Atyrau Kazakh. 30 E2
Atyrau admin. div. Kazakh. see
  Atyrauskaya Oblast'
Atyrau Oblast admin. div. Kazakh. see
  Atyrauskaya Oblast'
Atyrauskaya Oblast' admin. div. Kazakh.
  11 Q6
Aubagne France 24 G5
Aubenas France 24 G4
Aubrey Cliffs AZ U.S.A. 65 F3
Aubry Lake N.W.T. Canada 60 F3
Auburn r. Australia 57 E5
Auburn CA U.S.A. 65 B1
Auburn NE U.S.A. 63 H3
Auburn NY U.S.A. 64 C1
Auburn Range hills Australia 56 E5
Aubusson France 24 F4
Auch France 24 E5
Auchterarder U.K. 20 F4
Auckland N.Z. 59 E3
Auckland Islands N.Z. 53 G7
Audo mt. Eth. 48 E3
Audo Range mts Eth. see Audo
Augathella Australia 57 D5
Augher U.K. 21 E3
Aughnacloy U.K. 21 F3
Aughrim Ireland 21 F5
Augrabies S. Africa 50 E5
Augrabies Falls S. Africa 50 E5
Augrabies Falls National Park S. Africa
  50 E5
Augsburg Germany 17 M6
Augusta Australia 55 A8
Augusta Sicily Italy 26 F6
Augusta GA U.S.A. 63 K5
Augusta ME U.S.A. 63 N3
Augusta Auscorum France see Auch
Augusta Taurinorum Italy see Turin
Augusta Treverorum Germany see Trier
Augusta Vindelicorum Germany see
  Augsburg
Augusto de Lima Brazil 71 B2
Augustus, Mount Australia 55 B6
Aukštaitijos nacionalinis parkas nat. park
  Lith. 15 O9
Aulavik National Park N.W.T. Canada
  60 G2
Auld, Lake imp. l. Australia 54 C5
Auliye Ata Kazakh. see Taraz
Aulon Albania see Vlorë
Ault France 19 I8
Aumale Alg. see Sour el Ghozlane
Aundh India 38 B2
Aundhi India 38 D1
Aunglan Myanmar 37 H6
Auob watercourse Namibia/S. Africa 50 E4
Aura Fin. 15 M6
Auraiya India 36 D4
Aurangabad Bihar India 37 F4
Aurangabad Mahar. India 38 B2
Aure r. France 19 F9
Aurich Germany 17 K4
Aurigny i. Channel Is see Alderney
Aurilândia Brazil 71 A2
Aurillac France 24 F4
Aurora CO U.S.A. 62 G4
Aurora IL U.S.A. 63 J3
Aurora Island Vanuatu see Maéwo
Aurukun Australia 54 C2
Aus Namibia 50 C4
Auskerry i. U.K. 20 G1
Austin MN U.S.A. 63 I3
Austin NV U.S.A. 62 E4
Austin TX U.S.A. 62 H5
Austin, Lake imp. l. Australia 55 B6
Austintown OH U.S.A. 64 A2
Austral Downs Australia 56 B4
Australes, Îles is Fr. Polynesia see
  Tubuai Islands
Australia country Oceania 52 C4
Australian-Antarctic Basin sea feature
  S. Atlantic Ocean 74 C9
Australian Antarctic Territory Antarctica
  76 G2
Australian Capital Territory admin. div.
  Australia 58 D5
Austria country Europe 17 N7
Austvågøy i. Norway 14 I2

Autazes Brazil 69 G4
Autesiodorum France see Auxerre
Autti Fin. 14 O3
Auvergne reg. France 24 F4
Auvergne, Monts d' mts France 24 F4
Auxerre France 24 F3
Auxonne France 24 G3
Auyuittuq National Park Nunavut Canada
  61 L3
Auzangate, Nevado mt. Peru 68 D6
Ava NY U.S.A. 64 D1
Āvaj Iran 35 H4
Avallon France 24 F3
Avalon CA U.S.A. 65 E2
Avalon Peninsula Nfld. and Lab. Canada
  61 M5
Avān Iran 35 G3
Avarau atoll Cook Is see Palmerston
Avaré Brazil 71 A3
Avaricum France see Bourges
Avarua Cook Is 75 J7
Aveiro Port. 25 B3
Aveiro, Ria de est. Port. 25 B3
Avellino Italy 26 F4
Avenal CA U.S.A. 65 B2
Avenio France see Avignon
Aversa Italy 26 F4
Avesta Sweden 15 J6
Aveyron r. France 24 E4
Avezzano Italy 26 E3
Aviemore U.K. 20 F3
Avignon France 24 G5
Ávila Spain 25 D3
Avilés Spain 25 D2
Avis PA U.S.A. 64 C2
Avlama Dağı mt. Turkey 39 A1
Avlama Dağı mts Turkey 39 A1
Avlona Albania see Vlorë
Avnyugskiy Russia 12 J3
Avoca Australia 58 A6
Avoca r. Australia 58 A5
Avoca Ireland 21 F5
Avoca NY U.S.A. 64 C1
Avola Sicily Italy 26 F6
Avon r. England U.K. 19 E6
Avon r. England U.K. 19 E7
Avon r. England U.K. 19 F8
Avon r. Scotland U.K. 20 F3
Avon NY U.S.A. 64 C1
Avonmore r. Ireland 21 F5
Avonmore PA U.S.A. 64 B2
Avonmouth U.K. 19 E7
Avranches France 24 D2
Avsuyu Turkey 39 C1
Avuavu Solomon Is 53 G2
Avveel Fin. see Ivalo
Avvil Fin. see Ivalo
A'waj r. Syria 39 B3
Awakino N.Z. 59 E4
Awanui N.Z. 59 D2
Awārē Eth. 48 E3
'Awārid, Wādī al watercourse Syria 39 D2
Awarua Point N.Z. 59 B7
Āwash Eth. 48 E3
Āwash r. Eth. 48 D2
Awa-shima i. Japan 45 E5
Awash National Park Eth. 48 D3
Awasib Mountains Namibia 50 B3
Awat China 42 E4
Awatere r. N.Z. 59 E5
Awbārī Libya 46 E2
Awbārī, Idhān des. Libya 46 E2
Awbeg r. Ireland 21 D5
'Awdah, Hawr al imp. l. Iraq 35 G5
Aw Dheegle Somalia 47 H4
Awe, Loch l. U.K. 20 D4
Aweil South Sudan 47 F4
Awka Nigeria 46 D4
Axe r. England U.K. 19 D8
Axe r. England U.K. 19 E7
Axedale Australia 58 B6
Axel Heiberg Glacier Antarctica 76 I1
Axel Heiberg Island Nunavut Canada 61 I2
Axim Ghana 46 C4
Axminster U.K. 19 E8
Axum Eth. see Āksum
Ayachi, Jbel mt. Morocco 22 D5
Ayacucho Arg. 70 E5
Ayacucho Peru 68 D6
Ayadaw Myanmar 37 H5
Ayagoz Kazakh. 42 E3
Ayaguz Kazakh. see Ayagoz
Ayakkum Hu salt l. China 37 G1
Ayaköz Kazakh. see Ayagoz
Ayancık Turkey 34 D2
Ayang N. Korea 45 B5
Ayaş Turkey 34 D2
Aybas Kazakh. 13 K7
Aydar r. Ukr. 13 H6
Aydarko'li ko'li l. Uzbek. 33 K1
Aydere Turkm. 35 I3
Aydıncık Turkey 39 A1
Aydın Turkey 27 L6
Aydın Dağları mts Turkey 27 L5
Aydyñ Turkm. 35 I3
Ayelu vol. Eth. 32 F7
Ayer MA U.S.A. 64 E1
Ayers Rock h. Australia see Uluru
Ayeyarwady r. Myanmar see Irrawaddy
Ayila Ri'gyü mts China 36 D2
Áyios Dhimítrios Greece see
  Agios Dimitrios
Áyios Evstrátios i. Greece see
  Agios Efstratios
Áyios Nikólaos Greece see Agios Nikolaos
Áyios Yeóryios i. Greece see
  Agios Georgios
Aylesbury N.Z. 59 D6
Aylesbury U.K. 19 G7
Aylett VA U.S.A. 64 C4
Ayllón Spain 25 E3
Aylmer Ont. Canada 64 A1
Aylmer Lake N.W.T. Canada 60 H3
Aymangala India 38 C3
'Ayn al 'Abd well Saudi Arabia 35 H5
'Ayn al 'Arab Syria 39 D1
'Ayn al Baidā' Saudi Arabia 39 C2
'Ayn al Bayḍā' well Syria 39 C2
'Ayn al Ghazālah well Libya 34 A4
'Ayn al Maqfi spring Egypt 34 C6
'Ayn az Zaytūn Egypt 34 B6
'Ayn Dāllah spring Egypt 34 B6
'Ayn 'Īsá Syria 39 D1
'Ayn Tabaghbugh spring Egypt 34 B5
'Ayn Tumayrah spring Egypt 34 B5
Ayod South Sudan 32 D8
Ayon, Ostrov i. Russia 29 R3
'Ayoûn el 'Atroûs Mauritania 46 C3
Ayr Australia 56 D3
Ayr U.K. 20 E5
Ayr r. U.K. 20 E5
Ayr, Point of U.K. 18 D5
Ayrancı Turkey 39 D1
Ayre, Point of Isle of Man 18 C4
Aytos Bulg. 27 L3
Ayuthia Thai. see Ayutthaya
Ayutthaya Thai. 37 C4
Ayvacık Turkey 27 L5
Ayvalı Turkey 39 E1
Ayvalık Turkey 27 L5
Azad Kashmir admin. div. Pak. 36 C2
Azak Russia see Azov

Azamgarh India 37 E4
Azaouâd reg. Mali 46 C3
Azaouagh, Vallée de watercourse
  Mali/Niger 46 D3
Azaran Iran see Hashtrūd
Azärbaycan country Asia see Azerbaijan
Azärbaycan country Asia see Azerbaijan
Azare Nigeria 46 E3
Azawad reg. Mali 46 C3
A'zāz Syria 39 C1
Azbine mts Niger see Aïr, Massif de l'
Azdavay Turkey 34 D2
Azerbaijan country Asia 35 G2
Azerbaydzhanskaya S.S.R. country Asia see
  Azerbaijan
Azhibeksor, Ozero salt l. Kazakh. 31 I1
Azhikode India 38 B4
Aziziye Turkey see Pınarbaşı
Azogues Ecuador 68 C4
Azores terr. N. Atlantic Ocean 72 G3
Azores-Biscay Rise sea feature
  N. Atlantic Ocean 72 G2
Azotus Israel see Ashdod
Azov Russia 13 H7
Azov's'ke More sea Russia/Ukr. see
  Azov, Sea of
Azov, Sea of Russia/Ukr. 13 H7
Azovskoye More sea Russia/Ukr. see
  Azov, Sea of
Azraq, Bahr el r. Eth./Sudan see Blue Nile
Azraq, Qaşr al tourist site Jordan 39 C4
Azraq ash Shīshān Jordan 39 C4
Azrou Morocco 22 C5
Azuaga Spain 25 D4
Azuero, Península de pen. Panama 67 H7
Azul Arg. 70 E5
Azul, Cordillera mts Peru 68 C5
Azuma-san vol. Japan 45 F5
Azur, Côte d' coastal area France 24 H5
'Azza Gaza see Gaza
Azzaba Alg. 26 B6
Aż Zāhiriyah West Bank 39 B4
Aż Zahrān Saudi Arabia see Dhahran
Aż Zaqāzīq Egypt 34 C5
Az Zarbah Syria 39 C1
Az Zarqā' Jordan 39 C3
Za'tari (Zaatari) Jordan 39 C3
Az Zubayr Iraq 35 G5
Az Zuqur i. Yemen 32 F7

B

Baa Indon. 54 C2
Baabda Lebanon 39 B3
Ba'albek Lebanon 39 C2
Baan Baa Australia 58 D3
Baardheere Somalia 48 E3
Bab India 36 C4
Bāb, Köh-e mts Afgh. 36 B2
Baba Burnu pt Turkey 27 L5
Babadag mt. Azer. 35 H2
Babadag Romania 27 M2
Babaeski Turkey 27 L4
Babahoyo Ecuador 68 C4
Babai India 36 D5
Babai r. Nepal 37 E3
Bābā Kalān Iran 35 H5
Bāb al Mandab str. Africa/Asia 32 F7
Babanusa Sudan 32 C7
Babar i. Indon. 41 E8
Babar, Kepulauan is Indon. 54 E1
Babati Tanz. 49 D4
Babayevo Russia 12 H4
Babayurt Russia 13 J8
Babb MT U.S.A. 62 E1
Babel, Kepulauan is Indon. 41 E8
Babine r. B.C. Canada 60 E4
Babine Lake B.C. Canada 60 F4
Bābol Iran 35 I3
Bābolsar Iran 35 I3
Babongo Cameroon 47 E4
Baboon Point S. Africa 50 D7
Baboua Cent. Afr. Rep. 48 B3
Babruysk Belarus 13 F5
Babstovo Russia 44 C2
Babu China see Hezhou
Babuhri India 36 B4
Babusar Pass Pak. 36 C2
Babushkina, imeni Russia 12 I4
Babuyan i. Phil. 43 M9
Babuyan Channel Phil. 43 M9
Babuyan Islands Phil. 41 E6
Bacabal Brazil 69 J4
Bacan i. Indon. 41 E8
Bacău Romania 27 L1
Bacha China 44 D2
Bach Ice Shelf Antarctica 76 L2
Bachu China 42 D5
Back r. N.W.T./Nunavut Canada 61 I3
Bačka Palanka Serbia 27 H2
Backbone Mountain MD U.S.A. 64 B3
Backe Sweden 14 J5
Backstairs Passage Australia 57 B7
Bac Liêu Vietnam 31 J6
Bacolod Phil. 41 E6
Bacqueville-en-Caux France 19 H9
Bada mt. Eth. 48 D3
Badain Jaran Shamo des. China 42 I4
Badajoz Spain 25 C4
Badami India 38 B3
Badampahar India 37 F5
Badanah Saudi Arabia 35 F5
Badanjilin Shamo des. China see
  Badain Jaran Shamo
Badaojiang China see Baishan
Badarpur India 37 H4
Badaun India see Budaun
Badderen Norway 14 M2
Bademli Turkey see Aladağ
Bademli Geçidi pass Turkey 34 C3
Baden Austria 17 P6
Baden Switz. 24 I3
Baden-Baden Germany 17 L6
Bad Hersfeld Germany 17 L5
Badia Polesine Italy 26 D2
Badin Pak. 33 K5
Bādiyat ash Shām des. Asia see
  Syrian Desert
Badnawar India 38 B5
Badnera India 38 C1
Badnor India 36 C4
Badou Togo 46 D4
Badrah Iraq 35 G4
Badr Ḥunayn Saudi Arabia 32 E5
Bādūl Iran 35 I4
Bad Reichenhall Germany 17 N7
Bad Salzungen Germany 17 M5
Bad Schwartau Germany 17 M4
Bad Segeberg Germany 17 M4
Badu Australia 56 C1
Badulla Sri Lanka 38 D5
Badzhal'skiy Khrebet mts Russia 44 D2

Bae Colwyn U.K. see Colwyn Bay
Baeza Spain 25 E5
Bafatá Guinea-Bissau 46 B3
Baffa Pak. 36 C2
Baffin Bay Canada/Greenland 61 L2
Baffin Island Nunavut Canada 61 L3
Bafia Cameroon 46 E4
Bafing r. Africa 46 B3
Bafoulabé Mali 46 B3
Bafoussam Cameroon 46 E4
Bafq Iran 35 I5
Bafra Turkey 34 D2
Bafra Burnu pt Turkey 34 D2
Bāft Iran 35 I4
Bafwaboli Dem. Rep. Congo 48 C3
Bafwasende Dem. Rep. Congo 48 C3
Bagaha India 37 F4
Bagalkot India see Bagalkot
Bagamoyo Tanz. 49 D4
Bagan China 37 I2
Bagata Dem. Rep. Congo 48 B4
Bagdad AZ U.S.A. 65 F4
Bagdarin Russia 43 K2
Bagé Brazil 70 F4
Bagenalstown Ireland 21 F5
Bageshwar India 36 D3
Baggy Point U.K. 19 C7
Bagh India 38 B5
Bāgh, Chāh-e well Iran 35 I5
Bàgh a' Chaisteil U.K. see Castlebay
Baghak Pak. 36 A3
Baghdād Iraq 35 G4
Bāgh-e Malek Iran 35 H5
Bagherhat Bangl. see Bagerhat
Baghlān Afgh. 36 B1
Baghrān Afgh. 36 A2
Bağırsak r. Turkey 39 C1
Bağırsak Deresi r. Syria/Turkey see
  Sājūr, Nahr
Baglung Nepal 37 E3
Bagnères-de-Luchon France 24 E5
Bago Myanmar see Pegu
Bagrationovsk Russia 15 L9
Bagrax China see Bohu
Bagrax Hu l. China see Bosten Hu
Bagur, Cabo c. Spain see Begur, Cap de
Bagzane, Monts mts Niger 46 D3
Bahalda India 37 F5
Bahāmābād Iran see Rafsanjan
Bahamas, The country West Indies 67 I4
Baharampur India 37 G4
Bahardipur Pak. 36 B4
Bahariya Oasis oasis Egypt see
  Bahrīyah, Wāḥāt al
Bahawalnagar Pak. 36 C3
Bahawalpur Pak. 36 C3
Bahçe Adana Turkey 39 B1
Bahçe Osmaniye Turkey 34 E3
Baher Dar Eth. see Bahir Dar
Baheri India 36 D3
Bahia Brazil see Salvador
Bahia state Brazil 71 C1
Bahía, Islas de la is Hond. 67 G5
Bahía Blanca Arg. 70 D5
Bahía Laura Arg. 70 C7
Bahía Negra Para. 70 E2
Bahía Tortugas Mex. 66 B3
Bahir Dar Eth. 48 D2
Bahl India 36 C3
Bahla Oman 35 I5
Bahraich India 37 E4
Bahrain country Asia 32 H4
Bahrām Beyg Iran 35 H3
Bahrīyah, Wāḥāt al oasis Egypt 34 C5
Bahu Kalat Iran 35 J5
Bai India 37 H4
Baia Mare Romania 27 J1
Baicang China 37 G3
Baicheng Jilin China 44 A3
Baicheng Xinjiang China 42 E4
Baidoa Somalia see Baydhabo
Baidoi Co l. China 37 F2
Baie-aux-Feuilles Que. Canada see
  Tasiujaq
Baie-Comeau Que. Canada 63 N2
Baie-du-Poste Que. Canada see Mistissini
Baie-St-Paul Que. Canada 63 M2
Baihar India 37 E5
Baihe China 44 C4
Baiji Iraq see Bayjī
Baikal, Lake Russia 42 J2
Baikalu Shan mt. China 44 A1
Baikunthpur India 37 E5
Baile Átha Cliath Ireland see Dublin
Baile Átha Luain Ireland see Athlone
Baile Mhartainn U.K. 20 B3
Baile na Finne Ireland 21 D3
Băilești Romania 27 J2
Bailey Range hills Australia 55 C7
Bailieborough Ireland 21 F4
Baima Qinghai China 42 I6
Baima Xizang China see Baxoi
Bain r. U.K. 18 G5
Bainang China see Norkyung
Bainbridge GA U.S.A. 63 K6
Bainbridge NY U.S.A. 64 C1
Baindur India 38 B3
Baingoin China see Porong
Baiona Spain 25 B2
Baiquan China 44 B3
Bā'ir Jordan 39 C4
Bā'ir, Wādī watercourse Jordan/
  Saudi Arabia 39 C4
Bairab Co l. China 37 E2
Bairat India 36 D4
Baird Mountains AK U.S.A. 60 C3
Bairiki Kiribati 53 H5
Bairin Youqi China see Daban
Bairnsdale Australia 58 C6
Baisogala Lith. 15 M9
Baitadi Nepal 37 E3
Baitang China 37 I2
Baitou Shan mt. China/N. Korea 44 C4
Baiyin China 42 I5
Baiyuda Desert Sudan 32 D6
Baja Hungary 26 H1
Baja California pen. Mex. 66 A2
Bajawa Indon. 54 C2
Bajbay India 37 F3
Baj Baj India 37 G5
Bājil Yemen 32 F7
Bajo Caracoles Arg. 70 B7
Bajoga Nigeria 46 E3
Bajrakot India 37 E5
Bakala Cent. Afr. Rep. 47 F4
Bakanas Kazakh. 42 D4
Bakel Senegal 46 B3
Baker CA U.S.A. 65 D3
Baker MT U.S.A. 62 G2
Baker NV U.S.A. 65 E1
Baker OR U.S.A. 62 D3
Baker WV U.S.A. 64 B3
Baker, Mount vol. WA U.S.A. 62 C1
Baker Island terr. N. Pacific Ocean 53 I1

Baker Lake imp. l. Australia 55 D6
Baker Lake Nunavut Canada 61 I3
Baker Lake l. Nunavut Canada 61 I3
Bakersfield CA U.S.A. 65 C3
Bakhardok Turkm. see Bokurdak
Bakhasar India 36 B4
Bakhirevo Russia 44 C2
Bakhmach Ukr. 13 G6
Bakhma Dam Iraq see Bēkma, Sadd
Bakhtaran Iran see Kermānshāh
Bakhtegan, Daryācheh-ye l. Iran 35 I5
Baki Azer. see Baku
Bakı Azer. 35 H2
Bakırköy Turkey 27 M4
Bakkafjord Norway 14 K2
Bakloh India 36 D2
Bako Eth. 48 D3
Bakouma Cent. Afr. Rep. 48 C3
Baksan Russia 35 G2
Baku Dem. Rep. Congo 48 D3
Baky Azer. see Baku
Balā Turkey 34 D3
Bala U.K. 19 D6
Bala, Cerros de mts Bol. 68 E6
Balabac Strait Malaysia/Phil. 41 D7
Baladeh Māzandarān Iran 35 H3
Baladeh Māzandarān Iran 35 H3
Baladek Russia 44 D1
Balaghat India 38 D1
Balaghat Range hills India 38 B2
Balaka Malawi 49 D5
Balakän Azer. 35 G2
Balakhna Russia 12 I4
Balakhta Russia 42 G1
Balaklava Australia 57 B7
Balaklava Ukr. 34 D1
Balakleya Ukr. see Balakliya
Balakliya Ukr. 13 H6
Balakovo Russia 13 J5
Bala Lake l. U.K. 19 D6
Balaman India 36 B4
Balan India 36 B4
Balan Dağı h. Turkey 27 M6
Balanda Russia see Kalininsk
Balanda r. Russia 13 J6
Balanga Phil. 41 E6
Balangir India 38 D1
Balaözen r. Kazakh./Russia see Saryozen
Balarampur India see Balrampur
Bālā Shahr Iran 33 I4
Balashov Russia 13 I6
Balasore India see Baleshwar
Balaton, Lake Hungary 26 G1
Balatonboglár Hungary 26 G1
Balatonfüred Hungary 26 G1
Balbina Brazil 69 G4
Balbina, Represa de resr Brazil 69 G4
Balbriggan Ireland 21 F4
Balch Bulg. 27 M3
Balchik Bulg. 27 M3
Balclutha N.Z. 59 B8
Bald Mountain NV U.S.A. 65 E2
Baldwin PA U.S.A. 64 F2
Baldy Mountain h. Man. Canada 62 G1
Baldy Peak AZ U.S.A. 62 F5
Bâle Switz. see Basel
Baléa Mali 46 B3
Baleares is Spain see Balearic Islands
Baleares, Islas is Spain see Balearic Islands
Baleares Insulae is Spain see
  Balearic Islands
Balearic Islands is Spain 25 G4
Balears is Spain see Balearic Islands
Balears, Illes is Spain see Balearic Islands
Baleia, Ponta da pt Brazil 71 D2
Bale Mountains National Park Eth. 48 D3
Baleshwar India 37 F5
Balestrand Norway 15 E6
Balestrieri, Punta mt. Italy 26 C4
Baléyara Niger 46 D3
Balezino Russia 12 L4
Balfe's Creek Australia 56 D4
Balfour Downs Australia 54 C5
Balfron U.K. 20 E4
Balgo Australia 54 D5
Balguntay China 42 F4
Bali India 36 C4
Bali i. Indon. 41 D8
Bali, Laut sea Indon. 41 D8
Ballia India 37 F4
Baliapal India 37 F5
Balige N. Korea 45 B5
Baligurha India 38 D1
Balikesir Turkey 27 L5
Balıkpapan Indon. 41 D8
Balimila Reservoir India 38 D2
Balin P.N.G. 52 E2
Balin China 44 A2
Balingen Germany 17 L6
Balintore U.K. 20 F3
Balkanabat Turkm. 35 I3
Balkan Mountains Bulg./Serbia 27 J3
Balkash Kazakh. 42 D3
Balkassar Pak. 36 C2
Balkh r. Afgh. 36 A1
Balkhash Kazakh. 42 D3
Balkhash, Ozero l. Kazakh. see
  Balkhash, Lake
Balkuduk Kazakh. 13 J7
Ballachulish U.K. 20 D4
Balladonia Australia 55 C8
Balladoran Australia 58 D3
Ballaghaderreen Ireland 21 D4
Ballan Australia 58 B6
Ballangen Norway 14 J2
Ballantrae U.K. 20 E5
Ballarat Australia 58 A6
Ballard, Lake imp. l. Australia 55 C7
Ballarpur India 38 C2
Ballater U.K. 20 F3
Ballé Mali 46 C3
Ballena, Punta pt Chile 70 B3
Balleny Islands Antarctica 76 H2
Ballia India 37 F4
Ballina Australia 58 F2
Ballina Ireland 21 C3
Ballinafad Ireland 21 D4
Ballinamore Ireland 21 E3
Ballinasloe Ireland 21 D4
Ballindine Ireland 21 D4
Ballinger TX U.S.A. 63 H5
Ballinluig U.K. 20 F4
Ballinrobe Ireland 21 C4
Ballinskelligs Bay Ireland 21 B6
Ballintoy U.K. 21 F2
Ballsh Albania 27 H4
Ballston Spa NY U.S.A. 64 E1
Ballybay Ireland 21 F3
Ballybofey Ireland 21 E3
Ballybunion Ireland 21 C5
Ballycanew Ireland 21 F5
Ballycastle Ireland 21 C3
Ballycastle U.K. 21 F2
Ballyclare U.K. 21 G3
Ballyconnell Ireland 21 E3
Ballygar Ireland 21 D4
Ballygorman Ireland 21 E2
Ballyhaunis Ireland 21 D4
Ballyheigue Ireland 21 C5
Ballykelly U.K. 21 E2
Ballylynan Ireland 21 E5
Ballymacmague Ireland 21 E5
Ballymahon Ireland 21 E4

Ballymena U.K. 21 F3
Ballymoney U.K. 21 F2
Ballynahinch U.K. 21 G3
Ballyshannon Ireland 21 D3
Ballyteige Bay Ireland 21 F5
Ballyvaughan Ireland 21 C4
Ballyward Ireland 21 F3
Balmartin U.K. see Baile Mhartainn
Balmer U.K. see Barmer
Balochistan prov. Pak. 36 A3
Balombo Angola 49 B5
Balonne r. Australia 58 D2
Balotra India 36 C4
Balqash Kazakh. see Balkash
Balqash Köli l. Kazakh. see Balkhash, Lake
Balrampur India 37 E4
Balranald Australia 58 A5
Bals Romania 27 K2
Balsas Brazil 69 I5
Balta Ukr. 13 F7
Baltasound U.K. 20 [inset]
Baltay Russia 13 J5
Bălți Moldova 13 F7
Baltic Sea g. Europe 15 J5
Baltīm Egypt 34 C5
Baltim Egypt see Baltīm
Baltimore S. Africa 51 I2
Baltimore MD U.S.A. 64 C3
Baltinglass Ireland 21 F5
Baltiysk Russia 15 K9
Baltistan reg. Pak. 36 C2
Balurghat India 37 G4
Balvi Latvia 15 O8
Balya Turkey 27 L5
Balykchy Kyrg. 42 D4
Balykshi Kazakh. 30 E2
Balyqshy Kazakh. see Balykshi
Bam Iran 33 I4
Bamako Mali 46 C3
Bamba Mali 46 C3
Bambari Cent. Afr. Rep. 48 C3
Bamberg Germany 17 M6
Bambili Dem. Rep. Congo 48 C3
Bambio Cent. Afr. Rep. 48 B3
Bamboesberg mts S. Africa 51 H6
Bamboo Creek Australia 54 C5
Bambouti Cent. Afr. Rep. 48 C3
Bambuí Brazil 71 B3
Bamda China 37 I3
Bamenda Cameroon 46 E4
Bamiantong China see Muling
Bamingui Cent. Afr. Rep. 48 C3
Bamingui-Bangoran, Parc National du
  nat. park Cent. Afr. Rep. 48 B3
Bamor India 36 D4
Bamori India 38 C1
Bampton U.K. 19 D8
Bamrūd Iran 33 I3
Bāmyān Afgh. 36 A2
Bamyili Australia 54 F3
Banaba i. Kiribati 53 G2
Banabuiu, Açude resr Brazil 69 K5
Banagher Ireland 21 E4
Banalia Dem. Rep. Congo 48 C3
Banamana, Lagoa l. Moz. 51 K2
Banana Australia 56 E5
Bananal, Ilha do i. Brazil 69 H6
Banapur India 38 E2
Banas r. India 36 C4
Banaz Turkey 27 M5
Ban Ban Laos 42 I9
Banbridge U.K. 21 F3
Banbury U.K. 19 F6
Ban Cang Vietnam 42 I8
Banc d'Arguin, Parc National du nat. park
  Mauritania 46 B2
Banchory U.K. 20 G3
Bancroft Zambia see Chililabombwe
Banda Dem. Rep. Congo 48 C3
Banda India 36 E4
Banda, Kepulauan is Indon. 41 E8
Banda, Laut sea Indon. 41 F8
Banda Banda, Mount Australia 58 F3
Banda Daud Shah Pak. 36 B2
Bandama r. Côte d'Ivoire 46 C4
Bandar India see Machilipatnam
Bandar Moz. 49 D5
Bandar Abbas Iran see Bandar-e 'Abbās
Bandarban Bangl. 37 H5
Bandar-e 'Abbās Iran 33 I4
Bandar-e Anzalī Iran 35 H3
Bandar-e Büshehr Iran 35 H5
Bandar-e Dayyer Iran 35 H5
Bandar-e Deylam Iran 35 H5
Bandar-e Emām Khomeynī Iran 35 H5
Bandar-e Ganāveh Iran 35 H5
Bandar-e Heydarābād Iran 35 I5
Bandar-e Jāsk Iran 33 I4
Bandar-e Lengeh Iran 35 I5
Bandar-e Māhshahr Iran 35 H5
Bandar-e Nakhīlū Iran 35 I5
Bandar-e Pahlavī Iran see Bandar-e Anzalī
Bandar-e Shāh Iran see
  Bandar-e Torkaman
Bandar-e Shāhpūr Iran see
  Bandar-e Emām Khomeynī
Bandar-e Torkaman Iran 35 I3
Bandar Lampung Indon. 41 C8
Bandarpunch mt. India 36 D3
Banda Sea Indon. see Banda, Laut
Band-e Bamposht, Kūh-e mts Iran 33 J4
Bandeira Brazil 71 C1
Bandeirante Brazil 71 A1
Bandeiras, Pico de mt. Brazil 71 C3
Bandelierkop S. Africa 51 I2
Banderas, Bahía de b. Mex. 66 C4
Band-e Sar Qom Iran 35 I3
Bandhi Pak. 36 B4
Bandhogarh India 36 E5
Bandi r. India 36 C4
Bandiagara Mali 46 C3
Bandikui India 36 D4
Bandipur National Park India 38 C4
Bandırma Turkey 27 L4
Bandjarmasin Indon. see Banjarmasin
Bandon Ireland 21 D6
Ban Don Thai. see Surat Thani
Bandon r. Ireland 21 D6
Bandra India 38 B2
Bandundu Dem. Rep. Congo 48 B4
Bandung Indon. 41 C8
Bandya Australia 55 C6
Bāneh Iran 35 G3
Banera India 36 C4
Banes r. India 36 C4
Banff Alta Canada 62 D1
Banff U.K. 20 G3
Banfora Burkina Faso 46 C3
Banga Dem. Rep. Congo 49 C4
Bangalore India 38 C3
Bangalow Australia 58 F2
Bangaon India 37 G5
Bangassou Cent. Afr. Rep. 48 C3
Bangdag Co salt l. China 37 E2
Banggai Indon. 52 C2
Banggai, Kepulauan is Indon. 41 E8

Banggi i. Malaysia 41 D7
Banghāzī Libya see Benghazi
Bangka i. Indon. 41 C8
Bangko Indon. 41 C8
Bangkok Thai. 31 J5
Bangkor China 37 F3
Bangla state India see West Bengal
Bangladesh country Asia 37 G4
Bangolo Côte d'Ivoire 46 C4
Bangong Co salt l. China/India 36 D2
Bangor Northern Ireland U.K. 21 G3
Bangor Wales U.K. 18 C5
Bangor ME U.S.A. 63 N3
Bangor PA U.S.A. 64 D2
Bangor Erris Ireland 21 C3
Bangs, Mount AZ U.S.A. 65 F2
Bangsund Norway 14 G4
Bangued Phil. 43 M9
Bangui Cent. Afr. Rep. 48 B3
Bangweulu, Lake Zambia 49 C5
Banhā Egypt 34 C5
Banhine, Parque Nacional de nat. park Moz. 51 K2
Ban Houei Sai Laos see Houayxay
Bani, Jebel ridge Morocco 22 C6
Bania Cent. Afr. Rep. 48 B3
Bani-Bangou Niger 46 D3
Banifing r. Mali 46 C3
Banihal Pass and Tunnel India 36 C2
Banister r. VA U.S.A. 64 B4
Banī Suwayf Egypt 34 C5
Banī Walīd Libya 47 E1
Bāniyās Israel 39 B3
Bāniyās Syria 39 B2
Banja Luka Bos. & Herz. 26 G2
Banjarmasin Indon. 41 D8
Banjës, Liqeni i resr Albania 27 I4
Banjul Gambia 46 B3
Banka India 37 F4
Banka Banka Australia 54 F4
Bankapur India 38 B3
Bankass Mali 46 C3
Bankilaré Niger 46 D3
Banks Island N.W.T. Canada 60 F2
Banks Islands Vanuatu 53 G3
Banks Peninsula N.Z. 59 D6
Banks Strait Australia 57 [inset]
Bankura India 37 F5
Banmaw Myanmar see Bhamo
Banmo Myanmar see Bhamo
Bann r. Ireland 21 F5
Bann r. U.K. 21 F2
Banning CA U.S.A. 65 D4
Banningville Dem. Rep. Congo see Bandundu
Bannu Pak. 36 B2
Bano India 37 F5
Bañolas Spain see Banyoles
Ban Phôn-Hông Laos 42 I9
Bansi Bihar India 37 F4
Bansi Rajasthan India 36 C4
Bansi Uttar Prad. India 36 D4
Bansi Uttar Prad. India 37 E4
Bansihari India 37 G4
Banská Bystrica Slovakia 17 Q6
Banspani India 37 F5
Bansur India 36 D4
Banswara India 36 C5
Banteer Ireland 21 D5
Bantry Ireland 21 C6
Bantry Bay Ireland 21 C6
Bantval India 38 B3
Banyo Cameroon 46 E4
Banyoles Spain 25 H2
Banyuwangi Indon. 54 A2
Banzare Coast Antarctica 76 G2
Banzare Seamount sea feature Indian Ocean 73 N9
Banzart Tunisia see Bizerte
Banzyville Dem. Rep. Congo see Mobayi-Mbongo
Bao'an China see Shenzhen
Baochang China 43 L4
Baoding China 43 L5
Baoji China 42 J6
Baokang China 44 A3
Baolin China 44 C3
Baoqing China 44 D3
Baoro Cent. Afr. Rep. 48 B3
Baoshan China 42 H7
Baotou China 43 K4
Baoulé r. Mali 46 C3
Bap India 36 C4
Bapatla India 38 D3
Baq'ā' Saudi Arabia 35 F6
Baqbaq Egypt see Buqbuq
Baqên Xizang China 37 H2
Baqên Xizang China 37 H3
Ba'qūbah Iraq 35 G4
Bar Montenegro 27 H3
Bara Sudan 32 D7
Baraawe Somalia 48 E3
Barabanki India 36 E4
Bara Banki India see Barabanki
Baracaju r. Brazil 71 A1
Baracaldo Spain see Barakaldo
Baracoa Cuba 67 J4
Baradā, Nahr r. Syria 39 C3
Baradine Australia 58 D3
Baradine r. Australia 58 D3
Baragarh India see Bargarh
Barahona Dom. Rep. 67 J5
Barail Range mts India 37 H4
Baraka watercourse Eritrea/Sudan 47 G3
Barakaldo Spain 25 E2
Barakī Barak Afgh. 36 B2
Baralaba Australia 56 E5
Bara Lacha La India 36 D2
Baram India 37 F5
Baramati India 38 B2
Baramula India see Baramulla
Baramulla India 36 C2
Baran India 36 D4
Baran r. Pak. 36 B4
Barana Pak. 36 C3
Baranavichy Belarus 15 O10
Baranikha Russia 29 R3
Baranīs Egypt see Baranīs
Baranīs Egypt 32 E5
Barannda India 36 E4
Baranof Island AK U.S.A. 60 E4
Baranovichi Belarus see Baranavichy
Baranowicze Belarus see Baranavichy
Baraouéli Mali 46 C3
Barasat India 37 G5
Barat Daya, Kepulauan is Indon. 41 E8
Baraut India 36 D3
Barbacena Brazil 71 C3
Barbados country West Indies 67 M6
Barbar, Gebel el mt. Egypt see Barbar, Jabal
Barbar, Jabal mt. Egypt 39 A5
Barbastro Spain 25 G2
Barbate Spain 25 D5
Barberton S. Africa 51 J3
Barbezieux-St-Hilaire France 24 D4
Barbuda i. Antigua and Barbuda 67 L5
Barcaldine Australia 56 D4
Barce Libya see Al Marj
Barcelona Spain 25 H3
Barcelona Venez. 68 F1
Barcelonnette France 24 H4
Barcelos Brazil 68 F4
Barcino Spain see Barcelona
Barclay de Tolly atoll Fr. Polynesia see Raroia
Barclayville Liberia 46 C4
Barcoo watercourse Australia 56 C5
Barcoo Creek watercourse Australia see Cooper Creek
Barcoo National Park Australia see Welford National Park
Barcs Hungary 26 G2
Bärdä Azer. 35 G2
Bardaï Chad 47 E2
Bárðarbunga mt. Iceland 14 [inset 2]
Bardawil, Khabrat al salt pan Saudi Arabia 39 D4
Bardawīl, Sabkhat al lag. Egypt 39 A4
Barddhaman India 37 F5
Bardejov Slovakia 13 D6
Bardera Somalia see Baardheere
Bardhaman India see Barddhaman
Bardsey Island U.K. 19 C6
Bardsīr Iran 33 I4
Barðsneshorn pt Iceland 10 D2
Barduli Italy see Barletta
Bareilly India 36 D3
Barellan Australia 58 C5
Barentin France 19 H9
Barentsburg Svalbard 28 C2
Barents Sea Arctic Ocean 12 I1
Barentu Eritrea 32 E6
Barfleur, Pointe de pt France 19 F9
Bargarh India 37 E5
Bargrennan U.K. 20 E5
Barguna Bangl. 37 G5
Barhaj India 37 E4
Barham Australia 58 B5
Bari Italy 26 G4
Bariadi Tanz. 48 D4
Bari Doab lowland Pak. 33 L3
Barika Alg. 22 F4
Barinas Venez. 68 D2
Baripada India 37 F5
Bariri Brazil 71 A3
Bari Sadri India 36 C4
Barisal Bangl. 37 G5
Barisan, Pegunungan mts Indon. 41 C8
Barito r. Indon. 41 D8
Barium Italy see Bari
Barkal Bangl. 37 H5
Barkam China 42 I6
Barkan, Ra's-e pt Iran 35 H5
Barkava Latvia 15 O8
Barkly East S. Africa 51 H6
Barkly Homestead Australia 56 A3
Barkly-Oos S. Africa see Barkly East
Barkly Tableland reg. Australia 56 A3
Barkly-Wes S. Africa see Barkly West
Barkly West S. Africa 50 G5
Barkol China 42 G4
Barla Turkey 27 N5
Bârlad Romania 27 L1
Bar-le-Duc France 24 G2
Barlee, Lake imp. l. Australia 55 B7
Barlee Range hills Australia 55 A5
Barletta Italy 26 G4
Barlow Y.T. Canada 60 E3
Barmah Forest Australia 58 B5
Barmedman Australia 58 C5
Barmen-Elberfeld Germany see Wuppertal
Barmer India 36 B4
Barm Fīrūz, Kūh-e mt. Iran 35 H5
Barmouth U.K. 19 C6
Barnala India 36 C3
Barnard Castle U.K. 18 F4
Barnato Australia 58 B3
Barnaul Russia 42 E2
Barnegat Bay NJ U.S.A. 64 D3
Barnes Icecap Nunavut Canada 61 K2
Barneville-Carteret France 19 F9
Barnes Lake imp. l. Australia 58 B4
Barnsley U.K. 18 F5
Barnstable MA U.S.A. 64 F2
Barnstaple U.K. 19 C7
Barnstaple Bay U.K. 19 C7
Baro Nigeria 46 D4
Baroda Gujarat India see Vadodara
Baroda Madh. Prad. India 36 D4
Barons Range hills Australia 55 D6
Barpeta India 37 G4
Bar Pla Soi Thai. see Chon Buri
Barquisimeto Venez. 68 E1
Barra Brazil 69 J6
Barra i. U.K. 20 B4
Barra, Ponta da pt Moz. 51 L2
Barra, Sound of sea chan. U.K. 20 B3
Barraba Australia 58 E3
Barra Bonita Brazil 71 A3
Barracão do Barreto Brazil 69 G5
Barra do Bugres Brazil 69 G7
Barra do Corda Brazil 69 I5
Barra do Cuieté Brazil 71 C2
Barra do Garças Brazil 69 H7
Barra do Piraí Brazil 71 C3
Barra do São Manuel Brazil 69 G5
Barra do Turvo Brazil 71 A4
Barra Falsa, Ponta da pt Moz. 51 L2
Barraigh i. U.K. see Barra
Barra Mansa Brazil 71 B3
Barranca Peru 68 C4
Barranqueras Arg. 70 E3
Barranquilla Col. 68 D1
Barre MA U.S.A. 64 E1
Barre des Écrins mt. France 24 H4
Barreiras Brazil 69 J6
Barreirinha Brazil 69 G4
Barreirinhas Brazil 69 J4
Barreiro Port. 25 B4
Barreiros Brazil 69 K5
Barren Island Kiribati see Starbuck Island
Barretos Brazil 71 A3
Barrett, Mount h. Australia 54 D4
Barrhead U.K. 20 E5
Barrier Bay Antarctica 76 E2
Barrière B.C. Canada 62 C1
Barrier Range hills Australia 57 C6
Barrington, Mount Australia 58 E4
Barrington Tops National Park Australia 58 E4
Barringun Australia 58 B2
Barro Alto Brazil 71 A1
Barrocão Brazil 71 C2
Barron WI U.S.A. 63 I2
Barrow r. Ireland 21 F5
Barrow AK U.S.A. 60 C2
Barrow, Point AK U.S.A. 60 C2
Barrow Creek Australia 54 F5
Barrow-in-Furness U.K. 18 D4
Barrow Island Australia 54 A5
Barrow Range hills Australia 55 D6
Barrow Strait Nunavut Canada 61 I2
Barr Smith Range hills Australia 55 C6
Barry U.K. 19 D7
Barrydale S. Africa 50 E7
Barry Mountains Australia 58 C6
Barryville NY U.S.A. 64 D2
Barsalpur India 36 C3
Barshatas Kazakh. 42 D3
Barshi India see Barsi
Barsi India 38 B2
Barstow CA U.S.A. 65 D3
Barsur India 38 D2
Bar-sur-Aube France 24 G2
Barth Germany 17 N3
Bartica Guyana 69 G2
Bartın Turkey 34 D2
Bartle Frere, Mount Australia 56 D3
Barton-upon-Humber U.K. 18 G5
Bartoszyce Poland 17 R3
Barú, Volcán vol. Panama 67 H7
Barunga Australia see Bamyili
Barun-Torey, Ozero l. Russia 43 L2
Baruunturuun Mongolia 42 G3
Baruun-Urt Mongolia 43 K3
Baruva India 38 E2
Barwani India 36 C5
Barwéli Mali see Baraouéli
Barwon r. Australia 58 C3
Barygaza India see Bharuch
Barysaw Belarus 15 P9
Barysh Russia 13 J5
Basalt r. Australia 56 D3
Basankusu Dem. Rep. Congo 48 B3
Basar India 38 C2
Basarabi Romania 27 M2
Basargechar Armenia see Vardenis
Bascuñán, Cabo c. Chile 70 B3
Basel Switz. 24 H3
Bashanta Russia see Gorodovikovsk
Bāshī Iran 35 H5
Bashi Channel Phil./Taiwan 43 M8
Bashmakovo Russia 13 I5
Bāsht Iran 35 H5
Bashtanka Ukr. 13 G7
Basi Punjab India 36 D3
Basi Rajasthan India 36 D4
Basia India 37 F5
Basilan i. Phil. 41 E7
Basildon U.K. 19 H7
Basile, Pico vol. Equat. Guinea 46 D4
Basingstoke U.K. 19 F7
Basirhat India 37 G5
Basīţ, Ra's al pt Syria 39 B2
Başkale Turkey 35 G3
Baskatong, Réservoir resr Que. Canada 63 L2
Baskerville, Cape Australia 54 C4
Başkomutan Tarıhı Milli Parkı nat. park Turkey 27 N5
Başköy Turkey 39 A1
Baskunchak, Ozero l. Russia 13 J6
Basle Switz. see Basel
Basmat India 38 C2
Basoko Dem. Rep. Congo 48 C3
Basra Iraq 35 G5
Bassano Alta Canada 62 E1
Bassano del Grappa Italy 26 D2
Bassar Togo 46 D4
Bassas da India reef Indian Ocean 49 D6
Bassas de Pedro Padua Bank sea feature India 38 B3
Bassein Myanmar 42 G9
Basse-Normandie admin. reg. France 19 F9
Bassenthwaite Lake U.K. 18 D4
Basse Santa Su Gambia 46 B3
Basse-Terre Guadeloupe 67 L5
Basseterre St Kitts and Nevis 67 L5
Bassikounou Mauritania 46 C3
Bass Rock i. U.K. 20 G4
Bass Strait Australia 57 D8
Båstad Sweden 15 H8
Basti India 37 E4
Bastia Corsica France 24 I5
Bastioes r. Brazil 69 K5
Bastogne Belgium 17 J5
Bastrop LA U.S.A. 63 I5
Basuo China see Dongfang
Basutoland country Africa see Lesotho
Başyayla Turkey 39 A1
Bata Equat. Guinea 46 D4
Batabanó, Golfo de b. Cuba 67 H4
Batagay Russia 29 O3
Batala India 36 C3
Batalha Port. 25 B4
Batamay Russia 29 N3
Batan i. Phil. 43 M8
Batangafo Cent. Afr. Rep. 48 B3
Batangas Phil. 41 E6
Batan Islands Phil. 41 E5
Batavia Indon. see Jakarta
Batavia NY U.S.A. 64 B1
Bataysk Russia 13 H7
Batchawana Mountain h. Ont. Canada 63 K2
Bătdâmbâng Cambodia 31 J5
Batéké, Plateaux Congo 48 B4
Batemans Bay Australia 58 E5
Bates Range hills Australia 55 C6
Batesville AR U.S.A. 63 I4
Batetskiy Russia 12 F4
Bath U.K. 19 E7
Bath NY U.S.A. 64 C1
Batha watercourse Chad 47 E3
Bathgate U.K. 20 F5
Bathinda India 36 C3
Bathurst Australia 58 D4
Bathurst N.B. Canada 63 N2
Bathurst Gambia see Banjul
Bathurst S. Africa 51 H7
Bathurst, Cape N.W.T. Canada 60 F2
Bathurst, Lake Australia 58 D5
Bathurst Inlet inlet Nunavut Canada 60 H3
Bathurst Inlet (abandoned) Nunavut Canada 60 H3
Bathurst Island Australia 54 E2
Bathurst Island Nunavut Canada 61 I2
Batié Burkina Faso 46 C4
Batı Menteşe Dağları mts Turkey 27 L6
Batı Toroslar mts Turkey 27 N6
Batken Kyrg. 42 C5
Batkes Indon. 54 E1
Bāţlāq-e Gavkhūnī marsh Iran 35 I4
Batley U.K. 18 F5
Batlow Australia 58 D5
Batman Turkey 35 F3
Batna Alg. 22 F4
Baton Rouge LA U.S.A. 63 I5
Batouri Cameroon 47 E4
Batrā' tourist site Jordan see Petra
Batrā', Jabal al mt. Jordan 39 B5
Batroûn Lebanon 39 B2
Båtsfjord Norway 14 P1
Battambang Cambodia see Bătdâmbâng
Batticaloa Sri Lanka 38 D5
Battipaglia Italy 26 F4
Battle r. Alta/Sask. Canada 62 F1
Battle Creek MI U.S.A. 63 J3
Battle Mountain NV U.S.A. 62 D3
Battura Glacier Pak. 36 C1
Batu mt. Eth. 48 D3
Batu, Pulau-pulau is Indon. 41 B8
Batum Georgia see Batumi
Batumi Georgia 35 F2
Baturité Brazil 69 K4
Batyrevo Russia 13 J5
Batys Qazaqstan admin. div. Kazakh. see Zapadnyy Kazakhstan
Baubau Indon. 41 E8
Baucau East Timor 54 D2
Bauchi Nigeria 46 D3
Bauda India 38 E1
Baudh India see Bauda
Baugé-en-Anjou France 24 D3
Bauhinia Australia 56 E5
Baukau East Timor see Baucau
Baume-les-Dames France 24 H3
Baura Bangl. 37 G4
Bauru Brazil 71 A3
Bauska Latvia 15 N8
Bautino Kazakh. 35 H1
Bautzen Germany 17 O5
Bavānāt Iran 35 I5
Bavaria reg. Germany 17 M6
Bavda India 38 B2
Baviaanskloofberge mts S. Africa 50 F7
Bavla India 36 C5
Bavly Russia 11 Q5
Baw Myanmar 37 H5
Bawal India 36 D3
Baw Baw National Park Australia 58 C6
Bawdeswell U.K. 19 I6
Baxoi China 42 H6
Bay China see Baicheng
Bayamo Cuba 67 I4
Bayan Heilongjiang China 44 B3
Bayan Qinghai China 37 I2
Bayana India 36 D4
Bayan-Adarga Mongolia 43 K3
Bayanaul Kazakh. 42 D2
Bayanbulak China 42 E4
Bayanday Russia 42 J2
Bayan Gol China see Dengkou
Bayan Har Shan mts China 42 G5
Bayan Har Shankou pass China 37 I2
Bayanhongor Mongolia 42 I3
Bayan Hot China 42 J5
Bayanlū Iran 35 G4
Bayannur China 43 J4
Bayan Obo China 43 J4
Bayan Shutu China 43 K4
Bayantsagaan Mongolia 42 H3
Bayan Ul China 43 L4
Bayan-Uul Mongolia 43 K3
Bayat Turkey 27 N5
Bayāẓīyeh Iran 35 I4
Bayburt Turkey 35 F2
Bay City MI U.S.A. 63 K3
Bay City TX U.S.A. 63 H6
Baydaratskaya Guba Russia 28 H3
Baydhabo Somalia 48 E3
Bayerischer Wald mts Germany 17 N6
Bayerischer Wald, Nationalpark nat. park Germany 17 N6
Bayeux France 19 G9
Bayfield Ont. Canada 64 A1
Bayındır Turkey 27 L5
Bay Islands is Hond. see Bahía, Islas de la
Bayizhen China see Nyingchi
Bayjī Iraq 35 F4
Baykal, Ozero l. Russia see Baikal, Lake
Baykal-Amur Magistral Russia 44 C1
Baykal Range mts Russia see Baykal'skiy Khrebet
Baykal'skiy Khrebet mts Russia 43 J2
Baykan Turkey 35 F3
Bay-Khaak Russia 42 G2
Baykibashevo Russia 11 R4
Baykonur Kazakh. see Baykonyr
Baykonyr Kazakh. 42 A3
Baymak Russia 28 G4
Bayombong Phil. 41 E6
Bayona Spain see Baiona
Bayonne France 24 D5
Bayonne NJ U.S.A. 64 D2
Bayqongyr Kazakh. see Baykonyr
Bayram-Ali Turkm. see Baýramaly
Baýramaly Turkm. 33 J2
Bayramiç Turkey 27 L5
Bayreuth Germany 17 M6
Bayrūt Lebanon see Beirut
Bay Shore NY U.S.A. 64 E2
Bayston Hill U.K. 19 E6
Bayt Jālā West Bank 39 B4
Bayt Lahm West Bank see Bethlehem
Bay View N.Z. 59 F4
Bayy al Kabīr, Wādī watercourse Libya 47 E1
Baza Spain 25 E5
Baza, Sierra de mts Spain 25 E5
Bazardüzü Dağı mt. Azer./Russia see Bazardyuzyu, Gora
Bazardyuzyu, Gora mt. Azer./Russia 35 G2
Bāzār-e Māsāl Iran 35 H3
Bazarnyy Karabulak Russia 13 J5
Bazaruto, Ilha do i. Moz. 49 D6
Bazdar Pak. 33 K4
Bazhong China 42 J6
Bazhou China see Bazhong
Bazmān Iran 33 J4
Bazmān, Kūh-e mt. Iran 33 J4
Bcharré Lebanon 39 C2
Beachy Head hd U.K. 19 H8
Beacon NY U.S.A. 64 E2
Beacon Bay S. Africa 51 H7
Beaconsfield U.K. 19 G7
Beagle, Canal sea chan. Arg. 70 C8
Beagle Bank reef Australia 54 C3
Beagle Bay Australia 54 C4
Beagle Gulf Australia 54 E3
Bealanana Madag. 49 E5
Béal an Átha Ireland see Ballina
Béal an Mhuirthead Ireland 21 C3
Béal Átha na Sluaighe Ireland see Ballinasloe
Beale, Lake India 38 B2
Beaminster U.K. 19 E8
Bearalváhki Norway see Berlevåg
Beardmore Glacier Antarctica 76 H1
Bear Island Arctic Ocean see Bjørnøya
Bearma r. India 36 D4
Bearnaraigh i. U.K. see Berneray
Bear Paw Mountain MT U.S.A. 62 E2
Bearpaw Mountains MT U.S.A. 62 F2
Beas Dam India 36 C3
Beata, Cabo c. Dom. Rep. 67 J5
Beatrice NE U.S.A. 63 H3
Beatrice, Cape Australia 56 B2
Beatty NV U.S.A. 65 D2
Beaucaire France 24 G5
Beauchene Island Falkland Is 70 E8
Beaufort Australia 58 A6
Beaufort Sea Canada/U.S.A. 60 D2
Beaufort West S. Africa 50 F7
Beauly U.K. 20 E3
Beauly r. U.K. 20 E3
Beaumaris U.K. 18 C5
Beaumont N.Z. 59 B7
Beaumont TX U.S.A. 63 I5
Beaune France 24 G3
Beaupréau France 24 D3
Beauséjour Man. Canada 63 H1
Beauvais France 24 F2
Beaver r. Alta/Sask. Canada 60 H4
Beaver PA U.S.A. 64 A2
Beaver UT U.S.A. 65 F1
Beaver r. UT U.S.A. 65 F1
Beaver Creek Y.T. Canada 77 A2
Beaver Falls PA U.S.A. 64 A2
Beaver Hill Lake Man. Canada 63 H1
Beaver Island MI U.S.A. 63 J2
Beawar India 36 C4
Beazley Arg. 70 C4
Bebedouro Brazil 71 A3
Bebington U.K. 18 D5
Bêca China 37 I3
Beccles U.K. 19 I6
Bečej Serbia 27 I2
Becerreá Spain 25 C2
Béchar Alg. 22 D5
Bechuanaland country Africa see Botswana
Beckley WV U.S.A. 64 A4
Bedale U.K. 18 F4
Bedelē Eth. 48 D3
Bedford E. Cape S. Africa 51 H7
Bedford KwaZulu-Natal S. Africa 51 J5
Bedford U.K. 19 G6
Bedford IN U.S.A. 63 J4
Bedford PA U.S.A. 64 B2
Bedford VA U.S.A. 64 B4
Bedford, Cape Australia 56 D2
Bedford Downs Australia 54 D4
Bedgerebong Australia 58 C4
Bedi India 36 B5
Bedla India 36 C4
Bedlington U.K. 18 F3
Bedourie Australia 56 B5
Bedworth U.K. 19 F6
Beechworth Australia 58 C6
Beecroft Peninsula Australia 58 E5
Beed India see Bid
Beenleigh Australia 58 F1
Beersheba Israel 39 B4
Be'er Sheva' Israel see Beersheba
Be'ér Sheva', Naḥal watercourse Israel 39 B4
Beervlei Dam S. Africa 50 F7
Beerwah Australia 58 F1
Beetaloo Australia 54 F4
Beethoven Peninsula Antarctica 76 L2
Beeville TX U.S.A. 62 H6
Befori Dem. Rep. Congo 48 C3
Beg, Lough l. U.K. 21 F3
Bega Australia 58 D6
Begari r. Pak. 36 B3
Begicheva, Ostrov i. Russia see Bol'shoy Begichev, Ostrov
Begur, Cap de c. Spain 25 H3
Begusarai India 37 F4
Béhague, Pointe pt Fr. Guiana 69 H3
Behbahān Iran 35 H5
Behchokǫ̀ N.W.T. Canada 60 G3
Behrūsī Iran 35 I5
Behshahr Iran 35 I3
Bei'an China 44 B2
Beida Libya see Al Bayḍā'
Beiguan China see Anyang
Beihai China 43 J8
Bei Hulsan Hu salt l. China 37 H1
Beijing China 43 L5
Beijing mun. China 43 L4
Beik Myanmar see Myeik
Beinn an Oir h. U.K. 20 D5
Beinn an Tuirc h. U.K. 20 D5
Beinn Bheigeir h. U.K. 20 C5
Beinn Bhreac h. U.K. 20 D4
Beinn Dearg mt. U.K. 20 E3
Beinn Heasgarnich mt. U.K. 20 E4
Beinn Mholach h. U.K. 20 C2
Beinn Mhòr h. U.K. 20 B3
Beinn na Faoghlia i. U.K. see Benbecula
Beipiao China 43 M4
Beira Moz. 49 D5
Beirut Lebanon 39 B3
Bei Shan mts China 42 H4
Beitbridge Zimbabwe 49 C6
Beith U.K. 20 E5
Beja Port. 25 C4
Béja Tunisia 26 C6
Bejaïa Alg. 25 I5
Béjar Spain 25 D3
Bekaa val. Lebanon see El Béqaa
Békés Hungary 27 I1
Békéscsaba Hungary 27 I1
Bekily Madag. 49 E6
Bēkma, Sadd dam Iraq 35 G3
Bekovo Russia 13 I5
Bekwai Ghana 46 C4
Bela India 37 E4
Bela Pak. 33 K4
Belab r. Pak. 36 B3
Bela-Bela S. Africa 51 I3
Bélabo Cameroon 46 E4
Bela Crkva Serbia 27 I2
Belagavi India see Belgaum
Bel Air MD U.S.A. 64 C3
Belalcázar Spain 25 D4
Belapur India 38 B2
Belarus country Europe 13 E5
Belau country N. Pacific Ocean see Palau
Bela Vista Brazil 70 E2
Bela Vista Moz. 51 K4
Bela Vista de Goiás Brazil 71 A2
Belaya Glina Russia 13 I7
Belaya Kalitva Russia 13 I6
Belaya Kholunitsa Russia 12 K4
Belaya Tserkva Ukr. see Bila Tserkva
Belbédji Niger 46 D3
Bełchatów Poland 17 Q5
Belcher Islands Nunavut Canada 61 K4
Belcoo U.K. 21 E3
Beleapani reef India see Cherbaniani Reef
Belebey Russia 11 Q5
Beledweyne Somalia 48 E3
Belém Brazil 69 I4
Belém Novo Brazil 71 A5
Belén Arg. 70 C3
Belen Antalya Turkey 39 A1
Belen Hatay Turkey 39 C1
Belen NM U.S.A. 62 F5
Belep, Îles is New Caledonia 53 G3
Belev Russia 13 H5
Belfast U.K. 21 G3
Belfast ME U.S.A. 63 N3
Belfast Lough inlet U.K. 21 G3
Bēlfodiyo Eth. 48 D2
Belford U.K. 18 F3
Belfort France 24 H3
Belgaum India 38 B3
Belgian Congo country Africa see Congo, Democratic Republic of the
België country Europe see Belgium
Belgique country Europe see Belgium
Belgium country Europe 16 J5
Belgorod Russia 13 H6
Belgorod-Dnestrovskyy Ukr. see Bilhorod-Dnistrovs'kyy
Belgrade Serbia 27 I2
Belgrano II (Argentina) research stn Antarctica 76 A1
Belice r. Sicily Italy 26 E6
Belinskiy Russia 13 I5
Belinyu Indon. 41 C8
Belitung i. Indon. 41 C8
Belize Angola 49 B4
Belize Belize 66 G5
Belize country Central America 66 G5
Beljak Austria see Villach
Belkina, Mys pt Russia 44 E3
Bel'kovskiy, Ostrov i. Russia 29 O2
Bell Australia 58 E1
Bell r. Australia 58 D4
Bellac France 24 E3
Bellary India 38 C3
Bellata Australia 58 D2
Bella Unión Uruguay 70 E4
Bellbrook Australia 58 F3
Bell Cay reef Australia 56 E4
Belledonne mts France 24 G4
Bellefonte PA U.S.A. 64 C2
Belle Fourche SD U.S.A. 62 G3
Belle Fourche r. SD U.S.A. 62 G3
Belle Glade FL U.S.A. 63 K6
Belle-Île i. France 24 C3
Belle Isle i. Nfld. and Lab. Canada 61 M4
Belle Isle, Strait of Nfld. and Lab. Canada 61 M4
Belleville IL U.S.A. 63 J4
Bellevue WA U.S.A. 62 C2
Bellin Que. Canada see Kangirsuk
Bellingham U.K. 18 E3
Bellingham WA U.S.A. 62 C2
Bellingshausen (Russia) research stn Antarctica 76 A2
Bellingshausen Sea Antarctica 76 L2
Bellinzona Switz. 24 I3
Bellows Falls VT U.S.A. 64 E1
Bellpat Pak. 36 B3
Belluno Italy 26 E1
Bell Ville Arg. 70 D4
Bellville S. Africa 50 D7
Belmont Australia 58 E4
Belmont U.K. 20 [inset]
Belmont NY U.S.A. 64 B1
Belmonte Brazil 71 D1
Belmopan Belize 66 G5
Belmore, Mount h. Australia 58 F2
Belo Madag. 49 E6
Belo Campo Brazil 71 C1
Belogorsk Russia 44 C2
Belogorsk Ukr. see Bilohirs'k
Beloha Madag. 49 E6
Belo Horizonte Brazil 71 C2
Beloit WI U.S.A. 63 J3
Belokurikha Russia 42 E2
Belo Monte Brazil 69 H4
Belomorsk Russia 12 G2
Belonia India 37 G5
Belorechensk Russia 35 E1
Belorechenskaya Russia see Belorechensk
Belören Turkey 34 D3
Beloretsk Russia 28 G4
Belorussia country Europe see Belarus
Belorusskaya S.S.R. country Europe see Belarus
Belostok Poland see Białystok
Belot, Lac l. N.W.T. Canada 60 F3
Belo Tsiribihina Madag. 49 E5
Belovo Russia 42 F2
Beloyarskiy Russia 11 T3
Beloye, Ozero l. Russia 12 H3
Beloye More sea Russia see White Sea
Belozersk Russia 12 H3
Belpre OH U.S.A. 64 A3
Beltana Australia 57 B6
Belted Range mts NV U.S.A. 65 D2
Bel'ts' Moldova see Bălţi
Bel'tsy Moldova see Bălţi
Belukha, Gora mt. Kazakh./Russia 42 F3
Belush'ye Russia 12 J2
Belvidere NJ U.S.A. 64 D2
Belyando r. Australia 56 D4
Belyayevka Ukr. see Bilyayivka
Belyy Russia 12 G5
Belyy, Ostrov i. Russia 28 I2
Bemaraha, Plateau du Madag. 49 E5
Bembe Angola 49 B4
Bemidji MN U.S.A. 63 I2
Béna Burkina Faso 46 C3
Bena Dibele Dem. Rep. Congo 48 C4
Ben Alder mt. U.K. 20 E4
Benalla Australia 58 B6
Benares India see Varanasi
Ben Arous Tunisia 26 D6
Benavente Spain 25 D2
Ben Avon mt. U.K. 20 F3
Benbane Head hd U.K. 21 F2
Benbecula i. U.K. 20 B3
Ben Boyd National Park Australia 58 E6
Benburb U.K. 21 F3
Ben Chonzie h. U.K. 20 F4
Ben Cleuch h. U.K. 20 F4
Ben Cruachan mt. U.K. 20 D4
Bend OR U.S.A. 62 C3
Bendearg mt. S. Africa 51 H6
Bender Moldova 27 M1
Bender-Bayla Somalia 48 F3
Bendery Moldova see Bender
Bendigo Australia 58 B6
Bendoc Australia 58 D6
Bene Moz. 49 D5
Benenitra Madag. 49 E6
Benešov Czech Rep. 17 O6
Benevento Italy 26 F4
Beneventum Italy see Benevento
Benezette PA U.S.A. 64 B2
Bengal, Bay of sea Indian Ocean 31 H5
Bengaluru India see Bangalore
Bengamisa Dem. Rep. Congo 48 C3
Bengbu China 43 L6
Benghazi Libya 47 F1
Bengkulu Indon. 41 C8
Bengtsfors Sweden 15 H7
Benguela Angola 49 B5
Benha Egypt see Banhā
Ben Hiant h. U.K. 20 C4
Ben Hope h. U.K. 20 E2
Ben Horn h. U.K. 20 E2
Beni r. Bol. 68 E6
Beni Dem. Rep. Congo 48 C3
Beni Nepal 37 E3
Beni Abbès Alg. 22 D5
Benidorm Spain 25 F4
Beni Hammad, Al Qal'a tourist site Alg. 25 I6
Beni Mellal Morocco 22 C5
Benin country Africa 46 D4
Benin, Bight of g. Africa 46 D4
Benin City Nigeria 46 D4
Beni Saf Alg. 25 F6
Beni Snassen, Monts des mts Morocco 25 E6
Beni Suef Egypt see Banī Suwayf
Benito Juárez Arg. 70 E5
Benito Juárez Mex. 65 E4
Benjamin Constant Brazil 68 E4
Benjamín Hill Mex. 66 B2
Benjina Indon. 52 D2
Ben Klibreck h. U.K. 20 E2
Ben Lavin Nature Reserve S. Africa 51 I2
Ben Lawers mt. U.K. 20 E4
Ben Lomond mt. Australia 58 E3
Ben Lomond h. U.K. 20 E4
Ben Lomond National Park Australia 57 [inset]
Ben Macdui mt. U.K. 20 F3
Benmara Australia 56 B3
Ben More h. U.K. 20 C4
Ben More mt. U.K. 20 E4
Benmore, Lake N.Z. 59 C7
Ben More Assynt h. U.K. 20 E2
Bennäs Fin. 14 M5
Bennetta, Ostrov i. Russia 29 P2
Bennett Island Russia see Bennetta, Ostrov
Ben Nevis mt. U.K. 20 D4
Bennington NH U.S.A. 64 F1
Bennington VT U.S.A. 64 E1
Benoni S. Africa 51 I4
Bénoué, Parc National de la nat. park Cameroon 47 E4
Ben Rinnes h. U.K. 20 F3
Benson AZ U.S.A. 62 E5
Benteng Indon. 41 E8
Bentiu South Sudan 32 C8

Bent Jbaïl Lebanon 39 B3
Bentley U.K. 18 F5
Bento Gonçalves Brazil 71 A5
Benton CA U.S.A. 65 C2
Benton Harbor MI U.S.A. 63 J3
Bentonville AR U.S.A. 63 I4
Benue r. Nigeria 46 D4
Ben Vorlich h. U.K. 20 E4
Benwee Head hd Ireland 21 C3
Benwood WV U.S.A. 64 A2
Ben Wyvis mt. U.K. 20 E3
Benxi Liaoning China 44 A4
Benxi Liaoning China 44 B4
Beograd Serbia see Belgrade
Béoumi Côte d'Ivoire 46 C4
Beppu Japan 45 C6
Béqaa val. Lebanon see El Béqaa
Berach r. India 36 C4
Beraketa Madag. 49 E6
Berasia India 36 D5
Berat Albania 27 H4
Beravina Madag. 49 E5
Berber Sudan 32 D6
Berbera Somalia 48 E2
Berbérati Cent. Afr. Rep. 48 B3
Berchtesgaden, Nationalpark nat. park Germany 17 N7
Berck France 24 E1
Berdichev Ukr. see Berdychiv
Berdigestyakh Russia 29 N3
Berdyans'k Ukr. 13 H7
Berdychiv Ukr. 13 F6
Beregovo Ukr. see Berehove
Beregovoy Russia 44 B1
Berehove Ukr. 13 D6
Bereina P.N.G. 52 E2
Bere Island Ireland 21 C6
Bereket Turkm. 35 I3
Berekum Ghana 46 C4
Berenice Egypt see Baranīs
Berenice Libya see Benghazi
Berens River Man. Canada 63 H1
Bereza Belarus see Byaroza
Berezino Belarus see Byerazino
Berezivka Ukr. 13 F7
Berezne Ukr. 13 E6
Bereznik Russia 12 I3
Berezniki Russia 11 R4
Berezov Russia see Berezovo
Berezovka Russia 44 B2
Berezovka Ukr. see Berezivka
Berezovo Russia 11 T3
Berezovyy Russia 44 D2
Berga Spain 25 G2
Bergama Turkey 27 L5
Bergamo Italy 26 C2
Bergby Sweden 15 J6
Bergen Norway 15 D6
Bergen NY U.S.A. 64 C1
Bergen auf Rügen Germany 17 N3
Bergerac France 24 E4
Bergheim Germany 17 K5
Bergland Namibia 50 C2
Bergomum Italy see Bergamo
Bergoo WV U.S.A. 64 A3
Bergpark Wilhelmshöhe tourist site Germany 17 L5
Bergsjö Sweden 15 J6
Bergsviken Sweden 14 L4
Bergville S. Africa 51 I5
Berhampur India see Baharampur
Beringa, Ostrov i. Russia 29 R4
Beringovskiy Russia 29 S3
Bering Sea N. Pacific Ocean 29 S4
Bering Strait Russia/U.S.A. 29 U3
Berislav Ukr. see Beryslav
Berkåk Norway 14 G5
Berkane Morocco 25 E6
Berkeley CA U.S.A. 65 A2
Berkeley Springs WV U.S.A. 64 B3
Berkner Sub-glacial Island Antarctica 76 A1
Berkovitsa Bulg. 27 J3
Berkshire Downs hills U.K. 19 F7
Berkshire Hills MA U.S.A. 64 E1
Berlevåg Norway 14 P1
Berlin Germany 17 N4
Berlin MD U.S.A. 64 D3
Berlin PA U.S.A. 64 B3
Berlin Lake OH U.S.A. 64 A2
Bermagui Australia 58 E6
Bermejo r. Arg./Bol. 70 E3
Bermejo Bol. 68 F8
Bermen, Lac l. Que. Canada 61 L4
Bermuda terr. N. Atlantic Ocean 67 L2
Bermuda Rise sea feature N. Atlantic Ocean 72 D4
Bern Switz. 24 H3
Bernardino de Campos Brazil 71 A3
Bernardo O'Higgins (Chile) research stn Antarctica 76 A2
Bernardo O'Higgins, Parque Nacional nat. park Chile 70 B7
Bernasconi Arg. 70 D5
Berne Switz. see Bern
Berner Alpen mts Switz. 24 H3
Berneray i. Scotland U.K. 20 B3
Berneray i. Scotland U.K. 20 B4
Bernier Island Australia 55 A6
Bernina, Piz mt. Italy/Switz. 26 C1
Bernina Pass Switz. 24 J3
Beroea Greece see Veroia
Beroea Syria see Aleppo
Beroroha Madag. 49 E6
Beroun Czech Rep. 17 O6
Berounka r. Czech Rep. 17 O6
Berovina Madag. see Beravina
Berri Australia 57 C7
Berriane Alg. 22 E5
Berridale Australia 58 D6
Berriedale U.K. 20 F2
Berrigan Australia 58 B5
Berrima Australia 58 E5
Berrouaghia Alg. 25 H5
Berry Australia 58 E5
Berryessa, Lake CA U.S.A. 65 A1
Berry Head hd U.K. 19 D8
Berry Islands Bahamas 67 I3
Berryville VA U.S.A. 64 C3
Berseba Namibia 50 C4
Berté, Lac l. Que. Canada 63 N1
Berthoud Pass CO U.S.A. 62 F4
Bertolínia Brazil 69 J5
Bertoua Cameroon 46 E4
Bertraghboy Bay Ireland 21 C4
Beru atoll Kiribati 53 H2
Beruri Brazil 68 F4
Beruwala Sri Lanka 38 C5
Berwick Australia 58 B7
Berwick-upon-Tweed U.K. 18 E3
Berwyn hills U.K. 19 D6
Beryslav Ukr. 27 O1
Berytus Lebanon see Beirut
Besalampy Madag. 49 E5
Besançon France 24 H3
Beshneh Iran 35 I5
Besikama Indon. 54 D2
Beskra Alg. see Biskra
Beslan Russia 35 G2
Besnard Lake Sask. Canada 60 H4
Besni Turkey 34 E3
Besor, Naḥal watercourse Israel 39 B4
Besparmak Dağları mts Cyprus see Pentadaktylos Range
Bessbrook U.K. 21 F3
Bessemer AL U.S.A. 63 J5
Besshoky, Gora h. Kazakh. 35 I1
Besskorbnaya Russia 13 I7
Bessonovka Russia 13 J5
Betanzos Spain 25 B2
Bet Guvrin Israel 39 B4
Bethal S. Africa 51 I4
Bethanie Namibia 50 C4
Bethel Park PA U.S.A. 64 A2
Bethesda U.K. 18 C5
Bethesda MD U.S.A. 64 C3
Bethesda OH U.S.A. 64 A2
Bethlehem S. Africa 51 I5
Bethlehem PA U.S.A. 64 D2
Bethlehem West Bank 39 B4
Bethulie S. Africa 51 G6
Beti Pak. 36 B3
Betim Brazil 71 B2
Bet Lehem West Bank see Bethlehem
Betma India 36 C5
Betoota (abandoned) Australia 56 C5
Betpakdala plain Kazakh. 42 C3
Betroka Madag. 49 E6
Bet She'an Israel 39 B3
Betsiamites Que. Canada 63 N2
Betsukai Japan 44 G4
Bettiah India 37 F4
Bettyhill U.K. 20 E2
Bettystown Ireland 21 F4
Betul India 36 D5
Betwa r. India 36 D4
Betws-y-coed U.K. 19 D5
Beulah Australia 57 C7
Beult r. U.K. 19 H7
Beuthen Poland see Bytom
Beverley U.K. 18 G5
Beverly MA U.S.A. 64 F1
Beverly Hills CA U.S.A. 65 C3
Bexhill U.K. 19 H8
Bexley, Cape Nunavut Canada 60 G3
Beyce Turkey see Orhaneli
Bey Dağları mts Turkey 27 N6
Beykoz Turkey 27 M4
Beyla Guinea 46 C4
Beylagan Azer. see Beyläqan
Beyläqan Azer. 35 G3
Beyneu Kazakh. 30 E2
Beypazarı Turkey 27 N4
Beypınarı Turkey 34 E3
Beypore India 38 B4
Beyrouth Lebanon see Beirut
Beyşehir Turkey 34 C3
Beyşehir Gölü l. Turkey 34 C3
Beytonovo Russia 44 B1
Beytüşşebap Turkey 35 F3
Bezbozhnik Russia 12 K4
Bezhanitsy Russia 12 F4
Bezhetsk Russia 12 H4
Béziers France 24 F5
Bezmein Turkm. see Abadan
Bezwada India see Vijayawada
Bhabhar India 36 B4
Bhabhua India see Bhabua
Bhabua India 37 E4
Bhachau India 36 B5
Bhachbhar India 36 B4
Bhadgaon Nepal see Bhaktapur
Bhadohi India 37 E4
Bhadra India 36 C3
Bhadrachalam Road Station India see Kottagudem
Bhadrak India 37 F5
Bhadrakh India see Bhadrak
Bhadravati India 38 B3
Bhag Pak. 36 A3
Bhagalpur India 37 F4
Bhainsa India 38 C2
Bhainsdehi India 36 D5
Bhairab Bazar Bangl. 37 G4
Bhaktapur Nepal 37 F4
Bhalki India 38 C2
Bhamo Myanmar 42 H8
Bhamragarh India 38 D2
Bhandal India 36 C2
Bhandara India 36 D5
Bhanjanagar India 38 E2
Bhanrer Range hills India 36 D5
Bhaptiahi India 37 F4
Bharat country Asia see India
Bharati (India) research stn Antarctica 76 E2
Bharatpur India 36 D4
Bhareli r. India 37 H4
Bharuch India 36 C5
Bhatapara India 37 E5
Bhatarsaigh i. U.K. see Vatersay
Bhatghar Lake India 38 B2
Bhatinda India see Bathinda
Bhatnair India see Hanumangarh
Bhatpara India 37 G5
Bhaunagar India see Bhavnagar
Bhavani r. India 38 C4
Bhavani Sagar l. India 38 C4
Bhavnagar India 36 C5
Bhawana Pak. 36 C3
Bhawanipatna India 38 D2
Bhearnaraigh, Eilean i. U.K. see Berneray
Bheemavaram India see Bhimavaram
Bhekuzulu S. Africa 51 J4
Bhera Pak. 36 C2
Bhigvan India 38 B2
Bhikhna Thori Nepal 37 F4
Bhilai India 36 E5
Bhildi India 36 C4
Bhilwara India 36 C4
Bhima r. India 38 C2
Bhimar India 36 B4
Bhimavaram India 38 D2
Bhimlath India 36 E5
Bhind India 36 D4
Bhinga India 37 E4
Bhisho S. Africa 51 H7
Bhiwandi India 38 B2
Bhiwani India 36 D3
Bhogaipur India 36 D4
Bhojpur Nepal 37 F4
Bhola Bangl. 37 G5
Bhongweni S. Africa 51 I6
Bhopal India 36 D5
Bhopalpatnam India 38 D2
Bhrigukaccha India see Bharuch
Bhuban India 38 E1
Bhubaneshwar India 38 E1
Bhubaneswar India see Bhubaneshwar
Bhuj India 36 B5
Bhusawal India 36 C5
Bhutan country Asia 37 G4
Bhuttewala India 36 B4
Bia r. Ghana 46 C4
Biafo Glacier Pak. 36 C2
Biafra, Bight of g. Africa see Benin, Bight of
Biak Indon. 41 F8
Biak i. Indon. 41 F8
Biała Podlaska Poland 13 D5
Białogard Poland 17 O4
Białystok Poland 13 D5
Bianco, Monte mt. France/Italy see Blanc, Mont
Bianzhao China 44 A3
Biaora India 36 D5
Biarritz France 24 D5
Bibai Japan 44 F4
Bibbenluke Australia 58 D6
Bibbiena Italy 26 D3
Biberach an der Riß Germany 17 L6
Bibile Sri Lanka 38 D5
Biblos Lebanon see Jbail
Bicas Brazil 71 C3
Biçer Turkey 27 N5
Bicester U.K. 19 F7
Bichabhera India 36 C4
Bichevaya Russia 44 D3
Bichi r. Russia 44 E1
Bickerton Island Australia 56 B2
Bickleigh U.K. 19 D8
Bicuari, Parque Nacional do nat. park Angola 49 B5
Bid India 38 B2
Bida Nigeria 46 D4
Bidar India 38 C2
Biddeford ME U.S.A. 64 F1
Bidean nam Bian mt. U.K. 20 D4
Bideford U.K. 19 C7
Bideford Bay U.K. see Barnstaple Bay
Bidzhan Russia 44 C3
Bié Angola see Kuito
Bié, Planalto do Angola 49 B5
Biebrzański Park Narodowy nat. park Poland 15 M10
Bielawa Poland 17 P5
Biel/Bienne Switz. 24 H3
Bielefeld Germany 17 L4
Bielitz Poland see Bielsko-Biała
Biella Italy 26 C2
Bielsko-Biała Poland 17 Q6
Biên Hoa Vietnam 31 J5
Bienne Switz. see Biel/Bienne
Bienville, Lac l. Que. Canada 61 K4
Bierbank Australia 58 B1
Biesiesvlei S. Africa 51 G4
Bifoun Gabon 48 B4
Biga Turkey 27 L4
Bigadiç Turkey 27 M5
Biga Yarımadası pen. Turkey 27 L5
Big Bear Lake CA U.S.A. 65 D3
Big Bend Swaziland 51 J4
Bigbury-on-Sea U.K. 19 D8
Biger Nuur salt l. Mongolia 42 H3
Biggar Sask. Canada 62 F1
Biggar U.K. 20 F5
Bigge Island Australia 54 D3
Biggenden Australia 57 F5
Biggleswade U.K. 19 G6
Big Hole r. MT U.S.A. 62 E2
Bighorn r. MT/WY U.S.A. 62 F2
Bighorn Mountains WY U.S.A. 62 F3
Big Island Nunavut Canada 61 K3
Big Lake TX U.S.A. 62 G5
Bignona Senegal 46 B3
Big Pine CA U.S.A. 65 C2
Big Pine Peak CA U.S.A. 65 C3
Big Rapids MI U.S.A. 63 J3
Big River Sask. Canada 62 F1
Big Smokey Valley val. NV U.S.A. 65 D1
Big Spring TX U.S.A. 62 G5
Bigstone Lake Man. Canada 63 H1
Big Timber MT U.S.A. 62 F2
Big Trout Lake Ont. Canada 63 J1
Big Trout Lake Ont. Canada 63 I1
Bihać Bos. & Herz. 26 F2
Bihar state India 37 F4
Bihariganj India 37 F4
Bihar Sharif India 37 F4
Bihor, Vârful mt. Romania 27 J1
Bihoro Japan 44 G4
Bijagós, Arquipélago dos is Guinea-Bissau 46 B3
Bijapur India 36 D4
Bijapur India 38 B2
Bījār Iran 35 G4
Bijbehara India 36 C2
Bijeljina Bos. & Herz. 27 H2
Bijelo Polje Montenegro 27 H3
Bijie China 42 J7
Bijji India 38 D2
Bijnor India 36 D3
Bijnore India see Bijnor
Bikampur India 36 C4
Bikaner India 36 C3
Bikin Russia 44 D3
Bikin r. Russia 44 D3
Bikini atoll Marshall Is 74 H5
Bikori Sudan 32 D7
Bikoro Dem. Rep. Congo 48 B4
Bikou China 42 J6
Bikramganj India 37 F4
Bilād Banī Bū 'Alī Oman 33 I5
Bilaigarh India 38 D1
Bilara India 36 C4
Bilaspur Chhattisgarh India 37 E5
Bilaspur Hima. Prad. India 36 D3
Biläsuvar Azer. 35 H3
Bila Tserkva Ukr. 13 F6
Bilbao Spain 25 E2
Bilbays Egypt 34 C5
Bilbeis Egypt see Bilbays
Bilbo Spain see Bilbao
Bilecik Turkey 27 M4
Biłgoraj Poland 13 D6
Bilharamulo Tanz. 48 D4
Bilhaur India 36 E4
Bilhorod-Dnistrovs'kyy Ukr. 27 N1
Bili Dem. Rep. Congo 48 C3
Bilibino Russia 29 R3
Billabalong Australia 55 A6
Billabong Creek r. Australia see Moulamein Creek
Billericay U.K. 19 H7
Billiluna Australia 54 D4
Billingham U.K. 18 F4
Billings MT U.S.A. 62 F2
Billiton i. Indon. see Belitung
Bill of Portland hd U.K. 19 E8
Bill Williams r. AZ U.S.A. 65 E3
Bilma Niger 46 E3
Bilma, Grand Erg de des. Niger 46 E3
Bilo r. Russia see Belaya
Biloela Australia 56 E5
Bilohirs'k Ukr. 34 D1
Bilohir"ya Ukr. 13 E6
Biloku Guyana 69 G3
Biloli India 38 C2
Bilovods'k Ukr. 13 H6
Biloxi MS U.S.A. 63 J5
Bilpa Morea Claypan salt flat Australia 56 B5
Bilston U.K. 20 F5
Biltine Chad 47 F3
Bilto Norway 14 L2
Bilyayivka Ukr. 27 N1
Bima Indon. 54 B2
Bimberi, Mount Australia 58 D5
Bimbo 47 E4
Bimini Islands Bahamas 67 I3
Bimlipatam India 38 D2
Bina-Etawa India 36 D4
Binaija, Gunung mt. Indon. 41 E8
Binboğa Daği mt. Turkey 34 E3
Bincheng China see Binzhou
Bindebango Australia 58 C1
Bindle Australia 58 D1
Bindu Dem. Rep. Congo 49 B4
Bindura Zimbabwe 49 D5
Binéfar Spain 25 G3
Binga Zimbabwe 49 C5
Binga, Monte mt. Moz. 49 D5
Bingara Australia 58 E2
Bingaram i. India 38 B4
Bing Bong Australia 56 B2
Binghamton NY U.S.A. 64 D1
Bingöl Turkey 35 F3
Bingol Dağı mt. Turkey 35 F3
Binika India 37 E5
Binnaway Australia 58 D3
Binpur India 37 F5
Bint Jbeil Lebanon see Bent Jbaïl
Bintulu Sarawak Malaysia 41 D7
Binxian Heilongjiang China 44 B3
Binxian Shaanxi China 43 J6
Binya Australia 58 C5
Bin-Yauri Nigeria 46 D3
Binzhou Heilongjiang China see Binxian
Binzhou Shandong China 43 L5
Bioco i. Equat. Guinea see Bioko
Biograd na Moru Croatia 26 F3
Bioko i. Equat. Guinea 46 D4
Biokovo mts Croatia 26 G3
Biquinhas Brazil 71 B2
Bir India see Bid
Bira Russia 44 D2
Bi'r Abū Jady oasis Syria 39 D1
Birāk Libya 47 E2
Birakan Russia 44 C2
Bi'r al 'Abd Egypt 39 A4
Bi'r al Ḥalbā well Syria 39 D2
Bi'r al Jifjāfah well Egypt 39 A4
Bi'r al Khamsah well Egypt 34 B5
Bi'r al Māliḥah well Egypt 39 A5
Bi'r al Mulūsi Iraq 35 F4
Bi'r al Munbaṭiḥ well Syria 39 D2
Bi'r al Qaṭrānī well Egypt 34 B5
Bi'r al Ubbayiḍ well Egypt 34 B6
Bi'r an Nuṣf well Egypt see Bi'r an Nuṣṣ
Bi'r an Nuṣṣ well Egypt 34 B5
Bir Anzarane W. Sahara 46 B2
Birao Cent. Afr. Rep. 48 C2
Bi'r ar Rābiyah well Egypt 34 B5
Birata Turkm. 33 J1
Biratnagar Nepal 37 F4
Bi'r aṭ Ṭarfāwī well Libya 34 B5
Bi'r Başīrī well Syria 39 C2
Bi'r Bayḍā' well Egypt 39 B4
Bi'r Baylī well Egypt 34 B5
Bîr Beida well Egypt see Bi'r Bayḍā'
Bi'r Buṭaymān Syria 35 E3
Birch Mountains Y.T. Canada 60 G4
Birch River WV U.S.A. 64 A3
Bircot Eth. 48 E3
Bîr Dignâsh well Egypt see Bi'r Diqnāsh
Bi'r Diqnāsh well Egypt 34 B5
Birdsville Australia 57 B5
Birecik Turkey 34 E3
Bîr el 'Abd Egypt see Bi'r al 'Abd
Bir el Arbi well Alg. 25 I6
Bîr el Istabl well Egypt see Bi'r Iṣṭabl
Bîr el Khamsa well Egypt see Bi'r al Khamsah
Bîr el Nuṣṣ well Egypt see Bi'r an Nuṣṣ
Bîr el Obeiyiḍ well Egypt see Bi'r al Ubbayiḍ
Bîr el Qaṭrani well Egypt see Bi'r al Qaṭrānī
Bîr el Râbia well Egypt see Bi'r ar Rābiyah
Birendranagar Nepal see Surkhet
Bîr en Natrûn well Sudan 32 C6
Bireun Indon. 41 B7
Bi'r Fajr well Saudi Arabia 34 E5
Bi'r Fu'ād well Egypt 34 B5
Bîr Gifgâfa well Egypt see Bi'r al Jifjāfah
Bi'r Ḥajal well Syria 39 D2
Bi'r Ḥasanah well Egypt 39 A4
Bi'r Ḥayzān well Saudi Arabia 34 E6
Bi'r Ibn Hirmās Saudi Arabia see Al Bi'r
Birigui Brazil 71 A3
Bīrīn Syria 39 C2
Bi'r Iṣṭabl well Egypt 34 B5
Bīrjand Iran 33 I3
Bi'r Jubnī well Libya 34 B5
Birkāt Hamad well Iraq 35 G5
Birkenhead U.K. 18 D5
Birkirkara Malta 26 F7
Birksgate Range hills Australia 55 E6
Bîrlad Romania see Bârlad
Bi'r Lahfān well Egypt 39 A4
Bir Lahlou W. Sahara 46 C2
Birlik Kazakh. 42 C4
Birmingham U.K. 19 F6
Birmingham AL U.S.A. 63 J5
Bîr Mogreïn Mauritania 46 B2
Bi'r Muḥaymid al Wazwaz well Syria 39 D2
Bi'r Nāḥid oasis Egypt 34 C5
Birnin-Gwari Nigeria 46 D3
Birnin-Kebbi Nigeria 46 D3
Birnin Konni Niger 46 D3
Birobidzhan Russia 44 D2
Bi'r Qaṣīr as Sirr well Egypt 34 B5
Birr Ireland 21 E4
Bi'r Rawḍ Sālim well Egypt 39 A4
Birrie r. Australia 58 C2
Birrindudu Australia 54 E4
Bîr Rôd Sâlim well Egypt see Bi'r Rawḍ Sālim
Birsay U.K. 20 F1
Bi'r Shalatayn Egypt 32 E5
Bîr Shalatein Egypt see Bi'r Shalatayn
Birsk Russia 11 R4
Birstall U.K. 19 F6
Birthday Mountain h. Australia 56 C2
Biru China 37 H3
Birur India 38 B3
Biruxiong China see Biru
Biržai Lith. 15 N8
Bisalpur India 36 D3
Bisau India 36 C3
Bisbee AZ U.S.A. 62 F5
Biscay, Bay of sea France/Spain 24 B4
Biscay Abyssal Plain sea feature N. Atlantic Ocean 72 H3
Biscoe Islands Antarctica 76 L2
Biscotasi Lake Ont. Canada 63 K2
Bishbek Kyrg. see Bishkek
Bishenpur India see Bishnupur
Bishkek Kyrg. 42 C4
Bishnupur Manipur India 37 H4
Bishnupur W. Bengal India 37 F5
Bishop CA U.S.A. 65 C1
Bishop Auckland U.K. 18 F4
Bishop's Stortford U.K. 19 H7
Bishrī, Jabal hills Syria 39 D2
Bishui China 44 A1
Biskra Alg. 22 F5
Bismarck ND U.S.A. 62 G2
Bismarck Archipelago is P.N.G. 52 E2
Bismarck Range mts P.N.G. 52 E2
Bismarck Sea P.N.G. 52 E2
Bismil Turkey 35 F3
Bismo Norway 14 F6
Bispgården Sweden 14 J5
Bissa, Djebel mt. Alg. 25 G5
Bissamcuttak India 38 D2
Bissau Guinea-Bissau 46 B3
Bissaula Nigeria 46 E4
Bissett Man. Canada 63 H1
Bistcho Lake Alta Canada 60 G4
Bistrița Romania 27 K1
Bistrița r. Romania 27 L1
Bitburg Germany 17 K6
Bitche France 24 H2
Bithur India 36 E4
Bithynia reg. Turkey 27 M4
Bitkine Chad 47 E3
Bitlis Turkey 35 F3
Bitola Macedonia 27 I4
Bitolj Macedonia see Bitola
Bitonto Italy 26 G4
Bitra Par reef India 38 B4
Bitterfontein S. Africa 50 D6
Bitter Lakes Egypt 34 D5
Bitterroot r. MT U.S.A. 62 E2
Bitterroot Range mts ID U.S.A. 62 D2
Bitterwater CA U.S.A. 65 B2
Biu Nigeria 46 E3
Biwa-ko l. Japan 45 D6
Biwmaris U.K. see Beaumaris
Bïye K'obē Polis T'abīya Eth. 48 E2
Biysk Russia 42 F2
Bizana S. Africa 51 I6
Bizerta Tunisia see Bizerte
Bizerte Tunisia 26 C6
Bjargtangar hd Iceland 14 [inset 2]
Bjästa Sweden 14 K5
Bjelovar Croatia 26 G2
Bjerkvik Norway 14 J2
Bjerringbro Denmark 15 F8
Bjørgan Norway 14 G5
Björkliden Sweden 14 K2
Björklinge Sweden 15 J6
Bjorli Norway 14 F5
Björna Sweden 14 K5
Björneborg Fin. see Pori
Bjørnøya i. Arctic Ocean 28 C2
Bjurholm Sweden 14 K5
Bla Mali 46 C3
Black r. Vietnam 42 J8
Blackadder Water r. U.K. 20 G5
Blackall Australia 56 D5
Black Bourton U.K. 19 F7
Blackbull Australia 56 C3
Blackburn U.K. 18 E5
Blackbutt Australia 58 F1
Black Canyon gorge AZ U.S.A. 65 E3
Black Combe h. U.K. 18 D4
Blackdown Tableland National Park Australia 56 E4
Black Forest mts Germany 17 L7
Black Hill h. U.K. 18 F5
Black Hills SD U.S.A. 62 G3
Black Lake Sask. Canada 60 H4
Black Lake Sask. Canada 60 H4
Black Mountain Pak. 36 C2
Black Mountain hills U.K. 19 D7
Black Mountain AK U.S.A. 60 B3
Black Mountain CA U.S.A. 65 D3
Black Mountains hills U.K. 19 D7
Black Mountains AZ U.S.A. 65 E3
Black Nossob watercourse Namibia 50 D2
Black Pagoda India see Konarka
Blackpool U.K. 18 D5
Black Rock h. Jordan see 'Unāb, Jabal al
Blacksburg VA U.S.A. 64 A4
Black Sea Asia/Europe 13 H8
Blacksod Bay Ireland 21 B3
Blackstairs Mountains hills Ireland 21 F5
Blackstone VA U.S.A. 64 B4
Black Sugarloaf mt. Australia 58 E3
Blackville Australia 58 E3
Blackwater Australia 56 E4
Blackwater Ireland 21 F5
Blackwater r. Ireland 21 E5
Blackwater r. Ireland/U.K. 21 F3
Blackwater Reservoir U.K. 20 E4
Blackwood r. Australia 55 A8
Blackwood National Park Australia 56 D4
Bladensburg National Park Australia 56 C4
Blaenavon U.K. 19 D7
Blagodarnyy Russia 13 I7
Blagoevgrad Bulg. 27 J3
Blagoveshchensk Amurskaya Oblast' Russia 44 B2
Blagoveshchensk Respublika Bashkortostan Russia 11 R4
Blaine Lake Sask. Canada 62 F1
Blair Athol Australia 56 D4
Blair Atholl U.K. 20 F4
Blairgowrie U.K. 20 F4
Blakeney U.K. 19 I6
Blanc, Mont mt. France/Italy 24 H4
Blanca, Bahía b. Arg. 70 D5
Blanche, Lake imp. l. S.A. Australia 57 B6
Blanche, Lake imp. l. W.A. Australia 54 C5
Blanco r. Bol. 68 F6
Blanco, Cape OR U.S.A. 62 C3
Blanc-Sablon Que. Canada 61 M4
Bland r. Australia 58 C4
Bland VA U.S.A. 64 A4
Blanda r. Iceland 14 [inset 2]
Blandford Forum U.K. 19 E8
Blanes Spain 25 H3
Blanquilla, Isla i. Venez. 68 F1
Blansko Czech Rep. 17 P6
Blantyre Malawi 49 D5
Blarney Ireland 21 D6
Blåviksjön Sweden 14 K4
Blaye France 24 D4
Blayney Australia 58 D4
Blaze, Point Australia 54 E3
Blenheim N.Z. 59 D5
Blenheim Palace tourist site U.K. 19 F7
Blessington Lakes Ireland 21 F4
Bletchley U.K. 19 G6
Blida Alg. 25 H5
Bligh Water b. Fiji 53 H3
Blitta Togo 46 D4
Block Island RI U.S.A. 64 F2
Block Island Sound sea chan. RI U.S.A. 64 F2
Bloemfontein Free State S. Africa 51 H5
Bloemhof S. Africa 51 G4
Bloemhof Dam S. Africa 51 G4
Bloemhof Dam Nature Reserve S. Africa 51 G4
Blönduós Iceland 14 [inset 2]
Blongas Indon. 54 B2
Bloods Range mts Australia 55 E6
Bloodsworth Island MD U.S.A. 64 C3
Bloody Foreland pt Ireland 21 D2
Bloomington IL U.S.A. 63 J3
Bloomington IN U.S.A. 63 J4
Bloomsburg PA U.S.A. 64 C2
Blossburg PA U.S.A. 64 C2
Blosseville Kyst coastal area Greenland 61 P3
Blouberg S. Africa 51 I2
Blouberg Nature Reserve S. Africa 51 I2
Bloxham U.K. 19 F6
Blue Diamond NV U.S.A. 65 E2
Bluefield WV U.S.A. 64 A4
Bluefields Nicaragua 67 H6
Blue Knob h. PA U.S.A. 64 B2
Blue Mountain Pass Lesotho 51 H5
Blue Mountains Australia 58 D4
Blue Mountains OR U.S.A. 62 D2
Blue Mountains National Park Australia 58 E4
Blue Nile r. Eth./Sudan 47 G3
Bluenose Lake Nunavut Canada 60 G3
Blue Ridge VA U.S.A. 64 B4
Blue Ridge mts VA U.S.A. 64 A4
Blue Stack h. Ireland 21 D3
Blue Stack Mountains hills Ireland 21 D3
Bluestone Lake WV U.S.A. 64 A4
Bluff N.Z. 59 B8
Bluff Knoll mt. Australia 55 B8
Blumenau Brazil 71 A4
Blyde River Canyon Nature Reserve S. Africa 51 J3
Blyth England U.K. 18 F3
Blyth England U.K. 18 F5
Blythe CA U.S.A. 65 E4
Blytheville AR U.S.A. 63 J4
Bø Norway 15 F7
Bo Sierra Leone 46 B4
Boa Esperança Brazil 71 B3
Boali Cent. Afr. Rep. 48 B3
Boane Moz. 51 K4
Boa Nova Brazil 71 C1
Boatlaname Botswana 51 G2
Boa Viagem Brazil 69 K5
Boa Vista Brazil 68 F3
Boa Vista i. Cape Verde 46 [inset]
Bobadah Australia 58 C4
Bobai China 43 K8
Bobaomby, Tanjona c. Madag. 49 E5
Bobbili India 38 D2
Bobo-Dioulasso Burkina Faso 46 C3
Bobotov Kuk mt. Montenegro see Durmitor
Bobriki Russia see Novomoskovsk
Bobrinets Ukr. see Bobrynets'
Bobrov Russia 13 I6
Bobrovitsa Ukr. see Bobrovytsya
Bobrovytsya Ukr. 13 F6
Bobruysk Belarus see Babruysk
Bobrynets' Ukr. 13 G6
Bobuk Sudan 32 D7
Bobures Venez. 68 D2
Boby mt. Madag. 49 E6
Boca de Macareo Venez. 68 F2
Boca do Acre Brazil 68 E5
Boca do Jari Brazil 69 H4
Bocaiúva Brazil 71 C2
Bocaranga Cent. Afr. Rep. 48 B3
Bocas del Toro Panama 67 H7
Bochnia Poland 17 R6
Bochum Germany 17 K5
Bocoio Angola 49 B5
Boda Cent. Afr. Rep. 48 B3
Bodalla Australia 58 E6
Bodallin Australia 55 B7
Bodaybo Russia 29 M4
Boddam U.K. 20 H3
Bodega Head CA U.S.A. 65 A1
Bodélé reg. Chad 47 E3
Boden Sweden 14 L4
Bodenham U.K. 19 E6
Bodensee l. Germany/Switz. see Constance, Lake
Bodie (abandoned) CA U.S.A. 65 C1
Bodinayakkanur India 38 C4
Bodmin U.K. 19 C8
Bodmin Moor moorland U.K. 19 C8
Bodø Norway 14 I3
Bodoquena Brazil 69 G7
Bodoquena, Serra da hills Brazil 70 E2
Bodrum Turkey 27 L6
Bodträskfors Sweden 14 L3
Boende Dem. Rep. Congo 47 F5
Boffa Guinea 46 B3
Bogalusa LA U.S.A. 63 J5
Bogan r. Australia 58 C2
Bogandé Burkina Faso 46 C3
Bogan Gate Australia 58 C4
Boğazlıyan Turkey 34 D3
Bogcang Zangbo r. China 37 F3
Bogd Mongolia 42 I4
Bogda Shan mts China 42 F4
Boggabilla Australia 58 E2
Boggabri Australia 58 E3
Boggeragh Mountains hills Ireland 21 C5
Boghar Alg. 25 H6
Boghari Alg. see Ksar el Boukhari
Bognor Regis U.K. 19 G8
Bogodukhov Ukr. see Bohodukhiv
Bog of Allen reg. Ireland 21 E4
Bogong, Mount Australia 58 C6
Bogopol' Russia 44 D3
Bogoroditsk Russia 13 H5
Bogorodsk Russia 12 I4
Bogorodskoye Khabarovskiy Kray Russia 44 F1
Bogorodskoye Kirovskaya Oblast' Russia 12 K4
Bogotá Col. 68 D3
Bogotol Russia 28 J4
Bogoyavlenskoye Russia see Pervomayskiy
Bogra Bangl. 37 G4
Boguchany Russia 29 K4
Boguchar Russia 13 I6
Bogué Mauritania 46 B3
Bo Hai g. China 43 L5
Bohai Wan b. China 40 D4
Bohemian Forest mts Germany see Böhmer Wald
Bohlokong S. Africa 51 I5
Böhmer Wald mts Germany 17 N6
Bohodukhiv Ukr. 13 G6
Bohol Sea Phil. 41 E7
Bohu China 42 F4
Boiaçu Brazil 68 F4
Boichoko S. Africa 50 F5
Boikhutso S. Africa 51 H4
Boileau, Cape Australia 54 C4
Boim Brazil 69 G4
Boipeba, Ilha i. Brazil 71 D1
Bois r. Brazil 71 A2
Boise ID U.S.A. 62 D3
Boise City OK U.S.A. 62 G4
Boitumelong S. Africa 51 G4
Bojnūrd Iran 33 I2
Bokaak atoll Marshall Is see Taongi
Bokajan India 37 H4
Bokaro India 37 F5
Bokaro Reservoir India 37 F5
Bokatola Dem. Rep. Congo 48 B4
Boké Guinea 46 B3
Bokele Dem. Rep. Congo 48 C4
Bokhara r. Australia 58 C2
Boknafjorden sea chan. Norway 15 D7
Bokoko Dem. Rep. Congo 48 C3
Bokoro Chad 47 E3
Bokovskaya Russia 13 I6
Bokspits S. Africa 50 E4
Boktor Russia 44 E2
Bokurdak Turkm. 33 I2
Bol Chad 47 E3
Bolaiti Dem. Rep. Congo 47 F5
Bolama Guinea-Bissau 46 B3
Bolangir India see Balangir
Bolan Pass Pak. 36 A3
Bolbec France 24 E2
Bole China 42 E4
Bole Ghana 46 C4
Boleko Dem. Rep. Congo 48 B4
Bolen Russia 44 D2
Bolgar Respublika Tatarstan Russia 13 K5
Bolgatanga Ghana 46 C3
Bolgrad Ukr. see Bolhrad
Bolhrad Ukr. 27 M2
Boli China 44 C3
Bolia Dem. Rep. Congo 48 B4
Boliden Sweden 14 L4
Bolintin-Vale Romania 27 K2
Bolívar Peru 68 C5

Bolivar *NY* U.S.A. 64 B1
Bolívar, Pico *mt.* Venez. 68 D2
Bolivia *country* S. America 68 E7
Bolkhov Russia 13 H5
Bollène France 24 G4
Bollnäs Sweden 15 J6
Bollon Australia 58 C2
Bollstabruk Sweden 14 J5
Bolmen *l.* Sweden 15 H8
Bolobo Dem. Rep. Congo 48 B4
Bologna Italy 26 D2
Bolognesi Peru 68 D5
Bologoye Russia 12 G4
Bolokanang S. Africa 51 G5
Bolomba Dem. Rep. Congo 48 B3
Bolon' Russia 44 E2
Bolpur India 37 F5
Bolsena, Lago di *l.* Italy 26 D3
Bol'shakovo Russia 15 L9
Bol'shaya Chernigovka Russia 11 Q5
Bol'shaya Glushitsa Russia 13 K5
Bol'shaya Imandra, Ozero *l.* Russia 14 R3
Bol'shaya Kovriga, Gora *h.* Russia 12 K2
Bol'shaya Martynovka Russia 13 I7
Bol'shaya Tsarevshchina Russia *see* **Volzhskiy**
Bol'shevik, Ostrov *i.* Russia 29 L2
Bol'shezemel'skaya Tundra *lowland* Russia 12 L2
Bol'shiye Chirki Russia 12 J3
Bol'shoy Begichev, Ostrov *i.* Russia 77 E2
Bol'shoye Murashkino Russia 12 J5
Bol'shoy Irgiz *r.* Russia 13 J6
Bol'shoy Kamen' Russia 44 D4
Bol'shoy Kavkaz *mts* Asia/Europe *see* **Caucasus**
Bol'shoy Kundysh *r.* Russia 12 J4
Bol'shoy Lyakhovskiy, Ostrov *i.* Russia 29 P2
Bol'shoy Tokmak Kyrg. *see* **Tokmok**
Bol'shoy Tokmak Ukr. *see* **Tokmak**
Bolton U.K. 18 E5
Bolu Turkey 27 N4
Boluntay China 37 H1
Bolus Head *hd* Ireland 21 B6
Bolvadin Turkey 27 N5
Bolzano Italy 26 D1
Boma Dem. Rep. Congo 49 B4
Bomaderry Australia 58 E5
Bombala Australia 58 D6
Bombay India *see* **Mumbai**
Bombay Beach *CA* U.S.A. 65 E4
Bomberai, Semenanjung *pen.* Indon. 41 F8
Bomboma Dem. Rep. Congo 48 B3
Bom Comércio Brazil 68 E5
Bomdila India 37 H4
Bomi China 42 H7
Bomili Dem. Rep. Congo 48 C3
Bom Jardim de Goiás Brazil 71 A2
Bom Jesus Brazil 71 A5
Bom Jesus da Gurgueia, Serra do *hills* Brazil 69 J5
Bom Jesus da Lapa Brazil 71 C1
Bom Jesus do Norte Brazil 71 C3
Bømlo *i.* Norway 15 D7
Bomokandi *r.* Dem. Rep. Congo 48 C3
Bom Retiro Brazil 71 A4
Bom Sucesso Brazil 71 B3
Bon, Cap *c.* Tunisia 26 D6
Bona Alg. *see* **Annaba**
Bonāb *Āzarbāyjān-e Sharqī* Iran 35 G3
Bonāb *Zanjān* Iran 35 H3
Bon Air *VA* U.S.A. 64 C4
Bonaire *i.* West Indies 67 K6
Bonaparte Archipelago *is* Australia 54 D3
Bonar Bridge U.K. 20 E3
Bonavista Bay *Nfld. and Lab.* Canada 61 M5
Bonchester Bridge U.K. 20 G5
Bondo Dem. Rep. Congo 48 C3
Bondoukou Côte d'Ivoire 46 C4
Bondyuzhskiy Russia *see* **Mendeleyevsk**
Bône Alg. *see* **Annaba**
Bone, Teluk *b.* Indon. 41 E8
Bonerate, Kepulauan *is* Indon. 41 E8
Bo'ness U.K. 20 F4
Bonete, Cerro *mt.* Arg. 70 C3
Bonga Eth. 48 D3
Bongaigaon India 37 G4
Bongandanga Dem. Rep. Congo 48 C3
Bongani S. Africa 50 F5
Bongba China 36 E2
Bong Co *l.* China 37 G3
Bongo, Massif des *mts* Cent. Afr. Rep. 48 C3
Bongo, Serra do *mts* Angola 49 B4
Bongolava *mts* Madag. 49 E5
Bongor Chad 47 E3
Boni Mali 46 C3
Bonifacio *Corsica* France 24 I6
Bonifacio, Bocche di *str.* France/Italy *see* **Bonifacio, Strait of**
Bonifacio, Bouches de *str.* France/Italy *see* **Bonifacio, Strait of**
Bonifacio, Strait of France/Italy 24 I6
Bonin Islands Japan 45 F8
Bonn Germany 17 K5
Bonna Germany *see* **Bonn**
Bonnåsjøen Norway 14 I3
Bonners Ferry *ID* U.S.A. 62 D2
Bonneville France 24 H3
Bonnie Rock Australia 55 B7
Bonnyrigg U.K. 20 F5
Bonnyville *Alta* Canada 62 E1
Bononia Italy *see* **Bologna**
Bonorva *Sardinia* Italy 26 C4
Bonshaw Australia 58 E2
Bontebok National Park S. Africa 50 E8
Bonthe Sierra Leone 46 B4
Bontoc Phil. 41 E6
Bontosunggu Indon. 52 B2
Bontrug S. Africa 51 G7
Bonvouloir Islands P.N.G. 56 E1
Bonwapitse Botswana 51 H2
Boolba Australia 58 D2
Booligal Australia 58 B4
Boomer *WV* U.S.A. 64 A3
Boomi Australia 58 D2
Boonah Australia 58 F1
Boones Mill *VA* U.S.A. 64 B4
Booneville *MS* U.S.A. 63 J5
Böön Tsagaan Nuur *salt l.* Mongolia 42 H3
Boonville *CA* U.S.A. 65 A2
Boonville *NY* U.S.A. 64 D1
Boorabin National Park Australia 55 C7
Boorama Somalia 48 E3
Booroorban Australia 58 B5
Boorowa Australia 58 D5
Boort Australia 58 A6
Boothby, Cape Antarctica 76 D2
Boothia, Gulf of *Nunavut* Canada 61 J3
Boothia Peninsula *Nunavut* Canada 61 I2
Bootle U.K. 18 E5
Booué Gabon 48 B4
Boqê China 37 G3
Boqueirão, Serra do *hills* Brazil 69 J6
Bor Russia 12 J4
Bor Serbia 27 J2
Bor South Sudan 47 G4
Bor Turkey 34 D3
Bor, Lagh *watercourse* Kenya/Somalia 48 E3
Boraha, Nosy *i.* Madag. 49 F5
Borai India 38 D1
Borakalalo Nature Reserve S. Africa 51 H3
Boran Kazakh. 42 F3
Borås Sweden 15 H8
Borasambar India 38 D1
Borāzjān Iran 35 H5
Borba Brazil 69 G4
Borborema, Planalto da *plat.* Brazil 69 K5
Borçka Turkey 35 F2
Bor Dağı *mt.* Turkey 27 M6
Bordeaux France 24 D4
Borden Island *N.W.T./Nunavut* Canada 61 G2
Borden Peninsula *Nunavut* Canada 61 J2
Border Ranges National Park Australia 58 F2
Borðeyri Iceland 14 [inset 2]
Bordj Bou Arréridj Alg. 25 I5
Bordj Bounaama Alg. 25 G6
Bordj Flye Ste-Marie Alg. 46 C2
Bordj Messaouda Alg. 22 F5
Bordj Mokhtar Alg. 46 D2
Bordj Omar Driss Alg. *see* **Bordj Omer Driss**
Bordj Omer Driss Alg. 46 D2
Boreas Abyssal Plain *sea feature* Arctic Ocean 77 H1
Borgå Fin. *see* **Porvoo**
Borgarfjörður Iceland 14 [inset 2]
Borgarnes Iceland 14 [inset 2]
Børgefjell Nasjonalpark *nat. park* Norway 14 H4
Borgholm Sweden 15 J8
Borgo San Lorenzo Italy 26 D3
Bori India 38 C1
Bori *r.* India 36 C5
Borislav Ukr. *see* **Boryslav**
Borisoglebsk Russia 13 I6
Borisov Belarus *see* **Barysaw**
Borisovka Russia 13 H6
Borispol' Ukr. *see* **Boryspil'**
Bo River South Sudan 47 F4
Borja Peru 68 C4
Borkenes Norway 14 J2
Borkovskaya Russia 12 K2
Borlänge Sweden 15 I6
Borlaug Norway 15 E6
Borlu Turkey 27 M5
Borneo *i.* Asia 41 D7
Bornholm *i.* Denmark 15 I9
Bornova Turkey 27 L5
Borodino Russia 28 J3
Borodinskoye Russia 15 P6
Borogontsy Russia 29 O3
Borohoro Shan *mts* China 42 E4
Borok-Sulezhskiy Russia 12 H4
Boromo Burkina Faso 46 C3
Boron *CA* U.S.A. 65 D3
Borondi India 38 D2
Boroughbridge U.K. 18 F4
Borovichi Russia 12 G4
Borovoy *Kirovskaya Oblast'* Russia 12 K4
Borovoy *Respublika Kareliya* Russia 14 R4
Borovoy *Respublika Komi* Russia 12 L3
Borpeta India *see* **Barpeta**
Borrisokane Ireland 21 D5
Borroloola Australia 56 B3
Børsa Norway 14 G5
Borşa Romania 13 E7
Borsakelmas sho'rxogi *salt marsh* Uzbek. 35 J2
Borshchiv Ukr. 13 E6
Borshchovochnyy Khrebet *mts* Russia 43 J3
Bortala China *see* **Bole**
Borūjen Iran 35 H5
Borūjerd Iran 35 H4
Borve U.K. 20 B3
Boryslav Ukr. 13 D6
Boryspil' Ukr. 13 F6
Borzna Ukr. 13 G6
Borzya Russia 43 L2
Bosanska Dubica Bos. & Herz. 26 G2
Bosanska Gradiška Bos. & Herz. 26 G2
Bosanska Krupa Bos. & Herz. 26 G2
Bosanski Novi Bos. & Herz. 26 G2
Bosansko Grahovo Bos. & Herz. 26 G2
Boscawen Island Tonga *see* **Niuatoputopu**
Bose China *see* **Baise**
Boseong S. Korea 45 B6
Boshof S. Africa 51 G5
Bosna i Hercegovina *country* Europe *see* **Bosnia and Herzegovina**
Bosna Saray Bos. & Herz. *see* **Sarajevo**
Bosnia and Herzegovina *country* Europe 26 G2
Bosobogolo Pan *salt pan* Botswana 50 F3
Bosobolo Dem. Rep. Congo 48 B3
Bōsō-hantō *pen.* Japan 45 F6
Bosporus *str.* Turkey 27 M4
Bossangoa Cent. Afr. Rep. 48 B3
Bossembélé Cent. Afr. Rep. 48 B3
Bossiesvlei Namibia 50 C3
Bossut, Cape Australia 54 C4
Bostān Iran 35 G5
Bostan Pak. 36 A3
Bostānābād Iran 35 G3
Bosten Hu *l.* China 42 F4
Boston U.K. 19 G6
Boston *MA* U.S.A. 64 F1
Boston Mountains *AR* U.S.A. 63 I4
Boston Spa U.K. 18 F5
Botad India 36 B5
Botakara Kazakh. 42 C2
Botany Bay Australia 58 E4
Botev *mt.* Bulg. 27 K3
Botevgrad Bulg. 27 J3
Bothaville S. Africa 51 H4
Bothnia, Gulf of Fin./Sweden 15 K6
Botlikh Russia 35 G2
Botoşani Romania 13 E7
Botou China 43 L5
Botshabelo S. Africa 51 H5
Botswana *country* Africa 49 C6
Botte Donato, Monte *mt.* Italy 26 G5
Bottesford U.K. 18 G5
Bottrop Germany 17 K5
Botucatu Brazil 71 A3
Botuporã Brazil 71 C1
Bouaflé Côte d'Ivoire 46 C4
Bouaké Côte d'Ivoire 46 C4
Bouar Cent. Afr. Rep. 48 B3
Bou Arfa Morocco 22 D5
Bouba Ndjida, Parc National de *nat. park* Cameroon 47 E4
Bouca Cent. Afr. Rep. 48 B3
Boucaut Bay Australia 54 F3
Boucle du Baoulé, Parc National de la *nat. park* Mali 46 C3
Boudh India *see* **Bauda**
Bougaa Alg. 25 I5
Bougainville, Cape Australia 54 D3
Bougainville Island P.N.G. 52 F2
Bougainville Reef Australia 56 D2
Boughessa Mali 46 D3
Bougie Alg. *see* **Bejaïa**
Bougouni Mali 46 C3
Bougtob Alg. 22 E5
Bouillon Belgium 16 J6
Bouira Alg. 25 H5
Bou Izakarn Morocco 46 C2
Boujdour W. Sahara 46 B2
Boulder Australia 55 C7
Boulder *CO* U.S.A. 62 F3
Boulder Canyon *gorge NV* U.S.A. 65 E2
Boulder City *NV* U.S.A. 65 E3
Boulevard *CA* U.S.A. 65 D4
Boulia Australia 56 B4
Boulogne France *see* **Boulogne-sur-Mer**
Boulogne-Billancourt France 24 F2
Boulogne-sur-Mer France 24 E1
Boumerdès Alg. 25 H5
Bouna Côte d'Ivoire 46 C4
Bou Naceur, Jbel *mt.* Morocco 22 D5
Boû Nâga Mauritania 46 B3
Boundary Peak *NV* U.S.A. 65 C2
Boundiali Côte d'Ivoire 46 C4
Boundji Congo 48 B4
Bounty Islands N.Z. 53 H6
Bounty Trough *sea feature* S. Pacific Ocean 74 H9
Bourail New Caledonia 53 G4
Bourbon *reg.* France *see* **Bourbonnais**
Bourbon *terr.* Indian Ocean *see* **Réunion**
Bourbonnais *reg.* France 24 F3
Bourem Mali 46 C3
Bouressa Mali *see* **Boughessa**
Bourg-Achard France 19 H9
Bourganeuf France 24 E4
Bourg-en-Bresse France 24 G3
Bourges France 24 F3
Bourgogne *reg.* France *see* **Burgundy**
Bourgogne, Canal de France 24 G3
Bourke Australia 58 B3
Bourne U.K. 19 G6
Bournemouth U.K. 19 F8
Bourtoutou Chad 47 F3
Bou Saâda Alg. 25 I6
Bou Salem Tunisia 26 C6
Bouse *AZ* U.S.A. 65 E4
Bouse Wash *watercourse AZ* U.S.A. 65 E3
Boutilimit Mauritania 46 B3
Bouvet Island *terr.* S. Atlantic Ocean *see* **Bouvetøya**
Bouvetøya *terr.* S. Atlantic Ocean 72 I9
Bova Marina Italy 26 F5
Bow *r. Alta* Canada 62 E2
Bowa China *see* **Muli**
Bowden *WV* U.S.A. 64 B3
Bowditch *atoll* Tokelau *see* **Fakaofo**
Bowen Australia 56 E4
Bowen, Mount Australia 58 D6
Bowenville Australia 58 E1
Bowers Ridge *sea feature* Bering Sea 74 H2
Bowie Australia 56 D4
Bow Island *Alta* Canada 62 E2
Bowling Green *KY* U.S.A. 63 J4
Bowling Green *OH* U.S.A. 63 K3
Bowling Green *VA* U.S.A. 64 C3
Bowling Green Bay National Park Australia 56 D3
Bowman *ND* U.S.A. 62 G2
Bowman Island Antarctica 76 F2
Bowman Peninsula Antarctica 76 L2
Bowmore U.K. 20 C5
Bowo China *see* **Bomi**
Bowral Australia 58 E5
Boyabat Turkey 34 D2
Boyana *tourist site* Bulg. 27 J3
Boyd *r.* Australia 58 F2
Boyd Lagoon *imp. l.* Australia 55 D6
Boyers *PA* U.S.A. 64 B2
Boyle Ireland 21 D4
Boyne *r.* Ireland 21 F4
Boysun Uzbek. 33 K2
Boyuibe Bol. 68 F8
Böyük Qafqaz *mts* Asia/Europe *see* **Caucasus**
Bozcaada *i.* Turkey 27 L5
Bozdağ *mt.* Turkey 27 L5
Bozdağ *mt.* Turkey 39 C1
Boz Dağları *mts* Turkey 27 L5
Bozdoğan Turkey 27 M6
Bozeat U.K. 19 G6
Bozeman *MT* U.S.A. 62 E2
Bozen Italy *see* **Bolzano**
Bozoum Cent. Afr. Rep. 48 B3
Bozova Turkey 34 E3
Bozqūsh, Kūh-e *mts* Iran 35 G3
Bozüyük Turkey 27 N5
Bozyazı Turkey 39 A1
Bra Italy 26 B2
Brač *i.* Croatia 26 G3
Bracadale U.K. 20 C3
Bracadale, Loch *b.* U.K. 20 C3
Bracara Port. *see* **Braga**
Bracciano, Lago di *l.* Italy 26 E3
Bracebridge *Ont.* Canada 63 L2
Bräcke Sweden 14 I5
Bracknell U.K. 19 G7
Bradano *r.* Italy 26 G4
Bradenton *FL* U.S.A. 63 K6
Brades Montserrat 67 L5
Bradford U.K. 18 F5
Bradford *PA* U.S.A. 64 B2
Brady *TX* U.S.A. 62 H5
Brae U.K. 20 [inset]
Braemar U.K. 20 F3
Braga Port. 25 B3
Bragado Arg. 70 D5
Bragança Brazil 69 I4
Bragança Port. 25 C3
Bragança Paulista Brazil 71 B3
Brahin Belarus 13 F6
Brahmanbaria Bangl. 37 G5
Brahmapur India 38 E2
Brahmaputra *r.* China 42 F7
Brahmaputra *r.* China/India 40 B5
Brahmaputra *r.* India *see* **Dihang**
Brahmaur India 36 D2
Brăila Romania 27 L2
Brainerd *MN* U.S.A. 63 I2
Braintree U.K. 19 H7
Braithwaite Point Australia 54 F2
Brak *r.* S. Africa 51 I2
Brakwater Namibia 50 C2
Bramfield Australia 55 F8
Bramming Denmark 15 F9
Brämön *i.* Sweden 14 J5
Brampton *England* U.K. 18 E4
Brampton *England* U.K. 19 I6
Bramwell Australia 56 C2
Brancaster U.K. 19 H6
Branco *r.* Brazil 68 F4
Brandberg *mt.* Namibia 49 B6
Brandbu Norway 15 G6
Brande Denmark 15 F9
Brandenburg an der Havel Germany 17 N4
Brandfort S. Africa 51 H5
Brandon *Man.* Canada 62 H2
Brandon U.K. 19 H6
Brandon Head *hd* Ireland 21 B5
Brandon Mountain *h.* Ireland 21 B5
Brandvlei S. Africa 50 E6
Braniewo Poland 17 Q3
Bransfield Strait Antarctica 76 L2
Brantford *Ont.* Canada 64 A1
Branxton Australia 58 E4
Brasil *country* S. America *see* **Brazil**
Brasil, Planalto do *plat.* Brazil 69 J7
Brasiléia Brazil 68 E6
Brasília Brazil 71 B1
Brasília de Minas Brazil 71 B2
Braslav Belarus *see* **Braslaw**
Braslaw Belarus 15 O9
Braşov Romania 27 K2
Brassey, Mount Australia 55 F5
Brassey Range *hills* Australia 55 C6
Bratislava Slovakia 17 P6
Bratsk Russia 42 I1
Bratskoye Vodokhranilishche *resr* Russia 42 I1
Brattleboro *VT* U.S.A. 64 E1
Braunau am Inn Austria 17 N6
Braunschweig Germany 17 M4
Brava *i.* Cape Verde 46 [inset]
Brave *PA* U.S.A. 64 A3
Bråviken *inlet* Sweden 15 J7
Bravo, Cerro *mt.* Bol. 68 F7
Bravo del Norte, Río *r.* Mex. 62 H6
Bravo del Norte, Río *r.* Mex./U.S.A. *see* **Rio Grande**
Brawley *CA* U.S.A. 65 E4
Bray Ireland 21 F4
Bray Island *Nunavut* Canada 61 K3
Brazil *country* S. America 69 G5
Brazil Basin *sea feature* S. Atlantic Ocean 72 G7
Brazos *r. TX* U.S.A. 63 H6
Brazzaville Congo 49 B4
Brčko Bos. & Herz. 26 H2
Bré Ireland *see* **Bray**
Breadalbane Australia 56 B4
Breaksea Sound *inlet* N.Z. 59 A7
Bream Bay N.Z. 59 E2
Brechfa U.K. 19 C7
Brechin U.K. 20 G4
Břeclav Czech Rep. 17 P6
Brecon U.K. 19 D7
Brecon Beacons *reg.* U.K. 19 D7
Brecon Beacons National Park U.K. 19 D7
Breda Neth. 16 J5
Bredasdorp S. Africa 50 E8
Bredbo Australia 58 D5
Bredviken Sweden 14 I3
Bregenz Austria 17 L7
Breiðafjörður *b.* Iceland 14 [inset 2]
Breiðdalsvík Iceland 14 [inset 2]
Breivikbotn Norway 14 M1
Breizh *reg.* France *see* **Brittany**
Brejo Velho Brazil 71 C1
Brekstad Norway 14 F5
Bremen Germany 17 L4
Bremer Bay Australia 55 B8
Bremerhaven Germany 17 L4
Bremer Range *hills* Australia 55 C8
Bremersdorp Swaziland *see* **Manzini**
Brenham *TX* U.S.A. 63 H5
Brenna Norway 14 H4
Brennero, Passo di *pass* Austria/Italy *see* **Brenner Pass**
Brennerpaß *pass* Austria/Italy *see* **Brenner Pass**
Brenner Pass Austria/Italy 26 D1
Brentwood U.K. 19 H7
Brescia Italy 26 D2
Breslau Poland *see* **Wrocław**
Bresle *r.* France 19 I8
Bressanone Italy 26 D1
Bressay *i.* U.K. 20 [inset]
Bressuire France 24 D3
Brest Belarus 15 M10
Brest France 24 B2
Brest-Litovsk Belarus *see* **Brest**
Bretagne *reg.* France *see* **Brittany**
Breton Sound *b. LA* U.S.A. 63 J6
Brett, Cape N.Z. 59 E2
Bretton U.K. 18 E5
Breves Brazil 69 H4
Brewarrina Australia 58 C2
Brewster *OH* U.S.A. 64 A2
Brewster, Kap *c.* Greenland *see* **Kangikajik**
Brewster, Lake *imp. l.* Australia 58 B4
Breyten S. Africa 51 I4
Breytovo Russia 12 H4
Brezhnev Russia *see* **Naberezhnyye Chelny**
Brezno Slovakia 17 Q6
Brezovo Bulg. 27 K3
Brezovo Polje *plain* Croatia 26 G2
Bria Cent. Afr. Rep. 48 C3
Briançon France 24 H4
Brian Head *mt. UT* U.S.A. 65 F2
Bribbaree Australia 58 C5
Bribie Island Australia 58 F1
Briceni Moldova 13 E6
Brichany Moldova *see* **Briceni**
Brichen' Moldova *see* **Briceni**
Bridgend U.K. 19 D7
Bridge of Orchy U.K. 20 E4
Bridgeport *CA* U.S.A. 65 C1
Bridgeport *CT* U.S.A. 64 E2
Bridgeport *NE* U.S.A. 62 G3
Bridgeton *NJ* U.S.A. 64 D3
Bridgetown Australia 55 B8
Bridgetown Barbados 67 M6
Bridgeville *DE* U.S.A. 64 D3
Bridgewater *N.S.* Canada 63 O3
Bridgewater *NY* U.S.A. 64 D1
Bridgnorth U.K. 19 E6
Bridgwater U.K. 19 D7
Bridgwater Bay U.K. 19 D7
Bridlington U.K. 18 G4
Bridlington Bay U.K. 18 G4
Bridport Australia 57 [inset]
Bridport U.K. 19 E8
Brie *reg.* France 24 F2
Brieg Poland *see* **Brzeg**
Briery Knob *mt. WV* U.S.A. 64 A3
Brig Switz. 24 H3
Brigg U.K. 18 G5
Brigham City *UT* U.S.A. 62 E3
Brightlingsea U.K. 19 I7
Brighton U.K. 19 G8
Brighton *NY* U.S.A. 64 C1
Brignoles France 24 H5
Brikama Gambia 46 B3
Brindisi Italy 26 G4
Brioude France 24 F4
Brisbane Australia 58 F1
Brisbane Ranges National Park Australia 58 B6
Bristol U.K. 19 E7
Bristol *CT* U.S.A. 64 E2
Bristol *NH* U.S.A. 64 F1
Bristol *RI* U.S.A. 64 F2
Bristol *TN* U.S.A. 63 K4
Bristol Bay *AK* U.S.A. 60 B4
Bristol Channel *est.* U.K. 19 C7
Bristol Lake *CA* U.S.A. 65 E3
Britannia Island New Caledonia *see* **Maré**
British Antarctic Territory Antarctica 76 L2
British Columbia *prov.* Canada 62 C1
British Empire Range *mts Nunavut* Canada 61 J1
British Guiana *country* S. America *see* **Guyana**
British Honduras *country* Central America *see* **Belize**
British Indian Ocean Territory *terr.* Indian Ocean 73 M6
British Solomon Islands *country* S. Pacific Ocean *see* **Solomon Islands**
Brito Godins Angola *see* **Kiwaba N'zogi**
Brits S. Africa 51 H3
Britstown S. Africa 50 F6
Brittany *reg.* France 24 C2
Brive-la-Gaillarde France 24 E4
Briviesca Spain 25 E2
Brixham U.K. 19 D8
Brixia Italy *see* **Brescia**
Brlik Kazakh. *see* **Birlik**
Brno Czech Rep. 17 P6
Broach India *see* **Bharuch**
Broad *r. SC* U.S.A. 63 K5
Broadalbin *NY* U.S.A. 64 D1
Broad Arrow (abandoned) Australia 55 C7
Broadback *r. Que.* Canada 63 L1
Broad Bay U.K. *see* **Tuath, Loch a'**
Broadford Australia 58 B6
Broadford Ireland 21 D5
Broadford U.K. 20 D3
Broad Law *h.* U.K. 20 F5
Broadmere Australia 56 A3
Broad Sound *sea chan.* Australia 56 E4
Broadstairs U.K. 19 I7
Broadus *MT* U.S.A. 62 F2
Broadway *VA* U.S.A. 64 B3
Broadwood N.Z. 59 D2
Brochet *Man.* Canada 77 L3
Brochet, Lac *l. Man.* Canada 61 H4
Brochet, Lac au *l. Que.* Canada 63 N2
Brockman, Mount Australia 54 B5
Brockton *MA* U.S.A. 64 F1
Brockway *PA* U.S.A. 64 B2
Brodeur Peninsula *Nunavut* Canada 61 J2
Brodick U.K. 20 D5
Brodnica Poland 17 Q4
Brody Ukr. 13 E6
Brōghil, Kōtal-e Afgh. 36 C1
Broken Arrow *OK* U.S.A. 63 H4
Broken Bay Australia 58 E4
Broken Hill Australia 57 C6
Broken Hill Zambia *see* **Kabwe**
Broken Plateau *sea feature* Indian Ocean 73 O8
Brokopondo Suriname 69 G2
Brokopondo Stuwmeer *resr* Suriname *see* **Professor van Blommestein Meer**
Bromberg Poland *see* **Bydgoszcz**
Bromsgrove U.K. 19 E6
Brønderslev Denmark 15 F8
Brønnøysund Norway 14 H4
Brooke U.K. 19 I6
Brookhaven *MS* U.S.A. 63 I5
Brookings *OR* U.S.A. 62 C3
Brookings *SD* U.S.A. 63 H3
Brookline *MA* U.S.A. 64 F1
Brookneal *VA* U.S.A. 64 B4
Brooks *Alta* Canada 62 E1
Brooks Range *mts AK* U.S.A. 60 D3
Brookton Australia 55 B8
Brookville *PA* U.S.A. 64 B2
Broom, Loch *inlet* U.K. 20 D3
Broome Australia 54 C4
Brora U.K. 20 F2
Brora *r.* U.K. 20 F2
Brösarp Sweden 15 I9
Brosna *r.* Ireland 21 E4
Brough U.K. 18 E4
Brough Ness *pt* U.K. 20 G2
Broughshane U.K. 21 F3
Broughton Island *Nunavut* Canada *see* **Qikiqtarjuaq**
Broughton Islands Australia 58 F4
Brovary Ukr. 13 F6
Brovinia Australia 57 E5
Brovst Denmark 15 F8
Browne Range *hills* Australia 55 D6
Brownfield *TX* U.S.A. 62 G5
Brown Mountain *CA* U.S.A. 65 D3
Brownsville *PA* U.S.A. 64 B2
Brownsville *TN* U.S.A. 63 J4
Brownsville *TX* U.S.A. 63 H6
Brownwood *TX* U.S.A. 62 H5
Browse Island Australia 54 C3
Bruay-la-Buissière France 24 F1
Bruce Rock Australia 55 B7
Bruck an der Mur Austria 17 O7
Brue *r.* U.K. 19 E7
Bruges Belgium *see* **Brugge**
Brugge Belgium 16 I5
Bruin *PA* U.S.A. 64 B2
Bruini India 37 I3
Brūk, Wādī el *watercourse* Egypt *see* **Burūk, Wādī al**
Brukkaros Namibia 50 D3
Brûlé *Alta* Canada 62 D1
Brumado Brazil 71 C1
Brumunddal Norway 15 G6
Brundisium Italy *see* **Brindisi**
Brunei *country* Asia 41 D7
Brunei Brunei *see* **Bandar Seri Begawan**
Brunette Downs Australia 56 A3
Brunflo Sweden 14 I5
Brunico Italy 26 D1
Brünn Czech Rep. *see* **Brno**
Brunner, Lake N.Z. 59 C6
Brunswick Germany *see* **Braunschweig**
Brunswick *GA* U.S.A. 63 K5
Brunswick *MD* U.S.A. 64 C3
Brunswick *ME* U.S.A. 63 N3
Brunswick, Península de *pen.* Chile 70 B8
Brunswick Bay Australia 54 D3
Bruntál Czech Rep. 17 P6
Brunt Ice Shelf Antarctica 76 B2
Bruntville S. Africa 51 J5
Bruny Island Australia 57 [inset]
Brusa Turkey *see* **Bursa**
Brusenets Russia 12 I3
Brusque Brazil 71 A4
Brussel Belgium *see* **Brussels**
Brussels Belgium 16 J5
Bruthen Australia 58 C6
Bruxelles Belgium *see* **Brussels**
Bruzual Venez. 68 E2
Bryan *TX* U.S.A. 63 H5
Bryan, Mount *h.* Australia 57 B7
Bryan Coast Antarctica 76 L2
Bryansk *Bryanskaya Oblast'* Russia 13 G5
Bryansk *Respublika Dagestan* Russia 35 G1
Brynbuga U.K. *see* **Usk**
Bryne Norway 15 D7
Bryukhovetskaya Russia 13 H7
Brzeg Poland 17 P5
Brześć nad Bugiem Belarus *see* **Brest**
Bua *r.* Malawi 49 D5
Bu'aale Somalia 48 E3
Buala Solomon Is 53 F2
Buan S. Korea 45 B6
Būbiyān, Jazīrat Kuwait 35 H5
Bucak Turkey 27 N6
Bucaramanga Col. 68 D2
Buccaneer Archipelago *is* Australia 54 C4
Buchanan Liberia 46 B4
Buchanan *VA* U.S.A. 64 B4
Buchanan, Lake *imp. l.* Australia 56 D4
Buchan Gulf *Nunavut* Canada 61 K2
Bucharest Romania 27 L2
Bucheon S. Korea 45 B5
Buchon, Point *CA* U.S.A. 65 B3
Buchy France 19 I9
Bucin, Pasul *pass* Romania 27 K1
Buckambool Mountain *h.* Australia 58 B3
Buckeye *AZ* U.S.A. 62 E5
Buckhannon *WV* U.S.A. 64 A3
Buckhaven U.K. 20 F4
Buckie U.K. 20 G3
Buckingham U.K. 19 G6
Buckingham *VA* U.S.A. 64 B4
Buckingham Bay Australia 41 F9
Buckland Tableland *reg.* Australia 56 E5
Buckleboo Australia 55 G8
Buckle Island Antarctica 76 H2
Buckley *watercourse* Australia 56 B4
Buckley Bay Antarctica 76 G2
Buckskin Mountains *AZ* U.S.A. 65 F3
Bucureşti Romania *see* **Bucharest**
Buda-Kashalyova Belarus 13 F5
Budalin Myanmar 37 H5
Budapest Hungary 27 H1
Budaun India 36 D3
Budawang National Park Australia 58 E5
Budda Australia 58 B3
Budd Coast Antarctica 76 F2
Buddusò *Sardinia* Italy 26 C4
Bude U.K. 19 C8
Budennovsk Russia 13 J7
Buderim Australia 58 F1
Budīyah, Jabal *mts* Egypt 39 A5
Budongquan China 37 H2
Budoni *Sardinia* Italy 26 C4
Budweis Czech Rep. *see* **České Budějovice**
Buenaventura Col. 68 C3
Buena Vista *i.* N. Mariana Is *see* **Tinian**
Buena Vista *VA* U.S.A. 64 B4
Buendía, Embalse de *resr* Spain 25 E3
Buenos Aires Arg. 70 E4
Buenos Aires, Lago *l.* Arg./Chile 70 B7
Buerarema Brazil 71 D1
Buffalo *NY* U.S.A. 64 B1
Buffalo *SD* U.S.A. 62 G2
Buffalo *WY* U.S.A. 62 F3
Buffalo Narrows *Sask.* Canada 77 L3
Buffels *watercourse* S. Africa 50 C5
Buffels Drift S. Africa 51 H2
Buftea Romania 27 K2
Bug *r.* Poland 17 S5
Buga Col. 68 C3
Bugaldie Australia 58 D3
Bugdaýly Turkm. 35 I3
Bugojno Bos. & Herz. 26 G2
Bugrino Russia 12 K1
Bugt China 44 A2
Bugul'ma Russia 11 Q5
Bügür China *see* **Luntai**
Buguruslan Russia 11 Q5
Buhera Zimbabwe 49 D5
Buhuşi Romania 27 L1
Builth Wells U.K. 19 D6
Buin, Piz *mt.* Austria/Switz. 17 M7
Bui National Park Ghana 46 C4
Buinsk Russia 13 K5
Bū'īn Zahrā Iran 35 H4
Buitepos Namibia 50 D2
Bujanovac Serbia 27 I3
Bujumbura Burundi 48 C4
Bukachacha Russia 43 L2
Bukadaban Feng *mt.* China 37 G1
Buka Island P.N.G. 52 F2
Būkān Iran 35 G3
Būkand Iran 35 I5
Bukavu Dem. Rep. Congo 48 C4
Bukhoro Uzbek. *see* **Buxoro**
Bukittinggi Indon. 41 C8
Bukkapatnam India 38 C3
Bukoba Tanz. 48 D4
Bükreş Romania *see* **Bucharest**
Būl, Kūh-e *mt.* Iran 35 I5
Bülach Switz. 24 I3
Bulancak Turkey 34 E2
Bulandshahr India 36 D3
Bulanık Turkey 35 F3
Bulava Russia 44 F2
Bulawayo Zimbabwe 49 C6
Buldan Turkey 27 M5
Buldana India 38 C1
Buldhana India *see* **Buldana**
Bulembu Swaziland 51 J3
Bulgan *Bulgan* Mongolia 42 I3
Bulgan *Hovd* Mongolia 42 G3
Bulgar Russia *see* **Bolgar**
Bulgaria *country* Europe 27 K3
Bŭlgariya *country* Europe *see* **Bulgaria**
Bullawarra, Lake *imp. l.* Australia 58 A1
Buller *r.* N.Z. 59 C5
Buller, Mount Australia 58 C6
Bulleringa National Park Australia 56 C3
Bullfinch Australia 55 B7
Bullhead City *AZ* U.S.A. 65 E3
Bulli Australia 58 E5
Bullion Mountains *CA* U.S.A. 65 D3
Bullo *r.* Australia 54 E3
Bulloo Downs Australia 57 C6
Bulloo Lake *imp. l.* Australia 57 C6
Büllsport Namibia 50 C3
Bulman Australia 54 F3
Bulman Gorge Australia 54 F3
Buloke, Lake *dry lake* Australia 58 A6
Bulsar India *see* **Valsad**
Bultfontein S. Africa 51 H5
Bulukumba Indon. 41 E8
Bulun Russia 29 N2
Bulungu Dem. Rep. Congo 49 C4
Bulung'ur Uzbek. 42 B5
Bumba Dem. Rep. Congo 48 C3
Būmbah Libya 34 A4
Būmbah, Khalīj al *b.* Libya 34 A4
Bumpha Bum *mt.* Myanmar 37 I4
Buna Dem. Rep. Congo 48 B4
Buna Kenya 48 D3
Bunazi Tanz. 48 D4
Bunbury Australia 55 A8
Bunclody Ireland 21 F5
Buncrana Ireland 21 E2
Bunda Tanz. 48 D4
Bundaberg Australia 56 F5
Bundaleer Australia 58 C2
Bundarra Australia 58 E3
Bundi India 36 C4
Bundjalung National Park Australia 58 F2
Bundoran Ireland 21 D3
Bundukia South Sudan 47 G4
Bungay U.K. 19 I6
Bungendore Australia 58 D5
Bunger Hills Antarctica 76 F2
Bungle Bungle National Park Australia *see* **Purnululu National Park**
Bungo-suidō *sea chan.* Japan 45 D6
Bunguran, Kepulauan *is* Indon. *see* **Natuna, Kepulauan**
Bunguran, Pulau *i.* Indon. *see* **Natuna Besar**
Bunia Dem. Rep. Congo 48 D3
Bunianga Dem. Rep. Congo 48 C4
Buningonia *well* Australia 55 C7
Bunji Pak. 36 C2
Bunker Group *atolls* Australia 56 F4
Bunkeya Dem. Rep. Congo 49 C5
Bünsum China 37 E3
Bunya Mountains National Park Australia 58 E1
Bünyan Turkey 34 D3
Buôn Ma Thuột Vietnam 31 J5
Buor-Khaya, Guba *b.* Russia 29 O2
Bup *r.* China 37 F3
Buqayq Saudi Arabia *see* **Abqaiq**
Buqbuq Egypt 34 B5
Bura Kenya 48 D4
Buraan Somalia 48 E2
Buram Sudan 47 F3
Buran Kazakh. *see* **Boran**
Buranhaém *r.* Brazil 71 D2

Buranhém Brazil 71 C2
Burāq Syria 39 C3
Buray r. India 36 C5
Buraydah Saudi Arabia 32 F4
Burbank CA U.S.A. 65 C3
Burcher Australia 58 C4
Burco Somalia 48 E3
Burdigala France see Bordeaux
Burdur Turkey 27 N6
Burdur Gölü l. Turkey 27 N6
Burdwan India see Barddhaman
Burē Eth. 48 D2
Bure r. U.K. 19 I6
Bureå Sweden 14 L4
Bureinskiy Khrebet mts Russia 44 D2
Bureinskiy Zapovednik nature res. Russia 44 D2
Burewala Pak. 33 L3
Bureya r. Russia 44 C2
Bureya Range mts Russia see Bureinskiy Khrebet
Burford Ont. Canada 64 A1
Burgas Bulg. 27 L3
Burgeo Nfld. and Lab. Canada 61 M5
Burgersdorp S. Africa 51 H6
Burgersfort S. Africa 51 J3
Burges, Mount h. Australia 55 C7
Burgess Hill U.K. 19 G8
Burghausen Germany 17 N6
Burghead U.K. 20 F3
Burgio, Serra di h. Sicily Italy 26 F6
Burgos Mex. 62 H7
Burgos Spain 25 E2
Burgsvik Sweden 15 K8
Burgundy reg. France 24 G3
Burhan Budai Shan mts China 42 G5
Burhaniye Turkey 27 L5
Burhanpur India 36 D5
Burhar-Dhanpuri India 37 E5
Buri Brazil 71 A3
Buritama Brazil 71 A3
Buriti Alegre Brazil 71 A2
Buriti Bravo Brazil 69 J5
Buritirama Brazil 69 J6
Buritis Brazil 71 B1
Burj Aziz Khan Pak. 36 A3
Burke Island Antarctica 76 K2
Burke Pass N.Z. see Burkes Pass
Burkes Pass N.Z. 59 C7
Burketown Australia 56 B3
Burkeville VA U.S.A. 64 B4
Burkina country Africa see Burkina Faso
Burkina Faso country Africa 46 C3
Burley ID U.S.A. 62 E3
Burlington Ont. Canada 64 B1
Burlington CO U.S.A. 62 G4
Burlington IA U.S.A. 63 I3
Burlington VT U.S.A. 63 M3
Burma country Asia see Myanmar
Burmantovo Russia 11 S3
Burney, Monte vol. Chile 70 B8
Burnie Australia 57 [inset]
Burniston U.K. 18 G4
Burnley U.K. 18 E5
Burns OR U.S.A. 62 D3
Burnside r. Nunavut Canada 60 H3
Burnside, Lake imp. l. Australia 55 C6
Burns Lake B.C. Canada 60 F4
Burntisland U.K. 20 F4
Burntwood r. Man. Canada 61 I4
Burog Co l. China 37 F2
Burqin China 42 F3
Burqu' Jordan 39 D3
Burqu', Qaşr tourist site Jordan 39 C3
Burra Australia 57 B7
Burra i. U.K. 20 [inset]
Burravoe U.K. 20 [inset]
Burrel Albania 27 I4
Burrel CA U.S.A. 65 C2
Burren reg. Ireland 21 C4
Burrendong, Lake Australia 58 D4
Burren Junction Australia 58 D3
Burrewarra Point Australia 58 E5
Burrinjuck Australia 58 D5
Burrinjuck Reservoir Australia 58 D5
Burro, Serranías del mts Mex. 66 D3
Burro Creek watercourse AZ U.S.A. 65 F3
Burrowa Pine Mountain National Park Australia 58 C6
Burrow Head hd U.K. 20 E6
Burrundie Australia 54 E3
Bursa Turkey 27 M4
Būr Safāga Egypt see Būr Safājah
Būr Safājah Egypt 32 D4
Būr Sa'īd Egypt see Port Said
Būr Sa'īd Egypt see Port Said
Būr Sa'īd governorate Egypt see Būr Sa'īd
Būr Sa'īd governorate Egypt 39 A4
Būr Sudan Sudan see Port Sudan
Burton upon Trent U.K. 19 F6
Burträsk Sweden 14 L4
Burt Well Australia 55 F5
Buru i. Indon. 41 E8
Burūk, Wādī al watercourse Egypt 39 A4
Burullus, Baḥra el lag. Egypt see Burullus, Lake
Burullus, Buḥayrat al lag. Egypt see Burullus, Lake
Burullus, Lake lag. Egypt 34 C5
Burultokay China see Fuhai
Burūn, Ra's pt Egypt 39 A4
Burundi country Africa 48 C4
Burunniy Russia see Tsagan Aman
Bururi Burundi 48 C4
Burwash Landing Y.T. Canada 60 E3
Burwick U.K. 20 G2
Buryn' Ukr. 13 G6
Bury St Edmunds U.K. 19 H6
Burzil Pass Pak. 36 C2
Busambra, Rocca mt. Sicily Italy 26 E6
Busan S. Korea 45 C6
Busanga Dem. Rep. Congo 48 C4
Buseire Syria see Al Buşayrah
Bush r. U.K. 21 F2
Bushêngcaka China 37 E2
Bushenyi Uganda 48 D4
Bushire Iran see Bandar-e Būshehr
Bushmills U.K. 21 F2
Businga Dem. Rep. Congo 48 C3
Buşrá ash Shām Syria 39 C3
Busse Russia 44 B2
Busselton Australia 55 A8
Busto Arsizio Italy 26 C2
Buta Dem. Rep. Congo 48 C3
Butare Rwanda 48 C4
Butaritari atoll Kiribati 74 H5
Bute Australia 57 B7
Bute i. U.K. 20 D5
Butha-Buthe Lesotho 51 I5
Butha Qi China see Zalantun
Buthidaung Myanmar 37 H5
Butler PA U.S.A. 64 B2
Butlers Bridge Ireland 21 E3
Buton i. Indon. 41 E8
Butte MT U.S.A. 62 E2
Butterworth S. Africa see Gcuwa
Buttevant Ireland 21 D5
Butt of Lewis hd U.K. 20 C2
Button Bay Man. Canada 61 I4
Butuan Phil. 41 E7
Buturlinovka Russia 13 I6
Butwal Nepal 37 E4
Buulobarde Somalia 48 E3
Buur Gaabo Somalia 48 E4
Buurhabaka Somalia 48 E3
Buutsagaan Mongolia 42 H3
Buxar India 37 F4
Buxoro Uzbek. 33 J2
Buxton U.K. 18 F5
Buy Russia 12 I4
Buynaksk Russia 13 J8
Buyr Nuur l. Mongolia 43 L3
Büyükçekmece Turkey 34 C2
Büyük Egri Dağ mt. Turkey 39 A1
Büyükmenderes r. Turkey 27 L6
Buzău Romania 27 L2
Buzdyak Russia 11 Q5
Búzi Moz. 49 D5
Büzmeýin Turkm. see Abadan
Buzuluk Russia 11 Q5
Buzuluk r. Russia 13 I6
Buzzards Bay MA U.S.A. 64 F2
Byakar Bhutan see Jakar
Byala Bulg. 27 K3
Byala Slatina Bulg. 27 J3
Byalynichy Belarus 13 F5
Byarezina r. Belarus 13 F5
Byaroza Belarus 15 N10
Byblos tourist site Lebanon 39 B2
Bydgoszcz Poland 17 Q4
Byelorussia country Europe see Belarus
Byerazino Belarus 13 F5
Byeshankovichy Belarus 13 F5
Byesville OH U.S.A. 64 A3
Bygland Norway 15 E7
Bykhaw Belarus 13 F5
Bykhov Belarus see Bykhaw
Bykle Norway 15 E7
Bykovo Russia 13 J6
Bylot Island Nunavut Canada 61 K2
Byramgore Reef India 38 A4
Byrd Glacier Antarctica 76 H1
Byrkjelo Norway 15 E6
Byrock Australia 58 C3
Byron, Cape Australia 58 F2
Byron Bay Australia 58 F2
Byron Island Kiribati see Nikunau
Byrranga, Gory mts Russia 29 K2
Byske Sweden 14 L4
Byssa Russia 44 C1
Byssa r. Russia 44 C1
Bytom Poland 17 Q5
Bytów Poland 17 P3
Byurgyutli Turkm. 35 I3
Byzantium Turkey see İstanbul

C

Caacupé Para. 70 E3
Caatinga Brazil 71 B2
Caazapá Para. 70 E3
Caballas Peru 68 C6
Caballococha Peru 68 D4
Caballos Mesteños, Llano de los plain Mex. 66 D3
Cabanaconde Peru 68 D7
Cabanatuan Phil. 41 E6
Cabdul Qaadir Somalia 48 E2
Cabeceira Rio Manso Brazil 69 G7
Cabeceiras Brazil 71 B1
Cabeza del Buey Spain 25 D4
Cabezas Bol. 68 F7
Cabimas Venez. 68 D1
Cabinda Angola 49 B4
Cabinda prov. Angola 49 B5
Cabinet Inlet Antarctica 76 L2
Cabistra Turkey see Ereğli
Cabo Frio Brazil 71 C3
Cabo Frio, Ilha do i. Brazil 71 C3
Cabonga, Réservoir resr Que. Canada 63 L2
Caboolture Australia 58 F1
Cabo Orange, Parque Nacional de nat. park Brazil 69 H3
Cabo Pantoja Peru 68 C4
Cabora Bassa, Lake resr Moz. 49 D5
Cabo Raso Arg. 70 C6
Caborca Mex. 66 B2
Cabo San Lucas Mex. 66 C4
Cabot Strait Nfld. and Lab./N.S. Canada 61 L5
Cabourg France 19 G9
Cabo Verde country Africa see Cape Verde
Cabo Verde, Ilhas do is N. Atlantic Ocean 46 [inset]
Cabo Yubi Morocco see Tarfaya
Cabral, Serra do mts Brazil 71 B2
Căbrayıl Azer. 35 G3
Cabrera, Illa de i. Spain 25 H4
Cabrera, Sierra de la mts Spain 25 C2
Caçador Brazil 71 A4
Čačak Serbia 27 I3
Caccia, Capo c. Sardinia Italy 26 C4
Cacequi Brazil 70 F3
Cáceres Brazil 69 G7
Cáceres Spain 25 C4
Cache Creek B.C. Canada 62 C1
Cacheu Guinea-Bissau 46 B3
Cachi, Nevados de mts Arg. 70 C2
Cachimbo, Serra do hills Brazil 69 H5
Cachoeira Brazil 71 D1
Cachoeira Alta Brazil 71 A2
Cachoeira de Goiás Brazil 71 A2
Cachoeira do Arari Brazil 69 I4
Cachoeiro de Itapemirim Brazil 71 C3
Cacine Guinea-Bissau 46 B3
Caciporé, Cabo c. Brazil 69 H3
Cacolo Angola 49 B5
Caconda Angola 49 B4
Caçu Brazil 71 A2
Caculé Brazil 71 C1
Čadca Slovakia 17 Q6
Cadereyta Mex. 62 G6
Cadibarrawirracanna, Lake imp. l. Australia 57 A6
Cadillac MI U.S.A. 63 J3
Cádiz Spain 25 C5
Cadiz OH U.S.A. 64 A2
Cádiz, Golfo de g. Spain 25 C5
Cadiz Lake CA U.S.A. 65 E3
Cadotte Lake Alta Canada 60 G4
Caen France 24 D2
Caerdydd U.K. see Cardiff
Caerffili U.K. see Caerphilly
Caerfyrddin U.K. see Carmarthen
Caergybi U.K. see Holyhead
Caernarfon U.K. 19 C5
Caernarfon Bay U.K. 19 C5
Caernarvon U.K. see Caernarfon
Caerphilly U.K. 19 D7
Caesaraugusta Spain see Zaragoza
Caesarea Alg. see Cherchell
Caesarea Cappadociae Turkey see Kayseri
Caesarea Philippi Syria see Bāniyās
Caesarodunum France see Tours
Caesaromagus U.K. see Chelmsford
Caetité Brazil 71 C1
Cafayate Arg. 70 C3
Cafelândia Brazil 71 A3
Caffa Ukr. see Feodosiya
Cagayan de Oro Phil. 41 E7
Cagli Italy 26 E3
Cagliari Sardinia Italy 26 C5
Cagliari, Golfo di b. Sardinia Italy 26 C5
Çagyl Turkm. 35 I2
Cahama Angola 49 B5
Caha Mountains hills Ireland 21 C6
Cahermore Ireland 21 B6
Cahersiveen Ireland see Cahirsiveen
Cahir Ireland 21 E5
Cahirsiveen Ireland 21 B6
Cahora Bassa, Lago de resr Moz. see Cabora Bassa, Lake
Cahore Point Ireland 21 F5
Cahors France 24 E4
Cahuapanas Peru 68 C5
Cahul Moldova 27 M2
Caia Moz. 49 D5
Caiabis, Serra dos hills Brazil 69 G6
Caianda Angola 49 C5
Caiapó r. Brazil 71 A1
Caiapó, Serra do mts Brazil 71 A2
Caiapônia Brazil 71 A2
Caicara Venez. 68 E2
Caicos Islands Turks and Caicos Is 67 J4
Caicos Passage Bahamas/Turks and Caicos Is 67 J4
Caiguna Australia 55 D8
Caimodorro mt. Spain 25 F3
Caipe Arg. 70 C2
Caird Coast Antarctica 76 B1
Cairngorm Mountains U.K. 20 F3
Cairnryan U.K. 20 D6
Cairns Australia 56 D3
Cairnsmore of Carsphairn h. U.K. 20 E5
Cairo Egypt 34 C5
Caisleán an Bharraigh Ireland see Castlebar
Caiundo Angola 49 B5
Caiwarro (abandoned) Australia 58 B2
Cajamarca Peru 68 C5
Cajati Brazil 71 A4
Cajuru Brazil 71 B3
Čakovec Croatia 26 G1
Çal Turkey 27 M5
Cala S. Africa 51 H6
Calabar Nigeria 46 D4
Calabria, Parco Nazionale della nat. park Italy 26 G5
Calafat Romania 27 J3
Calagurris Spain see Calahorra
Calahorra Spain 25 F2
Calai Angola 49 B5
Calais France 24 E1
Calais ME U.S.A. 63 N2
Calalasteo, Sierra de mts Arg. 70 C3
Calama Brazil 68 F5
Calama Chile 70 C2
Calamar Col. 68 D1
Calamian Group is Phil. 41 D6
Calamocha Spain 25 F3
Calandula Angola 49 B4
Calapan Phil. 41 E6
Călărași Romania 27 L2
Calatayud Spain 25 F3
Calayan i. Phil. 43 M9
Calbayog Phil. 41 E6
Calçoene Brazil 69 H3
Calcutta India see Kolkata
Caldas da Rainha Port. 25 B4
Caldas Novas Brazil 69 I7
Caldera Chile 70 B3
Caldervale Australia 56 D5
Caldew r. U.K. 18 E4
Caldwell ID U.S.A. 62 D3
Caldwell OH U.S.A. 64 A3
Caledon r. Lesotho/S. Africa 51 H6
Caledon S. Africa 50 D8
Caledon Bay Australia 56 B2
Caledonia Ont. Canada 64 B1
Caledonia admin. div. U.K. see Scotland
Caleta el Cobre Chile 70 B2
Calexico CA U.S.A. 65 E4
Calf of Man i. Isle of Man 18 C4
Calgary Alta Canada 62 E1
Cali Col. 68 C3
Calicut India see Kozhikode
Caliente NV U.S.A. 65 E2
California PA U.S.A. 64 B2
California state U.S.A. 62 C3
California, Golfo de g. Mex. see California, Gulf of
California, Gulf of Mex. 66 B2
California Aqueduct canal CA U.S.A. 65 B2
Cälilabad Azer. 35 H3
Calingasta Arg. 70 C4
Calipatria CA U.S.A. 65 E4
Calistoga CA U.S.A. 65 A1
Calkiní Mex. 66 F4
Callabonna, Lake imp. l. Australia 57 C6
Callan Ireland 21 E5
Callan r. U.K. 21 F3
Callander U.K. 20 E4
Callao Peru 68 C6
Callicoon NY U.S.A. 64 D2
Callington U.K. 19 C8
Calliope Australia 56 E5
Callipolis Turkey see Gallipoli
Caloundra Australia 58 F1
Caltagirone Sicily Italy 26 F6
Caltanissetta Sicily Italy 26 F6
Calucinga Angola 49 B5
Calulo Angola 49 B4
Calunga Angola 49 B5
Caluquembe Angola 49 B5
Caluula Somalia 48 F2
Caluula, Raas pt Somalia 48 F2
Calvados Chain is P.N.G. 56 F1
Calvert Hills Australia 56 B3
Calvi Corsica France 26 I5
Calvià Spain 25 H4
Calvinia S. Africa 50 D6
Calvo, Monte mt. Italy 26 F4
Cam r. U.K. 19 H6
Camaçari Brazil 71 D1
Camache Reservoir CA U.S.A. 65 B1
Camacho Mex. 66 D4
Camacuio Angola 49 B5
Camacupa Angola 49 B5
Camagüey Cuba 67 I4
Camagüey, Archipiélago de is Cuba 67 I4
Camamu Brazil 71 D1
Camaná Peru 68 D7
Camanongue Angola 49 C5
Camapuã Brazil 69 H7
Camaquã Brazil 70 F4
Çamardı Turkey 34 D3
Camargo Bol. 68 E8
Camargue reg. France 24 G5
Camarillo CA U.S.A. 65 C3
Camarones Arg. 70 C6
Camarones, Bahía b. Arg. 70 C6
Ca Mau Vietnam 31 J6
Ca Mau, Mui c. Vietnam 31 J6
Cambay India see Khambhat
Cambay, Gulf of India see Khambhat, Gulf of
Camberley U.K. 19 G7
Cambodia country Asia 31 J5
Camboriú Brazil 71 A4
Camborne U.K. 19 B8
Cambrai France 24 F1
Cambria admin. div. U.K. see Wales
Cambrian Mountains hills U.K. 19 D6
Cambridge Ont. Canada 64 A1
Cambridge N.Z. 59 E3
Cambridge U.K. 19 H6
Cambridge MA U.S.A. 64 F1
Cambridge MD U.S.A. 64 C3
Cambridge MN U.S.A. 63 I2
Cambridge NY U.S.A. 64 E1
Cambridge OH U.S.A. 63 K3
Cambridge Bay Nunavut Canada 61 H3
Cambrien, Lac l. Que. Canada 61 L4
Cambulo Angola 49 C4
Cambundi-Catembo Angola 49 B5
Cambuquira Brazil 71 B3
Cam Co l. China 37 E2
Camdeboo National Park S. Africa 50 G7
Camden AR U.S.A. 63 I5
Camden NJ U.S.A. 64 D3
Camden NY U.S.A. 64 D1
Cameia Angola 49 C5
Cameia, Parque Nacional da nat. park Angola 49 C5
Cameron Island Nunavut Canada 61 H2
Cameron Park CA U.S.A. 65 B1
Cameroon country Africa 46 E4
Cameroon, Mount vol. Cameroon see Cameroun, Mont
Cameroon Highlands slope Cameroon/Nigeria 46 E4
Caméroun country Africa see Cameroon
Cameroun, Mont vol. Cameroon 46 D4
Cametá Brazil 69 I4
Camiña Chile 68 E7
Camiri Bol. 68 F8
Camisea Peru 68 D6
Camocim Brazil 69 J4
Camooweal Australia 56 B3
Camooweal Caves National Park Australia 56 B4
Campana, Isla i. Chile 70 A7
Campbell S. Africa 50 F5
Campbell, Cape N.Z. 59 E5
Campbell, Mount h. Australia 54 E5
Campbell Island N.Z. 74 H9
Campbell Plateau sea feature S. Pacific Ocean 74 H9
Campbell Range hills Australia 54 D3
Campbell River B.C. Canada 62 B1
Campbellton N.B. Canada 63 N2
Campbelltown Australia 58 E5
Campbeltown U.K. 20 D5
Campeche Mex. 66 F5
Campeche, Bahía de g. Mex. 66 F5
Camperdown Australia 58 A7
Câmpina Romania 27 K2
Campina Grande Brazil 69 K5
Campinas Brazil 71 B3
Campina Verde Brazil 71 A2
Campo Cameroon 46 D4
Campobasso Italy 26 F4
Campo Belo Brazil 71 B3
Campo Belo do Sul Brazil 71 A4
Campo de Diauarum Brazil 69 H6
Campo Florido Brazil 71 A2
Campo Gallo Arg. 70 D3
Campo Grande Brazil 70 F2
Campo Largo Brazil 71 A4
Campo Maior Brazil 69 J4
Campo Maior Port. 25 C4
Campo Mourão Brazil 70 F2
Campos Altos Brazil 71 B2
Campos dos Goytacazes Brazil 71 C3
Campos Novos Brazil 71 A4
Campos Sales Brazil 69 J5
Câmpulung Romania 27 K2
Câmpulung Moldovenesc Romania 27 K1
Camrose Alta Canada 62 E1
Camrose U.K. 19 B7
Camsell Portage Sask. Canada 60 H4
Camulodunum U.K. see Colchester
Çan Turkey 27 L4
Canaã dos Carajás Brazil 69 H5
Canaan CT U.S.A. 64 E1
Canabrava Brazil 71 B2
Canacona India 38 B3
Canada country N. America 60 H4
Canada Basin sea feature Arctic Ocean 77 A1
Canadian TX U.S.A. 62 G4
Canadian r. U.S.A. 62 H4
Canadian Abyssal Plain sea feature Antarctica 77 A1
Cañadón Grande, Sierra mts Arg. 70 C7
Canaima, Parque Nacional nat. park Venez. 68 F2
Çanakkale Turkey 27 L4
Çanakkale Boğazı str. Turkey see Dardanelles
Canalejas Arg. 70 C5
Cañamares Spain 25 E3
Canandaigua NY U.S.A. 64 C1
Cananea Mex. 66 B2
Cananéia Brazil 71 B4
Canápolis Brazil 71 A2
Cañar Ecuador 68 C4
Canarias terr. N. Atlantic Ocean see Canary Islands
Canárias, Ilha das i. Brazil 69 J4
Canarias, Islas terr. N. Atlantic Ocean see Canary Islands
Canarreos, Archipiélago de los is Cuba 67 H4
Canary Islands terr. N. Atlantic Ocean 46 B2
Canastota NY U.S.A. 64 D1
Canastra, Serra da mts Goiás Brazil 71 A1
Canastra, Serra da mts Minas Gerais Brazil 71 B2
Canatiba Brazil 71 C1
Canatlán Mex. 66 D4
Canaveral, Cape FL U.S.A. 63 K6
Cañaveras Spain 25 E3
Canavieiras Brazil 71 D1
Canbelego Australia 58 C3
Canberra Australia 58 D5
Cancún Mex. 67 G4
Çandar Turkey see Kastamonu
Çandarlı Turkey 27 L5
Candia Greece see Iraklion
Cândido de Abreu Brazil 71 A4
Çandır Turkey 34 D2
Candle Lake Sask. Canada 62 F1
Candlewood, Lake CT U.S.A. 64 E2
Cane r. Australia 54 A5
Canea Greece see Chania
Canela Brazil 71 A5
Canelones Uruguay 70 E4
Cangallo Peru 68 D6
Cangamba Angola 49 B5
Cangandala, Parque Nacional de nat. park Angola 49 B4
Cangbu r. China see Brahmaputra
Cango Caves S. Africa 50 F7
Cangola Angola 49 B4
Canguaretama Brazil 69 K5
Canguçu Brazil 70 F4
Canguçu, Serra do hills Brazil 70 F4
Cangzhou China 43 L5
Caniapiscau Que. Canada 61 L4
Caniapiscau r. Que. Canada 61 L4
Caniapiscau, Réservoir de resr Que. Canada 61 K4
Caniçado Moz. see Guija
Canicattì Sicily Italy 26 E6
Canindé Brazil 69 K4
Canisteo r. NY U.S.A. 64 C1
Canisteo Peninsula Antarctica 76 K2
Çankırı Turkey 34 D2
Canna Australia 55 A7
Canna i. U.K. 20 C3
Cannanore India see Kannur
Cannanore Islands India 38 B4
Cannes France 24 H5
Cannock U.K. 19 E6
Cann River Australia 58 D6
Canoas Brazil 71 A5
Canõas, Rio das r. Brazil 71 A4
Canoeiros Brazil 71 B2
Canoinhas Brazil 71 A4
Canoona Australia 56 E4
Canora Sask. Canada 62 G1
Canowindra Australia 58 D4
Cantabrian Mountains Spain see Cantábrica, Cordillera
Cantábrica, Cordillera mts Spain 25 D2
Cantábrico, Mar sea Spain 25 C2
Cantagalo Brazil 71 C3
Canterbury U.K. 19 I7
Canterbury Bight b. N.Z. 59 C7
Canterbury Plains N.Z. 59 C6
Cần Thơ Vietnam 31 J5
Cantil CA U.S.A. 65 D3
Canton MS U.S.A. 63 J5
Canton OH U.S.A. 64 A2
Canton PA U.S.A. 64 C2
Canton Island atoll Kiribati see Kanton
Cantuaria U.K. see Canterbury
Canunda National Park Australia 57 C8
Canutama Brazil 68 F5
Canvey Island U.K. 19 H7
Cany-Barville France 19 H9
Canyon TX U.S.A. 62 G4
Canyon Ferry Lake MT U.S.A. 62 E2
Cao Bằng Vietnam 31 J4
Caohu China 42 E4
Caoshi China 44 B4
Caozhou China see Heze
Çapakçur Turkey see Bingöl
Capanaparo r. Venez. 68 E2
Capanema Brazil 69 I4
Capão Bonito Brazil 71 A4
Caparaó, Serra do mts Brazil 71 C3
Cape r. Australia 56 D4
Cape Arid National Park Australia 55 C8
Cape Barren Island Australia 57 [inset]
Cape Basin sea feature S. Atlantic Ocean 72 I8
Cape Breton Island N.S. Canada 61 L5
Cape Charles VA U.S.A. 64 C4
Cape Coast Ghana 46 C4
Cape Coast Castle Ghana see Cape Coast
Cape Cod Bay MA U.S.A. 64 F2
Cape Cod National Seashore nature res. MA U.S.A. 64 G2
Cape Crawford Australia 56 A3
Cape Dorset Nunavut Canada 61 K3
Cape Girardeau MO U.S.A. 63 J4
Cape Johnson Depth sea feature N. Pacific Ocean 74 E5
Cape Juby Morocco see Tarfaya
Cape Krusenstern National Monument nat. park AK U.S.A. 60 B3
Capel Australia 55 A8
Cape Le Grand National Park Australia 55 C8
Capelinha Brazil 71 C2
Capella Australia 56 E4
Capelongo Angola see Kuvango
Cape May NJ U.S.A. 64 D3
Cape May Court House NJ U.S.A. 64 D3
Cape May Point NJ U.S.A. 64 D3
Cape Melville National Park Australia 56 D2
Capenda-Camulemba Angola 49 B4
Cape Palmerston National Park Australia 56 E4
Cape Range National Park Australia 54 A5
Cape Town S. Africa 50 D7
Cape Tribulation National Park Australia 56 D2
Cape Upstart National Park Australia 56 D3
Cape Verde country Africa 46 [inset]
Cape Verde Basin sea feature N. Atlantic Ocean 72 F5
Cape Verde Plateau sea feature N. Atlantic Ocean 72 F4
Cape York Peninsula Australia 56 C2
Cap-Haïtien Haiti 67 J5
Capim r. Brazil 69 I4
Capivara, Represa resr Brazil 71 A3
Čapljina Bos. & Herz. 26 G3
Cappoquin Ireland 21 E5
Capraia, Isola di i. Italy 26 C3
Caprara, Punta pt Sardinia Italy 26 C4
Capri, Isola di i. Italy 26 F4
Capricorn Channel Australia 56 E4
Capricorn Group atolls Australia 56 F4
Caprivi Strip reg. Namibia 49 C5
Capsa Tunisia see Gafsa
Captina r. OH U.S.A. 64 A3
Capuava Brazil 71 A4
Caquetá r. Col. 68 E4
Caracal Romania 27 K2
Caracas Venez. 68 E1
Caraguatatuba Brazil 71 B3
Caraí Brazil 71 C2
Carajás, Serra dos hills Brazil 69 H5
Carales Sardinia Italy see Cagliari
Caralis Sardinia Italy see Cagliari
Carandaí Brazil 71 C3
Caransebeș Romania 27 J2
Caraquet N.B. Canada 63 N2
Caratasca, Laguna de lag. Hond. 67 H5
Caratinga Brazil 71 C2
Carauari Brazil 68 E4
Caravaca de la Cruz Spain 25 F4
Caravelas Brazil 71 D2
Carbó Mex. 66 B3
Carbon, Cap c. Alg. 25 F6
Carbonara, Capo c. Sardinia Italy 26 C5
Carbondale PA U.S.A. 64 D2
Carbonia Sardinia Italy 26 C5
Carbonita Brazil 71 C2
Carcaixent Spain 25 F4
Carcassonne France 24 F5
Cardamom Hills India 38 C4
Cárdenas Cuba 67 H4
Cárdenas Mex. 66 E4
Cardenyabba watercourse Australia 58 A2
Çardi Turkey see Harmancık
Cardiel, Lago l. Arg. 70 B7
Cardiff U.K. 19 D7
Cardiff MD U.S.A. 64 C3
Cardigan U.K. 19 C6
Cardigan Bay U.K. 19 C6
Cardoso Brazil 71 A3
Cardoso, Ilha do i. Brazil 71 B4
Carei Romania 27 J1
Carentan France 24 D2
Carey, Lake imp. l. Australia 55 C7
Cargados Carajos Islands Mauritius 73 L7
Carhaix-Plouguer France 24 C2
Cariacica Brazil 71 C3
Cariamanga Ecuador 68 C4
Caribbean Sea N. Atlantic Ocean 67 H5
Caribou ME U.S.A. 63 N2
Caribou Lake Ont. Canada 61 J4
Caribou Mountains Alta Canada 60 G4
Carinda Australia 58 C3
Cariñena Spain 25 F3
Carinhanha r. Brazil 71 C1
Carlabhagh U.K. see Carloway
Carletonville S. Africa 51 H4
Carlingford Lough inlet Ireland/U.K. 21 F3
Carlini (Argentina) research stn Antarctica 76 A2
Carlisle U.K. 18 E4
Carlisle NY U.S.A. 64 D1
Carlisle PA U.S.A. 64 C2
Carlisle Lakes imp. l. Australia 55 D7
Carlit, Pic mt. France 24 E5
Carlos Chagas Brazil 71 C2
Carlow Ireland 21 F5
Carloway U.K. 20 C2
Carlsbad Czech Rep. see Karlovy Vary
Carlsbad CA U.S.A. 65 D4
Carlsbad NM U.S.A. 62 G5
Carlsberg Ridge sea feature Indian Ocean 73 L5
Carlson Inlet Antarctica 76 L1
Carlton Hill Australia 54 E3
Carluke U.K. 20 F5
Carlyle Sask. Canada 62 G2
Carmacks Y.T. Canada 60 E3
Carmagnola Italy 26 B2
Carman Man. Canada 62 H2
Carmana Iran see Kermān
Carmarthen U.K. 19 C7
Carmarthen Bay U.K. 19 C7
Carmaux France 24 F4
Carmel NY U.S.A. 64 E2
Carmel, Mount h. Israel 39 B3
Carmel Head hd U.K. 18 C5
Carmel Valley CA U.S.A. 65 B2
Carmen, Isla i. Mex. 66 B3
Carmen de Patagones Arg. 70 D6
Carmichael CA U.S.A. 65 B1
Carmo da Cachoeira Brazil 71 B3
Carmo do Paranaíba Brazil 71 B2
Carmona Angola see Uíge
Carmona Spain 25 D5
Carnac France 24 C3
Carnamah Australia 55 A7
Carnarvon Australia 55 A6
Carnarvon S. Africa 50 F6
Carnarvon National Park Australia 56 D5
Carnarvon Range hills Australia 55 C6
Carnarvon Range mts Australia 56 E5
Carn Dearg h. U.K. 20 E3
Carndonagh Ireland 21 E2
Carnegie Australia 55 C6
Carnegie, Lake imp. l. Australia 55 C6
Carn Eige mt. U.K. 20 D3
Carnes Australia 55 F7
Carney Island Antarctica 76 J2
Carnforth U.K. 18 E4
Carn Glas-choire h. U.K. 20 F3
Carnlough U.K. 21 G3
Carn nan Gabhar mt. U.K. 20 F4
Carn Odhar h. U.K. 20 E3
Carnot Cent. Afr. Rep. 48 B3
Carnoustie U.K. 20 G4
Carnsore Point Ireland 21 F5
Carnwath U.K. 20 F5
Carola Cay reef Australia 56 F3
Carolina Brazil 69 I5
Carolina S. Africa 51 J4
Caroline Island atoll Kiribati 75 J6
Caroline Islands N. Pacific Ocean 41 G7
Caroline Peak N.Z. 59 A7
Caroline Range hills Australia 54 D4
Caroní r. Venez. 68 F2
Carpathian Mountains Europe 13 C6
Carpații mts Europe see Carpathian Mountains
Carpații Meridionali mts Romania see Transylvanian Alps
Carpații Occidentali mts Romania 27 J2
Carpentaria, Gulf of Australia 56 B2
Carpentras France 24 G4
Carpi Italy 26 D2
Carpinteria CA U.S.A. 65 C3
Carra, Lough l. Ireland 21 C4
Carraig na Siuire Ireland see Carrick-on-Suir
Carrantuohill mt. Ireland 21 C6
Carrara Italy 26 D2
Carrasco, Parque Nacional nat. park Bol. 68 F7
Carrathool Australia 58 B5
Carrhae Turkey see Harran
Carrickfergus U.K. 21 G3
Carrickmacross Ireland 21 F4
Carrick-on-Shannon Ireland 21 D4
Carrick-on-Suir Ireland 21 E5
Carrigallen Ireland 21 E4
Carrigtohill Ireland 21 D6
Carrington ND U.S.A. 62 H2
Carrizal Bajo Chile 70 B3
Carrizo Springs TX U.S.A. 62 H6
Carrizozo NM U.S.A. 62 F5
Carroll IA U.S.A. 63 I3
Carrollton GA U.S.A. 63 J5
Carrollton OH U.S.A. 64 A2
Carrolltown PA U.S.A. 64 B2
Carron r. U.K. 20 E3
Carrowmore Lake Ireland 21 C3
Çarşamba Turkey 34 E2
Carson City NV U.S.A. 65 C1
Carson Escarpment Australia 54 D3
Carson Lake NV U.S.A. 65 C1
Carstensz Pyramid mt. Indon. see Jaya, Puncak
Carstensz-top mt. Indon. see Jaya, Puncak
Cartagena Col. 68 C1
Cartagena Spain 25 F5
Carteret Group is P.N.G. see Kilinailau Islands
Carteret Island Solomon Is see Malaita
Carthage tourist site Tunisia 26 D6
Carthage MO U.S.A. 63 I4
Carthago tourist site Tunisia see Carthage
Carthago Nova Spain see Cartagena
Cartier Island Australia 54 C3
Cartmel U.K. 18 E4
Cartwright Nfld. and Lab. Canada 61 M4
Caruaru Brazil 69 K5
Carúpano Venez. 68 F1
Caryapundy Swamp Australia 57 C6
Casablanca Morocco 22 C5
Casa Branca Brazil 71 B3
Casa de Piedra, Embalse resr Arg. 70 C5
Casa Grande AZ U.S.A. 62 E5
Casale Monferrato Italy 26 C2
Casalmaggiore Italy 26 D2
Casca Brazil 71 A5
Cascade Australia 55 C8
Cascade r. N.Z. 59 B7
Cascade Point N.Z. 59 B7
Cascade Range mts Canada/U.S.A. 60 F5
Cascais Port. 25 B4
Cascavel Brazil 70 F2
Caserta Italy 26 F4
Casey (Australia) research stn Antarctica 76 F2
Casey Bay Antarctica 76 D2
Caseyr, Raas c. Somalia see Gwardafuy, Gees
Cashel Ireland 21 E5
Cashmere Australia 58 D1
Casino Australia 58 F2
Casiquiare, Canal r. Venez. 68 E3
Casnewydd U.K. see Newport

Caspe Spain 25 F3
Casper WY U.S.A. 62 F3
Caspian Lowland Kazakh./Russia 30 D2
Caspian Sea l. Asia/Europe 35 H1
Cass WV U.S.A. 64 B3
Cassacatiza Moz. 49 D5
Cassadaga NY U.S.A. 64 B1
Cassaigne Alg. see Sidi Ali
Cassamba Angola 49 C5
Cássia Brazil 71 B3
Cassiar Mountains B.C. Canada 60 E3
Cassilândia Brazil 71 A2
Cassilis Australia 58 D4
Cassino Italy 26 E4
Cassley r. U.K. 20 E3
Cassongue Angola 49 B5
Castanhal Brazil 69 I4
Castanho Brazil 68 F5
Castaños Mex. 66 D3
Castelfranco Veneto Italy 26 D2
Castell-nedd U.K. see Neath
Castell Newydd Emlyn U.K. see Newcastle Emlyn
Castellón Spain see Castellón de la Plana
Castellón de la Plana Spain 25 F4
Castelo Branco Port. 25 C4
Castelo de Vide Port. 25 C4
Casteltermini Sicily Italy 26 E6
Castelvetrano Sicily Italy 26 E6
Castiglione della Pescaia Italy 26 D3
Castilla y León reg. Spain 24 B6
Castlebar Ireland 21 C4
Castlebay U.K. 20 B4
Castlebellingham Ireland 21 F4
Castleblayney Ireland 21 F3
Castlebridge Ireland 21 F5
Castle Carrock U.K. 18 E4
Castle Cary U.K. 19 E7
Castlederg U.K. 21 E3
Castledermot Ireland 21 F5
Castle Dome Mountains AZ U.S.A. 65 E4
Castle Donington U.K. 19 F6
Castle Douglas U.K. 20 F6
Castleford U.K. 18 F5
Castlegar B.C. Canada 62 D2
Castlegregory Ireland 21 B5
Castleisland Ireland 21 C5
Castlemaine Australia 58 B6
Castlemaine Ireland 21 C5
Castlemartyr Ireland 21 D6
Castle Mountain CA U.S.A. 65 B3
Castlepoint N.Z. 59 F5
Castlepollard Ireland 21 E4
Castlerea Ireland 21 D4
Castlereagh r. Australia 58 C3
Castle Rock CO U.S.A. 62 G4
Castletown Ireland 21 E5
Castletown Isle of Man 18 C4
Castra Regina Germany see Regensburg
Castres France 24 F5
Castries St Lucia 67 L6
Castro Brazil 71 A4
Castro Chile 70 B6
Castro Alves Brazil 71 D1
Castro Verde Port. 25 B5
Castroville CA U.S.A. 65 B2
Çat Turkey 35 F3
Catacaos Peru 68 B5
Cataguases Brazil 71 C3
Çatak Turkey 35 F3
Catalão Brazil 71 B2
Çatalca Yarımadası pen. Turkey 27 M4
Çatal Hüyük tourist site Turkey 34 D3
Catalonia aut. comm. Spain see Cataluña
Cataluña aut. comm. Spain 25 G3
Catalunya aut. comm. Spain see Cataluña
Catamarca Arg. 70 C3
Catana Sicily Italy see Catania
Catanduanes i. Phil. 41 E6
Catanduva Brazil 71 A3
Catania Sicily Italy 26 F6
Catanzaro Italy 26 G5
Catarina, Raso da hills Brazil 69 K5
Catarman Phil. 41 E6
Catastrophe, Cape Australia 57 A7
Cataxa Moz. 49 D5
Catbalogan Phil. 41 E6
Catembe Moz. 51 K4
Catengue Angola 49 B5
Catete Angola 49 B4
Cathair Dónall Ireland 21 B6
Cathcart Australia 58 D6
Cathcart S. Africa 51 H7
Cathedral Peak S. Africa 51 I5
Cathedral Rock National Park Australia 58 F3
Catheys Valley CA U.S.A. 65 B2
Catió Guinea-Bissau 46 B3
Catisimiña Venez. 68 F3
Cat Island Bahamas 67 I4
Cat Lake Ont. Canada 63 I1
Catoche, Cabo c. Mex. 67 G4
Cato Island and Bank reef Australia 56 F4
Catriló Arg. 70 D5
Catskill NY U.S.A. 64 E1
Catskill Mountains NY U.S.A. 64 D1
Catuane Moz. 51 K4
Caubvick, Mount Nfld. and Lab. Canada 61 L4
Cauca r. Col. 67 J7
Caucaia Brazil 69 K4
Caucasia Col. 68 C2
Caucasus mts Asia/Europe 35 F2
Câu Giat Vietnam 42 J9
Caulonia Italy 26 G5
Caungula Angola 49 B4
Cauquenes Chile 70 B5
Cavaglià Italy 26 C2
Cavalcante, Serra do hills Brazil 71 B1
Cavan Ireland 21 E4
Çavdır Turkey 27 M6
Caveira r. Brazil 71 C1
Caviana, Ilha i. Brazil 69 H3
Cawdor U.K. 20 F3
Cawnpore India see Kanpur
Cawston U.K. 19 I6
Caxias Brazil 69 J4
Caxias do Sul Brazil 71 A5
Caxito Angola 49 B4
Çay Turkey 27 N5
Cayambe, Volcán vol. Ecuador 68 C3
Çaybaşı Turkey see Çayeli
Çaycuma Turkey 27 O4
Çayeli Turkey 35 F2
Cayenne Fr. Guiana 69 H3
Cayeux-sur-Mer France 19 I8
Çayırhan Turkey 27 N4
Cayman Brac i. Cayman Is 67 I5
Cayman Islands terr. West Indies 67 H5
Cayman Trench sea feature Caribbean Sea 72 C4
Caynaba Somalia 48 E3
Cayucos CA U.S.A. 65 B3
Cayuga Ont. Canada 64 B1
Cayuga Lake NY U.S.A. 64 C1
Cazê China 37 F3
Cazenovia NY U.S.A. 64 D1
Cazombo Angola 49 C5
Ceadâr-Lunga Moldova see Ciadîr-Lunga
Ceananus Mór Ireland see Kells
Ceann a Deas na Hearadh pen. U.K. see South Harris
Ceará Brazil see Fortaleza
Ceara Abyssal Plain sea feature S. Atlantic Ocean 72 F6
Ceatharlach Ireland see Carlow
Ceballos Mex. 66 D3
Cebu Phil. 41 E6
Čechy reg. Czech Rep. 17 N6
Cecil Plains Australia 58 E1
Cecil Rhodes, Mount h. Australia 55 C6
Cecina Italy 26 D3
Cedar City UT U.S.A. 65 F2
Cedar Island VA U.S.A. 64 D4
Cedar Lake Man. Canada 62 G1
Cedar Rapids IA U.S.A. 63 I3
Cedar Run NJ U.S.A. 64 D3
Cedarville S. Africa 51 I6
Cedros, Isla i. Mex. 66 A3
Ceduna Australia 55 F8
Ceeldheere Somalia 48 E3
Ceerigaabo Somalia 48 E2
Cefalù Sicily Italy 26 F5
Cegléd Hungary 27 H1
Cêgnê China 37 H2
Çekerek Turkey 34 D2
Çekiçler Turkm. 35 I3
Celaya Mex. 66 D4
Celbridge Ireland 21 F4
Celebes i. Indon. 41 E8
Celebes Basin sea feature Pacific Ocean 74 E5
Celebes Sea Indon./Phil. 41 E7
Celestún Mex. 66 F4
Celje Slovenia 26 F1
Celle Germany 17 M4
Celovec Austria see Klagenfurt am Wörthersee
Celtic Sea Ireland/U.K. 16 D5
Celtic Shelf sea feature N. Atlantic Ocean 72 H2
Cenderawasih, Teluk b. Indon. 41 F8
Çendir r. Turkm. 35 I3
Centane S. Africa 51 I7
Centenary Zimbabwe 49 D5
Centereach NY U.S.A. 64 E2
Centerville WV U.S.A. 64 A3
Centrafricaine, République country Africa see Central African Republic
Central admin. dist. Botswana 51 H2
Central, Cordillera mts Col. 68 C3
Central, Cordillera mts Peru 68 C6
Central African Empire country Africa see Central African Republic
Central African Republic country Africa 48 B3
Central Brahui Range mts Pak. 33 K4
Central City NE U.S.A. 62 H3
Central Kalahari Game Reserve nature res. Botswana 50 F2
Central Kara Rise sea feature Arctic Ocean 77 F1
Central Makran Range mts Pak. 33 J4
Central Mount Stuart h. Australia 54 F5
Central Pacific Basin sea feature Pacific Ocean 74 H5
Central Provinces state India see Madhya Pradesh
Central Range mts P.N.G. 52 E2
Central Russian Upland hills Russia 13 H5
Central Siberian Plateau Russia 29 M3
Central Square NY U.S.A. 64 C1
Centreville MD U.S.A. 64 C3
Ceos i. Greece see Tzia
Cephaloedium Sicily Italy see Cefalù
Cephalonia i. Greece 27 I5
Ceram i. Indon. see Seram
Cerbat Mountains AZ U.S.A. 65 E3
Ceres Arg. 70 D3
Ceres Brazil 71 A1
Ceres S. Africa 50 D7
Ceres CA U.S.A. 65 B2
Céret France 24 F5
Cerezo de Abajo Spain 25 E3
Cerignola Italy 26 F4
Cerigo i. Greece see Kythira
Cêringgolêb China see Dongco
Çerkeş Turkey 34 D2
Çerkeşli Turkey 27 M4
Çermik Turkey 35 E3
Cernăuţi Ukr. see Chernivtsi
Cernavodă Romania 27 M2
Cerralvo, Isla i. Mex. 66 C4
Cërrik Albania 27 H4
Cerritos Mex. 66 D4
Cerro Azul Brazil 71 A4
Cerro de Pasco Peru 68 C6
Cerros Colorados, Embalse resr Arg. 70 C5
Cervantes, Cerro mt. Arg. 70 B8
Cervati, Monte mt. Italy 26 F4
Cervione Corsica France 24 I5
Cervo Spain 25 C2
Cesena Italy 26 E2
Cēsis Latvia 15 N8
Česká Republika country Europe see Czech Republic
České Budějovice Czech Rep. 17 O6
Českomoravská vysočina hills Czech Rep. 17 O6
Český Krumlov Czech Rep. 17 O6
Český les mts Czech Rep./Germany 17 N6
Çeşme Turkey 27 L5
Cessnock Australia 58 E4
Cetatea Albă Ukr. see Bilhorod-Dnistrovs'kyy
Cetinje Montenegro 26 H3
Cetraro Italy 26 F5
Ceuta N. Africa 25 D6
Ceva-i-Ra reef Fiji 53 H4
Cévennes mts France 24 F5
Cévennes, Parc National des nat. park France 24 F4
Cevizli Turkey 39 C1
Cevizlik Turkey see Maçka
Ceyhan Turkey 34 D3
Ceyhan r. Turkey 39 B1
Ceyhan Boğazı r. mouth Turkey 39 B1
Ceylanpınar Turkey 35 F3
Ceylon country Asia see Sri Lanka
Chābahār Iran 33 J4
Chabrol i. New Caledonia see Lifou
Chabug China 37 E2
Chabyêr Caka salt l. China 37 F3
Chachapoyas Peru 68 C5
Chacharan Pak. 36 B3
Chaco Boreal reg. Para. 70 E2
Chad country Africa 47 E3
Chad, Lake Africa 47 E3
Chadaasan Mongolia 42 I3
Chadan Russia 42 G2
Chadibe Botswana 51 H2
Chadron NE U.S.A. 62 G3
Chadyr-Lunga Moldova see Ciadîr-Lunga
Chaeryŏng N. Korea 45 B5
Chagai Pak. 33 J4
Chagdo Kangri mt. China 37 F2
Chaghcharān Afgh. 36 A2
Chagny France 24 G3
Chagoda Russia 12 G4
Chagos Archipelago is B.I.O.T. 73 M6
Chagos-Laccadive Ridge sea feature Indian Ocean 73 M6
Chagos Trench sea feature Indian Ocean 73 M6
Chagoyan Russia 44 C1
Chahār Kent Afgh. 36 A1
Chahbounia Alg. 25 H6
Chāh-e Bāzargānī Iran 35 I5
Chāh Kūh Iran 35 I5
Chaibasa India 37 F5
Chainjoin Co l. China 37 F2
Chaitén Chile 70 B6
Chajarí Arg. 70 E4
Chakai India 37 F4
Chak Amru Pak. 36 C2
Chakar r. Pak. 36 B3
Chakaria Bangl. 37 H5
Chakdarra Pak. 36 C2
Chakku Pak. 36 A4
Chakonipau, Lac l. Que. Canada 61 L4
Chakoria Bangl. see Chakaria
Chakvi Georgia 35 F2
Chala Peru 68 D7
Chalatenango El Salvador 66 G6
Chaláua Moz. 49 D5
Chalaxung China 37 I2
Chalcedon Turkey see Kadıköy
Chalengkou China 42 G5
Chaleur Bay inlet N.B./Que. Canada 63 N2
Chaleurs, Baie des inlet N.B./Que. Canada see Chaleur Bay
Chalisgaon India 38 B1
Chalki i. Greece 27 L6
Chalkida Greece 27 J5
Challakere India 38 C3
Challans France 24 D3
Challapata Bol. 68 E7
Challenger Deep sea feature N. Pacific Ocean 74 F5
Challenger Fracture Zone sea feature S. Pacific Ocean 74 M8
Challis ID U.S.A. 62 E3
Châlons-en-Champagne France 24 G2
Châlons-sur-Marne France see Châlons-en-Champagne
Chalon-sur-Saône France 24 G3
Chālūs Iran 35 H3
Cham, Kūh-e h. Iran 35 H4
Chamaico Arg. 70 D5
Chamais Bay Namibia 50 B4
Chaman Pak. 30 F3
Chaman Bīd Iran 35 J3
Chamarajanagar India 38 C4
Chamba India 36 D2
Chamba Tanz. 49 D5
Chambal r. India 36 D4
Chamberlain r. Australia 54 D4
Chamberlain SD U.S.A. 62 H3
Chambersburg PA U.S.A. 64 C3
Chambéry France 24 G4
Chambeshi r. Zambia 49 C5
Chambi, Jebel mt. Tunisia 26 C7
Chamdo China see Qamdo
Chamechaude mt. France 24 G4
Chamoli India see Gopeshwar
Chamonix-Mont-Blanc France 24 H4
Champa India 37 E5
Champagne Castle mt. S. Africa 51 I5
Champagne Humide reg. France 24 G2
Champagne Pouilleuse reg. France 24 F2
Champagnole France 24 G3
Champagny Islands Australia 54 D3
Champaign IL U.S.A. 63 J3
Champhai India 37 H5
Champlain VA U.S.A. 64 C3
Champlain, Lake Canada/U.S.A. 61 K5
Champotón Mex. 66 F5
Chamzinka Russia 13 J5
Chanak Turkey see Çanakkale
Chañaral Chile 70 B3
Chanda India see Chandrapur
Chandalar r. AK U.S.A. 60 D3
Chandausi India 36 D3
Chandbali India 37 F5
Chanderi India 36 D4
Chandigarh India 36 D3
Chandil India 37 F5
Chandler AZ U.S.A. 62 E5
Chandod India 36 C5
Chandpur Bangl. 37 G5
Chandpur India 36 D3
Chandragiri India 38 C3
Chandrapur India 38 C2
Chandvad India 38 B1
Changane r. Moz. 51 K3
Changbai China 44 C4
Changbai Shan mts China/N. Korea 44 B4
Chang Cheng research stn Antarctica see Great Wall
Changchow Fujian China see Zhangzhou
Changchow Jiangsu China see Changzhou
Changchun China 44 B4
Changchunling China 44 B3
Changde China 43 K7
Changgo China 37 F3
Changhua Taiwan see Zhanghua
Changhwa Taiwan see Zhanghua
Changji China 42 F4
Changjin-ho resr N. Korea 45 B4
Changkiang China see Zhanjiang
Changlang India 37 H4
Changling China 44 A3
Changlung India 33 M3
Changma China 42 H5
Changngoi China 37 F3
Changnyŏn N. Korea 45 B5
Ch'ang-pai Shan mts China/N. Korea see Changbai Shan
Changsan-got pt N. Korea 45 B5
Changsha China 43 K7
Changteh China see Changde
Changting China 44 C3
Changwon S. Korea 45 C6
Changyŏn N. Korea 45 B5
Changzhi China 43 K5
Changzhou China 43 L6
Chañi, Nevado de mt. Arg. 70 C2
Chania Greece 27 K7
Chanion, Kolpos b. Greece 27 J7
Channapatna India 38 C3
Channel Islands English Chan. 19 E9
Channel Islands CA U.S.A. 65 C4
Channel Islands National Park CA U.S.A. 65 C3
Channel-Port-aux-Basques Nfld. and Lab. Canada 61 M5
Channel Tunnel France/U.K. 19 I7
Chantada Spain 25 C2
Chanthaburi Thai. 31 J5
Chantilly France 24 F2
Chanuwala Pak. 36 C2
Chany, Ozero salt l. Russia 28 I4
Chaor He r. China 44 A3
Chaowula Shan mt. China 37 I2
Chaoyang Heilongjiang China see Jiayin
Chaoyang Liaoning China 43 M4
Chaoyang Nei Mongol China 44 B2
Chaoyang Hu l. China 37 F2
Chaozhong China 44 A2
Chaozhou China 43 L8
Chapada Diamantina, Parque Nacional nat. park Brazil 71 C1
Chapada dos Veadeiros, Parque Nacional da nat. park Brazil 71 B1
Chapak Goẕar Afgh. 36 A1
Chapala, Laguna de l. Mex. 66 D4
Chāpārī, Kōtal-e Afgh. 36 A2
Chapayevo Kazakh. 30 E1
Chapayevsk Russia 13 K5
Chapecó Brazil 70 F3
Chapecó r. Brazil 70 F3
Chapel-en-le-Frith U.K. 18 F5
Chapeltown U.K. 18 F5
Chapleau Ont. Canada 63 K2
Chaplygin Russia 13 H5
Chappell Islands Australia 57 [inset]
Chapra Bihar India 37 F4
Chapra Jharkhand India see Chatra
Charagua Bol. 68 F7
Charcas Mex. 66 D4
Charcot Island Antarctica 76 L2
Chard U.K. 19 E8
Chardara Kazakh. see Shardara
Chardara, Step' plain Kazakh. see Shardara, Step'
Chardon OH U.S.A. 64 A2
Chardzhev Turkm. see Türkmenabat
Chardzhou Turkm. see Türkmenabat
Charef Alg. 25 H6
Charef, Oued watercourse Morocco 22 D5
Charente r. France 24 D4
Chari r. Cameroon/Chad 47 E3
Chārīkār Afgh. 36 B2
Chärjew Turkm. see Türkmenabat
Charkayuvom Russia 12 L2
Charkhlik China see Ruoqiang
Charleroi Belgium 16 J5
Charles, Cape VA U.S.A. 64 D4
Charles City IA U.S.A. 63 I3
Charles City VA U.S.A. 64 C4
Charles Hill Botswana 50 E2
Charles Island Galápagos Ecuador see Floreana, Isla
Charles Point Australia 54 E3
Charleston N.Z. 59 C5
Charleston SC U.S.A. 63 L5
Charleston WV U.S.A. 63 K4
Charleston Peak NV U.S.A. 65 E2
Charlestown Ireland 21 D4
Charlestown NH U.S.A. 64 E1
Charlestown RI U.S.A. 64 F2
Charles Town WV U.S.A. 64 C3
Charleville Australia 57 D5
Charleville Ireland 21 D5
Charleville-Mézières France 24 G2
Charlie, Dome Antarctica 76 F2
Charlotte NC U.S.A. 63 K4
Charlotte Amalie Virgin Is (U.S.A.) 67 L5
Charlotte Harbor b. FL U.S.A. 63 K6
Charlottesville VA U.S.A. 64 B3
Charlottetown P.E.I. Canada 61 L5
Charlton Australia 58 A6
Charlton Island Nunavut Canada 63 L1
Charsadda Pak. 36 B2
Charshangngy Turkm. see Köýtendag
Charters Towers Australia 56 D4
Chartres France 24 E2
Chas India 37 F5
Chase B.C. Canada 62 D1
Chashmeh-ye Palasi Iran 35 I4
Chashniki Belarus 13 F5
Chaslands Mistake c. N.Z. 59 B8
Chasŏng N. Korea 44 B4
Chasseral mt. Switz. 17 K7
Chassiron, Pointe de pt France 24 D3
Chastab, Kūh-e mts Iran 35 I4
Chāt Iran 35 I3
Chatanika AK U.S.A. 60 D3
Châteaubriant France 24 D3
Château-du-Loir France 24 E3
Châteaudun France 24 E2
Châteaulin France 24 B2
Châteaumeillant France 24 F3
Châteauneuf-sur-Loire France 24 F3
Châteauroux France 24 E3
Château-Thierry France 24 F2
Châtellerault France 24 E3
Chatham U.K. 19 H7
Chatham MA U.S.A. 64 G2
Chatham NY U.S.A. 64 E1
Chatham PA U.S.A. 64 D3
Chatham VA U.S.A. 64 B4
Chatham, Isla i. Chile 70 B8
Chatham Island Galápagos Ecuador see San Cristóbal, Isla
Chatham Island N.Z. 53 I6
Chatham Island Samoa see Savai'i
Chatham Islands N.Z. 53 I6
Chatham Rise sea feature S. Pacific Ocean 74 I8
Châtillon-sur-Seine France 24 G3
Chatkal Range mts Kyrg./Uzbek. 33 L1
Chatra India 37 F4
Chatra Nepal 37 F4
Chatsworth NJ U.S.A. 64 D3
Chattagam Bangl. see Chittagong
Chattanooga TN U.S.A. 63 J4
Chattarpur India see Chhatarpur
Chatteris U.K. 19 H6
Chattisgarh state India see Chhattisgarh
Chatyr-Tash Kyrg. 33 M1
Chauhtan India 36 B4
Chauk Myanmar 37 H5
Chaumont France 24 G2
Chaunskaya Guba b. Russia 29 R3
Chauny France 24 F2
Chausy Belarus see Chavusy
Chautauqua, Lake NY U.S.A. 64 B1
Chauter Pak. 36 A3
Chavakachcheri Sri Lanka 38 D4
Chavakkad India 38 B4
Chaves Port. 25 C3
Chavusy Belarus 13 F5
Chayatyn, Khrebet ridge Russia 44 E1
Chayevo Russia 12 H4
Chaykovskiy Russia 11 Q4
Chazhegovo Russia 12 L3
Cheadle U.K. 19 F6
Cheat r. WV U.S.A. 64 B3
Cheb Czech Rep. 17 N5
Chebba Tunisia 26 D7
Cheboksarskoye Vodokhranilishche resr Russia 12 J5
Cheboksary Russia 12 J4
Cheboygan MI U.S.A. 63 K2
Chechen', Ostrov i. Russia 13 J8
Cheddar U.K. 19 E7
Cheektowaga NY U.S.A. 64 B1
Cheepie Australia 58 B1
Cheetham, Cape Antarctica 76 H2
Chefchaouene Morocco 25 D6
Chefoo China see Yantai
Chefornak AK U.S.A. 60 B3
Chefu Moz. 51 K2
Chegdomyn Russia 44 D2
Chegga Mauritania 46 C2
Chegutu Zimbabwe 49 D5
Chehalis WA U.S.A. 62 C2
Chehel Chashmeh, Kūh-e mt. Iran 35 G4
Cheju S. Korea see Jeju
Chekhov Moskovskaya Oblast' Russia 13 H5
Chekhov Sakhalinskaya Oblast' Russia 44 F3
Chekiang prov. China see Zhejiang
Chekichler Turkm. see Çekiçler
Chekunda Russia 44 D2
Chela, Serra da mts Angola 49 B5
Chelan, Lake WA U.S.A. 62 C2
Cheleken Turkm. see Hazar
Cheline Moz. 51 L2
Chelkar Kazakh. see Shalkar
Chełm Poland 13 D6
Chelmer r. U.K. 19 H7
Chełmno Poland 17 Q4
Chelmsford U.K. 19 H7
Cheltenham U.K. 19 E7
Chelva Spain 25 F4
Chelyabinsk Russia 28 H4
Chemba Moz. 49 D5
Chêm Co l. China 36 D2
Chemnitz Germany 17 N5
Chemulpo S. Korea see Incheon
Chenab r. India/Pak. 36 B3
Chenachane, Oued watercourse Alg. 46 C2
Chendir r. Turkm. see Çendir
Chengalpattu India 38 D3
Chengchow China see Zhengzhou
Chengde China 43 L4
Chengdu China 42 I6
Chengjiang China see Taihe
Chengjiang Fossil Site tourist site China 42 I8
Chengtu China see Chengdu
Chengxian China 42 J6
Chenkaladi Sri Lanka 38 D5
Chennai India 38 D3
Chenqing China 44 B2
Chenqingqiao China see Chenqing
Chenstokhov Poland see Częstochowa
Chenzhou China 43 K7
Cheonan S. Korea 45 B5
Cheongdo S. Korea 45 C6
Cheongju S. Korea 45 B5
Chepén Peru 68 C5
Chepes Arg. 70 C4
Chepo Panama 67 I7
Chepstow U.K. 19 E7
Cheptsa r. Russia 12 K4
Cher r. France 24 E3
Chera state India see Kerala
Cherbaniani Reef India 38 A3
Cherbourg-Octeville France 24 D2
Cherchell Alg. 25 H5
Cherchen China see Qiemo
Cherdakly Russia 13 K5
Cherdyn' Russia 11 R3
Chereapani reef India see Byramgore Reef
Cheremkhovo Russia 42 I2
Cheremshany Russia 44 D3
Cheremukhovka Russia 12 K4
Cherepanovo Russia 42 E2
Cherepovets Russia 12 H4
Cherevkovo Russia 12 J3
Chergui, Chott ech imp. l. Alg. 22 D5
Chéria Alg. 26 B7
Cheriton VA U.S.A. 64 D4
Cheriyakara, Suheli India 38 B4
Cheriyam atoll India 38 B4
Cherkassy Ukr. see Cherkasy
Cherkasy Ukr. 13 G6
Cherkessk Russia 13 I7
Cherla India 38 D2
Chernaya Russia 12 M1
Chernaya r. Russia 12 M1
Chernigov Ukr. see Chernihiv
Chernigovka Russia 44 D3
Chernihiv Ukr. 13 F6
Cherninivka Ukr. 13 H7
Chernivtsi Ukr. 13 E6
Chernobyl' Ukr. see Chornobyl'
Chernogorsk Russia 42 G2
Chernovtsy Ukr. see Chernivtsi
Chernoye More sea Asia/Europe see Black Sea
Chernushka Russia 11 R4
Chernyakhiv Ukr. 13 F6
Chernyakhovsk Russia 13 D5
Chernyanka Russia 13 H6
Chernyayevo Russia 44 B1
Chernyshevsk Russia 43 L2
Chernyshevskiy Russia 29 M3
Chernyshkovskiy Russia 13 I6
Chernyye Zemli reg. Russia 13 J7
Chernyy Irtysh r. China/Kazakh. see Ertix He
Chernyy Porog Russia 12 G3
Chernyy Yar Russia 13 J6
Cherrapunji India 37 G4
Cherry Hill NJ U.S.A. 64 D3
Cherry Island Solomon Is 53 G3
Cherry Lake CA U.S.A. 65 C1
Cherskiy Russia 77 C2
Cherskiy Range mts Russia see Cherskogo, Khrebet
Cherskogo, Khrebet mts Respublika Sakha (Yakutiya) Russia 29 P3
Cherskogo, Khrebet mts Zabaykal'skiy Kray Russia 43 K2
Chertkov Ukr. see Chortkiv
Chertkovo Russia 13 I6
Cherven Bryag Bulg. 27 K3
Chervonoarmeyskoye Ukr. see Vil'nyans'k
Chervonoarmiys'k Donets'ka Oblast' Ukr. see Krasnoarmiys'k
Chervonoarmiys'k Rivnens'ka Oblast' Ukr. see Radyvyliv
Chervonograd Ukr. see Chervonohrad
Chervonohrad Ukr. 13 E6
Chervyen' Belarus 13 F5
Cherwell r. U.K. 19 F7
Cherykaw Belarus 13 F5
Chesapeake VA U.S.A. 64 C4
Chesapeake Bay MD/VA U.S.A. 64 C3
Chesham U.K. 19 G7
Cheshire Plain U.K. 18 E5
Cheshskaya Guba b. Russia 12 J2
Cheshunt U.K. 19 G7
Chesnokovka Russia see Novoaltaysk
Chester U.K. 18 E5
Chester SC U.S.A. 63 K5
Chester r. MD U.S.A. 64 C3
Chesterfield U.K. 18 F5
Chesterfield VA U.S.A. 64 C4
Chesterfield, Îles is New Caledonia 53 F3
Chesterfield Inlet Nunavut Canada 61 I3
Chesterfield Inlet inlet Nunavut Canada 61 I3
Chester-le-Street U.K. 18 F4
Chestertown MD U.S.A. 64 C3
Chestertown NY U.S.A. 64 E1
Chestnut Ridge PA U.S.A. 64 B2
Chesuncook Lake ME U.S.A. 63 N2
Chetaïbi Alg. 26 B6
Chetlat i. India 38 B4
Chetumal Mex. 66 G5
Chetwynd B.C. Canada 60 F4
Cheviot N.Z. 59 D6
Cheviot Hills U.K. 18 E3
Cheviot Range hills Australia 56 C5
Cheyenne WY U.S.A. 62 G3
Cheyenne r. SD U.S.A. 62 G3
Cheyenne Wells CO U.S.A. 62 G4
Cheyne Bay Australia 55 B8
Cheyur India 38 D3
Chhapra India see Chapra
Chhata India 36 D4
Chhatak Bangl. 37 G4
Chhatarpur Jharkhand India 37 F4
Chhatarpur Madh. Prad. India 36 D4
Chhatr Pak. 36 B3
Chhatrapur India 38 E2
Chhattisgarh state India 37 E5
Chhindwara India 36 D5
Chhitkul India see Chitkul
Chhukha Bhutan 37 G4
Chiai Taiwan see Jiayi
Chiamboni Somalia 48 E4
Chiange Angola 49 B5
Chiang Mai Thai. 31 I5
Chiang Rai Thai. 31 I5
Chiari Italy 26 C2
Chiautla Mex. 66 E5
Chiavenna Italy 26 C1
Chiayi Taiwan see Jiayi
Chiba Japan 45 F6
Chibi China 43 K7
Chibia Angola 49 B5
Chibizovka Russia see Zherdevka
Chiboma Moz. 49 D6
Chibougamau Que. Canada 63 M2
Chibuto Moz. 51 K3
Chibuzhang Co l. China 37 G2
Chicacole India see Srikakulam
Chicago IL U.S.A. 63 J3
Chichagof Island AK U.S.A. 60 E4
Chichaoua Morocco 22 C5
Chichatka Russia 44 A1
Chichester U.K. 19 G8
Chichester Range mts Australia 54 B5
Chichgarh India 38 D1
Chichibu Japan 45 E6
Chichibu-Tama Kokuritsu-kōen Japan 45 E6
Chichijima-rettō is Japan 45 F8
Chickasha OK U.S.A. 62 H4
Chiclana de la Frontera Spain 25 C5
Chiclayo Peru 68 C5
Chico r. Arg. 70 C6
Chico CA U.S.A. 62 C4
Chicomo Moz. 51 L3
Chicopee MA U.S.A. 64 E1
Chicoutimi Que. Canada 61 K5
Chicualacuala Moz. 51 J2
Chidambaram India 38 C4
Chidenguele Moz. 51 L3
Chidley, Cape Nfld. and Lab./Nunavut Canada 61 L3
Chido China see Sêndo
Chiducuane Moz. 51 L3
Chiemsee l. Germany 17 N7
Chiengmai Thai. see Chiang Mai
Chieti Italy 26 F3
Chifeng China 43 L4
Chifre, Serra do mts Brazil 71 C2
Chiginagak Volcano, Mount AK U.S.A. 60 C4
Chigu China 37 G3
Chigubo Moz. 51 K2
Chigu Co l. China 37 G3
Chihli, Gulf of China see Bo Hai
Chihuahua Mex. 66 C3
Chikalda India 36 D5
Chikhli India 38 C1
Chikishlyar Turkm. see Çekiçler
Chikmagalur India 38 B3
Chikodi India 38 B2
Chilanko r. B.C. Canada 62 C1
Chilas Pak. 36 C2
Chilaw Sri Lanka 38 C5
Childers Australia 56 F5
Childress TX U.S.A. 62 G5
Chile country S. America 70 B4
Chile Basin sea feature S. Pacific Ocean 75 O8
Chile Chico Chile 70 B7
Chile Rise sea feature S. Pacific Ocean 75 O8
Chilgir Russia 13 J7
Chilia-Nouă Ukr. see Kiliya
Chilika Lake India 38 E2
Chililabombwe Zambia 49 C5
Chilko Lake B.C. Canada 62 C1
Chillán Chile 70 B5
Chillicothe MO U.S.A. 63 I4
Chillicothe OH U.S.A. 63 K4
Chilliwack B.C. Canada 62 C2
Chilo India 36 C4
Chiloé, Isla de i. Chile 70 B6
Chiloé, Isla Grande de i. Chile see Chiloé, Isla de
Chilpancingo Mex. 66 E5
Chilpancingo de los Bravos Mex. see Chilpancingo
Chilpi Pak. 36 C1
Chiltern Hills U.K. 19 G7
Chiluage Angola 49 C4
Chilubi Zambia 49 C5
Chilung Taiwan 43 M7
Chilwa, Lake Malawi 49 D5
Chimala Tanz. 49 D4
Chimaltenango Guat. 66 F6
Chimbas Arg. 70 C4
Chimborazo mt. Ecuador 68 C4
Chimbote Peru 68 C5
Chimboy Uzbek. 33 I1
Chimishliya Moldova see Cimişlia
Chimkent Kazakh. see Shymkent
Chimoio Moz. 49 D5
Chimtargha, Qullai mt. Tajik. 33 K2
Chimtorga, Gora mt. Tajik. see Chimtargha, Qullai
China country Asia 42 H5
China, Republic of country Asia see Taiwan
China Lake CA U.S.A. 65 D3
Chinandega Nicaragua 66 G6
China Point CA U.S.A. 65 C4
Chincha Alta Peru 68 C6
Chinchaga r. Alta Canada 60 G4
Chinchilla Australia 58 E1
Chincholi India 38 C2
Chinchorro, Banco sea feature Mex. 67 G5
Chincoteague Bay MD/VA U.S.A. 64 D4
Chinde Moz. 49 D5
Chindwin r. Myanmar 37 H5
Chinese Turkestan aut. reg. China see Xinjiang Uygur Zizhiqu
Chinghai prov. China see Qinghai
Chingleput India see Chengalpattu
Chingola Zambia 49 C5
Chinguar Angola 49 B5
Chinguetti Mauritania 46 B2
Chinhoyi Zimbabwe 49 D5
Chini India see Kalpa
Chining China see Jining
Chiniot Pak. 33 L3
Chinju S. Korea 45 C6
Chinle AZ U.S.A. 62 F4
Chinnamp'o N. Korea see Namp'o
Chinnur India 38 C2
Chino Creek watercourse AZ U.S.A. 65 F3
Chinon France 24 E3
Chinook Trough sea feature N. Pacific Ocean 74 I3
Chino Valley AZ U.S.A. 62 E5
Chinsali Zambia 49 D5
Chintamani India 38 C3
Chioggia Italy 26 E2
Chios Greece 27 L5
Chios i. Greece 27 K5
Chipata Zambia 49 D5
Chipchihua, Sierra de mts Arg. 70 C6
Chipindo Angola 49 B5
Chipinga Zimbabwe see Chipinge
Chipinge Zimbabwe 49 D6
Chippenham U.K. 19 E7

Chipping Norton U.K. 19 F7
Chipping Sodbury U.K. 19 E7
Chipurupalle Andhra Prad. India 38 D2
Chipurupalle Andhra Prad. India 38 D2
Chiquinquirá Col. 68 D2
Chir r. Russia 13 I6
Chirada India 38 D3
Chirala India 38 D3
Chīras Afgh. 36 A2
Chirchiq Uzbek. 33 K1
Chiredzi Zimbabwe 49 D6
Chirfa Niger 46 E2
Chiricahua Peak AZ U.S.A. 62 F5
Chirikof Island AK U.S.A. 60 C4
Chiriquí, Golfo de b. Panama 67 H7
Chiriquí, Volcán de vol. Panama see Barú, Volcán
Chirk U.K. 19 D6
Chirnside U.K. 20 G5
Chirripó mt. Costa Rica 67 H7
Chisamba Zambia 49 C5
Chisasibi Que. Canada 61 K4
Chishima-retto is Russia see Kuril Islands
Chishtian Pak. 33 L4
Chishui China 42 J7
Chisimaio Somalia see Kismaayo
Chişinău Moldova 27 M1
Chistopol' Russia 12 K5
Chita Russia 43 K2
Chitado Angola 49 B5
Chitaldrug India see Chitradurga
Chitalwana India 36 B4
Chitambo Zambia 49 D5
Chita Oblast admin. div. Russia see Chitinskaya Oblast'
Chitato Angola 49 C4
Chitembo Angola 49 B5
Chitina AK U.S.A. 60 D3
Chitinskaya Oblast' admin. div. Russia 44 A1
Chitipa Malawi 49 D4
Chitkul India 36 D3
Chitobe Moz. 49 D6
Chitoor India see Chittoor
Chitor India see Chittaurgarh
Chitose Japan 44 F4
Chitradurga India 38 C3
Chitrakoot India 36 E4
Chitrakut India see Chitrakoot
Chitral Pak. 33 L2
Chitral r. Pak. 36 B2
Chitravati r. India 38 C3
Chitré Panama 67 H7
Chitrod India 36 B5
Chittagong Bangl. 37 G5
Chittaurgarh India 36 C4
Chittoor India 38 C3
Chittor India see Chittoor
Chittorgarh India see Chittaurgarh
Chittur India 38 C4
Chitungwiza Zimbabwe 49 D5
Chiume Angola 49 C5
Chivasso Italy 26 B2
Chivhu Zimbabwe 49 D5
Chizarira National Park Zimbabwe 49 C5
Chizu Japan 45 D6
Chkalov Russia see Orenburg
Chkalovsk Russia 12 I4
Chkalovskoye Russia 44 D3
Chlef Alg. 25 G5
Chlef, Oued r. Alg. 25 G5
Chloride AZ U.S.A. 65 E3
Chlya, Ozero l. Russia 44 F1
Chobe National Park Botswana 49 C5
Choele Choel Arg. 70 C5
Chogar r. Russia 44 D1
Chogori Feng mt. China/Pakistan see K2
Chograyskoye Vodokhranilishche resr Russia 13 J7
Choiseul i. Solomon Is 53 F2
Choix Mex. 66 C3
Chojnice Poland 17 P4
Chōkai-san vol. Japan 45 F5
Ch'ok'ē mts Eth. 48 D2
Ch'ok'ē Mountains Eth. see Ch'ok'ē
Ch'ok'ē Terara mt. Eth. 48 D2
Chokola mt. China 36 E3
Choksum China 37 F3
Chokue Moz. see Chókwè
Chokurdakh Russia 29 P2
Chókwè Moz. 51 K3
Cholame CA U.S.A. 65 B3
Cholet France 24 D3
Choluteca Hond. 67 G6
Choma Zambia 49 C5
Chomo Ganggar mt. China 37 G3
Chomo Lhari mt. China/Bhutan 37 G4
Chomutov Czech Rep. 17 N5
Chon Buri Thai. 31 J5
Ch'ŏnch'ŏn N. Korea 44 B4
Chone Ecuador 68 B4
Ch'ŏngch'ŏn-gang r. N. Korea 45 B5
Chonggye China see Qonggyai
Ch'ŏngjin N. Korea 44 C4
Chongkü China 37 I3
Chongming Dao i. China 43 M6
Chongoroi Angola 49 B5
Chŏngp'yŏng N. Korea 45 B5
Chongqing China 42 J7
Chongqing mun. China 42 J6
Chongwe Zambia 49 C5
Chonguene Moz. 51 K3
Chonos, Archipiélago de los is Chile 70 A6
Cho Oyu mt. China/Nepal 37 F3
Chopda India 36 C5
Chor Pak. 36 B4
Chora Sfakion Greece 27 K7
Chorley U.K. 18 E5
Chornobyl' Ukr. 13 F6
Chornomors'ke Ukr. 27 O2
Chortkiv Ukr. 13 E6
Ch'osan N. Korea 44 B4
Chōshi Japan 45 F6
Chosŏn country Asia see South Korea
Chosŏn-minjujuŭi-inmin-konghwaguk country Asia see North Korea
Choszczno Poland 17 O4
Chota Peru 68 C5
Chota Sinchula mt. India 37 G4
Choti Pak. 36 B3
Choûm Mauritania 46 B2
Chowchilla CA U.S.A. 65 B2
Choybalsan Mongolia 43 K3
Choyr Mongolia 43 J3
Chřiby hills Czech Rep. 17 P6
Chrissiesmeer S. Africa 51 J4
Christchurch N.Z. 59 D6
Christchurch U.K. 19 F8
Christian, Cape Nunavut Canada 61 L2
Christiana S. Africa 51 G4
Christiania Norway see Oslo
Christiansburg VA U.S.A. 64 A4
Christianshåb Greenland see Qasigiannguit
Christina, Mount N.Z. 59 B7
Christmas Island terr. Indian Ocean 41 C9
Christopher, Lake imp. l. Australia 55 D6
Chrudim Czech Rep. 17 O6
Chrysochou Bay Cyprus 39 A2
Chrysochous, Kolpos b. Cyprus see Chrysochou Bay
Chu Kazakh. see Shu
Chuadanga Bangl. 37 G5
Chuali, Lago l. Moz. 51 K3
Chuanhui China see Zhoukou
Chubarovka Ukr. see Polohy
Chubartau Kazakh. see Barshatas
Chūbu-Sangaku Kokuritsu-kōen Japan 45 E5
Chuchkovo Russia 13 I5
Chuckwalla Mountains CA U.S.A. 65 E4
Chudniv Ukr. 13 F6
Chudovo Russia 12 F4
Chudskoye, Ozero l. Estonia/Russia see Peipus, Lake
Chugach Mountains AK U.S.A. 60 D3
Chūgoku-sanchi mts Japan 45 D6
Chugqênsumdo China see Jigzhi
Chuguchak China see Tacheng
Chuguyev Ukr. see Chuhuyiv
Chuguyevka Russia 44 D3
Chuhuyiv Ukr. 13 H6
Chujiang China see Shimen
Chukchagirskoye, Ozero l. Russia 44 E1
Chukchi Abyssal Plain sea feature Arctic Ocean 77 B1
Chukchi Peninsula Russia see Chukotskiy Poluostrov
Chukchi Plateau sea feature Arctic Ocean 77 B1
Chukchi Sea Russia/U.S.A. 29 T3
Chukhloma Russia 12 I4
Chukotskiy, Mys c. Russia 60 A3
Chukotskiy Poluostrov pen. Russia 29 T3
Chulakkurgan Kazakh. see Sholakkorgan
Chulaktau Kazakh. see Karatau
Chulasa Russia 12 J2
Chula Vista CA U.S.A. 65 D4
Chulucanas Peru 68 B5
Chulung Pass Pak. 36 D2
Chulym Russia 28 J4
Chumar India 36 D2
Chumbicha Arg. 70 C3
Chumda China 37 I2
Chumikan Russia 29 O4
Chumphon Thai. 31 I5
Chunar India 37 E4
Chuncheon S. Korea 45 B5
Chunga Zambia 49 C5
Chung-hua Jen-min Kung-ho-kuo country Asia see China
Chung-hua Min-kuo country Asia see Taiwan
Chungju S. Korea 45 B5
Chungking China see Chongqing
Ch'ungmu S. Korea see Tongyeong
Chŭngsan N. Korea 45 B5
Chunian Pak. 36 C3
Chunskiy Russia 42 H1
Chunya r. Russia 29 K3
Chupa Russia 14 R3
Chūplū Iran 35 G3
Chuquicamata Chile 70 C2
Chur Switz. 24 I3
Churachandpur India 37 H4
Churapcha Russia 29 O3
Churchill Man. Canada 61 I4
Churchill r. Man. Canada 61 I4
Churchill r. Nfld. and Lab. Canada 61 L4
Churchill, Cape Man. Canada 61 I4
Churchill Mountains Antarctica 76 H1
Churchville VA U.S.A. 64 B3
Churia Ghati Hills Nepal 37 F4
Churu India 36 C3
Churún-Merú waterfall Venez. see Angel Falls
Chushul India 36 D2
Chusovaya r. Russia 11 R4
Chusovoy Russia 11 R4
Chust Ukr. see Khust
Chute-des-Passes Que. Canada 63 M2
Chutia Assam India 37 H4
Chutia Jharkhand India 37 F5
Chuuk is Micronesia 74 G5
Chuxiong China 42 I7
Chüy r. Kazakh./Kyrg. see Shu
Chymyshliya Moldova see Cimişlia
Chyulu Hills National Park Kenya 48 D4
Ciadâr-Lunga Moldova see Ciadîr-Lunga
Ciadîr-Lunga Moldova 27 M1
Cianorte Brazil 70 F2
Čićarija mts Croatia 26 E2
Cide Turkey 34 D2
Ciechanów Poland 17 R4
Ciego de Ávila Cuba 67 I4
Ciénaga Col. 68 D1
Cienfuegos Cuba 67 H4
Cieza Spain 25 F4
Çiftlik Turkey see Kelkit
Cifuentes Spain 25 E3
Cigüela r. Spain 25 E4
Cihanbeyli Turkey 34 D3
Cíjara, Embalse de resr Spain 25 D4
Cilacap Indon. 41 C8
Çıldır Turkey 35 F2
Çıldır Gölü l. Turkey 35 F2
Çıldıroba Turkey 39 C1
Cilento, Vallo di Diano e Alburni, Parco Nazionale del nat. park Italy 26 F4
Cilician Gates pass Turkey see Gülek Boğazı
Cill Airne Ireland see Killarney
Cill Chainnigh Ireland see Kilkenny
Cill Mhantáin Ireland see Wicklow
Çilmämmetgum des. Turkm. 35 I2
Cilo Dağı mt. Turkey 35 G3
Çilov Adası i. Azer. 35 H2
Cimarron r. OK U.S.A. 62 H4
Cimişlia Moldova 27 M1
Cimone, Monte mt. Italy 26 D2
Cîmpina Romania see Câmpina
Cîmpulung Romania see Câmpulung
Cîmpulung Moldovenesc Romania see Câmpulung Moldovenesc
Çınar Turkey 35 F3
Cinca r. Spain 25 G3
Cincinnati OH U.S.A. 63 K4
Cinco de Outubro Angola see Xá-Muteba
Cinderford U.K. 19 E7
Çine Turkey 27 M6
Cintalapa Mex. 66 F5
Cinto, Monte mt. France 24 I5
Ciping China 43 K7
Circeo, Parco Nazionale del nat. park Italy 26 E4
Circle AK U.S.A. 60 D3
Cirebon Indon. 41 C8
Cirencester U.K. 19 F7
Cirò Marina Italy 26 G5
Cirta Alg. see Constantine
Cisne, Islas del is Caribbean Sea 67 H5
Citlaltépetl vol. Mex. see Orizaba, Pico de
Čitluk Bos. & Herz. 26 G3
Citrus Heights CA U.S.A. 65 B1
Città di Castello Italy 26 E3
Ciucaş, Vârful mt. Romania 27 K2
Ciudad Acuña Mex. 62 G6
Ciudad Altamirano Mex. 66 D5
Ciudad Bolívar Venez. 68 F2
Ciudad Camargo Mex. 66 C3
Ciudad Constitución Mex. 66 B3
Ciudad del Carmen Mex. 66 F5
Ciudad Delicias Mex. 66 C3
Ciudad de Panamá Panama see Panama City
Ciudad de Valles Mex. 66 E4
Ciudad Flores Guat. see Flores
Ciudad Guayana Venez. 68 F2
Ciudad Guzmán Mex. 66 D5
Ciudad Juárez Mex. 66 C2
Ciudad Mante Mex. 66 E4
Ciudad Obregón Mex. 66 C3
Ciudad Real Spain 25 E4
Ciudad Río Bravo Mex. 62 H6
Ciudad Rodrigo Spain 25 C3
Ciudad Trujillo Dom. Rep. see Santo Domingo
Ciudad Victoria Mex. 66 E4
Ciutadella Spain 25 H3
Cıva Burnu pt Turkey 34 E2
Cividale del Friuli Italy 26 E1
Civitanova Marche Italy 26 E3
Civitavecchia Italy 26 D3
Çivril Turkey 27 M5
Cizre Turkey 35 F3
Clacton-on-Sea U.K. 19 I7
Clady U.K. 21 E3
Claire, Lake Alta Canada 60 G4
Clairfontaine Alg. see El Aouinet
Clamecy France 24 F3
Clane Ireland 21 F4
Clanwilliam Dam S. Africa 50 D7
Clara Ireland 21 E4
Claraville Australia 56 C3
Clare N.S.W. Australia 58 A4
Clare S.A. Australia 57 B7
Clare r. Ireland 21 C4
Clarecastle Ireland 21 D5
Clare Island Ireland 21 B4
Claremont NH U.S.A. 64 E1
Claremorris Ireland 21 D4
Clarence r. Australia 58 F2
Clarence N.Z. 59 D6
Clarence Island Antarctica 76 A2
Clarence Town Bahamas 63 M7
Clarendon PA U.S.A. 64 B2
Clarenville Nfld. and Lab. Canada 61 M5
Claresholm Alta Canada 62 E1
Clarie Coast Antarctica see Wilkes Coast
Clarington OH U.S.A. 64 A3
Clarion PA U.S.A. 64 B2
Clarion r. PA U.S.A. 64 B2
Clarión, Isla i. Mex. 66 B5
Clarkebury S. Africa 51 I6
Clarke Range mts Australia 56 D4
Clarke River Australia 56 D3
Clark Mountain CA U.S.A. 65 E3
Clarksburg WV U.S.A. 64 A3
Clarksdale MS U.S.A. 63 I5
Clarksville AR U.S.A. 63 I4
Clarksville TN U.S.A. 63 J4
Claro r. Goiás Brazil 71 A2
Claro r. Mato Grosso Brazil 71 A1
Clashmore Ireland 21 E5
Claudy U.K. 21 E3
Clay WV U.S.A. 64 A3
Clayhole Wash watercourse AZ U.S.A. 65 F2
Clayton DE U.S.A. 64 D3
Clayton NM U.S.A. 62 G4
Claytor Lake VA U.S.A. 64 A4
Clear, Cape Ireland 21 C6
Clearco WV U.S.A. 64 A3
Clear Creek Ont. Canada 64 A1
Cleare, Cape AK U.S.A. 60 D4
Clearfield PA U.S.A. 64 B2
Clear Island Ireland 21 C6
Clear Lake IA U.S.A. 63 I3
Clear Lake CA U.S.A. 65 A1
Clear Lake UT U.S.A. 65 F1
Clearwater r. Alta/Sask. Canada 60 G4
Clearwater FL U.S.A. 63 K6
Cleburne TX U.S.A. 63 H5
Cleethorpes U.K. 18 G5
Clendenin WV U.S.A. 64 A3
Clendening Lake OH U.S.A. 64 A2
Clères France 19 I9
Clerke Reef Australia 54 B4
Clermont Australia 56 D4
Clermont-Ferrand France 24 F4
Cles Italy 26 D1
Clevedon U.K. 19 E7
Cleveland MS U.S.A. 63 I5
Cleveland OH U.S.A. 64 A2
Cleveland TN U.S.A. 63 K4
Cleveland, Cape Australia 56 D3
Cleveland, Mount MT U.S.A. 62 E2
Cleveland Heights OH U.S.A. 64 A2
Cleveland Hills U.K. 18 F4
Cleveleys U.K. 18 D5
Clew Bay Ireland 21 C4
Clifden Ireland 21 B4
Cliffoney Ireland 21 D3
Clifton Australia 58 E1
Clifton AZ U.S.A. 62 F5
Clifton Beach Australia 56 D3
Clifton Forge VA U.S.A. 64 B4
Clifton Park NY U.S.A. 64 E1
Clinton Ont. Canada 64 A1
Clinton IA U.S.A. 63 I3
Clinton OK U.S.A. 62 H4
Clipperton, Île terr. N. Pacific Ocean 75 M5
Clisham h. U.K. 20 C3
Clitheroe U.K. 18 E5
Cliza Bol. 68 E7
Clocolan S. Africa 51 H5
Cloghan Ireland 21 E4
Clonakilty Ireland 21 D6
Clonbern Ireland 21 D4
Cloncurry Australia 56 C4
Cloncurry r. Australia 56 C3
Clones Ireland 21 E3
Clonmel Ireland 21 E5
Clonygowan Ireland 21 E4
Cloonbannin Ireland 21 C5
Clooneagh Ireland 21 E4
Cloud Peak WY U.S.A. 62 F3
Cloverdale CA U.S.A. 65 A1
Clovis CA U.S.A. 65 C2
Clovis NM U.S.A. 62 G5
Cluain Meala Ireland see Clonmel
Cluanie, Loch l. U.K. 20 D3
Cluff Lake Mine Sask. Canada 60 H4
Cluj-Napoca Romania 27 J1
Clun U.K. 19 D6
Clunes Australia 58 A6
Cluny Australia 56 B5
Cluses France 24 H3
Clutterbuck Hills h. Australia 55 D6
Clwydian Range hills U.K. 18 D5
Clyde r. U.K. 20 E5
Clyde NY U.S.A. 64 C1
Clyde, Firth of est. U.K. 20 E5
Clydebank U.K. 20 E5
Clyde River Nunavut Canada 61 L2
Côa r. Port. 25 C3
Coachella CA U.S.A. 65 D4
Coaldale (abandoned) NV U.S.A. 65 D1
Coalinga CA U.S.A. 65 B2
Coalport PA U.S.A. 64 B2
Coal River B.C. Canada 60 F4
Coal Valley val. NV U.S.A. 65 E2
Coalville U.K. 19 F6
Coari Brazil 68 F4
Coari r. Brazil 68 F4
Coarsegold CA U.S.A. 65 C2
Coastal Plain U.S.A. 63 I5
Coast Mountains B.C. Canada 60 F4
Coast Ranges hills Australia 57 E5
Coast Ranges mts CA U.S.A. 65 B2
Coatbridge U.K. 20 E5
Coatesville PA U.S.A. 64 D3
Coats Island Nunavut Canada 61 J3
Coats Land reg. Antarctica 76 A1
Coatzacoalcos Mex. 66 F5
Cobar Australia 58 B3
Cobargo Australia 58 D6
Cobden Australia 58 A7
Cobh Ireland 21 D6
Cobija Bol. 68 E6
Coblenz Germany see Koblenz
Cobleskill NY U.S.A. 64 D1
Cobourg Peninsula Australia 54 F2
Cobra Australia 55 B6
Cobram Australia 58 B5
Coburg Germany 17 M5
Coburg Island Nunavut Canada 61 K2
Coca Ecuador 68 C4
Coca Spain 25 D3
Cocalinho Brazil 71 A1
Cocanada India see Kakinada
Cochabamba Bol. 68 E7
Cochin India see Kochi
Cochrane Alta Canada 62 E1
Cochrane Ont. Canada 63 K2
Cockburn Australia 57 C7
Cockburnspath U.K. 20 G5
Cockburn Town Turks and Caicos Is see Grand Turk
Cockermouth U.K. 18 D4
Cocklebiddy Australia 55 D8
Cockscomb mt. S. Africa 50 G7
Coco r. Hond./Nicaragua 67 H6
Coco, Isla de i. N. Pacific Ocean 67 G7
Cocobeach Gabon 48 A3
Coconino Plateau AZ U.S.A. 65 F3
Cocopara National Park Australia 58 C5
Cocos Brazil 71 B1
Cocos (Keeling) Islands terr. Indian Ocean 41 B9
Cocos Basin sea feature Indian Ocean 73 O5
Cocos Ridge sea feature N. Pacific Ocean 75 O5
Cocuy, Sierra Nevada del mt. Col. 68 D2
Cod, Cape MA U.S.A. 64 F2
Codajás Brazil 68 F4
Codfish Island N.Z. 59 A8
Codigoro Italy 26 E2
Cod Island Nfld. and Lab. Canada 61 L4
Codlea Romania 27 K2
Codó Brazil 69 J4
Codsall U.K. 19 E6
Cod's Head hd Ireland 21 B6
Cody WY U.S.A. 62 F3
Coen Australia 56 C2
Coeur d'Alene ID U.S.A. 62 D2
Coffee Bay S. Africa 51 I6
Coffee Cultural Landscape of Colombia tourist site Col. 68 C2
Coffeyville KS U.S.A. 63 H4
Coffin Bay Australia 57 A7
Coffin Bay National Park Australia 57 A7
Coffs Harbour Australia 58 F3
Cofimvaba S. Africa 51 H7
Cognac France 24 D4
Cogo Equat. Guinea 46 D4
Coguno Moz. 51 L3
Cohoes NY U.S.A. 64 E1
Cohuna Australia 58 B5
Coiba, Isla de i. Panama 67 H7
Coigeach, Rubha pt U.K. 20 D2
Coihaique Chile 70 B7
Coimbatore India 38 C4
Coimbra Port. 25 B3
Coipasa, Salar de salt flat Bol. 68 E7
Coire Switz. see Chur
Colac Australia 58 A7
Colair Lake India see Kolleru Lake
Colatina Brazil 71 C2
Colby KS U.S.A. 62 G4
Colchester U.K. 19 H7
Colchester CT U.S.A. 64 E2
Cold Bay AK U.S.A. 60 B4
Coldingham U.K. 20 G5
Coldstream U.K. 20 G5
Coleambally Australia 58 B5
Coleman r. Australia 56 C2
Coleman TX U.S.A. 62 H5
Çölemerik Turkey see Hakkâri
Colenso S. Africa 51 I5
Cole Peninsula Antarctica 76 L2
Coleraine Australia 57 C8
Coleraine U.K. 21 F2
Coles, Punta de pt Peru 68 D7
Coles Bay Australia 57 [inset]
Colesberg S. Africa 51 G6
Colfax CA U.S.A. 65 B1
Colhué Huapí, Lago l. Arg. 70 C7
Coligny S. Africa 51 H4
Colima Mex. 66 D5
Colima, Nevado de vol. Mex. 66 D5
Coll i. U.K. 20 C4
Collado Villalba Spain 25 E3
Collarenebri Australia 58 D2
Collerina Australia 58 C2
Collie N.S.W. Australia 58 D3
Collie W.A. Australia 55 B8
Collier Bay Australia 54 D4
Collier Range National Park Australia 55 B6
Collingwood N.Z. 59 D5
Collins Glacier Antarctica 76 E2
Collinson Peninsula Nunavut Canada 61 H2
Collipulli Chile 70 B5
Collooney Ireland 21 D3
Colmar France 24 H2
Colmenar Viejo Spain 25 E3
Colmonell U.K. 20 E5
Colne r. U.K. 19 H7
Cologne Germany 17 K5
Colomb-Béchar Alg. see Béchar
Colômbia Brazil 71 A3
Colombia country S. America 68 D3
Colombian Basin sea feature S. Atlantic Ocean 72 C5
Colombo Sri Lanka 38 C5
Colomiers France 24 E5
Colón Buenos Aires Arg. 70 D4
Colón Entre Ríos Arg. 70 E4
Colón Panama 67 I7
Colón, Archipiélago de is Ecuador see Galapagos Islands
Colona Australia 55 F7
Colonelganj India 37 E4
Colônia r. Brazil 71 D1
Colonia Agrippina Germany see Cologne
Colonia Julia Fenestris Italy see Fano
Colonia Las Heras Arg. 70 C7
Colonial Heights VA U.S.A. 64 C4
Colonna, Capo c. Italy 26 G5
Colonsay i. U.K. 20 C4
Colorado r. Arg. 70 D5
Colorado r. Mex./U.S.A. 65 F2
Colorado r. TX U.S.A. 62 H6
Colorado state U.S.A. 62 F4
Colorado City AZ U.S.A. 65 F2
Colorado Desert CA U.S.A. 65 D4
Colorado Plateau CO U.S.A. 62 F4
Colorado River Aqueduct canal CA U.S.A. 65 E3
Colorado Springs CO U.S.A. 62 G4
Colossae Turkey see Honaz
Colotlán Mex. 66 D4
Colquiri Bol. 68 E7
Colsterworth U.K. 19 G6
Colstrip MT U.S.A. 62 F2
Coltishall U.K. 19 I6
Colton CA U.S.A. 65 D3
Columbia MD U.S.A. 64 C3
Columbia MO U.S.A. 63 I4
Columbia PA U.S.A. 64 C2
Columbia SC U.S.A. 63 K5
Columbia TN U.S.A. 63 J4
Columbia r. WA U.S.A. 62 C2
Columbia, District of admin. dist. U.S.A. 64 C3
Columbia, Mount Alta/B.C. Canada 62 D1
Columbia Mountains B.C. Canada 62 C1
Columbia Plateau U.S.A. 62 D2
Columbine, Cape S. Africa 50 C7
Columbus GA U.S.A. 63 K5
Columbus IN U.S.A. 63 J4
Columbus MS U.S.A. 63 J5
Columbus NE U.S.A. 63 H3
Columbus NM U.S.A. 62 F5
Columbus OH U.S.A. 63 K4
Columbus Salt Marsh NV U.S.A. 65 C1
Colusa CA U.S.A. 65 A1
Colville N.Z. 59 E3
Colville r. AK U.S.A. 60 C2
Colville Channel N.Z. 59 E3
Colville Lake N.W.T. Canada 60 F3
Colwyn Bay U.K. 18 D5
Comacchio Italy 26 E2
Comacchio, Valli di lag. Italy 26 E2
Comai China 37 G3
Comalcalco Mex. 66 F5
Comandante Ferraz (Brazil) research stn Antarctica 76 A2
Comandante Salas Arg. 70 C4
Comăneşti Romania 27 L1
Combarbalá Chile 70 B4
Comber U.K. 21 G3
Combermere Bay Myanmar 37 H6
Combomune Moz. 51 K2
Comboyne Australia 58 F3
Comencho, Lac l. Que. Canada 63 L1
Comendador Dom. Rep. see Elías Piña
Comendador Gomes Brazil 71 A2
Comeragh Mountains hills Ireland 21 E5
Comercinho Brazil 71 C2
Cometela Moz. 51 L1
Comilla Bangl. 37 G5
Comino, Capo c. Sardinia Italy 26 C4
Comitán de Domínguez Mex. 66 F5
Commack NY U.S.A. 64 E2
Commentry France 24 F3
Committee Bay Nunavut Canada 61 J3
Commonwealth Territory admin. div. Australia see Jervis Bay Territory
Como Italy 26 C2
Como, Lago di Italy see Como, Lake
Como, Lake Italy 26 C2
Como Chamling l. China 37 G3
Comodoro Rivadavia Arg. 70 C7
Comoé, Parc National de la nat. park Côte d'Ivoire 46 C4
Comores country Africa see Comoros
Comorin, Cape India 38 C4
Comoro Islands country Africa see Comoros
Comoros country Africa 49 E5
Compiègne France 24 F2
Comprida, Ilha i. Brazil 71 B4
Comrat Moldova 27 M1
Comrie U.K. 20 F4
Cona China 37 G4
Conakry Guinea 46 B4
Cona Niyeo Arg. 70 C6
Conceição r. Brazil 71 B2
Conceição da Barra Brazil 71 D2
Conceição do Araguaia Brazil 69 I5
Conceição do Mato Dentro Brazil 71 C2
Concepción Chile 70 B5
Concepción Mex. 66 D4
Concepción Para. 70 E2
Concepción de la Vega Dom. Rep. see La Vega
Conception, Point CA U.S.A. 65 B3
Conchos r. Chihuahua Mex. 66 D3
Conchos r. Nuevo León/Tamaulipas Mex. 66 E4
Concord CA U.S.A. 65 A2
Concord NH U.S.A. 64 F1
Concordia Arg. 70 E4
Concordia Peru 68 D4
Concordia S. Africa 50 C5
Concordia KS U.S.A. 62 H4
Concordia (France/Italy) research stn 76 G2
Concord Peak Afgh. 36 C1
Condamine Australia 58 E1
Condamine r. Australia 58 D1
Condeúba Brazil 71 C1
Condobolin Australia 58 C4
Condom France 24 E5
Cóndor, Cordillera del mts Ecuador/Peru 68 C4
Conegliano Italy 26 E2
Conemaugh r. PA U.S.A. 64 B2
Conesus Lake NY U.S.A. 64 C1
Conflict Group is P.N.G. 56 E1
Confoederatio Helvetica country Europe see Switzerland
Confusion Range mts UT U.S.A. 65 F1
Congdü China 37 F3
Congleton U.K. 18 E5
Congo country Africa 48 B4
Congo (Brazzaville) country Africa see Congo
Congo (Kinshasa) country Africa see Congo, Democratic Republic of the
Congo, Democratic Republic of the country Africa 48 C4
Congo, Republic of country Africa see Congo
Congo Basin Dem. Rep. Congo 48 C4
Congo Cone sea feature S. Atlantic Ocean 72 I6
Congo Free State country Africa see Congo, Democratic Republic of the
Congonhas Brazil 71 C3
Congress AZ U.S.A. 65 F3
Conimbla National Park Australia 58 D4
Coningsby U.K. 19 G5
Coniston U.K. 18 D4
Conjuboy Australia 56 D3
Conn, Lough l. Ireland 21 C3
Connacht reg. Ireland 21 C4
Connaught reg. Ireland see Connacht
Conneaut OH U.S.A. 64 A2
Connecticut state U.S.A. 64 E2
Connemara reg. Ireland 21 C4
Connemara National Park Ireland 21 C4
Connors Range hills Australia 56 E4
Conoble Australia 58 B4
Conquista Brazil 71 B2
Conrad MT U.S.A. 62 E2
Conrad Rise sea feature Southern Ocean 73 K9
Conroe TX U.S.A. 63 H5
Conselheiro Lafaiete Brazil 71 C3
Consett U.K. 18 F4
Constance Germany see Konstanz
Constance, Lake Germany/Switz. 17 L7
Constância dos Baetas Brazil 68 F5
Constanţa Romania 27 M2
Constantia tourist site Cyprus see Salamis
Constantia Germany see Konstanz
Constantina Spain 25 D5
Constantine Alg. 22 F4
Constantine, Cape AK U.S.A. 60 C4
Constantinople Turkey see İstanbul
Contamana Peru 68 C5
Contas r. Brazil 71 D1
Contria Brazil 71 B2
Contwoyto Lake N.W.T./Nunavut Canada 60 G3
Convención Col. 68 D2
Conway U.K. see Conwy
Conway AR U.S.A. 63 I4
Conway, Cape Australia 56 E4
Conway, Lake imp. l. Australia 57 A6
Conway National Park Australia 56 E4
Conway Reef Fiji see Ceva-i-Ra
Conwy U.K. 18 D5
Conwy r. U.K. 19 D5
Coober Pedy Australia 55 F7
Cooch Behar India see Koch Bihar
Coochbehar India see Koch Bihar
Cook Australia 55 E7
Cook, Grand Récif de reef New Caledonia 53 G3
Cook, Mount N.Z. see Aoraki/Mount Cook
Cookhouse S. Africa 51 G7
Cook Ice Shelf Antarctica 76 H2
Cook Inlet sea chan. AK U.S.A. 60 C3
Cook Islands terr. S. Pacific Ocean 74 J7
Cooksburg NY U.S.A. 64 D1
Cooks Passage Australia 56 D2
Cookstown U.K. 21 F3
Cook Strait N.Z. 59 E5
Cooktown Australia 56 D2
Coolabah Australia 58 C3
Cooladdi Australia 58 B1
Coolah Australia 58 D3
Coolamon Australia 58 C5
Coolgardie Australia 55 C7
Coolibah Australia 54 E3
Coolum Beach Australia 57 F5
Cooma Australia 58 D6
Coombah Australia 57 C7
Coonabarabran Australia 58 D3
Coonamble Australia 58 D3
Coondambo Australia 57 A6
Coondapoor India see Kundapura
Coongoola Australia 58 B1
Cooper Creek watercourse Australia 57 B6
Coopernook Australia 58 F3
Cooperstown NY U.S.A. 64 D1
Coopracambra National Park Australia 58 D6
Coorabie Australia 55 F7
Coorong National Park Australia 57 B8
Coorow Australia 55 B7
Coos Bay OR U.S.A. 62 C3
Cootamundra Australia 58 D5
Cootehill Ireland 21 E3
Cooyar Australia 58 E1
Copala Mex. 66 E5
Copenhagen Denmark 15 H9
Copertino Italy 26 H4
Copeton Reservoir Australia 58 E2
Copiapó Chile 70 B3
Copley Australia 57 B6
Copparo Italy 26 D2
Coppermine Nunavut Canada see Kugluktuk
Coppermine r. N.W.T./Nunavut Canada 77 L2
Copperton S. Africa 50 F5
Coqên Xizang China 37 F3
Coqên Xizang China 37 F3
Coquilhatville Dem. Rep. Congo see Mbandaka
Coquille i. Micronesia see Pikelot
Coquimbo Chile 70 B3
Corabia Romania 27 K3
Coração de Jesus Brazil 71 B2
Coracesium Turkey see Alanya
Coraki Australia 58 F2
Coral Bay Australia 55 A5
Coral Harbour Nunavut Canada 61 J3
Coral Sea S. Pacific Ocean 52 F3
Coral Sea Basin S. Pacific Ocean 74 G6
Coral Sea Islands Territory terr. Australia 52 F3
Corangamite, Lake Australia 58 A7
Corat Azer. 35 H2
Corbett National Park India 36 D3
Corby U.K. 19 G6
Corcaigh Ireland see Cork
Corcoran CA U.S.A. 65 C2
Corcovado, Golfo de sea chan. Chile 70 B6
Corcyra i. Greece see Corfu
Cordele GA U.S.A. 63 K5
Cordelia CA U.S.A. 65 A1
Cordilheiras, Serra das hills Brazil 69 I5
Cordillera Azul, Parque Nacional nat. park Peru 68 C5
Cordillera de los Picachos, Parque Nacional nat. park Col. 68 D3
Cordillo Downs Australia 57 C5
Cordisburgo Brazil 71 B2
Córdoba Arg. 70 D4
Córdoba Mex. 66 E5
Córdoba Spain 25 D5
Córdoba, Sierras de mts Arg. 70 D4
Cordova Spain see Córdoba
Cordova AK U.S.A. 60 D3
Corduba Spain see Córdoba
Corfu i. Greece 27 H5
Coria Spain 25 C4
Coribe Brazil 71 B1
Coricudgy mt. Australia 58 E4
Corigliano Calabro Italy 26 G5
Coringa Islands Australia 56 E3
Corinium U.K. see Cirencester
Corinth Greece 27 J6
Corinth MS U.S.A. 63 J5
Corinth NY U.S.A. 64 E1
Corinth, Gulf of sea chan. Greece 27 J5
Corinthus Greece see Corinth
Corinto Brazil 71 B2
Cork Ireland 21 D6
Corleone Sicily Italy 26 E6
Çorlu Turkey 27 L4
Cormeilles France 19 H9
Cornelia S. Africa 51 I4
Cornélio Procópio Brazil 71 A3
Cornélios Brazil 71 A5
Corner Brook Nfld. and Lab. Canada 61 M5
Corner Inlet b. Australia 58 C7
Corner Seamounts sea feature N. Atlantic Ocean 72 E3
Corneto Italy see Tarquinia
Corning NY U.S.A. 64 C1
Cornish watercourse Australia 56 D4
Corn Islands is Nicaragua see Maíz, Islas del
Corno di Campo mt. Italy/Switz. 24 J3
Corno Grande mt. Italy 26 E3
Cornwall Ont. Canada 63 M2

Cornwallis Island Nunavut Canada 61 I2
Cornwall Island Nunavut Canada 61 I2
Coro Venez. 68 E1
Coroaci Brazil 71 C2
Coroatá Brazil 69 J4
Corofin Ireland 21 C5
Coromandel Brazil 71 B2
Coromandel Coast India 38 D4
Coromandel Peninsula N.Z. 59 E3
Coromandel Range hills N.Z. 59 E3
Corona CA U.S.A. 65 D4
Coronado CA U.S.A. 65 D4
Coronado, Bahía de b. Costa Rica 67 H7
Coronation Gulf Nunavut Canada 60 G3
Coronation Island S. Atlantic Ocean 76 A2
Coronda Arg. 70 D4
Coronel Fabriciano Brazil 71 C2
Coronel Oviedo Para. 70 E3
Coronel Pringles Arg. 70 D5
Coronel Suárez Arg. 70 D5
Coropuna, Nudo mt. Peru 68 D7
Çorovodë Albania 27 I4
Corowa Australia 58 C5
Corpus Christi TX U.S.A. 63 H6
Corque Bol. 68 E7
Corral de Cantos mt. Spain 25 D4
Corrandibby Range hills Australia 55 A6
Corrente Brazil 69 I6
Corrente r. Bahia Brazil 71 C1
Corrente r. Minas Gerais Brazil 71 A2
Correntes Brazil 69 H7
Correntina Brazil 71 B1
Correntina r. Brazil see Éguas
Corrib, Lough l. Ireland 21 C4
Corrientes Arg. 70 E3
Corrientes, Cabo c. Col. 68 C2
Corrientes, Cabo c. Mex. 66 C4
Corrigin Australia 55 B8
Corris U.K. 19 D6
Corry PA U.S.A. 64 B2
Corse i. France see Corsica
Corse, Cap c. Corsica France 24 I5
Corsham U.K. 19 E7
Corsica i. France 24 I5
Corsicana TX U.S.A. 63 H5
Corte Corsica France 24 I5
Cortegana Spain 25 C5
Cortes, Sea of g. Mex. see California, Gulf of
Cortez CO U.S.A. 62 F4
Cortina d'Ampezzo Italy 26 E1
Cortland NY U.S.A. 64 C1
Corton U.K. 19 I6
Cortona Italy 26 D3
Coruche Port. 25 B4
Çoruh Turkey see Artvin
Çoruh r. Turkey 35 F2
Çorum Turkey 34 D2
Corumbá Brazil 69 G7
Corumbá r. Brazil 71 A2
Corumbá de Goiás Brazil 71 A1
Corumbaíba Brazil 71 A2
Corumbaú, Ponta pt Brazil 71 D2
Corunna Spain see A Coruña
Corvallis OR U.S.A. 62 C3
Corwen U.K. 19 D6
Coryville PA U.S.A. 64 B2
Cos i. Greece see Kos
Cosentia Italy see Cosenza
Cosenza Italy 26 G5
Cosne-Cours-sur-Loire France 24 F3
Costa Blanca coastal area Spain 25 F4
Costa Brava coastal area Spain 25 H3
Costa de la Luz coastal area Spain 25 C5
Costa del Sol coastal area Spain 25 D5
Costa de Miskitos coastal area Nicaragua see Mosquitos, Costa de
Costa Marques Brazil 68 F6
Costa Rica Brazil 69 H7
Costa Rica country Central America 67 H6
Costa Rica Mex. 66 C4
Costa Verde coastal area Spain 25 C2
Costermansville Dem. Rep. Congo see Bukavu
Costești Romania 27 K2
Cotabato Phil. 41 E7
Cotagaita Bol. 68 E8
Cotahuasi Peru 68 D7
Côte d'Ivoire country Africa 46 C4
Côte Française de Somalis country Africa see Djibouti
Cotentin pen. France 19 F9
Cothi r. U.K. 19 C7
Cotiaeum Turkey see Kütahya
Cotiella mt. Spain 25 G2
Cotonou Benin 46 D4
Cotopaxi, Volcán vol. Ecuador 68 C4
Cotswold Hills U.K. 19 E7
Cottage Grove OR U.S.A. 62 C3
Cottbus Germany 17 O5
Cottenham U.K. 19 H6
Cottian Alps mts France/Italy 24 H4
Cottica Suriname 69 H3
Cottiennes, Alpes mts France/Italy see Cottian Alps
Coubre, Pointe de la pt France 24 D4
Coudersport PA U.S.A. 64 B2
Couedic, Cape du Australia 57 B8
Coulman Island Antarctica 76 H2
Coulterville CA U.S.A. 65 B2
Council Bluffs IA U.S.A. 63 H3
Councillor Island Australia 57 [inset]
Courland Lagoon b. Lith./Russia 15 L9
Courtenay B.C. Canada 62 C2
Courtmacsherry Ireland 21 D6
Courtmacsherry Bay Ireland 21 D6
Courtown Ireland 21 F5
Courtrai Belgium see Kortrijk
Coutances France 24 D2
Cove Fort UT U.S.A. 65 F1
Cove Mountains hills PA U.S.A. 64 B3
Coventry U.K. 19 F6
Covesville VA U.S.A. 64 B4
Covilhã Port. 25 C3
Covington VA U.S.A. 64 A4
Cowal, Lake dry lake Australia 58 C4
Cowan, Lake imp. l. Australia 55 C7
Cowargarzê China 37 I2
Cowcowing Lakes imp. l. Australia 55 B7
Cowdenbeath U.K. 20 F4
Cowell Australia 57 B7
Cowes U.K. 19 F8
Cowley Australia 58 B1
Cowper Point N.W.T. Canada 61 G2
Cowra Australia 58 D4
Cox r. Australia 56 A2
Coxá r. Brazil 71 B1
Coxen Hole Hond. see Roatán
Coxilha de Santana hills Brazil/Uruguay 70 E4
Coxilha Grande hills Brazil 70 F3
Coxim Brazil 69 H7
Cox's Bazar Bangl. 37 G5
Coyhaique Chile see Coihaique
Coyote Lake CA U.S.A. 65 D3
Coyote Peak h. AZ U.S.A. 65 E4
Cozhê Xizang China 37 F2
Cozhê Xizang China 37 F3
Cozie, Alpi mts France/Italy see Cottian Alps
Cozumel Mex. 67 G4
Cozumel, Isla de i. Mex. 67 G4
Craboon Australia 58 D4
Cracovia Poland see Kraków
Cracow Australia 56 E5
Cracow Poland see Kraków
Cradle Mountain Lake St Clair National Park Australia 57 [inset]
Cradock S. Africa 51 G7
Craig U.K. 20 D3
Craig CO U.S.A. 62 F3
Craigavon U.K. 21 F3
Craigieburn Australia 58 B6
Craignure U.K. 20 D4
Craigsville WV U.S.A. 64 A3
Crail U.K. 20 G4
Crailsheim Germany 17 M6
Craiova Romania 27 J2
Cramlington U.K. 18 F3
Cranberry Portage Man. Canada 62 G1
Cranborne Chase for. U.K. 19 E8
Cranbourne Australia 58 B7
Cranbrook B.C. Canada 62 D2
Cranston RI U.S.A. 64 F2
Cranz Russia see Zelenogradsk
Crary Ice Rise Antarctica 76 I1
Crary Mountains Antarctica 76 J1
Crateús Brazil 69 J5
Crato Brazil 69 K5
Crawley U.K. 19 G7
Creag Meagaidh mt. U.K. 20 E4
Credenhill U.K. 19 E6
Crediton U.K. 19 D8
Creel Mex. 66 C3
Cree Lake Sask. Canada 60 H4
Crema Italy 26 C2
Cremona Italy 26 D2
Crépy-en-Valois France 24 F2
Cres i. Croatia 26 F2
Crescent City CA U.S.A. 62 C3
Crescent Head Australia 58 F3
Cressy Australia 58 A7
Creston B.C. Canada 62 D2
Creston IA U.S.A. 63 I3
Crestview FL U.S.A. 63 J5
Creswick Australia 58 A6
Creta i. Greece see Crete
Crete i. Greece 27 K7
Creus, Cap de c. Spain 25 H2
Creuse r. France 24 E3
Crevasse Valley Glacier Antarctica 76 J1
Crewe U.K. 19 E5
Crewe VA U.S.A. 64 B4
Crewkerne U.K. 19 E8
Crianlarich U.K. 20 E4
Criccieth U.K. 19 C6
Criciúma Brazil 71 A5
Crieff U.K. 20 F4
Criffel h. U.K. 20 F6
Criffell h. U.K. see Criffel
Crikvenica Croatia 26 F2
Crimea disp. terr. Europe 13 G7
Crimea pen. Ukr. 9
Crimond U.K. 20 H3
Crisfield MD U.S.A. 64 D4
Cristalândia Brazil 69 I6
Cristalina Brazil 71 B2
Cristalino r. Brazil see Mariembero
Cristóbal Colón, Pico mt. Col. 68 D1
Crixás Brazil 71 A1
Crixás Açu r. Brazil 71 A1
Crixás Mirim r. Brazil 71 A1
Crna Gora country Europe see Montenegro
Crni Vrh mt. Serbia 27 J2
Črnomelj Slovenia 26 F2
Croagh Patrick h. Ireland 21 C4
Croajingolong National Park Australia 58 D6
Croatia country Europe 26 G2
Crocker, Banjaran mts Malaysia 41 D7
Croker Island Australia 54 F2
Cromarty U.K. 20 E3
Cromarty Firth est. U.K. 20 E3
Cromer U.K. 19 I6
Crook U.K. 18 F4
Crooked Island Bahamas 67 J4
Crooked Island Passage Bahamas 67 J4
Crookston MN U.S.A. 63 H2
Crookwell Australia 58 D5
Croom Ireland 21 D5
Croppa Creek Australia 58 E2
Crosby U.K. 18 D5
Crosby ND U.S.A. 62 G2
Cross City FL U.S.A. 63 K6
Cross Fell h. U.K. 18 E4
Crossgar U.K. 21 G3
Crosshaven Ireland 21 D6
Cross Inn U.K. 19 C6
Cross Lake Man. Canada 61 I4
Cross Lake NY U.S.A. 64 C1
Crossmaglen U.K. 21 F3
Crossman Peak AZ U.S.A. 65 E3
Croton Italy see Crotone
Crotone Italy 26 G5
Crouch r. U.K. 19 H7
Crowal watercourse Australia 58 C3
Crowborough U.K. 19 H7
Crowdy Bay National Park Australia 58 F3
Crowland U.K. 19 G6
Crowley, Lake CA U.S.A. 65 C2
Crown Prince Olav Coast Antarctica 76 D2
Crown Princess Martha Coast Antarctica 76 B1
Crows Nest Australia 58 F1
Croydon Australia 56 C3
Crozet VA U.S.A. 64 B3
Crozet, Îles is Indian Ocean 73 L9
Crozet Basin sea feature Indian Ocean 73 M8
Crozet Plateau sea feature Indian Ocean 73 K8
Crozon France 24 B2
Cruden Bay U.K. 20 H3
Crumlin U.K. 21 F3
Crusheen Ireland 21 D5
Cruz Alta Brazil 70 F3
Cruz del Eje Arg. 70 D4
Cruzeiro Brazil 71 B3
Cruzeiro do Sul Brazil 68 D5
Crystal City TX U.S.A. 62 H6
Crystal Falls MI U.S.A. 63 J2
Csongrád Hungary 27 I1
Cuamba Moz. 49 D5
Cuando r. Angola/Zambia 49 C5
Cuangar Angola 49 B5
Cuango Angola 49 B4
Cuanza r. Angola 49 B4
Cuatro Ciénegas Mex. 66 D3
Cuauhtémoc Mex. 62 F6
Cuba NY U.S.A. 64 B1
Cuba country West Indies 67 H4
Cubal Angola 49 B5
Cubango r. Angola/Namibia 49 C5
Cubatão Brazil 71 B3
Çubuk Turkey 34 D2
Cuchi Angola 49 B5
Cuchilla Grande hills Uruguay 70 E4
Cucuí Brazil 68 E3
Cúcuta Col. 68 D2
Cudal Australia 58 D4
Cuddalore India 38 C4
Cuddapah India see Kadapa
Cuddeback Lake CA U.S.A. 65 D3
Cue Australia 55 B6
Cuéllar Spain 25 D3
Cuemba Angola 49 B5
Cuenca Ecuador 68 C4
Cuenca Spain 25 E3
Cuenca, Serranía de mts Spain 25 E3
Cuernavaca Mex. 66 E5
Cuervos Mex. 65 E4
Cugir Romania 27 J2
Cuiabá Amazonas Brazil 69 G5
Cuiabá Mato Grosso Brazil 69 G7
Cuiabá r. Brazil 69 G7
Cuilcagh h. Ireland/U.K. 21 E3
Cuillin Hills U.K. 20 C3
Cuillin Sound sea chan. U.K. 20 C3
Cuilo Angola 49 B4
Cuiluan China 44 C3
Cuité r. Brazil 71 C2
Cuito r. Angola 49 C5
Cuito Cuanavale Angola 49 B5
Çukurova plat. Turkey 39 B1
Culcairn Australia 58 C5
Culebra, Sierra de la mts Spain 25 C3
Culfa Azer. 35 G3
Culgoa r. Australia 58 C2
Culiacán Mex. 66 C4
Culiacán Rosales Mex. see Culiacán
Cullen U.K. 20 G3
Cullen Point Australia 56 C1
Cullera Spain 25 F4
Cullivoe U.K. 20 [inset]
Cullman AL U.S.A. 63 J5
Cullybackey U.K. 21 F3
Cul Mòr h. U.K. 20 D2
Culpeper VA U.S.A. 64 C3
Cultural Landscape of the Serra de Tramuntana tourist site Spain 25 H4
Cultural Sites of Al Ain tourist site U.A.E. 33 I5
Culuene r. Brazil 69 H6
Culver, Point Australia 55 D8
Culverden N.Z. 59 D6
Cumaná Venez. 68 F1
Cumari Brazil 71 A2
Cumbal, Nevado de vol. Col. 68 C3
Cumberland MD U.S.A. 64 B3
Cumberland VA U.S.A. 64 B4
Cumberland Lake Sask. Canada 62 G1
Cumberland Peninsula Nunavut Canada 61 L3
Cumberland Plateau KY/TN U.S.A. 63 J4
Cumberland Sound sea chan. Nunavut Canada 61 L3
Cumbernauld U.K. 20 F5
Cumbum India 38 C3
Cummins Australia 57 A7
Cummins Range hills Australia 54 D4
Cumnock Australia 58 D4
Cumnock U.K. 20 E5
Çumra Turkey 34 D3
Cumuruxatiba Brazil 71 D2
Cunderdin Australia 55 B7
Cuneo Italy 26 B2
Cunnamulla Australia 58 B2
Cunningsburgh U.K. 20 [inset]
Cupar U.K. 20 F4
Cupica, Golfo de b. Col. 68 C2
Curaçá Brazil 69 K5
Curaçá r. Brazil 68 D4
Curaçao i. West Indies 67 K6
Curaray r. Ecuador 68 D4
Curdlawidny Lagoon imp. l. Australia 57 B6
Curia Switz. see Chur
Curicó Chile 70 B4
Curitiba Brazil 71 A4
Curitibanos Brazil 71 A4
Curlewis Australia 58 E3
Curnamona Australia 57 B6
Currabubula Australia 58 E3
Currais Novos Brazil 69 K5
Currane, Lough l. Ireland 21 B6
Currant NV U.S.A. 65 E1
Curranyalpa Australia 58 B3
Currawilla Australia 56 C5
Currawinya National Park Australia 58 B2
Currie Australia 52 E5
Currockbilly, Mount Australia 58 E5
Curtis Channel Australia 56 F5
Curtis Island Australia 56 E4
Curtis Island N.Z. 53 I5
Curuá r. Brazil 69 H5
Curupira, Serra mts Brazil/Venez. 68 F3
Cururupu Brazil 69 J4
Curvelo Brazil 71 B2
Cusco Peru 68 D6
Cushendall U.K. 21 F2
Cushendun U.K. 21 F2
Cut Bank MT U.S.A. 62 E2
Cuthbertson Falls Australia 54 F3
Cuttaburra Creek r. Australia 58 B2
Cuttack India 38 E1
Cuvelai Angola 49 B5
Cuxhaven Germany 17 L4
Cuya Chile 68 D7
Cuyahoga Falls OH U.S.A. 64 A2
Cuyama CA U.S.A. 65 C3
Cuyama r. CA U.S.A. 65 B3
Cuyuni r. Guyana 69 G2
Cuzco Peru see Cusco
Cwmbrân U.K. 19 D7
Cyangugu Rwanda 48 C4
Cyclades is Greece 27 K6
Cydonia Greece see Chania
Cymru admin. div. U.K. see Wales
Cypress Hills Alta/Sask. Canada 62 E2
Cyprus country Asia 39 A2
Cyrenaica reg. Libya 47 F2
Cythera i. Greece see Kythira
Czechia country Europe see Czech Republic
Czech Republic country Europe 17 O6
Czernowitz Ukr. see Chernivtsi
Czersk Poland 17 P4
Częstochowa Poland 17 Q5

D

Đa, Sông r. Vietnam see Black
Da'an China 44 B3
Ḑabāb, Jabal aḑ mt. Jordan 39 B4
Dabakala Côte d'Ivoire 46 C4
Daban China 43 L4
Daba Shan mts China 43 J6
Dabhoi India 36 C5
Ḑab'ī, Wādī aḑ watercourse Jordan 39 C4
Dablana India 36 C4
Dabola Guinea 46 B3
Dabqig China 43 J5
Dąbrowa Górnicza Poland 17 Q5
Dabs Nur l. China 44 A3
Dabusu Pao l. China see Dabs Nur
Dacca Bangl. see Dhaka
Dachau Germany 17 M6
Dachuan China see Dazhou
Dadaab Kenya 48 E3
Daday Turkey 34 D2
Dadohae Haesang National Park S. Korea 45 B6
Dadong China see Donggang
Dadra India see Achalpur
Dadu Pak. 33 K4
Daecheong-do i. S. Korea 45 B5
Daegu S. Korea 45 C6
Daeheuksan-gundo is S. Korea 45 B6
Daejeon S. Korea 45 B5
Daejeong S. Korea 45 B6
Daejŏn S. Korea see Daejeon
Daet Phil. 41 E6
Dafla Hills India 37 H4
Dagana Senegal 46 B3
Dagcagoin China see Zoigê
Dağlıq Qarabağ disp. terr. Azer. see Nagorno-Karabakh
Daglung China 37 G3
Dagö i. Estonia see Hiiumaa
Dagon Myanmar see Rangoon
Daguokui Shan mt. China 44 C3
Dagupan Phil. 41 E6
Dagzê China 37 G3
Dagzê Co salt l. China 37 F3
Dahalach, Isole is Eritrea see Dahlak Archipelago
Dahana des. Saudi Arabia see Ad Dahnā'
Dahe China 44 D3
Daheiding Shan mt. China 44 C3
Dahei Shan mts China 44 B4
Dahej India 36 C5
Da Hinggan Ling mts China 44 A2
Dahlak Archipelago is Eritrea 32 F6
Dahlak Marine National Park Eritrea 32 F6
Dahm, Ramlat des. Saudi Arabia/Yemen 32 G6
Dahmani Tunisia 26 C7
Dahod India 36 C5
Dahomey country Africa see Benin
Dahongliutan Aksai Chin 36 D2
Dahra Senegal see Dara
Dahūk/Dihok Iraq 35 F3
Dai i. Indon. 54 E1
Dailekh Nepal 37 E3
Dailly U.K. 20 E5
Daimiel Spain 25 E4
Daingean Uí Chúis Ireland 21 B5
Dainkognubma China 37 I2
Daintree National Park Australia 56 D3
Dair, Jebel ed mt. Sudan 32 D7
Dairen China see Dalian
Dai-sen vol. Japan 45 D6
Daisetsu-zan Kokuritsu-kōen Japan 44 F4
Daiyun Shan mts China 43 L7
Dajarra Australia 56 B4
Da Juh China 37 H1
Dakar Senegal 46 B3
Dākhilah, Wāḩāt ad oasis Egypt 32 C4
Dakhla W. Sahara 46 B2
Dakhla Oasis oasis Egypt see Dākhilah, Wāḩāt ad
Dakol'ka r. Belarus 13 F5
Dakor India 36 C5
Dakoro Niger 46 D3
Đakovica Kosovo see Gjakovë
Đakovo Croatia 26 H2
Daktuy Russia 44 B1
Dala Angola 49 C5
Dalaba Guinea 46 B3
Dalai China see Da'an
Dalain Hob China 42 I4
Dālakī Iran 35 H5
Dalälven r. Sweden 15 J6
Dalaman Turkey 27 M6
Dalandzadgad Mongolia 42 I4
Dalap-Uliga-Darrit Marshall Is see Delap-Uliga-Djarrit
Đa Lat Vietnam 31 J5
Dalatando Angola see N'dalatando
Dalaud India 36 C5
Dalauda India 36 C5
Dalbandin Pak. 33 J4
Dalbeattie U.K. 20 F6
Dalbeg Australia 56 D4
Dalby Australia 58 E1
Dalby Isle of Man 18 C4
Dale Hordaland Norway 15 D6
Dale Sogn og Fjordane Norway 15 D6
Dale City VA U.S.A. 64 C3
Dale Hollow Lake TN U.S.A. 63 J4
Dalet Myanmar 37 H6
Daletme Myanmar 37 H5
Dalfors Sweden 15 I6
Dalgety Australia 58 D6
Dalgety r. Australia 55 A6
Dalhart TX U.S.A. 62 G4
Dalhousie, Cape N.W.T. Canada 60 F2
Dali China 42 I7
Dalian China 43 M5
Dalin China 44 A4
Dalizi China 44 B4
Dalkeith U.K. 20 F5
Dallas TX U.S.A. 63 H5
Dalles City OR U.S.A. see The Dalles
Dall Island AK U.S.A. 60 E4
Dalmacija reg. Bos. & Herz./Croatia see Dalmatia
Dalmatia reg. Bos. & Herz./Croatia 30 A2
Dalmau India 36 E4
Dalmellington U.K. 20 E5
Dalmi India 37 F5
Dal'negorsk Russia 44 D3
Dal'nerechensk Russia 44 D3
Dal'niye Zelentsy Russia 12 H1
Dalny China see Dalian
Daloa Côte d'Ivoire 46 C4
Dalol (abandoned) Eth. 32 F7
Daloloia Group is P.N.G. 56 E1
Dalry U.K. 20 E5
Dalrymple U.K. 20 E5
Dalrymple, Lake Australia 56 D4
Daltenganj India see Daltonganj
Dalton S. Africa 51 J5
Dalton GA U.S.A. 63 K5
Dalton MA U.S.A. 64 E1
Dalton PA U.S.A. 64 D2
Daltonganj India 37 F4
Dalton-in-Furness U.K. 18 D4
Daly r. Australia 54 E3
Daly City CA U.S.A. 65 A2
Daly River Australia 54 E3
Daly Waters Australia 54 F4
Damagaram Takaya Niger 46 D3
Daman India 38 B1
Daman and Diu union terr. India 38 A1
Damanhūr Egypt 34 C5
Damanhûr Egypt see Damanhūr
Damão India see Daman
Damar i. Indon. 41 E8
Damara Cent. Afr. Rep. 48 B3
Damaraland reg. Namibia 49 B6
Damas Syria see Damascus
Damascus Syria 39 C3
Damaturu Nigeria 46 E3
Damāvand Iran 35 I4
Damāvand, Qolleh-ye mt. Iran 35 I4
Dambulla Sri Lanka 38 D5
Dāmghān Iran 35 I3
Damianópolis Brazil 71 B1
Damietta Egypt see Dumyāţ
Dāmiyā Jordan 39 B3
Damjong China 37 H2
Damlasu Turkey 39 D1
Dammam Saudi Arabia 32 H4
Damoh India 36 D5
Damour Lebanon 39 B3
Dampier Archipelago is Australia 54 B5
Dampier Island P.N.G. see Karkar Island
Dampier Land pen. Australia 54 C4
Dampier Strait P.N.G. 52 E2
Dampir, Selat sea chan. Indon. 41 F8
Damqoq Zangbo r. China 37 F3
Dam Qu r. China 37 H2
Damxoi China see Comai
Damxung China see Gongtang
Ḑānā Jordan 39 B4
Dana Nepal 37 E3
Danakil reg. Africa 48 E2
Danané Côte d'Ivoire 46 C4
Đa Năng Vietnam 31 J5
Danata Turkm. 35 I3
Danbury CT U.S.A. 64 E2
Danby VT U.S.A. 64 E1
Danby Lake CA U.S.A. 65 E3
Dandaragan Australia 55 A7
Dande Eth. 48 D3
Dandeldhura Nepal 36 E3
Dandeli India 38 B3
Dandong China 45 B4
Dandot Pak. 36 C2
Dane r. U.K. 18 E5
Daneborg Greenland 77 I2
Danese WV U.S.A. 64 A4
Dangara Tajik. see Danghara
Dangbi Russia 44 C3
Dangchengwan China see Subei
Danger Islands atoll Cook Is see Pukapuka
Danger Point S. Africa 50 D8
Danghara Tajik. 33 K2
Danghe Nanshan mts China 42 G5
Dang La pass China see Tanggula Shankou
Dangla Shan mts China see Tanggula Shan
Dangqên China 37 G3
Dangriga Belize 66 G5
Daniëlskuil S. Africa 50 F5
Danilov Russia 12 I4
Danilovka Russia 13 J6
Danilovskaya Vozvyshennost' hills Russia 12 H4
Danjiangkou China 43 K6
Danjo-guntō is Japan 45 C6
Dankhar India 36 D2
Dankov Russia 13 H5
Danlí Hond. 67 G6
Danmark country Europe see Denmark
Dannebrog Ø i. Greenland see Qillak
Dannevirke N.Z. 59 F5
Dannhauser S. Africa 51 J5
Dano Burkina Faso 46 C3
Dansville NY U.S.A. 64 C1
Danta India 36 C4
Dantan India 37 F5
Dantevada India see Dantewada
Dantewada India 38 D2
Dantewara India see Dantewada
Danube r. Europe 13 F7
Danube Delta Romania/Ukr. 27 M2
Danville IL U.S.A. 63 J3
Danville PA U.S.A. 64 C2
Danville VA U.S.A. 63 L4
Danzig Poland see Gdańsk
Danzig, Gulf of Poland/Russia see Gdańsk, Gulf of
Dao Tay Sa is S. China Sea see Paracel Islands
Daoud Alg. see Aïn Beïda
Daoukro Côte d'Ivoire 46 C4
Dapaong Togo 46 D3
Dapha Bum mt. India 37 I4
Dapitan Phil. 41 E7
Daporijo India 37 H4
Da Qaidam China 42 H5
Daqing China 44 B3
Dara Senegal 46 B3
Dar'ā Syria 39 C3
Dāra, Gebel mt. Egypt see Dārah, Jabal
Dārāb Iran 35 I5
Dārah, Jabal mt. Egypt 34 D6
Dārākūyeh Iran 35 I5
Dārān Iran 35 H4
Darazo Nigeria 46 E3
Darbhanga India 37 F4
Dardanelles str. Turkey 27 L4
Dardania country Europe see Kosovo
Dardo China see Kangding
Dar el Beida Morocco see Casablanca
Darende Turkey 34 E3
Dar es Salaam Tanz. 49 D4
Darfo Boario Terme Italy 26 D2
Dargai Pak. 36 B2
Dargaville N.Z. 59 D2
Dargo Australia 58 C6
Dargo Zangbo r. China 37 F3
Darhan Mongolia 42 J3
Darién, Golfo del g. Col. 68 C2
Darién, Parque Nacional de nat. park Panama 67 I7
Dariganga Mongolia 43 K3
Darjeeling India see Darjiling
Darjiling India 37 G4
Darkhazineh Iran 35 H5
Darling r. Australia 58 B3
Darling Downs hills Australia 58 D1
Darling Range hills Australia 55 A8
Darlington U.K. 18 F4
Darlington Point Australia 58 C5
Darlot, Lake imp. l. Australia 55 C6
Darłowo Poland 17 P3
Darma Pass China/India 36 E3
Darmstadt Germany 17 L6
Darnah Libya 34 A4
Darnall S. Africa 51 J5
Darnick Australia 58 A4
Darnley, Cape Antarctica 76 E2
Daroca Spain 25 F3
Darovskoy Russia 12 J4
Darr watercourse Australia 56 C4
Darreh-ye Bāhābād Iran 35 I5
Darsi India 38 C3
Dart r. U.K. 19 D8
Dartang China see Baqên
Dartford U.K. 19 H7
Dartmoor Australia 57 C8
Dartmoor hills U.K. 19 C8
Dartmoor National Park U.K. 19 D8
Dartmouth N.S. Canada 63 O3
Dartmouth U.K. 19 D8
Dartmouth, Lake imp. l. Australia 57 D5
Dartmouth Reservoir Australia 58 C6
Darton U.K. 18 F5
Daru P.N.G. 52 E2
Daru Sierra Leone 46 B4
Darwāzagēy Afgh. 36 A3
Darwen U.K. 18 E5
Darwin Australia 54 E3
Darwin, Monte mt. Chile 70 C8
Daryācheh-ye Orūmīyeh salt l. Iran see Urmia, Lake
Dar"yalyktakyr, Ravnina plain Kazakh. 42 A3
Dar"yoi Amu r. Asia see Amudar'ya
Darzāb Afgh. 36 A2
Dasada India 36 B5
Dashhowuz Turkm. see Daşoguz
Dashkesan Azer. see Daşkäsän
Dashkhovuz Turkm. see Daşoguz
Dashköpri Turkm. see Daşköpri
Dasht Iran 35 J3
Daska Pak. 36 C2
Daşkäsän Azer. 35 G2
Daşköpri Turkm. 33 J2
Daşoguz Turkm. see Daşoguz
Daşoguz Turkm. 30 E2
Daspar mt. Pak. 36 C1
Datça Turkey 27 L6
Date Japan 44 F4
Date Creek watercourse AZ U.S.A. 65 F3
Dateland AZ U.S.A. 65 F4
Datha India 36 C5
Datia India 36 D4
Datong Heilongjiang China 44 B3
Datong Shanxi China 43 K4
Datong He r. China 42 I5
Dattapur India 38 C1
Daudkandi Bangl. 37 G5
Daugava r. Latvia 15 N8
Daugavpils Latvia 15 O9
Daulatabad India 38 B2
Daulatabad Iran see Malāyer
Daulatpur Bangl. 37 G5
Daungyu r. Myanmar 37 H5
Dauphin Man. Canada 62 G1
Dauphiné reg. France 24 G4
Dauphiné, Alpes du mts France 24 G4
Dauphin Lake Man. Canada 62 H1
Daurie Creek r. Australia 55 A6
Dausa India 36 D4
Dava U.K. 20 F3
Davanagere India see Davangere
Davangere India 38 B3
Davao Phil. 41 E7
Davel S. Africa 51 I4
Davenport IA U.S.A. 63 I3
Davenport Downs Australia 56 C5
Davenport Range hills Australia 54 F5
Daventry U.K. 19 F6
Daveyton S. Africa 51 I4
David Panama 67 H7
David Glacier Antarctica 76 H1
Davidson Sask. Canada 62 F1
Davidson, Mount h. Australia 54 E5
Davis r. Australia 54 C5
Davis CA U.S.A. 65 B1
Davis WV U.S.A. 64 B3
Davis (Australia) research stn Antarctica 76 E2
Davis, Mount h. PA U.S.A. 64 B3
Davis Bay Antarctica 76 G2
Davis Dam AZ U.S.A. 65 E3
Davis Inlet (abandoned) Nfld. and Lab. Canada 61 L4
Davis Sea Antarctica 76 F2
Davis Strait Canada/Greenland 61 M3
Davlekanovo Russia 11 Q5
Davos Switz. 24 I3
Dawa Co l. China 37 F3
Dawa Wenz r. Eth. 48 E3
Dawaxung China 37 F3
Dawei Myanmar 31 I5
Dawera i. Indon. 54 E1
Dawmat al Jandal Saudi Arabia 35 E5
Dawo China see Maqên
Dawqah Oman 33 H6
Dawson r. Australia 56 E4
Dawson Y.T. Canada 60 E3
Dawson Creek B.C. Canada 60 F4
Dawsons Landing B.C. Canada 62 B1
Dawu China see Maqên
Dawukou China see Shizuishan
Dax France 24 D5
Daxian China see Dazhou
Daxing'an Ling mts China see Da Hinggan Ling
Da Xueshan mts China 31 J3
Dayan China see Lijiang
Dayangshu China 44 B2
Dayao China 42 I7
Daylesford Australia 58 B6
Daylight Pass NV U.S.A. 65 D2
Dayong China see Zhangjiajie
Dayr Abū Sa'īd Jordan 39 B3
Dayr az Zawr Syria 35 F4
Dayr Ḩāfir Syria 39 C1
Dayrī', Wādī watercourse Saudi Arabia 35 F6
Dayton OH U.S.A. 63 K4
Dayton VA U.S.A. 64 B3
Daytona Beach FL U.S.A. 63 K6
Dazhou China 43 J6
De Aar S. Africa 50 G6
Dead r. Ireland 21 D5
Deadman Lake CA U.S.A. 65 D3
Dead Mountains NV U.S.A. 65 E3
Dead Sea salt l. Asia 39 B4
Deakin Australia 55 E7
Deal U.K. 19 I7
Dealesville S. Africa 51 G5
Dean, Forest of U.K. 19 E7
Deán Funes Arg. 70 D4
Deanuvuotna inlet Norway see Tanafjorden
Dearne r. U.K. 18 F5
Dease Lake B.C. Canada 60 F4
Dease Strait Nunavut Canada 60 H3
Death Valley depr. CA U.S.A. 65 D2
Death Valley Junction CA U.S.A. 65 D2
Death Valley National Park CA U.S.A. 65 D2
Deauville France 24 E2
De Baai S. Africa see Port Elizabeth
Debar Macedonia 27 I4
Debenham U.K. 19 I6
Débo, Lac l. Mali 46 C3
Deborah East, Lake imp. l. Australia 55 B7
Deborah West, Lake imp. l. Australia 55 B7
Debrecen Hungary 27 I1
Debre Markos Eth. 32 E7
Debre Tabor Eth. 32 E7
Debre Zeyit Eth. 48 D3
Decatur AL U.S.A. 63 J5
Decatur IL U.S.A. 63 J4
Deccan plat. India 38 C2
Deception Bay Australia 58 F1
Děčín Czech Rep. 17 O5
Decorah IA U.S.A. 63 I3
Deddington U.K. 19 F7
Dedegöl Dağları mts Turkey 27 N6
Dedo de Deus mt. Brazil 71 B4
Dédougou Burkina Faso 46 C3
Dedovichi Russia 12 F4
Dedu China see Wudalianchi
Dee r. Ireland 21 F4
Dee est. U.K. 18 D5
Dee r. England/Wales U.K. 19 D5
Dee r. Scotland U.K. 20 G3
Deel r. Cork/Limerick Ireland 21 D5
Deel r. Meath/Westmeath Ireland 21 F4
Deep Creek Lake MD U.S.A. 64 B3
Deepwater Australia 58 E2
Deeri Somalia 48 E3
Deering AK U.S.A. 60 B3
Deering, Mount Australia 55 E6
Deer Island AK U.S.A. 60 B4
Deer Lodge MT U.S.A. 62 E2
Deesa India see Disa
Defensores del Chaco, Parque Nacional nat. park Para. 70 D2
Degana India 36 C4
Degeh Bur Eth. 48 E3
Degema Nigeria 46 D4
Deggendorf Germany 17 N6
Degh r. Pak. 36 C3
De Grey r. Australia 54 B5
Degtevo Russia 13 I6

Ende Indon. 41 E8
Endeavour Strait Australia 56 C1
Endeh Indon. see Ende
Enderby Land reg. Antarctica 76 D2
Endicott NY U.S.A. 64 C1
Endicott Mountains AK U.S.A. 60 C3
EnenKio terr. N. Pacific Ocean see Wake Island
Energodar Ukr. see Enerhodar
Enerhodar Ukr. 13 G7
Enewetak atoll Marshall Is 74 G5
Enez Turkey 27 L4
Enfe Lebanon 39 B2
Enfião, Ponta do pt Angola 49 B5
Enfidaville Tunisia 26 D6
Engan Norway 14 F5
Engaru Japan 44 F3
En Gedi Israel 39 B4
Engel's Russia 13 J6
Enggano i. Indon. 41 C8
England admin. div. U.K. 19 E6
English Bazar India see Ingraj Bazar
English Channel France/U.K. 19 F9
English Coast Antarctica 76 L2
Engozero Russia 12 G2
Enhlalakahle S. Africa 51 J5
Enid OK U.S.A. 62 H4
Eniwa Japan 44 F4
Eniwetok atoll Marshall Is see Enewetak
Enkeldoorn Zimbabwe see Chivhu
Enköping Sweden 15 J7
Enna Sicily Italy 26 F6
Ennadai Lake Nunavut Canada 61 H3
En Nahud Sudan 32 C7
Ennedi, Massif mts Chad 47 F3
Ennell, Lough l. Ireland 21 E4
Enngonia Australia 58 B2
Ennis Ireland 21 D5
Ennis TX U.S.A. 63 H5
Enniscorthy Ireland 21 F5
Enniskillen U.K. 21 E3
Ennistymon Ireland 21 C5
Enn Nâqoûra Lebanon 39 B3
Enns r. Austria 17 O6
Eno Fin. 14 Q5
Enoch UT U.S.A. 65 F2
Enontekiö Fin. 14 M2
Ensay Australia 58 C6
Enschede Neth. 17 K4
Ensenada Mex. 66 A2
Enshi China 43 J6
Entebbe Uganda 48 D3
Enterprise N.W.T. Canada 60 G3
Enterprise UT U.S.A. 65 F2
Entre Rios Bol. 68 F8
Entre Rios Brazil 69 H5
Entre Rios de Minas Brazil 71 B3
Entroncamento Port. 25 B4
Enugu Nigeria 46 D4
Enurmino Russia 29 T3
Envira Brazil 68 D5
Envira r. Brazil 68 D5
'En Yahav Israel 39 B4
Enyamba Dem. Rep. Congo 48 C4
Eochaill Ireland see Youghal
Epéna Congo 48 B3
Ephrata PA U.S.A. 64 C2
Épi i. Vanuatu 53 G3
Epidamnus Albania see Durrës
Épinal France 24 H2
Episkopi Bay Cyprus 39 A2
Episkopis, Kolpos b. Cyprus see Episkopi Bay
ePitoli S. Africa see Pretoria
Epomeo, Monte vol. Italy 26 E4
Epping U.K. 19 H7
Epping Forest National Park Australia 56 D4
Eppynt, Mynydd hills U.K. 19 D6
Epsom U.K. 19 G7
Eqlīd Iran 35 I5
Equatorial Guinea country Africa 46 D4
Équeurdreville-Hainneville France 19 F9
Erac Creek watercourse Australia 58 B1
Erandol India 38 B1
Erawadi r. Myanmar see Irrawaddy
Erbaa Turkey 34 E2
Erbeskopf h. Germany 17 K6
Erbet Iraq 35 G4
Erciş Turkey 35 F3
Erciyes Dağı mt. Turkey 34 D3
Érd Hungary 26 H1
Erdaobaihe China see Baihe
Erdaogou Bingzhan China 37 H2
Erdao Jiang r. China 44 B4
Erdek Turkey 27 L4
Erdemli Turkey 39 B1
Erdenedalay Mongolia 42 I3
Erdenet Mongolia 42 I3
Erdenetsagaan Mongolia 43 L3
Erdi reg. Chad 47 F3
Erdniyevskiy Russia 13 J7
Erebus, Mount vol. Antarctica 76 H1
Erechim Brazil 70 F3
Ereentsav Mongolia 43 L3
Ereğli Konya Turkey 34 D3
Ereğli Zonguldak Turkey 27 N4
Erego Moz. see Errego
Erei, Monti mts Sicily Italy 26 F6
Erementaū Kazakh. see Yereymentau
Erenhot China 43 K4
Erepucu, Lago de l. Brazil 69 G4
Erevan Armenia see Yerevan
Erfurt Germany 17 M5
Ergani Turkey 35 E3
'Erg Chech des. Alg./Mali 46 C2
Ergene r. Turkey 27 L4
Ērgļi Latvia 15 N8
Ergu China 44 C3
Ergun China 43 M2
Ergun He r. China/Russia see Argun'
Ergun Youqi China see Ergun
Ergun Zuoqi China see Gegen Gol
Erhulai China 44 B4
Eriboll, Loch inlet U.K. 20 E2
Ericht r. U.K. 20 F4
Ericht, Loch l. U.K. 20 E4
Erie PA U.S.A. 64 A1
Erie, Lake Canada/U.S.A. 64 A1
'Erîgât des. Mali 46 C3
Erik Eriksenstretet sea chan. Svalbard 28 D2
Erimo-misaki c. Japan 44 F4
Erinpura Road India 36 C4
Eriskay i. U.K. 20 B3
Eritrea country Africa 32 E6
Erlangen Germany 17 M6
Erldunda Australia 55 F6
Erlistoun watercourse Australia 55 C6
Erlong Shan mt. China 44 C4
Erlongshan Shuiku resr China 44 B4
Ermak Kazakh. see Aksu
Ermelo S. Africa 51 I4
Ermenek Turkey 39 A1
Ermenek r. Turkey 39 A1
Ermont Egypt see Armant
Ermoupoli Greece 27 K6
Ernakulam India 38 C4
Erne r. Ireland/U.K. 21 D3
Ernest Giles Range hills Australia 55 C6
Erode India 38 C4
Eromanga Australia 57 C5
Erongo admin. reg. Namibia 50 B1
Errabiddy Hills Australia 55 A6
Er Rachidia Morocco 22 D5
Errego Moz. 49 D5
Er Remla Tunisia 26 D7
Er Renk South Sudan 32 D7
Errigal h. Ireland 21 D2
Errinundra National Park Australia 58 D6
Erris Head hd Ireland 21 B3
Erromango i. Vanuatu 53 G3
Erronan i. Vanuatu see Futuna
Erseka Albania see Ersekë
Ersekë Albania 27 I4
Ersmark Sweden 14 L5
Ertai China 42 G3
Ertil' Russia 13 I6
Ertis r. Kazakh./Russia see Irtysh
Ertix He r. China/Kazakh. 42 F3
Ērtra country Africa see Eritrea
Eruh Turkey 35 F3
Eryuan China 42 H7
Erzerum Turkey see Erzurum
Erzgebirge mts Czech Rep./Germany 17 N5
Erzhan China 44 B2
Erzin Turkey 39 C1
Erzincan Turkey 35 E3
Erzurum Turkey 35 F3
Esa-ala P.N.G. 56 E1
Esan-misaki pt Japan 44 F4
Esashi Japan 44 F3
Esbjerg Denmark 15 F9
Esbo Fin. see Espoo
Escalante Desert UT U.S.A. 65 F2
Escalón Mex. 66 D3
Escanaba MI U.S.A. 63 J2
Escárcega Mex. 66 F5
Escatrón Spain 25 F3
Eschscholtz atoll Marshall Is see Bikini
Eschwege Germany 17 M5
Escondido CA U.S.A. 65 D4
Escuinapa Mex. 66 C4
Escuintla Guat. 66 F6
Eséka Cameroon 46 E4
Eşen Turkey 27 M6
Esenguly Turkm. 35 I3
Esenguly Döwlet Gorugy nature res. Turkm. 35 I3
Eşfahān Iran 35 H4
Eshkanān Iran 35 I6
Eshowe S. Africa 51 J5
eSikhaleni S. Africa 51 J5
Esil Kazakh. see Yesil'
Esil r. Kazakh./Russia see Yesil'
Esk Australia 58 F1
Esk r. Australia 57 [inset]
Esk r. U.K. 18 D4
Eskdalemuir U.K. 20 F5
Esker Nfld. and Lab. Canada 61 L4
Eskifjörður Iceland 14 [inset 2]
Eski Gediz Turkey 27 M5
Eskilstuna Sweden 15 J7
Eskimo Lakes N.W.T. Canada 60 E3
Eskimo Point Nunavut Canada see Arviat
Eskipazar Turkey 34 D2
Eskişehir Turkey 27 N5
Esla r. Spain 25 C3
Eslāmābād-e Gharb Iran 35 G4
Esler Dağı mt. Turkey 27 M6
Eslöv Sweden 15 H9
Eşme Turkey 27 M5
Esmeraldas Ecuador 68 C3
Esmont VA U.S.A. 64 B4
Espakeh Iran 33 J4
Espalion France 24 F4
España country Europe see Spain
Espanola Ont. Canada 63 K2
Esperance Australia 55 C8
Esperance Bay Australia 55 C8
Esperanza Arg. 70 B8
Esperanza Mex. 62 F6
Esperanza (Argentina) research stn Antarctica 76 A2
Espichel, Cabo c. Port. 25 B4
Espigão, Serra do mts Brazil 71 A4
Espigüete mt. Spain 25 D2
Espinhaço, Serra do mts Brazil 71 C2
Espinosa Brazil 71 C1
Espírito Santo Brazil see Vila Velha
Espírito Santo state Brazil 71 C2
Espírito Santo do Pinhal Brazil 71 B3
Espiritu Santo i. Vanuatu 53 G3
Espíritu Santo, Isla i. Mex. 62 E7
Espoo Fin. 15 N6
Espuña mt. Spain 25 F5
Esquel Arg. 70 B6
Essaouira Morocco 46 C1
Essen Germany 17 K5
Essequibo r. Guyana 69 G2
Essex CA U.S.A. 65 E3
Essex MD U.S.A. 64 C3
Es-Smara W. Sahara 46 B2
Esso Russia 29 Q4
Essoyla Russia 12 G3
Estados, Isla de los i. Arg. 70 D8
Estahbān Iran 35 I5
Estância Brazil 69 K6
Estats, Pic d' mt. France/Spain 24 E5
Estcourt S. Africa 51 I5
Estelí Nicaragua 67 G6
Estella Spain 25 E2
Estepa Spain 25 D5
Estepona Spain 25 D5
Esteras de Medinaceli Spain 25 E3
Esterhazy Sask. Canada 62 G1
Estero Bay CA U.S.A. 65 B3
Esteros Para. 70 D2
Estevan Sask. Canada 62 G2
Estherville IA U.S.A. 63 I3
Eston Sask. Canada 62 F1
Estonia country Europe 15 N7
Estonskaya S.S.R. country Europe see Estonia
Estrela Brazil 71 A5
Estrela, Serra da mts Port. 25 C3
Estrela do Sul Brazil 71 B2
Estrella mt. Spain 25 E4
Estremoz Port. 25 C4
Estrondo, Serra hills Brazil 69 I5
Etadunna Australia 57 B6
Etah India 36 D4
Étampes France 24 F2
Étaples France 24 E1
Etawah Rajasthan India 36 D4
Etawah Uttar Prad. India 36 D4
Ethandakukhanya S. Africa 51 J4
Ethel Creek Australia 55 C5
E'Thembini S. Africa 50 F5
Ethiopia country Africa 48 D3
Etimesgut Turkey 34 D3
Etive, Loch inlet U.K. 20 D4
Etna, Mount vol. Sicily Italy 26 F6
Etne Norway 15 D7
Etobicoke Ont. Canada 64 B1
Etolin Strait AK U.S.A. 60 B3
Etorofu-tō i. Russia see Iturup, Ostrov
Etosha National Park Namibia 49 B5
Etosha Pan salt pan Namibia 49 B5
Etoumbi Congo 48 B3
Etrek r. Iran/Turkm. see Atrek
Etrek Turkm. 35 I3
Étrépagny France 19 I9
Étretat France 19 H9
Ettelbruck Lux. 17 K6
Ettrick Water r. U.K. 20 F5
Euabalong Australia 58 C4
Euboea i. Greece see Evvoia
Eucla Australia 55 E7
Euclid OH U.S.A. 64 A2
Euclides da Cunha Brazil 69 K6
Eucumbene, Lake Australia 58 D6
Eudunda Australia 57 B7
Eufaula Lake resr OK U.S.A. 63 H4
Eugene OR U.S.A. 62 C3
Eugenia, Punta pt Mex. 66 A3
Eugowra Australia 58 D4
Eulo Australia 58 B2
Eumungerie Australia 58 D3
Eungella Australia 56 E4
Eungella National Park Australia 56 E4
Euphrates r. Asia 32 F3
Eura Fin. 15 M6
Eureka CA U.S.A. 62 C3
Eureka MT U.S.A. 62 D2
Eureka NV U.S.A. 62 D4
Eureka Sound sea chan. Nunavut Canada 61 J2
Eureka Valley val. CA U.S.A. 65 D2
Euriowie Australia 57 C6
Euroa Australia 58 B6
Eurombah Australia 57 E5
Eurombah Creek r. Australia 57 E5
Europa, Île i. Indian Ocean 49 E6
Europa, Punta de pt Gibraltar see Europa Point
Europa Point Gibraltar 25 D5
Eva Downs Australia 54 F4
Evans, Lac l. Que. Canada 63 L1
Evans City PA U.S.A. 64 A2
Evans Head Australia 58 F2
Evans Head hd Australia 58 F2
Evans Ice Stream Antarctica 76 L1
Evanston WY U.S.A. 62 E3
Evansville IN U.S.A. 63 J4
Eva Perón Arg. see La Plata
Evaton S. Africa 51 H4
Evaz Iran 35 I6
Evensk Russia 29 Q3
Everard, Lake imp. l. Australia 57 A6
Everard, Mount Australia 55 F5
Everard Range hills Australia 55 F6
Everek Turkey see Develi
Everest, Mount China/Nepal 37 F4
Everett PA U.S.A. 64 B2
Everett WA U.S.A. 62 C2
Everglades swamp FL U.S.A. 63 K6
Evesham Australia 56 C4
Evesham U.K. 19 F6
Evesham, Vale of val. U.K. 19 F6
Evijärvi Fin. 14 M5
Evje Norway 15 E7
Évora Port. 25 C4
Evoron, Ozero l. Russia 44 E2
Évreux France 24 E2
Evros r. Bulg. see Maritsa
Evros r. Turkey see Meriç
Evrotas r. Greece 27 J6
Evrychou Cyprus 39 A2
Evrykhou Cyprus see Evrychou
Evvoia i. Greece 27 K5
Ewan Australia 56 D3
Ewaso Ngiro r. Kenya 48 E3
Ewe, Loch b. U.K. 20 D3
Ewo Congo 48 B4
Exaltación Bol. 68 E6
Excelsior S. Africa 51 H5
Excelsior Mountain CA U.S.A. 65 C1
Excelsior Mountains NV U.S.A. 65 C1
Exe r. U.K. 19 D8
Exeter Australia 58 E5
Exeter Ont. Canada 64 A1
Exeter U.K. 19 D8
Exeter CA U.S.A. 65 C2
Exeter NH U.S.A. 64 F1
Exminster U.K. 19 D8
Exmoor hills U.K. 19 D7
Exmoor National Park U.K. 19 D7
Exmore VA U.S.A. 64 D4
Exmouth Australia 54 A5
Exmouth U.K. 19 D8
Exmouth, Mount Australia 58 D3
Exmouth Gulf Australia 54 A5
Exmouth Plateau sea feature Indian Ocean 73 P7
Expedition National Park Australia 56 E5
Expedition Range mts Australia 56 E5
Exton PA U.S.A. 64 D2
Extremadura aut. comm. Spain 25 D4
Exuma Cays is Bahamas 67 I4
Eyasi, Lake salt l. Tanz. 48 D4
Eyawadi r. Myanmar see Irrawaddy
Eye U.K. 19 I6
Eyeleneborsk Russia 11 S3
Eyemouth U.K. 20 G5
Eyjafjörður inlet Iceland 14 [inset 2]
Eyl Somalia 48 E3
Eylau Russia see Bagrationovsk
Eynsham U.K. 19 F7
Eyre Creek watercourse Australia 56 B5
Eyre Mountains N.Z. 59 B7
Eyre Peninsula Australia 57 A7
Eysturoy i. Faroe Is 14 [inset 1]
Ezakheni S. Africa 51 J5
Ezenzeleni S. Africa 51 I4
Ezequiel Ramos Mexía, Embalse resr Arg. 70 C5
Ezhou China 43 K6
Ezhva Russia 12 K3
Ezine Turkey 27 L5
Ezo i. Japan see Hokkaidō
Ezousa r. Cyprus 39 A2

F

Faaborg Denmark 15 G9
Faadhippolhu Maldives 38 B5
Faafxadhuun Somalia 48 E3
Fåborg Denmark see Faaborg
Fabriano Italy 26 E3
Fachi Niger 46 E3
Fada Chad 47 F3
Fada-N'Gourma Burkina Faso 46 D3
Fadghāmī Syria 35 F4
Fadiffolu Atoll Maldives see Faadhippolhu
Fadippolu Atoll Maldives see Faadhippolhu
Faenza Italy 26 D2
Færoerne terr. N. Atlantic Ocean see Faroe Islands
Faeroes terr. N. Atlantic Ocean see Faroe Islands
Făgăraş Romania 27 K2
Fagatogo American Samoa 53 I3
Fagersta Sweden 15 I7
Fagurhólsmýri Iceland 14 [inset 2]
Fagwir South Sudan 32 D8
Fahraj Iran 35 I5
Fā'id Egypt 34 D5
Fairbanks AK U.S.A. 60 D3
Fairchance PA U.S.A. 64 B3
Fairfax VA U.S.A. 64 C3
Fairfield CA U.S.A. 65 A1
Fair Haven VT U.S.A. 64 E1
Fair Head hd U.K. 21 F2
Fair Isle i. U.K. 20 H1
Fairmont MN U.S.A. 63 I3
Fairmont WV U.S.A. 64 A3
Fairview Australia 56 D2
Fairview PA U.S.A. 64 A1
Fairweather, Mount Canada/U.S.A. 60 E4
Faisalabad Pak. 33 L3
Faith SD U.S.A. 62 G2
Faīẕābād Afgh. 36 B1
Faizabad Afgh. see Faīẕābād
Faizabad India 37 E4
Fakaofo atoll Tokelau 53 I2
Fakaofu atoll Tokelau see Fakaofo
Fakenham U.K. 19 H6
Fåker Sweden 14 I5
Fakfak Indon. 41 F8
Fakhrābād Iran 35 I5
Fakiragram India 37 G4
Fako vol. Cameroon see Cameroun, Mont
Fal r. U.K. 19 C8
Falaba Sierra Leone 46 B4
Falam Myanmar 37 H5
Falāvarjān Iran 35 H4
Falenki Russia 12 K4
Falkenberg Sweden 15 H8
Falkirk U.K. 20 F5
Falkland U.K. 20 F4
Falkland Escarpment sea feature S. Atlantic Ocean 72 E9
Falkland Islands terr. S. Atlantic Ocean 70 E8
Falkland Plateau sea feature S. Atlantic Ocean 72 E9
Falkland Sound sea chan. Falkland Is 70 D8
Falköping Sweden 15 H7
Fallbrook CA U.S.A. 65 D4
Fallieres Coast Antarctica 76 L2
Fallon NV U.S.A. 62 D4
Fall River MA U.S.A. 64 F2
Fall River Pass CO U.S.A. 62 F3
Falmouth U.K. 19 B8
Falmouth VA U.S.A. 64 C3
False Bay S. Africa 50 D8
False Point India 37 F5
Falster i. Denmark 15 G9
Fălticeni Romania 13 E7
Falun Sweden 15 I6
Famagusta Cyprus 39 A2
Famagusta Bay Cyprus see Ammochostos Bay
Fāmenīn Iran 35 H4
Fame Range hills Australia 55 C6
Family Well Australia 54 D5
Fāmūr, Daryācheh-ye l. Iran 35 H5
Fana Mali 46 C3
Fanad Head hd Ireland 21 E2
Fandriana Madag. 49 E6
Fane r. Ireland 21 F4
Fangxian China 43 K6
Fangzheng China 44 C3
Fannich, Loch l. U.K. 20 D3
Fano Italy 26 E3
Fanum Fortunae Italy see Fano
Faqīh Aḥmadān Iran 35 H5
Faraba Mali 46 B3
Faradofay Madag. see Tôlañaro
Farafangana Madag. 49 E6
Farāfirah, Wāḥāt al oasis Egypt 32 C4
Farafra Oasis oasis Egypt see Farāfirah, Wāḥāt al
Farāh Afgh. 33 J3
Faraḥābād Iran see Khezerābād
Farallones de Cali, Parque Nacional nat. park Col. 68 C3
Faranah Guinea 46 B3
Fararah Oman 33 I6
Farasān, Jazā'ir is Saudi Arabia 32 F6
Faraulep atoll Micronesia 41 G7
Fareham U.K. 19 F8
Farewell, Cape Greenland 61 N3
Farewell, Cape N.Z. 59 D5
Farewell Spit N.Z. 59 D5
Färgelanda Sweden 15 H7
Farghona Uzbek. see Farg'ona
Fargo ND U.S.A. 62 H2
Farg'ona Uzbek. 33 L1
Faribault MN U.S.A. 63 I3
Faribault, Lac l. Que. Canada 61 K4
Faridabad India 36 D3
Faridkot India 36 C3
Faridpur Bangl. 37 G5
Farīmān Iran 33 I2
Farkhār Afgh. 36 B1
Farkhar Afgh. see Farkhār
Farmahīn Iran 35 H4
Farmington ME U.S.A. 63 M3
Farmington NH U.S.A. 64 F1
Farmington NM U.S.A. 62 F4
Farmville VA U.S.A. 64 B4
Farnborough U.K. 19 G7
Farne Islands U.K. 18 F3
Farnham U.K. 19 G7
Farnham, Lake imp. l. Australia 55 D6
Farnham, Mount B.C. Canada 62 D1
Faro Brazil 69 G4
Faro Port. 25 C5
Fårö i. Sweden 15 K8
Faroe - Iceland Ridge sea feature Arctic Ocean 77 I2
Faroe Islands terr. N. Atlantic Ocean 14 [inset 1]
Fårösund Sweden 15 K8
Farquhar Group is Seychelles 49 F5
Farquharson Tableland hills Australia 55 C6
Farrāshband Iran 35 I5
Farr Bay Antarctica 76 F2
Farrukhabad India see Fatehgarh
Farsund Norway 15 E7
Farwell TX U.S.A. 62 G5
Fasā Iran 35 I5
Fasano Italy 26 G4
Faşikan Geçidi pass Turkey 39 A1
Fastiv Ukr. 13 F6
Fastov Ukr. see Fastiv
Fatehabad India 36 C3
Fatehgarh India 36 D4
Fatehpur Rajasthan India 36 C4
Fatehpur Uttar Prad. India 36 E4
Fatick Senegal 46 B3
Fattoilep atoll Micronesia see Faraulep
Faughan r. U.K. 21 E2
Fauresmith S. Africa 51 G5
Fauske Norway 14 I3
Fawley U.K. 19 F8
Faxaflói b. Iceland 14 [inset 2]
Faxälven r. Sweden 14 J5
Faya Chad 47 E3
Fayetteville AR U.S.A. 63 I4
Fayetteville NC U.S.A. 63 L4
Fayetteville WV U.S.A. 64 A3
Fāyid Egypt see Fā'id
Faylakah i. Kuwait 35 H5
Fazao Malfakassa, Parc National de nat. park Togo 46 D4
Fazilka India 36 C3
Fdérik Mauritania 46 B2
Fead Group is P.N.G. see Nuguria Islands
Feale r. Ireland 21 C5
Fear, Cape NC U.S.A. 63 L5
Featherston N.Z. 59 E5
Feathertop, Mount Australia 58 C6
Fécamp France 24 E2
Federal District admin. dist. Brazil see Distrito Federal
Federalsburg MD U.S.A. 64 D3
Federated Malay States country Asia see Malaysia
Fedusar India 36 C4
Fehmarn i. Germany 17 M3
Feia, Lagoa lag. Brazil 71 C3
Feijó Brazil 68 D5
Feilding N.Z. 59 E5
Feio r. Brazil see Aguapeí
Feira de Santana Brazil 71 D1
Fejd el Abiod pass Alg. 26 B6
Feke Turkey 34 D3
Felanitx Spain 25 H4
Feldberg mt. Germany 17 L7
Feldkirch Austria 17 L7
Feldkirchen in Kärnten Austria 17 O7
Felipe C. Puerto Mex. 66 G5
Felixlândia Brazil 71 B2
Felixstowe U.K. 19 I7
Felixton S. Africa 51 J5
Fellowsville WV U.S.A. 64 B3
Felsina Italy see Bologna
Felton DE U.S.A. 64 D3
Feltre Italy 26 D1
Femunden l. Norway 14 G5
Femundsmarka Nasjonalpark nat. park Norway 14 H5
Fenaio, Punta del pt Italy 26 D3
Fener Burnu hd Turkey 39 B1
Fénérive Madag. see Fenoarivo Atsinanana
Fengari mt. Greece 27 K4
Fengguang China 44 B3
Fengman China 44 B4
Fengxian China 42 J6
Fengxiang Heilongjiang China see Luobei
Fengxiang Yunnan China see Lincang
Fengyuan Taiwan 43 M8
Fengzhen China 43 K4
Feni Bangl. 37 G5
Feni Islands P.N.G. 52 F2
Feno, Capo di c. Corsica France 24 I6
Fenoarivo Atsinanana Madag. 49 E5
Fenua Ura atoll Fr. Polynesia see Manuae
Feodosiya Ukr. 34 D1
Fer, Cap de c. Alg. 26 B6
Férai Greece see Feres
Ferdows Iran 33 I3
Feres Greece 27 L4
Fergus Falls MN U.S.A. 63 H2
Fergusson Island P.N.G. 52 F2
Fériana Tunisia 26 C7
Ferizaj Kosovo 27 I3
Ferkessédougou Côte d'Ivoire 46 C4
Fermo Italy 26 E3
Fermont Que. Canada 61 L4
Fermoselle Spain 25 C3
Fermoy Ireland 21 D5
Fernandina, Isla i. Galápagos Ecuador 68 [inset]
Fernandina Beach FL U.S.A. 63 K5
Fernando de Magallanes, Parque Nacional nat. park Chile 70 B8
Fernando de Noronha i. Brazil 72 F6
Fernandópolis Brazil 71 A3
Fernando Poó i. Equat. Guinea see Bioko
Fernão Dias Brazil 71 B2
Ferndown U.K. 19 F8
Fernlee Australia 58 C2
Ferns Ireland 21 F5
Ferozepore India see Firozpur
Ferrara Italy 26 D2
Ferreira Gomes Brazil 69 H3
Ferro, Capo c. Sardinia Italy 26 C4
Ferrol Spain 25 B2
Ferros Brazil 71 C2
Ferryville Tunisia see Menzel Bourguiba
Fert-tavi nat. park Hungary 26 G1
Fès Morocco 22 D5
Feshi Dem. Rep. Congo 49 B4
Fété Bowé Senegal 46 B3
Fethard Ireland 21 E5
Fethiye Malatya Turkey see Yazıhan
Fethiye Muğla Turkey 27 M6
Fethiye Körfezi b. Turkey 27 M6
Fetisovo Kazakh. 35 I2
Fetlar i. U.K. 20 [inset]
Fettercairn U.K. 20 G4
Feuilles, Rivière aux r. Que. Canada 61 K4
Fevral'sk Russia 44 C1
Fevzipaşa Turkey 34 E3
Fez Morocco see Fès
Fezzan reg. Libya 46 E2
Ffestiniog U.K. 19 D6
Fianarantsoa Madag. 49 E6
Fichē Eth. 48 D3
Fier Albania 27 H4
Fiery Creek r. Australia 56 B3
Fife Ness pt U.K. 20 G4
Fifield Australia 58 C4
Figeac France 24 F4
Figueira da Foz Port. 25 B3
Figueras Spain see Figueres
Figueres Spain 25 H2
Figuig Morocco 22 D5
Figuil Cameroon 47 E4
Fiji country S. Pacific Ocean 53 H3
Fīk' Eth. 48 E3
Filadelfia Para. 70 D2
Filchner Ice Shelf Antarctica 76 A1
Filey U.K. 18 G4
Filibe Bulg. see Plovdiv
Filingué Niger 46 D3
Filipinas country Asia see Philippines
Filippiada Greece 27 I5
Filipstad Sweden 15 I7
Fillan Norway 14 F5
Fillmore CA U.S.A. 65 C3
Fillmore UT U.S.A. 65 F1
Fīltu Eth. 48 E3
Fimbul Ice Shelf Antarctica 76 C2
Findhorn r. U.K. 20 F3
Findlay OH U.S.A. 63 K3
Fīn-e 'Olyā Iran 35 H4
Finger Lakes NY U.S.A. 64 C1
Finike Turkey 27 N6
Finike Körfezi b. Turkey 27 N6
Finisterre Spain see Fisterra
Finisterre, Cabo c. Spain see Finisterre, Cape
Finisterre, Cape Spain 25 B2
Finke watercourse Australia 56 A5
Finke, Mount h. Australia 55 F7
Finke Bay Australia 54 E3
Finke Gorge National Park Australia 55 F6
Finland country Europe 14 O5
Finland, Gulf of Europe 15 M7
Finlay r. B.C. Canada 60 F4
Finn r. Ireland 21 E3
Finnigan, Mount Australia 56 D2
Finniss, Cape Australia 55 F8
Finnmarksvidda reg. Norway 14 H2
Finnsnes Norway 14 J2
Finspång Sweden 15 I7
Fintona U.K. 21 E3
Finucane Range hills Australia 56 C4
Fionn Loch l. U.K. 20 D3
Fionnphort U.K. 20 C4
Fiordland National Park N.Z. 59 A7
Firat r. Asia see Euphrates
Firebaugh CA U.S.A. 65 B2
Firenze Italy see Florence
Firk, Sha'īb watercourse Iraq 35 G5
Firmat Arg. 70 D4
Firminy France 24 G4
Firmum Italy see Fermo
Firmum Picenum Italy see Fermo
Firovo Russia 12 G4
Firozabad India 36 D4
Firozpur India 36 C3
Fīrūzābād Iran 35 I5
Fīrūzkūh Iran 35 I4
Fischersbrunn Namibia 50 B3
Fish watercourse Namibia 50 C5
Fisher (abandoned) Australia 55 E7
Fisher Bay Antarctica 76 G2
Fisher Glacier Antarctica 76 E2
Fishers Island NY U.S.A. 64 F2
Fisher Strait Nunavut Canada 61 J3
Fishguard U.K. 19 C7
Fishing Creek MD U.S.A. 64 C3
Fiske, Cape Antarctica 76 L2
Fiskenæsset Greenland see Qeqertarsuatsiaat
Fismes France 24 F2
Fisterra Spain 25 B2
Fisterra, Cabo c. Spain see Finisterre, Cape
Fitri, Lac l. Chad 47 E3
Fitzgerald River National Park Australia 55 B8
Fitz Roy Arg. 70 C7
Fitzroy r. Australia 54 C4
Fitz Roy, Cerro mt. Arg. 70 B7
Fitzroy Crossing Australia 54 D4
Fiume Croatia see Rijeka
Fivemiletown U.K. 21 E3
Five Points CA U.S.A. 65 B2
Fizi Dem. Rep. Congo 49 C4
Fizuli Azer. see Füzuli
Flå Norway 15 F6
Flagstaff S. Africa 51 I6
Flagstaff AZ U.S.A. 62 E4
Flamborough Head hd U.K. 18 G4
Flaminksvlei salt pan S. Africa 50 E6
Flannan Isles U.K. 20 B2
Flåsjön l. Sweden 14 I4
Flathead r. U.S.A. 62 E2
Flathead Lake MT U.S.A. 62 E2
Flattery, Cape Australia 56 D2
Flattery, Cape WA U.S.A. 62 C2
Fleetwood Australia 56 D4
Fleetwood U.K. 18 D5
Fleetwood PA U.S.A. 64 D2
Flekkefjord Norway 15 E7
Flemington NJ U.S.A. 64 D2
Flen Sweden 15 J7
Flensburg Germany 17 L3
Flers France 24 D2
Fletcher Peninsula Antarctica 76 L2
Flinders r. Australia 56 C3
Flinders Chase National Park Australia 57 B7
Flinders Group National Park Australia 56 D2
Flinders Island Australia 57 [inset]
Flinders Passage Australia 56 E3
Flinders Ranges mts Australia 57 B7
Flinders Ranges National Park Australia 57 B6
Flinders Reefs Australia 56 E3
Flin Flon Man. Canada 62 G1
Flint U.K. 18 D5
Flint MI U.S.A. 63 K3
Flint Island Kiribati 75 J6
Flinton Australia 58 D1
Flisa Norway 15 H6
Flissingskiy, Mys c. Russia 28 H2
Flodden U.K. 18 E3
Flood Range mts Antarctica 76 J1
Flora r. Australia 54 E3
Florac France 24 F4
Flora Reef Australia 56 D3
Floreana, Isla i. Galápagos Ecuador 68 [inset]
Florence Italy 26 D3
Florence AL U.S.A. 63 J5
Florence AZ U.S.A. 62 E5
Florence SC U.S.A. 63 L5
Florencia Col. 68 C3
Florentia Italy see Florence
Florentino Ameghino, Embalse resr Arg. 70 C6
Flores r. Arg. 70 E5
Flores Guat. 66 G5
Flores i. Indon. 41 E8
Flores, Laut sea Indon. 41 D8
Floresta Brazil 69 K5
Floriano Brazil 69 J5
Florianópolis Brazil 71 A4
Florida Uruguay 70 E4
Florida state U.S.A. 63 K5
Florida, Straits of Bahamas/U.S.A. 67 H4
Florida Islands Solomon Is 53 G2
Florida Keys is FL U.S.A. 63 K7
Florin CA U.S.A. 65 B1
Florina Greece 27 I4
Florø Norway 15 D6
Floyd VA U.S.A. 64 A4
Floyd, Mount AZ U.S.A. 65 F3
Flushing Neth. see Vlissingen
Fly r. P.N.G. 52 E2
Flying Fish, Cape Antarctica 76 K2
Foam Lake Sask. Canada 62 G1
Foča Bos. & Herz. 26 H3
Foça Turkey 27 L5
Fochabers U.K. 20 F3
Focşani Romania 27 L2
Foggia Italy 26 F4
Fogo i. Cape Verde 46 [inset]
Foinaven h. U.K. 20 E2
Foix France 24 E5
Folda sea chan. Norway 14 I3
Foldereid Norway 14 H4
Foldfjorden sea chan. Norway 14 G4
Folegandros i. Greece 27 K6
Foleyet Ont. Canada 63 K2
Foley Island Nunavut Canada 61 K3
Foligno Italy 26 E3
Folkestone U.K. 19 I7
Folkingham U.K. 19 G6
Folkston GA U.S.A. 63 K5
Folldal Norway 14 G5
Follonica Italy 26 D3
Folsom Lake CA U.S.A. 65 B1
Fomboni Comoros 49 E5
Fomin Russia 13 I7
Fominskaya Russia 12 K2
Fominskoye Russia 12 I4
Fonda NY U.S.A. 64 D1
Fond-du-Lac Sask. Canada 60 H4
Fond du Lac WI U.S.A. 63 J3
Fondevila Spain 25 B3
Fondi Italy 26 E4
Fonni Sardinia Italy 26 C4
Fonsagrada Spain see A Fonsagrada
Fonseca, Golfo do b. Central America 66 G6
Fonte Boa Brazil 68 E4
Fontur pt Iceland 14 [inset 2]
Foochow China see Fuzhou
Foraker, Mount AK U.S.A. 60 C3
Foraulep atoll Micronesia see Faraulep
Forbes Australia 58 D4
Forchheim Germany 17 M6
Ford City CA U.S.A. 65 C3

Georga, Zemlya i. Russia 28 F1
George r. Que. Canada 61 L4
George S. Africa 50 F7
George, Lake Australia 58 D5
George, Lake NY U.S.A. 64 E1
George Land i. Russia see Georga, Zemlya
Georges Mills NH U.S.A. 64 E1
George Sound inlet N.Z. 59 A7
Georgetown Australia 56 C3
George Town Cayman Is 67 H5
Georgetown Guyana 69 G2
George Town Malaysia 41 C7
Georgetown DE U.S.A. 64 D3
Georgetown SC U.S.A. 63 L5
Georgetown TX U.S.A. 62 H5
George VI Sound sea chan. Antarctica 76 L2
George V Land reg. Antarctica 76 G2
Georgia country Asia 35 F2
Georgia state U.S.A. 63 K5
Georgian Bay Ont. Canada 63 K2
Georgienne, Baie b. Ont. Canada see Georgian Bay
Georgina watercourse Australia 56 B5
Georgiu-Dezh Russia see Liski
Georgiyevka Vostochnyy Kazakhstan Kazakh. 42 E3
Georgiyevka Zhambylskaya Oblast' Kazakh. see Korday
Georgiyevsk Russia 13 I7
Georgiyevskoye Russia 12 J4
Georg von Neumayer research stn Antarctica see Neumayer III
Gera Germany 17 N5
Geral, Serra mts Brazil 71 A4
Geral de Goiás, Serra hills Brazil 71 B1
Geraldine N.Z. 59 C7
Geral do Paraná, Serra hills Brazil 71 B1
Geraldton Australia 55 A7
Gerar, Naḥal watercourse Israel 39 B4
Gercüş Turkey 35 F3
Gerede Turkey 34 D2
Germania country Europe see Germany
Germanicea Turkey see Kahramanmaraş
German South-West Africa country Africa see Namibia
Germany country Europe 17 L5
Germersheim Germany 17 L6
Germī Iran 35 H3
Gerona Spain see Girona
Gerrit Denys is P.N.G. see Lihir Group
Gers r. France 24 E4
Gersoppa India 38 B3
Géryville Alg. see El Bayadh
Gêrzê China 37 F2
Gerze Turkey 34 D2
Gesoriacum France see Boulogne-sur-Mer
Gestro Wenz, Wabē r. Eth. 30 D6
Gettysburg PA U.S.A. 64 C3
Gettysburg SD U.S.A. 62 H2
Gettysburg National Military Park nat. park PA U.S.A. 64 C3
Getz Ice Shelf Antarctica 76 J2
Geumeo-do i. S. Korea 45 B6
Geurie Australia 58 D4
Gevaş Turkey 35 F3
Gevgelija Macedonia 27 J4
Gēwārām Band Afgh. 36 A3
Gexto Spain see Algorta
Gey Iran see Nīkshahr
Geyikli Turkey 27 L5
Geylegphug Bhutan 37 G4
Geysdorp S. Africa 51 G4
Geyserville CA U.S.A. 65 A1
Geyve Turkey 27 N4
Ghaap Plateau S. Africa 50 F4
Ghāb, Wādī al r. Syria 39 C2
Ghabāghib Syria 39 C3
Ghabeish Sudan 32 C7
Ghadaf, Wādī al watercourse Jordan 39 C4
Ghadamés Libya see Ghadāmis
Ghadāmis Libya 46 D1
Ghaghara r. India 37 F4
Ghaibi Dero Pak. 36 A4
Ghana country Africa 46 C4
Ghantila India 36 B5
Ghanwā Saudi Arabia 32 G4
Ghanzi Botswana 49 C6
Ghanzi admin. dist. Botswana 50 F2
Ghap'an Armenia see Kapan
Ghardaïa Alg. 22 E5
Gharghoda India 38 D1
Ghârib, Gebel mt. Egypt see Ghārib, Jabal
Ghārib, Jabal mt. Egypt 34 D5
Gharm Tajik. 33 L2
Gharqābād Iran 35 H4
Gharwa India see Garhwa
Gharyān Libya 47 E1
Ghāt Libya 46 E2
Ghatgaon India 37 F5
Ghatol India 36 C5
Ghawdex i. Malta see Gozo
Ghazal, Bahr el watercourse Chad 47 E3
Ghazaouet Alg. 25 F6
Ghaziabad India 36 D3
Ghazi Ghat Pak. 36 B3
Ghazipur India 37 E4
Ghazna Afgh. see Ghaznī
Ghaznī Afgh. 36 B2
Ghaznī Rōd r. Afgh. 36 A2
Ghazzah Gaza see Gaza
Ghent Belgium 16 I5
Gheorghe Gheorghiu-Dej Romania see Onești
Gheorgheni Romania 27 K1
Gherla Romania 27 J1
Ghijduwon Uzbek. see G'ijduvon
Ghīnah, Wādī al watercourse Saudi Arabia 39 D4
Ghisonaccia Corsica France 24 I5
Ghōriyān Afgh. 33 J3
Ghotaru India 36 B4
Ghotki Pak. 33 K4
Ghudamis Libya see Ghadāmis
Ghugri r. India 37 F4
Ghurayfah h. Saudi Arabia 39 C4
Ghūrī Iran 35 I5
Ghuwayṭah, Nafūd al des. Saudi Arabia 39 D5
Ghuzor Uzbek. see G'uzor
Giaginskaya Russia 35 F1
Gialias r. Cyprus 39 A2
Giannisada i. Greece 27 L7
Giannitsa Greece 27 J4
Giant's Castle mt. S. Africa 51 I5
Giant's Causeway lava field U.K. 21 F2
Giarre Sicily Italy 26 F6
Gibb r. Australia 54 D3
Gibeon Namibia 50 C3
Gibraltar terr. Europe 25 D5
Gibraltar, Strait of Morocco/Spain 25 C6
Gibraltar Range National Park Australia 58 F2
Gibson Australia 55 C8
Gibson Desert Australia 55 C6
Gichgeniyn Nuruu mts Mongolia 42 G3
Giddalur India 38 C3
Gīddi, Gebel el h. Egypt see Jiddī, Jabal al
Gīdolē Eth. 47 G4
Gien France 24 F3
Gießen Germany 17 L5
Gifford r. Nunavut Canada 61 J2
Gifu Japan 45 E6
Gigha i. U.K. 20 D5
Gīgīga Eth. see Jijiga
G'ijduvon Uzbek. 33 J1
Gijón Spain see Gijón/Xixón
Gijón/Xixón Spain 25 D2
Gila r. AZ U.S.A. 65 E4
Gila Bend AZ U.S.A. 65 F4
Gila Bend Mountains AZ U.S.A. 65 F4
Gīlān-e Gharb Iran 35 G4
Gilbert r. Australia 56 C3
Gilbert Islands Kiribati 74 H5
Gilbert Islands country Pacific Ocean see Kiribati
Gilbert Ridge sea feature Pacific Ocean 74 H6
Gilbert River Australia 56 C3
Gilbués Brazil 69 I5
Gil Chashmeh Iran 35 J4
Gilé Moz. 49 D5
Gilead reg. Jordan 39 B3
Giles Creek r. Australia 54 E4
Gilgai Australia 58 E2
Gilgandra Australia 58 D3
Gil Gil Creek r. Australia 58 D2
Gilgit Pak. 36 C2
Gilgit r. Pak. 33 L2
Gilgit-Baltistan admin. div. Pak. 36 C1
Gilgunnia Australia 58 C4
Gilındire Turkey see Aydıncık
Gillam Man. Canada 61 I4
Gillen, Lake imp. l. Australia 55 D6
Gilles, Lake imp. l. Australia 57 B7
Gillett PA U.S.A. 64 C2
Gillette WY U.S.A. 62 F3
Gilliat Australia 56 C4
Gillingham England U.K. 19 E7
Gillingham England U.K. 19 H7
Gilling West U.K. 18 F4
Gilmour Island Nunavut Canada 61 K4
Gilroy CA U.S.A. 65 B2
Gīmbī Eth. 48 D3
Gimcheon S. Korea 45 C5
Gimhae S. Korea 45 C6
Gimhwa S. Korea 45 B5
Gimli Man. Canada 63 H1
Gimol'skoye, Ozero l. Russia 12 G3
Ginebra, Laguna l. Bol. 68 E6
Gineifa Egypt see Junayfah
Gin Gin Australia 56 E5
Gingin Australia 55 A7
Gīnīr Eth. 48 E3
Ginosa Italy 26 G4
Ginzo de Limia Spain see Xinzo de Limia
Gioia del Colle Italy 26 G4
Gippsland reg. Australia 58 B7
Girā, Wādī watercourse Egypt see Jirā', Wādī
Girard PA U.S.A. 64 A1
Giresun Turkey 34 E2
Girgenti Sicily Italy see Agrigento
Giridh India see Giridih
Giridih India 37 F4
Girilambone Australia 58 C3
Girishk Afgh. 33 J3
Girna r. India 36 C5
Gir National Park India 36 B5
Girne Cyprus see Kyrenia
Girón Ecuador 68 C4
Giron Sweden see Kiruna
Girona Spain 25 H3
Gironde est. France 24 D4
Girot Pak. 36 C2
Girral Australia 58 C4
Girraween National Park Australia 58 E2
Girvan U.K. 20 E5
Girvas Russia 12 G3
Gisborne N.Z. 59 G4
Gislaved Sweden 15 H8
Gissar Range mts Tajik./Uzbek. 33 K2
Gissarskiy Khrebet mts Tajik./Uzbek. see Gissar Range
Gitarama Rwanda 48 C4
Gitega Burundi 48 C4
Giuba r. Somalia see Jubba
Giulianova Italy 26 E3
Giurgiu Romania 27 K3
Giuvala, Pasul pass Romania 27 K2
Gīvar Iran 35 J3
Givors France 24 G4
Giyani S. Africa 51 J2
Giza Egypt 34 C5
Gizhiga Russia 29 R3
Gjakovë Kosovo 27 I3
Gjilan Kosovo 27 I3
Gjirokastër Albania 27 I4
Gjirokastra Albania see Gjirokastër
Gjoa Haven Nunavut Canada 61 I3
Gjøra Norway 14 F5
Gjøvik Norway 15 G6
Gkinas, Akrotirio pt Greece 27 M6
Glace Bay N.S. Canada 61 M5
Glacier Bay National Park and Preserve AK U.S.A. 60 E4
Glacier Peak vol. WA U.S.A. 62 C2
Gladstad Norway 14 G4
Gladstone Australia 56 E4
Gladys VA U.S.A. 64 B4
Glamis U.K. 20 F4
Glamis CA U.S.A. 65 E4
Glamoč Bos. & Herz. 26 G2
Glanton U.K. 18 F3
Glasgow U.K. 20 E5
Glasgow KY U.S.A. 63 J4
Glasgow MT U.S.A. 62 F2
Glasgow VA U.S.A. 64 B4
Glass, Loch l. U.K. 20 E3
Glass Mountain CA U.S.A. 65 C2
Glastonbury U.K. 19 E7
Glazov Russia 12 L4
Gleiwitz Poland see Gliwice
Glen Allen VA U.S.A. 64 C4
Glen Alpine Dam S. Africa 51 I2
Glenamaddy Ireland 21 D4
Glenamoy r. Ireland 21 C3
Glenbawn, Lake Australia 58 E4
Glencoe Ont. Canada 64 A1
Glencoe S. Africa 51 J5
Glendale AZ U.S.A. 62 E5
Glendale CA U.S.A. 65 C3
Glendale UT U.S.A. 65 F2
Glendale Lake PA U.S.A. 64 B2
Glen Davis Australia 58 E4
Glenden Australia 56 E4
Glendive MT U.S.A. 62 G2
Glenfield NY U.S.A. 64 D1
Glengavlen Ireland 21 E3
Glengyle Australia 56 B5
Glen Innes Australia 58 E2
Glenluce U.K. 20 E6
Glen More val. U.K. 20 E3
Glenmorgan Australia 58 D1
Glennallen AK U.S.A. 60 D3
Glenore Australia 56 C3
Glenormiston Australia 56 B4
Glenreagh Australia 58 F3
Glenrothes U.K. 20 F4
Glens Falls NY U.S.A. 64 E1
Glen Shee val. U.K. 20 F4
Glenties Ireland 21 D3
Glenveagh National Park Ireland 21 E2
Glenville WV U.S.A. 64 A3
Glenwood Springs CO U.S.A. 62 F4
Glevum U.K. see Gloucester
Glittertinden mt. Norway 15 F6
Gliwice Poland 17 Q5
Globe AZ U.S.A. 62 E5
Glogau Poland see Głogów
Głogów Poland 17 P5
Glomfjord Norway 14 H3
Glomma r. Norway 14 G7
Glommersträsk Sweden 14 K4
Glorieuses, Îles is Indian Ocean 49 E5
Glorioso Islands Indian Ocean see Glorieuses, Îles
Gloucester Australia 58 E3
Gloucester U.K. 19 E7
Gloucester MA U.S.A. 64 F1
Gloucester VA U.S.A. 64 C4
Gloversville NY U.S.A. 64 D1
Glubinnoye Russia 44 D3
Glubokiy Krasnoyarskiy Kray Russia 42 H2
Glubokiy Rostovskaya Oblast' Russia 13 I6
Glubokoye Belarus see Hlybokaye
Glubokoye Kazakh. 42 E2
Gluggarnir h. Faroe Is 14 [inset 1]
Glukhov Ukr. see Hlukhiv
Glusburn U.K. 18 F5
Glynebwy U.K. see Ebbw Vale
Gmelinka Russia 13 J6
Gmünd Austria 17 O6
Gmunden Austria 17 N7
Gnarp Sweden 15 J5
Gnesen Poland see Gniezno
Gniezno Poland 17 P4
Gnjilane Kosovo see Gjilan
Gnowangerup Australia 55 B8
Gnows Nest Range hills Australia 55 B7
Goa India 38 B3
Goa state India 38 B3
Goageb Namibia 50 C4
Goalen Head hd Australia 58 E6
Goalpara India 37 G4
Goat Fell h. U.K. 20 D5
Goba Eth. 48 E3
Gobabis Namibia 50 D2
Gobannium U.K. see Abergavenny
Gobas Namibia 50 D4
Gobi Desert des. China/Mongolia 42 J4
Gobindpur India 37 F5
Gobō Japan 45 D6
Gochas Namibia 50 D3
Godalming U.K. 19 G7
Godavari r. India 38 D2
Godavari, Cape India 38 D2
Godda India 37 F4
Godē Eth. 48 E3
Godere Eth. 48 E3
Goderich Ont. Canada 63 K3
Goderville France 19 H9
Godhavn Greenland see Qeqertarsuaq
Godhra India 36 C5
Gods r. Man. Canada 61 I4
Gods Lake Man. Canada 63 I1
Godthåb Greenland see Nuuk
Godwin-Austen, Mount China/Pakistan see K2
Goedgegun Swaziland see Nhlangano
Goegap Nature Reserve S. Africa 50 D5
Goélands, Lac aux l. Que. Canada 61 L4
Gogra r. India see Ghaghara
Goheung S. Korea 45 B6
Goiana Brazil 69 L5
Goiandira Brazil 71 A2
Goianésia Brazil 71 A1
Goiânia Brazil 71 A2
Goiás Brazil 71 A1
Goiás state Brazil 71 A2
Goidhoo Maldives 38 B5
Goioerê Brazil 70 F2
Gojra Pak. 36 C3
Gokak India 38 B2
Gokarn India 38 B3
Gök Çay r. Turkey 39 A1
Gökçeada i. Turkey 27 K4
Gökdere r. Turkey 39 A1
Goklenkuy, Solonchak salt l. Turkm. 35 J2
Gökova Körfezi b. Turkey 27 L6
Göksun Turkey 34 E3
Göksu Parkı Turkey 39 A1
Gokwe Zimbabwe 49 C5
Gol Norway 15 F6
Golaghat India 37 H4
Gölbaşı Turkey 34 E3
Gölcük Turkey 27 M4
Gold PA U.S.A. 64 C2
Gołdap Poland 17 S3
Gold Coast country Africa see Ghana
Gold Coast Australia 58 F2
Golden Bay N.Z. 59 D5
Golden Gate Highlands National Park S. Africa 51 I5
Golden Hinde mt. B.C. Canada 62 B2
Goldfield NV U.S.A. 65 D2
Goldsboro NC U.S.A. 63 L4
Goldstone Lake CA U.S.A. 65 D3
Goldsworthy (abandoned) Australia 54 B5
Goldvein VA U.S.A. 64 C3
Göle Turkey 35 F2
Goleta CA U.S.A. 65 C3
Golets-Davydov, Gora mt. Russia 43 J2
Gölgeli Dağları mts Turkey 27 M6
Golingka China see Gongbo'gyamda
Gölköy Turkey 34 E2
Gollel Swaziland see Lavumisa
Golmud China 42 G5
Golovnino Russia 44 G4
Golpāyegān Iran 35 H4
Gölpazarı Turkey 27 N4
Golspie U.K. 20 F3
Golyama Syutkya mt. Bulg. 27 K4
Golyam Persenk mt. Bulg. 27 K4
Golyshi Russia see Vetluzhskiy
Goma Dem. Rep. Congo 48 C4
Gōmal Kēlay Afgh. 36 B2
Gomang Co salt l. China 37 G3
Gomati r. India 33 N4
Gombe Nigeria 46 E3
Gombe r. Tanz. 49 D4
Gombi Nigeria 46 E3
Gombroon Iran see Bandar-e 'Abbās
Gomel' Belarus see Homyel'
Gómez Palacio Mex. 66 D3
Gomīsh Tappeh Iran 35 I3
Gomo Co salt l. China 37 F2
Gonaïves Haiti 67 J5
Gonarezhou National Park Zimbabwe 49 D6
Gonâve, Île de la i. Haiti 67 J5
Gonbad, Chāh-e well Iran 35 I4
Gonbad-e Kāvūs Iran 35 I3
Gonda India 37 E4
Gondal India 36 B5
Gondar Eth. see Gonder
Gonder Eth. 48 D2
Gondia India see Gondiya
Gondiya India 36 E5
Gönen Turkey 27 L4
Gonfreville-l'Orcher France 19 H9
Gongbalou China see Gamba
Gongbo'gyamda China 37 H3
Gongchang China see Longxi
Gongga Shan mt. China 42 I7
Gonghe China 42 I5
Gongogi r. Brazil 71 D1
Gongolgon Australia 58 C3
Gongtang China 37 G3
Gonjog China see Coqên
Gonzales CA U.S.A. 65 B2
Gonzales TX U.S.A. 63 H6
Gonzha Russia 44 B1
Goochland VA U.S.A. 64 C4
Goodenough, Cape Antarctica 76 G2
Goodenough Island P.N.G. 52 F2
Good Hope, Cape of S. Africa 50 D8
Goodooga Australia 58 C2
Goodspeed Nunataks Antarctica 76 E2
Goole U.K. 18 G5
Goolgowi Australia 58 B5
Goolma Australia 58 D4
Gooloogong Australia 58 D4
Goomalling Australia 55 B7
Goombalie Australia 58 B2
Goondiwindi Australia 58 E2
Goongarrie, Lake imp. l. Australia 55 C7
Goongarrie National Park Australia 55 C7
Goonyella Australia 56 D4
Goorly, Lake imp. l. Australia 55 B7
Goose Bay Nfld. and Lab. Canada see Happy Valley-Goose Bay
Goose Lake CA U.S.A. 62 C3
Gooty India 38 C3
Gopalganj Bangl. 37 G5
Gopalganj India 37 F4
Gopeshwar India 36 D3
Göppingen Germany 17 L6
Gorakhpur India 37 E4
Goražde Bos. & Herz. 26 H3
Gorczański Park Narodowy nat. park Poland 17 R6
Gördes Turkey 27 M5
Gordil Cent. Afr. Rep. 48 C3
Gordon U.K. 20 G5
Gordon, Lake Australia 57 [inset]
Gordon Downs Australia 54 E4
Gordon Lake PA U.S.A. 64 B3
Gordonsville VA U.S.A. 64 B3
Goré Chad 47 E4
Gorē Eth. 48 D3
Gore N.Z. 59 B8
Gore VA U.S.A. 64 B3
Gorebridge U.K. 20 F5
Gore Point AK U.S.A. 60 C4
Gorey Ireland 21 F5
Gorgān Iran 35 I3
Gorgān, Khalīj-e Iran 35 I3
Gorge Range hills Australia 54 B5
Gorgona, Isla i. Col. 68 C3
Gori Georgia 32 F1
Goris Armenia 35 G3
Gorizia Italy 26 E2
Gorki Belarus see Horki
Gor'kiy Russia see Nizhniy Novgorod
Gor'kovskoye Vodokhranilishche resr Russia 12 I4
Gorlice Poland 13 D6
Görlitz Germany 17 O5
Gorlovka Ukr. see Horlivka
Gorna Dzhumaya Bulg. see Blagoevgrad
Gorna Oryahovitsa Bulg. 27 K3
Gornji Milanovac Serbia 27 I2
Gornji Vakuf Bos. & Herz. 26 G3
Gorno-Altaysk Russia 42 F2
Gornotrakiyska Nizina lowland Bulg. 27 K3
Gornozavodsk Permskiy Kray Russia 11 R4
Gornozavodsk Sakhalinskaya Oblast' Russia 44 F3
Gornyak Russia 42 E2
Gornyy Russia 13 K6
Gornyye Klyuchi Russia 44 D3
Goro i. Fiji see Koro
Gorodenka Ukr. see Horodenka
Gorodets Russia 12 I4
Gorodishche Penzenskaya Oblast' Russia 13 J5
Gorodishche Volgogradskaya Oblast' Russia 13 J6
Gorodok Belarus see Haradok
Gorodok Russia see Zakamensk
Gorodok Khmel'nyts'ka Oblast' Ukr. see Horodok
Gorodok L'vivs'ka Oblast' Ukr. see Horodok
Gorodovikovsk Russia 13 I7
Goroka P.N.G. 52 E2
Gorokhovets Russia 12 I4
Gorom Gorom Burkina Faso 46 C3
Gorongosa mt. Moz. 49 D5
Gorongosa, Parque Nacional da nat. park Moz. 49 D5
Gorontalo Indon. 41 E7
Gorshechnoye Russia 13 H6
Gort Ireland 21 D4
Gort an Choirce Ireland 21 D2
Gorutuba r. Brazil 71 C1
Goryachiy Klyuch Russia 35 E1
Goryeong S. Korea 45 C6
Gorzów Wielkopolski Poland 17 O4
Gosainthan mt. China see Xixabangma Feng
Gosforth U.K. 18 F3
Goshen CA U.S.A. 65 C2
Goshen NH U.S.A. 64 E1
Goshen NY U.S.A. 64 D2
Goshen VA U.S.A. 64 B4
Goshoba Turkm. see Goşoba
Goşoba Turkm. 35 I2
Gospić Croatia 26 F2
Gosport U.K. 19 F8
Gossi Mali 46 C3
Gostivar Macedonia 27 I4
Göteborg Sweden see Gothenburg
Götene Sweden 15 H7
Gotenhafen Poland see Gdynia
Gotha Germany 17 M5
Gothenburg Sweden 15 G8
Gotland i. Sweden 15 K8
Gotō-rettō is Japan 45 C6
Gotse Delchev Bulg. 27 J4
Gotska Sandön i. Sweden 15 K7
Gōtsu Japan 45 D6
Göttingen Germany 17 L5
Gott Peak B.C. Canada 62 C1
Gottwaldow Czech Rep. see Zlín
Gouda Neth. 16 J4
Goudiri Senegal 46 B3
Goudoumaria Niger 46 E3
Goûgaram Niger 46 D3
Gough Island S. Atlantic Ocean 72 H8
Gouin, Réservoir resr Que. Canada 63 M2
Goulburn Australia 58 D5
Goulburn r. N.S.W. Australia 58 E4
Goulburn r. Vic. Australia 58 B6
Goulburn Islands Australia 54 F2
Goulburn River National Park Australia 58 E4
Gould Coast Antarctica 76 J1
Goulou atoll Micronesia see Ngulu
Goundam Mali 46 C3
Goundi Chad 47 E4
Gouraya Alg. 25 G5
Gourcy Burkina Faso 46 C3
Gourdon France 24 E4
Gouré Niger 46 E3
Gouripur Bangl. 37 G4
Gourits r. S. Africa 50 E8
Gourma-Rharous Mali 46 C3
Gournay-en-Bray France 24 E2
Governador Valadares Brazil 71 C2
Governor's Harbour Bahamas 67 I3
Govĭ Altayn Nuruu mts Mongolia 42 H4
Govind Ballash Pant Sagar resr India 37 E4
Gowanda NY U.S.A. 64 B1
Gowan Range hills Australia 56 D5
Gowna, Lough l. Ireland 21 E4
Goya Arg. 70 E3
Göyçay Azer. 35 G2
Goyder watercourse Australia 55 F6
Göygöl Azer. 35 G2
Goýmatdag hills Turkm. 35 I2
Goymatdag hills Turkm. see Goýmatdag
Göynük Turkey 27 N4
Goyoum Cameroon 46 E4
Goz-Beïda Chad 47 F3
Gozha Co salt l. China 36 E2
Gözkaya Turkey 39 C1
Gozo i. Malta 26 F6
Graaff-Reinet S. Africa 50 G7
Grabo Côte d'Ivoire 46 C4
Grabouw S. Africa 50 D8
Gračac Croatia 26 F2
Gradaús, Serra dos hills Brazil 69 H5
Gradiška Bos. & Herz. see Bosanska Gradiška
Grafton Australia 58 F2
Grafton WV U.S.A. 64 A3
Grafton, Cape Australia 56 D3
Grafton, Mount NV U.S.A. 65 E1
Grafton Passage Australia 56 D3
Graham TX U.S.A. 62 H5
Graham Bell Island Russia see Greem-Bell, Ostrov
Graham Island B.C. Canada 60 E4
Graham Island Nunavut Canada 61 I2
Graham Land pen. Antarctica 76 L2
Grahamstown S. Africa 51 H7
Grahovo Bos. & Herz. see Bosansko Grahovo
Graigue Ireland 21 F5
Grajaú Brazil 69 I5
Grajaú r. Brazil 69 J4
Grammos mt. Greece 27 I4
Grampian Mountains U.K. 20 E4
Grampians National Park Australia 57 C8
Granada Nicaragua 67 G6
Granada Spain 25 E5
Granard Ireland 21 E4
Granby Que. Canada 63 M2
Gran Canaria i. Canary Is 46 B2
Gran Chaco reg. Arg./Para. 70 D3
Grand r. MO U.S.A. 62 J3
Grand Atlas mts Morocco see Haut Atlas
Grand Bahama i. Bahamas 67 I3
Grand Ballon mt. France 17 K7
Grand Bank Nfld. and Lab. Canada 61 M5
Grand Banks of Newfoundland sea feature N. Atlantic Ocean 72 E3
Grand-Bassam Côte d'Ivoire 46 C4
Grand Bend Ont. Canada 64 A1
Grand Canal China 43 L5
Grand Canal Ireland 21 E4
Grand Canary i. Canary Is see Gran Canaria
Grand Canyon AZ U.S.A. 62 E4
Grand Canyon gorge AZ U.S.A. 65 F2
Grand Canyon National Park AZ U.S.A. 65 F2
Grand Cayman i. Cayman Is 67 H5
Grand Drumont mt. France 17 K7
Grande r. Bahia Brazil 71 B1
Grande r. São Paulo Brazil 71 A3
Grande, Bahía b. Arg. 70 C8
Grande, Ilha i. Brazil 71 B3
Grande Comore i. Comoros see Ngazidja
Grande de Matagalpa r. Nicaragua 67 H6
Grande Prairie Alta Canada 60 G4
Grand Erg Occidental des. Alg. 22 D5
Grand Erg Oriental des. Alg. 22 F6
Grande-Rivière Que. Canada 63 O2
Grandes, Salinas salt flat Arg. 70 C4
Grande Terre i. S. Pacific Ocean 53 G4
Grand Falls N.B. Canada 63 N2
Grand Falls-Windsor Nfld. and Lab. Canada 61 M5
Grand Forks ND U.S.A. 63 H2
Grand Gorge NY U.S.A. 64 D1
Grandioznyy, Pik mt. Russia 42 H2
Grand Island NE U.S.A. 62 H3
Grand Isle LA U.S.A. 63 I6
Grand Junction CO U.S.A. 62 F4
Grand-Lahou Côte d'Ivoire 46 C4
Grand Lake N.B. Canada 63 N2
Grand Manan Island N.B. Canada 63 N3
Grand Marais MN U.S.A. 63 I2
Grândola Port. 25 B4
Grand Passage New Caledonia 53 G3
Grand Rapids Man. Canada 62 H1
Grand Rapids MI U.S.A. 63 J3
Grand Rapids MN U.S.A. 63 I2
Grand-Sault N.B. Canada see Grand Falls
Grand St-Bernard, Col du pass Italy/Switz. see Great St Bernard Pass
Grand Teton mt. WY U.S.A. 62 E3
Grand Turk Turks and Caicos Is 67 J4
Grand Wash Cliffs mts AZ U.S.A. 65 E3
Grange Ireland 21 E6
Grängesberg Sweden 15 I6
Grangeville ID U.S.A. 62 D2
Granite Mountains CA U.S.A. 65 E3
Granite Mountains CA U.S.A. 65 E4
Granite Peak MT U.S.A. 62 F2
Granitola, Capo c. Sicily Italy 26 E6
Granja Brazil 69 J4
Gran Laguna Salada l. Arg. 70 C6
Gränna Sweden 15 I7
Gran Paradiso mt. Italy 26 B2
Gran Paradiso, Parco Nazionale del nat. park Italy 26 B2
Gran Pilastro mt. Austria/Italy 17 M7
Gran San Bernardo, Colle del pass Italy/Switz. see Great St Bernard Pass
Gran Sasso e Monti della Laga, Parco Nazionale del nat. park Italy 26 E3
Grantham U.K. 19 G6
Grant Island Antarctica 76 J2
Grantown-on-Spey U.K. 20 F3
Grant Range mts NV U.S.A. 65 E1
Grants NM U.S.A. 62 F4
Grants Pass OR U.S.A. 62 C3
Grantsville WV U.S.A. 64 A3
Grantville PA U.S.A. 64 C2
Granville France 24 D2
Granville NY U.S.A. 64 E1
Granville Lake Man. Canada 61 H4
Grão Mogol Brazil 71 C2
Grapevine Mountains NV U.S.A. 65 D2
Graskop S. Africa 51 J3
Grasplatz Namibia 50 B4
Grasse France 24 H5
Grassflat PA U.S.A. 64 B2
Grassington U.K. 18 F4
Grass Valley CA U.S.A. 65 B1
Grästorp Sweden 15 H7
Graudenz Poland see Grudziądz
Graus Spain 25 G2
Gravataí Brazil 71 A5
Grave, Pointe de pt France 24 D4
Gravelotte S. Africa 51 J2
Gravesend Australia 58 E2
Gravesend U.K. 19 H7
Gravina in Puglia Italy 26 G4
Gray France 24 G3
Grays U.K. 19 H7
Graz Austria 17 O7
Great Abaco i. Bahamas 67 I3
Great Australian Bight g. Australia 55 E8
Great Baddow U.K. 19 H7
Great Bahama Bank sea feature Bahamas 67 I3
Great Barrier Island N.Z. 59 E3
Great Barrier Reef Australia 56 D1
Great Barrier Reef Marine Park (Cairns Section) Australia 56 D3
Great Barrier Reef Marine Park (Capricor Section) Australia 56 E4
Great Barrier Reef Marine Park (Central Section) Australia 56 E3
Great Barrier Reef Marine Park (Far Nort Section) Australia 56 D2
Great Barrington MA U.S.A. 64 E1
Great Basalt Wall National Park Australia 56 D3
Great Basin NV U.S.A. 62 D4
Great Basin National Park NV U.S.A. 65 E1
Great Bear Lake N.W.T. Canada 60 G3
Great Belt sea chan. Denmark 15 G9
Great Bend KS U.S.A. 62 H4
Great Bitter Lake Egypt 39 A4
Great Blasket Island Ireland 21 B5
Great Britain i. U.K. 16 G4
Great Clifton U.K. 18 D4
Great Cumbrae i. U.K. 20 E5
Great Dividing Range mts Australia 58 B6
Great Eastern Erg des. Alg. see Grand Erg Oriental
Greater Antarctica reg. Antarctica see East Antarctica
Greater Antilles is Caribbean Sea 67 H4
Greater Khingan Mountains China see Da Hinggan Ling
Great Exuma i. Bahamas 67 I4
Great Falls MT U.S.A. 62 E2
Great Fish r. S. Africa 51 H7
Great Fish Point S. Africa 51 H7
Great Fish River Reserve Complex nature res. S. Africa 51 H7
Great Gandak r. India 37 F4
Great Ganges atoll Cook Is see Manihiki
Great Inagua i. Bahamas 67 J4
Great Karoo plat. S. Africa 50 F7
Great Kei r. S. Africa 51 I7
Great Lake Australia 57 [inset]
Great Malvern U.K. 19 E6
Great Meteor Tablemount sea feature N. Atlantic Ocean 72 G4
Great Namaqualand reg. Namibia 50 C4
Great Nicobar i. India 31 I6
Great Ormes Head hd U.K. 18 D5
Great Ouse r. U.K. 19 H6
Great Oyster Bay Australia 57 [inset]
Great Palm Islands Australia 56 D3
Great Point MA U.S.A. 64 F2
Great Rift Valley Africa 48 D4
Great Ruaha r. Tanz. 49 D4
Great Sacandaga Lake NY U.S.A. 64 D1
Great St Bernard Pass Italy/Switz. 26 B2
Great Salt Lake UT U.S.A. 62 E3
Great Salt Lake Desert UT U.S.A. 62 E3
Great Sand Sea des. Egypt/Libya 34 B5
Great Sandy Desert Australia 54 C5
Great Sandy Island Australia see Fraser Island
Great Sandy National Park Australia 57 F5
Great Sea Reef Fiji 53 H3
Great Slave Lake N.W.T. Canada 60 G3
Greatstone-on-Sea U.K. 19 H8
Great Stour r. U.K. 19 I7
Great Torrington U.K. 19 C8
Great Victoria Desert Australia 55 E7
Great Wall (China) research stn Antarctica 76 A2
Great Wall tourist site China 43 L4
Great Waltham U.K. 19 H7
Great Western Erg des. Alg. see Grand Erg Occidental
Great Whernside h. U.K. 18 F4
Great Yarmouth U.K. 19 I6
Grebenkovskiy Ukr. see Hrebinka
Grebyonka Ukr. see Hrebinka
Greco, Cape Cyprus see Greko, Cape
Gredos, Sierra de mts Spain 25 D3
Greece country Europe 27 I5
Greece NY U.S.A. 64 C1
Greeley CO U.S.A. 62 G3
Greem-Bell, Ostrov i. Russia 28 H1
Green r. WY U.S.A. 62 F4
Green Bay WI U.S.A. 63 J3
Green Bay b. WI U.S.A. 63 J2
Greenbrier r. WV U.S.A. 64 A4
Green Cape Australia 58 E6
Greencastle U.K. 21 F3
Greene NY U.S.A. 64 D1
Greeneville TN U.S.A. 63 K4
Greenfield CA U.S.A. 65 B2
Greenfield MA U.S.A. 64 E1
Green Head hd Australia 55 A7
Greenhill Island Australia 54 F2
Green Lake Sask. Canada 62 F1
Greenland terr. N. America 61 N3
Greenland Basin sea feature Arctic Ocean 77 I2
Greenland Fracture Zone sea feature Arctic Ocean 77 I1
Greenland Sea Greenland/Svalbard 28 A2
Greenlaw U.K. 20 G5
Green Line Cyprus 39 A2
Greenock U.K. 20 E5
Greenore Ireland 21 F3
Greenport NY U.S.A. 64 E2
Green River WY U.S.A. 62 F3
Greensburg PA U.S.A. 64 B2
Greenstone Point U.K. 20 D3
Greenville Liberia 46 C4
Greenville AL U.S.A. 63 J5
Greenville MS U.S.A. 63 I5
Greenville NH U.S.A. 64 F1
Greenville PA U.S.A. 64 A2
Greenville SC U.S.A. 63 K5
Greenville TX U.S.A. 63 H5
Greenwich atoll Micronesia see Kapingamarangi
Greenwich CT U.S.A. 64 E2
Greenwood SC U.S.A. 63 K5
Gregory r. Australia 56 B3
Gregory, Lake imp. l. S.A. Australia 57 B6
Gregory, Lake imp. l. W.A. Australia 54 D5
Gregory, Lake imp. l. W.A. Australia 55 B6
Gregory Downs Australia 56 B3
Gregory National Park Australia 54 E4
Gregory Range hills Qld Australia 56 C3
Gregory Range hills W.A. Australia 54 C5
Greifswald Germany 17 N3
Greko, Cape Cyprus 39 B2
Gremyachinsk Russia 11 R4
Grenå Denmark see Grenaa
Grenaa Denmark 15 G8
Grenada MS U.S.A. 63 J5
Grenada country West Indies 67 L6
Grenade France 24 E5
Grenen spit Denmark 15 G8
Grenfell Australia 58 D4
Grenfell Sask. Canada 62 G1
Grenoble France 24 G4

Grense-Jakobselv Norway 14 Q2
Grenville, Cape Australia 56 C1
Grenville Island Fiji see Rotuma
Greshak Pak. 36 A4
Gressåmoen Nasjonalpark nat. park Norway 14 H4
Greta r. U.K. 18 E4
Gretna U.K. 20 F6
Gretna VA U.S.A. 64 B4
Grevena Greece 27 I4
Grevesmühlen Germany 17 M4
Grey, Cape Australia 56 C1
Greybull WY U.S.A. 62 F3
Grey Hunter Peak Y.T. Canada 60 D3
Greymouth N.Z. 59 C6
Greytown S. Africa 51 J5
Gribanovskiy Russia 13 I6
Griffin GA U.S.A. 63 K5
Griffith Australia 58 C5
Grim, Cape Australia 57 [inset]
Grimari Cent. Afr. Rep. 48 C3
Grimsby U.K. 18 G5
Grimshaw Alta Canada 60 G4
Grímsey i. Iceland 14 [inset 2]
Grimstad Norway 15 F7
Grindavík Iceland 14 [inset 2]
Grímsstaðir Iceland 14 [inset 2]
Grindsted Denmark 15 F9
Grindul Chituc spit Romania 27 M2
Grinnell Peninsula Nunavut Canada 61 I2
Griqualand East reg. S. Africa 51 I6
Griqualand West reg. S. Africa 51 F5
Griquatown S. Africa 50 F5
Grise Fiord Nunavut Canada 61 J2
Grishino Ukr. see Krasnoarmiys'k
Gris Nez, Cap c. France 19 I8
Gritley U.K. 20 G2
Groblersdal S. Africa 51 I3
Groblershoop S. Africa 50 F5
Grodno Belarus see Hrodna
Groen watercourse N. Cape S. Africa 50 F6
Groen watercourse Northern Cape/Western Cape S. Africa 50 C6
Groix, Île de i. France 24 C3
Grombalia Tunisia 26 D6
Grong Norway 14 H4
Groningen Neth. 17 N4
Grønland terr. N. America see Greenland
Groot-Aar Pan salt pan S. Africa 50 E4
Groot Berg r. S. Africa 50 D7
Groot Brakrivier S. Africa 50 F8
Grootdraaidam dam S. Africa 51 I4
Grootdrink S. Africa 50 E5
Groote Eylandt i. Australia 56 B2
Grootfontein Namibia 49 B5
Groot Karas Berg plat. Namibia 50 D4
Groot Letaba r. S. Africa 51 J2
Groot Marico S. Africa 51 H3
Groot Swartberge mts S. Africa 50 E7
Grootvloer salt pan S. Africa 50 E5
Groot Winterberg mt. S. Africa 51 H7
Gross Barmen Namibia 50 C2
Großer Rachel mt. Germany 17 N6
Grosser Speikkogel mt. Austria 17 O7
Grosseto Italy 26 D3
Grossevichi Russia 44 E3
Groß-Gerau Germany 17 L6
Großglockner mt. Austria 17 N7
Gross Ums Namibia 50 D2
Großvenediger mt. Austria 17 N7
Grottoes VA U.S.A. 64 B3
Groundhog r. Ont. Canada 63 K2
Grove Mountains Antarctica 76 E2
Grover Beach CA U.S.A. 65 F4
Growler Mountains AZ U.S.A. 65 F4
Groznyy Russia 13 J8
Grubišno Polje Croatia 26 G2
Grudovo Bulg. see Sredets
Grudziądz Poland 17 Q4
Grünau Namibia 50 D4
Grünberg Poland see Zielona Góra
Grundarfjörður Iceland 14 [inset 2]
Gruzinskaya S.S.R. country Asia see Georgia
Gryazi Russia 13 H5
Gryazovets Russia 12 I4
Gryfice Poland 17 O4
Gryfino Poland 17 O4
Gryfów Śląski Poland 17 O5
Gryllefjord Norway 14 J2
Grytviken S. Georgia 70 I8
Gua India 37 F5
Guacanayabo, Golfo de b. Cuba 67 I4
Guadajoz r. Spain 25 D5
Guadalajara Mex. 66 D4
Guadalajara Spain 25 E3
Guadalcanal i. Solomon Is 53 G3
Guadalete r. Spain 25 C5
Guadalope r. Spain 25 F3
Guadalquivir r. Spain 25 D5
Guadalupe i. Mex. 66 A3
Guadalupe, Sierra de mts Spain 25 D4
Guadalupe Peak TX U.S.A. 62 G5
Guadalupe Victoria Mex. 62 G7
Guadarrama, Sierra de mts Spain 25 D3
Guadeloupe terr. West Indies 67 L5
Guadeloupe Passage Caribbean Sea 67 L5
Guadiana r. Port./Spain 25 C5
Guadix Spain 25 E5
Guafo, Isla i. Chile 70 B6
Guaíba Brazil 71 A5
Guaiçuí Brazil 71 B2
Guaíra Brazil 71 A3
Guajira, Península de la pen. Col. 68 D1
Gualala CA U.S.A. 65 A1
Gualeguay Arg. 70 E4
Gualeguaychu Arg. 70 E4
Gualicho, Salina salt flat Arg. 70 C6
Guam terr. N. Pacific Ocean 41 G6
Guamblin, Isla i. Chile 70 A6
Guampí, Sierra de mts Venez. 68 E2
Guamúchil Mex. 66 C3
Guanabacoa Cuba 67 H4
Guanaja Venez. 68 E7
Guanambi Brazil 71 C1
Guanare Venez. 68 E2
Guane Cuba 67 H4
Guangdong prov. China 43 K8
Guanghua China see Laohekou
Guangxi aut. reg. China see Guangxi Zhuangzu Zizhiqu
Guangxi Zhuangzu Zizhiqu aut. reg. China 43 J8
Guangyuan China 42 J6
Guangzhou China 43 K8
Guanhães Brazil 71 C2
Guanipa r. Venez. 68 F2
Guanshui China 44 B4
Guantánamo Cuba 67 I4
Guapé Brazil 71 B3
Guapi Col. 68 C3
Guaporé r. Bol./Brazil 68 E6
Guaporé Brazil 71 A5
Guaqui Bol. 68 E7
Guará r. Brazil 71 B1
Guarabira Brazil 69 K5
Guaranda Ecuador 68 C4

Guarapari Brazil 71 C3
Guarapuava Brazil 71 A4
Guararapes Brazil 71 A3
Guaratinguetá Brazil 71 B3
Guaratuba Brazil 71 A4
Guaratuba, Baía de b. Brazil 71 A4
Guarda Port. 25 C3
Guardafui, Cape Somalia see Gwardafuy, Gees
Guardiagrele Italy 26 F3
Guardo Spain 25 D2
Guárico, del Embalse resr Venez. 68 E2
Guarujá Brazil 71 B3
Guasave Mex. 62 F6
Guasdualito Venez. 68 D2
Guatemala country Central America 66 F5
Guatemala City Guat. 66 F6
Guaviare r. Col. 68 E3
Guaxupé Brazil 71 B3
Guayaquil Ecuador 68 C4
Guayaquil, Golfo de g. Ecuador 68 B4
Guaymas Mex. 66 B3
Guazhou China 42 H4
Guba Eth. 48 D3
Gubakha Russia 11 R4
Gubbi India 38 C3
Gubbio Italy 26 E3
Gubkin Russia 13 H5
Gucheng China 43 K6
Gudari India 38 D2
Gudbrandsdalen val. Norway 15 F6
Gudermes Russia 13 J8
Gudivada India 38 D2
Gudiyattam India 38 C3
Gudur Andhra Prad. India 38 C3
Gudur Andhra Prad. India 38 C3
Gudvangen Norway 15 E6
Gudzhal r. Russia 44 D2
Guéckédou Guinea 46 B4
Guelma Alg. 26 B6
Guelmim Morocco 46 B2
Guelph Ont. Canada 64 A1
Guerara Alg. 22 E5
Guercif Morocco 22 D5
Guéret France 24 E3
Guernsey terr. Channel Is 19 E9
Guérou Mauritania 46 B3
Guerrah Et-Tarf salt pan Alg. 26 B7
Guerrero Negro Mex. 62 E6
Guers, Lac l. Que. Canada 61 L4
Gueugnon France 24 G3
Gügé mt. Eth. 48 D3
Gügerd, Küh-e mts Iran 35 I4
Guiana Basin sea feature N. Atlantic Ocean 72 E5
Guidan-Roumji Niger 46 D3
Guider Cameroon 47 E4
Guidonia Montecelio Italy 26 E4
Guigang China 43 J8
Guiglo Côte d'Ivoire 46 C4
Guija Moz. 51 K3
Guildford U.K. 19 G7
Guilherme Capelo Angola see Cacongo
Guilin China 43 K7
Guillaume-Delisle, Lac l. Que. Canada 61 K4
Guimarães Brazil 69 J4
Guimarães Port. 25 B3
Guinea country Africa 46 B3
Guinea, Gulf of Africa 46 D4
Guinea Basin sea feature N. Atlantic Ocean 72 H5
Guinea-Bissau country Africa 46 B3
Guinea-Conakry country Africa see Guinea
Guinea Ecuatorial country Africa see Equatorial Guinea
Guiné-Bissau country Africa see Guinea-Bissau
Guinée country Africa see Guinea
Guînes France 24 C2
Guingamp France 24 C2
Guipavas France 24 B2
Guiratinga Brazil 69 H7
Guiyang China 42 J7
Guizhou prov. China 42 J7
Gujarat state India 36 C5
Gujar Khan Pak. 36 C2
Gujerat state India see Gujarat
Gujranwala Pak. 33 L3
Gujrat Pak. 33 L3
Gukovo Russia 13 H6
Gulabgarh India 36 D2
Gulbarga India 38 C2
Gul'cha Kyrg. see Gülchö
Gülchö Kyrg. 42 C4
Gülcihan Turkey 39 B1
Gulian China see Yushu
Guliston Uzbek. 33 L1
Guliya Shan mt. China 44 A2
Gulja China see Yining
Gul Kach Pak. 36 B3
Gul'kevichi Russia 35 F1
Gull Lake Sask. Canada 62 F1
Gullträsk Sweden 14 L3
Güllük Körfezi b. Turkey 27 L6
Gülnar Turkey 39 B1
Gulu Uganda 48 D3
Guluwuru Island Australia 56 B1
Gulyayevskiye Koshki, Ostrova is Russia 12 L1
Guma China see Pishan
Gumal r. Pak. 33 L3
Gumare Botswana 49 C5
Gumbaz Pak. 36 A3
Gumbinnen Russia see Gusev
Gumdag Turkm. 35 I3
Gumel Nigeria 46 D3
Gümgüm Turkey see Varto
Gumi S. Korea 45 C5
Gumla India 37 F5
Gümüşhacıköy Turkey 34 D2
Gümüşhane Turkey 35 E2
Guna India 36 D4
Guna Terara mt. Eth. 32 E7
Gunbar Australia 58 C5
Gunbower Australia 58 B6
Güncang China 37 H3
Gundabooka National Park Australia 57 D6
Gundagai Australia 58 D5
Güney Turkey 27 M5
Güneydoğu Toroslar mts Turkey 34 F3
Gungu Dem. Rep. Congo 49 B4
Gunib Russia 35 G2
Gunisao r. Man. Canada 61 M4
Gunnaur India 36 D3
Gunnbjørn Fjeld nunatak Greenland 61 P3
Gunnedah Australia 58 E3
Gunning Australia 58 D5
Gunnison CO U.S.A. 62 F4
Gunsan S. Korea 45 B5
Guntakal India 38 C3
Guntur India 38 D2
Gunungsitoli Indon. 41 B7
Günyüzü Turkey 39 C1
Gunza Angola see Porto Amboim
Günzburg Germany 17 M6
Guovdageaidnu Norway see Kautokeino

Gupis Pak. 36 C1
Gurbantünggüt Shamo des. China 42 F4
Gurdaspur India 36 C2
Gurdzhaani Georgia see Gurjaani
Güre Turkey 27 M5
Gurgan Iran see Gorgān
Gurgaon India 36 D3
Gurgei, Jebel mt. Sudan 47 F3
Gurha India 36 B4
Guri, Embalse de resr Venez. 68 F2
Gurinhatã Brazil 71 A2
Gurjaani Georgia 35 G2
Guro Moz. 49 D5
Guru China 37 G3
Gurué Moz. 49 D5
Gurupá Brazil 69 H4
Gurupi Brazil 69 I6
Gurupi r. Brazil 69 I4
Gurupi, Serra do hills Brazil 69 I4
Guru Sikhar mt. India 36 C4
Guruzala India 38 C2
Gur'yev Kazakh. see Atyrau
Gur'yevsk Russia 15 L9
Gur'yevskaya Oblast' admin. div. Kazakh. see Atyrauskaya Oblast'
Gusau Nigeria 46 D3
Gusev Russia 15 M9
Gushan China 45 A5
Gusino Russia 13 F5
Gusinoozersk Russia 42 J2
Gus'-Khrustal'nyy Russia 12 I5
Guspini Sardinia Italy 26 C5
Gustav Holm, Kap c. Greenland see Tasiilap Karra
Gustine CA U.S.A. 65 B2
Güstrow Germany 17 N4
Gütersloh Germany 17 L5
Gutsuo China 37 F3
Guwahati India 37 G4
Guwlumayak Turkm. see Guwlumäýak
Guwlumäýak Turkm. 35 I2
Guyana country S. America 69 G2
Guyane Française terr. S. America see French Guiana
Guyang China 43 K3
Guyenne reg. France 24 D4
Guy Fawkes River National Park Australia 58 F3
Guymon OK U.S.A. 62 G4
Guyra Australia 58 E3
Guyuan Hebei China 43 K4
Guyuan Ningxia China 42 J5
Güzeloluk Turkey 39 B1
Güzelyurt Cyprus see Morfou
Guzmán Mex. 66 E5
Guzmán, Lago de l. Mex. 66 C2
G'uzor Uzbek. 33 K2
Gvardeysk Russia 15 M9
Gvasyugi Russia 44 E3
Gwa Myanmar 42 G9
Gwabegar Australia 58 D3
Gwadar Pak. 33 J4
Gwaii Haanas B.C. Canada 60 E4
Gwaii Haanas National Park Reserve and Haida Heritage Site B.C. Canada 60 E4
Gwal Haidarzai Pak. 36 B3
Gwalior India 36 D4
Gwanda Zimbabwe 49 C6
Gwane Dem. Rep. Congo 48 C3
Gwangcheon S. Korea 45 B5
Gwangju S. Korea 45 B6
Gwardafuy, Gees c. Somalia 48 F2
Gweebarra Bay Ireland 21 D3
Gwelo Zimbabwe see Gweru
Gwêr Iraq 35 F3
Gweru Zimbabwe 49 C5
Gweta Botswana 49 C6
Gwoza Nigeria 46 E3
Gwydir r. Australia 58 D2
Gyablung China 37 H3
Gyaca China 37 H3
Gya'gya China see Saga
Gyaijêpozhanggê China see Zhidoi
Gya'nyima China see Gyanyima
Gya'Qu r. China 37 H3
Gyaisi China see Jiulong
Gyali i. Greece 27 L6
Gyamotang China see Dêngqên
Gyamug China 36 E2
Gyandzha Azer. see Gäncä
Gyangkar China see Dinggyê
Gyangnyi Caka salt l. China 37 F2
Gyangrang China 37 F3
Gyangtse China see Gyangzê
Gyangzê China 37 G3
Gyaring China 37 I2
Gyaring Co l. China 37 F3
Gyaring Hu l. China 42 H6
Gyaros i. Greece 27 K6
Gyarubtang China 42 G6
Gydan, Khrebet mts Russia see Kolymskoye Nagor'ye
Gydan Peninsula Russia 28 I2
Gydanskiy Poluostrov pen. Russia see Gydan Peninsula
Gyêgu China see Yushu
Gyêmdong China 37 H3
Gyimda China 37 H3
Gyirong Xizang China 37 F3
Gyirong Xizang China 37 F3
Gyiza China 37 H2
Gyldenløve Fjord inlet Greenland see Umiiviip Kangertiva
Gympie Australia 57 F5
Gyöngyös Hungary 17 Q7
Gyôr Hungary 26 G1
Gypsumville Man. Canada 62 H1
Gyrfalcon Islands Que. Canada 61 L4
Gytheio Greece 27 J6
Gyula Hungary 27 I1
Gyulafehérvár Romania see Alba Iulia
Gyümai China see Tarlag
Gyumri Armenia 35 G2
Gzhatsk Russia see Gagarin

H

Haa Bhutan 37 G4
Haa-Alif Atoll Maldives see Ihavandhippolhu
Ha'apai Group is Tonga 53 I3
Haapajärvi Fin. 14 N5
Haapavesi Fin. 14 N4
Haapsalu Estonia 15 M7
Ha 'Arava watercourse Israel/Jordan see 'Arabah, Wādī al
Ha'Arava, Nahal watercourse Israel/Jordan see Jayb, Wādī al
Haarlem Neth. 16 J4
Haarstrang ridge S. Africa 50 F7
Hab r. Pak. 36 A4
Habahe China 42 F3
Habana Cuba see Havana
Habarane Sri Lanka 38 D4
Habaswein Kenya 48 D3
Habay Alta Canada 60 G3
Habban Yemen 32 G7
Ḩabbānīyah, Hawr al l. Iraq 35 F4
Hab Chauki Pak. 36 A4
Habra India 37 G5
Hachijō-jima i. Japan 45 E6
Hachinohe Japan 44 F4
Hacıköy Turkey see Çekerek

Hacıqabul Azer. 35 H2
Hack, Mount Australia 57 B6
Hackberry AZ U.S.A. 65 F3
Hackensack NJ U.S.A. 64 D2
Hacufera Moz. 49 D6
Ḩadabat al Jilf al Kabīr plat. Egypt see Jilf al Kabīr, Ḩadabat al
Hadagalli India 38 B3
Hadayang China 44 B2
Hadd, Ra's al pt Oman 33 I5
Haddington U.K. 20 G5
Hadejia Nigeria 46 E3
Hadera Israel 39 B3
Hadera, Naḩal r. Israel 39 B3
Haderslev Denmark 15 F9
Hadhramaut reg. Yemen see Ḩadramawt
Ḩādī, Jabal al mts Jordan 39 C4
Hadim Turkey 34 D3
Hadleigh U.K. 19 H6
Hadong S. Korea 45 B6
Ḩadraj, Wādī watercourse Saudi Arabia 39 C4
Ḩadramawt reg. Yemen 48 G6
Hadranum Sicily Italy see Adrano
Hadrian's Wall tourist site U.K. 18 E4
Hadrumetum Tunisia see Sousse
Hadsund Denmark 15 G8
Hadych Ukr. 13 G6
Haeju N. Korea 45 B5
Haeju-man b. N. Korea 45 B5
Haenam S. Korea 45 B6
Haenertsburg S. Africa 51 I2
Haerbin China see Harbin
Ḩafar al Bāṭin Saudi Arabia 32 G4
Hafik Turkey 34 E3
Ḩafirah, Qā' al salt pan Jordan 39 C4
Hafizabad Pak. 36 C2
Haflong India 37 H4
Hafnarfjörður Iceland 14 [inset 2]
Hafren r. U.K. see Severn
Haftgel Iran 35 H5
Hafursfjörður b. Iceland 14 [inset 2]
Haga Myanmar see Haka
Hagar Nish Plateau Eritrea 32 E6
Hagåtña Guam 41 G6
Hagen Germany 17 K5
Hagerstown MD U.S.A. 64 C3
Hagfors Sweden 15 H6
Hagi Japan 45 C6
Ha Giang Vietnam 31 J4
Hagley U.K. 19 E6
Hag's Head hd Ireland 21 C5
Hague, Cap de la c. France 24 D2
Haguenau France 24 H2
Hahajima-rettō is Japan 45 F8
Hai Tanz. 47 D5
Haib watercourse Namibia 50 C5
Haibowan China see Wuhai
Haicheng China 45 A4
Haida Gwaii B.C. Canada 60 E4
Haifa Israel 39 B3
Haifa, Bay of Israel 39 B3
Haig Australia 55 D7
Haikakan country Asia see Armenia
Haikou China 43 K8
Ḩā'il Saudi Arabia 35 F6
Hailin China 44 C3
Hailong China see Meihekou
Hailsham U.K. 19 H8
Hailun China 44 B3
Hailuoto i. Fin. 14 N4
Hainan prov. China 43 J9
Hainan Dao i. China 43 K9
Hainan Strait China 43 J9
Haines AK U.S.A. 60 E3
Haines Junction Y.T. Canada 60 E3
Hai Phong Vietnam see Hai Phong
Haiphong Vietnam 31 J4
Haiqing China 44 D3
Haitan Dao i. China 43 L7
Haiti country West Indies 67 J5
Haiwee Reservoir CA U.S.A. 65 D2
Haiya Sudan 32 E6
Haiyan China 42 I5
Haiyang Dao i. China 45 A5
Haizhou Wan b. China 43 L6
Hajdúböszörmény Hungary 27 I1
Hajeb El Ayoun Tunisia 26 C7
Hajhir mt. Yemen 33 H7
Haji Mahesar Pak. 36 A3
Hajipur India 37 F4
Hajjah Yemen 32 F6
Ḩajjī 'Alī Qolī, Kavīr-e salt pan Iran 35 I4
Ḩājjīābād Fārs Iran 35 I5
Ḩājjīābād Yazd Iran 35 I4
Hakha Myanmar see Haka
Hakkâri Turkey 35 F3
Hakkas Sweden 14 L3
Hakken-zan mt. Japan 45 D6
Hako-dake mt. Japan 44 F3
Hakodate Japan 44 F3
Hakos Mountains Namibia 50 C2
Hakseen Pan salt pan S. Africa 50 E4
Hakui Japan 45 E5
Haku-san mt. Japan 45 E5
HaNegev des. Israel see Negev
HaNeqarot, Naḩal watercourse Israel 39 B4
Halab Syria see Aleppo
Ḩalabjah/Ḩelebce Iraq 35 G4
Halaç Turkm. see Halaç
Halaç Turkm. 33 J2
Halahai China 44 B3
Ḩalā'ib Sudan 32 E5
Halaib Triangle disp. terr. Egypt/Sudan 32 E5
Halāl, Gebel h. Egypt see Hilāl, Jabal
Ḩalāniyāt, Juzur al is Oman 33 I6
Halba Lebanon 39 C2
Halberstadt Germany 17 M5
Halcon, Mount Phil. 41 G4
Halden Norway 15 G7
Haldensleben Germany 17 M4
Haldia India 37 G5
Haldwani India 36 D3
Hale watercourse Australia 56 A5
Ḩāleh Iran 35 H5
Haleparki Deresi r. Syria/Turkey see Quwayq, Nahr
Halesowen U.K. 19 E6
Halesworth U.K. 19 I6
Half Assini Ghana 46 C4
Halfmoon Bay N.Z. 59 B8
Halfway Ireland 21 D6
Halia India 37 E4
Ḩalībīyah Syria 39 E4
Halicarnassus Turkey see Bodrum
Halifax N.S. Canada 61 L5
Halifax U.K. 18 F5
Halifax, Mount Australia 56 D3
Ḩalīmah mt. Lebanon/Syria 39 C2
Halkirk U.K. 20 F2
Halla S. Korea see Gülchö
Ḩalla Sweden 14 J5
Halla-san National Park S. Korea 45 B6
Halladale r. U.K. 20 F2
Halle (Saale) Germany 17 M5
Halleflors Sweden 15 I7
Hallein Austria 17 N7
Hallett, Cape Antarctica 76 H2
Halley (U.K.) research stn Antarctica 76 B1
Hallgreen, Mount Antarctica 76 B2
Hall Islands Micronesia 74 G5
Hällnäs Sweden 14 K4
Hallock MN U.S.A. 63 H2

Hall Peninsula Nunavut Canada 61 L3
Hallsberg Sweden 15 I7
Halls Creek Australia 54 D4
Hallstead PA U.S.A. 64 D2
Hallviken Sweden 14 I5
Halmahera i. Indon. 41 E7
Halmstad Sweden 15 H8
Hals Denmark 15 G8
Hälsingborg Sweden see Helsingborg
Halsua Fin. 14 N5
Haltwhistle U.K. 18 E4
Haly, Mount Australia 58 E1
Hama Syria 39 C2
Hamada Japan 45 D6
Hamadān Iran 35 H4
Hamah Syria 39 C2
Hamam Turkey see Haci
Hamamatsu Japan 45 E6
Hamar Norway 15 G6
Ḩamāta, Gebel mt. Egypt see Ḩamāṭah, Jabal
Ḩamāṭah, Jabal mt. Egypt 32 D5
Hamatonbetsu Japan 44 F3
Hambantota Sri Lanka 38 D5
Hambleton Hills U.K. 18 F4
Hamburg Germany 17 L4
Hamburg S. Africa 51 H7
Hamburg NY U.S.A. 64 B1
Hamburgisches Wattenmeer, Nationalpark nat. park Germany 17 L4
Ḩamḑ, Wādī al watercourse Saudi Arabia 32 E4
Hamden CT U.S.A. 64 E2
Hämeenlinna Fin. 15 N6
HaMelah, Yam salt l. Asia see Dead Sea
Hamelin Australia 55 A6
Hameln Germany 17 L4
Hamersley Range mts Australia 54 B5
Hamhŭng N. Korea 45 B5
Hami China 42 G4
Hamid Sudan 32 D5
Hamilton Qld Australia 56 C4
Hamilton S.A. Australia 57 A5
Hamilton Vic. Australia 57 C8
Hamilton watercourse Qld Australia 56 B4
Hamilton watercourse S.A. Australia 57 A5
Hamilton Bermuda 67 L2
Hamilton Ont. Canada 64 B1
Hamilton N.Z. 59 E3
Hamilton U.K. 20 E5
Hamilton MT U.S.A. 62 E3
Hamilton NY U.S.A. 64 D1
Hamilton, Mount CA U.S.A. 65 B2
Hamilton, Mount NV U.S.A. 65 E1
Hamilton Mountain h. NY U.S.A. 64 D1
Hamīm, Wādī al watercourse Libya 23 I5
Hamina Fin. 15 O6
Hamirpur Hima. Prad. India 36 D3
Hamirpur Uttar Prad. India 36 E4
Hamitabat Turkey see Isparta
Hamju N. Korea 45 B5
Hamm Germany 17 K5
Ḩammām al 'Alīl Iraq 35 F3
Hammam Boughrara Alg. 25 F6
Ḩammām, Hawr al imp. l. Iraq 35 G5
Hammamet Tunisia 26 D6
Hammamet, Golfe de g. Tunisia 26 D6
Ḩammār, Hawr al imp. l. Iraq 35 G5
Hammarstrand Sweden 14 J5
Hammerdal Sweden 14 I5
Hammerfest Norway 14 M1
Hammonton NJ U.S.A. 64 D3
Hampden Sydney VA U.S.A. 64 B4
Hampshire Downs hills U.K. 19 F7
Hampton NH U.S.A. 64 F1
Hampton VA U.S.A. 64 C4
Hampton Tableland reg. Australia 55 D8
Ḩamrāʾ, Al Ḩamādah al plat. Libya 48 E2
Ḩamrāʾ, Birkat al well Saudi Arabia 35 F5
Ḩamrā watercourse Syria/Turkey see Ḩimār, Wādī al
Hamrat esh Sheikh Sudan 32 C7
Hamta Pass India 36 D2
Hämün-e Lowrah dry lake Afgh./Pak. see Lora, Hāmūn-i-
Hāmūn Şāberī, Daryācheh-ye imp. l. Afgh./Iran 33 J3
Hamur Turkey 35 G3
Hamwic U.K. see Southampton
Hanahai watercourse Botswana/Namibia 50 F2
Ḩanak Saudi Arabia 32 E4
Hanakpınar Turkey see Çınar
Hanamaki Japan 45 F5
Hanang mt. Tanz. 49 D4
Hanbin China see Ankang
Hancheng China 43 K5
Hancock MD U.S.A. 64 B3
Hancock NY U.S.A. 64 D2
Handa Island U.K. 20 D2
Handan China 43 K5
Handeni Tanz. 49 D4
Hanford CA U.S.A. 65 C2
Hangayn Nuruu mts Mongolia 42 H3
Hangchow China see Hangzhou
Hangö Fin. see Hanko
Hangya China 42 H5
Hangzhou China 43 M6
Hangzhou Wan b. China 43 M6
Hani Turkey 35 F3
Hanish Kabir i. Yemen see Suyūl Ḩanīsh
Hankey S. Africa 51 G7
Hanko Fin. 15 M7
Hanle India 36 D2
Hann, Mount h. Australia 54 D3
Hanna Alta Canada 60 H4
Hannibal MO U.S.A. 63 I4
Hannover Germany 17 L4
Hann Range mts Australia 55 F5
Hanöbukten b. Sweden 15 I9
Hanoi Vietnam see Ha Nôi
Ha Nôi Vietnam 31 J4
Hanover Germany see Hannover
Hanover S. Africa 50 G6
Hanover NH U.S.A. 64 E1
Hanover VA U.S.A. 64 C4
Hansen Mountains Antarctica 76 D2
Hansi India 36 D3
Hanstholm Denmark 15 F8
Hantsavichy Belarus 15 O10
Hanumangarh India 36 C3
Hanwood Australia 58 C5
Hanyin China 43 J5
Hanzhong China 42 J5
Hao atoll Fr. Polynesia 75 K7
Haora India 37 G5
Haparanda Sweden 14 N4
Happy Valley-Goose Bay Nfld. and Lab. Canada 61 L4
Ḩaql Saudi Arabia 39 B5
Ḩarad, Jabal al mt. Jordan 39 C5
Ḩaraḑ Saudi Arabia 32 G5
Haradok Belarus 13 F5
Ḩaraḑ watercourse Syria/Turkey see Ḩimār, Wādī al — no
Haramachi Japan 45 F5
Haramukh mt. India 36 C2
Haran Turkey see Harran

Harappa Road Pak. 36 C3
Harar Eth. see Härer
Harare Zimbabwe 49 D5
Ḩarāsīs, Jiddat al des. Oman 33 I6
Ḩarāt Iran 35 I5
Haraze-Mangueigne Chad 47 F3
Harbin China 44 B3
Harboi Hills Pak. 36 A3
Harchoka India 37 E5
Harda India 36 D5
Harda Khas India see Harda
Hardangerfjorden sea chan. Norway 15 D7
Hardangervidda plat. Norway 15 E6
Hardangervidda Nasjonalpark nat. park Norway 15 E6
Hardap admin. reg. Namibia 50 C3
Hardap Dam Namibia 50 C3
Hardap Recreation Resort nature res. Namibia 50 C3
Hardeveld mts S. Africa 50 D6
Hardin MT U.S.A. 62 F2
Harding S. Africa 51 I6
Harding Range hills Australia 55 B6
Hardisty Alta Canada 60 H4
Hardwar India see Haridwar
Hareiðin, Wādī watercourse Egypt see Ḩurayḑin, Wādī
Harf el Mreffi mt. Lebanon 39 B3
Hargeisa Somalia see Hargeysa
Hargele Eth. 48 E3
Hargeysa Somalia 48 E3
Harghita-Mădăraş, Vârful mt. Romania 27 K1
Harhorin Mongolia 42 I3
Har Hu l. China 42 H5
Haricha, Hamâda El des. Mali 46 C2
Haridwar India 36 D3
Harif, Har mt. Israel 39 B4
Harihar India 38 B3
Harihari N.Z. 59 C6
Hariharpur India 38 B3
Hārim Syria 39 C1
Harima-nada b. Japan 45 D6
Haringhat r. Bangl. 37 G5
Ḩarīr, Wādī adh r. Syria 39 C3
Ḩarī Rōd r. Afgh./Iran 33 J2
Harjavalta Fin. 15 M6
Harlech U.K. 19 C6
Harleston U.K. 19 I6
Harlow U.K. 19 H7
Harlowton MT U.S.A. 62 F2
Harman WV U.S.A. 64 B3
Harmancık Turkey 27 M5
Harmanli Bulg. 27 K4
Harnai India 38 B2
Harnai Pak. 36 A3
Harney Basin OR U.S.A. 62 C3
Härnösand Sweden 14 J5
Har Nuur l. Mongolia 42 H3
Haroldswick U.K. 20 [inset]
Harper Liberia 46 C4
Harper, Mount AK U.S.A. 60 D3
Harper Lake CA U.S.A. 65 D3
Harrai India 36 D5
Harran Turkey 39 D1
Harricana, Rivière d' r. Ont./Que. Canada 63 L1
Harrington Australia 58 F3
Harrington DE U.S.A. 64 D3
Harris, Lake imp. l. Australia 57 A6
Harris, Mount Australia 55 E6
Harrisburg PA U.S.A. 64 C2
Harrismith Australia 55 B8
Harrison AR U.S.A. 63 I4
Harrison, Cape Nfld. and Lab. Canada 61 M4
Harrison Bay AK U.S.A. 60 C2
Harrisonburg VA U.S.A. 64 B3
Harrisonville MO U.S.A. 63 I4
Harrisville PA U.S.A. 64 A2
Harrisville WV U.S.A. 64 A3
Harrodsville N.Z. see Otorohanga
Harrogate U.K. 18 F5
Har Sai Shan mt. China 37 I2
Harsin Iran 35 G4
Harşit r. Turkey 34 E2
Hârşova Romania 27 L2
Harstad Norway 14 J2
Harsud India 36 D5
Hart r. Y.T. Canada 60 E3
Hartbees watercourse S. Africa 50 E5
Hartberg Austria 17 O7
Harteigan mt. Norway 15 E6
Harter Fell h. U.K. 18 E4
Hartford CT U.S.A. 64 E2
Hartland U.K. 19 C8
Hartland Point U.K. 19 C7
Hartlepool U.K. 18 F4
Hartley Zimbabwe see Chegutu
Hartley Bay B.C. Canada 60 F4
Hartola Fin. 15 O6
Harts r. S. Africa 51 G5
Härtsfeld hills Germany 17 M6
Harts Range mts Australia 55 F5
Hartswater S. Africa 50 G4
Har Us Nuur l. Mongolia 42 G3
Harvey Australia 55 A8
Harvey ND U.S.A. 62 G2
Harwich U.K. 19 I7
Haryana state India 36 D3
Harz hills Germany 17 M5
Har Zin Israel 39 B4
Ḩaşāh, Wādī al watercourse Jordan 39 B4
Ḩaşāh, Wādī al watercourse Jordan/Saudi Arabia 39 B5
Hāsānabad Azer. 35 H3
Ḩasanah, Wādī watercourse Egypt 39 A4
Hasan Dağı mts Turkey 34 D3
Hasan Guli Turkm. see Esenguly
Hasankeyf Turkey 35 F3
Hasanur India 38 C4
Hasardag mt. Turkm. 35 J3
Hasbaiya Lebanon 39 B3
Hasbaya Lebanon see Hasbaïya
HaSharon plain Israel 39 B3
Hashtgerd Iran 35 H4
Hashtpar Iran see Tālesh
Hashtrūd Iran 35 H3
Haskovo Bulg. 27 K4
Haslemere U.K. 19 G7
Hăşmaşul Mare mt. Romania 27 K1
Ḩaşş, Jabal al hills Syria 39 C1
Hassan India 38 C3
Hasselt Belgium 16 J5
Hassi Bel Guebbour Alg. 46 D2
Hassi Messaoud Alg. 22 F5
Hässleholm Sweden 15 H8
Hastings r. Australia 58 F3
Hastings N.Z. 59 F4
Hastings U.K. 19 H8
Hastings NE U.S.A. 62 H3
Hata India 37 E4
Hatanbulag Mongolia 43 J4
Hatay Turkey see Antakya
Hatay prov. Turkey 39 C1
Hatch UT U.S.A. 65 F2

Hatches Creek (abandoned) Australia 56 A4
Hatfield Australia 58 A4
Hatfield U.K. 18 G5
Hatgal Mongolia 42 I2
Hath India 38 D1
Hat Head National Park Australia 58 F3
Hathras India 36 D4
Hatisar Bhutan see Geylegphug
Hatod India 36 C5
Hato Hud East Timor see Hatudo
Hatra Iraq 35 F4
Hattah Australia 57 C7
Hattah Kulkyne National Park Australia 57 C7
Hatteras, Cape NC U.S.A. 63 L4
Hatteras Abyssal Plain sea feature S. Atlantic Ocean 72 D4
Hattfjelldal Norway 14 H4
Hattiesburg MS U.S.A. 63 J5
Hatudo East Timor 54 D2
Hat Yai Thai. 31 J6
Haud reg. Eth. 48 E3
Hauge Norway 15 E7
Haugesund Norway 15 D7
Haukeligrend Norway 15 E7
Haukipudas Fin. 14 N4
Haukivesi l. Fin. 14 P5
Hauraki Gulf N.Z. 59 E3
Haut Atlas mts Morocco 22 C5
Haute-Normandie admin. reg. France 19 I9
Haute-Volta country Africa see Burkina Faso
Haut-Folin h. France 24 G3
Hauts Plateaux Alg. 22 D5
Havana Cuba 67 H4
Havant U.K. 19 G8
Havasu, Lake AZ/CA U.S.A. 65 E3
Havel r. Germany 17 M4
Havelock N.Z. 59 D5
Havelock Swaziland see Bulembu
Havelock Falls Australia 54 F3
Havelock North N.Z. 59 F4
Haverfordwest U.K. 19 C7
Haverhill MA U.S.A. 64 F1
Haveri India 38 B3
Havlíčkův Brod Czech Rep. 17 O6
Havøysund Norway 14 N1
Havran Turkey 27 L5
Havre MT U.S.A. 62 F2
Havre Rock i. Kermadec Is 53 I5
Havre-St-Pierre Que. Canada 63 O1
Havza Turkey 34 D2
Hawai'i i. HI U.S.A. 62 [inset]
Hawai'ian Islands N. Pacific Ocean 74 I4
Hawaiian Ridge sea feature N. Pacific Ocean 74 I4
Ḩawallī Kuwait 35 H5
Hawarden U.K. 18 D5
Hawea, Lake N.Z. 59 B7
Hawera N.Z. 59 E4
Hawes U.K. 18 E4
Hawick U.K. 20 G5
Ḩawīzah, Hawr al imp. l. Iraq 35 G5
Hawkdun Range mts N.Z. 59 B7
Hawke Bay N.Z. 59 F4
Hawkins Peak UT U.S.A. 65 F2
Hawlēr Iraq see Arbīl/Hewlêr
Hawley PA U.S.A. 64 D2
Ḩawrān, Wādī watercourse Iraq 35 F4
Hawston S. Africa 50 D8
Hawthorne NV U.S.A. 65 C1
Haxby U.K. 18 F4
Hay Australia 58 B5
Hay watercourse Australia 56 B5
Hay r. Alta/N.W.T. Canada 60 G3
Hayachine-san mt. Japan 45 F5
Hayastan country Asia see Armenia
Haydān, Wādī al r. Jordan 39 B4
Hayes r. Nunavut Canada 61 I3
Hayes Halvø pen. Greenland 61 L2
Hayfield Reservoir CA U.S.A. 65 E4
Hayl, Wādī watercourse Syria 39 C3
Hayl, Wādī al watercourse Syria 39 D2
Hayle U.K. 19 B8
Haymā' Oman 33 I6
Haymana Turkey 34 D3
Haymarket VA U.S.A. 64 C3
Hay-on-Wye U.K. 19 D6
Hayrabolu Turkey 27 L4
Hay River N.W.T. Canada 60 G3
Hays KS U.S.A. 62 H4
Hays Yemen 32 F7
Haysyn Ukr. 13 F6
Ḩayţān, Jabal h. Egypt 39 A4
Hayward CA U.S.A. 65 A2
Haywards Heath U.K. 19 G8
Hazar Turkm. 35 I3
Hazaribag India see Hazaribagh
Hazaribagh India 37 F5
Hazaribagh Range mts India 37 E5
Hazār Masjed, Kūh-e mts Iran 33 I2
Hazelton B.C. Canada 60 F4
Hazen Strait N.W.T./Nunavut Canada 61 G2
Hazleton PA U.S.A. 64 D2
Hazlett, Lake imp. l. Australia 54 E5
Ḩazm al Jawf Yemen 32 F6
Ḩazrat-e Sulţān Afgh. 36 A1
H. Bouchard Arg. 70 D4
Headford Ireland 21 C4
Headingly Australia 56 B4
Head of Bight b. Australia 55 E7
Healdsburg CA U.S.A. 65 A1
Healesville Australia 58 B6
Healy AK U.S.A. 60 D3
Heanor U.K. 19 F5
Heard Island Indian Ocean 73 M9
Heard Island and McDonald Islands terr. Indian Ocean 73 M9
Hearst Ont. Canada 63 K2
Hearst Island Antarctica 76 L2
Heart of Neolithic Orkney tourist site U.K. 20 F1
Heathcote Australia 58 B6
Heathfield U.K. 19 H8
Heathsville VA U.S.A. 64 C4
Hebei prov. China 43 L5
Hebel Australia 58 C2
Heber City UT U.S.A. 62 E3
Hebron Nfld. and Lab. Canada 61 L4
Hebron West Bank 39 B4
Hecate Strait B.C. Canada 60 E4
Hechi China 43 J8
Hede Sweden 14 H5
Hedemora Sweden 15 I6
Ḩefa Israel see Haifa
Ḩefa, Mifraz Israel see Haifa, Bay of
Hefei China 43 L6
Hegang China 44 C3
Heidan r. Jordan see Haydān, Wādī al
Heide Germany 17 L3
Heide Namibia 50 C2
Heidelberg Germany 17 L6
Heidelberg S. Africa 51 I4
Heihe China 44 B2
Heilbron S. Africa 51 H4
Heilbronn Germany 17 L6
Heiligenhafen Germany 17 M3
Heilongjiang prov. China 44 C3
Heilong Jiang r. China 44 F1
Heilong Jiang r. China/Russia 40 F3
Heilungkiang prov. China see Heilongjiang
Heinola Fin. 15 O6
Heirnkut Myanmar 37 H4
Heishi Beihu l. China 37 E2
Heisker Islands U.K. see Monach Islands
Heiţān, Gebel h. Egypt see Ḩayţān, Jabal
Hejaz reg. Saudi Arabia see Hijaz
Hekimhan Turkey 34 E3
Hekla vol. Iceland 14 [inset 2]
Hekou China 42 I5
Helagsfjället mt. Sweden 14 H5
Helan Shan mts China 42 J5
Helena MT U.S.A. 62 E2
Helensburgh U.K. 20 E4
Helen Springs Australia 54 F4
Ḩelez Israel 39 B4
Helgoland i. Germany 17 K3
Helgoländer Bucht g. Germany 17 L3
Heligoland i. Germany see Helgoland
Heligoland Bight g. Germany see Helgoländer Bucht
Heliopolis Lebanon see Ba'albek
Helixi China see Ningguo
Hella Iceland 14 [inset 2]
Helland Norway 14 J2
Hellas country Europe see Greece
Helleh r. Iran 35 H5
Hellespont str. Turkey see Dardanelles
Hellhole Gorge National Park Australia 56 D5
Hellín Spain 25 F4
Hellinikon tourist site Greece 34 A3
Hell-Ville Madag. see Andoany
Helmand r. Afgh. 36 A2
Helmantica Spain see Salamanca
Helmeringhausen Namibia 50 C3
Helmond Neth. 17 J5
Helmsdale U.K. 20 F2
Helmsdale r. U.K. 20 F2
Helmstedt Germany 17 M4
Helong China 44 C4
Helsingborg Sweden 15 H8
Helsingfors Fin. see Helsinki
Helsingør Denmark 15 H8
Helsinki Fin. 15 N6
Helston U.K. 19 B8
Helvécia Brazil 71 D2
Helvetic Republic country Europe see Switzerland
Helwân Egypt see Ḩulwān
Hemel Hempstead U.K. 19 G7
Hemet CA U.S.A. 65 D4
Hemlock Lake NY U.S.A. 64 C1
Hemsby U.K. 19 I6
Hemse Sweden 15 K8
Henan prov. China 43 K6
Henares r. Spain 25 E3
Henashi-zaki pt Japan 45 E4
Henbury Australia 55 F6
Hendek Turkey 27 N4
Henderson NC U.S.A. 63 L4
Henderson NV U.S.A. 65 E2
Henderson TX U.S.A. 63 I5
Henderson Island Pitcairn Is 75 L7
Henderville atoll Kiribati see Aranuka
Hendon U.K. 19 G7
Hendorābī, Jazīreh-ye i. Iran 35 I6
Hendy-Gwyn U.K. see Whitland
Hengduan Shan mts China 42 H7
Hengelo Neth. 17 K4
Hengnan China see Hengyang
Hengshan China 44 C3
Hengshui China 43 L5
Hengxian China 43 J8
Hengyang China 43 K7
Hengzhou China see Hengxian
Heniches'k Ukr. 13 G7
Henley N.Z. 59 C7
Henley-on-Thames U.K. 19 G7
Henlopen, Cape DE U.S.A. 64 D3
Hennenman S. Africa 51 H4
Henniker NH U.S.A. 64 F1
Henrietta Maria, Cape Ont. Canada 61 J4
Henrique de Carvalho Angola see Saurimo
Henry, Cape NC U.S.A. 64 C4
Henry Ice Rise Antarctica 76 A1
Henryk Arctowski research stn Antarctica see Arctowski
Henry Kater, Cape Nunavut Canada 61 L3
Hensall Ont. Canada 64 A1
Henshaw, Lake CA U.S.A. 65 D4
Henteyn Nuruu mts Mongolia 43 J3
Hentiesbaai Namibia 50 B2
Henty Australia 58 C5
Henzada Myanmar see Hinthada
Heptanesus is Greece see Ionian Islands
Heraclea Turkey see Ereğli
Heraclea Pontica Turkey see Ereğli
Heraklion Greece see Iraklion
Herald Cays atolls Australia 56 E3
Herāt Afgh. 33 J3
Hérault r. France 24 F5
Herbert Downs Australia 56 B4
Herbert River Falls National Park Australia 56 D3
Herbert Wash imp. l. Australia 55 D6
Hercules Dome Antarctica 76 K1
Hereford U.K. 19 E6
Hereford TX U.S.A. 62 G5
Hereheretue atoll Fr. Polynesia 75 K7
Herford Germany 17 L4
Herīs Iran 35 G3
Herisau Switz. 24 I3
Herkimer NY U.S.A. 64 D1
Herlen Gol r. China/Mongolia 43 L3
Herlen He r. China/Mongolia see Herlen Gol
Herm i. Channel Is 19 E9
Herma Ness hd U.K. 20 [inset]
Hermanus S. Africa 50 D8
Hermel Lebanon 39 C2
Hermes, Cape S. Africa 51 I6
Hermidale Australia 58 C3
Hermite, Islas is Chile 70 C9
Hermit Islands P.N.G. 52 E2
Hermon, Mount Lebanon/Syria 39 B3
Hermonthis Egypt see Armant
Hermopolis Magna Egypt see Al Ashmūnayn
Hermosillo Mex. 66 B3
Hernandarias Para. 70 F3
Herndon CA U.S.A. 65 C2
Herndon PA U.S.A. 64 C2
Herndon WV U.S.A. 64 A4
Herne Bay U.K. 19 I7
Herning Denmark 15 F8
Heroica Nogales Mex. see Nogales
Heroica Puebla de Zaragoza Mex. see Puebla
Hérouville-St-Clair France 19 G9
Herowābād Iran see Khalkhāl
Herrera del Duque Spain 25 D4
Hershey PA U.S.A. 64 C2
Hertford U.K. 19 G7
Hertzogville S. Africa 51 G5
Hervey Islands Cook Is 75 J7
Herzliyya Israel 39 B3
Heşār Būshehr Iran 35 H5
Heşār Zanjān Iran 35 H3
Heshan China 43 J8
Hesperia CA U.S.A. 65 D3
Hesselberg h. Germany 17 M6
Hetton U.K. 18 E4
Hettstedt Germany 17 M5
Hève, Cap de la c. France 19 H9
Hevron West Bank see Hebron
Hexham U.K. 18 E4
Hexian China see Hezhou
Heydebreck Poland see Kędzierzyn-Koźle
Heysham U.K. 18 E4
Heyshope Dam S. Africa 51 J4
Heywood U.K. 18 E5
Heze China 43 L5
Hezhou China 43 K8
Hezuo China 42 I5
Hezuozhen China see Hezuo
Hibbing MN U.S.A. 63 I2
Hibbs, Point Australia 57 [inset]
Hibernia Reef Australia 54 C3
Hicks, Point Australia 58 D6
Hicks Bay N.Z. 59 G3
Hidaka Japan 44 F4
Hidaka-sanmyaku mts Japan 44 F4
Hidalgo Mex. 62 H7
Hidalgo del Parral Mex. 66 C3
Hidrolândia Brazil 71 A2
Hierosolyma Israel/West Bank see Jerusalem
Higashi-suidō str. Japan 45 C6
Higgins Bay NY U.S.A. 64 D1
High Atlas mts Morocco see Haut Atlas
High Desert OR U.S.A. 62 C3
Highland Peak CA U.S.A. 65 C1
Highland Peak NV U.S.A. 65 E2
Highlands NJ U.S.A. 64 E2
Highland Springs VA U.S.A. 64 C4
High Level Alta Canada 60 G4
High Point NC U.S.A. 63 L4
High Point h. NJ U.S.A. 64 D2
High Prairie Alta Canada 60 G4
High River Alta Canada 62 E1
High Tatras mts Poland/Slovakia see Tatra Mountains
High Wycombe U.K. 19 G7
Higüey Dom. Rep. 67 K5
Hiiumaa i. Estonia 15 M7
Hijānah, Buḩayrat al salt pan Syria 39 C3
Hijaz reg. Saudi Arabia 32 E4
Ḩikmah, Ra's al pt Egypt 34 B5
Hiko NV U.S.A. 65 E2
Hikone Japan 45 E6
Hikurangi mt. N.Z. 59 G3
Hila Indon. 54 D1
Hilāl, Jabal h. Egypt 39 A4
Hilāl, Ra's al pt Libya 32 B3
Hilary Coast Antarctica 76 H1
Hildale UT U.S.A. 65 F2
Hildesheim Germany 17 L4
Hillah Iraq 35 G4
Hill End Australia 58 D4
Hillerød Denmark 15 H9
Hillgrove Australia 56 D3
Hillside Australia 54 B5
Hillston Australia 58 B4
Hilton Australia 56 B4
Hilton S. Africa 51 J5
Hilton NY U.S.A. 64 C1
Hilton Head Island SC U.S.A. 63 K5
Hilvan Turkey 34 E3
Hilversum Neth. 16 J4
Himachal Pradesh state India 36 D3
Himalaya mts Asia 36 D2
Himalchul mt. Nepal 37 F3
Himanka Fin. 14 M4
Ḩimār, Wādī al watercourse Syria/Turkey 39 D1
Himarë Albania 27 H4
Himatnagar India 36 C5
Himeji Japan 45 D6
Ḩimş Syria see Homs
Ḩimş, Baḩrat resr Syria see Qaţţīnah, Buḩayrat
Hinchinbrook Island Australia 56 D3
Hinckley U.K. 19 F6
Hinckley Reservoir NY U.S.A. 64 D1
Hindaun India 36 D4
Hinderwell U.K. 18 G4
Hindley U.K. 18 E5
Hindmarsh, Lake dry lake Australia 57 C8
Hindu Kush mts Afgh./Pak. 33 K3
Hindupur India 38 C3
Hinesville GA U.S.A. 63 K5
Hinganghat India 38 C1
Hingoli India 38 C2
Hınıs Turkey 35 F3
Hinnøya i. Norway 14 I2
Hinojosa del Duque Spain 25 D4
Hinsdale NH U.S.A. 64 E1
Hinthada Myanmar 42 H9
Hinton WV U.S.A. 64 A4
Hiort i. U.K. see St Kilda
Hipponium Italy see Vibo Valentia
Hippo Regius Alg. see Annaba
Hippo Zarytus Tunisia see Bizerte
Hirabit Dağ mt. Turkey 35 G3
Hiraizumi tourist site Japan 45 F5
Hirakud Dam India 37 E5
Hirakud Reservoir India 37 E5
Hirapur India 36 D4
Hiriyur India 38 C3
Hirosaki Japan 44 F4
Hiroshima Japan 45 D6
Hirschberg mt. Germany 17 M7
Hirschberg Poland see Jelenia Góra
Hirson France 24 G2
Hîrşova Romania see Hârşova
Hirta is U.K. see St Kilda
Hirtshals Denmark 15 F8
Hisar India 36 C3
Hisarköy Turkey see Domaniç
Hisarönü Turkey 27 O4
Ḩisb, Sha'īb watercourse Iraq 35 G5
Ḩisbān Jordan 39 B4
Hisor Tizmasi mts Tajik./Uzbek. see Gissar Range
Hispalis Spain see Seville
Hispania country Europe see Spain
Hispaniola i. Caribbean Sea 67 J4
Hispur Glacier Pak. 36 C1
Hissar India see Hisar
Hisua India 37 F4
Ḩisyah Syria 39 C2
Hīt Iraq 35 F4
Hitachi Japan 45 F5
Hitachinaka Japan 45 F5
Hitra i. Norway 14 F5
Hiva Oa i. Fr. Polynesia 75 K6
Hixson Cay reef Australia 56 F4
Hiyyon, Naḩal watercourse Israel 39 B4
Hizan Turkey 35 F3
Hjälmaren l. Sweden 15 I7
Hjerkinn Norway 14 F5
Hjo Sweden 15 I7
Hjørring Denmark 15 G8
Hkakabo Razi mt. China/Myanmar 42 H7
Hlaingdet Myanmar 37 I5
Hlane Royal National Park Swaziland 51 J4
Hlatikulu Swaziland 51 J4
Hlohlowane S. Africa 51 H5
Hlotse Lesotho 51 I5
Hluhluwe-Umfolozi Park nature res. S. Africa 51 J5
Hlukhiv Ukr. 13 G6
Hlusha Belarus 13 F5
Hlybokaye Belarus 15 O9
Ho Ghana 46 D4
Hoachanas Namibia 50 D2
Hoang Sa is S. China Sea see Paracel Islands
Hobart Australia 57 [inset]
Hobart OK U.S.A. 62 H4
Hobbs NM U.S.A. 62 G5
Hobbs Coast Antarctica 76 J1
Hobiganj Bangl. see Habiganj
Hobro Denmark 15 F8
Hobyo Somalia 48 E3
Hochfeiler mt. Austria/Italy see Gran Pilastro
Hochfeld Namibia 49 B6
Hô Chi Minh Vietnam see Ho Chi Minh City
Ho Chi Minh City Vietnam 31 J5
Hochschwab mt. Austria 17 O7
Hochschwab mts Austria 17 O7
Hôd reg. Mauritania 46 C3
Hoddesdon U.K. 19 G7
Hodeidah Yemen 32 F7
Hodgson Downs Australia 54 F3
Hódmezővásárhely Hungary 27 I1
Hodna, Chott el salt l. Alg. 25 I6
Hodo-dan pt N. Korea 45 B5
Hoeryŏng N. Korea 44 C4
Hof Germany 17 M5
Hofmeyr S. Africa 51 G6
Höfn Iceland 14 [inset 2]
Hofors Sweden 15 J6
Hofsjökull Iceland 14 [inset 2]
Hofsós Iceland 14 [inset 2]
Hōfu Japan 45 C6
Höganäs Sweden 15 H8
Hogan Group is Australia 58 C7
Hoggar plat. Alg. see Ahaggar
Hog Island VA U.S.A. 64 D4
Högsby Sweden 15 J8
Hohensalza Poland see Inowrocław
Hoher Dachstein mt. Austria 17 N7
Hohe Tauern mts Austria 17 N7
Hohhot China 43 K4
Höhmorït Mongolia 42 G3
Hohneck mt. France 24 H2
Hoh Sai Hu l. China 37 H2
Hoh Xil Hu salt l. China 37 G2
Hoh Xil Shan mts China 37 G2
Hoima Uganda 48 D3
Hojagala Turkm. 35 J3
Hojai India 37 H4
Højryggen mts Greenland 61 M2
Hokitika N.Z. 59 C6
Hokkaidō i. Japan 44 F4
Hokksund Norway 15 F7
Hol Norway 15 F6
Holbæk Denmark 15 G9
Holbeach U.K. 19 H6
Holbrook Australia 58 C5
Holbrook AZ U.S.A. 62 E5
Holden UT U.S.A. 65 F1
Holdrege NE U.S.A. 62 H3
Holguín Cuba 67 I4
Holin He r. China 44 B3
Höljes Sweden 15 H6
Holland country Europe see Netherlands
Holland NY U.S.A. 64 B1
Hollandia Indon. see Jayapura
Hollick-Kenyon Peninsula Antarctica 76 L2
Hollick-Kenyon Plateau Antarctica 76 K1
Hollidaysburg PA U.S.A. 64 B2
Hollister CA U.S.A. 65 B2
Holly Springs MS U.S.A. 63 J5
Hollywood CA U.S.A. 65 C4
Hollywood FL U.S.A. 63 K6
Holm Norway 14 H4
Holmes Reef Australia 56 D3
Holmes Summit Antarctica 76 B1
Holmestrand Norway 15 G7
Holmgard Russia see Velikiy Novgorod
Holm Ø i. Greenland see Kiatassuaq
Holmön i. Sweden 14 L5
Holmsund Sweden 14 L5
Ḩolon Israel 39 B3
Holoog Namibia 50 C4
Holothuria Banks reef Australia 54 D3
Holroyd r. Australia 56 C2
Holstebro Denmark 15 F8
Holsteinsborg Greenland see Sisimiut
Holston r. TN U.S.A. 63 K4
Holsworthy U.K. 19 C8
Holt U.K. 19 I6
Holycross Ireland 21 E5
Holy Cross AK U.S.A. 60 C3
Holyhead U.K. 18 C5
Holyhead Bay U.K. 18 C5
Holy Island England U.K. 18 F3
Holy Island Wales U.K. 18 C5
Holyoke CO U.S.A. 62 G3
Holy See Europe see Vatican City
Holywell U.K. 18 D5
Holzkirchen Germany 17 M7
Homāyūnshahr Iran see Khomeynīshahr
Hombori Mali 46 C3
Home Bay Nunavut Canada 61 L3
Homer NY U.S.A. 64 C1
Homestead Australia 56 D4
Homnabad India 38 C2
Homoine Moz. 51 L2
Homs Libya see Al Khums
Homs Syria 39 C2
Homyel' Belarus 13 F5
Honan prov. China see Henan
Honavar India 38 B3
Honawad India 38 B2
Honaz Turkey 27 M6
Hondeklipbaai S. Africa 50 C6
Hondo TX U.S.A. 62 H6
Honduras country Central America 67 G6
Hønefoss Norway 15 G6
Honesdale PA U.S.A. 64 D2
Honey Lake salt l. CA U.S.A. 62 C3
Honeyoye Lake NY U.S.A. 64 C1
Honfleur France 24 E2
Hông, Sông r. Vietnam see Red
Honghe Hani Rice Terraces tourist site China 42 I8
Hongjiang China 43 J7
Hong Kong H.K. China 43 K8
Hong Kong aut. reg. China 43 K8
Hongliuwan China see Aksay
Hongliuyuan China 42 H4
Hongshilazi China 44 B4
Hongwŏn N. Korea 45 B4
Hongxing China 44 A3
Hongze Hu l. China 43 L6
Honiara Solomon Is 53 F2
Honiton U.K. 19 D8
Honkajoki Fin. 15 M6
Honningsvåg Norway 14 N1
Honolulu HI U.S.A. 62 [inset]
Honshū i. Japan 45 D6
Hood, Mount vol. OR U.S.A. 62 C2
Hood Point Australia 55 B8
Hood Point P.N.G. 56 D1
Hoogeveen Neth. 17 K4
Hooghly r. mouth India see Hugli
Hook Head hd Ireland 21 F5
Hook Reef Australia 56 E3
Hooper Bay AK U.S.A. 77 B2
Hooper Island MD U.S.A. 64 C3
Hoopstad S. Africa 51 G4
Höör Sweden 15 H9
Hoorn Neth. 16 J4
Hoosick NY U.S.A. 64 E1
Hoover Dam AZ/NV U.S.A. 65 E2
Hopa Turkey 35 F2
Hope B.C. Canada 62 C2
Hope r. N.Z. 59 D6
Hope AR U.S.A. 63 I5
Hope, Lake imp. l. Australia 55 C8
Hope, Point AK U.S.A. 60 B3
Hopedale Nfld. and Lab. Canada 61 L4
Hopefield S. Africa 50 D7
Hopei prov. China see Hebei
Hope Saddle pass N.Z. 59 D5
Hopes Advance, Cap c. Que. Canada 61 L3
Hopetoun Australia 57 C7
Hopetown S. Africa 50 G5
Hopewell VA U.S.A. 64 C4
Hopewell Islands Nunavut Canada 61 K4
Hopkins r. Australia 57 C8
Hopkins, Lake imp. l. Australia 55 E6
Hopkinsville KY U.S.A. 63 J4
Hopland CA U.S.A. 65 A1
Horasan Turkey 35 F2
Hörby Sweden 15 H9
Horizon Deep sea feature S. Pacific Ocean 74 I7
Horki Belarus 13 F5
Horlick Mountains Antarctica 76 K1
Horlivka Ukr. 13 H6
Hormuz, Strait of Iran/Oman 33 I4
Horn Austria 17 O6
Horn c. Iceland 14 [inset 2]
Horn, Cape Chile 70 C9
Horn, Îles de is Wallis and Futuna Is 53 I3
Hornavan l. Sweden 14 J3
Horncastle U.K. 18 G5
Horndal Sweden 15 J6
Horne, Îles de is Wallis and Futuna Is see Horn, Îles de
Hörnefors Sweden 14 K5
Hornell NY U.S.A. 64 C1
Hornepayne Ont. Canada 63 K2
Hornisgrinde mt. Germany 17 L6
Hornkranz Namibia 50 C2
Hornos, Cabo de Chile see Horn, Cape
Hornsby Australia 58 E4
Hornsea U.K. 18 G5
Hornslandet pen. Sweden 15 J6
Horodenka Ukr. 13 E6
Horodnya Ukr. 13 F6
Horodok Khmel'nyts'ka Oblast' Ukr. 13 E6
Horodok L'vivs'ka Oblast' Ukr. 13 D6
Horokanai Japan 44 F3
Horoshiri-dake mt. Japan 44 F4
Horqin Youyi Qianqi China see Ulanhot
Horqin Zuoyi Houqi China see Ganjig
Horqin Zuoyi Zhongqi China see Baokang
Horrabridge U.K. 19 C8
Horrocks Australia 55 A7
Horru China 37 G3
Horseheads NY U.S.A. 64 C1
Horseleap Ireland 21 D4
Horsens Denmark 15 F9
Horseshoe Bend Australia 55 F6
Horseshoe Seamounts sea feature N. Atlantic Ocean 72 G3
Horsham Australia 57 C8
Horsham U.K. 19 G7
Horten Norway 15 G7
Hortobágyi nat. park Hungary 27 I1
Horton r. N.W.T. Canada 60 F3
Ḩoseynābād Iran 35 G4
Ḩoseynīyeh Iran 35 H5
Hoshangabad India 36 D5
Hoshiarpur India 36 C3
Hospet India 38 C3
Hospital Ireland 21 D5
Hotagen r. Sweden 14 I5
Hotahudo East Timor see Hatudo
Hotan China 36 E1
Hotazel S. Africa 50 F4
Hot Creek Range mts NV U.S.A. 65 D1
Hotgi India 38 C2
Hotham r. Australia 55 B8
Hoting Sweden 14 J4
Hot Springs AR U.S.A. 63 I5
Hot Springs NM U.S.A. see Truth or Consequences
Hot Springs SD U.S.A. 62 G3
Hottah Lake N.W.T. Canada 60 G3
Hottentots Bay Namibia 50 B4
Hottentots Point Namibia 50 B4
Houayxay Laos 42 I8
Houghton MI U.S.A. 63 J2
Houghton NY U.S.A. 64 B1
Houghton le Spring U.K. 18 F4
Houma China 43 K5
Houma LA U.S.A. 63 I6
Houston TX U.S.A. 63 H6
Houtman Abrolhos is Australia 55 A7
Houton U.K. 20 F2
Houwater S. Africa 50 F6
Hovd Mongolia 42 G3
Hove U.K. 19 G8
Hoveton U.K. 19 I6
Hovmantorp Sweden 15 I8
Hövsgöl Nuur l. Mongolia 42 I2
Howar, Wadi watercourse Sudan 32 C6
Howard Australia 56 F5
Howard PA U.S.A. 64 C2
Howden U.K. 18 G5
Howe, Cape Australia 58 D6
Howe, Mount Antarctica 76 J1
Howick S. Africa 51 J5
Howland Island terr. N. Pacific Ocean 53 I1
Howlong Australia 58 C5
Howrah India see Haora
Howth Ireland 21 F4
Howz i-Mian i-Tak Iran 35 I4
Höxter Germany 17 L5
Hoy i. U.K. 20 F2
Høyanger Norway 15 E6
Hoyerswerda Germany 17 O5
Høylandet Norway 14 H4
Höytiäinen l. Fin. 14 P5
Hpapun Myanmar 42 H9
Hpungan Pass India/Myanmar 37 I4
Hradec Králové Czech Rep. 17 O5
Hrasnica Bos. & Herz. 26 H3
Hrazdan Armenia 35 G2
Hrebinka Ukr. 13 G6
Hrodna Belarus 15 M10
Hrvatska country Europe see Croatia
Hrvatsko Grahovo Bos. & Herz. see Bosansko Grahovo
Hsiang Kang H.K. China see Hong Kong
Hsin-chia-p'o country Asia see Singapore
Hsin-chia-p'o Sing. see Singapore
Hsinchu Taiwan see Xinzhu
Hsinking China see Changchun
Hsipaw Myanmar 42 H8
Hsi-sha Ch'ün-tao is S. China Sea see Paracel Islands
Huab watercourse Namibia 49 B6
Huacho Peru 68 C6
Huachuan China 44 C3
Huade China 43 K4
Huadian China 44 B4
Huai'an China 43 L6
Huaibei China 43 L6
Huaide China 44 B4
Huaihua China 43 J7
Huailillas mt. Peru 68 C5
Huainan China 43 L6
Huaiyin China see Huai'an
Huajialing China 42 I5
Huajuápan de León Mex. 66 E5
Hualapai Peak AZ U.S.A. 65 F3
Hualian Taiwan 43 M8
Hualien Taiwan see Hualian
Huallaga r. Peru 68 C5
Huambo Angola 49 B5
Huanan China 44 C3
Huancane Peru 68 E7
Huancavelica Peru 68 C6
Huancayo Peru 68 C6
Huangcaoba China see Xingyi
Huangchuan China 43 L6
Huang Hai sea N. Pacific Ocean see Yellow Sea
Huang He r. China see Yellow
Huangshan China 43 L7
Huangshi China 43 L6
Huangtu Gaoyuan plat. China 43 J5
Huanren China 44 B4
Huánuco Peru 68 C5
Huaraz Peru 68 C5
Huarmey Peru 68 C6
Huascarán, Nevado de mt. Peru 68 C5
Huasco Chile 70 B3
Huashugou China see Sanchakou
Huashulinzi China 44 B4
Huatabampo Mex. 66 C3
Huazangsi China see Tianzhu
Hubballi India see Hubli
Hubei prov. China 43 K6
Hubli India 38 B3
Hucknall U.K. 19 F5
Huddersfield U.K. 18 F5
Huder China 44 A2
Hudiksvall Sweden 15 J6
Hudson MA U.S.A. 64 F1
Hudson MD U.S.A. 64 C3
Hudson NY U.S.A. 64 E1
Hudson r. NY U.S.A. 64 E2
Hudson, Baie d' sea Canada see Hudson Bay
Hudson, Détroit d' str. Nunavut/Que. Canada see Hudson Strait
Hudson Bay Sask. Canada 62 G1
Hudson Bay sea Canada 61 J4
Hudson Falls NY U.S.A. 64 E1
Hudson Island Tuvalu see Nanumanga
Hudson Mountains Antarctica 76 K2
Hudson Strait Nunavut/Que. Canada 61 K3
Huê Vietnam 31 J5
Huehuetenango Guat. 66 F5
Huehueto, Cerro mt. Mex. 66 C4
Huelva Spain 25 C5
Huentelauquén Chile 70 B4
Huércal-Overa Spain 25 F5
Huesca Spain 25 F2
Huéscar Spain 25 E5
Hughenden Australia 56 D4
Hughes (abandoned) Australia 55 E7
Hughson CA U.S.A. 65 B2
Hugli r. mouth India 37 F5
Hugli-Chinsurah India 37 G5
Hugo OK U.S.A. 63 H5
Huhehot China see Hohhot
Huhhot China see Hohhot
Huhudi S. Africa 50 G4
Hui'anpu China 42 J5
Huiarau Range mts N.Z. 59 F4
Huib-Hoch Plateau Namibia 50 C4
Huila, Nevado de vol. Col. 68 C3
Huíla, Planalto da Angola 49 B5
Huili China 42 I7
Huimanguillo Mex. 66 F5
Huiten Nur l. China 37 G2
Huittinen Fin. 15 M6
Huiyang China see Huizhou
Huize China 42 I7
Huizhou China 43 K8
Hujr Saudi Arabia 32 F4
Hukawng Valley Myanmar 37 I4
Hukuntsi Botswana 50 E2
Hulan China 44 B3
Hulan Ergi China 44 A3
Ḩulayfah Saudi Arabia 32 F4
Ḩulayḩilah well Syria 39 D2
Hulin China 44 D3
Hull Que. Canada 63 L2
Hull U.K. see Kingston upon Hull
Hull Island atoll Kiribati see Orona
Hultsfred Sweden 15 I8
Hulun China see Hulun Buir
Hulun Buir China 43 L3
Hulun Nur l. China 43 L3
Ḩulwān Egypt 34 C5
Huma China 44 B2
Humahuaca Arg. 70 C2
Humaitá Brazil 68 F5
Humber, Mouth of the U.K. 18 H5
Humboldt Sask. Canada 62 F1
Humboldt r. NV U.S.A. 60 G5
Humeburn Australia 58 B1
Hume Reservoir Australia 58 C5
Humphrey Island atoll Cook Is see Manihiki
Humphreys, Mount CA U.S.A. 65 C2
Humphreys Peak AZ U.S.A. 62 E4
Hūn Libya 47 E2
Húnaflói b. Iceland 14 [inset 2]
Hunan prov. China 43 K7
Hunedoara Romania 27 J2
Hungary country Europe 23 H2
Hungerford Australia 58 B2
Hŭngnam N. Korea 45 B5
Hunjiang China see Baishan
Huns Mountains Namibia 50 C4
Hunstanton U.K. 19 H6
Hunte r. Germany 17 L4
Hunter r. Australia 58 E4
Hunter Island Australia 57 [inset]
Hunter Island S. Pacific Ocean 53 H4
Hunter Islands Australia 57 [inset]
Huntingdon U.K. 19 G6
Huntingdon PA U.S.A. 64 C2
Huntington IN U.S.A. 63 J3
Huntington WV U.S.A. 63 K4
Huntington Beach CA U.S.A. 65 C4
Huntly N.Z. 59 E3
Huntly U.K. 20 G3
Huntsville Ont. Canada 63 L2
Huntsville AL U.S.A. 63 J5
Huntsville TX U.S.A. 63 H5
Hunza reg. Pak. 36 C1
Huolin He r. China see Holin He
Huolongmen China 44 B2
Huonville Australia 57 [inset]
Hupeh prov. China see Hubei
Hupnik r. Turkey 39 C1
Ḩuraydīn, Wādī watercourse Egypt 39 A4
Hurd Island Kiribati see Arorae
Hüren Tovon Uul mt. Mongolia 42 H4
Hurghada Egypt see Al Ghurdaqah
Hurler's Cross Ireland 21 D5
Huron CA U.S.A. 65 B2
Huron SD U.S.A. 62 H3
Huron, Lake Canada/U.S.A. 64 A1
Hurricane UT U.S.A. 65 F2

Kalmytskaya Avtonomnaya Oblast' aut. rep. Russia see Kalmykiya-Khalm'g-Tangch, Respublika
Kalnai India 37 E5
Kalodnaye Belarus 15 O11
Kalol India 36 C5
Kalomo Zambia 49 C5
Kalone Peak B.C. Canada 60 F4
Kalpa India 36 D3
Kalpeni atoll India 38 B4
Kalpetta India 38 C4
Kalpi India 36 D4
Kaltag AK U.S.A. 60 C3
Kaltukatjara Australia 55 E6
Kaluga Russia 13 H5
Kalundborg Denmark 15 G9
Kalush Ukr. 13 E6
Kalvakol India 38 C2
Kälviä Fin. 14 M5
Kal'ya Russia 11 R3
Kalyan India 38 B2
Kalyandurg India 33 M7
Kalyansingapuram India 38 D2
Kalyazin Russia 12 H4
Kalymnos i. Greece 27 L6
Kama Dem. Rep. Congo 48 C4
Kama r. Russia 12 L4
Kamaishi Japan 45 F5
Kamalamai Nepal 37 F4
Kamalia Pak. 36 C3
Kaman Turkey 34 D3
Kamanjab Namibia 49 B5
Kamarān i. Yemen 32 F6
Kamaran Island Yemen see Kamarān
Kamaron Sierra Leone 46 B4
Kamasin India 36 E4
Kambalda Australia 55 C7
Kambam India 38 C4
Kambara i. Fiji see Kabara
Kambia Sierra Leone 46 B4
Kambing, Pulau i. East Timor see Ataúro, Ilha de
Kambo-san mt. N. Korea see Kwanmo-bong
Kambove Dem. Rep. Congo 49 C5
Kambūt Libya 34 B5
Kamchatka, Poluostrov pen. Russia see Kamchatka Peninsula
Kamchatka Basin sea feature Bering Sea 74 H2
Kamchatka Peninsula Russia 29 Q4
Kamchia r. Bulg. 27 L3
Kameia, Parque Nacional de nat. park Angola see Cameia, Parque Nacional da
Kamelik r. Russia 13 K5
Kamen', Gory mts Russia 28 K3
Kamenets-Podol'skiy Ukr. see Kam"yanets'-Podil's'kyy
Kamenitsa mt. Bulg. 27 J4
Kamenjak, Rt pt Croatia 26 E2
Kamenka Arkhangel'skaya Oblast' Russia 12 J2
Kamenka Penzenskaya Oblast' Russia 13 J5
Kamenka Primorskiy Kray Russia 44 E3
Kamenka-Bugskaya Ukr. see Kam"yanka-Buz'ka
Kamenka-Strumilovskaya Ukr. see Kam"yanka-Buz'ka
Kamen'-na-Obi Russia 42 E2
Kamennogorsk Russia 15 P6
Kamennomostskiy Russia 35 F1
Kamenolomni Russia 13 I7
Kamenongue Angola see Camanongue
Kamen'-Rybolov Russia 44 D3
Kamenskoye Russia 29 R3
Kamenskoye Ukr. see Dniprodzerzhyns'k
Kamensk-Shakhtinskiy Russia 13 I6
Kamensk-Ural'skiy Russia 28 H4
Kamet mt. China 36 D3
Kamiesberge mts S. Africa 50 D6
Kamieskroon S. Africa 50 C6
Kamileroi Australia 56 C3
Kamina Dem. Rep. Congo 49 C4
Kaminak Lake Nunavut Canada 61 I3
Kaminuriak Lake Nunavut Canada see Qamanirjuaq Lake
Kamishihoro Japan 44 F4
Kamloops B.C. Canada 62 C1
Kamo Armenia see Gavarr
Kamoke Pak. 36 C3
Kamonia Dem. Rep. Congo 49 C4
Kampala Uganda 48 D3
Kampara India 38 D1
Kampene Dem. Rep. Congo 48 C4
Kampinoski Park Narodowy nat. park Poland 17 R4
Kâmpóng Cham Cambodia 31 J5
Kâmpóng Saôm Cambodia see Sihanoukville
Kâmpóng Spœ Cambodia 31 J5
Kâmpóng Thum Cambodia 31 J5
Kâmpôt Cambodia 31 J5
Kampuchea country Asia see Cambodia
Kamrau, Teluk b. Indon. 41 F8
Kamsack Sask. Canada 62 G1
Kamskoye Vodokhranilishche resr Russia 11 R4
Kamsuuma Somalia 48 E3
Kamuli Uganda 48 D3
Kam"yanets'-Podil's'kyy Ukr. 13 E6
Kam"yanka-Buz'ka Ukr. 13 E6
Kamyanyets Belarus 15 M10
Kāmyārān Iran 35 G4
Kamyshin Russia 13 J6
Kamyzyak Russia 13 K7
Kanab UT U.S.A. 62 E4
Kanab Creek r. AZ U.S.A. 65 F2
Kanak Pak. 36 A3
Kananga Dem. Rep. Congo 49 C4
Kanangra-Boyd National Park Australia 58 E4
Kanarak India see Konarka
Kanarraville UT U.S.A. 65 F2
Kanas watercourse Namibia 50 C4
Kanash Russia 12 J5
Kanauj India see Kannauj
Kanazawa Japan 45 E5
Kanbalu Myanmar 37 H5
Kanchanjanga mt. India/Nepal see Kangchenjunga
Kanchipuram India 38 C3
Kand mt. Pak. 36 A3
Kanda Pak. 36 A3
Kandahār Afgh. 36 A3
Kandalaksha Russia 12 G2
Kandalakshskiy Zaliv g. Russia 12 G2
Kandar Indon. 54 E2
Kandavu i. Fiji see Kadavu
Kandavu Passage Fiji see Kadavu Passage
Kandé Togo 46 D4
Kandh Kot Pak. 36 B3
Kandi Benin 46 D3
Kandi India 38 C2
Kandiaro Pak. 36 B4
Kandıra Turkey 27 N4
Kandos Australia 58 D4
Kandreho Madag. 49 E5
Kandukur India 38 C3
Kandy Sri Lanka 38 D5
Kandyagash Kazakh. 28 G5
Kane PA U.S.A. 64 B2
Kane Bassin b. Greenland 77 K1
Kaneh watercourse Iran 35 I6
Kaneti Pak. 36 A3
Kanevskaya Russia 13 H7
Kang Botswana 50 F2
Kangaamiut Greenland 61 M3
Kangaarsussuaq c. Greenland 61 K2
Kangaba Mali 46 C3
Kangal Turkey 34 E3
Kangandala, Parque Nacional de nat. park Angola see Cangandala, Parque Nacional de
Kangar Malaysia 41 C7
Kangaroo Island Australia 57 B7
Kangaroo Point Australia 56 B3
Kangaslampi Fin. 14 P5
Kangasniemi Fin. 14 O6
Kangāvar Iran 35 G4
Kangchenjunga mt. India/Nepal 37 G4
Kangding China 42 I6
Kangean, Kepulauan is Indon. 41 D8
Kangen r. South Sudan 47 G4
Kangerlussuaq Greenland 61 M3
Kangerlussuaq inlet Greenland 61 M3
Kangersuatsiaq Greenland 61 M2
Kangertittivaq sea chan. Greenland 61 P2
Kanggye N. Korea 44 B4
Kangikajik c. Greenland 61 P2
Kangirsuk Que. Canada 61 K3
Kangmar China 37 F3
Kango Gabon 48 B3
Kangping China 44 A4
Kangri Karpo La China/India 37 I3
Kangrinboqê Feng mt. China 36 E3
Kangsangdobdê China see Xainza
Kangto mt. China/India 37 H4
Kangtog China 37 F2
Kanigiri India 38 C3
Kanin, Poluostrov pen. Russia 12 J2
Kanin Nos Russia 77 G2
Kanin Nos, Mys c. Russia 12 I1
Kaninskiy Bereg coastal area Russia 12 I2
Kanjiroba mt. Nepal 37 E3
Kankaanpää Fin. 15 M6
Kankakee IL U.S.A. 63 J3
Kankan Guinea 46 C3
Kanker India 38 D1
Kankesanturai Sri Lanka 38 D4
Kankossa Mauritania 46 B3
Kannauj India 36 D4
Kanniya Kumari c. India see Comorin, Cape
Kannonkoski Fin. 14 N5
Kannur India 38 B4
Kannus Fin. 14 M5
Kano Nigeria 46 D3
Kanonpunt pt S. Africa 50 E8
Kanosh UT U.S.A. 65 F1
Kanovlei Namibia 49 B5
Kanoya Japan 45 C7
Kanpur Odisha India 38 E1
Kanpur Uttar Prad. India 36 E4
Kansas r. KS U.S.A. 62 I4
Kansas state U.S.A. 62 H4
Kansas City KS U.S.A. 63 I4
Kansk Russia 29 K4
Kansu prov. China see Gansu
Kantara h. Cyprus 39 A2
Kantavu i. Fiji see Kadavu
Kantchari Burkina Faso 46 D3
Kantemirovka Russia 13 H6
Kanthi India 37 F5
Kantishna r. AK U.S.A. 60 C3
Kanton atoll Kiribati 53 I2
Kanturk Ireland 21 D5
Kanuku Mountains Guyana 69 G3
Kanur India 38 C3
Kanus Namibia 50 D4
Kanyakubja India see Kannauj
Kanyamazane S. Africa 51 J3
Kanye Botswana 51 G3
Kaohsiung Taiwan see Gaoxiong
Kaokoveld plat. Namibia 49 B5
Kaolack Senegal 46 B3
Kaoma Zambia 49 C5
Kaouadja Cent. Afr. Rep. 48 C3
Kapa S. Africa see Cape Town
Kapan Armenia 35 G3
Kapanga Dem. Rep. Congo 49 C4
Kaparhā Iran 35 H5
Kapatu Zambia 49 D4
Kap Dan Greenland see Kulusuk
Kapello, Akrotirio pt Greece 27 J6
Kapellskär Sweden 15 K7
Kapelskär Sweden see Kapellskär
Kapingamarangi atoll Micronesia 74 G5
Kapingamarangi Rise sea feature N. Pacific Ocean 74 G5
Kapıorman Dağları mts Turkey 27 N4
Kapip Pak. 36 B3
Kapiri Mposhi Zambia 49 C5
Kapisillit Greenland 61 M3
Kapiskau r. Ont. Canada 63 K1
Kapiti Island N.Z. 59 E5
Kaplankyr, Chink esc. Asia 35 I2
Kaplankyr Döwlet Gorugy nature res. Turkm. 35 J2
Kapoeta South Sudan 47 G4
Kaposvár Hungary 26 G1
Kappeln Germany 17 L3
Kapshagay Kazakh. 42 D4
Kapshagay, Vodokhranilishche resr Kazakh. 42 D4
Kapsukas Lith. see Marijampol
Kaptai Bangl. 37 H5
Kapuriya India 36 C4
Kapurthala India 36 C3
Kapuskasing Ont. Canada 63 K2
Kapustin Yar Russia 13 J6
Kaputar mt. Australia 58 E3
Kaputir Kenya 48 D3
Kapuvár Hungary 26 G1
Kapydzhik, Gora mt. Armenia/Azer. see Qazangödağ
Kapyl' Belarus 15 O10
Kara India 36 E4
Kara Togo 46 D4
Kara r. Turkey 35 F3
Kara-Balta Kyrg. 42 C4
Karabalyk Kazakh. 30 F1
Karabaur, Uval hills Kazakh./Uzbek. 35 I2
Karabekaul' Turkm. see Garabekewül
Karabiga Turkey 27 L4
Kara-Bogaz-Gol, Proliv sea chan. Turkm. see Garabogazköl Bogazy
Kara-Bogaz-Gol'skiy Zaliv b. Turkm. see Garabogazköl Aýlagy
Karabük Turkey 34 D2
Karaburun Turkey 27 L5
Karabutak Kazakh. 28 H5
Karacabey Turkey 27 M4
Karacaköy Turkey 27 M4
Karacalı Dağ mt. Turkey 35 E3
Karaçal Tepe mt. Turkey 39 A1
Karacasu Turkey 27 M6
Karaca Yarımadası pen. Turkey 27 N6
Karachayevsk Russia 13 I8
Karachev Russia 13 G5
Karachi Pak. 33 K5
Karacurun Turkey see Hilvan
Karad India 38 B2
Kara Dağ h. Turkey 39 D1
Kara Dağ mt. Turkey 34 D3
Kara Deniz sea Asia/Europe see Black Sea
Karagan Russia 44 A1
Karagandy Kazakh. 42 C3
Karagayly Kazakh. 42 D3
Karaginskiy Zaliv b. Russia 29 R4
Karagiye, Vpadina depr. Kazakh. 35 H2
Karagola India 37 F4
Karahallı Turkey 27 M5
Karahasanlı Turkey 34 D3
Karaikal India 38 C4
Karaikkudi India 38 C4
Karaisalı Turkey 34 D3
Karaitivu i. Sri Lanka 38 C4
Karaj Iran 35 H4
Karak Jordan see Al Karak
Karakalli Turkey see Özalp
Karakax China see Moyu
Karakax He r. China 36 E1
Karaklis Armenia see Vanadzor
Karakoçan Turkey 35 F3
Kara-Köl Kyrg. 31 G2
Karakol Kyrg. 42 D4
Karakoram Pass China/India 36 D2
Karakoram Range mts Asia 33 M2
Kara K'orē Eth. 48 D2
Karakorum Range mts Asia see Karakoram Range
Karaköse Turkey see Ağrı
Kara Kul' Kyrg. see Kara-Köl
Karakul', Ozero l. Tajik. see Qarokŭl
Kara Kum des. Turkm. see Karakum Desert
Karakum, Peski Kazakh. see Karakum Desert
Karakum Desert Kazakh. 30 E2
Karakum Desert Turkm. 30 F3
Karakurt Turkey 35 F2
Karakuş Dağı ridge Turkey 27 N5
Karal Chad 47 E3
Karala Estonia 15 L7
Karalundi Australia 55 B6
Karaman Turkey 34 D3
Karaman prov. Turkey 39 A1
Karamanlı Turkey 27 M6
Karamay China 42 E3
Karambar Pass Afgh./Pak. 36 C1
Karamea N.Z. 59 D5
Karamea Bight b. N.Z. 59 C5
Karamiran China 37 F1
Karamiran Shankou pass China 37 F1
Karamürsel Turkey 27 M4
Karamyshevo Russia 15 P8
Karān i. Saudi Arabia 35 H6
Karangasem Indon. 54 A2
Karanja India 38 C1
Karanjia India 36 E5
Karapınar Gaziantep Turkey 39 C1
Karapınar Konya Turkey 34 D3
!Karas admin. reg. Namibia 50 C4
Karasay China 37 E1
Karasburg Namibia 50 D5
Kara Sea Russia 28 I2
Kárášjohka Norway see Karasjok
Karasjok Norway 14 N2
Kara Strait Russia see Karskiye Vorota, Proliv
Karasu r. Syria/Turkey 39 C1
Karasu Bitlis Turkey see Hizan
Karasu Sakarya Turkey 27 N4
Karasu r. Turkey 35 F3
Karasubazar Ukr. see Bilohirs'k
Karasuk Russia 28 I4
Karataş Turkey 39 B1
Karataş Burnu hd Turkey see Fener Burnu
Karatau Kazakh. 42 C4
Karatau, Khrebet mts Kazakh. 42 B4
Karatax Shan mts China 36 E2
Karatepe Turkey 39 A1
Karatsu Japan 45 C6
Karaudanawa Guyana 69 G3
Karauli India 36 D4
Karavan Kyrg. see Kerben
Karavostasi Cyprus 39 A2
Karayılan Turkey 39 C1
Karayulgun China 42 E4
Karazhal Kazakh. 42 C3
Karbalā' Iraq 35 G4
Karcag Hungary 27 I1
Kardhítsa Greece see Karditsa
Karditsa Greece 27 I5
Kärdla Estonia 15 M7
Kardzhali Bulg. 27 K4
Karee S. Africa 51 H5
Kareeberge mts S. Africa 50 E6
Kareima Sudan 32 D6
Kareli India 36 D5
Karelia aut. rep. Russia see Kareliya, Respublika
Kareliya, Respublika aut. rep. Russia 14 R5
Karel'skaya A.S.S.R. aut. rep. Russia see Kareliya, Respublika
Karel'skiy Bereg coastal area Russia 12 G2
Karema Tanz. 49 D4
Karera India 36 D4
Karesuando Sweden 14 M2
Kargalinskaya Russia 35 G2
Kargalinski Russia see Kargalinskaya
Kargapazarı Dağları mts Turkey 35 F3
Karghalik China see Yecheng
Kargı Turkey 34 D2
Kargil India 36 D2
Kargilik China see Yecheng
Kargıpınarı Turkey 39 B1
Kargopol' Russia 12 H3
Kari Nigeria 46 E3
Kariba Zimbabwe 49 C5
Kariba, Lake resr Zambia/Zimbabwe 49 C5
Kariba Dam Zambia/Zimbabwe 49 C5
Kariba-yama vol. Japan 44 E4
Karibib Namibia 50 B1
Karigasniemi Fin. 14 N2
Karijini National Park Australia 55 B5
Karijoki Fin. 14 L5
Karikachi-tōge pass Japan 44 F4
Karikari, Cape N.Z. 59 D2
Karimata, Selat str. Indon. 41 C8
Karimganj India 37 H4
Karimnagar India 38 C2
Káristos Greece see Karystos
Karjat Mahar. India 38 B2
Karjat Mahar. India 38 B2
Karkaraly Kazakh. 42 D3
Karkar Island P.N.G. 52 E2
Karkh Pak. 36 A4
Karkinits'ka Zatoka g. Ukr. 27 O2
Kärkölä Fin. 15 N6
Karkonoski Park Narodowy nat. park Czech Rep./Poland see Krkonošský národní park
Karksi-Nuia Estonia 15 N7
Karkūk Iraq see Kirkūk
Karlachi Pak. 36 B2
Karlholmsbruk Sweden 15 J6
Karlik Shan mts China 42 G4
Karlıova Turkey 35 F3
Karlivka Ukr. 13 G6
Karl Marks, Qullai mt. Tajik. 36 C1
Karl-Marx-Stadt Germany see Chemnitz
Karlovac Croatia 26 F2
Karlovka Ukr. see Karlivka
Karlovo Bulg. 27 K3
Karlovy Vary Czech Rep. 17 N5
Karlsborg Sweden 15 I7
Karlsburg Romania see Alba Iulia
Karlshamn Sweden 15 I8
Karlskoga Sweden 15 I7
Karlskrona Sweden 15 I8
Karlsruhe Germany 17 L6
Karlstad Sweden 15 H7
Karluk AK U.S.A. 60 C4
Karmala India 38 B2
Karmel, Har h. Israel see Carmel, Mount
Karmona Spain see Córdoba
Karmøy i. Norway 15 D7
Karmpur Pak. 36 C3
Karnal India 36 D3
Karnaphuli Reservoir Bangl. 37 H5
Karnataka state India 38 B3
Karnavati India see Ahmadabad
Karnobat Bulg. 27 L3
Karodi Pak. 36 A4
Karoi Zimbabwe 49 C5
Karo La pass China 37 G3
Karong India 37 H4
Karonga Malawi 49 D4
Karonie Australia 55 C7
Karoo National Park S. Africa 50 F7
Karoonda Australia 57 B7
Karora Eritrea 32 E6
Káros i. Greece see Keros
Karossa, Tanjung pt Indon. 54 B2
Karpasia pen. Cyprus 39 B2
Karpas Peninsula Cyprus see Karpasia
Karpathos i. Greece 27 L7
Karpathou, Steno sea chan. Greece 27 L6
Karpaty mts Europe see Carpathian Mountains
Karpenisi Greece 27 I5
Karpilovka Belarus see Aktsyabrski
Karpinsk Russia 11 S4
Karpogory Russia 12 J2
Karpuz r. Turkey 39 A1
Karratha Australia 54 B5
Karroo plat. S. Africa see Great Karoo
Kars Turkey 35 F2
Kärsämäki Fin. 14 N5
Kārsava Latvia 15 O8
Karshi Uzbek. see Qarshi
Karskiye Vorota, Proliv str. Russia 28 G3
Karskoye More sea Russia see Kara Sea
Karstula Fin. 14 N5
Karsu Turkey 39 C1
Karsun Russia 13 J5
Kartal Turkey 27 M4
Kartaly Russia 28 H4
Kartayel' Russia 12 L2
Karttula Fin. 14 O5
Karumba Australia 56 C3
Karumbhar Island India 36 B5
Karūn, Rūd-e r. Iran 35 H5
Karuni Indon. 54 B2
Karur India 38 C4
Karvia Fin. 14 M5
Karviná Czech Rep. 17 Q6
Karwar India 38 B3
Karyagino Azer. see Füzuli
Karymskoye Russia 43 K2
Karynzharyk, Peski des. Kazakh. 35 I2
Karystos Greece 27 K5
Kaş Turkey 27 M6
Kasa India 38 B2
Kasaba Turkey see Turgutlu
Kasaï, Plateau du Dem. Rep. Congo 49 C4
Kasaji Dem. Rep. Congo 49 C5
Kasama Zambia 49 D5
Kasane Botswana 49 C5
Kasaragod India 38 B3
Kasargod India see Kasaragod
Kasargode India see Kasaragod
Kasatkino Russia 44 C2
Kasba Lake N.W.T. Canada 61 H3
Kasba Tadla Morocco 22 C5
Kasenga Dem. Rep. Congo 49 C5
Kasengu Dem. Rep. Congo 49 C4
Kasese Dem. Rep. Congo 48 C4
Kasese Uganda 48 D3
Kasevo Russia see Neftekamsk
Kasganj India 36 D4
Kāshān Iran 35 H4
Kashary Russia 13 I6
Kashgar China see Kashi
Kashi China 42 D5
Kashihara Japan 45 D6
Kashima-nada b. Japan 45 F5
Kashin Russia 12 H4
Kashipur India 36 D3
Kashira Russia 13 H5
Kashiwazaki Japan 45 E5
Kashkarantsy Russia 12 H2
Kāshmar Iran 33 I2
Kashmir reg. Asia 36 D2
Kashmir, Vale of reg. India 36 C2
Kashyr Kazakh. 42 D2
Kashyukulu Dem. Rep. Congo 49 C4
Kasi India see Varanasi
Kāsīgar Afgh. 36 B2
Kasimov Russia 13 I5
Kaskinen Fin. 14 L5
Kaskö Fin. see Kaskinen
Kasongo Dem. Rep. Congo 49 C4
Kasongo-Lunda Dem. Rep. Congo 49 B4
Kasos i. Greece 27 L7
Kaspīy Mangy Oypaty lowland Kazakh./Russia see Caspian Lowland
Kaspiysk Russia 35 G2
Kaspiyskiy Russia see Lagan'
Kaspiyskoye More l. Asia/Europe see Caspian Sea
Kassa Slovakia see Košice
Kassala Sudan 32 E6
Kassandras, Akrotirio pt Greece 27 J5
Kassandras, Kolpos b. Greece 27 J4
Kassel Germany 17 L5
Kasserine Tunisia 26 C7
Kastamonu Turkey 34 D2
Kastéllion Greece see Kissamos
Kastellorizon i. Greece see Megisti
Kastoria Greece 27 I4
Kastornoye Russia 13 H6
Kastsyukovichy Belarus 13 G5
Kasulu Tanz. 49 D4
Kasumkent Russia 35 H2
Kasungu Malawi 49 D5
Kasungu National Park Malawi 49 D5
Kasur Pak. 36 C3
Katâdtlit Nunât terr. N. America see Greenland
Katahdin, Mount ME U.S.A. 63 N2
Katah Sang Srah Afgh. 36 A2
Kataklik India 36 D2
Katako-Kombe Dem. Rep. Congo 48 C4
Katakwi Uganda 48 D3
Katana India 36 C5
Katangi India 36 D5
Katanning Australia 55 B8
Katavi National Park Tanz. 49 D4
Katea Dem. Rep. Congo 49 C4
Katerini Greece 27 J4
Katesh Tanz. 49 D4
Kate's Needle mt. Canada/U.S.A. 60 E4
Katete Zambia 49 D5
Katherîna, Gebel mt. Egypt see Kātrīnā, Jabal
Katherine Australia 54 F3
Katherine Gorge National Park Australia see Nitmiluk National Park
Kathiawar pen. India 36 B5
Kathihar India see Katihar
Kathiraveli Sri Lanka 38 D4
Kathiwara India 36 C5
Kathleen Falls Australia 54 E3
Kathmandu Nepal 37 F4
Kathu S. Africa 50 F4
Kathua India 36 C2
Kati Mali 46 C3
Katihar India 37 F4
Katikati S. Africa 51 H7
Katima Mulilo Namibia 49 C5
Katiola Côte d'Ivoire 46 C4
Kā Tiritiri o te Moana mts N.Z. see Southern Alps
Kati Thanda-Lake Eyre Australia 57 B6
Kati Thanda-Lake Eyre (North) Australia 57 B6
Kati Thanda-Lake Eyre (South) Australia 57 B6
Kati Thanda-Lake Eyre National Park Australia 57 B6
Katkop Hills S. Africa 50 E6
Katlehong S. Africa 51 I4
Katmai National Park and Preserve AK U.S.A. 60 C4
Katmandu Nepal see Kathmandu
Katni India 36 E5
Kato Achaïa Greece 27 I5
Katoomba Australia 58 E4
Katowice Poland 17 Q5
Katoya India 37 G5
Katrancık Dağı mts Turkey 27 M6
Kātrīnā, Jabal mt. Egypt 34 D5
Katrine, Loch l. U.K. 20 E4
Katrineholm Sweden 15 J7
Katse Dam Lesotho 51 I5
Katsina Nigeria 46 D3
Katsina-Ala Nigeria 46 D4
Katsuura Japan 45 F6
Kattamudda Well Australia 54 D5
Kattaqo'rg'on Uzbek. 33 K2
Kattaqŭrghon Uzbek. see Kattaqo'rg'on
Kattegat str. Denmark/Sweden 15 G8
Kattowitz Poland see Katowice
Katumbar India 36 D4
Katunino Russia 12 J4
Katuri Pak. 36 B3
Katwa India see Katoya
Kaua'i i. HI U.S.A. 75 J4
Kauhajoki Fin. 14 M5
Kauhava Fin. 14 M5
Kaukkwè Hills Myanmar 37 I4
Kaukonen Fin. 14 N3
Kaunas Lith. 15 M9
Kaunata Latvia 15 O8
Kaundy, Vpadina depr. Kazakh. 35 I2
Kaunia Bangl. 37 G4
Kaura-Namoda Nigeria 46 D3
Kaustinen Fin. 14 M5
Kautokeino Norway 14 M2
Kavadarci Macedonia 27 J4
Kavak Turkey 34 E2
Kavaklıdere Turkey 27 M6
Kavala Greece 27 K4
Kavalas, Kolpos b. Greece 27 K4
Kavalerovo Russia 44 D3
Kavali India 38 C3
Kavango Zambezi Transfrontier Conservation Area res. Africa 50 C4
Kavār Iran 35 I5
Kavaratti India 38 B4
Kavaratti atoll India 38 B4
Kavarna Bulg. 27 M3
Kavendou, Mont mt. Guinea 46 B3
Kaveri r. India 38 C4
Kavīr Iran 35 H4
Kavīr, Dasht-e des. Iran 35 I4
Kavkasioni mts Asia/Europe see Caucasus
Kawagoe Japan 45 E6
Kawaguchi Japan 45 E6
Kawakawa N.Z. 59 E2
Kawambwa Zambia 49 C4
Kawana Zambia 49 C5
Kawardha India 36 E5
Kawasaki Japan 45 E6
Kawau Island N.Z. 59 E3
Kawerau N.Z. 59 F4
Kawhia N.Z. 59 E4
Kawhia Harbour N.Z. 59 E4
Kawich Peak NV U.S.A. 65 E2
Kawich Range mts NV U.S.A. 65 D2
Kawlin Myanmar 37 H5
Kawm Umbū Egypt 32 D5
Kaxgar China see Kashi
Kaxgar He r. China 33 M2
Kax He r. China 42 E4
Kaxtexi Shan mts China 37 E1
Kaya Burkina Faso 46 C3
Kayadibi Turkey 34 E3
Kayankulam India 38 C4
Kayar India 38 C2
Kaydak, Sor dry lake Kazakh. 35 I1
Kaydanovo Belarus see Dzyarzhynsk
Kayembe-Mukulu Dem. Rep. Congo 49 C4
Kayenta AZ U.S.A. 62 E4
Kayes Mali 46 B3
Kaylahgay (abandoned) Afgh. 36 B2
Kaymaz Turkey 27 N5
Kaynar Kazakh. 42 D3
Kaynar Turkey 34 E3
Kayseri Turkey 34 D3
Kayuyu Dem. Rep. Congo 48 C4
Kazach'ye Russia 29 O2
Kazakh Azer. see Qazax
Kazakhskaya S.S.R. country Asia see Kazakhstan
Kazakhskiy Zaliv b. Kazakh. 35 I2
Kazakhstan country Asia 30 F2
Kazakhstan Kazakh. see Aksay
Kazakh Steppe plain Kazakh. see Saryarka
Kazakstan country Asia see Kazakhstan
Kazan' Russia 12 K5
Kazandzhik Turkm. see Bereket
Kazanka r. Russia 12 K5
Kazanlak Bulg. 27 K3
Kazanlı Turkey 39 B1
Kazan-rettō is Japan see Volcano Islands
Kazatin Ukr. see Kozyatyn
Kazbek mt. Georgia/Russia 13 J8
Kaz Dağı mts Turkey 27 L5
Kāzerūn Iran 35 H5
Kazhym Russia 12 K3
Kazidi Tajik. see Qozide
Kazi Magomed Azer. see Hacıqabul
Kazincbarcika Hungary 13 D6
Kaziranga National Park India 37 H4
K'azreti Georgia 35 G2
Kaztalovka Kazakh. 11 P6
Kazym r. Russia 11 T3
Kazym-Mys Russia 11 T3
Keady U.K. 21 F3
Kéamu i. Vanuatu see Anatom
Kearney NE U.S.A. 62 H3
Keban Turkey 34 E3
Keban Barajı resr Turkey 34 E3
Kébémèr Senegal 46 B3
Kebili Tunisia 22 F5
Kebīr, Nahr al r. Lebanon/Syria 39 B2
Kebkabiya Sudan 47 F3
Kebnekaise mt. Sweden 14 K3
Kebock Head hd U.K. 20 C2
K'ebrī Dehar Eth. 48 E3
Kechika r. B.C. Canada 77 A3
Keçiborlu Turkey 27 N6
Kecskemét Hungary 27 H1
Keda Georgia 35 F2
Kdainiai Lith. 15 M9
Kedairu Passage Fiji see Kadavu Passage
Kedong China 44 B3
Kédougou Senegal 46 B3
Kedva r. Russia 12 L2
Kędzierzyn-Koźle Poland 17 Q5
Keele r. Y.T. Canada 60 F3
Keele Peak Y.T. Canada 60 E3
Keeler CA U.S.A. 65 D2
Keeling Islands terr. Indian Ocean see Cocos (Keeling) Islands
Keen, Mount h. U.K. 20 G4
Keene CA U.S.A. 65 C3
Keene NH U.S.A. 64 E1
Keeper Hill h. Ireland 21 D5
Keepit, Lake resr Australia 58 E3
Keep River National Park Australia 54 E3
Keer-weer, Cape Australia 56 C2
Keetmanshoop Namibia 50 D4
Keewatin Ont. Canada 63 I2
Kefallinía i. Greece see Cephalonia
Kefallonia i. Greece see Cephalonia
Kefamenanu Indon. 41 E8
Kefe Ukr. see Feodosiya
Keffi Nigeria 46 D4
Keflavík Iceland 14 [inset 2]
Kegalla Sri Lanka 38 D5
Kegen Kazakh. 42 D4
Keg River Alta Canada 60 G4
Kegul'ta Russia 13 J7
Kehra Estonia 15 N7
Keighley U.K. 18 F5
Keila Estonia 15 N7
Keimoes S. Africa 50 E5
Keitele Fin. 14 O5
Keitele l. Fin. 14 O5
Keith Australia 57 C8
Keith U.K. 20 G3
Kékes mt. Hungary 17 R7
Kekri India 36 C4
Kelaa i. Maldives 38 B5
K'elafo Eth. 48 E3
Kelibia Tunisia 26 D6
Kelif Uzboýy marsh Turkm. 33 J2
Kelkit Turkey 35 E2
Kelkit r. Turkey 34 E2
Kéllé Congo 48 B4
Keller Lake N.W.T. Canada 60 F3
Kellett, Cape N.W.T. Canada 60 F2
Kelloselkä Fin. 14 P3
Kells Ireland 21 F4
Kells r. U.K. 21 F3
Kelly Range hills Australia 55 C6
Kelm Lith. 15 M9
Kélo Chad 47 E4
Kelowna B.C. Canada 62 D2
Kelseyville CA U.S.A. 65 A1
Kelso U.K. 20 G5
Kelso (abandoned) CA U.S.A. 65 E3
Keluang Malaysia 41 C7
Kelvington Sask. Canada 62 G1
Kem' Russia 12 G2
Kem' r. Russia 12 G2
Ke Macina Mali see Macina
Kemah Turkey 34 E3
Kemaliye Turkey 34 E3
Kemalpaşa Turkey 27 L5
Kemano (abandoned) B.C. Canada 60 F4
Kembé Cent. Afr. Rep. 48 C3
Kemeneshát hills Hungary 26 G1
Kemer Antalya Turkey 27 N6
Kemer Muğla Turkey 27 M6
Kemer Barajı resr Turkey 27 M6
Kemerovo Russia 28 J4
Kemi Fin. 14 N4
Kemijärvi Fin. 14 O3
Kemijärvi l. Fin. 14 O3
Kemijoki r. Fin. 14 N4
Kemiö Fin. see Kimito
Kemir Turkm. see Keymir
Kemmerer WY U.S.A. 62 E3
Kemnay U.K. 20 G3
Kemp Coast reg. Antarctica see Kemp Land
Kempele Fin. 14 N4
Kemp Land reg. Antarctica 76 D2
Kemp Peninsula Antarctica 76 A2
Kempsey Australia 58 F3
Kempt, Lac l. Que. Canada 63 M2
Kempten (Allgäu) Germany 17 M7
Kempton Park S. Africa 51 I4
Ken r. India 36 E4
Kenai AK U.S.A. 60 C3
Kenai Fiords National Park AK U.S.A. 60 C4
Kenai Mountains AK U.S.A. 60 C4
Kenâyis, Râs el pt Egypt see Ḥikmah, Ra's al
Kenbridge VA U.S.A. 64 B4
Kendal U.K. 18 E4
Kendall Australia 58 F3
Kendall, Cape Nunavut Canada 61 J3
Kendari Indon. 41 E8
Kendawangan Indon. 41 D8
Kendégué Chad 47 E3
Kendirli-Kiyasan, Plato plat. Kazakh. 35 I2
Kendrapara India 37 F5
Kendraparha India see Kendrapara
Kendujhar India see Kendujhargarh
Kendujhargarh India 37 F5
Kendyrlisor, Solonchak salt l. Kazakh. 35 I2
Kenebri Australia 58 D3
Kenema Sierra Leone 46 B4
Kenge Dem. Rep. Congo 49 B4
Kenhardt S. Africa 50 E5
Kéniéba Mali 46 B3
Kenitra Morocco 22 C5
Kenmare Ireland 21 C6
Kenmare River inlet Ireland 21 B6
Kenmore NY U.S.A. 64 B1
Kennebunkport ME U.S.A. 64 F1
Kennedy, Cape FL U.S.A. see Canaveral, Cape
Kennedy Range National Park Australia 55 A6
Kennet r. U.K. 19 G7
Kenneth Range hills Australia 55 B5
Kennewick WA U.S.A. 62 D2
Kenn Reef Australia 56 F4
Kenora Ont. Canada 63 I2
Kenosha WI U.S.A. 63 J3
Kenozero, Ozero l. Russia 12 H3
Kent r. U.K. 18 E4
Kent OH U.S.A. 64 A2
Kent VA U.S.A. 64 A4
Kentani S. Africa see Centane
Kent Group is Australia 57 [inset]
Kent Peninsula Nunavut Canada 60 H3
Kentucky state U.S.A. 63 K4
Kenya country Africa 48 D3
Kenya, Mount Kenya 48 D4
Keokuk IA U.S.A. 63 I3
Keoladeo National Park India 36 D4
Keonjhar India see Kendujhargarh
Keonjhargarh India see Kendujhargarh
Kepina r. Russia 12 I2
Keppel Bay Australia 56 E4
Kepsut Turkey 27 M5
Kera India 37 F5
Kerala state India 38 B4

Kohlu Pak. 36 B3
Kohtla-Järve Estonia 15 O7
Koidu Sierra Leone see Koidu-Sefadu
Koidu-Sefadu Sierra Leone 46 B4
Koilkonda India 38 C2
Koin N. Korea 45 B4
Koin r. Russia 12 K3
Kojonup Australia 55 B8
Kökar Fin. 15 L7
Kokchetav Kazakh. see Kokshetau
Kokemäenjoki r. Fin. 15 L6
Kokerboom Namibia 50 D5
Kokkilai Sri Lanka 38 D4
Kokkola Fin. 14 M5
Koko Nigeria 46 D3
Kokomo IN U.S.A. 63 J3
Kokong Botswana 50 F3
Kokosi S. Africa 51 H4
Kokpekty Kazakh. 42 E3
Koksan N. Korea 45 B5
Kokshaal-Tau, Khrebet mts China/Kyrg. see Kakshaal-Too
Koksharka Russia 12 J4
Kokshetau Kazakh. 31 F1
Kokstad S. Africa 51 I6
Kokterek Kazakh. 13 K6
Koktokay China see Fuyun
Kola Russia 14 R2
Kolachi r. Pak. 36 A4
Kolahoi mt. India 36 C2
Kolaka Indon. 41 E8
Kola Peninsula Russia 12 H2
Kolar Chhattisgarh India 38 D2
Kolar Karnataka India 38 C3
Kolaras India 36 D4
Kolar Gold Fields India 38 C3
Kolari Fin. 14 M3
Kolarovgrad Bulg. see Shumen
Kolasib India 37 H4
Kolayat India 36 C4
Kolberg Poland see Kołobrzeg
Kol'chugino Russia 12 H4
Kolda Senegal 46 B3
Kolding Denmark 15 F9
Kole Kasaï-Oriental Dem. Rep. Congo 48 C4
Kole Orientale Dem. Rep. Congo 48 C3
Koléa Alg. 25 H5
Koler Sweden 14 L4
Kolguyev, Ostrov i. Russia 12 K1
Kolhan reg. India 37 F5
Kolhapur India 38 B2
Kolikata India see Kolkata
Kõljala Estonia 15 M7
Kolkasrags pt Latvia 15 M8
Kolkata India 37 G5
Kolkhozabad Khatlon Tajik. see Kolkhozobod
Kolkhozabad Khatlon Tajik. see Vose'
Kolkhozobod Tajik. 33 K2
Kollam India 38 C4
Kolleru Lake India 38 D2
Kolmanskop (abandoned) Namibia 50 B4
Köln Germany see Cologne
Kołobrzeg Poland 17 O3
Kologriv Russia 12 J4
Kolokani Mali 46 C3
Kolombangara i. Solomon Is 53 F2
Kolomea Ukr. see Kolomyya
Kolomna Russia 13 H5
Kołomyja Ukr. see Kolomyya
Kolomyya Ukr. 13 E6
Kolondiéba Mali 46 C3
Kolonedale Indon. 52 C2
Koloni Cyprus 39 A2
Kolonkwaneng Botswana 50 E4
Kolozsvár Romania see Cluj-Napoca
Kolpashevo Russia 28 J4
Kol'skiy Poluostrov pen. Russia see Kola Peninsula
Kölük Turkey see Kâhta
Koluli Eritrea 32 F7
Kolva r. Russia 12 M2
Kolvan India 38 B2
Kolvereid Norway 14 G4
Kolvik Norway 14 N1
Kolvitskoye, Ozero l. Russia 14 R3
Kolwezi Dem. Rep. Congo 49 C5
Kolyma r. Russia 29 R3
Kolyma Lowland Russia see Kolymskaya Nizmennost'
Kolyma Range mts Russia see Kolymskoye Nagor'ye
Kolymskaya Nizmennost' lowland Russia 29 Q3
Kolymskoye Nagor'ye mts Russia 29 R3
Kolyshley Russia 13 J5
Kom mt. Bulg. 27 J3
Komadugu-Gana watercourse Nigeria 46 E3
Komaggas S. Africa 50 C5
Komaki Japan 45 E6
Komandnaya, Gora mt. Russia 44 E2
Komandorskiye Ostrova is Russia 29 R4
Komárno Slovakia 17 Q7
Komati r. Swaziland 51 J3
Komatipoort S. Africa 51 J3
Komatsu Japan 45 E5
Komba i. Indon. 54 C1
Komga S. Africa 51 H7
Komintern Ukr. see Marhanets'
Kominternivs'ke Ukr. 27 N1
Komiža Croatia 26 G3
Komló Hungary 26 H1
Kommunarsk Ukr. see Alchevs'k
Komodo, Taman Nasional Indon. 54 B2
Kôm Ombo Egypt see Kawm Umbū
Komono Congo 48 B4
Komotini Greece 27 K4
Kompong Cham Cambodia see Kâmpóng Cham
Kompong Som Cambodia see Sihanoukville
Kompong Speu Cambodia see Kâmpóng Spœ
Kompong Thom Cambodia see Kâmpóng Thum
Komrat Moldova see Comrat
Komsberg mts S. Africa 50 E7
Komsomol Kazakh. see Karabalyk
Komsomolets Kazakh. see Karabalyk
Komsomolets, Ostrov i. Russia 28 K1
Komsomol's'k Ukr. 13 G6
Komsomol'skiy Chukotskiy Avtonomnyy Okrug Russia 77 C2
Komsomol'skiy Khanty-Mansiyskiy Avtonomnyy Okrug-Yugra Russia see Yugorsk
Komsomol'skiy Respublika Kalmykiya-Khalm'g-Tangch Russia 13 J7
Komsomol'sk-na-Amure Russia 44 E2
Komsomol'skoye Russia 13 J6
Kömürlü Turkey 35 F2
Kon India 37 E4
Konacık Turkey 39 B1
Konada India 38 D2
Konarak India see Konarka
Konarka India 37 F6
Konch India 36 D4
Kondagaon India 38 D2
Kondinin Australia 55 B8
Kondinskoye Russia see Oktyabr'skoye
Kondoa Tanz. 49 D4
Kondol' Russia 13 J5
Kondopoga Russia 12 G3
Kondoz Afgh. see Kunduz
Kondrovo Russia 13 G5
Köneürgenç Turkm. see Köneürgenç
Köneürgenç Turkm. 33 I1
Kong Cameroon 46 E4
Kong Christian IX Land reg. Greenland 61 O3
Kong Christian X Land reg. Greenland 61 P2
Kongelab atoll Marshall Is see Rongelap
Kong Frederik IX Land reg. Greenland 61 M3
Kong Frederik VI Kyst coastal area Greenland 61 N3
Kongolo Dem. Rep. Congo 49 C4
Kongor South Sudan 47 G4
Kong Oscars Fjord inlet Greenland 61 P2
Kongoussi Burkina Faso 46 C3
Kongsberg Norway 15 F7
Kongsvinger Norway 15 H6
Kongur Shan mt. China 42 D5
Königsberg Russia see Kaliningrad
Konin Poland 17 Q4
Konjic Bos. & Herz. 26 G3
Konkiep watercourse Namibia 50 C5
Konnevesi Fin. 14 O5
Konosha Russia 12 I3
Konotop Ukr. 13 G6
Konpara India 37 E5
Konqi He r. China 42 F4
Konso Eth. 48 D3
Konstantinograd Ukr. see Krasnohrad
Konstantinovka Russia 44 B2
Konstantinovka Ukr. see Kostyantynivka
Konstanz Germany 17 L7
Kontiolahti Fin. 14 P5
Konttila Fin. 14 O4
Könugard Ukr. see Kiev
Konushin, Mys pt Russia 12 I2
Konya Turkey 34 D3
Konzhakovskiy Kamen', Gora mt. Russia 11 R4
Kooch Bihar India see Koch Bihar
Kookynie Australia 55 C7
Koolyanobbing Australia 55 B7
Koondrook Australia 58 B5
Koorawatha Australia 58 D5
Koordarrie Australia 54 A5
Kootenay Lake B.C. Canada 62 D2
Kootjieskolk S. Africa 50 E6
Kópasker Iceland 14 [inset 2]
Kopbirlik Kazakh. 42 D3
Koper Slovenia 26 E2
Kopet Dag mts Iran/Turkm. 33 I2
Kopet-Dag, Khrebet mts Iran/Turkm. see Kopet Dag
Köpetdag Gershi mts Iran/Turkm. see Kopet Dag
Kopili r. India 37 G4
Köping Sweden 15 J7
Köpmanholmen Sweden 14 K5
Kopong Botswana 51 G3
Koppal India 38 C3
Koppang Norway 15 G6
Kopparberg Sweden 15 I7
Koppeh Dāgh mts Iran/Turkm. see Kopet Dag
Koppi r. Russia 44 F2
Koppies S. Africa 51 H4
Koppieskraal Pan salt pan S. Africa 50 E4
Koprivnica Croatia 26 G1
Köprülü Turkey 39 A1
Köprülü Kanyon Milli Parkı nat. park Turkey 27 N6
Kopyl' Belarus see Kapyl'
Kora India 36 E4
Korablino Russia 13 I5
K'orahē Eth. 48 E3
Koramlik China 37 F1
Korangal India 38 C2
Korangi Pak. 36 A4
Koraput India 38 D2
Korat Thai. see Nakhon Ratchasima
Koratla India 38 C2
Korba India 37 E5
Korçë Albania 27 I4
Korčula Croatia 26 G3
Korčula i. Croatia 26 G3
Korčulanski Kanal sea chan. Croatia 26 G3
Korday Kazakh. 42 C4
Kord Küy Iran 35 I3
Korea, North country Asia 45 B5
Korea, South country Asia 45 B5
Korea Bay g. China/N. Korea 45 B5
Korea Strait Japan/S. Korea 45 C6
Koregaon India 38 B2
Korenovsk Russia 35 E1
Korenovskaya Russia see Korenovsk
Korepino Russia 11 R3
Korets' Ukr. 13 E6
Körfez Turkey 27 M4
Korff Ice Rise Antarctica 76 L1
Korfovskiy Russia 44 D2
Korgalzhyn Kazakh. 42 C2
Korgen Norway 14 H3
Korhogo Côte d'Ivoire 46 C4
Koribundu Sierra Leone 46 B4
Kori Creek inlet India 36 B5
Korinthiakos Kolpos sea chan. Greece see Corinth, Gulf of
Korinthos Greece see Corinth
Kőris-hegy h. Hungary 26 G1
Koritnik mt. Albania 27 I3
Koritsa Albania see Korçë
Kōriyama Japan 45 F5
Korkuteli Turkey 27 N6
Korla China 42 F4
Kormakitis, Cape Cyprus 39 A2
Körmend Hungary 26 G1
Kornati, Nacionalni Park nat. park Croatia 26 F3
Korneyevka Russia 13 K6
Koro Côte d'Ivoire 46 C4
Koro i. Fiji 53 H3
Koro Mali 46 C3
Köroğlu Dağları mts Turkey 27 O4
Köroğlu Tepesi mt. Turkey 34 D2
Korogwe Tanz. 49 D4
Koroneia, Limni l. Greece 27 J4
Korong Vale Australia 58 A6
Koror Palau 41 F7
Koro Sea sea Fiji 53 H3
Korosten' Ukr. 13 F6
Korostyshiv Ukr. 13 F6
Koro Toro Chad 47 E3
Korpilahti Fin. 14 N5
Korpo Fin. 15 L6
Korppoo Fin. see Korpo
Korsakov Russia 44 F3
Korsnäs Fin. 14 L5
Korsør Denmark 15 G9
Korsun'-Shevchenkivs'kyy Ukr. 13 F6
Korsun'-Shevchenkovskiy Ukr. see Korsun'-Shevchenkivs'kyy
Korsze Poland 17 R3
Kortesjärvi Fin. 14 M5
Korti Sudan 32 D6
Kortkeros Russia 12 K3
Kortrijk Belgium 16 I5
Korvala Fin. 14 O3
Koryakskaya Sopka, Vulkan vol. Russia 29 Q4
Koryakskoye Nagor'ye mts Russia 29 S3
Koryazhma Russia 12 J3
Kos i. Greece 27 L6
Kosa Russia 11 Q4
Kosam India 36 E4
Kosan N. Korea 45 B5
Kościan Poland 17 P4
Kosciusko, Mount Australia see Kosciuszko, Mount
Kosciuszko, Mount Australia 58 D6
Kosciuszko National Park Australia 58 D6
Köse Turkey 35 E2
Köseçobanlı Turkey 39 A1
Kosgi India 38 C2
Kosh-Agach Russia 42 F3
Koshikijima-rettō is Japan 45 C7
Koshki Russia 13 K5
Kosi Bay S. Africa 51 K4
Košice Slovakia 13 D6
Kosigi India 38 C3
Koskullskulle Sweden 14 L3
Köslin Poland see Koszalin
Kosma r. Russia 12 K2
Kosŏng N. Korea 45 C5
Kosova country Europe see Kosovo
Kosovo country Europe 27 I3
Kosovo-Metohija country Europe see Kosovo
Kosovska Mitrovica Kosovo see Mitrovicë
Kosrae atoll Micronesia 74 G5
Kosta-Khetagurovo Russia see Nazran'
Kostanay Kazakh. 30 F1
Kostenets Bulg. 27 J3
Kosti Sudan 32 D7
Kostinbrod Bulg. 27 J3
Kostino Russia 28 J3
Kostomuksha Russia 12 F2
Kostopil' Ukr. 13 E6
Kostopol' Ukr. see Kostopil'
Kostroma Russia 12 I4
Kostrzyn nad Odrą Poland 17 O4
Kostyantynivka Ukr. 13 H6
Kostyukovichi Belarus see Kastsyukovichy
Kos'yu Russia 11 R2
Koszalin Poland 17 P3
Kőszeg Hungary 26 G1
Kota Andhra Prad. India 38 D3
Kota Chhattisgarh India 37 E5
Kota Rajasthan India 36 C4
Kota Baharu Malaysia see Kota Bharu
Kotabaru Indon. 41 D8
Kota Bharu Malaysia 41 C7
Kot Addu Pak. 36 B3
Kota Kinabalu Sabah Malaysia 41 D7
Kotaparh India 38 D2
Kot Diji Pak. 36 B4
Kotel'nich Russia 12 K4
Kotel'nikovo Russia 13 I7
Kotel'nyy, Ostrov i. Russia 29 O2
Kotgar India 38 D2
Kotgarh India 36 D3
Kothagudem India see Kottagudem
Kotido Uganda 47 G4
Kotikovo Russia 44 D3
Kotka Fin. 15 O6
Kot Kapura India 36 C3
Kotkino Russia 12 K2
Kotlas Russia 12 J3
Kotli Pak. 36 C2
Kotlik AK U.S.A. 60 B3
Kötlutangi pt Iceland 14 [inset 2]
Kotly Russia 15 P7
Kotovo Russia 13 J6
Kotovsk Russia 13 I5
Kotra India 36 C4
Kotra Pak. 36 A3
Kotri r. India 38 D2
Kot Sarae Pak. 36 A5
Kottagudem India 38 D2
Kottarakara India 38 C4
Kottayam India 38 C4
Kotte Sri Lanka see Sri Jayewardenepura Kotte
Kotto r. Cent. Afr. Rep. 48 C3
Kotturu India 38 C3
Kotuy r. Russia 29 L2
Kotzebue AK U.S.A. 60 B3
Kotzebue Sound sea chan. AK U.S.A. 60 B3
Kouango Cent. Afr. Rep. 48 C3
Koubia Guinea 46 B3
Koudougou Burkina Faso 46 C3
Kouebokkeveld mts S. Africa 50 D7
Koufey Niger 46 E3
Koufonisi i. Greece 27 L7
Kougaberge mts S. Africa 50 F7
Koukdjuak, Great Plain of the Nunavut Canada 61 K3
Koukourou r. Cent. Afr. Rep. 48 B3
Koulikoro Mali 46 C3
Koumac New Caledonia 53 G4
Koumpentoum Senegal 46 B3
Koumra Chad 47 E4
Koundâra Guinea 46 B3
Koupéla Burkina Faso 46 C3
Kourou Fr. Guiana 69 H2
Kouroussa Guinea 46 C3
Kousséri Cameroon 47 E3
Koutiala Mali 46 C3
Kouvola Fin. 15 O6
Kovallberget Sweden 14 J4
Kovdor Russia 12 F2
Kovel' Ukr. 13 E6
Kovernino Russia 12 I4
Kovilpatti India 38 C4
Kovno Lith. see Kaunas
Kovrov Russia 12 I4
Kovylkino Russia 13 I5
Kovzhskoye, Ozero l. Russia 12 H3
Kowanyama Australia 56 C2
Kowŏn N. Korea 45 B5
Kōyama-misaki pt Japan 45 C6
Koyamutthoor India see Coimbatore
Köyceğiz Turkey 27 M6
Koygorodok Russia 12 K3
Koyna Reservoir India 38 B2
Köytendag Turkm. 33 K2
Koyuk AK U.S.A. 60 B3
Koyukuk r. AK U.S.A. 60 C3
Koyulhisar Turkey 34 E2
Kozağacı Turkey see Günyüzü
Kō-zaki pt Japan 45 C6
Kozan Turkey 34 D3
Kozani Greece 27 I4
Kozara mts Bos. & Herz. 26 G2
Kozara, Nacionalni Park nat. park Bos. & Herz. 26 G2
Kozarska Dubica Bos. & Herz. see Bosanska Dubica
Kozelets' Ukr. 13 F6
Kozel'sk Russia 13 G5
Kozhikode India 38 B4
Kozhva Russia 12 M2
Kozlu Turkey 27 N4
Kozly Russia 12 H2
Koz'modem'yansk Russia 12 J4
Kožuf mts Greece/Macedonia 27 J4
Kōzu-shima i. Japan 45 E6
Kozyatyn Ukr. 13 F6
Kpandae Ghana 46 C4
Krabi Thai. 31 I6
Krâchéh Cambodia 31 J5
Kraddsele Sweden 14 J4
Kragerø Norway 15 F7
Kragujevac Serbia 27 I2
Krakau Poland see Kraków
Kraków Poland 17 Q5
Kralendijk Bonaire 67 K6
Kramators'k Ukr. 13 H6
Kramfors Sweden 14 J5
Kranidi Greece 27 J6
Kranj Slovenia 26 F1
Kranskop S. Africa 51 J5
Krasavino Russia 12 J3
Krasilov Ukr. see Krasyliv
Krasino Russia 28 G2
Kraskino Russia 44 C4
Krāslava Latvia 15 O9
Krasnaya Gorbatka Russia 12 I5
Krasnoarmeysk Russia 13 J6
Krasnoarmeysk Ukr. see Krasnoarmiys'k
Krasnoarmiys'k Ukr. 13 H6
Krasnoborsk Russia 12 J3
Krasnodar Russia 13 H7
Krasnodar Kray admin. div. Russia see Krasnodarskiy Kray
Krasnodarskiy Kray admin. div. Russia 34 E1
Krasnodon Ukr. 13 H6
Krasnogorodsk Russia 15 P8
Krasnogorsk Russia 44 F2
Krasnogorskoye Russia 12 L4
Krasnograd Ukr. see Krasnohrad
Krasnogvardeysk Uzbek. see Bulung'ur
Krasnogvardeyskoye Russia 13 I7
Krasnohrad Ukr. 13 G6
Krasnohvardiys'ke Ukr. 13 G7
Krasnokamsk Russia 11 R4
Krasnoperekops'k Ukr. 13 G7
Krasnopol'ye Russia 44 F2
Krasnorechenskiy Russia 44 D3
Krasnoslobodsk Russia 13 I5
Krasnotur'insk Russia 11 S4
Krasnoufimsk Russia 11 R4
Krasnovishersk Russia 11 R3
Krasnovodsk Turkm. see Türkmenbaşy
Krasnovodsk, Mys pt Turkm. 35 I3
Krasnovodskoye Plato plat. Turkm. 35 I2
Krasnowodsk Aylagy b. Turkm. see Türkmenbaşy Aýlagy
Krasnoyarovo Russia 44 C2
Krasnoyarsk Russia 28 K4
Krasnoyarskoye Vodokhranilishche resr Russia 42 G2
Krasnoye Lipetskaya Oblast' Russia 13 H5
Krasnoye Respublika Kalmykiya-Khalm'g-Tangch Russia see Ulan Erge
Krasnoznamenskiy Kazakh. see Yegindykol'
Krasnoznamenskoye Kazakh. see Yegindykol'
Krasnyy Russia 13 F5
Krasnyy Chikoy Russia 43 J2
Krasnyye Baki Russia 12 J4
Krasnyy Kamyshanik Russia see Komsomol'skiy
Krasnyy Kholm Russia 12 H4
Krasnyy Kut Russia 13 J6
Krasnyy Luch Ukr. 13 H6
Krasnyy Lyman Ukr. 13 H6
Krasnyy Yar Russia 13 K7
Krasyliv Ukr. 13 E6
Kratie Cambodia see Krâchéh
Kraulshavn Greenland see Nuussuaq
Kraynovka Russia 13 J8
Krefeld Germany 17 K5
Kremenchug Ukr. see Kremenchuk
Kremenchugskoye Vodokhranilishche resr Ukr. see Kremenchuts'ke Vodoskhovyshche
Kremenchuk Ukr. 13 G6
Kremenchuts'ke Vodoskhovyshche resr Ukr. 13 G6
Křemešník h. Czech Rep. 17 O6
Kremges Ukr. see Svitlovods'k
Kremmydi, Akrotirio pt Greece 27 J6
Krems Austria see Krems an der Donau
Krems an der Donau Austria 17 O6
Kresta, Zaliv g. Russia 29 T3
Kresttsy Russia 12 G4
Kretinga Lith. 15 L9
Kreva Belarus 15 O9
Kribi Cameroon 46 D4
Krichev Belarus see Krychaw
Krikellos Greece 27 I5
Kril'on, Mys c. Russia 44 F3
Krishna India 38 C2
Krishna r. India 38 D2
Krishnanagar India 37 G5
Krishnarajanagara India 38 C3
Krishnaraja Sagara l. India 38 C3
Kristiania Norway see Oslo
Kristiansand Norway 15 E7
Kristianstad Sweden 15 I8
Kristiansund Norway 14 E5
Kristiinankaupunki Fin. see Kristinestad
Kristinehamn Sweden 15 I7
Kristinestad Fin. 14 L5
Kristinopol' Ukr. see Chervonohrad
Kriti i. Greece see Crete
Kritiko Pelagos sea Greece 27 K6
Krivoy Rog Ukr. see Kryvyy Rih
Križevci Croatia 26 G1
Krk i. Croatia 26 F2
Krka, Nacionalni Park nat. park Croatia 26 F3
Krkonošský národní park nat. park Czech Rep./Poland 17 O5
Krokom Sweden 14 I5
Krokstadøra Norway 14 F5
Krokstranda Norway 14 I3
Krolevets' Ukr. 13 G6
Kronoby Fin. 14 M5
Kronprins Christian Land reg. Greenland 77 I1
Kronprins Frederik Bjerge nunataks Greenland 61 O3
Kronshtadt Russia 15 P7
Kronstadt Romania see Braşov
Kronstadt Russia see Kronshtadt
Kroonstad S. Africa 51 H4
Kropotkin Russia 13 I7
Krosno Poland 13 D6
Krotoszyn Poland 17 P5
Kruger National Park S. Africa 51 J2
Kruglikovo Russia 44 D2
Kruglyakov Russia see Oktyabr'skiy
Krui Indon. 41 C8
Kruisfontein S. Africa 50 G8
Kruja Albania see Krujë
Krujë Albania 27 H4
Krumovgrad Bulg. 27 K4
Krungkao Thai. see Ayutthaya
Krung Thep Thai. see Bangkok
Krupa Bos. & Herz. see Bosanska Krupa
Krupa na Uni Bos. & Herz. see Bosanska Krupa
Krupki Belarus 13 F5
Krusenstern, Cape AK U.S.A. 60 B3
Kruševac Serbia 27 I3
Krychaw Belarus 13 F5
Krylov Seamount sea feature N. Atlantic Ocean 72 G4
Krym' pen. Ukr. see Crimea
Krymsk Russia 13 H7
Krymskaya Russia see Krymsk
Kryms'kyy Pivostriv pen. Ukr. see Crimea
Krystynopol Ukr. see Chervonohrad
Kryvyy Rih Ukr. 13 G7
Ksabi Alg. 22 D6
Ksar Chellala Alg. 25 H6
Ksar el Boukhari Alg. 25 H6
Ksar el Kebir Morocco 25 D6
Ksar-es-Souk Morocco see Er Rachidia
Ksenofontova Russia 11 R3
Kshirpai India 37 F5
Ksour Essaf Tunisia 26 D7
Kstovo Russia 12 J4
Kū', Jabal al h. Saudi Arabia 32 G4
Kuaidamao China see Tonghua
Kuala Dungun Malaysia see Dungun
Kuala Lipis Malaysia 41 C7
Kuala Lumpur Malaysia 41 C7
Kuala Terengganu Malaysia 41 C7
Kuandian China 44 B4
Kuantan Malaysia 41 C7
Kuba Azer. see Quba
Kuban' r. Russia 13 H7
Kubār Syria 35 E4
Kubaybāt Syria 39 C2
Kubaysah Iraq 35 F4
Kubenskoye, Ozero l. Russia 12 H4
Kubrat Bulg. 27 L3
Kuchema Russia 12 I2
Kuching Sarawak Malaysia 41 D7
Kucing Sarawak Malaysia see Kuching
Kuçovë Albania 27 H4
Kuda India 36 B5
Kudal India 38 B3
Kudat Sabah Malaysia 41 D7
Kudligi India 38 C3
Kudremukh mt. India 38 B3
Kudymkar Russia 11 Q4
Ku'erqisi China see Fuyun
Kufstein Austria 17 N7
Kugaaruk Nunavut Canada 61 J3
Kugesi Russia 12 J4
Kugka Lhai China 37 G3
Kugluktuk Nunavut Canada 60 G3
Kugmallit Bay N.W.T. Canada 77 A2
Kūh, Khār mt. Iran 35 I5
Kūh, Shīr mt. Iran 35 I5
Kuhanbokano mt. China 37 E3
Kūhdasht Iran 35 G4
Kūhhā-ye Zagros mts Iran see Zagros Mountains
Kūhīn Iran 35 H3
Kuhmo Fin. 14 P4
Kuhmoinen Fin. 15 N6
Kūhrān, Kūh-e mt. Iran 33 I4
Kuis Namibia 50 C3
Kuiseb watercourse Namibia 50 B2
Kuito Angola 49 B5
Kuitun China see Kuytun
Kuivaniemi Fin. 14 N4
Kujang N. Korea 45 B5
Kuji Japan 45 F4
Kujū-san vol. Japan 45 C6
Kukan Russia 44 D2
Kukës Albania 27 I3
Kukesi Albania see Kukës
Kukmor Russia 12 K4
Kukshi India 36 C5
Kukunuru India 38 D2
Kula Turkey 27 M5
Kulaisila India 37 F5
Kula Kangri mt. China/Bhutan 37 G3
Kulandy Kazakh. 28 G5
Kular Russia 29 O2
Kuldīga Latvia 15 L8
Kuldja China see Yining
Kul'dur Russia 44 C2
Kule Botswana 50 E2
Kulebaki Russia 13 I5
Kulgera Australia 55 F6
Kulikovo Russia 12 J3
Kulin Australia 55 B8
Kulja Australia 55 B7
Kulkyne watercourse Australia 58 B3
Kullu India 36 D3
Kulmbach Germany 17 M5
Kŭlob Tajik. 33 K2
Kuloy Russia 12 I3
Kuloy r. Russia 12 I2
Kulp Turkey 35 F3
Kul'sary Kazakh. 30 E2
Kulu India see Kullu
Kulu Turkey 34 D3
Kulunda Russia 42 D2
Kulundinskaya Ravnina plain Kazakh./Russia 42 D2
Kulundinskoye, Ozero salt l. Russia 42 D2
Kulusuk Greenland 61 O3
Kulwin Australia 57 C7
Kulyab Tajik. see Kŭlob
Kuma r. Russia 13 J7
Kumagaya Japan 45 E5
Kumalar Dağı mts Turkey 27 N5
Kumamoto Japan 45 C6
Kumano Japan 45 E6
Kumanovo Macedonia 27 I3
Kumara Russia 44 B2
Kumasi Ghana 46 C4
Kumayri Armenia see Gyumri
Kumba Cameroon 46 D4
Kumbakonam India 38 C4
Kumbet Turkey 27 N5
Kumbharli Ghat mt. India 38 B2
Kumbla India 38 B3
Kumchuru Botswana 50 F2
Kum-Dag Turkm. see Gumdag
Kumdah Saudi Arabia 32 G5
Kumel well Iran 35 I4
Kumeny Russia 12 K4
Kumertau Russia 28 G4
Kumgang-san mt. N. Korea 45 C5
Kumguri India 37 G4
Kumi Uganda 47 G4
Kumla Sweden 15 I7
Kumlu Turkey 39 C1
Kumo Nigeria 46 E3
Kumon Range mts Myanmar 42 H7
Kums Namibia 50 D5
Kumta India 38 B3
Kumu Dem. Rep. Congo 48 C3
Kumukh Russia 35 G2
Kumul China see Hami
Kumund India 38 D1
Kumylzhenskaya Russia see Kumylzhenskiy
Kumylzhenskiy Russia 13 I6
Kunar Sīnd r. Afgh. 36 B2
Kunashir, Ostrov i. Russia 44 G3
Kunashirskiy Proliv sea chan. Japan/Russia see Nemuro-kaikyō
Kunchuk Tso salt l. China 37 E2
Kunda Estonia 15 O7
Kunda India 37 E4
Kundapura India 38 B3
Kundelungu, Parc National de nat. park Dem. Rep. Congo 49 C5
Kundelungu Ouest, Parc National de nat. park Dem. Rep. Congo 49 C5
Kundia India 36 C4
Kunduz Afgh. 36 B1
Kunene r. Angola see Cunene
Kuneneng admin. dist. Botswana see Kweneng
Künes China see Xinyuan
Kungälv Sweden 15 G8
Kungsbacka Sweden 15 H8
Kungshamn Sweden 15 G7
Kungu Dem. Rep. Congo 48 B3
Kungur mt. China see Kongur Shan
Kungur Russia 11 R4
Kuni r. India 38 C2
Kunié i. New Caledonia see Pins, Île des
Kunigal India 38 C3
Kunimi-dake mt. Japan 45 C6
Kunkavav India 36 B5
Kunlun Shan mts China 36 D1
Kunlun Shankou pass China 37 H2
Kunming China 42 I7
Kununurra Australia 54 E3
Kun'ya Russia 12 F4
Kunya-Urgench Turkm. see Köneürgenç
Kuohijärvi l. Fin. 15 N6
Kuoloyarvi Russia 14 P3
Kuopio Fin. 14 O5
Kuortane Fin. 14 M5
Kupa r. Croatia/Slovenia 26 G2
Kupang Indon. 41 E9
Kupari India 37 F5
Kupiškis Lith. 15 N9
Kupreanof Island AK U.S.A. 60 E4
Kupwara India 36 C2
Kup"yans'k Ukr. 13 H6
Kuqa China 42 E4
Kuragino Russia 42 G2
Kurakh Russia 13 J8
Kurama Range mts Asia 33 K1
Kuraminskiy Khrebet mts Asia see Kurama Range
Kurashiki Japan 45 D6
Kurasia India 37 E5
Kurayn i. Saudi Arabia 35 H6
Kurayoshi Japan 45 D6
Kurchatov Russia 13 G6
Kürd, Köh-e mt. Afgh. 36 A2
Kürdämir Azer. 35 H2
Kurdistan reg. Asia 35 F3
Kure Japan 45 D6
Küre Turkey 34 D2
Kure Atoll HI U.S.A. 74 I4
Kuressaare Estonia 15 M7
Kurgal'dzhino Kazakh. see Korgalzhyn
Kurgal'dzhinskiy Kazakh. see Korgalzhyn
Kurgan Russia 28 H4
Kurganinsk Russia 35 F1
Kurgannaya Russia see Kurganinsk
Kurgantyube Tajik. see Qŭrghonteppa
Kuri India 36 B4
Kuria Muria Islands Oman see Ḥalāniyāt, Juzur al
Kuridala (abandoned) Australia 56 C4
Kurigram Bangl. 37 G4
Kurikka Fin. 14 M5
Kuril Basin sea feature Sea of Okhotsk 74 F2
Kuril Islands Russia 44 H3
Kurilovka Russia 13 K6
Kuril'sk Russia 44 G3
Kuril'skiye Ostrova is Russia see Kuril Islands
Kuril Trench sea feature N. Pacific Ocean 74 F3
Kurkino Russia 13 H5
Kurmashkino Kazakh. see Kurshim
Kurmuk Sudan 32 D7
Kurnool India 38 C3
Kurow N.Z. 59 C7
Kurram Pak. 36 B2
Kurri Kurri Australia 58 E4
Kursavka Russia 35 F1
Kurshim Kazakh. 42 E3
Kürshim Kazakh. see Kurshim
Kurshskiy Zaliv b. Lith./Russia see Courland Lagoon
Kuršių marios b. Lith./Russia see Courland Lagoon
Kursk Russia 13 H6
Kurskaya Russia 35 G1
Kurskiy Zaliv b. Lith./Russia see Courland Lagoon
Kurşunlu Turkey 34 D2
Kurtalan Turkey 35 F3
Kurtoğlu Burnu pt Turkey 27 M6
Kurtpınar Turkey 39 B1
Kurucaşile Turkey 34 D2
Kuruçay Turkey 34 E3
Kurukshetra India 36 D3
Kuruk Tag mts China 42 F4
Kuruman S. Africa 50 F4
Kuruman watercourse S. Africa 50 E4
Kurume Japan 45 C6
Kurumkan Russia 43 K2
Kurunegala Sri Lanka 38 D5
Kurupam India 38 D2
Kurush, Jebel hills Sudan 32 D5
Kur'ya Russia 11 R3
Kuryk Kazakh. 35 H2
Kuşadası Turkey 27 L6
Kuşadası, Gulf of b. Turkey 27 L6
Kusaie atoll Micronesia see Kosrae
Kusary Azer. see Qusar
Kuşcenneti nat. park Turkey 39 B1
Kuschke Nature Reserve S. Africa 51 I3
Kuş Gölü l. Turkey 27 L4
Kushalgarh India 36 C5
Kushchevskaya Russia 13 H7
Kushimoto Japan 45 D6
Kushiro Japan 44 G4
Kushka Turkm. see Serhetabat
Kushkopola Russia 12 J3
Kushtagi India 38 C3
Kushtia Bangl. 37 G5
Kuskan Turkey 39 A1
Kuskokwim r. AK U.S.A. 60 B3
Kuskokwim Bay AK U.S.A. 60 B4
Kuskokwim Mountains AK U.S.A. 60 C3
Kuşluyan Turkey see Gölköy
Kusmuryn Kazakh. 30 F1
Kusŏng N. Korea 45 B5
Kustanay Kazakh. see Kostanay
Küstence Romania see Constanţa
Kustia Bangl. see Kushtia
Küt 'Abdollāh Iran 35 H5
Kütahya Turkey 27 M5
Kutaisi Georgia 35 F2
Kut-al-Imara Iraq see Al Küt
Kutan Russia 13 J7
Kutaraja Indon. see Banda Aceh
Kutch, Gulf of India see Kachchh, Gulf of
Kutch, Rann of marsh India see Kachchh, Rann of
Kutchan Japan 44 F4
Kutina Croatia 26 G2
Kutjevo Croatia 26 G2
Kutno Poland 17 Q4
Kutru India 38 D2
Küt Seyyed Na'im Iran 35 H5
Kutu Dem. Rep. Congo 48 B4
Kutubdia Island Bangl. 37 G5
Kutum Sudan 47 F3
Kutztown PA U.S.A. 64 D2
Kuujjua r. N.W.T. Canada 60 G2
Kuujjuaq Que. Canada 61 L4
Kuujjuarapik Que. Canada 61 K4
Kuusamo Fin. 14 P4
Kuusankoski Fin. 15 O6

Kuvango Angola 49 B5
Kuvshinovo Russia 12 G4
Kuwait country Asia 32 G4
Kuwait Kuwait 35 G5
Kuwajleen atoll Marshall Is see Kwajalein
Kūyah/Koye Iraq 35 G3
Kuybyshev Novosibirskaya Oblast' Russia 28 I4
Kuybyshev Respublika Tatarstan Russia see Bolgar
Kuybyshev Samarskaya Oblast' Russia see Samara
Kuybysheve Ukr. 13 H7
Kuybyshevka-Vostochnaya Russia see Belogorsk
Kuybyshevskoye Vodokhranilishche resr Russia 13 K5
Kuyeda Russia 11 R4
Kuygan Kazakh. 42 C3
Kuytun China 42 E4
Kuytun Russia 42 I2
Kuyucak Turkey 27 M6
Kuzino Russia 11 R4
Kuznechnoye Russia 15 P6
Kuznetsk Russia 13 J5
Kuznetsovo Russia 44 E3
Kuznetsovs'k Ukr. 13 E6
Kuzovatovo Russia 13 J5
Kvænangen sea chan. Norway 14 L1
Kvaløya i. Norway 14 K2
Kvalsund Norway 14 M1
Kvarnerić sea chan. Croatia 26 F2
Kvitøya i. Svalbard 28 E2
Kwa r. Dem. Rep. Congo see Kasaï
Kwabhaca S. Africa see Mount Frere
Kwadelen atoll Marshall Is see Kwajalein
KwaDukuza S. Africa 51 J5
Kwajalein atoll Marshall Is 74 H5
Kwale Nigeria 46 D4
KwaMashu S. Africa 51 J5
KwaMhlanga S. Africa 51 I3
Kwa Mtoro Tanz. 49 D4
Kwangchow China see Guangzhou
Kwangsi Chuang Autonomous Region aut. reg. China see Guangxi Zhuangzu Zizhiqu
Kwangtung prov. China see Guangdong
Kwanmo-bong mt. N. Korea 44 C4
KwaNobuhle S. Africa 51 G7
KwaNojoli S. Africa 51 G7
Kwanonqubela S. Africa 51 H7
KwaNonzame S. Africa 50 G6
Kwanza r. Angola see Cuanza
Kwatarkwashi Nigeria 46 D3
Kwatinidubu S. Africa 51 H7
KwaZamokhule S. Africa 51 I4
KwaZamukucinga S. Africa 50 G7
Kwazamuxolo S. Africa 50 G6
KwaZanele S. Africa 51 I4
KwaZulu-Natal prov. S. Africa 51 J5
Kweichow prov. China see Guizhou
Kweiyang China see Guiyang
Kwekwe Zimbabwe 49 C5
Kweneng admin. dist. Botswana 50 G2
Kwenge r. Dem. Rep. Congo 49 B4
Kwezi-Naledi S. Africa 51 H6
Kwidzyn Poland 17 Q4
Kwikila P.N.G. 52 E2
Kwilu r. Angola/Dem. Rep. Congo 49 B4
Kwoka mt. Indon. 41 F8
Kyabra Australia 57 C5
Kyabram Australia 58 B6
Kyakhta Russia 42 J2
Kyalite Australia 58 A5
Kyancutta Australia 55 F8
Kyangin Myanmar 37 I6
Kyangngoin China 37 H3
Kyaukpadaung Myanmar 37 H5
Kyaukpyu Myanmar 37 H6
Kyaukse Myanmar 37 I5
Kyauktaw Myanmar 37 H5
Kybartai Lith. 15 M9
Kyêbxang Co l. China 37 G2
Kyela Tanz. 49 D4
Kyelang India 36 D2
Kyidaunggan Myanmar 37 I6
Kyiv Ukr. see Kiev
Kyivs'ke Vodoskhovyshche resr Ukr. 13 F6
Kyklades is Greece see Cyclades
Kyle of Lochalsh U.K. 20 D3
Kyllini mt. Greece 27 J6
Kymi Greece 27 K5
Kymis, Akrotirio pt Greece 27 K5
Kynazhegubskoye Vodokhranilishche l. Russia 14 R3
Kyneton Australia 58 B6
Kynuna Australia 56 C4
Kyoga, Lake Uganda 48 D3
Kyōga-misaki pt Japan 45 D6
Kyogle Australia 58 F2
Kyōto Japan 45 D6
Kyparissia Greece 27 I6
Kypros country Asia see Cyprus
Kyra Russia 43 K3
Kyra Panagia i. Greece 27 K5
Kyrenia Cyprus 39 A2
Kyrenia Mountains Cyprus see Pentadaktylos Range
Kyrgyz Ala-Too mts Kazakh./Kyrg. see Kirghiz Range
Kyrgyzstan country Asia 31 G2
Kyrksæterøra Norway 14 F5
Kyrta Russia 11 R3
Kyssa Russia 12 J2
Kytalyktakh Russia 29 O3
Kythira i. Greece 27 J6
Kythnos i. Greece 27 K6
Kyunglung China 36 E3
Kyunhla Myanmar 37 H5
Kyuquot B.C. Canada 62 B1
Kyurdamir Azer. see Kürdämir
Kyūshū i. Japan 45 C7
Kyushu-Palau Ridge sea feature N. Pacific Ocean 74 F4
Kyustendil Bulg. 27 J3
Kywong Australia 58 C5
Kyyev Ukr. see Kiev
Kyyiv Ukr. see Kiev
Kyyjärvi Fin. 14 N5
Kyzyl Russia 42 G2
Kyzyl-Burun Azer. see Siyäzän
Kyzyl-Kiya Kyrg. see Kyzyl-Kyya
Kyzylkum, Peski des. Kazakh./Uzbek. see Kyzylkum Desert
Kyzylkum Desert Kazakh./Uzbek. 30 F2
Kyzyl-Kyya Kyrg. 42 C4
Kyzyl-Mazhalyk Russia 42 G2
Kyzylorda Kazakh. 42 B4
Kyzylrabot Tajik. see Qizilrabot
Kyzylsay Kazakh. 35 I2
Kyzylysor Kazakh. 35 H1
Kyzylzhar Kazakh. 42 B3
Kzyl-Dzhar Kazakh. see Kyzylzhar
Kzyl-Orda Kazakh. see Kyzylorda
Kzyltu Kazakh. see Kishkenekol'

L

Laagri Estonia 15 N7
La Angostura, Presa de resr Mex. 66 F5
Laanila Fin. 14 O2
Laascaanood Somalia 48 E3
Laasqoray Somalia 48 E2
Laâyoune W. Sahara 46 B2
La Banda Arg. 70 D3
Labasa Fiji 53 H3
La Baule-Escoublac France 24 C3
Labé Guinea 46 B3
Labinsk Russia 13 I7
Labouheyre France 24 D4
Laboulaye Arg. 70 D4
Labozhskoye Russia 12 L2
Labrador reg. Nfld. and Lab. Canada 61 L4
Labrador City Nfld. and Lab. Canada 61 L4
Labrador Sea Canada/Greenland 61 M3
Lábrea Brazil 68 F5
Labudalin China see Ergun
Labuhanbilik Indon. 41 C7
Labuna Indon. 41 E8
Labyrinth, Lake imp. l. Australia 57 A6
Labytnangi Russia 28 H3
Laç Albania 27 H4
La Calle Alg. see El Kala
La Cañiza Spain see A Cañiza
La Capelle France 24 F2
La Carlota Arg. 70 D4
La Carolina Spain 25 E4
Lăcăuți, Vârful mt. Romania 27 L2
Laccadive, Minicoy and Amindivi Islands union terr. India see Lakshadweep
Laccadive Islands is India see Lakshadweep
Lac du Bonnet Man. Canada 63 H1
Lacedaemon Greece see Sparti
La Ceiba Hond. 67 G5
Lacepede Bay Australia 57 B8
Lacepede Islands Australia 54 C4
Lacha, Ozero l. Russia 12 H3
Lachlan r. Australia 58 A5
La Chorrera Panama 67 I7
Lachute Que. Canada 63 M2
Laçın Azer. 35 G3
La Ciotat France 24 G5
Lac La Biche Alta Canada 60 G4
Lac la Martre N.W.T. Canada see Whatî
Lacombe Alta Canada 62 E1
Laconi Sardinia Italy 26 C5
Laconia NH U.S.A. 64 F1
La Coruña Spain see A Coruña
La Crosse WI U.S.A. 63 I3
La Cruz Mex. 66 C4
La Cuesta Mex. 62 G6
Ladainha Brazil 71 C2
Ladakh reg. India/Pak. 36 D2
Ladakh Range mts India 36 D2
Ladik Turkey 34 D2
Ladnun India 36 C4
Ladoga, Lake Russia 12 F3
Ladozhskoye Ozero l. Russia see Ladoga, Lake
Ladrones terr. N. Pacific Ocean see Northern Mariana Islands
Ladu mt. India 37 H4
Ladva-Vetka Russia 12 G3
Ladybank U.K. 20 F4
Ladybrand S. Africa 51 H5
Lady Frere S. Africa 51 H6
Lady Grey S. Africa 51 H6
Ladysmith S. Africa 51 I5
Ladzhanurges Georgia see Lajanurp'ekhi
Lae P.N.G. 52 E2
Lærdalsøyri Norway 15 E6
La Esmeralda Bol. 68 F8
Læsø i. Denmark 15 G8
Lafayette Alg. see Bougaa
Lafayette IN U.S.A. 63 J3
Lafayette LA U.S.A. 63 I5
Lafia Nigeria 46 D4
Lafiagi Nigeria 46 D4
La Flèche France 24 D3
Laforge Que. Canada 61 K4
Lāft Iran 33 I4
La Galite i. Tunisia 26 C6
Lagan' Russia 13 J7
Lagan r. U.K. 21 G3
Lagarto Brazil 69 K6
Lågen r. Norway 15 G7
Lages Brazil 71 A4
Lagg U.K. 20 D5
Laggan U.K. 20 E3
Laghouat Alg. 22 E5
Lagkor Co salt l. China 37 F2
Lago Agrio Ecuador see Nueva Loja
Lagoa Santa Brazil 71 C2
Lagoa Vermelha Brazil 71 A5
Lagodekhi Georgia 35 G2
Lagolândia Brazil 71 A1
La Gomera i. Canary Is 46 B2
Lagos Nigeria 46 D4
Lagos Port. 25 B5
Lagosa Tanz. 49 C4
La Grande OR U.S.A. 62 D2
La Grande 3, Réservoir resr Que. Canada 61 K4
La Grande 4, Réservoir resr Que. Canada 61 K4
La Grange Australia 54 C4
La Grange CA U.S.A. 65 B2
La Grange GA U.S.A. 63 J5
La Gran Sabana plat. Venez. 68 F2
La Grita Venez. 68 D2
Laguna Brazil 71 A5
Laguna, Picacho de la mt. Mex. 66 B4
Laguna Dam AZ/CA U.S.A. 65 E4
Laguna Mountains CA U.S.A. 65 D4
Lagunas Chile 70 C2
Laguna San Rafael, Parque Nacional nat. park Chile 70 B7
Laha China 44 B2
La Habana Cuba see Havana
La Habra CA U.S.A. 65 D4
Lahad Datu Sabah Malaysia 41 D7
Laharpur India 36 E4
Lahat Indon. 41 C8
Lahe Myanmar 37 H4
Lahemaa rahvuspark nat. park Estonia 15 N7
Laḥij Yemen 32 F7
Lāhījān Iran 35 H3
Laholm Sweden 15 H8
Lahore Pak. 33 L3
Lahri Pak. 36 B3
Lāhrūd Iran 35 G3
Lahti Fin. 15 N6
Laï Chad 47 E4
Laibach Slovenia see Ljubljana
Laidley Australia 58 F1
L'Aigle France 24 E2
Laihia Fin. 14 M5
Laimakuri India 37 H4
Laimos, Akrotirio pt Greece 27 J5
Laingsburg S. Africa 50 E7
Lainioälven r. Sweden 14 M3
Lairg U.K. 20 E2
Laishevo Russia 12 K5
Laitila Fin. 15 L6
Laives Italy 26 D1
Laiwu China 43 L5
Laiyang China 43 M5
Laizhou China 43 L5
Laizhou Wan b. China 43 L5
Lajamanu Australia 54 E4
Lajanurp'ekhi Georgia 35 F2
Lajeado Brazil 71 A5
Lajes Brazil 69 K5
La Junta Mex. 62 F6
La Junta CO U.S.A. 62 G4
Lakadiya India 36 B5
La Kagera, Parc National de nat. park Rwanda see Akagera National Park
L'Akagera, Parc National de nat. park Rwanda see Akagera National Park
Lakeba i. Fiji 53 I3
Lake Bardawil Reserve nature res. Egypt 39 A4
Lake Bolac Australia 58 A6
Lake Cargelligo Australia 58 C4
Lake Cathie Australia 58 F3
Lake Charles LA U.S.A. 63 I5
Lake City FL U.S.A. 63 K5
Lake Clark National Park and Preserve AK U.S.A. 60 C3
Lake District National Park U.K. 18 D4
Lake Eildon National Park Australia 58 B6
Lakefield Australia 56 D2
Lake Gairdner National Park Australia 57 B7
Lake George NY U.S.A. 64 E1
Lake Grace Australia 55 B8
Lake Harbour Nunavut Canada see Kimmirut
Lake Havasu City AZ U.S.A. 65 E3
Lakehurst NJ U.S.A. 64 D2
Lake Isabella CA U.S.A. 65 C3
Lake King Australia 55 B8
Lakeland FL U.S.A. 63 K6
Lakemba i. Fiji see Lakeba
Lake Nash Australia 56 B4
Lake Paringa N.Z. 59 B6
Lake Pleasant NY U.S.A. 64 D1
Lakeport CA U.S.A. 65 A1
Lake Providence LA U.S.A. 63 I5
Lakes Entrance Australia 58 D6
Lakeside VA U.S.A. 64 C4
Lakes of Ounianga tourist site Chad 47 F3
Lake Tabourie Australia 58 E5
Lake Tekapo N.Z. 59 C7
Lake Torrens National Park Australia 57 B6
Lakeview OR U.S.A. 62 C3
Lakewood NJ U.S.A. 64 D2
Lakewood NY U.S.A. 64 B1
Lakha India 36 B4
Lakhdenpokh'ya Russia 14 Q6
Lakhimpur Assam India see North Lakhimpur
Lakhimpur Uttar Prad. India 36 E4
Lakhisarai India 37 F4
Lakhish, Naḥal r. Israel 39 B4
Lakhnadon India 36 D5
Lakhpat India 36 B5
Lakhtar India 36 B5
Lakki Marwat Pak. 33 L3
Lakonikos Kolpos b. Greece 27 J6
Lakor i. Indon. 54 E2
Lakota Côte d'Ivoire 46 C4
Laksefjorden sea chan. Norway 14 O1
Lakselv Norway 14 N1
Lakshadweep India 38 B4
Lakshadweep union terr. India 38 B4
Lakshettipet India 38 C2
Lakshmipur Bangl. 37 G5
Laksmipur Bangl. see Lakshmipur
Lalaghat India 37 H4
Lalbara India 38 D1
L'Alcora Spain 25 F3
Lalganj India 37 F4
Lālī Iran 35 H4
La Ligua Chile 70 B4
Laliki Indon. 54 D1
Lalin China 44 B3
Lalín Spain 25 B2
La Línea de la Concepción Spain 25 D5
Lalin He r. China 44 B3
Lalitpur India 36 D4
Lalitpur Nepal see Patan
Lalmanirhat Bangl. see Lalmonirhat
Lalmonirhat Bangl. 37 G4
La Loche Sask. Canada 60 H4
La Louvière Belgium 16 J5
Lal'sk Russia 12 J3
Lalung La pass China 37 F3
Lama Bangl. 37 H5
La Macarena, Parque Nacional nat. park Col. 68 D3
La Maddalena Sardinia Italy 26 C4
Lamadian China 44 B3
Lamadianzi China see Lamadian
La Mancha reg. Spain 25 E4
La Manche str. France/U.K. see English Channel
Lamar CO U.S.A. 62 G4
La Marmora, Punta mt. Sardinia Italy 26 C5
La Martre, Lac l. N.W.T. Canada 60 G3
Lamas r. Turkey 39 B1
Lambaréné Gabon 48 B4
Lambasa Fiji see Labasa
Lambayeque Peru 68 C5
Lambay Island Ireland 21 G4
Lambert atoll Marshall Is see Ailinglaplap
Lambert Glacier Antarctica 76 E2
Lambert's Bay S. Africa 50 D7
Lambeth Ont. Canada 64 A1
Lambi India 36 C3
Lambourn Downs hills U.K. 19 F7
Lamego Port. 25 C3
La Merced Arg. 70 C3
La Merced Peru 68 C6
Lāmerd Iran 35 I6
Lameroo Australia 57 C7
La Mesa CA U.S.A. 65 D4
Lamesa TX U.S.A. 62 G5
Lamia Greece 27 J5
Lamington National Park Australia 58 F2
Lammerlaw Range mts N.Z. 59 B7
Lammermuir Hills U.K. 20 G5
Lammhult Sweden 15 I8
Lammi Fin. 15 N6
Lamont CA U.S.A. 65 C3
La Montaña de Covadonga, Parque Nacional de nat. park Spain see Picos de Europa, Parque Nacional de los
Lampang Thai. 31 I5
Lampazos Mex. 62 G6
Lampedusa, Isola di i. Sicily Italy 26 E7
Lampeter U.K. 19 C6
Lampsacus Turkey see Lâpseki
Lamu Kenya 48 E4
Lamu Myanmar 37 H6
Lanark U.K. 20 F5
Lancang Jiang r. China see Mekong
Lancaster U.K. 18 E4
Lancaster CA U.S.A. 65 C3
Lancaster PA U.S.A. 64 C2
Lancaster SC U.S.A. 63 K5
Lancaster VA U.S.A. 64 C4
Lancaster Canal U.K. 18 E5
Lancaster Sound str. Nunavut Canada 61 J2
Lanchow China see Lanzhou
Landana Angola see Cacongo
Landau an der Isar Germany 17 N6
Landeck Austria 17 M7
Landeh Iran 35 H5
Lander watercourse Australia 54 E5
Lander WY U.S.A. 62 F3
Landhi Pak. 36 A4
Landor Australia 55 B6
Landsberg Poland see Gorzów Wielkopolski
Landsberg am Lech Germany 17 M6
Land's End pt U.K. 19 B8
Landshut Germany 17 N6
Landskrona Sweden 15 H9
Lanesborough Ireland 21 E4
La'nga Co l. China 36 E3
Langar Afgh. 36 B2
Langberg mts S. Africa 50 F5
Langdon ND U.S.A. 62 H2
Langeac France 24 F4
Langeberg mts S. Africa 50 D7
Langeland i. Denmark 15 G9
Längelmäki Fin. 15 N6
Langenthal Switz. 24 H3
Langesund Norway 15 F7
Langfang China 43 L5
Langgar China 37 H3
Langjan Nature Reserve S. Africa 51 I2
Langjökull Iceland 14 [inset 2]
Langklip S. Africa 50 E5
Langlo Crossing Australia 57 D5
Langøya i. Norway 14 I2
Langphu mt. China 37 F3
Langport U.K. 19 E7
Langqên Zangbo r. China 36 D3
Langres France 24 G3
Langres, Plateau de France 24 G3
Langru China 36 D1
Langsa Indon. 41 B7
Långsele Sweden 14 J5
Lang Sơn Vietnam 42 J8
Langtang National Park Nepal 37 F3
Langting India 37 H4
Langtoft U.K. 18 G4
Languedoc reg. France 24 E5
Långvattnet Sweden 14 L4
Lanigan Sask. Canada 62 F1
Lanín, Parque Nacional nat. park Arg. 70 B5
Lanín, Volcán vol. Arg./Chile 70 B5
Lanji India 36 E5
Lanka country Asia see Sri Lanka
Länkäran Azer. 35 H3
Lannion France 24 C2
Lansån Sweden 14 M3
Lansing MI U.S.A. 63 K3
Lanxi China 44 B3
Lan Yu i. Taiwan 43 M8
Lanzarote i. Canary Is 46 B2
Lanzhou China 42 I5
Lanzi China 44 A3
Laoag City Phil. 41 E6
Lao Cai Vietnam 31 J4
Laodicea Syria see Latakia
Laodicea Turkey see Denizli
Laodicea ad Lycum Turkey see Denizli
Laodicea ad Mare Syria see Latakia
Laohekou China 43 K6
Laojunmiao China 42 H5
Lao Ling mts China 44 B4
Lao Mangnai China 42 G5
Laon France 24 F2
La Oroya Peru 68 C6
Laos country Asia 41 C6
Laotougou China 44 C4
Laotu Dingzi mt. China 44 B4
Laowohi pass India see Khardung La
Laoye Ling mts Heilongjiang/Jilin China 44 C4
Laoye Ling mts Jilin China 44 B4
Lapa Brazil 71 A4
La Palma i. Canary Is 46 B2
La Palma Panama 67 I7
La Palma del Condado Spain 25 C5
La Panza Range mts CA U.S.A. 65 B3
La Paragua Venez. 68 F2
La Paya, Parque Nacional nat. park Col. 68 D3
La Paz Arg. 70 E4
La Paz Bol. 68 E7
La Paz Hond. 66 G6
La Paz Mex. 66 B4
La Pedrera Col. 68 E4
La Pérouse Strait Japan/Russia 44 F3
La Pesca Mex. 66 E4
Lapinlahti Fin. 14 O5
Lapithos Cyprus 39 A2
La Plata Arg. 70 E4
La Plata MD U.S.A. 64 C3
La Plata, Isla i. Ecuador 68 B4
La Plata, Río de sea chan. Arg./Uruguay 70 E4
Lapmežciems Latvia 15 M8
La Pola Spain 25 D2
La Pola Siero Spain 25 D2
Lapominka Russia 12 I2
Laporte PA U.S.A. 64 C2
Lappajärvi Fin. 14 M5
Lappajärvi l. Fin. 14 M5
Lappeenranta Fin. 15 P6
Läppi Fin. 15 L6
Lappland reg. Europe 14 K3
Lâpseki Turkey 27 L4
Laptevo Russia see Yasnogorsk
Laptev Sea Russia 29 N2
Lapua Fin. 14 M5
Lapurdum France see Bayonne
Laqiya Arbain well Sudan 32 C5
La Quiaca Arg. 70 C2
L'Aquila Italy 26 E3
La Quinta CA U.S.A. 65 D4
Lār Iran 35 I6
Larache Morocco 25 C6
Laramie WY U.S.A. 62 F3
Laramie Mountains WY U.S.A. 62 F3
Laranda Turkey see Karaman
Laranjal Paulista Brazil 71 B3
Laranjeiras do Sul Brazil 70 F3
Laranjinha r. Brazil 71 A3
Larantuka Indon. 41 E8
Larat Indon. 54 E1
Larat i. Indon. 41 F8
Larba Alg. 25 H5
Lärbro Sweden 15 K8
L'Ardenne, Plateau de plat. Belgium see Ardennes
Laredo Spain 25 E2
Laredo TX U.S.A. 62 H6
La Reina Adelaida, Archipiélago de is Chile 70 B8
Largeau Chad see Faya
Largs U.K. 20 E5
L'Ariana Tunisia 26 D6
La Rioja Arg. 70 C3
La Rioja aut. comm. Spain 25 E2
Larisa Greece 27 J5
Larissa Greece see Larisa
Larkana Pak. 33 K4
Lark Passage Australia 56 D2
Larnaca Cyprus 39 A2
Larnaka Cyprus see Larnaca
Larnaka Bay Cyprus 39 A2
Larnakos, Kolpos b. Cyprus see Larnaka Bay
Larne U.K. 21 G3
La Robla Spain 25 D2
La Rochelle France 24 D3
La Roche-sur-Yon France 24 D3
La Roda Spain 25 E4
La Romana Dom. Rep. 67 K5
La Ronge Sask. Canada 60 H4
La Ronge, Lac l. Sask. Canada 60 H4
Larrey Point Australia 54 B4
Larrimah Australia 54 F3
Lars Christensen Coast Antarctica 76 E2
Larsen Ice Shelf Antarctica 76 L2
Larsmo Fin. 14 M5
Larvik Norway 15 G7
Las Anod Somalia see Laascaanood
La Sarre Que. Canada 63 L2
Las Cruces CA U.S.A. 65 B3
Las Cruces NM U.S.A. 62 F5
La Selle, Pic mt. Haiti 67 J5
La Serena Chile 70 B3
La Seu d'Urgell Spain 25 G2
Las Flores Arg. 70 E5
Las Heras Arg. 70 C4
Lashio Shan Myanmar 42 H8
Lashio Myanmar 31 I4
Lashkar India 36 D4
Lashkar Gāh Afgh. 33 J3
Las Juntas Chile 70 C3
Las Lomitas Arg. 70 D2
Las Marismas marsh Spain 25 C5
Las Martinetas Arg. 70 C7
Las Minas, Cerro de mt. Hond. 66 G6
La Société, Archipel de is Fr. Polynesia see Society Islands
Las Palmas de Gran Canaria Canary Is 46 B2
Las Petas Bol. 69 G7
La Spezia Italy 26 C2
Las Plumas Arg. 70 C6
Laspur Pak. 36 C1
Lassance Brazil 71 B2
Las Tablas Panama 67 H7
Las Termas Arg. 70 D3
Last Mountain Lake Sask. Canada 62 F1
Las Tórtolas, Cerro mt. Chile 70 C3
Lastoursville Gabon 48 B4
Lastovo i. Croatia 26 G3
Las Tres Vírgenes, Volcán vol. Mex. 66 B3
Las Tunas Cuba 67 I4
Las Varas Chihuahua Mex. 66 C3
Las Varas Nayarit Mex. 66 C4
Las Varillas Arg. 70 D4
Las Vegas NM U.S.A. 62 F4
Las Vegas NV U.S.A. 65 E2
Las Villuercas mt. Spain 25 D4
Latacunga Ecuador 68 C4
Latady Island Antarctica 76 L2
Latakia Syria 39 B2
La Teste-de-Buch France 24 D4
Latham Australia 55 B7
Latheron U.K. 20 F2
Lathi India 36 B4
Latho India 36 D2
Lathrop CA U.S.A. 65 B2
Latina Italy 26 E4
La Tortuga, Isla i. Venez. 68 E1
Laṭrūn West Bank 39 B4
Lattaquié Syria see Latakia
La Tuque Que. Canada 63 M2
Latur India 38 C2
Latvia country Europe 15 N8
Latvija country Europe see Latvia
Latviyskaya S.S.R. country Europe see Latvia
Lauca, Parque Nacional nat. park Chile 68 E7
Lauchhammer Germany 17 N5
Lauder U.K. 20 G5
Laudio Spain 25 E2
Laufen Switz. 24 H3
Lauge Koch Kyst reg. Greenland 61 L2
Laughlen, Mount Australia 55 F5
Lauka Estonia 15 M7
Launceston Australia 57 [inset]
Launceston U.K. 19 C8
Laune r. Ireland 21 C5
La Unión Bol. 68 F7
Laura Australia 56 D2
Laurel DE U.S.A. 64 D3
Laurel MS U.S.A. 63 J5
Laureldale PA U.S.A. 64 D2
Laurel Hill hills PA U.S.A. 64 B3
Laurencekirk U.K. 20 G4
Laurieton Australia 58 F3
Laurinburg NC U.S.A. 63 L5
Lauru i. Solomon Is see Choiseul
Lausanne Switz. 24 H3
Laut i. Indon. 41 D8
Laut Bali sea Indon. see Bali, Laut
Lautem East Timor 54 D2
Laut Flores sea Indon. see Flores, Laut
Lautoka Fiji 53 H3
Laut Sawu sea Indon. see Sawu, Laut
Lauvuskylä Fin. 14 P5
Laval France 24 D2
La Vall d'Uixó Spain 25 F4
Lāvān, Jazīreh-ye i. Iran 35 I6
Lavapié, Punta pt Chile 70 B5
Lāvar Iran 35 H5
Laveaga Peak CA U.S.A. 65 B2
La Vega Dom. Rep. 67 J5
Laverton Australia 55 C7
La Vila Joíosa Spain see Villajoyosa-La Vila Joiosa
La Viña Peru 68 C5
Lavongal i. P.N.G. see New Hanover
Lavras Brazil 71 B3
Lavumisa Swaziland 51 J4
Lavushi-Manda National Park Zambia 49 D5
Lawa India 36 C4
Lawa Myanmar 37 I4
Lawa Pak. 36 B2
Law Dome Antarctica 76 F2
Lawn Hill National Park Australia 56 B3
Lawra Ghana 46 C3
Lawrence KS U.S.A. 63 H4
Lawrence MA U.S.A. 64 F1
Lawrenceburg TN U.S.A. 63 J4
Lawrence Wells, Mount h. Australia 55 C6
Lawton OK U.S.A. 62 H5
Lawz, Jabal al mt. Saudi Arabia 34 D5
Laxå Sweden 15 I7
Laxey Isle of Man 18 C4
Laxo U.K. 20 [inset]
Laya r. Russia 12 M2
Laydennyy, Mys c. Russia 12 J1
Laylā Saudi Arabia 32 G5
Laylā salt pan Saudi Arabia 39 D4
Laysan Island HI U.S.A. 74 I4
Layyah Pak. 33 L3
Lazarev Russia 44 F1
Lazarevac Serbia 27 I2
Lázaro Cárdenas Mex. 66 D5
Lazcano Uruguay 70 F4
Lazdijai Lith. 15 M9
Lazo Primorskiy Kray Russia 44 D4
Lazo Respublika Sakha (Yakutiya) Russia 29 O3
Lead SD U.S.A. 62 G3
Leader Water r. U.K. 20 G5
Leadville Australia 58 D4
Leaf Bay Que. Canada see Tasiujaq
Leane, Lough l. Ireland 21 C5
Leap Ireland 21 C6
Leatherhead U.K. 19 G7
Leavitt Peak CA U.S.A. 65 C1
Lebanon country Asia 39 B2
Lebanon MO U.S.A. 63 I4
Lebanon NH U.S.A. 64 E1
Lebanon PA U.S.A. 64 C2
Lebanon Mountains Lebanon see Liban, Jebel
Lebec CA U.S.A. 65 C3
Lebedyan' Russia 13 H5
Le Blanc France 24 E3
Lębork Poland 17 P3
Lebowakgomo S. Africa 51 I3
Lebrija Spain 25 C5
Łebsko, Jezioro lag. Poland 17 P3
Lebu Chile 70 B5
Lebyazh'ye Kazakh. see Akku
Lebyazh'ye Russia 12 K4
Le Caire Egypt see Cairo
Lecce Italy 26 H4
Lecco Italy 26 C2
Lech r. Austria/Germany 17 M7
Lechaina Greece 27 I6
Lechang China 43 K7
Le Chasseron mt. Switz. 24 H3
Lechtaler Alpen mts Austria 17 M7
Leck Germany 17 L3
Le Creusot France 24 G3
Le Crotoy France 19 I8
Lectoure France 24 E5
Ledbury U.K. 19 E6
Ledesma Spain 25 D3
Ledmore U.K. 20 E2
Ledmozero Russia 14 R4
Le Dorat France 24 E3
Lee r. Ireland 21 D6
Lee MA U.S.A. 64 E1
Leech Lake MN U.S.A. 63 I2
Leeds U.K. 18 F5
Leedstown U.K. 19 B8
Leek U.K. 19 E5
Leesburg VA U.S.A. 64 C3
Lee Steere Range hills Australia 55 C6
Leesville LA U.S.A. 63 I5
Leesville Lake OH U.S.A. 64 A2
Leesville Lake VA U.S.A. 64 B4
Leeton Australia 58 C5
Leeu-Gamka S. Africa 50 E7
Leeuwarden Neth. 17 J4
Leeuwin, Cape Australia 55 A8
Leeuwin-Naturaliste National Park Australia 55 A8
Lee Vining CA U.S.A. 65 C2
Leeward Islands Caribbean Sea 67 L5
Lefka Cyprus 39 A2
Lefkada Greece 27 I5
Lefkada i. Greece 27 I5
Lefkás Greece see Lefkada
Lefke Cyprus see Lefka
Lefkimmi Greece 27 I5
Lefkoniko Cyprus see Lefkonikon
Lefkonikon Cyprus 39 A2
Lefkoşa Cyprus see Nicosia
Lefkosia Cyprus see Nicosia
Lefroy, Lake imp. l. Australia 55 C7
Legges Tor mt. Australia 57 [inset]
Leghorn Italy see Livorno
Legnago Italy 26 D2
Legnica Poland 17 P5
Le Grand CA U.S.A. 65 B2
Leguna Australia 54 E3
Leh India 36 D2
Le Havre France 24 E2
Lehighton PA U.S.A. 64 D2
Lehmo Fin. 14 P5
Lehtimäki Fin. 14 M5
Lehututu Botswana 50 E2
Leibnitz Austria 17 O7
Leicester U.K. 19 F6
Leichhardt r. Australia 52 B3
Leichhardt Falls Australia 56 B3
Leichhardt Range mts Australia 56 D4
Leiden Neth. 16 J4
Leigh N.Z. 59 E3
Leigh U.K. 18 E5
Leighton Buzzard U.K. 19 G7
Leinster Australia 55 C6
Leinster reg. Ireland 21 F4
Leinster, Mount h. Ireland 21 F5
Leipsoi i. Greece 27 L6
Leipzig Germany 17 N5
Leiranger Norway 14 I3
Leiria Port. 25 B4
Leirvik Norway 15 D7
Leisler, Mount h. Australia 55 E5
Leith Hill h. U.K. 19 G7
Leiva, Cerro mt. Col. 68 D3
Leixlip Ireland 21 F4
Leiyang China 43 K7
Leizhou Bandao pen. China 43 J8
Leka Norway 14 G4
Lékana Congo 48 B4
Le Kef Tunisia 26 C6
Lekhainá Greece see Lechaina
Lekkersing S. Africa 50 C5
Lékoni Gabon 48 B4
Leksand Sweden 15 I6
Leksozero, Ozero l. Russia 14 Q5
Lélouma Guinea 46 B3
Lelystad Neth. 16 J4
Le Maire, Estrecho de sea chan. Arg. 70 C9
Léman, Lac l. France/Switz. see Geneva, Lake
Le Mans France 24 E2
Le Mars IA U.S.A. 63 H3
Lemberg Ukr. see L'viv
Lemdiyya Alg. see Médéa
Leme Brazil 71 B3
Lemesos Cyprus see Limassol
Lemi Fin. 15 O6
Lemieux Islands Nunavut Canada 61 L3
Lemmenjoen kansallispuisto nat. park Fin. 14 N2
Lemmon SD U.S.A. 62 G2
Lemnos i. Greece see Limnos
Lemoncove CA U.S.A. 65 C2
Lemoore CA U.S.A. 65 C2
Le Moyne, Lac l. Que. Canada 61 L4
Lemro r. Myanmar 37 H5
Lemtybozh Russia 11 R3
Le Murge hills Italy 26 G4
Lemvig Denmark 15 F8
Lem"yu r. Russia 12 M3
Lena r. Russia 29 N2
Lenadoon Point Ireland 21 C3
Lena Pillars Nature Park tourist site Russia 29 N3
Lenchung Tso salt l. China 37 E2
Lençóis Brazil 71 C1
Lençóis Maranhenses, Parque Nacional dos nat. park Brazil 69 J4
Lendery Russia 12 F3
Le Neubourg France 19 H9
Lenglong Ling mts China 42 I5
Lengshuijiang China 43 K7
Lenham U.K. 19 H7
Lenhovda Sweden 15 I8
Lenin, Qullai mt. Kyrg./Tajik. see Lenin Peak
Lenina, Pik mt. Kyrg./Tajik. see Lenin Peak
Leninabad Tajik. see Khŭjand
Leninakan Armenia see Gyumri
Lenin Atyndagy Choku mt. Kyrg./Tajik. see Lenin Peak

Lenine Ukr. 34 D1
Leningrad Russia see St Petersburg
Leningrad Oblast admin. div. Russia see Leningradskaya Oblast'
Leningradskaya Russia 13 H7
Leningradskaya Oblast' admin. div. Russia 15 R7
Leningradskiy Russia 29 S3
Lenino Ukr. see Lenine
Leninobod Tajik. see Khŭjand
Lenin Peak Kyrg./Tajik. 42 C5
Leninsk Kazakh. see Baykonyr
Leninsk Russia 13 J6
Leninskiy Russia 13 H5
Leninsk-Kuznetskiy Russia 28 J4
Leninskoye Kirovskaya Oblast' Russia 12 J4
Leninskoye Yevreyskaya Avtonomnaya Oblast' Russia 44 D3
Lenkoran' Azer. see Länkäran
Lenox MA U.S.A. 64 E1
Lens France 24 F1
Lensk Russia 29 M3
Lenti Hungary 26 G1
Lentini Sicily Italy 26 F6
Léo Burkina Faso 46 C3
Leoben Austria 17 O7
Leodhais, Eilean i. U.K. see Lewis, Isle of
Leominster U.K. 19 E6
Leominster MA U.S.A. 64 F1
León Mex. 66 D4
León Nicaragua 67 G6
León Spain 25 D2
Leonardtown MD U.S.A. 64 C3
Leonardville Namibia 50 D2
Leongatha Australia 58 B7
Leonidio Greece 27 J6
Leonidovo Russia 44 F2
Leonora Australia 55 C7
Leopold WV U.S.A. 64 A3
Leopold and Astrid Coast Antarctica see King Leopold and Queen Astrid Coast
Léopold II, Lac l. Dem. Rep. Congo see Mai-Ndombe, Lac
Leopoldina Brazil 71 C3
Leopoldo de Bulhões Brazil 71 A2
Léopoldville Dem. Rep. Congo see Kinshasa
Lepalale S. Africa see Lephalale
Lepaya Latvia see Liepāja
Lepel' Belarus see Lyepyel'
Lephalala r. S. Africa 51 H2
Lephalale S. Africa 51 H2
Lephepe Botswana 51 G2
Lephoi S. Africa 51 G6
Leping China 43 L7
Lepontine Alps mts Italy/Switz. 26 C1
Leppävirta Fin. 14 O5
Lepsa Kazakh. see Lepsi
Lepsi Kazakh. 42 D3
Le Puy France see Le Puy-en-Velay
Le Puy-en-Velay France 24 F4
Lerala Botswana 51 H2
Leratswana S. Africa 51 H5
Léré Mali 46 C3
Leribe Lesotho see Hlotse
Lérida Col. 68 D4
Lérida Spain see Lleida
Lerik Azer. 35 H3
Lerma Spain 25 E2
Lermontov Russia 35 F1
Lermontovka Russia 44 D3
Lermontovskiy Russia see Lermontov
Leros i. Greece 27 L6
Le Roy NY U.S.A. 64 C1
Le Roy, Lac l. Que. Canada 61 K4
Lerum Sweden 15 H8
Lerwick U.K. 20 [inset]
Les Amirantes is Seychelles see Amirante Islands
Lesbos i. Greece 27 K5
Les Cayes Haiti 67 J5
Leshan China 42 I7
Leshukonskoye Russia 12 J2
Lesi watercourse South Sudan 47 F4
Leskhimstroy Ukr. see Syeverodonets'k
Leskovac Serbia 27 I3
Lesneven France 24 B2
Lesnoy Kirovskaya Oblast' Russia 12 L4
Lesnoy Murmanskaya Oblast' Russia see Umba
Lesnoye Russia 12 G4
Lesogorskoye Russia 44 F2
Lesopil'noye Russia 44 D3
Lesosibirsk Russia 28 K4
Lesotho country Africa 51 I5
Lesozavodsk Russia 44 D3
L'Espérance Rock i. Kermadec Is 53 I5
Les Pieux France 19 F9
Les Sables-d'Olonne France 24 D3
Lesser Antarctica reg. Antarctica see West Antarctica
Lesser Antilles is Caribbean Sea 67 K6
Lesser Caucasus mts Asia 35 F2
Lesser Himalaya mts India/Nepal 36 D3
Lesser Khingan Mountains China see Xiao Hinggan Ling
Lesser Slave Lake Alta Canada 60 G4
Lester WV U.S.A. 64 A4
Lestijärvi Fin. 14 N5
Les Vans France 24 G4
Lesvos i. Greece see Lesbos
Leszno Poland 17 P5
Letaba S. Africa 51 J2
Letchworth Garden City U.K. 19 G7
Le Télégraphe h. France 24 G3
Leteri India 36 D4
Letha Range mts Myanmar 37 H5
Lethbridge Alta Canada 62 E2
Leti i. Indon. 54 D2
Leti, Kepulauan is Indon. 41 E8
Leticia Col. 68 E4
Letlhakeng Botswana 51 G3
Letnerechenskiy Russia 12 G2
Letniy Navolok Russia 12 H2
Le Touquet-Paris-Plage France 19 I8
Letpadan Myanmar 42 H9
Le Tréport France 24 E1
Letsitele S. Africa 51 J2
Letsopa S. Africa 51 G4
Letterkenny Ireland 21 E3
Lëtzebuerg country Europe see Luxembourg
Léua Angola 49 C5
Leucas Greece see Lefkada
Leucate, Étang de l. France 24 F5
Leuchars U.K. 20 G4
Leukas Greece see Lefkada
Leunovo Russia 12 I2
Leura Australia 56 E4
Leuven Belgium 16 J5
Levanger Norway 14 G5
Levante, Riviera di coastal area Italy 26 C2
Levanto Italy 26 C2
Levashi Russia 13 J8
Levelland TX U.S.A. 62 G5
Leven England U.K. 18 G5
Leven Scotland U.K. 20 G4
Leven, Loch l. U.K. 20 F4
Lévêque, Cape Australia 54 C4
Leverkusen Germany 17 K5
Lévézou mts France 24 F4
Levice Slovakia 17 Q6
Levin N.Z. 59 E5
Levitha i. Greece 27 L6
Levittown NY U.S.A. 64 E2
Levittown PA U.S.A. 64 D2
Levkás i. Greece see Lefkada
Levkímmi Greece see Lefkimmi
Levskigrad Bulg. see Karlovo
Lev Tolstoy Russia 13 H5
Lévy, Cap c. France 19 F9
Lewe Myanmar 37 I6
Lewerberg mt. S. Africa 50 C5
Lewes U.K. 19 H8
Lewes DE U.S.A. 64 D3
Lewis, Isle of i. U.K. 20 C2
Lewis, Lake imp. l. Australia 54 F5
Lewisburg PA U.S.A. 64 C2
Lewisburg WV U.S.A. 64 A4
Lewis Pass N.Z. 59 D6
Lewis Range hills Australia 54 E5
Lewis Range mts MT U.S.A. 62 E2
Lewiston ID U.S.A. 62 D2
Lewistown MT U.S.A. 62 F2
Lewistown PA U.S.A. 64 C2
Lexington KY U.S.A. 63 K4
Lexington NE U.S.A. 62 H3
Lexington VA U.S.A. 64 B4
Lexington Park MD U.S.A. 64 C3
Leyden Neth. see Leiden
Leyla Dāgh mt. Iran 35 G3
Lezha Albania see Lezhë
Lezhë Albania 27 H4
L'gov Russia 13 G6
Lharigarbo China 37 G2
Lhasa China 37 G3
Lhasoi China 37 H3
Lhatog China 37 I3
Lhaviyani Atoll Maldives see Faadhippolhu
Lhazê Xizang China 37 F3
Lhazê Xizang China 37 H3
Lhazhong China 37 F3
Lhoma China 37 G3
Lhorong China 37 H3
Lhotse mt. China/Nepal 37 F4
Lhozhag China 37 G3
Lhuentse Bhutan 37 G4
Lhünzê China 42 G7
Lhünzhub China see Poindo
Liakoura mt. Greece 27 J5
Liancourt Rocks i. N. Pacific Ocean 45 C5
Liandu China see Lishui
Liangdaohe China see Zaring
Liangzhou China see Wuwei
Lianhe China see Qianjiang
Lianjiang China see Xingguo
Lianshan China 43 M4
Lianyin China 44 A1
Lianyungang China 43 L6
Liaocheng China 43 L5
Liaodong Bandao pen. China 43 M4
Liaodong Wan b. China 43 M4
Liao He r. China 44 A4
Liaoning prov. China 44 A4
Liaoyang China 44 A4
Liaoyuan China 44 B4
Liaozhong China 44 A4
Liapades Greece 27 H5
Liard r. N.W.T. Canada 60 F3
Liari Pak. 36 A4
Liathach mt. U.K. 20 D3
Liban country Asia see Lebanon
Liban, Jebel mts Lebanon 39 C2
Libau Latvia see Liepāja
Libby MT U.S.A. 62 D2
Libenge Dem. Rep. Congo 48 B3
Liberal KS U.S.A. 62 G4
Liberdade Brazil 71 B3
Liberec Czech Rep. 17 O5
Liberia country Africa 46 C4
Liberia Costa Rica 67 G6
Liberty NY U.S.A. 64 D2
Liberty Lake MD U.S.A. 64 C3
Libni, Gebel h. Egypt see Libnī, Jabal
Libnī, Jabal h. Egypt 39 A4
Libode S. Africa 51 I6
Libourne France 24 D4
Libral Well Australia 54 D5
Libreville Gabon 48 A3
Libya country Africa 47 E2
Libyan Desert Egypt/Libya 32 C5
Libyan Plateau Egypt 34 B5
Licantén Chile 70 B4
Licata Sicily Italy 26 E6
Lice Turkey 35 F3
Lichas hills Greece 27 J5
Lichfield U.K. 19 F6
Lichinga Moz. 49 D5
Lichtenburg S. Africa 51 H4
Lida Belarus 15 N10
Liddel Water r. U.K. 20 G5
Lidfontein Namibia 50 D3
Lidköping Sweden 15 H7
Lidsjöberg Sweden 14 I4
Liebig, Mount Australia 55 E5
Liechtenstein country Europe 24 I3
Liège Belgium 17 J5
Liegnitz Poland see Legnica
Lieksa Fin. 14 Q5
Lielupe r. Latvia 15 N8
Lielvärde Latvia 15 N8
Lienart Dem. Rep. Congo 48 C3
Lienchung i. Taiwan see Mazu Dao
Lienz Austria 17 N7
Liepāja Latvia 15 L8
Liepaya Latvia see Liepāja
Lietuva country Europe see Lithuania
Liezen Austria 17 O7
Liffey r. Ireland 21 F4
Lifford Ireland 21 E3
Lifi Mahuida mt. Arg. 70 C6
Lifou i. New Caledonia 53 G4
Lifu i. New Caledonia see Lifou
Līgatne Latvia 15 N8
Lightning Ridge Australia 58 C2
Ligonha r. Moz. 49 D5
Ligure, Mar sea France/Italy see Ligurian Sea
Ligurian Sea France/Italy 26 C3
Ligurienne, Mer sea France/Italy see Ligurian Sea
Ligurta AZ U.S.A. 65 E4
Lihir Group is P.N.G. 52 F2
Lihou Reef and Cays Australia 56 E3
Liivi laht b. Estonia/Latvia see Riga, Gulf of
Lijiang China 42 I7
Lika reg. Croatia 26 F2
Likasi Dem. Rep. Congo 49 C5
Likati Dem. Rep. Congo 48 C3
Likhachevo Ukr. see Pervomays'kyy
Likhachyovo Ukr. see Pervomays'kyy
Likhapani India 37 H4
Likhás hills Greece see Lichas
Likhoslavl' Russia 12 G4
Liku Indon. 41 C7
Likupang Russia 12 I4
L'Île-Rousse Corsica France 24 I5
Lilla Pak. 36 C2
Lilla Edet Sweden 15 H7
Lille France 24 F1
Lille Bælt sea chan. Denmark see Little Belt
Lillebonne France 19 H9
Lillehammer Norway 15 G6
Lillesand Norway 15 F7
Lillestrøm Norway 15 G7
Lillholmsjö Sweden 14 I5
Lillian, Point h. Australia 55 D6
Lillooet B.C. Canada 62 C1
Lilongwe Malawi 49 D5
Lilydale Australia 57 B7
Lima Peru 68 C6
Lima NY U.S.A. 64 C1
Lima OH U.S.A. 63 K3
Lima Duarte Brazil 71 C3
Liman Russia 13 J7
Limar Indon. 54 D1
Limassol Cyprus 39 A2
Limavady U.K. 21 F2
Limay r. Arg. 70 C5
Limbaži Latvia 15 N8
Limbunya Australia 54 E4
Lime Acres S. Africa 50 F5
Limeira Brazil 71 B3
Limerick Ireland 21 D5
Limingen Norway 14 H4
Limingen l. Norway 14 H4
Liminka Fin. 14 N4
Limmen Bight b. Australia 56 B2
Limmen National Park Australia 54 F3
Limnos i. Greece 27 K5
Limoeiro Brazil 69 K5
Limoges France 24 E4
Limón Costa Rica see Puerto Limón
Limon CO U.S.A. 62 G4
Limonlu Turkey 39 B1
Limonum France see Poitiers
Limousin reg. France 24 E4
Limoux France 24 F5
Limpopo prov. S. Africa 51 I2
Limpopo r. S. Africa/Zimbabwe 51 K3
Līnah well Saudi Arabia 35 F5
Linakhamari Russia 14 Q2
Linares Chile 70 B5
Linares Mex. 66 E4
Linares Spain 25 E4
Lincang China 42 I8
Linchuan China see Fuzhou
Linck Nunataks nunataks Antarctica 76 K1
Lincoln Arg. 70 D4
Lincoln U.K. 18 G5
Lincoln CA U.S.A. 65 B1
Lincoln IL U.S.A. 63 J3
Lincoln NE U.S.A. 63 H3
Lincoln National Park Australia 57 A7
Lincoln Sea Canada/Greenland 77 J1
Lincolnshire Wolds hills U.K. 18 G5
Linda, Serra hills Brazil 71 C1
Linda Creek watercourse Australia 56 B4
Lindau (Bodensee) Germany 17 L7
Lindeman Group is Australia 56 E4
Linden Guyana 69 G2
Lindesnes c. Norway 15 E7
Líndhos Greece see Lindos
Lindi r. Dem. Rep. Congo 48 C3
Lindi Tanz. 49 D4
Lindian China 44 B3
Lindisfarne i. U.K. see Holy Island
Lindley S. Africa 51 H4
Lindos Greece 23 J4
Lindsay CA U.S.A. 65 C2
Lindside WV U.S.A. 64 A4
Lindum U.K. see Lincoln
Line Islands Kiribati 75 J5
Linesville PA U.S.A. 64 A2
Linfen China 43 K5
Lingampet India 38 C2
Linganamakki Reservoir India 38 B3
Lingcheng China see Lingshui
Lingelethu S. Africa 51 H7
Lingen (Ems) Germany 17 K4
Lingga, Kepulauan is Indon. 41 C8
Lingling China 43 K7
Lingomo Dem. Rep. Congo 48 C3
Lingshui China 43 J9
Lingsugur India 38 C2
Linguère Senegal 46 B3
Lingxia China 44 A3
Lingzi Tang plain Aksai Chin 36 D2
Linhai China 43 M7
Linhares Brazil 71 C2
Linhpa Myanmar 37 H4
Linjiang China 44 B4
Linköping Sweden 15 I7
Linkou China 44 C3
Linlithgow U.K. 20 F5
Linnansaaren kansallispuisto nat. park Fin. 14 P5
Linnhe, Loch inlet U.K. 20 D4
Linosa, Isola di i. Sicily Italy 26 E7
Lins Brazil 71 A3
Lintao China 42 I5
Linton ND U.S.A. 62 G2
Linxi China 43 L4
Linxia China 42 I5
Linyi Shandong China 43 L5
Linyi Shandong China 43 L5
Linz Austria 17 O6
Lion, Golfe du g. France 24 F5
Lions, Gulf of France see Lion, Golfe du
Lioua Chad 47 E3
Lipari Sicily Italy 26 F5
Lipari, Isole is Italy 26 F5
Lipetsk Russia 13 H5
Lipin Bor Russia 12 H3
Lipova Romania 27 I1
Lipovtsy Russia 44 C3
Lipsoi i. Greece see Leipsoi
Lipti Lekh pass Nepal 36 E3
Liptrap, Cape Australia 58 B7
Lira Uganda 48 D3
Liranga Congo 48 B4
Lircay Peru 68 D6
Lisala Dem. Rep. Congo 48 C3
Lisbellaw U.K. 21 E3
Lisboa Port. see Lisbon
Lisbon Port. 25 B4
Lisbon OH U.S.A. 64 A2
Lisburn U.K. 21 F3
Liscannor Bay Ireland 21 C5
Lisdoonvarna Ireland 21 C4
Lishi China see Dingnan
Lishu China 44 B4
Lishui China 43 L7
Lisichansk Ukr. see Lysychans'k
Lisieux France 24 E2
Liskeard U.K. 19 C8
Liski Russia 13 H6
Lismore Australia 58 F2
Lismore Ireland 21 E5
Lisnarrick U.K. 21 E3
Lisnaskea U.K. 21 E3
Liss mt. Saudi Arabia 39 D4
Lissa Poland see Leszno
Lister, Mount Antarctica 76 H1
Listowel Ireland 21 C5
Lit Sweden 14 I5
Litang Guangxi China 43 J8
Litang Sichuan China 42 I6
Līṭānī, Nahr el r. Lebanon 39 B3
Litchfield CT U.S.A. 64 E2
Lit-et-Mixe France 24 D4
Lithgow Australia 58 E4
Lithino, Akrotirio pt Greece 27 K7
Lithuania country Europe 15 M9
Lititz PA U.S.A. 64 C2
Litoměřice Czech Rep. 17 O5
Litovko Russia 44 D2
Litovskaya S.S.R. country Europe see Lithuania
Little Abaco i. Bahamas 67 I3
Little Andaman i. India 31 I5
Little Barrier i. N.Z. 59 E3
Little Belt sea chan. Denmark 15 F9
Little Bitter Lake Egypt 39 A4
Little Cayman i. Cayman Is 67 H5
Little Creek Peak UT U.S.A. 65 F2
Little Desert National Park Australia 57 C8
Little Egg Harbor inlet NJ U.S.A. 64 D3
Little Falls MN U.S.A. 63 I2
Littlefield AZ U.S.A. 65 F2
Littlefield TX U.S.A. 62 G5
Littlehampton U.K. 19 G8
Little Karas Berg plat. Namibia 50 D4
Little Karoo plat. S. Africa 50 E7
Little Lake CA U.S.A. 65 D3
Little Mecatina r. Nfld. and Lab./Que. Canada see Petit Mécatina
Little Minch sea chan. U.K. 20 B3
Little Namaqualand reg. S. Africa see Namaqualand
Little Ouse r. U.K. 19 H6
Little Pamir mts Asia 36 C1
Little Rock AR U.S.A. 63 I5
Littlerock CA U.S.A. 65 D3
Little Salt Lake UT U.S.A. 65 F2
Little Sandy Desert Australia 55 B5
Little Tibet reg. India/Pak. see Ladakh
Little Valley NY U.S.A. 64 B1
Litunde Moz. 49 D5
Liu'an China see Lu'an
Liuchow China see Liuzhou
Liuhe China 44 B4
Liukesong China 44 B3
Liupanshui China 42 I7
Liuwa Plain National Park Zambia 49 C5
Liuzhan China 44 B2
Liuzhou China 43 J8
Livadeia Greece 27 J5
Līvāni Latvia 15 O8
Liveringa Australia 52 C3
Livermore CA U.S.A. 65 B2
Livermore, Mount TX U.S.A. 62 G5
Liverpool Australia 58 E4
Liverpool N.S. Canada 63 O3
Liverpool U.K. 18 E5
Liverpool Bay N.W.T. Canada 60 E3
Liverpool Plains Australia 58 E3
Liverpool Range mts Australia 58 D3
Livingston U.K. 20 F5
Livingston MT U.S.A. 62 E2
Livingston TX U.S.A. 63 I5
Livingston, Lake TX U.S.A. 63 H5
Livingstone Zambia 49 C5
Livingston Island Antarctica 76 L2
Livingston Manor NY U.S.A. 64 D2
Livno Bos. & Herz. 26 G3
Livny Russia 13 H5
Livojoki r. Fin. 14 O4
Livonia NY U.S.A. 64 C1
Livorno Italy 26 D3
Livramento de Nossa Senhora Brazil 71 C1
Liwā', Wādī al watercourse Syria 39 C3
Liwale Tanz. 49 D4
Lixus Morocco see Larache
Lizard U.K. 19 B9
Lizarda Brazil 69 I5
Lizard Point U.K. 19 B9
Lizarra Spain see Estella
Lizemores WV U.S.A. 64 A3
Ljouwert Neth. see Leeuwarden
Ljubljana Slovenia 26 F1
Ljugarn Sweden 15 K8
Ljungan r. Sweden 14 J5
Ljungaverk Sweden 14 J5
Ljungby Sweden 15 H8
Ljusdal Sweden 15 J6
Ljusnan r. Sweden 15 J6
Ljusne Sweden 15 J6
Llaima, Volcán vol. Chile 70 B5
Llanandras U.K. see Presteigne
Llanbadarn Fawr U.K. 19 C6
Llanbedr Pont Steffan U.K. see Lampeter
Llanbister U.K. 19 D6
Llandeilo U.K. 19 D7
Llandissilio U.K. 19 C7
Llandovery U.K. 19 D7
Llandrindod Wells U.K. 19 D6
Llandudno U.K. 18 D5
Llandysul U.K. 19 C6
Llanegwad U.K. 19 C7
Llanelli U.K. 19 C7
Llanfair Caereinion U.K. 19 D6
Llanfair-ym-Muallt U.K. see Builth Wells
Llangefni U.K. 18 C5
Llangollen U.K. 19 D6
Llangurig U.K. 19 D6
Llanllyfni U.K. 19 C5
Llannerch-y-medd U.K. 18 C5
Llannor U.K. 19 C6
Llano Estacado plain NM/TX U.S.A. 62 G5
Llanos plain Col./Venez. 68 E2
Llanquihue, Lago l. Chile 70 B6
Llanrhystud U.K. 19 C6
Llantrisant U.K. 19 D7
Llanuwchllyn U.K. 19 D6
Llanwnog U.K. 19 D6
Llanymddyfri U.K. see Llandovery
Llay U.K. 19 D5
Lleida Spain 25 G3
Llerena Spain 25 C4
Llíria Spain 25 F4
Llodio Spain see Laudio
Lloyd George, Mount B.C. Canada 60 F4
Lloyd Lake Sask. Canada 60 H4
Lloydminster Alta/Sask. Canada 62 E1
Lluchmayor Spain see Llucmajor
Llucmajor Spain 25 H4
Llullaillaco, Volcán vol. Chile 70 C2
Loa r. Chile 70 B2
Loban' r. Russia 12 K4
Lobatejo mt. Spain 25 D5
Lobatse Botswana 51 G3
Lobaye r. Cent. Afr. Rep. 48 B3
Loberia Arg. 70 E5
Lobito Angola 49 B5
Lobos Arg. 70 E5
Lobos de Tierra, Isla i. Peru 68 B5
Lochaline U.K. 20 D4
Loch Baghasdail U.K. see Lochboisdale
Lochboisdale U.K. 20 B3
Lochcarron U.K. 20 D3
Lochearnhead U.K. 20 E4
Lochern National Park Australia 56 C5
Loches France 24 E3
Loch Garman Ireland see Wexford
Lochgelly U.K. 20 F4
Lochgilphead U.K. 20 D4
Lochinver U.K. 20 D2
Loch Lomond and the Trossachs National Park U.K. 20 E4
Lochmaddy U.K. 20 B3
Lochnagar mt. U.K. 20 F4
Loch nam Madadh U.K. see Lochmaddy
Loch Raven Reservoir MD U.S.A. 64 C3
Lochy, Loch l. U.K. 20 E4
Lock Australia 57 A7
Lockerbie U.K. 20 F5
Lockhart Australia 58 C5
Lock Haven PA U.S.A. 64 C2
Lockport NY U.S.A. 64 B1
Lod Israel 39 B4
Loddon r. Australia 58 A5
Lodève France 24 F5
Lodeynoye Pole Russia 12 G3
Lodhikheda India 36 D5
Lodhran Pak. 33 K3
Lodi Italy 26 C2
Lodi CA U.S.A. 65 B1
Lødingen Norway 14 I2
Lodja Dem. Rep. Congo 48 C4
Lodomeria Russia see Vladimir
Lodrani India 36 B5
Lodwar Kenya 48 D3
Łódź Poland 17 Q5
Loeriesfontein S. Africa 50 D6
Lofoten is Norway 14 H2
Lofusa South Sudan 47 G4
Log Russia 13 I6
Loga Niger 46 D3
Logan UT U.S.A. 62 E3
Logan, Mount Y.T. Canada 60 D3
Logan Creek r. Australia 56 D4
Logatec Slovenia 26 F2
Logroño Spain 25 E2
Lohardaga India 37 F5
Loharu India 36 C3
Lohatlha S. Africa 50 F5
Lohawat India 36 C4
Lohil r. China/India see Zayü Qu
Lohiniva Fin. 14 N3
Lohit r. India 37 H4
Lohjanjärvi l. Fin. 15 M6
Lohtaja Fin. 14 M4
Loi-lem Myanmar 42 H8
Loimaa Fin. 15 M6
Loipyet Hills Myanmar 37 I4
Loire r. France 24 C3
Loja Ecuador 68 C4
Loja Spain 25 D5
Lokan tekojärvi resr Fin. 14 O3
Lokchim r. Russia 12 K3
Lokgwabe Botswana 50 E3
Lokichar Kenya 30 C6
Lokichokio Kenya 48 D3
Løkken Denmark 15 F8
Løkken Norway 14 F5
Loknya Russia 12 F4
Lokoja Nigeria 46 D4
Lokolama Dem. Rep. Congo 48 B4
Lokossa Benin 46 D4
Lokot' Russia 13 G5
Loktak Lake India 37 H4
Lol South Sudan 47 F4
Lola Guinea 46 C4
Loliondo Tanz. 48 D4
Lolland i. Denmark 15 G9
Lolwane S. Africa 50 F4
Lom Bulg. 27 J3
Lom Norway 15 F6
Lomami r. Dem. Rep. Congo 48 C3
Lomar Pass Afgh. 36 A2
Lomas, Bahía de b. Chile 70 C8
Lomas de Zamora Arg. 70 E4
Lombarda, Serra hills Brazil 69 H3
Lomblen i. Indon. 54 C2
Lombok Indon. 54 B2
Lombok i. Indon. 41 D8
Lombok, Selat sea chan. Indon. 54 A2
Lomé Togo 46 D4
Lomela Dem. Rep. Congo 48 C4
Lomela r. Dem. Rep. Congo 47 F5
Lomond, Loch l. U.K. 20 E4
Lomonosov Russia 15 P7
Lomonosov Ridge sea feature Arctic Ocean 77 B1
Lomovoye Russia 12 I2
Lompoc CA U.S.A. 65 B3
Łomża Poland 17 S4
Lonar India 38 C2
Londa Bangl. 37 G5
Londa India 38 B3
Londinières France 19 I9
Londinium U.K. see London
Londoko Russia 44 D2
London Ont. Canada 64 A1
London U.K. 19 G7
London KY U.S.A. 63 K4
Londonderry U.K. 21 E3
Londonderry VT U.S.A. 64 E1
Londonderry, Cape Australia 54 D3
Londrina Brazil 71 A3
Lone Pine CA U.S.A. 65 C2
Longa Angola 49 B5
Longa, Proliv sea chan. Russia 29 S2
Long Ashton U.K. 19 E7
Longbao China 37 I2
Long Bay NC U.S.A. 63 L5
Longbeach N.Z. 59 C7
Long Beach CA U.S.A. 65 C4
Long Branch NJ U.S.A. 64 E2
Long Eaton U.K. 19 F6
Longford Ireland 21 E4
Longhoughton U.K. 18 F3
Longhurst, Mount Antarctica 76 H1
Long Island Bahamas 67 I4
Long Island P.N.G. 52 E2
Long Island NY U.S.A. 64 E2
Long Island Sound sea chan. CT/NY U.S.A. 64 E2
Longjiang China 44 A3
Longlac Ont. Canada 63 J2
Longmeadow MA U.S.A. 64 E1
Long Melford U.K. 19 H6
Longmen China 44 B2
Longmont CO U.S.A. 62 F3
Longnan China 43 K8
Long Point Ont. Canada 64 A1
Long Point Ont. Canada 64 A1
Long Point N.Z. 59 B8
Long Point Bay Ont. Canada 64 A1
Long Preston U.K. 18 E4
Long Range Mountains Nfld. and Lab. Canada 61 M5
Longreach Australia 56 D4
Long Stratton U.K. 19 I6
Longtown U.K. 18 E3
Longuyon France 24 G2
Longview TX U.S.A. 63 I5
Longwangmiao China 44 D3
Longwei Co l. China 37 G2
Longxi China 42 I6
Longxingchang China see Wuyuan
Long Xuyên Vietnam 31 J5
Longyan China 43 L7
Longyearbyen Svalbard 28 C2
Longzhen China 44 B2
Lönsboda Sweden 15 I8
Lons-le-Saunier France 24 G3
Lonton Myanmar 37 I4
Loochoo Islands Japan see Ryukyu Islands
Lookout, Cape NC U.S.A. 63 L5
Lookout, Point Australia 58 F1
Lookout Point Australia 55 B8
Loolmalasin vol. crater Tanz. 48 D4
Loongana Australia 55 D7
Loop Head hd Ireland 21 C5
Lop China 36 E1
Lopasnya Russia see Chekhov
Lopatina, Gora mt. Russia 44 F2
Lop Buri Thai. 31 J5
Lopez, Cap c. Gabon 48 A4
Lop Nur salt flat China 42 G4
Lopphavet b. Norway 14 L1
Loptyuga Russia 12 K3
Lora r. Venez. 68 D2
Lora, Hāmūn-i- dry lake Afgh./Pak. 33 K4
Lora del Río Spain 25 D5
Lorain OH U.S.A. 61 J5
Loralai Pak. 33 K3
Loralai r. Pak. 36 B3
Lorca Spain 25 F5
Lordegān Iran 35 H5
Lord Howe Atoll Solomon Is see Ontong Java Atoll
Lord Howe Island Australia 53 F5
Lord Howe Rise sea feature S. Pacific Ocean 74 G7
Lordsburg NM U.S.A. 62 F5
Lore East Timor 54 D2
Lorena Brazil 71 B3
Loreto Brazil 69 I5
Loreto Mex. 62 E6
Lorient France 24 C3
Lorn, Firth of est. U.K. 20 D4
Lorne Australia 56 D5
Lorne watercourse Australia 56 B3
Lorrain, Plateau France 24 H2
Lorraine Australia 56 B3
Lorraine reg. France 24 G2
Losal India 36 C4
Los Alamos CA U.S.A. 65 B3
Los Alamos NM U.S.A. 62 F4
Los Alerces, Parque Nacional nat. park Arg. 70 B6
Los Ángeles Chile 70 B5
Los Angeles CA U.S.A. 65 C3
Los Angeles Aqueduct canal CA U.S.A. 65 C3
Los Banos CA U.S.A. 65 B2
Los Blancos Arg. 70 D2
Los Glaciares, Parque Nacional nat. park Arg. 70 B8
Lošinj i. Croatia 26 F2
Los Juríes Arg. 70 D3
Los Katíos, Parque Nacional nat. park Col. 67 I7
Loskop Dam S. Africa 51 I3
Los Menucos Arg. 70 C6
Los Mochis Mex. 66 C3
Losombo Dem. Rep. Congo 48 B3
Los Roques, Islas is Venez. 68 E1
Lossie r. U.K. 20 F3
Lossiemouth U.K. 20 F3
Lost Creek WV U.S.A. 64 A3
Los Teques Venez. 68 E1
Los Testigos is Venez. 68 F1
Lost Hills CA U.S.A. 65 C3
Lostwithiel U.K. 19 C8
Los Vilos Chile 70 B4
Lot r. France 24 E4
Lota Chile 70 B5
Lothringen reg. France see Lorraine
Lotikipi Plain Kenya/South Sudan 48 D3
Loto Dem. Rep. Congo 48 C4
Lotsane r. Botswana 51 I2
Lot's Wife i. Japan see Sōfu-gan
Louangnamtha Laos 40 C5
Louangphabang Laos 41 C6
Loubomo Congo 49 B4
Loudéac France 24 C2
Louga Senegal 46 B3
Loughborough U.K. 19 F6
Lougheed Island Nunavut Canada 61 H2
Loughor r. U.K. 19 C7
Loughrea Ireland 21 D4
Loughton U.K. 19 H7
Louhans France 24 G3
Louisa VA U.S.A. 64 C3
Louisburgh Ireland 21 C4
Louis-Gentil Morocco see Youssoufia
Louisiade Archipelago is P.N.G. 52 F3
Louisiana state U.S.A. 63 I5
Louis Trichardt S. Africa see Makhado
Louisville KY U.S.A. 63 J4
Louisville Ridge sea feature S. Pacific Ocean 74 I8
Loukhi Russia 14 R3
Loukoléla Congo 48 B4
Loukouo Congo 47 E5
Loulé Port. 25 B5
Loum Cameroon 46 D4
Louny Czech Rep. 17 N5
Loups Marins, Lacs des lakes Que. Canada 61 K4
Lourdes France 24 D5
Lourenço Marques Moz. see Maputo
Lousã Port. 25 B3
Loushan China 44 C3
Louth Australia 58 B3
Louth U.K. 18 G5
Loutra Aidipsou Greece 27 J5
Louvain Belgium see Leuven
Louviers France 19 I9
Louwater-Suid Namibia 50 C2
Louwsburg S. Africa 51 J4
Lövånger Sweden 14 L4
Lovat' r. Russia 12 F4
Lovech Bulg. 27 K3
Loveland CO U.S.A. 62 F3
Lovelock NV U.S.A. 62 D3
Loviisa Fin. 15 O6
Lovington NM U.S.A. 62 G5
Lovozero Russia 12 G1
Lóvua Lunda Norte Angola 49 C4
Lóvua Moxico Angola 49 C5
Low, Cape Nunavut Canada 61 J3
Lowa Dem. Rep. Congo 48 C4
Lowa r. Dem. Rep. Congo 48 C4
Lowarai Pass Pak. 36 B2
Lowell MA U.S.A. 64 F1
Lower California pen. Mex. see Baja California
Lower Glenelg National Park Australia 57 C8
Lower Granite Gorge AZ U.S.A. 65 F3
Lower Hutt N.Z. 59 E5
Lower Lake CA U.S.A. 65 A1
Lower Lough Erne l. U.K. 21 E3
Lower Tunguska r. Russia see Nizhnyaya Tunguska
Lower Zambezi National Park Zambia 49 C5
Lowestoft U.K. 19 I6
Łowicz Poland 17 Q4
Low Island Kiribati see Starbuck Island
Lowther Hills U.K. 20 F5
Lowville NY U.S.A. 63 L3
Loxton Australia 57 C7
Loyal, Loch l. U.K. 20 E2
Loyalsock Creek r. PA U.S.A. 64 C2
Loyalty Islands New Caledonia see Loyauté, Îles
Loyang China see Luoyang
Loyauté, Îles is New Caledonia 53 G4
Loyev Belarus see Loyew
Loyew Belarus 13 F6
Lozère, Mont mt. France 24 F4
Loznica Serbia 27 H2
Lozova Ukr. 13 H6
Lozovaya Ukr. see Lozova
Lua r. Dem. Rep. Congo 48 B3
Luacano Angola 49 C5
Lu'an China 43 L6
Luanda Angola 49 B4
Luang Namtha Laos see Louangnamtha

Mamison Pass Georgia/Russia see Klukhorskiy, Pereval
Mamit India 37 H5
Mammoth Reservoir CA U.S.A. 65 C2
Mamonas Brazil 71 C1
Mamoré r. Bol./Brazil 68 E6
Mamou Guinea 46 B3
Mampikony Madag. 49 E5
Mampong Ghana 46 C4
Mamuju Indon. 52 B2
Mamuno Botswana 50 E2
Man Côte d'Ivoire 46 C4
Man India 38 B2
Man r. India 38 B2
Man, Isle of terr. Irish Sea 18 C4
Manacapuru Brazil 68 F4
Manacor Spain 25 H4
Manado Indon. 41 E7
Managua Nicaragua 67 G6
Manakara Madag. 49 E6
Manakau mt. N.Z. 59 D6
Manākhah Yemen 32 F6
Manama Bahrain 32 H4
Manamadurai India 38 C4
Mana Maroka National Park S. Africa 51 H5
Manamelkudi India 38 C4
Manam Island P.N.G. 52 E2
Mananara Avaratra Madag. 49 E5
Manangoora Australia 56 B3
Mananjary Madag. 49 E6
Manantali, Lac de l. Mali 46 B3
Manantenina Madag. 49 E6
Mana Pass China/India 36 D3
Mana Pools National Park Zimbabwe 49 C5
Manapouri, Lake N.Z. 59 A7
Manasa India 36 C4
Manas He r. China 42 F3
Manas Hu l. China 42 F3
Manaslu mt. Nepal 37 F3
Manas National Park nature res. Bhutan 37 G4
Manassas VA U.S.A. 64 C3
Manastir Macedonia see Bitola
Man-aung Kyun Myanmar 42 G9
Manaus Brazil 68 F4
Manavgat Turkey 34 C3
Manbazar India 37 F5
Manbij Syria 39 C1
Manby U.K. 18 H5
Manchar India 38 B2
Manchester U.K. 18 E5
Manchester CT U.S.A. 64 E2
Manchester MD U.S.A. 64 C3
Manchester NH U.S.A. 64 F1
Manchester VT U.S.A. 64 E1
Mancılık Turkey 34 E3
Mand, Rūd-e r. Iran 35 H5
Manda Tanz. 49 D4
Manda, Jabal mt. South Sudan 47 F4
Manda, Parc National de nat. park Chad 47 E4
Mandabe Madag. 49 E6
Mandal Norway 15 E7
Mandala, Puncak mt. Indon. 41 G8
Mandalay Myanmar 37 I5
Mandale Myanmar see Mandalay
Mandalgovĭ Mongolia 42 J3
Mandalī Iraq 35 G4
Mandal-Ovoo Mongolia 42 I4
Mandalt China 43 K4
Mandan ND U.S.A. 62 G2
Mandas Sardinia Italy 26 C5
Mandasa India 38 E2
Mandasor India see Mandsaur
Mandav Hills India 36 B5
Mandera Kenya 48 E3
Manderfield UT U.S.A. 65 F1
Mandeville Jamaica 67 I5
Mandeville N.Z. 59 B7
Mandha India 36 B4
Mandhoúdhíon Greece see Mantoudi
Mandi India 36 D3
Mandiana Guinea 46 C3
Mandié Moz. 49 D5
Mandini S. Africa 51 J5
Mandira Dam India 37 F5
Mandla India 36 E5
Mandleshwar India 36 C5
Mandrael India 36 D4
Mandritsara Madag. 49 E5
Mandsaur India 36 C4
Mandurah Australia 55 A8
Manduria Italy 26 G4
Mandvi India 36 B5
Mandya India 38 C3
Manerbio Italy 26 D2
Manevychi Ukr. 13 E6
Manfalūṭ Egypt 34 C6
Manfredonia Italy 26 F4
Manfredonia, Golfo di g. Italy 26 G4
Manga Brazil 71 C1
Manga Burkina Faso 46 C3
Mangabeiras, Serra das hills Brazil 69 I6
Mangai Dem. Rep. Congo 48 B4
Mangaia i. Cook Is 75 J7
Mangakino N.Z. 59 E4
Mangalagiri India 38 D2
Mangalia Romania 27 M3
Mangalmé Chad 47 E3
Mangalore India 38 B3
Mangaluru India see Mangalore
Mangaon India 38 B2
Mangareva Islands Fr. Polynesia see Gambier, Îles
Mangaung Free State S. Africa see Bloemfontein
Mangaung Free State S. Africa 51 H5
Mangawan India 37 E4
Mangea i. Cook Is see Mangaia
Mangghyshlaq Kazakh. see Mangistau
Mangghystaū Kazakh. see Mangistau
Mangghystaū admin. div. Kazakh. see Mangystauskaya Oblast'
Mangghyt Uzbek. see Mang'it
Manghāl Afgh. 33 J3
Manghit Uzbek. see Mang'it
Mangin Range mts Myanmar see Mingin Range
Mangistau Kazakh. 35 H2
Mang'it Uzbek. 33 J1
Mangla Bangl. see Mongla
Mangla Pak. 36 C2
Mangnai China 42 G5
Mangochi Malawi 49 D5
Mangoky r. Madag. 49 E6
Mangole i. Indon. 41 E8
Mangoli India 38 B2
Mangotsfield U.K. 19 E7
Mangqystaū Shyghanaghy b. Kazakh. see Mangystau, Zaliv
Mangrol India 36 B5
Mangrul India 38 C1
Mangshi China 42 H8
Mangualde Port. 25 C3
Manguéni, Plateau du Niger 46 E2
Mangui China 44 A2
Mangula Zimbabwe see Mhangura
Mangyshlak Kazakh. see Mangistau
Mangyshlak Oblast admin. div. Kazakh. see Mangystauskaya Oblast'
Mangyshlakskaya Oblast' admin. div. Kazakh. see Mangystauskaya Oblast'
Mangystau Kazakh. see Mangistau
Mangystau, Poluostrov pen. Kazakh. 35 H1
Mangystau, Zaliv b. Kazakh. 35 H1
Mangystauskaya Oblast' admin. div. Kazakh. 35 I2
Manhā Brazil 71 B1
Manhattan KS U.S.A. 63 H4
Manhica Moz. 51 K3
Manhoca Moz. 51 K4
Manhuaçu Brazil 71 C3
Manhuaçu r. Brazil 71 C2
Mani China 37 F2
Mania r. Madag. 49 E5
Maniago Italy 26 E1
Manicouagan r. Que. Canada 63 N2
Manicouagan, Petit Lac l. Que. Canada 61 L4
Manicouagan, Réservoir resr Que. Canada 63 N1
Manīfah Saudi Arabia 35 H6
Manihiki atoll Cook Is 74 J6
Maniitsoq Greenland 61 M3
Manikchhari Bangl. 37 H5
Manikgarh India see Rajura
Manila Phil. 41 E6
Manildra Australia 58 D4
Manilla Australia 58 E3
Maningrida Australia 54 F3
Manipur India see Imphal
Manipur state India 37 H4
Manisa Turkey 27 L5
Manistee MI U.S.A. 63 J3
Manitoba prov. Canada 62 H1
Manitoba, Lake Man. Canada 61 I4
Manitou Beach NY U.S.A. 64 C1
Manitou Islands MI U.S.A. 63 J2
Manitoulin Island Ont. Canada 63 K2
Manitowoc WI U.S.A. 63 J3
Maniwaki Que. Canada 63 L2
Manizales Col. 68 C2
Manja Madag. 49 E6
Manjarabad India 38 B3
Manjeri India 38 C4
Manjhand Pak. 36 B4
Manjhi India 37 F4
Manjra r. India 38 C2
Mankaiana Swaziland see Mankayane
Mankato MN U.S.A. 63 I3
Mankayane Swaziland 51 J4
Mankera Pak. 36 B3
Mankono Côte d'Ivoire 46 C4
Manlay Mongolia 42 J4
Manley Hot Springs AK U.S.A. 60 C3
Manmad India 38 B1
Mann r. Australia 54 F3
Mann, Mount Australia 55 E6
Mannahill Australia 57 B7
Mannar Sri Lanka 38 C4
Mannar, Gulf of India/Sri Lanka 38 C4
Manneru r. India 38 D3
Mannheim Germany 17 L6
Mannicolo Islands Solomon Is see Vanikoro Islands
Manning r. Australia 58 F3
Manning Alta Canada 60 G4
Mannington WV U.S.A. 64 A3
Manningtree U.K. 19 I7
Mann Ranges mts Australia 55 E6
Mannsville NY U.S.A. 64 C1
Mannu, Capo c. Sardinia Italy 26 C4
Manoel Ribas Brazil 71 A4
Manoel Vitorino Brazil 71 C1
Man-of-War Rocks is HI U.S.A. see Gardner Pinnacles
Manoharpur India 36 D4
Manohar Thana India 36 D4
Manokotak AK U.S.A. 60 C4
Manokwari Indon. 41 F8
Manosque France 24 G5
Manouane, Lac l. Que. Canada 63 M1
Manovo-Gounda Saint Floris, Parc National du nat. park Cent. Afr. Rep. 48 C3
Manp'o N. Korea 44 B4
Manra i. Kiribati 53 I2
Manresa Spain 25 G3
Mansa Gujarat India 36 C5
Mansa Punjab India 36 C3
Mansa Zambia 49 C5
Mansa Konko Gambia 46 B3
Mansehra Pak. 33 L3
Mansel Island Nunavut Canada 61 K3
Mansfield Australia 58 C6
Mansfield U.K. 19 F5
Mansfield LA U.S.A. 63 I5
Mansfield OH U.S.A. 63 K3
Mansfield PA U.S.A. 64 C2
Mansi Myanmar 37 H4
Manso r. Brazil see Mortes, Rio das
Manta Ecuador 68 B4
Mantaro r. Peru 68 D6
Manteca CA U.S.A. 65 B2
Mantena Brazil 71 C2
Mantes-la-Jolie France 24 E2
Mantiqueira, Serra da mts Brazil 71 B3
Mantoudi Greece 27 J5
Mantova Italy see Mantua
Mäntsälä Fin. 15 N6
Mänttä Fin. 14 N5
Mantua Italy 26 D2
Mantuan Downs Australia 56 D5
Manturovo Russia 12 J4
Mäntyharju Fin. 15 O6
Mäntyjärvi Fin. 14 O3
Manú Peru 68 D6
Manu, Parque Nacional del nat. park Peru 68 D6
Manuae atoll Fr. Polynesia 75 J7
Manu'a Islands American Samoa 53 I3
Manuelzinho Brazil 69 H5
Manui i. Indon. 41 E8
Manukau N.Z. 59 E3
Manukau Harbour N.Z. 59 E3
Manunda watercourse Australia 57 B7
Manus Island P.N.G. 52 E2
Manvi India 38 C3
Many LA U.S.A. 63 I5
Manyakatana S. Africa 51 J3
Manyana Botswana 51 G3
Manyas Turkey 27 L4
Manyas Gölü l. Turkey see Kuş Gölü
Manyoni Tanz. 49 D4
Manzai Pak. 36 B2
Manzanares Spain 25 E4
Manzanillo Cuba 67 I4
Manzanillo Mex. 66 D5
Manzhouli China 43 L3
Manzini Swaziland 51 J4
Mao Chad 47 E3
Maó Spain 25 I4
Maoke, Pegunungan mts Indon. 41 F8
Maokeng S. Africa 51 H4
Maokui Shan mt. China 44 A4
Maolin China 44 A4
Maoming China 43 K8
Maopora i. Indon. 54 D1
Mapai Moz. 51 J2
Mapam Yumco l. China 37 E3
Mapanza Zambia 49 C5
Maphodi S. Africa 51 G6
Mapimí, Bolsón de des. Mex. 66 D3
Mapinhane Moz. 51 L2
Mapiri Bol. 68 E7
Maple Creek Sask. Canada 62 F2
Mapmaker Seamounts sea feature N. Pacific Ocean 74 H4
Mapoon Australia 56 C1
Mapoteng Lesotho 51 H5
Mapuera r. Brazil 69 G4
Mapulanguene Moz. 51 K3
Mapungubwe National Park S. Africa 51 I2
Maputo Moz. 51 K3
Maputo prov. Moz. 51 K3
Maputo r. Moz./S. Africa 51 K4
Maputo, Baía de b. Moz. 51 K4
Maputsoe Lesotho 51 H5
Maqanshy Kazakh. see Makanshy
Maqar an Na'am well Iraq 35 F5
Maqat Kazakh. see Makat
Maqên China 42 I6
Maqên Kangri mt. China 42 H6
Maqnā Saudi Arabia 34 D5
Maqteïr reg. Mauritania 46 B2
Ma Qu r. China see Yellow
Maquan He r. China see Damqoq Zangbo
Maquela do Zombo Angola 49 B4
Maquinchao Arg. 70 C6
Mar, Serra do mts Rio de Janeiro/São Paulo Brazil 71 B3
Mar, Serra do mts Rio Grande do Sul/Santa Catarina Brazil 71 A5
Mara India 37 E5
Mara S. Africa 51 I2
Maraã Brazil 68 E4
Marabá Brazil 69 I5
Maraboon, Lake resr Australia 56 E4
Maracá, Ilha de i. Brazil 69 H3
Maracaibo Venez. 68 D1
Maracaibo, Lago de Venez. see Maracaibo, Lake
Maracaibo, Lake Venez. 68 D2
Maracaju Brazil 70 E2
Maracaju, Serra de hills Brazil 70 E2
Maracanda Uzbek. see Samarqand
Maracás Brazil 71 C1
Maracás, Chapada de hills Brazil 71 C1
Maracay Venez. 68 E1
Marādah Libya 47 E2
Maradi Niger 46 D3
Marāgheh Iran 35 G3
Marahuaca, Cerro mt. Venez. 68 E3
Marajó, Baía de est. Brazil 69 I4
Marajó, Ilha de i. Brazil 69 H4
Marakele National Park S. Africa 51 H3
Maralal Kenya 48 D3
Maralbashi China see Bachu
Maralinga Australia 55 E7
Maralwexi China see Bachu
Maramasike i. Solomon Is 53 G2
Maramba Zambia see Livingstone
Marambio (Argentina) research stn Antarctica 76 A2
Marand Iran 35 G3
Marandellas Zimbabwe see Marondera
Maranhão r. Brazil 71 A1
Maranoa r. Australia 58 D1
Marañón r. Peru 68 D4
Marão Moz. 51 L3
Marão mt. Port. 25 C3
Mara Rosa Brazil 71 A1
Maraş Turkey see Kahramanmaraş
Marathon NY U.S.A. 64 C1
Maraú Brazil 71 D1
Marbella Spain 25 D5
Marble Bar Australia 54 B5
Marble Hall S. Africa 51 I3
Marbul Pass India 36 C2
Marburg Germany 17 L5
Marburg S. Africa 51 J6
Marburg Slovenia see Maribor
Marca, Ponta do pt Angola 49 B5
Marcali Hungary 26 G1
Marcelino Ramos Brazil 71 A4
March U.K. 19 H6
Marche reg. France 24 E3
Marchena Spain 25 D5
Marchinbar Island Australia 56 B1
Mar Chiquita, Laguna l. Arg. 70 D4
Marchtrenk Austria 17 O6
Marcona Peru 68 C7
Marcus Baker, Mount AK U.S.A. 60 D3
Marcy, Mount NY U.S.A. 63 M3
Mardan Pak. 33 L3
Mar del Plata Arg. 70 E5
Mardin Turkey 35 F3
Maré i. New Caledonia 53 G4
Maree, Loch l. U.K. 20 D3
Marevo Russia 12 G4
Marfa TX U.S.A. 62 G5
Marganets Ukr. see Marhanets'
Margao India 38 B3
Margaret r. Australia 54 D4
Margaret watercourse Australia 57 B6
Margaret, Mount h. Australia 54 B5
Margaret River Australia 55 A8
Margaretville NY U.S.A. 64 D1
Margarita, Isla de i. Venez. 68 F1
Margaritovo Russia 44 D4
Margate U.K. 19 I7
Margeride, Monts de la mts France 24 F4
Margherita, Lake Eth. see Abaya, Lake
Margherita Peak Dem. Rep. Congo/Uganda 48 C3
Marghilon Uzbek. see Marg'ilon
Marg'ilon Uzbek. 33 L1
Mārgō, Dasht-e des. Afgh. 33 J3
Mārgo, Dasht-i des. Afgh. see Mārgō, Dasht-e
Margog Caka l. China 37 F2
Marguerite, Pic mt. Dem. Rep. Congo/Uganda see Margherita Peak
Marguerite Bay Antarctica 76 L2
Margyang China 37 G3
Marhaj Khalīl Iraq 35 G4
Marhanets' Ukr. 13 G7
Marhoum Alg. 22 D5
Maria atoll Fr. Polynesia 75 J7
María Elena Chile 70 C2
Maria Island Australia 56 A2
Maria Island National Park Australia 57 [inset]
Mariala National Park Australia 57 D5
Mariana Brazil 71 C3
Mariana Ridge sea feature N. Pacific Ocean 74 F4
Mariana Trench sea feature N. Pacific Ocean 74 F5
Mariani India 37 H4
Mariánica, Cordillera mts Spain see Morena, Sierra
Marianna AR U.S.A. 63 I5
Marianna FL U.S.A. 63 J5
Mariano Machado Angola see Ganda
Mariánské Lázně Czech Rep. 17 N6
Marías, Islas is Mex. 66 C4
Mariato, Punta pt Panama 67 H7
Maria van Diemen, Cape N.Z. 59 D2
Ma'rib Yemen 32 G6
Maribor Slovenia 26 F1
Marica r. Bulg. see Maritsa
Maricopa CA U.S.A. 65 C3
Maridi South Sudan 47 F4
Marie Byrd Land reg. Antarctica 76 J1
Marie-Galante i. Guadeloupe 67 L5
Mariehamn Fin. 15 K6
Mariembero r. Brazil 71 A1
Marienbad Czech Rep. see Mariánské Lázně
Marienburg Poland see Malbork
Mariental Namibia 50 C3
Marienwerder Poland see Kwidzyn
Mariestad Sweden 15 H7
Marietta GA U.S.A. 63 K5
Marietta OH U.S.A. 64 A3
Marignane France 24 G5
Marii, Mys pt Russia 40 G2
Mariinsk Russia 28 J4
Mariinskiy Posad Russia 12 J4
Marijampolė Lith. 15 M9
Marília Brazil 71 A3
Marillana Australia 54 B5
Marimba Angola 49 B4
Marín Spain 25 B2
Marina CA U.S.A. 65 B2
Marina di Gioiosa Ionica Italy 26 G5
Mar'ina Gorka Belarus see Mar"ina Horka
Mar"ina Horka Belarus 15 P10
Marinette WI U.S.A. 63 J2
Maringá Brazil 71 A3
Maringa r. Dem. Rep. Congo 48 B3
Marinha Grande Port. 25 B4
Marion IN U.S.A. 63 J3
Marion OH U.S.A. 63 K3
Marion SC U.S.A. 63 L5
Marion VA U.S.A. 63 K4
Marion, Lake SC U.S.A. 63 K5
Marion Reef Australia 56 F3
Maripa Venez. 68 E2
Mariposa CA U.S.A. 65 C2
Mariscal José Félix Estigarribia Para. 70 D2
Maritime Alps mts France/Italy 24 H4
Maritime Kray admin. div. Russia see Primorskiy Kray
Maritimes, Alpes mts France/Italy see Maritime Alps
Marittime, Alpi mts France/Italy see Maritime Alps
Mariupol' Ukr. 13 H7
Mariusa, Parque Nacional nat. park Venez. 68 F2
Marīvān Iran 35 G4
Marjan Afgh. see Mashōrēy
Marjayoûn Lebanon 39 B3
Marka Somalia 48 E3
Markala Mali 46 C3
Markaryd Sweden 15 H8
Markaz-e Sayyidābād Afgh. 36 B2
Marken S. Africa 51 I2
Markermeer l. Neth. 16 J4
Market Deeping U.K. 19 G6
Market Drayton U.K. 19 E6
Market Harborough U.K. 19 G6
Markethill U.K. 21 F3
Market Weighton U.K. 18 G5
Markha r. Russia 29 M3
Markit China 33 M2
Markleeville CA U.S.A. 65 C1
Markounda Cent. Afr. Rep. 48 B3
Markovo Russia 29 S3
Marks Russia 13 J6
Marla Australia 55 F6
Marlborough Downs hills U.K. 19 F7
Marlinton WV U.S.A. 64 A3
Marlo Australia 58 D6
Marmagao India 38 B3
Marmande France 24 E4
Marmara, Sea of g. Turkey 27 M4
Marmara Denizi g. Turkey see Marmara, Sea of
Marmara Gölü l. Turkey 27 M5
Marmarica reg. Libya 34 B5
Marmaris Turkey 27 M6
Marmion, Lake salt l. Australia 55 C7
Marmolada mt. Italy 26 D1
Marne r. France 24 F2
Marne-la-Vallée France 24 F2
Maroantsetra Madag. 49 E5
Maroc country Africa see Morocco
Marol Pak. 36 D2
Maromokotro mt. Madag. 49 E5
Marondera Zimbabwe 49 D5
Maroochydore Australia 58 F1
Maroonah Australia 55 A5
Marosvás>01a>rhely Romania see Târgu Mureş
Marot Pak. 36 C3
Maroua Cameroon 47 E3
Marovoay Madag. 49 E5
Marqadah Syria 35 F4
Marquard S. Africa 51 H5
Marquesas Islands Fr. Polynesia 75 K6
Marquette MI U.S.A. 63 J2
Marquise France 19 I8
Marquises, Îles is Fr. Polynesia see Marquesas Islands
Marra Australia 58 A3
Marra r. Australia 58 C3
Marra, Jebel mt. Sudan 47 F3
Marra, Jebel Sudan 47 F3
Marracuene Moz. 51 K3
Marrakech Morocco 22 C5
Marrakesh Morocco see Marrakech
Marrangua, Lagoa l. Moz. 51 L3
Marrar Australia 58 C5
Marrawah Australia 57 [inset]
Marree Australia 57 B6
Marruecos country Africa see Morocco
Marrupa Moz. 49 D5
Marryat Australia 55 F6
Marsá al 'Alam Egypt 32 D4
Marsa 'Alam Egypt see Marsá al 'Alam
Marsá al Burayqah Libya 47 E1
Marsabit Kenya 48 D3
Marsala Sicily Italy 26 E6
Marsá Maṭrūḥ Egypt 34 B5
Marsciano Italy 26 E3
Marsden Australia 58 C4
Marseille France 24 G5
Marseilles France see Marseille
Marsfjället mt. Sweden 14 I4
Marshall watercourse Australia 56 B4
Marshall MN U.S.A. 63 H3
Marshall MO U.S.A. 63 I4
Marshall TX U.S.A. 63 I5
Marshall Islands country N. Pacific Ocean 74 H5
Marshalltown IA U.S.A. 63 I3
Marsh Harbour Bahamas 67 I3
Marsh Island LA U.S.A. 63 I6
Märsta Sweden 15 J7
Marsyaty Russia 11 S3
Martapura Indon. 41 D8
Martha's Vineyard i. MA U.S.A. 64 F2
Martigny Switz. 24 H3
Martim Vaz, Ilhas is S. Atlantic Ocean see Martin Vas, Ilhas
Martin Slovakia 17 Q6
Martin SD U.S.A. 62 G3
Martinez Lake AZ U.S.A. 65 E4
Martinho Campos Brazil 71 B2
Martinique terr. West Indies 67 L6
Martinique Passage Dominica/Martinique 67 L5
Martin Peninsula Antarctica 76 K2
Martinsburg WV U.S.A. 64 C3
Martins Ferry OH U.S.A. 64 A2
Martinsville VA U.S.A. 63 L4
Martin Vas, Ilhas is S. Atlantic Ocean 72 G7
Martin Vaz Islands S. Atlantic Ocean see Martin Vas, Ilhas
Martök Kazakh. see Martok
Martok Kazakh. 30 E1
Marton N.Z. 59 E5
Martorell Spain 25 G3
Martos Spain 25 E5
Martuni Armenia 35 G2
Ma'rūf Afgh. 36 A3
Maruim Brazil 69 K6
Marukhis Ughelt'ekhili pass Georgia/Russia 35 F2
Marulan Australia 58 D5
Marvast Iran 35 I5
Marvdasht Iran 35 I5
Marvejols France 24 F4
Mary r. Australia 54 E3
Mary Turkm. 30 F3
Maryborough Qld Australia 57 F5
Maryborough Vic. Australia 58 A6
Marydale S. Africa 50 F5
Maryland state U.S.A. 64 C3
Maryport U.K. 18 D4
Marysville CA U.S.A. 65 B1
Marysville KS U.S.A. 63 H4
Maryvale N.T. Australia 55 F6
Maryvale Qld Australia 56 D3
Maryville MO U.S.A. 63 I3
Maryville TN U.S.A. 63 K4
Marzagão Brazil 71 A2
Masada tourist site Israel 39 B4
Masai Steppe plain Tanz. 49 D4
Masaka Uganda 48 D4
Masakhane S. Africa 51 H6
Masallı Azer. 35 H3
Masan S. Korea 45 C6
Masasi Tanz. 49 D5
Masavi Bol. 68 F7
Masbate i. Phil. 41 E6
Mascara Alg. 25 G6
Mascarene Basin sea feature Indian Ocean 73 L7
Mascarene Plain sea feature Indian Ocean 73 L7
Mascarene Ridge sea feature Indian Ocean 73 L6
Mascote Brazil 71 D1
Masela Indon. 54 E2
Masela i. Indon. 54 E2
Maseru Lesotho 51 H5
Mashai Lesotho 51 I5
Masherbrum mt. Pak. 36 D2
Mashhad Iran 33 I2
Mashishing S. Africa 51 J3
Mashkel, Hamun-i- salt flat Pak. 33 J4
Mashōrēy Afgh. 36 B2
Masi Norway 14 M2
Masibambane S. Africa 51 H6
Masīlah, Wādī al watercourse Yemen 32 H6
Masilo S. Africa 51 H5
Masi-Manimba Dem. Rep. Congo 49 B4
Masindi Uganda 48 D3
Masinyusane S. Africa 50 F6
Masira, Gulf of Oman see Maşīrah, Khalīj
Maşīrah, Jazīrat i. Oman 33 I5
Maşīrah, Khalīj b. Oman 33 I6
Masira Island Oman see Maşīrah, Jazīrat
Masjed Soleymān Iran 35 H5
Mask, Lough l. Ireland 21 C4
Maslovo Russia 11 S3
Masoala, Tanjona c. Madag. 49 F5
Mason, Lake imp. l. Australia 55 B6
Mason Bay N.Z. 59 A8
Mason City IA U.S.A. 63 I3
Masontown PA U.S.A. 64 B3
Masqaṭ Oman see Muscat
Massa Italy 26 D2
Massachusetts state U.S.A. 64 E1
Massachusetts Bay MA U.S.A. 64 F1
Massafra Italy 26 G4
Massakory Chad 47 E3
Massa Marittima Italy 26 D3
Massangena Moz. 49 D6
Massango Angola 49 B4
Massawa Eritrea 32 E6
Massenya Chad 47 E3
Masset B.C. Canada 60 E4
Massif Central mts France 24 F4
Massilia France see Marseille
Massillon OH U.S.A. 64 A2
Massinga Moz. 51 L2
Massingir Moz. 51 K2
Massingir, Barragem de resr Moz. 51 K2
Masson Island Antarctica 76 F2
Masteksay Kazakh. 13 K6
Masterton N.Z. 59 E5
Mastung Pak. 30 F4
Mastūrah Saudi Arabia 32 E5
Masty Belarus 15 N10
Masuda Japan 45 C6
Masuku Gabon see Franceville
Masulipatam India see Machilipatnam
Masulipatnam India see Machilipatnam
Masuna i. American Samoa see Tutuila
Masvingo Zimbabwe 49 D6
Masvingo prov. Zimbabwe 51 J1
Maswa Tanz. 48 D4
Maşyāf Syria 39 C2
Matabeleland South prov. Zimbabwe 51 I1
Matad Mongolia 43 L3
Matadi Dem. Rep. Congo 49 B4
Matagalpa Nicaragua 67 G6
Matagami Que. Canada 63 L2
Matagami, Lac l. Que. Canada 63 L2
Matagorda Island TX U.S.A. 63 H6
Matakana Island N.Z. 59 F3
Matala Angola 49 B5
Maṭāli', Jabal mt. Saudi Arabia 35 F6
Matam Senegal 46 B3
Matamey Niger 46 D3
Matamoros PA U.S.A. 64 D2
Matamoros Coahuila Mex. 66 D3
Matamoros Tamaulipas Mex. 66 E3
Matandu r. Tanz. 49 D4
Matane Que. Canada 63 N2
Matanzas Cuba 67 H4
Matapan, Cape c. Greece see Tainaro, Akrotirio
Matara Sri Lanka 38 D5
Mataram Indon. 41 D8
Matarani Peru 68 D7
Mataranka Australia 54 F3
Mataripe Brazil 71 D1
Mataró Spain 25 H3
Matatiele S. Africa 51 I6
Matatila Reservoir India 36 D4
Mataura N.Z. 59 B8
Matā'utu Wallis and Futuna Is 53 I3
Mata-Utu Wallis and Futuna Is see Matā'utu
Matawai N.Z. 59 F4
Matay Kazakh. 42 D3
Mategua Bol. 68 F6
Matehuala Mex. 66 D4
Matemanga Tanz. 49 D5
Matera Italy 26 G4
Mateur Tunisia 26 C6
Mathaji India 36 B4
Mathews VA U.S.A. 64 C4
Mathis TX U.S.A. 62 H6
Mathoura Australia 58 B5
Mathura India 36 D4
Mati Phil. 41 E7
Matiali India 37 G4
Matias Cardoso Brazil 71 C1
Matías Romero Mex. 66 E5
Matin India 37 E5
Matla r. India 37 G5
Matlabas r. S. Africa 51 H2
Matli Pak. 36 B4
Matlock U.K. 19 F5
Mato, Cerro mt. Venez. 68 E2
Matobo Hills Zimbabwe 49 C6
Mato Grosso state Brazil 71 A1
Mato Grosso, Planalto do plat. Brazil 69 H7
Matopo Hills Zimbabwe see Matobo Hills
Matos Costa Brazil 71 A4
Matosinhos Port. 25 B3
Mato Verde Brazil 71 C1
Matroosberg mt. S. Africa 50 D7
Matsesta Russia 35 E2
Matsue Japan 45 D6
Matsumoto Japan 45 E5
Matsu Tao i. Taiwan see Mazu Dao
Matsuyama Japan 45 D6
Mattagami r. Ont. Canada 63 K1
Matterhorn mt. Italy/Switz. 26 B2
Matterhorn mt. NV U.S.A. 62 D3
Matthew Town Bahamas 67 J4
Matturai Sri Lanka see Matara
Matuku i. Fiji 53 H3
Matumbo Angola 49 B5
Maturín Venez. 68 F2
Matusadona National Park Zimbabwe 49 C5
Matwabeng S. Africa 51 H5
Maty Island P.N.G. see Wuvulu Island
Mau India see Maunath Bhanjan
Maúa Moz. 49 D5
Maubourguet France 24 E5
Mauchline U.K. 20 E5
Maudaha India 36 E4
Maude Australia 57 D7
Maud Seamount sea feature S. Atlantic Ocean 72 I10
Mau-é-ele Moz. see Marão
Maués Brazil 69 G4
Maughold Head hd Isle of Man 18 C4
Maui i. HI U.S.A. 62 [inset]
Maukkadaw Myanmar 37 H5
Maule r. Chile 70 B5
Maulvi Bazar Bangl. see Moulvibazar
Maumere Indon. 54 C2
Maumturk Mountains hills Ireland 21 C4
Maun Botswana 49 C5
Maunath Bhanjan India 37 E4
Maunatlala Botswana 51 H2
Maungaturoto N.Z. 59 E3
Maungdaw Myanmar 37 H5
Mauriac France 24 F4
Maurice country Indian Ocean see Mauritius
Maurice, Lake imp. l. Australia 55 E7
Mauritania country Africa 46 B3
Mauritanie country Africa see Mauritania
Mauritius country Indian Ocean 73 L7
Maurs France 24 F4
Mava Dem. Rep. Congo 48 C3
Mavago Moz. 49 D5
Mavanza Moz. 51 L2
Mavinga Angola 49 C5
Mavrovo nat. park Macedonia 27 I4
Mavume Moz. 51 L2
Mavuya S. Africa 51 H6
Mawana India 36 D3
Mawanga Dem. Rep. Congo 49 B4
Mawjib, Wādī al r. Jordan 39 B4
Mawkmai Myanmar 42 H8
Mawlaik Myanmar 37 H5
Mawlamyaing Myanmar 31 I5
Mawlamyine Myanmar see Mawlamyaing
Mawqaq Saudi Arabia 35 F6
Mawson (Australia) research stn Antarctica 76 E2
Mawson Coast Antarctica 76 E2
Mawson Escarpment Antarctica 76 E2
Mawson Peninsula Antarctica 76 H2
Mawza' Yemen 32 F7
Maxán Arg. 70 C3
Maxia, Punta mt. Sardinia Italy 26 C5
Maxixe Moz. 51 L2
Maxmo Fin. 14 M5
May, Isle of i. U.K. 20 G4
Maya r. Russia 29 O3
Mayaguana i. Bahamas 67 J4
Mayagüez Puerto Rico 67 K5
Mayahi Niger 46 D3
Mayak Russia 44 E2
Mayakovskiy, Qullai mt. Tajik. 36 B1
Mayakovskogo, Pik mt. Tajik. see Mayakovskiy, Qullai
Mayama Congo 48 B4
Maya Mountains Belize/Guat. 66 G5
Mayar h. U.K. 20 F4
Maybeury WV U.S.A. 64 A4
Maybole U.K. 20 E5
Maych'ew Eth. 48 D2
Maydān Shahr Afgh. see Maīdān Shahr
Maydh Somalia 32 G7
Maydos Turkey see Eceabat
Mayenne France 24 D2
Mayenne r. France 24 D3
Mayêr Kangri mt. China 37 F2
Mayfield N.Z. 59 C6
Mayi He r. China 44 C3
Maykop Russia 13 I7
Mayna Respublika Khakasiya Russia 28 K4
Mayna Ul'yanovskaya Oblast' Russia 13 J5
Mayni India 38 B2
Mayo Alim Cameroon 46 E4
Mayoko Congo 48 B4
Mayor, Puig mt. Spain see Major, Puig
Mayor Island N.Z. 59 F3
Mayor Pablo Lagerenza Para. 70 D1
Mayotte terr. Africa 49 E5
Mayskiy Amurskaya Oblast' Russia 44 C1
Mayskiy Kabardino-Balkarskaya Respublika Russia 35 G2
Mays Landing NJ U.S.A. 64 D3
Mayumba Gabon 48 B4
Mayum La pass China 37 E3
Mayuram India 38 C4
Mayville NY U.S.A. 64 B1
Mazabuka Zambia 49 C5
Mazaca Turkey see Kayseri
Mazagan Morocco see El Jadida
Mazar China 36 D1
Mazār, Kōh-e mt. Afgh. 36 A2
Mazara, Val di reg. Sicily Italy 26 E6
Mazara del Vallo Sicily Italy 26 E6
Mazār-e Sharīf Afgh. 36 A1
Mazatán Mex. 62 E6
Mazatlán Mex. 66 C4
Mazdaj Iran 35 H4
Mažeikiai Lith. 15 M8
Mazocruz Peru 68 E7
Mazomora Tanz. 49 D4
Mazu Dao i. Taiwan 43 M7
Mazunga Zimbabwe 49 C6

Moble watercourse Australia 58 B1
Mobridge SD U.S.A. 62 G2
Mobutu, Lake Dem. Rep. Congo/Uganda see Albert, Lake
Mobutu Sese Seko, Lake Dem. Rep. Congo/ Uganda see Albert, Lake
Moca Geçidi pass Turkey 39 A1
Moçambique country Africa see Mozambique
Moçambique Moz. 49 E5
Moçâmedes Angola see Namibe
Mocha Yemen 32 F7
Mocha, Isla i. Chile 70 B5
Mochirma, Parque Nacional nat. park Venez. 68 F1
Mochudi Botswana 51 H3
Mochudi admin. dist. Botswana see Kgatleng
Mocimboa da Praia Moz. 49 E5
Mockträsk Sweden 14 L4
Mocoa Col. 68 C3
Mococa Brazil 71 B3
Mocoduene Moz. 51 L2
Moctezuma Chihuahua Mex. 66 C2
Moctezuma San Luis Potosí Mex. 66 D4
Mocuba Moz. 49 D5
Modane France 24 H4
Modder r. S. Africa 51 G5
Modena Italy 26 D2
Modena UT U.S.A. 65 F2
Modesto CA U.S.A. 65 B2
Modesto Lake CA U.S.A. 65 B2
Modimolle S. Africa 51 I3
Modjadjiskloof S. Africa 51 J2
Modung China 37 I3
Moe Australia 58 C7
Moel Sych h. U.K. 19 D6
Moelv Norway 15 G6
Moen Norway 14 K2
Moeraki Point N.Z. 59 C7
Moero, Lake Dem. Rep. Congo/Zambia see Mweru, Lake
Moffat U.K. 20 F5
Moga India 36 C3
Mogadishu Somalia 48 E3
Mogador Morocco see Essaouira
Mogadore Reservoir OH U.S.A. 64 A2
Moganyaka S. Africa 51 I3
Mogaung Myanmar 42 H7
Mogdy Russia 44 D2
Mogi das Cruzes Brazil 71 B3
Mogilev Belarus see Mahilyow
Mogilev Podol'skiy Ukr. see Mohyliv-Podil's'kyy
Mogi Mirim Brazil 71 B3
Mogiquiçaba Brazil 71 D2
Mogocha Russia 43 L2
Mogod mts Tunisia 26 C6
Mogoditshane Botswana 51 G3
Mogontiacum Germany see Mainz
Mogroum Chad 47 E3
Moguqi China 44 A3
Mogwadi S. Africa 51 I2
Mogwadi r. S. Africa 51 I2
Mogwase S. Africa 51 H3
Mogzon Russia 43 K2
Mohács Hungary 26 H2
Mohaka r. N.Z. 59 F4
Mohala India 38 D1
Mohale Dam Lesotho 51 I5
Mohale's Hoek Lesotho 51 H6
Mohali India 36 D3
Moḩammadābād Iran 33 I4
Mohammadia Alg. 25 G6
Mohan r. India/Nepal 36 E3
Mohana India 36 D4
Mohave, Lake NV U.S.A. 65 E3
Mohawk r. NY U.S.A. 64 E1
Mohawk Mountains AZ U.S.A. 65 F4
Mohenjo Daro tourist site Pak. 36 B4
Moher, Cliffs of Ireland 21 C5
Mohill Ireland 21 E4
Mohon Peak AZ U.S.A. 65 F3
Mohoro Tanz. 49 D4
Mohyliv-Podil's'kyy Ukr. 13 E6
Moi Norway 15 E7
Moijabana Botswana 51 H2
Moincêr China 36 E3
Moine Moz. 51 K3
Moinești Romania 27 L1
Mointy Kazakh. see Moyynty
Mo i Rana Norway 14 I3
Mõisaküla Estonia 15 N7
Moissac France 24 E4
Mojave CA U.S.A. 65 C3
Mojave r. CA U.S.A. 65 D3
Mojave Desert CA U.S.A. 65 D3
Mojiang China 42 I8
Mojos, Llanos de plain Bol. 68 E6
Moju r. Brazil 69 I4
Mokama India 37 F4
Mokau N.Z. 59 E4
Mokau r. N.Z. 59 E4
Mokelumne r. CA U.S.A. 65 B1
Mokelumne Aqueduct canal CA U.S.A. 65 B1
Mokh, Gowd-e l. Iran 35 I5
Mokhoabong Pass Lesotho 51 I5
Mokhotlong Lesotho 51 I5
Moknine Tunisia 26 D7
Mokohinau Islands N.Z. 59 E2
Mokokchung India 37 H4
Mokolo Cameroon 47 E3
Mokolo r. S. Africa 51 H2
Mokopane S. Africa 51 I3
Mokpo S. Korea 45 B6
Mokrous Russia 13 J6
Moksha r. Russia 13 I5
Mokshan Russia 13 J5
Mõksy Fin. 14 N5
Mōktama, Gulf of Myanmar see Mottama, Gulf of
Mokundurra India see Mukandwara
Mokwa Nigeria 46 D4
Molatón mt. Spain 25 F4
Moldavia country Europe see Moldova
Moldavskaya S.S.R. country Europe see Moldova
Molde Norway 14 E5
Moldjord Norway 14 I3
Moldova country Europe 13 F7
Moldoveanu, Vârful mt. Romania 27 K2
Moldovei de Sud, Câmpia plain Moldova 27 M1
Molen r. S. Africa 51 I4
Mole National Park Ghana 46 C4
Molepolole Botswana 51 G3
Moltai Lith. 15 N9
Molfetta Italy 26 G4
Molière Alg. see Bordj Bounaama
Molihong Shan mt. China see Morihong Shan
Molina de Aragón Spain 25 F3
Moling mt. India 37 H3
Molkom Sweden 15 H7
Mollagara Turkm. 35 I3
Mollakara Turkm. see Mollagara
Mol Len mt. India 37 H4
Mollendo Peru 68 D7
Mölnlycke Sweden 15 H8
Molochnyy Russia 14 R2
Molodechno Belarus see Maladzyechna
Moloma r. Russia 12 K4
Molong Australia 58 D4
Molopo watercourse Botswana/S. Africa 50 E5
Molotov Russia see Perm'
Molotovsk Arkhangel'skaya Oblast' Russia see Severodvinsk
Molotovsk Kirovskaya Oblast' Russia see Nolinsk
Moloundou Cameroon 47 E4
Molson Lake Man. Canada 63 H1
Moluccas is Indon. 41 E8
Molucca Sea sea Indon. see Maluku, Laut
Moma Moz. 49 D5
Moma r. Russia 29 P3
Momba Australia 58 A3
Mombaça Brazil 69 K5
Mombasa Kenya 48 D4
Mombetsu Hokkaidō Japan see Monbetsu
Mombetsu Hokkaidō Japan see Hidaka
Mombi New India 37 H4
Momchilgrad Bulg. 27 K4
Momī, Rhiy di- pt Yemen 33 H7
Mompós Col. 68 D2
Møn i. Denmark 15 H9
Mon India 37 H4
Mona terr. Irish Sea see Isle of Man
Monach, Sound of sea chan. U.K. 20 B3
Monach Islands U.K. 20 B3
Monaco country Europe 24 H5
Monaco Basin sea feature N. Atlantic Ocean 72 G4
Monadhliath Mountains U.K. 20 E3
Monaghan Ireland 21 F3
Mona Passage Dom. Rep./Puerto Rico 67 K5
Monapo Moz. 49 E5
Monar, Loch l. U.K. 20 D3
Monarch Pass CO U.S.A. 62 F4
Monastir Macedonia see Bitola
Monastir Tunisia 26 D7
Monastyrishche Ukr. see Monastyryshche
Monastyryshche Ukr. 13 F6
Monbetsu Japan 44 F3
Moncalieri Italy 26 B2
Moncayo mt. Spain 25 F3
Monchegorsk Russia 12 G2
Mönchengladbach Germany 17 K5
Monchique Port. 25 B5
Monclova Mex. 66 D3
Moncton N.B. Canada 63 O2
Mondego r. Port. 25 B3
Mondo Chad 47 E3
Mondovì Italy 26 B2
Mondragone Italy 26 E4
Mondy Russia 42 I2
Monemvasia Greece 27 J6
Monessen PA U.S.A. 64 B2
Moneygall Ireland 21 E5
Moneymore U.K. 21 F3
Monfalcone Italy 26 E2
Monfalut Egypt see Manfalūṭ
Monforte de Lemos Spain 25 C2
Monga Dem. Rep. Congo 48 C3
Mongala r. Dem. Rep. Congo 48 B3
Mongar Bhutan 37 G4
Mongbwalu Dem. Rep. Congo 48 D3
Mông Cai Vietnam 31 J4
Mongers Lake imp. l. Australia 55 B7
Monghyr India see Munger
Mongla Bangl. 37 G5
Mong Lin Myanmar 42 I8
Mong Long Myanmar 37 I5
Mongo Chad 47 E3
Mongolia country Asia 42 I3
Mongol Uls country Asia see Mongolia
Mongora Pak. 33 L3
Mongour h. U.K. 20 G4
Mongu Zambia 49 C5
Monguno Nigeria 46 E3
Mönhhaan Mongolia 43 K3
Mönh Hayrhan Uul mt. Mongolia 42 G3
Moniaive U.K. 20 F5
Monitor Mountain NV U.S.A. 65 D1
Monitor Range mts NV U.S.A. 65 D1
Monivea Ireland 21 D4
Monkey Bay Malawi 49 D5
Monkira Australia 56 C5
Monkton Ont. Canada 64 A1
Monmouth U.K. 19 E7
Monnow r. U.K. 19 E7
Mono, Punta pt Nicaragua 67 H6
Mono Lake CA U.S.A. 65 C1
Monolithos Greece 27 L6
Monomoy Point MA U.S.A. 64 F2
Monopoli Italy 26 G4
Monreal del Campo Spain 25 F3
Monreale Sicily Italy 26 E5
Monroe LA U.S.A. 63 I5
Monroeton PA U.S.A. 64 C2
Monrovia Liberia 46 B4
Mons Belgium 16 I5
Monselice Italy 26 D2
Montagne d'Ambre, Parc National de nat. park Madag. 49 E5
Montagu S. Africa 50 E7
Montague Range hills Australia 55 B6
Montalto mt. Italy 26 F5
Montalto Uffugo Italy 26 G5
Montana Bulg. 27 J3
Montana state U.S.A. 62 F2
Montanhas do Tumucumaque, Parque Nacional nat. park 69 H3
Montargis France 24 F3
Montauban France 24 E4
Montauk NY U.S.A. 64 F2
Montauk Point NY U.S.A. 64 F2
Mont-aux-Sources mt. Lesotho 51 I5
Montbard France 24 G3
Montblanc Spain 25 G3
Montblanch Spain see Montblanc
Montbrison France 24 G4
Montceau-les-Mines France 24 G3
Mont-de-Marsan France 24 D5
Montdidier France 24 F2
Monte Alegre Brazil 69 H4
Monte Alegre de Goiás Brazil 71 B1
Monte Alegre de Minas Brazil 71 A2
Monte Azul Brazil 71 C1
Monte Azul Paulista Brazil 71 A3
Montebello Islands Australia 54 A5
Montebelluna Italy 26 E2
Monte-Carlo Monaco 24 H5
Monte Cristi Dom. Rep. 67 J5
Monte Cristo S. Africa 51 H2
Monte Dourado Brazil 69 H4
Montego Bay Jamaica 67 I5
Montélimar France 24 G4
Monte Lindo r. Para. 70 E2
Montemorelos Mex. 66 E3
Montemor-o-Novo Port. 25 B4
Montenegro country Europe 26 H3
Montepulciano Italy 26 D3
Monte Quemado Arg. 70 D3
Montereau-Fault-Yonne France 24 F2
Monterey Mex. see Monterrey
Monterey CA U.S.A. 65 B2
Monterey VA U.S.A. 64 B3
Monterey Bay CA U.S.A. 65 A2
Montería Col. 68 C2
Monteros Arg. 70 C3
Monterrey Baja California Mex. 65 E4
Monterrey Nuevo León Mex. 66 D3
Montesano sulla Marcellana Italy 26 F4
Monte Santo Brazil 69 K6
Monte Santu, Capo di c. Sardinia Italy 26 C4
Montes Claros Brazil 71 C2
Montesilvano Italy 26 F3
Montevarchi Italy 26 D3
Montevideo Uruguay 70 E4
Montezuma Peak NV U.S.A. 65 D2
Montgomery U.K. 19 D6
Montgomery AL U.S.A. 63 J5
Montgomery WV U.S.A. 64 A3
Montgomery Islands Australia 54 C3
Monthey Switz. 24 H3
Monticello NY U.S.A. 64 D2
Monticello UT U.S.A. 62 F4
Montieri, Poggio di mt. Italy 26 D3
Montignac France 24 E4
Montilla Spain 25 D5
Monti Sibillini, Parco Nazionale dei nat. park Italy 26 E3
Montividiu Brazil 71 A2
Montivilliers France 19 H9
Mont-Laurier Que. Canada 63 L2
Montluçon France 24 F3
Montmagny Que. Canada 63 M2
Montmorillon France 24 E3
Monto Australia 56 E5
Montour Falls NY U.S.A. 64 C1
Montpelier VT U.S.A. 63 M3
Montpellier France 24 F5
Montréal Que. Canada 61 K5
Montreal Lake Sask. Canada 62 F1
Montreuil France 19 I8
Montreux Switz. 24 H3
Montrose well S. Africa 50 E4
Montrose U.K. 20 G4
Montrose CO U.S.A. 62 F4
Montrose PA U.S.A. 64 D2
Montross VA U.S.A. 64 C3
Mont-St-Aignan France 19 I9
Montserrat terr. West Indies 67 L5
Monywa Myanmar 37 H5
Monza Italy 26 C2
Monze, Cape c. Pak. see Muari, Ras
Monzón Spain 25 G3
Mooi r. S. Africa 51 J5
Mooifontein Namibia 50 C4
Mookane Botswana 51 H2
Mookgophong S. Africa 51 I3
Mookgopong S. Africa see Mookgophong
Moolawatana Australia 57 B6
Moomba Australia 57 C6
Moomin Creek r. Australia 58 D2
Moonaree Australia 57 A6
Moonbi Range mts Australia 58 E3
Moonda Lake imp. l. Australia 57 C5
Moonie Australia 58 E1
Moonie r. Australia 58 D2
Moora Australia 55 B7
Mooraberree Australia 56 C5
Moore r. Australia 55 A7
Moore, Lake imp. l. Australia 55 B7
Moore Embayment b. Antarctica 76 H1
Moorefield WV U.S.A. 64 B3
Moore Reef Australia 56 E3
Moore River National Park Australia 55 A7
Moorfoot Hills U.K. 20 F5
Moorhead MN U.S.A. 63 H2
Moornanyah Lake imp. l. Australia 58 A4
Mooroopna Australia 58 B6
Moorreesburg S. Africa 50 D7
Moorrinya National Park Australia 56 D4
Moose r. Ont. Canada 63 K1
Moose Factory Ont. Canada 63 K1
Moosehead Lake ME U.S.A. 63 N2
Moose Jaw Sask. Canada 62 F1
Moosomin Sask. Canada 62 G1
Moosonee Ont. Canada 63 K1
Mootwingee National Park Australia 57 C6
Mopane S. Africa 51 I2
Mopeia Moz. 49 D5
Mopipi Botswana 49 C6
Mopti Mali 46 C3
Moquegua Peru 68 D7
Mora Cameroon 47 E3
Mora Spain 25 E4
Mora Sweden 15 I6
Moradabad India 36 D3
Morada Nova Brazil 69 K5
Moraleda, Canal sea chan. Chile 70 B6
Moram India 38 C2
Moramanga Madag. 49 E5
Moranbah Australia 56 E4
Morang Nepal see Biratnagar
Morar, Loch l. U.K. 20 D4
Morari, Tso l. India 36 D2
Moratuwa Sri Lanka 38 C5
Morava reg. Czech Rep. 17 P6
Moravia NY U.S.A. 64 C1
Morawa Australia 55 A7
Moray Firth b. U.K. 20 E3
Moray Range hills Australia 54 E3
Morbeng S. Africa see Morebeng
Morbi India 36 B5
Morcenx France 24 D4
Mordaga China 43 M2
Mor Dağı mt. Turkey 35 G3
Morden Man. Canada 62 H2
Mordovo Russia 13 I5
Morebeng S. Africa 51 I2
Morecambe U.K. 18 E4
Morecambe Bay U.K. 18 D4
Moree Australia 58 D2
Morehead P.N.G. 52 E2
Morehead City NC U.S.A. 67 I2
More Laptevykh sea Russia see Laptev Sea
Morelia Mex. 66 D5
Morella Australia 56 C4
Morella Spain 25 F3
Morena India 36 D4
Morena, Sierra mts Spain 25 C5
Moreni Romania 27 K2
Moreno Valley CA U.S.A. 65 D4
Moresby, Mount B.C. Canada 60 E4
Moresby Island B.C. Canada see Gwaii Haanas
Moreswe Pan salt pan Botswana 50 G2
Moreton Bay Australia 58 F1
Moreton-in-Marsh U.K. 19 F7
Moreton Island Australia 58 F1
Moreton Island National Park Australia 58 F1
Morez France 24 H3
Morfou Cyprus 39 A2
Morfou Bay Cyprus 39 A2
Morgan Hill CA U.S.A. 65 B2
Morganton NC U.S.A. 63 K4
Morgantown WV U.S.A. 64 B3
Morgenzon S. Africa 51 I4
Morges Switz. 24 H3
Morghāb, Daryā-ye r. Afgh. 36 A2
Morhar r. India 37 F4
Mori China 42 G4
Mori Japan 44 F4
Moriah, Mount NV U.S.A. 65 E1
Moriarty's Range hills Australia 58 B2
Morice Lake B.C. Canada 60 F4
Morichal Col. 68 D3
Morihong Shan mt. China 44 B4
Morija Lesotho 51 H5
Morin Dawa China see Nirji
Morioka Japan 45 F5
Morisset Australia 58 E4
Moriyoshi-zan vol. Japan 45 F5
Morjärv Sweden 14 M3
Morki Russia 12 K4
Morlaix France 24 C2
Morley U.K. 18 F5
Mormugao India see Marmagao
Morne Diablotins vol. Dominica 67 L5
Morney watercourse Australia 56 C5
Mornington, Isla i. Chile 70 A7
Mornington Abyssal Plain sea feature S. Atlantic Ocean 72 C9
Mornington Island Australia 56 B3
Mornington Peninsula National Park Australia 58 B7
Moro Pak. 36 A4
Morobe P.N.G. 52 E2
Morocco country Africa 46 C1
Morococala mt. Bol. 68 E7
Morogoro Tanz. 49 D4
Moro Gulf Phil. 41 E7
Morojaneng S. Africa 51 H5
Morokweng S. Africa 50 F4
Morombe Madag. 49 E6
Mörön Mongolia 42 I3
Morondava Madag. 49 E6
Morón de la Frontera Spain 25 D5
Moroni Comoros 49 E5
Moron Us He r. China see Tongtian He
Morotai i. Indon. 41 E7
Moroto Uganda 48 D3
Morozovsk Russia 13 I6
Morpeth Ont. Canada 64 A1
Morpeth U.K. 18 F3
Morphou Cyprus see Morfou
Morrinhos Brazil 71 A2
Morris Man. Canada 63 H2
Morris PA U.S.A. 64 C2
Morristown AZ U.S.A. 65 F4
Morristown NJ U.S.A. 64 D2
Morristown TN U.S.A. 63 K4
Morrisville NY U.S.A. 64 D1
Morro Brazil 71 B2
Morro Bay CA U.S.A. 65 B3
Morro do Chapéu Brazil 69 J6
Morro Grande h. Brazil 69 H4
Morrosquillo, Golfo de b. Col. 68 C2
Morrumbene Moz. 51 L2
Morse, Cape Antarctica 76 G2
Morshanka Russia see Morshansk
Morshansk Russia 13 I5
Morsott Alg. 26 C7
Mort watercourse Australia 56 C4
Mortagne-au-Perche France 24 E2
Mortagne-sur-Sèvre France 24 D3
Mortara Italy 26 C2
Mortehoe U.K. 19 C7
Morteros Arg. 70 D4
Mortes, Rio das r. Brazil 71 A1
Mortlake Australia 58 A7
Mortlock Islands Micronesia 74 G5
Mortlock Islands P.N.G. see Takuu Islands
Morton U.K. 19 G6
Morton National Park Australia 58 E5
Morundah Australia 58 C5
Morupule Botswana 51 H2
Moruroa atoll Fr. Polynesia see Mururoa
Moruya Australia 58 E5
Morven Australia 57 D5
Morven h. U.K. 20 F2
Morvern reg. U.K. 20 D4
Morvi India see Morbi
Morwell Australia 58 C7
Morzhovets, Ostrov i. Russia 12 I2
Mosbach Germany 17 L6
Mosborough U.K. 18 F5
Moscow Russia 12 H5
Moscow ID U.S.A. 62 D2
Moscow PA U.S.A. 64 D2
Moscow University Ice Shelf Antarctica 76 G2
Moselebe watercourse Botswana 50 F3
Moselle r. France 24 H2
Moses Lake WA U.S.A. 62 D2
Mosgiel N.Z. 59 C7
Moshaweng watercourse S. Africa 50 F4
Moshchnyy, Ostrov i. Russia 15 O7
Moshi Tanz. 48 D4
Mosh'yuga Russia 12 L2
Mosi-oa-Tunya waterfall Zambia/ Zimbabwe see Victoria Falls
Mosjøen Norway 14 H4
Moskal'vo Russia 44 F1
Moskenesøy i. Norway 14 H3
Moskva Russia see Moscow
Mosonmagyaróvár Hungary 17 P7
Mosquera Col. 68 C3
Mosquito r. Brazil 71 C1
Mosquito Creek Lake OH U.S.A. 64 A2
Mosquitos, Costa de coastal area Nicaragua 67 H6
Mosquitos, Golfo de los b. Panama 67 H7
Moss Norway 15 G7
Mossâmedes Angola see Namibe
Mossat U.K. 20 G3
Mossburn N.Z. 59 B7
Mosselbaai S. Africa see Mossel Bay
Mossel Bay S. Africa 50 F8
Mossel Bay b. S. Africa 50 F8
Mossgiel Australia 58 B4
Mossman Australia 56 D3
Mossoró Brazil 69 K5
Moss Vale Australia 58 E5
Most Czech Rep. 17 N5
Mostaganem Alg. 25 G6
Mostar Bos. & Herz. 26 G3
Mostovskoy Russia 35 F1
Mosty Belarus see Masty
Mosul Iraq 35 F3
Møsvatnet l. Norway 15 F7
Motala Sweden 15 I7
Motaze Moz. 51 K3
Motetema S. Africa 51 I3
Moth India 36 D4
Motherwell U.K. 20 F5
Motian Ling h. China 44 A4
Motihari India 37 F4
Motilla del Palancar Spain 25 F4
Motiti Island N.Z. 59 F3
Motokwe Botswana 50 F3
Motril Spain 25 E5
Motru Romania 27 J2
Mottama, Gulf of Myanmar 31 I5
Motu Ihupuku i. N.Z. see Campbell Island
Motul Mex. 66 G4
Mouaskar Alg. see Mascara
Moudjéria Mauritania 46 B3
Moudros Greece 27 K5
Mouhijärvi Fin. 15 M6
Mouila Gabon 48 B4
Moulamein Australia 58 B5
Moulamein Creek r. Australia 58 A5
Moulavibazar Bangl. see Moulvibazar
Mould Bay N.W.T. Canada 60 G2
Moulèngui Binza Gabon 48 B4
Moulins France 24 F3
Moulouya r. Morocco 22 D4
Moultrie GA U.S.A. 63 K5
Moultrie, Lake SC U.S.A. 63 L5
Moulvibazar Bangl. 37 G4
Moundou Chad 47 E4
Moundsville WV U.S.A. 64 A3
Mount Abu India 36 C4
Mountain Home AR U.S.A. 63 I4
Mountain Home ID U.S.A. 62 D3
Mountain Lake Park MD U.S.A. 64 B3
Mountain Zebra National Park S. Africa 51 G7
Mount Aspiring National Park N.Z. 59 B7
Mount Ayliff S. Africa 51 I6
Mountbellew Ireland 21 D4
Mount Buffalo National Park Australia 58 C6
Mount Carmel Junction UT U.S.A. 65 F2
Mount Coolon Australia 56 D4
Mount Darwin Zimbabwe 49 D5
Mount Denison Australia 54 F5
Mount Dutton Australia 57 A5
Mount Eba Australia 57 A6
Mount Elgon National Park Uganda 48 D3
Mount Fletcher S. Africa 51 I6
Mount Frankland National Park Australia 55 B8
Mount Frere S. Africa 51 I6
Mount Gambier Australia 57 C8
Mount Hagen P.N.G. 52 E2
Mount Hamiguitan Range Wildlife Sanctuary tourist site Phil. 41 E7
Mount Holly NJ U.S.A. 64 D3
Mount Hope Australia 58 B4
Mount Hope WV U.S.A. 64 A4
Mount Howitt Australia 57 C5
Mount Isa Australia 56 B4
Mount Jackson VA U.S.A. 64 B3
Mount Jewett PA U.S.A. 64 B2
Mount Joy PA U.S.A. 64 C2
Mount Kaputar National Park Australia 58 E3
Mount Keith Australia 55 C6
Mount Lofty Range mts Australia 57 B7
Mount Magnet Australia 55 B7
Mount Manara Australia 58 A4
Mount McKinley National Park AK U.S.A. see Denali National Park and Preserve
Mountmellick Ireland 21 E4
Mount Moorosi Lesotho 51 H6
Mount Morgan Australia 56 E4
Mount Morris NY U.S.A. 64 C1
Mount Murchison Australia 58 A3
Mount Nebo WV U.S.A. 64 A3
Mount Pleasant IA U.S.A. 63 I3
Mount Pleasant MI U.S.A. 63 K3
Mount Pleasant TX U.S.A. 63 I5
Mount Remarkable National Park Australia 57 B7
Mount Rogers National Recreation Area park VA U.S.A. 64 A4
Mount Sanford Australia 54 E4
Mount's Bay U.K. 19 B8
Mount Shasta CA U.S.A. 62 C3
Mountsorrel U.K. 19 F6
Mount Swan Australia 56 A4
Mount Union PA U.S.A. 64 C2
Mount Vernon Australia 55 B6
Mount Vernon IL U.S.A. 63 J4
Mount Vernon WA U.S.A. 62 C2
Mount William National Park Australia 57 [inset]
Mount Willoughby Australia 55 F6
Moura Australia 56 E5
Moura Brazil 68 F4
Moura Port. 25 C4
Mourdi, Dépression du depr. Chad 47 F3
Mourdiah Mali 46 C3
Mourne r. U.K. 21 E3
Mourne Mountains hills U.K. 21 F3
Mousa i. U.K. 20 [inset]
Mouscron Belgium 16 I5
Mousgougou Chad 48 B2
Moussafoyo Chad 47 E4
Moussoro Chad 47 E3
Moutamba Congo 48 B4
Moutong Indon. 41 E7
Mouydir, Monts du plat. Alg. 46 D2
Mowbullan, Mount Australia 58 E1
Moy r. Ireland 21 C3
Moyale Eth. 48 D3
Moyen Atlas mts Morocco 22 C5
Moyen Congo country Africa see Congo
Moyeni Lesotho 51 H6
Moynalyk Russia 42 H2
Moyo i. Indon. 54 B2
Moyobamba Peru 68 C5
Moyola r. U.K. 21 F3
Moyu China 36 D1
Moyynkum Kazakh. 42 C4
Moyynkum, Peski des. Kazakh. 42 B4
Moyynty Kazakh. 28 I5
Mozambique country Africa 49 D6
Mozambique Channel Africa 49 E6
Mozambique Ridge sea feature Indian Ocean 73 K7
Mozdok Russia 13 J8
Mozhaysk Russia 13 H5
Mozhga Russia 12 L4
Mozyr' Belarus see Mazyr
Mpaathutlwa Pan salt pan Botswana 50 E3
Mpanda Tanz. 49 D4
Mpen India 37 I4
Mpika Zambia 49 D5
Mpolweni S. Africa 51 J5
Mporokoso Zambia 49 D4
Mpulungu Zambia 49 D4
Mpumalanga prov. S. Africa 51 I4
Mpunde mt. Tanz. 49 D4
Mpwapwa Tanz. 49 D4
Mqanduli S. Africa 51 I6
Mqinvartsveri mt. Georgia/Russia see Kazbek
Mrauk-U Myanmar 37 H5
Mrewa Zimbabwe see Murehwa
Mrkonjić-Grad Bos. & Herz. 26 G2
M'Saken Tunisia 26 D7
Mshinskaya Russia 15 P7
M'Sila Alg. 25 I6
Msta r. Russia 12 F4
Mstislavl' Belarus see Mstsislaw
Mstsislaw Belarus 13 F5
Mtelo Kenya 48 D3
Mthatha S. Africa 51 I6
Mtoko Zimbabwe see Mutoko
Mtorwi Tanz. 49 D4
Mtsensk Russia 13 H5
Mts'ire Kavkasioni Asia see Lesser Caucasus
Mtubatuba S. Africa 51 K5
Mtunzini S. Africa 51 J5
Mtwara Tanz. 49 E5
Mu r. Myanmar 37 H5
Mu'āb, Jibāl reg. Jordan see Moab
Muanda Dem. Rep. Congo 49 B4
Muang Khoua Laos 42 I8
Muang Pakxan Laos see Pakxan
Muang Sing Laos 42 I8
Muang Thai country Asia see Thailand
Muari, Ras c. Pak. 36 A4
Mu'ayqil, Khashm al h. Saudi Arabia 35 H6
Mubarek Uzbek. see Muborak
Mubarraz well Saudi Arabia 35 F5
Mubende Uganda 48 D3
Mubi Nigeria 46 E3
Muborak Uzbek. 33 K2
Mucajaí, Serra do mts Brazil 68 F3
Muccan Australia 54 C5
Muchinga Escarpment Zambia 49 D5
Muck i. U.K. 20 C4
Mucojo Moz. 49 E5
Muconda Angola 49 C5
Mucubela Moz. 49 D5
Mucugê Brazil 71 C1
Mucur Turkey 34 D3
Mucuri Brazil 71 D2
Mucuri r. Brazil 71 D2
Mudabidri India 38 B3
Mudan China see Heze
Mudanjiang China 44 C3
Mudan Jiang r. China 44 C3
Mudan Ling mts China 44 B4
Mudanya Turkey 27 M4
Mudaysīsāt, Jabal al h. Jordan 39 C4
Muddus nationalpark nat. park Sweden 14 K3
Muddy r. NV U.S.A. 65 E2
Muddy Peak NV U.S.A. 65 E2
Mudgal India 38 C3
Mudgee Australia 58 D4
Mudhol India 38 B2
Mudigere India 38 B3
Mud Lake NV U.S.A. 65 D2
Mudraya country Africa see Egypt
Mudurnu Turkey 27 N4
Mud'yuga Russia 12 H3
Mueda Moz. 49 D5
Mueller Range hills Australia 54 D4
Muftyuga Russia 12 J2
Mufulira Zambia 49 C5
Mufumbwe Zambia 49 C5
Muğan Düzü lowland Azer. 35 H3
Mugarripug China 37 F2
Mughalbhin Pak. see Jati
Mughal Kot Pak. 36 B3
Mughal Sarai India 37 E4
Mūghār Iran 35 I4
Mughayrā' Saudi Arabia 39 C5
Muğla Turkey 27 M6
Mugxung China 37 H2
Mūḩ, Sabkhat imp. l. Syria 39 D2
Muhammad Ashraf Pak. 36 B4
Muhammad Qol Sudan 32 E5
Muhammarah Iran see Khorramshahr
Muhashsham, Wādī al watercourse Egypt 39 B4
Muḩaysh, Wādī al watercourse Jordan 39 C5
Muhaysin Syria 39 D1
Mühlhausen/Thüringen Germany 17 M5
Mühlig-Hofmann Mountains Antarctica 76 C2
Muhos Fin. 14 N4
Muḩradah Syria 39 C2
Mui Bai Bung c. Vietnam see Ca Mau, Mui
Muié Angola 49 C5
Muineachán Ireland see Monaghan
Muirkirk U.K. 20 E5
Muir of Ord U.K. 20 E3
Muite Moz. 49 D5
Mūjān, Chāh-e well Iran 35 I4
Muji China 36 D1
Muju S. Korea 45 B5
Mukacheve Ukr. 13 D6
Mukachevo Ukr. see Mukacheve
Mukalla Yemen 32 G7
Mukandwara India 36 D4
Mukden China see Shenyang
Mukhen Russia 44 E2
Mukhino Russia 44 B1
Mukhtuya Russia see Lensk
Mukinbudin Australia 55 B7
Mukojima-rettō is Japan 45 F8
Muktsar India 36 C3
Mula r. India 38 B2
Mulan China 44 C3
Mulanje, Mount Malawi 49 D5
Mulapula, Lake imp. l. Australia 57 B6
Mulayz, Wādī al watercourse Egypt 39 A4
Mulchatna r. AK U.S.A. 60 C3
Mulde r. Germany 17 N5
Mulegé Mex. 66 B3
Mules i. Indon. 54 C2
Muleshoe TX U.S.A. 62 G5
Mulga Park Australia 55 E6
Mulgathing Australia 55 F7
Mulhacén mt. Spain 25 E5
Mülhausen France see Mulhouse
Mulhouse France 24 H3
Muli China 42 I7
Muli Russia see Vysokogorniy
Muling Heilongjiang China 44 C3
Muling Heilongjiang China 44 C3
Muling He r. China 44 D3
Mull i. U.K. 20 D4
Mull, Sound of sea chan. U.K. 20 C4
Mullaghcleevaun h. Ireland 21 F4
Mullaittivu Sri Lanka 38 D4
Mullaley Australia 58 D3
Mullengudgery Australia 58 C3
Mullens WV U.S.A. 64 A4
Muller watercourse Australia 54 F5
Mullewa Australia 55 A7
Mullica r. NJ U.S.A. 64 D3
Mullingar Ireland 21 E4
Mullion Creek Australia 58 D4
Mull of Galloway c. U.K. 20 E6
Mull of Kintyre hd U.K. 20 D5
Mull of Oa hd U.K. 20 C5
Mullumbimby Australia 58 F2
Mulobezi Zambia 49 C5
Mulshi Lake India 38 B2
Multai India 36 D5
Multan Pak. 33 L3
Multia Fin. 14 N5
Mulug India 38 C2
Mumbai India 38 B2
Mumbil Australia 58 D4
Mumbwa Zambia 49 C5
Muna Mex. 66 G4
Muna r. Russia 29 N3
Munabao Pak. 36 B4
Munaðarnes Iceland 14 [inset 2]
München Germany see Munich
München-Gladbach Germany see Mönchengladbach
Muncoonie West, Lake imp. l. Australia 56 B5
Muncy PA U.S.A. 64 C2
Munda Pak. 36 B3
Mundel Lake Sri Lanka 38 C5
Mundesley U.K. 19 I6
Mundford U.K. 19 H6
Mundiwindi (abandoned) Australia 55 C5
Mundra India 36 B5
Mundrabilla Australia 52 C5
Mundubbera Australia 57 E5
Mundwa India 36 C4
Mungallala Australia 57 D5
Mungana Australia 56 D3
Mungap-do i. S. Korea 45 B5
Mungári Moz. 49 D5
Mungbere Dem. Rep. Congo 48 C3
Mungeli India 37 E5
Munger India 37 F4
Mu Nggava i. Solomon Is see Rennell
Mungindi Australia 58 D2
Mungla Bangl. see Mongla
Mungo Angola 49 B5
Mungo, Lake Australia 58 A4

Nendo i. Solomon Is 53 G3
Nene r. U.K. 19 H6
Nenjiang China 44 B2
Nen Jiang r. China 44 B3
Neosho MO U.S.A. 63 I4
Nepal country Asia 37 E3
Nepalganj Nepal 37 E3
Nepean, Point Australia 58 B7
Nephi UT U.S.A. 62 E4
Nephin h. Ireland 21 C3
Nephin Beg Range hills Ireland 21 C3
Nepisiguit r. N.B. Canada 63 N2
Nepoko r. Dem. Rep. Congo 48 C3
Nérac France 24 E4
Nerang Australia 58 F1
Nera Tso l. China 37 H3
Nerchinsk Russia 43 L2
Nerekhta Russia 12 I4
Neretva r. Bos. & Herz./Croatia 26 G3
Nêri Pünco l. China 37 G3
Neriquinha Angola 49 C5
Nerl' r. Russia 12 H4
Nerópolis Brazil 71 A2
Neryungri Russia 29 N4
Nes Norway 15 F6
Nes' Russia 12 J2
Nesbyen Norway 15 F6
Neskaupstaður Iceland 14 [inset 2]
Nesna Norway 14 H3
Nesri India 38 B2
Ness r. U.K. 20 E3
Ness, Loch l. U.K. 20 E3
Nesvizh Belarus see Nyasvizh
Netanya Israel 39 B3
Netherlands country Europe 16 J4
Netrakona Bangl. 37 G4
Netrokona Bangl. see Netrakona
Nettilling Lake Nunavut Canada 61 K3
Neubrandenburg Germany 17 N4
Neuchâtel Switz. 24 H3
Neuchâtel, Lac de l. Switz. 24 H3
Neufchâteau France 24 G2
Neufchâtel-en-Bray France 24 E2
Neufchâtel-Hardelot France 19 I8
Neuhausen Russia see Gur'yevsk
Neukuhren Russia see Pionerskiy
Neumayer III (Germany) research stn Antarctica 76 B2
Neumünster Germany 17 L3
Neunkirchen Austria 17 P7
Neunkirchen Germany 17 K6
Neuquén Arg. 70 C5
Neuruppin Germany 17 N4
Neu Sandez Poland see Nowy Sącz
Neusiedler See l. Austria/Hungary 17 P7
Neusiedler See Seewinkel, Nationalpark nat. park Austria 17 P7
Neustrelitz Germany 17 N4
Neuville-lès-Dieppe France 19 I9
Neuwied Germany 17 K5
Nevada MO U.S.A. 63 I4
Nevada state U.S.A. 62 D4
Nevada, Sierra mts Spain 25 E5
Nevada, Sierra mts CA U.S.A. 62 C3
Nevado, Cerro mt. Arg. 70 C5
Nevado, Sierra del mts Arg. 70 C5
Nevasa India 38 B2
Nevatim Israel 39 B4
Nevdubstroy Russia see Kirovsk
Nevel' Russia 12 F4
Nevel'sk Russia 44 F3
Never Russia 44 B1
Nevers France 24 F3
Nevertire Australia 58 C3
Nevesinje Bos. & Herz. 26 H3
Nevinnomyssk Russia 13 I7
Nevşehir Turkey 34 D3
Nevskoye Russia 44 D3
New r. CA U.S.A. 65 E4
New r. WV U.S.A. 64 A4
Newala Tanz. 49 D5
New Albany IN U.S.A. 63 J4
New Amsterdam Guyana 69 G2
New Angledool Australia 58 C2
Newark DE U.S.A. 64 D3
Newark NJ U.S.A. 64 D2
Newark NY U.S.A. 64 C1
Newark-on-Trent U.K. 19 G5
New Bedford MA U.S.A. 64 F2
New Berlin NY U.S.A. 64 D1
New Bern NC U.S.A. 63 L4
Newberry SC U.S.A. 63 K5
Newberry Springs CA U.S.A. 65 D3
New Bethlehem PA U.S.A. 64 B2
Newbiggin-by-the-Sea U.K. 18 F3
New Bloomfield PA U.S.A. 64 C2
New Boston TX U.S.A. 63 I5
New Braunfels TX U.S.A. 62 H6
Newbridge Ireland 21 E4
New Britain i. P.N.G. 52 E2
New Britain CT U.S.A. 64 E2
New Britain Trench sea feature S. Pacific Ocean 74 G6
New Brunswick prov. Canada 63 N2
New Brunswick NJ U.S.A. 64 D2
Newburgh U.K. 20 G3
Newburgh NY U.S.A. 64 D2
Newbury U.K. 19 F7
Newburyport MA U.S.A. 64 F1
Newby Bridge U.K. 18 E4
New Caledonia terr. S. Pacific Ocean 53 G4
New Caledonia Trough sea feature Tasman Sea 74 G7
Newcastle Australia 58 E4
Newcastle Ireland 21 F4
Newcastle S. Africa 51 I4
Newcastle U.K. 21 G3
New Castle PA U.S.A. 64 A2
Newcastle UT U.S.A. 65 F2
New Castle VA U.S.A. 64 A4
Newcastle WY U.S.A. 62 G3
Newcastle Emlyn U.K. 19 C6
Newcastle-under-Lyme U.K. 19 E5
Newcastle upon Tyne U.K. 18 F4
Newcastle Waters Australia 54 F4
Newcastle West Ireland 21 C5
Newchwang China see Yingkou
New City NY U.S.A. 64 E2
New Cumberland WV U.S.A. 64 A2
New Cumnock U.K. 20 E5
New Deer U.K. 20 G3
New Delhi India 36 D3
New Don Pedro Reservoir CA U.S.A. 65 B2
Newell, Lake imp. l. Australia 55 D6
New England National Park Australia 58 F3
New England Range mts Australia 58 E3
New England Seamounts sea feature N. Atlantic Ocean 72 E3
Newenham, Cape AK U.S.A. 60 B4
Newent U.K. 19 E7
Newfane NY U.S.A. 64 B1
Newfane VT U.S.A. 64 E1
Newfoundland i. Nfld. and Lab. Canada 61 M5
Newfoundland prov. Canada see Newfoundland and Labrador
Newfoundland and Labrador prov. Canada 61 M4
New Galloway U.K. 20 E5
New Georgia i. Solomon Is 53 F2
New Georgia Islands Solomon Is 53 F2
New Georgia Sound sea chan. Solomon Is 53 F2
New Guinea i. Indon./P.N.G. 41 G8
New Halfa Sudan 32 E6
New Hampshire state U.S.A. 64 F1
New Hanover i. P.N.G. 52 F2
Newhaven U.K. 19 H8
New Haven CT U.S.A. 64 E2
New Hebrides country S. Pacific Ocean see Vanuatu
New Hebrides Trench sea feature S. Pacific Ocean 74 H7
New Iberia LA U.S.A. 63 I5
Newinn Ireland 21 E5
New Ireland i. P.N.G. 52 F2
New Jersey state U.S.A. 64 D3
New Kensington PA U.S.A. 64 B2
New Kent VA U.S.A. 64 C4
New Lanark U.K. 20 F5
Newland Range hills Australia 55 C7
New Liskeard Ont. Canada 63 L2
New London CT U.S.A. 64 E2
Newman Australia 55 B5
Newman CA U.S.A. 65 B2
Newmarket Ireland 21 C5
Newmarket U.K. 19 H6
New Market VA U.S.A. 64 B3
Newmarket-on-Fergus Ireland 21 D5
New Martinsville WV U.S.A. 64 A3
New Mexico state U.S.A. 62 F5
New Milford PA U.S.A. 64 D2
New Orleans LA U.S.A. 63 I6
New Philadelphia OH U.S.A. 64 A2
New Pitsligo U.K. 20 G3
New Plymouth N.Z. 59 E4
Newport Mayo Ireland 21 C4
Newport Tipperary Ireland 21 D5
Newport England U.K. 19 E6
Newport England U.K. 19 F8
Newport Wales U.K. 19 D7
Newport AR U.S.A. 63 I4
Newport NH U.S.A. 64 E1
Newport NJ U.S.A. 64 D3
Newport OR U.S.A. 62 C3
Newport RI U.S.A. 64 F2
Newport VT U.S.A. 63 M3
Newport WA U.S.A. 62 D2
Newport Beach CA U.S.A. 65 D4
Newport News VA U.S.A. 64 C4
Newport Pagnell U.K. 19 G6
Newquay U.K. 19 B8
New Roads LA U.S.A. 63 I5
New Rochelle NY U.S.A. 64 E2
New Romney U.K. 19 H8
New Ross Ireland 21 F5
Newry Australia 54 E4
Newry U.K. 21 F3
New Siberia Islands Russia 29 P2
New South Wales state Australia 58 C4
New Stanton PA U.S.A. 64 B2
Newton U.K. 18 E5
Newton IA U.S.A. 63 I3
Newton KS U.S.A. 63 H4
Newton MA U.S.A. 64 F1
Newton NJ U.S.A. 64 D2
Newton Abbot U.K. 19 D8
Newton Mearns U.K. 20 E5
Newton Stewart U.K. 20 E6
Newtown Ireland 21 D5
Newtown England U.K. 19 E6
Newtown Wales U.K. 19 D6
New Town ND U.S.A. 62 G2
Newtownabbey U.K. 21 G3
Newtownards U.K. 21 G3
Newtownbarry Ireland see Bunclody
Newtownbutler U.K. 21 E3
Newtown Mount Kennedy Ireland 21 F4
Newtown St Boswells U.K. 20 G5
Newtownstewart U.K. 21 E3
New Ulm MN U.S.A. 63 I3
Newville PA U.S.A. 64 C2
New York NY U.S.A. 64 E2
New York state U.S.A. 64 D1
New Zealand country Oceania 59 D5
Nexø Denmark 15 I9
Neya Russia 12 I4
Neyrīz Iran 35 I5
Neyshābūr Iran 33 I2
Nezhin Ukr. see Nizhyn
Ngabé Congo 48 B4
Ngagahtawng Myanmar 37 I4
Ngagau mt. Tanz. 49 D4
Ngalu Indon. 54 C2
Ngamring China 37 F3
Ngangla Ringco salt l. China 37 E3
Nganglong Kangri mt. China 36 E2
Nganglong Kangri mts China 36 E2
Ngangzê Co salt l. China 37 F3
Ngangzê Shan mts China 37 F3
Ngaoundal Cameroon 46 E4
Ngaoundéré Cameroon 47 E4
Ngape Myanmar 37 H5
Ngarrab China see Gyaca
Ngau i. Fiji see Gau
Ngawa China see Aba
Ngazidja i. Comoros 49 E5
Ngcobo S. Africa 51 H6
Ngga Pulu mt. Indon. see Jaya, Puncak
Ngilmina Indon. 54 D2
Ngiva Angola see Ondjiva
Ngo Congo 48 B4
Ngoako Ramalepe S. Africa see Modjadjiskloof
Ngoin, Co salt l. China 37 G3
Ngoko r. Cameroon/Congo 47 E4
Ngom Qu r. China see Ji Qu
Ngoqumaima China 37 F2
Ngoring China 37 I2
Ngoring Hu l. China 37 I2
Ngourti Niger 46 E3
Ngqamakhwe S. Africa 51 H7
Nguigmi Niger 46 E3
Nguiu Australia 54 E2
Ngukurr Australia 54 F3
Ngulu atoll Micronesia 41 F7
Ngunza Angola see Sumbe
Ngunza-Kabolu Angola see Sumbe
Nguru Nigeria 46 E3
Ngwaketse admin. dist. Botswana see Southern
Ngwane country Africa see Swaziland
Ngwathe S. Africa 51 H4
Ngwavuma r. S. Africa/Swaziland 51 K4
Ngwelezana S. Africa 51 J5
Nhachengue Moz. 51 L2
Nhamalabué Moz. 49 D5
Nha Trang Vietnam 31 J5
Nhecolândia Brazil 69 G7
Nhill Australia 57 C8
Nhlangano Swaziland 51 J4
Nhow i. Fiji see Gau
Nhulunbuy Australia 56 B2
Niafounké Mali 46 C3
Niagara Falls Ont. Canada 64 B1
Niagara Falls NY U.S.A. 64 B1
Niagara-on-the-Lake Ont. Canada 64 B1
Niagzu Aksai Chin 36 D2
Niakaramandougou Côte d'Ivoire 46 C4
Niamey Niger 46 D3
Niangara Dem. Rep. Congo 48 C3
Niangay, Lac l. Mali 46 C3
Nianzishan China 44 A3
Nias i. Indon. 41 B7
Niassa, Lago l. Africa see Nyasa, Lake
Nibil Well Australia 54 D5
Nīca Latvia 15 L8
Nicaragua country Central America 67 G6
Nicaragua, Lake Nicaragua 67 G6
Nicastro Italy 26 G5
Nice France 24 H5
Nice CA U.S.A. 65 A1
Nicephorium Syria see Ar Raqqah
Nicholson r. Australia 56 B3
Nicholson Range hills Australia 55 B6
Nicobar Islands India 31 I6
Nicolaus CA U.S.A. 65 B1
Nicomedia Turkey see İzmit
Nicosia Cyprus 39 A2
Nicoya, Península de pen. Costa Rica 67 G7
Nida Lith. 15 L9
Nidagunda India 38 C2
Nidd r. U.K. 18 F4
Nidzica Poland 17 R4
Niebüll Germany 17 L3
Niedere Tauern mts Austria 17 N7
Niedersächsisches Wattenmeer, Nationalpark nat. park Germany 16 K4
Niefang Equat. Guinea 46 E4
Niellé Côte d'Ivoire 46 C3
Nienburg (Weser) Germany 17 L4
Nieuw Nickerie Suriname 69 G2
Nieuwoudtville S. Africa 50 D6
Niğde Turkey 34 D3
Niger country Africa 46 D3
Niger r. Africa 46 D4
Niger, Mouths of the Nigeria 46 D4
Niger Cone sea feature S. Atlantic Ocean 72 I5
Nigeria country Africa 46 D4
Nighthawk Lake Ont. Canada 63 K2
Nigrita Greece 27 J4
Nihing Pak. 36 A3
Nihon country Asia see Japan
Niigata Japan 45 E5
Niihama Japan 45 D6
Nii-jima i. Japan 45 E6
Niimi Japan 45 D6
Niitsu Japan 45 E5
Nijil, Wādī watercourse Jordan 39 B4
Nijmegen Neth. 17 J5
Nikel' Russia 12 F1
Nikki Benin 46 D4
Nikkō Japan 45 E5
Nikkō Kokuritsu-kōen Japan 45 E5
Nikolayev Ukr. see Mykolayiv
Nikolayevka Russia 13 J5
Nikolayevsk Russia 13 J6
Nikolayevskiy Russia see Nikolayevsk
Nikolayevsk-na-Amure Russia 44 F1
Nikol'sk Russia 12 J4
Nikol'skiy Kazakh. see Satpayev
Nikol'skoye Kamchatskiy Kray Russia 29 R4
Nikol'skoye Vologodskaya Oblast' Russia see Sheksna
Nikopol' Ukr. 13 G7
Niksar Turkey 34 E2
Nīkshahr Iran 33 J4
Nikšić Montenegro 26 H3
Nikumaroro atoll Kiribati 53 I2
Nikunau i. Kiribati 53 H2
Nīl, Bahr el r. Africa see Nile
Nilagiri India 37 F5
Niland CA U.S.A. 65 E4
Nilang India see Nelang
Nilanga India 38 C2
Nilaveli Sri Lanka 38 D4
Nile r. Africa 34 C5
Niles OH U.S.A. 64 A2
Nilgiri Hills India 38 C4
Nīl Kōtal Afgh. 36 A2
Nilphamari Bangl. 37 G4
Nilsiä Fin. 14 P5
Nimach India see Neemuch
Niman r. Russia 44 D2
Nimba, Monts mt. Africa see Richard-Molard, Mont
Nimbal India 38 B2
Nimberra Well Australia 55 C5
Nimelen r. Russia 44 E1
Nîmes France 24 G5
Nimmitabel Australia 57 E8
Nimrod Glacier Antarctica 76 H1
Nimu India 36 D2
Nimule South Sudan 47 G4
Nimwegen Neth. see Nijmegen
Nindigully Australia 58 D2
Nine Degree Channel India 38 B4
Nine Islands P.N.G. see Kilinailau Islands
Ninetyeast Ridge sea feature Indian Ocean 73 N8
Ninety Mile Beach Australia 58 C7
Ninety Mile Beach N.Z. 59 D2
Nineveh NY U.S.A. 64 D1
Ningaloo Coast tourist site Australia 55 A5
Ning'an China 44 C3
Ningbo China 43 M7
Ningde China 43 L7
Ningguo China 43 L6
Ninghsia Hui Autonomous Region aut. reg. China see Ningxia Huizu Zizhiqu
Ningjiang China see Songyuan
Ningjing Shan mts China 42 H6
Ningnan China 42 I7
Ningwu China 43 K5
Ningxia aut. reg. China see Ningxia Huizu Zizhiqu
Ningxia Huizu Zizhiqu aut. reg. China 42 J5
Ningxian China 43 J5
Ninh Binh Vietnam 42 J8
Ninnis Glacier Antarctica 76 G2
Ninnis Glacier Tongue Antarctica 76 H2
Ninohe Japan 45 F4
Niobrara r. NE U.S.A. 62 H3
Niokolo Koba, Parc National du nat. park Senegal 46 B3
Niono Mali 46 C3
Nioro Mali 46 C3
Niort France 24 D3
Nipani India 38 B2
Niphad India 38 B1
Nipigon Ont. Canada 61 J5
Nipigon, Lake Ont. Canada 61 J5
Nipissing, Lake Ont. Canada 63 L2
Nippon country Asia see Japan
Nippon Hai sea N. Pacific Ocean see Japan, Sea of
Nipton CA U.S.A. 65 E3
Niquelândia Brazil 71 A1
Nīr Iran 35 G3
Nir Iran 35 I5
Nira r. India 38 B2
Nirji China 44 B2
Nirmal India 38 C2
Nirmali India 37 F4
Nirmal Range hills India 38 C2
Niš Serbia 27 I3
Nisa Port. 25 C4
Nisarpur India 38 B1
Niscemi Sicily Italy 26 F6
Nīshāpūr Iran see Neyshābūr
Nishino-shima vol. Japan 45 F8
Nishi-Sonogi-hantō pen. Japan 45 C6
Nisibis Turkey see Nusaybin
Nísiros i. Greece see Nisyros
Nissan r. Sweden 15 H8
Nistru r. Moldova see Dniester
Nistru r. Ukr. see Dniester
Nisyros i. Greece 27 L6
Niṭā Saudi Arabia 35 H6
Nitendi i. Solomon Is see Nendo
Niterói Brazil 71 C3
Nith r. U.K. 20 F5
Nitibe East Timor 54 D2
Niti Pass China/India 36 D3
Niti Shankou pass China/India see Niti Pass
Nitmiluk National Park Australia 54 F3
Nitra Slovakia 17 Q6
Niuafo'ou i. Tonga 53 I3
Niuatoputopu i. Tonga 53 I3
Niue terr. S. Pacific Ocean 53 J3
Niulakita i. Tuvalu 53 H3
Niutao i. Tuvalu 53 H2
Nivala Fin. 14 N5
Nive watercourse Australia 56 D5
Niwai India 36 C4
Niwas India 36 E5
Nixia China see Sêrxü
Niya China see Minfeng
Niya He r. China 37 E1
Nizamabad India 38 C2
Nizam Sagar l. India 38 C2
Nizhnedevitsk Russia 13 H6
Nizhnekamsk Russia 12 K5
Nizhnekamskoye Vodokhranilishche resr Russia 11 Q4
Nizhnekolymsk Russia 29 R3
Nizhnetambovskoye Russia 44 E2
Nizhneudinsk Russia 42 H2
Nizhnevartovsk Russia 28 I3
Nizhnevolzhsk Russia see Narimanov
Nizhneyansk Russia 29 O2
Nizhniy Baskunchak Russia 13 J6
Nizhniye Kresty Russia see Cherskiy
Nizhniy Lomov Russia 13 I5
Nizhniy Novgorod Russia 12 I4
Nizhniy Odes Russia 12 L3
Nizhniy Tagil Russia 11 R4
Nizhnyaya Mola Russia 12 J2
Nizhnyaya Omra Russia 12 L3
Nizhnyaya Pirenga, Ozero l. Russia 14 R3
Nizhnyaya Tunguska r. Russia 28 J3
Nizhnyaya Tura Russia 11 R4
Nizhyn Ukr. 13 F6
Nizina Mazowiecka reg. Poland 17 R4
Nizip Turkey 39 C1
Nízke Tatry, Národný park nat. park Slovakia 17 Q6
Nizwā Oman see Nazwá
Nizza France see Nice
Njallavarri mt. Norway 14 L2
Njavve Sweden 14 K3
Njombe Tanz. 49 D4
Njurundabommen Sweden 14 J5
Nkambe Cameroon 46 E4
Nkandla S. Africa 51 J5
Nkawkaw Ghana 46 C4
Nkhata Bay Malawi 49 D5
Nkhotakota Malawi 49 D5
Nkondwe Tanz. 49 D4
Nkongsamba Cameroon 46 D4
N'Koutal, Tizi pass Alg. 25 I5
Nkululeko S. Africa 51 H6
Nkwenkwezi S. Africa 51 H7
Noakhali Bangl. 37 G5
Noatak r. AK U.S.A. 60 B3
Nobber Ireland 21 F4
Nobeoka Japan 45 C6
Noboribetsu Japan 44 F4
Noccundra Australia 57 C5
Nockatunga Australia 57 C5
Noel Kempff Mercado, Parque Nacional nat. park Bol. 68 F6
Nogales Mex. 66 B2
Nogales AZ U.S.A. 62 E5
Nōgata Japan 45 C6
Nogent-le-Rotrou France 24 E2
Noginsk Russia 12 H5
Nogliki Russia 44 F2
Nogoa r. Australia 56 E4
Nohar India 36 C3
Noheji Japan 44 F4
Noida India 36 D3
Noirmoutier, Île de i. France 24 C3
Noirmoutier-en-l'Île France 24 C3
Nōkis Uzbek. see Nukus
Nok Kundi Pak. 33 J4
Nokou Chad 47 E3
Nokrek Peak India 37 G4
Nola Cent. Afr. Rep. 48 B3
Nolinsk Russia 12 K4
No Mans Land i. MA U.S.A. 64 F2
Nome AK U.S.A. 60 B3
Nomgon Mongolia 42 J4
Nomhon China 37 I1
Nomoi Islands Micronesia see Mortlock Islands
Nomonde S. Africa 51 H6
Nomzha Russia 12 I4
Nondweni S. Africa 51 J5
Nong'an China 44 B3
Nongoma S. Africa 51 J4
Nongstoin India 37 G4
Nonidas Namibia 50 B2
Nonni r. China see Nen Jiang
Nonning Australia 57 B7
Nonouti atoll Kiribati 53 H2
Nonzwakazi S. Africa 50 G6
Noolyeanna Lake imp. l. Australia 57 B5
Noondie, Lake imp. l. Australia 55 B7
Noonkanbah Australia 54 D4
Noonthorangee Range hills Australia 57 C6
Noorama Creek watercourse Australia 58 B1
Nora r. Russia 44 C2
Noranda Que. Canada 63 L2
Nor-Bayazet Armenia see Gavarr
Norberg Sweden 15 I6
Nord Greenland see Station Nord
Nordaustlandet i. Svalbard 28 D2
Norden Germany 17 K4
Nordenshel'da, Arkhipelag is Russia 28 K2
Nordenskjold Archipelago is Russia see Nordenshel'da, Arkhipelag
Norderstedt Germany 17 M4
Nordfjordeid Norway 14 D6
Nordfold Norway 14 I3
Nordfriesische Inseln Germany see North Frisian Islands
Nordhausen Germany 17 M5
Nordkapp c. Norway see North Cape
Nordkinnhalvøya i. Norway 14 O1
Nordkjosbotn Norway 14 K2
Nordli Norway 14 H4
Nordmaling Sweden 14 K5
Nord- og Østgrønland, Nationalparken i nat. park Greenland 61 O2
Nordostrundingen c. Greenland 77 I1
Nord-Ostsee-Kanal Germany see Kiel Canal
Norðoyar is Faroe Is 10 E3
Nordre Strømfjord inlet Greenland see Nassuttooq
Nordvik Russia 29 M2
Nore r. Ireland 21 F5
Nore, Pic de mt. France 24 F5
Noreg country Europe see Norway
Norfolk NE U.S.A. 63 H3
Norfolk VA U.S.A. 64 C4
Norfolk Island terr. S. Pacific Ocean 53 G4
Norfolk Island Ridge sea feature Tasman Sea 74 H7
Norge country Europe see Norway
Norheimsund Norway 15 E6
Noril'sk Russia 28 J3
Norkyung China 37 G3
Norma Co l. China 37 G2
Norman OK U.S.A. 63 H4
Normanby Island P.N.G. 56 E1
Normandes, Îles is English Chan. see Channel Islands
Normandia Brazil 69 G3
Normandie reg. France see Normandy
Normandie, Collines de hills France 24 D2
Normandy reg. France 24 D2
Normanton Australia 56 C3
Ñorquinco Arg. 70 B6
Norra Kvarken str. Fin./Sweden 14 L5
Norra Storfjället mts Sweden 14 I4
Norristown PA U.S.A. 64 D2
Norrköping Sweden 15 J7
Norrtälje Sweden 15 K7
Norseman Australia 55 C8
Norsjö Sweden 14 K4
Norsk Russia 44 C1
Norsup Vanuatu 53 G3
Norte, Punta pt Arg. 70 E5
Norte, Serra do hills Brazil 69 G6
Nortelândia Brazil 69 G6
North, Cape Antarctica 76 H2
Northallerton U.K. 18 F4
Northam Australia 55 B7
Northampton Australia 52 B4
Northampton U.K. 19 G6
Northampton MA U.S.A. 64 E1
Northampton PA U.S.A. 64 D2
North Anna r. VA U.S.A. 64 C4
North Atlantic Ocean Atlantic Ocean 63 O4
North Australian Basin sea feature Indian Ocean 73 P6
North Battleford Sask. Canada 62 F1
North Bay Ont. Canada 63 L2
North Berwick U.K. 20 G4
North Berwick ME U.S.A. 64 F1
North Bourke Australia 58 B3
North Canton OH U.S.A. 64 A2
North Cape Norway 14 N1
North Cape N.Z. 59 D2
North Cape AK U.S.A. 60 A4
North Caribou Lake Ont. Canada 63 I1
North Carolina state U.S.A. 63 L4
North Channel lake channel Ont. Canada 63 K2
North Channel U.K. 21 G2
Northcliffe Glacier Antarctica 76 F2
North Collins NY U.S.A. 64 B1
North Dakota state U.S.A. 62 G2
North Downs hills U.K. 19 G7
North East PA U.S.A. 64 B1
Northeast Foreland c. Greenland see Nordostrundingen
North-East Frontier Agency state India see Arunachal Pradesh
Northeast Pacific Basin sea feature N. Pacific Ocean 75 J4
North Edwards CA U.S.A. 65 D3
Northern prov. S. Africa see Limpopo
Northern Areas admin. div. Pak. see Gilgit-Baltistan
Northern Cape prov. S. Africa 50 D5
Northern Donets r. Russia/Ukr. see Severskiy Donets
Northern Dvina r. Russia see Severnaya Dvina
Northern Ireland prov. U.K. 21 F3
Northern Lau Group is Fiji 53 I3
Northern Mariana Islands terr. N. Pacific Ocean 41 G6
Northern Rhodesia country Africa see Zambia
Northern Sporades is Greece see Voreies Sporades
Northern Territory admin. div. Australia 52 D3
Northern Transvaal prov. S. Africa see Limpopo
North Esk r. U.K. 20 G4
North Foreland c. U.K. 19 I7
North Fork CA U.S.A. 65 C2
North Fork Pass Y.T. Canada 60 E3
North Frisian Islands Germany 17 L3
North Geomagnetic Pole Arctic Ocean 61 K2
North Grimston U.K. 18 G4
North Haven CT U.S.A. 64 E2
North Head hd N.Z. 59 E3
North Horr Kenya 48 D3
North Island N.Z. 59 D4
North Kingsville OH U.S.A. 64 A2
North Knife Lake Man. Canada 61 I4
North Korea country Asia 45 B5
North Lakhimpur India 37 H4
North Las Vegas NV U.S.A. 65 E2
North Luangwa National Park Zambia 49 D5
North Magnetic Pole Canada 77 A1
North Malosmadulu Atoll Maldives see Maalhosmadulu Uthuruburi
North Palisade mt. CA U.S.A. 65 C2
North Perry OH U.S.A. 64 A2
North Platte NE U.S.A. 62 G3
North Platte r. NE U.S.A. 62 G3
North Pole Arctic Ocean 77 I1
North Rona i. U.K. see Rona
North Ronaldsay i. U.K. 20 G1
North Ronaldsay Firth sea chan. U.K. 20 G1
North Saskatchewan r. Alta/Sask. Canada 62 F1
North Sea Europe 16 H2
North Shields U.K. 18 F3
North Shoshone Peak NV U.S.A. 65 D1
North Siberian Lowland Russia 28 L2
North Siberian Lowland Russia 77 E2
North Sinai governorate Egypt see Shamāl Sīnā'
North Slope plain AK U.S.A. 60 D3
North Somercotes U.K. 18 H5
North Spirit Lake Ont. Canada 63 I1
North Stradbroke Island Australia 58 F1
North Sunderland U.K. 18 F3
North Syracuse NY U.S.A. 64 C1
North Taranaki Bight b. N.Z. 59 E4
Northton U.K. 20 B3
North Tonawanda NY U.S.A. 64 B1
North Trap reef N.Z. 59 A8
North Tyne r. U.K. 18 E4
North Uist i. U.K. 20 B3
Northumberland National Park U.K. 18 E3
Northumberland Strait N.B./N.S. Canada 63 O2
Northville NY U.S.A. 64 D1
North Walsham U.K. 19 I6
North West prov. S. Africa 50 G4
Northwest Atlantic Mid-Ocean Channel N. Atlantic Ocean 72 E1
North West Cape Australia 54 A5
North West Frontier prov. Pak. see Khyber Pakhtunkhwa
North West Nelson Forest Park nat. park N.Z. see Kahurangi National Park
Northwest Pacific Basin sea feature N. Pacific Ocean 74 G3
Northwest Territories admin. div. Canada 60 H3
Northwich U.K. 18 E5
North Wildwood NJ U.S.A. 64 D3
Northwind Ridge sea feature Arctic Ocean 77 B1
Northwood NH U.S.A. 64 F1
North York Moors moorland U.K. 18 G4
North York Moors National Park U.K. 18 G4
Norton U.K. 18 G4
Norton de Matos Angola see Balombo
Norton Sound sea chan. AK U.S.A. 60 B3
Norvegia, Cape Antarctica 76 B2
Norwalk CT U.S.A. 64 E2
Norwalk OH U.S.A. 63 K3
Norway country Europe 14 E6
Norway House Man. Canada 62 H1
Norwegian Basin sea feature N. Atlantic Ocean 72 H1
Norwegian Bay Nunavut Canada 61 I2
Norwegian Sea N. Atlantic Ocean 77 H2
Norwich Ont. Canada 64 A1
Norwich U.K. 19 I6
Norwich CT U.S.A. 64 E2
Norwich NY U.S.A. 64 D1
Noshiro Japan 45 F4
Nosovaya Russia 12 L1
Noşratābād Iran 33 I4
Noss, Isle of i. U.K. 20 [inset]
Nossebro Sweden 15 H7
Notch Peak UT U.S.A. 65 F1
Noteć r. Poland 17 O4
Noto, Golfo di g. Sicily Italy 26 F6
Notodden Norway 15 F7
Noto-hantō pen. Japan 45 E5
Notre-Dame, Monts mts Que. Canada 63 N2
Notre Dame Bay Nfld. and Lab. Canada 61 M5
Notre-Dame-de-Koartac Que. Canada see Quaqtaq
Nottaway r. Que. Canada 63 L1
Nottingham U.K. 19 F6
Nottingham Island Nunavut Canada 61 K3
Nottoway r. VA U.S.A. 64 C4
Nouabalé-Ndoki, Parc National de nat. park Congo 48 B3
Nouâdhibou Mauritania 46 B2
Nouâdhibou, Râs c. Mauritania 46 B2
Nouakchott Mauritania 46 B3
Nouâmghâr Mauritania 46 B3
Nouméa New Caledonia 53 G4
Nouna Burkina Faso 46 C3
Noupoort S. Africa 50 G6
Nousu Fin. 14 P3
Nouveau-Brunswick prov. Canada see New Brunswick
Nouveau-Comptoir Que. Canada see Wemindji
Nouvelle Calédonie terr. S. Pacific Ocean see New Caledonia
Nouvelle-France, Cap de c. Que. Canada 61 K3
Nouvelles Hébrides country S. Pacific Ocean see Vanuatu
Nova América Brazil 71 A1
Nova Chaves Angola see Muconda
Nova Freixa Moz. see Cuamba
Nova Friburgo Brazil 71 C3
Nova Gaia Angola see Cambundi-Catembo
Nova Goa India see Panaji
Nova Gradiška Croatia 26 G2
Nova Iguaçu Brazil 71 C3
Nova Kakhovka Ukr. 27 O1
Nova Lima Brazil 71 C2
Nova Lisboa Angola see Huambo
Novalukoml' Belarus 13 F5
Nova Mambone Moz. 49 D6
Nova Nabúri Moz. 49 D5
Nova Odesa Ukr. 13 F7
Nova Ponte Brazil 71 B2
Nova Ponte, Represa resr Brazil 71 B2
Novara Italy 26 C2
Nova Roma Brazil 71 B1
Nova Scotia prov. Canada 63 N3
Novato CA U.S.A. 65 A1
Nova Trento Brazil 71 A4
Nova Venécia Brazil 71 C2
Nova Xavantina Brazil 69 H6
Novaya Kakhovka Ukr. see Nova Kakhovka
Novaya Ladoga Russia 12 G3
Novaya Lyalya Russia 11 S4
Novaya Odessa Ukr. see Nova Odesa
Novaya Sibir', Ostrov i. Russia 29 P2
Novaya Zemlya is Russia 28 G2
Nova Zagora Bulg. 27 L3
Novelda Spain 25 F4
Nové Zámky Slovakia 17 Q7
Novgorod Russia see Velikiy Novgorod
Novgorod-Severskiy Ukr. see Novhorod-Sivers'kyy
Novgorod-Volynskiy Ukr. see Novohrad-Volyns'kyy
Novhorod-Sivers'kyy Ukr. 13 G6
Novi Grad Bos. & Herz. see Bosanski Novi
Novi Iskar Bulg. 27 J3
Novikovo Russia 44 F3
Novi Kritsim Bulg. see Stamboliyski
Novi Ligure Italy 26 C2
Novi Pazar Bulg. 27 L3
Novi Pazar Serbia 27 I3
Novi Sad Serbia 27 H2
Novo Acre Brazil 71 C1
Novoaltaysk Russia 42 E2
Novoanninskiy Russia 13 I6
Novo Aripuanã Brazil 68 F5
Novoazovs'k Ukr. 13 H7
Novocheboksarsk Russia 12 J4
Novocherkassk Russia 13 I7
Novo Cruzeiro Brazil 71 C2
Novodugino Russia 12 G5
Novodvinsk Russia 12 I2
Novoekonomicheskoye Ukr. see Dymytrov
Novogeorgiyevka Russia 44 B2
Novogrudok Belarus see Navahrudak
Novo Hamburgo Brazil 71 A5
Novohradské hory mts Czech Rep. 17 O6
Novohrad-Volyns'kyy Ukr. 13 E6
Novokhopersk Russia 13 I6
Novokiyevskiy Uval Russia 44 C2
Novokubansk Russia 35 F1
Novokubanskiy Russia see Novokubansk
Novokuybyshevsk Russia 13 K5
Novokuznetsk Russia 42 F2
Novolazarevskaya (Russia) research stn Antarctica 76 C2
Novolukoml' Belarus see Novalukoml'
Novo mesto Slovenia 26 F2
Novomikhaylovskiy Russia 34 E1
Novomoskovsk Russia 13 H5
Novomoskovs'k Ukr. 13 G6
Novonikolayevsk Russia see Novosibirsk
Novonikolayevskiy Russia 13 I6

Oshogbo Nigeria see Osogbo
Oshtorān Kūh mt. Iran 35 H4
Ōshū Japan 45 F5
Oshwe Dem. Rep. Congo 48 B4
Osijek Croatia 26 H2
Osimo Italy 26 E3
Osipenko Ukr. see Berdyans'k
Osipovichi Belarus see Asipovichy
Osiyan India 36 C4
oSizweni S. Africa 51 J4
Osječenica mts Bos. & Herz. 26 G2
Ösjön l. Sweden 14 I5
Oskarshamn Sweden 15 J8
Öskemen Kazakh. see Ust'-Kamenogorsk
Oslo Norway 15 G7
Oslofjorden sea chan. Norway 15 G7
Osmanabad India 38 C2
Osmancık Turkey 34 D2
Osmaneli Turkey 27 M4
Osmaniye Turkey 34 E3
Osmannagar India 38 C2
Os'mino Russia 15 P7
Osnabrück Germany 17 L4
Osnaburg atoll Fr. Polynesia see Mururoa
Osogbo Nigeria 46 D4
Osogovska Planina mts Bulg./Macedonia 27 J3
Osogovske Planine mts Bulg./Macedonia see Osogovska Planina
Osogovski Planini mts Bulg./Macedonia see Osogovska Planina
Osorno Chile 70 B6
Osorno Spain 25 D2
Osoyoos B.C. Canada 62 D2
Osøyro Norway 15 D6
Osprey Reef Australia 56 D2
Oss Neth. 17 J5
Ossa, Mount Australia 57 [inset]
Ossining NY U.S.A. 64 E2
Ossora Russia 29 R4
Ostashkov Russia 12 G4
Ostend Belgium 16 I5
Ostende Belgium see Ostend
Østerbymo Sweden 15 I8
Österdalälven r. Sweden 15 H6
Østerdalen val. Norway 15 G5
Österreich country Europe see Austria
Östersund Sweden 14 I5
Ostfriesische Inseln Germany see East Frisian Islands
Östhammar Sweden 15 K6
Ostrava Czech Rep. 17 Q6
Ostróda Poland 17 Q4
Ostrogozhsk Russia 13 H6
Ostrov Russia 12 F4
Ostrovets Poland see Ostrowiec Świętokrzyski
Ostrovnoy Russia 77 G2
Ostrovskoye Russia 12 I4
Ostrov Vrangelya i. Russia see Wrangel Island
Ostrów Poland see Ostrów Wielkopolski
Ostrowiec Poland see Ostrowiec Świętokrzyski
Ostrowiec Świętokrzyski Poland 13 D6
Ostrów Mazowiecka Poland 17 R4
Ostrowo Poland see Ostrów Wielkopolski
Ostrów Wielkopolski Poland 17 P5
Ōsumi-shotō is Japan 45 C7
Osuna Spain 25 D5
Oswego NY U.S.A. 64 C1
Oswestry U.K. 19 D6
Otago Peninsula N.Z. 59 C7
Otahiti i. Fr. Polynesia see Tahiti
Otaki N.Z. 59 E5
Otanmäki Fin. 14 O4
Otaru Japan 44 F4
Otavi Namibia 49 B5
Ōtawara Japan 45 F5
Otdia atoll Marshall Is see Wotje
Otematata N.Z. 59 C7
Otepää Estonia 15 O7
Otgon Tenger Uul mt. Mongolia 42 H3
oThongathi S. Africa 51 J5
Otira N.Z. 59 C6
Otjinene Namibia 49 B6
Otjiwarongo Namibia 49 B6
Otjozondjupa admin. reg. Namibia 50 C1
Otley U.K. 18 F5
Otorohanga N.Z. 59 E4
Otpor Russia see Zabaykal'sk
Otradnoye Russia see Otradnyy
Otradnyy Russia 13 K5
Otranto Italy 26 H4
Otranto, Strait of Albania/Italy 26 H4
Otrogovo Russia see Stepnoye
Otrozhnyy Russia 29 S3
Otsego Lake NY U.S.A. 64 D1
Ōtsu Japan 45 D6
Otta Norway 15 F6
Ottawa Ont. Canada 61 K5
Ottawa r. Ont./Que. Canada 63 M2
Ottawa IL U.S.A. 63 J3
Ottawa KS U.S.A. 63 H4
Ottawa Islands Nunavut Canada 61 J4
Otter r. U.K. 19 D8
Otterburn U.K. 18 E3
Otter Rapids Ont. Canada 63 K1
Ottumwa IA U.S.A. 63 I3
Otukpo Nigeria 46 D4
Oturkpo Nigeria see Otukpo
Otuzco Peru 68 C5
Otway, Cape Australia 58 A7
Otway National Park Australia 58 A7
Ouachita Mountains AR/OK U.S.A. 63 I5
Ouadda Cent. Afr. Rep. 48 C3
Ouaddaï reg. Chad 47 F3
Ouagadougou Burkina Faso 46 C3
Ouahigouya Burkina Faso 46 C3
Ouahran Alg. see Oran
Ouaka r. Cent. Afr. Rep. 48 B3
Oualâta Mauritania 46 C3
Oualâta, Dahr hills Mauritania 46 C3
Ouallam Niger 46 D3
Ouanda Djallé Cent. Afr. Rep. 48 C3
Ouando Cent. Afr. Rep. 48 C3
Ouango Cent. Afr. Rep. 48 C3
Ouara r. Cent. Afr. Rep. 48 C3
Ouarâne reg. Mauritania 46 C2
Ouargaye Burkina Faso 46 D3
Ouargla Alg. 22 F5
Ouarogou Burkina Faso see Ouargaye
Ouarzazate Morocco 22 C5
Oubangui r. Cent. Afr. Rep./Dem. Rep. Congo see Ubangi
Oubergpas pass S. Africa 50 G7
Oudtshoorn S. Africa 50 F7
Oued Tlélat Alg. 25 F6
Oued Zem Morocco 22 C5
Oued Zénati Alg. 26 B6
Ouessant, Île d' i. France 24 B2
Ouesso Congo 48 B3
Ouezzane Morocco 25 D6
Oughter, Lough l. Ireland 21 E3
Ouguati Namibia 50 B1
Ouistreham France 19 G9
Oujda Morocco 25 F6
Oujeft Mauritania 46 B3
Oulainen Fin. 14 N4
Oulangan kansallispuisto nat. park Fin. 14 P3
Ouled Djellal Alg. 25 I6
Ouled Farès Alg. 25 G5
Ouled Naïl, Monts des mts Alg. 25 H6
Oulu Fin. 14 N4
Oulujärvi l. Fin. 14 O4
Oulujoki r. Fin. 14 N4
Oulunsalo Fin. 14 N4
Oulx Italy 26 B2
Oum-Chalouba Chad 47 F3
Oum el Bouaghi Alg. 26 B7
Oum-Hadjer Chad 47 E3
Ounasjoki r. Fin. 14 N3
Oundle U.K. 19 G6
Ounianga Kébir Chad 47 F3
Our, Vallée de l' val. Germany/Lux. 17 K6
Oura, Akrotirio pt Greece 27 L5
Ourense Spain 25 C2
Ouricuri Brazil 69 J5
Ourinhos Brazil 71 A3
Ouro r. Brazil 71 A1
Ouro Preto Brazil 71 C3
Ous Russia 11 S3
Ouse r. England U.K. 18 G5
Ouse r. England U.K. 19 H8
Outaouais, Rivière des r. Ont./Que. Canada see Ottawa
Outapi Namibia 49 B5
Outardes Quatre, Réservoir resr Que. Canada 63 N1
Outer Hebrides is U.K. 20 B3
Outer Mongolia country Asia see Mongolia
Outer Santa Barbara Channel CA U.S.A. 65 C4
Outjo Namibia 49 B6
Outlook Sask. Canada 62 F1
Outokumpu Fin. 14 P5
Out Skerries is U.K. 20 [inset]
Ouvéa atoll New Caledonia 53 G4
Ouyen Australia 57 C7
Ouzel r. U.K. 19 G6
Ovace, Punta d' mt. Corsica France 24 I6
Ovacık Turkey 39 A1
Ovada Italy 26 C2
Ovalle Chile 70 B4
Ovamboland reg. Namibia 49 B5
Ovan Gabon 48 B3
Ovar Port. 25 B3
Överkalix Sweden 14 M3
Overlander Roadhouse Australia 55 A6
Overton NV U.S.A. 65 E2
Övertorneå Sweden 14 M3
Överum Sweden 15 J8
Ovid NY U.S.A. 64 C1
Oviedo Spain 25 D2
Øvre Anárjohka Nasjonalpark nat. park Norway 14 N2
Øvre Dividal Nasjonalpark nat. park Norway 14 K2
Øvre Rendal Norway 15 G6
Ovruch Ukr. 13 F6
Ovsyanka Russia 44 B1
Owando Congo 48 B4
Owa Rafa i. Solomon Is see Santa Ana
Owasco Lake NY U.S.A. 64 C1
Owase Japan 45 E6
Owatonna MN U.S.A. 63 I3
Owego NY U.S.A. 64 C1
Owel, Lough l. Ireland 21 E4
Owenmore r. Mayo Ireland 21 C3
Owenmore r. Sligo Ireland 21 D3
Owenreagh r. U.K. 21 E3
Owen River N.Z. 59 D5
Owens r. CA U.S.A. 65 D2
Owensboro KY U.S.A. 63 J4
Owens Lake CA U.S.A. 65 D2
Owen Sound Ont. Canada 63 K3
Owen Stanley Range mts P.N.G. 52 E2
Owerri Nigeria 46 D4
Owo Nigeria 46 D4
Owyhee NV U.S.A. 62 D3
Owyhee r. OR U.S.A. 62 D3
Öxarfjörður b. Iceland 14 [inset 2]
Oxelösund Sweden 15 J7
Oxford N.Z. 59 D6
Oxford U.K. 19 F7
Oxford MD U.S.A. 64 C3
Oxford MS U.S.A. 63 J5
Oxford NY U.S.A. 64 D1
Oxford Lake Man. Canada 63 H1
Oxley Australia 58 B5
Oxleys Peak Australia 58 E3
Oxley Wild Rivers National Park Australia 58 F3
Ox Mountains hills Ireland 21 C4
Oxnard CA U.S.A. 65 C3
Oxus r. Asia see Amudar'ya
Øya Norway 14 H3
Oyama Japan 45 E5
Oyapock r. Brazil/Fr. Guiana 69 H3
Oyem Gabon 48 B3
Oyen Alta Canada 62 E1
Oykel r. U.K. 20 E3
Oyo Nigeria 46 D4
Oyonnax France 24 G3
Oyster Rocks is India 38 B3
Oytograk China 37 E1
Oyukludağı mt. Turkey 39 A1
Oyyaylak China 37 E1
Özalp Turkey 35 G3
Ozark AL U.S.A. 63 J5
Ozark Plateau MO U.S.A. 63 I4
Ozarks, Lake of the MO U.S.A. 63 I4
O'zbekiston country Asia see Uzbekistan
Özen Kazakh. see Kyzylsay
Ozernovskiy Russia 29 Q4
Ozernyy Russia 13 G5
Ozerpakh Russia 44 F1
Ozersk Russia 15 M9
Ozerskiy Russia 44 F3
Ozery Russia 13 H5
Ozeryane Russia 44 C2
Ozieri Sardinia Italy 26 C4
Ozinki Russia 13 K6
Oznachennoye Russia see Sayanogorsk
Ozuki Japan 45 C6

P

Paamiut Greenland 61 N3
Paanayarvi Natsional'nyy Park nat. park Russia 14 Q3
Paanopa i. Kiribati see Banaba
Paarl S. Africa 50 D7
Paatsjoki r. Europe see Patsoyoki
Paballelo S. Africa 50 E5
P'abal-li N. Korea 44 C4
Pabbay i. U.K. 20 B3
Pabianice Poland 17 Q5
Pabianitz Poland see Pabianice
Pabna Bangl. 37 G4
Pabrad Lith. 15 N9
Pab Range mts Pak. 33 K4
Pacaás Novos, Parque Nacional nat. park Brazil 68 F6
Pacaraimã, Serra mts S. America see Pakaraima Mountains
Pacasmayo Peru 68 C5
Pachagarh Bangl. see Panchagarh
Pachala South Sudan 47 G4
Pachikha Russia 12 J3
Pachino Sicily Italy 26 F6
Pachmarhi India 36 D5
Pachor India 36 D5
Pachora India 38 B1
Pachpadra India 36 C4
Pachuca Mex. 66 E4
Pachuca de Soto Mex. see Pachuca
Pacific-Antarctic Ridge sea feature S. Pacific Ocean 75 J9
Pacific Grove CA U.S.A. 65 B2
Pacific Ocean 74
Packsaddle Australia 57 C6
Pacoval Brazil 69 H4
Pacuí r. Brazil 71 B2
Paczków Poland 17 P5
Padali Russia see Amursk
Padampur India 36 C3
Padang Indon. 41 C8
Padany Russia 12 G3
Padatha, Kūh-e mt. Iran 35 H4
Padcaya Bol. 68 F8
Paddington Australia 58 B4
Paden City WV U.S.A. 64 A3
Paderborn Germany 17 L5
Padeşu, Vârful mt. Romania 27 J2
Padibyu Myanmar 37 I5
Padilla Bol. 68 F7
Padjelanta nationalpark nat. park Sweden 14 J3
Padova Italy see Padua
Padrão, Ponta pt Angola 49 B4
Padrauna India 37 F4
Padre Island TX U.S.A. 63 H6
Padstow U.K. 19 C8
Padsvillye Belarus 15 O9
Padua India 38 D2
Padua Italy 26 D2
Paducah KY U.S.A. 63 J4
Paducah TX U.S.A. 62 G5
Padum India 36 D2
Paegam N. Korea 44 C4
Paektu-san mt. China/N. Korea see Baitou Shan
Pafos Cyprus see Paphos
Pafuri Moz. 51 J2
Pag Croatia 26 F2
Pag i. Croatia 26 F2
Paga Indon. 54 C2
Pagadian Phil. 41 E7
Pagai Selatan i. Indon. 41 C8
Pagalu i. Equat. Guinea see Annobón
Pagan i. N. Mariana Is 41 G6
Pagasitikos Kolpos b. Greece 27 J5
Paget, Mount S. Georgia 70 I8
Paget Cay reef Australia 56 F3
Pagon i. N. Mariana Is see Pagan
Pagosa Springs CO U.S.A. 62 F4
Pahlgam India 36 C2
Pahranagat Range mts NV U.S.A. 65 E2
Pahrump NV U.S.A. 65 E2
Pahuj r. India 36 D4
Pahute Mesa plat. NV U.S.A. 65 D2
Paicines CA U.S.A. 65 B2
Paide Estonia 15 N7
Paignton U.K. 19 D8
Päijänne l. Fin. 15 N6
Paikü Co l. China 37 F3
Paimio Fin. 15 M6
Painel Brazil 71 A4
Painesville OH U.S.A. 64 A2
Pains Brazil 71 B3
Painted Rock Dam AZ U.S.A. 65 F4
Paint Hills Que. Canada see Wemindji
Paisley U.K. 20 E5
Paita Peru 68 B5
Paiva Couceiro Angola see Quipungo
Pajala Sweden 14 M3
Pakala India 38 C3
Pakangyi Myanmar 37 H5
Pakaraima Mountains Guyana 67 M8
Pakaraima Mountains S. America 68 F3
Pakaur India see Pakur
Pakhachi Russia 29 R3
Pakhoi China see Beihai
Paki Nigeria 46 D3
Pakistan country Asia 33 J4
Pakxampho Thai. see Nakhon Sawan
Pakokku Myanmar 37 H5
Pakpattan Pak. 36 C3
Pakruojis Lith. 15 M9
Paks Hungary 26 H1
Pakse Laos see Pakxé
Pakur India 37 F4
Pakxan Laos 42 I9
Pakxé Laos 41 C6
Pala Chad 47 E4
Palaestinia reg. Asia see Palestine
Palaiochora Greece 27 J7
Palaiseau France 24 F2
Palakkad India 38 C4
Palakkat India see Palakkad
Palamakoloi Botswana 50 F2
Palamau India see Palamu
Palamós Spain 25 H3
Palamu India 37 F5
Palana Russia 29 Q4
Palandur India 38 D1
Palani India 38 C4
Palanpur India 36 C4
Palapye Botswana 51 H2
Palatka Russia 29 Q3
Palatka FL U.S.A. 63 K6
Palau country N. Pacific Ocean 41 F7
Palau Islands Palau 41 F7
Palawan i. Phil. 41 D7
Palawan Trough sea feature N. Pacific Ocean 74 D5
Palayankottai India 38 C4
Palchal Lake India 38 D2
Paldiski Estonia 15 N7
Palekh Russia 12 I4
Palembang Indon. 41 C8
Palena Chile 70 B6
Palencia Spain 25 D2
Palermo Sicily Italy 26 E5
Palestine reg. Asia 39 B3
Palestine TX U.S.A. 63 H5
Paletwa Myanmar 37 H5
Palezgir Chauki Pak. 36 B3
Palghat India see Palakkad
Palgrave, Mount h. Australia 55 A5
Palhoça Brazil 71 A4
Pali Chhattisgarh India 38 D1
Pali Mahar. India 38 B2
Pali Rajasthan India 36 C4
Palikir Micronesia 74 G5
Palimé Togo 46 D4
Palinuro, Capo c. Italy 26 F4
Paliouri, Akrotirio pt Greece 27 J5
Palitana India 36 B5
Palivere Estonia 15 M7
Palk Bay Sri Lanka 38 C4
Palkino Russia 15 P8
Palkonda Range hills India 38 C3
Palk Strait India/Sri Lanka 38 C4
Palla Bianca mt. Austria/Italy see Weißkugel
Pallamallawa Australia 58 E2
Pallas Green New Ireland 21 D5
Pallasovka Russia 13 J6
Pallas-Yllästunturin kansallispuisto nat. park Fin. 14 M2
Pallavaram India 38 D3
Palliser, Cape N.Z. 59 E5
Palliser, Îles is Fr. Polynesia 75 K7
Palliser Bay N.Z. 59 E5
Pallu India 36 C3
Palma r. Brazil 71 B1
Palma del Río Spain 25 D5
Palma de Mallorca Spain 25 H4
Palmaner India 38 C3
Palmares Brazil 69 K5
Palmares do Sul Brazil 71 A5
Palmas Brazil 71 A4
Palmas 68 I6
Palmas, Cape Liberia 46 C4
Palmdale CA U.S.A. 65 C3
Palmeira Brazil 71 A4
Palmeira das Missões Brazil 70 F3
Palmeira dos Índios Brazil 69 K5
Palmeirais Brazil 69 J5
Palmeiras Brazil 71 C1
Palmeirinhas, Ponta das pt Angola 49 B4
Palmer (U.S.A.) research stn Antarctica 76 L2
Palmer r. Australia 56 C3
Palmer watercourse Australia 55 F6
Palmer AK U.S.A. 60 D3
Palmer Land reg. Antarctica 76 L2
Palmerston N.T. Australia see Darwin
Palmerston N.T. Australia 54 E3
Palmerston atoll Cook Is 53 J3
Palmerston N.Z. 59 C7
Palmerston North N.Z. 59 E5
Palmerton PA U.S.A. 64 D2
Palmerville Australia 56 D2
Palmi Italy 26 F5
Palmira Col. 68 C3
Palm Springs CA U.S.A. 65 D4
Palmyra Syria see Tadmur
Palmyra VA U.S.A. 64 B4
Palmyra Atoll terr. N. Pacific Ocean 74 J5
Palmyras Point India 37 F5
Palni Hills India 38 C4
Palo Alto CA U.S.A. 65 A2
Paloich South Sudan 32 D7
Palojärvi Fin. 14 M2
Palojoensuu Fin. 14 M2
Palomaa Fin. 14 O2
Palomar Mountain CA U.S.A. 65 D4
Paloncha India 38 D2
Palopo Indon. 41 E8
Palos, Cabo de c. Spain 25 F5
Palo Verde CA U.S.A. 65 E4
Paltamo Fin. 14 O4
Palu Indon. 41 D8
Palu i. Indon. 41 E8
Palu Turkey 35 E3
Palwal India 36 D3
Palwancha India see Paloncha
Palyeskaya Nizina marsh Belarus/Ukr. see Pripet Marshes
Pamana i. Indon. 54 C2
Pambarra Moz. 51 L1
Pambula Australia 58 D6
Pamidi India 38 C3
Pamiers France 24 E5
Pamir mts Asia 33 L2
Pamlico Sound sea chan. NC U.S.A. 63 L4
Pampa de Infierno Arg. 70 D3
Pampas reg. Arg. 70 D5
Pampeluna Spain see Pamplona
Pamphylia reg. Turkey 27 N6
Pamplin VA U.S.A. 64 B4
Pamplona Col. 68 D2
Pamplona Spain 25 F2
Pamukova Turkey 27 N4
Pamzal India 36 D2
Panaca NV U.S.A. 65 E2
Panagyurishte Bulg. 27 K3
Panaji India 38 B3
Panama country Central America 67 H7
Panamá Panama see Panama City
Panamá, Canal de Panama 67 I7
Panamá, Golfo de Panama see Panama, Gulf of
Panama, Gulf of Panama 67 I7
Panama, Isthmus of Panama 67 I7
Panamá, Istmo de Panama see Panama, Isthmus of
Panama City Panama 67 I7
Panama City FL U.S.A. 63 J5
Panamint Range mts CA U.S.A. 65 D2
Panamint Valley val. CA U.S.A. 65 D2
Panao Peru 68 C5
Panarea, Isola i. Italy 26 F5
Panay i. Phil. 41 E6
Pancake Range mts NV U.S.A. 65 E1
Pančevo Serbia 27 I2
Panchagarh Bangl. 37 G4
Pancsova Serbia see Pančevo
Panda Moz. 51 L3
Pandeiros r. Brazil 71 B1
Pandharpur India 38 B2
Pandy U.K. 19 E7
Paneas Syria see Bāniyās
Panevėžys Lith. 15 N9
Panfilov Kazakh. see Zharkent
Pangi Range mts Pak. 36 C2
Pangkalanbuun Indon. 41 D8
Pangkalpinang Indon. 41 C8
Pangnirtung Nunavut Canada 61 L3
Pangody Russia 28 I3
Pangong Tso salt l. China/India see Bangong Co
Pangu He r. China 44 B1
Panguitch UT U.S.A. 65 F2
Panipat India 36 D3
Panir Pak. 36 A3
Panj Tajik. 36 B1
Panjāb Afgh. 36 A2
Panjim India see Panaji
Panjnad r. Pak. 36 B3
Pankakoski Fin. 14 Q5
Panna India 36 E4
Panna reg. India 36 D4
Pannawonica Australia 54 B5
Pano Lefkara Cyprus 39 A2
Panorama Brazil 71 A3
Panormus Sicily Italy see Palermo
Panshi China 44 B4
Pantanal marsh Brazil 69 G7
Pantanal Matogrossense, Parque Nacional do nat. park Brazil 69 G7
Pantar i. Indon. 54 D2
Pantelaria Sicily Italy see Pantelleria
Pantelleria Sicily Italy 26 D6
Pantelleria, Isola di i. Sicily Italy 26 E6
Pantha Myanmar 37 H5
Panth Piploda India 36 C5
Panticapaeum Ukr. see Kerch
Pánuco Mex. 66 E4
Panwari India 36 D4
Panzhihua China 42 I7
Panzi Dem. Rep. Congo 49 B4
Paola Italy 26 G5
Paoua Cent. Afr. Rep. 48 B3
Pápa Hungary 26 G1
Papa, Monte del mt. Italy 26 F4
Papagni r. India 38 C3
Papakura N.Z. 59 E3
Papanasam India 38 C4
Papantla Mex. 66 E4
Paparoa National Park N.Z. 59 C6
Papa Stour i. U.K. 20 [inset]
Papa Westray i. U.K. 20 G1
Papay i. U.K. see Papa Westray
Papeete Fr. Polynesia 75 K7
Papenburg Germany 17 K4
Paphos Cyprus 39 A2
Paphus Cyprus see Paphos
Papoose Lake NV U.S.A. 65 E2
Papua, Gulf of P.N.G. 52 E2
Papua New Guinea country Oceania 52 E2
Par U.K. 19 C8
Pará r. Brazil 71 B2
Pará, Rio do r. Brazil 69 I4
Paraburdoo Australia 55 B5
Paracatu Brazil 71 B2
Paracatu r. Brazil 71 B2
Paracel Islands S. China Sea 41 D6
Parachilna Australia 57 B6
Paraćin Serbia 27 I3
Paracuru Brazil 69 K4
Pará de Minas Brazil 71 B2
Paradise CA U.S.A. 62 C4
Paradise Peak NV U.S.A. 65 D1
Paradwip India 37 F5
Paraetonium Egypt see Marsá Maţrūḩ
Paragominas Brazil 69 I4
Paragould AR U.S.A. 63 I4
Paragua i. Phil. see Palawan
Paraguaçu Paulista Brazil 71 A3
Paraguay r. Arg./Para. 70 E3
Paraguay country S. America 70 E2
Paraíba do Sul r. Brazil 71 C3
Parainen Fin. see Pargas
Paraíso do Tocantins Brazil 69 I6
Paraisópolis Brazil 71 B3
Parak Iran 35 I6
Parakou Benin 46 D4
Paralakhemundi India 38 E2
Paralkot India 38 D2
Paramagudi India see Paramakkudi
Paramakkudi India 38 C4
Paramaribo Suriname 69 G2
Paramillo, Parque Nacional nat. park Col. 68 C2
Paramirim Brazil 71 C1
Paramo Frontino mt. Col. 68 C2
Paramus NJ U.S.A. 64 D2
Paramushir, Ostrov i. Russia 29 Q4
Paran, Naḥal watercourse Israel 39 B4
Paraná Arg. 70 D4
Paranã Brazil 71 B1
Paranã r. Brazil 71 A1
Paraná state Brazil 71 A4
Paraná r. S. America 70 E4
Paranã, Serra do hills Brazil 71 B1
Paranaguá Brazil 71 A4
Paranaíba Brazil 71 A2
Paranaíba r. Brazil 71 A3
Paranapiacaba, Serra mts Brazil 71 A4
Paranavaí Brazil 70 F2
Parangi Aru r. Sri Lanka 38 D4
Parang Pass India 36 D2
Parângul Mare, Vârful mt. Romania 27 J2
Parantan Sri Lanka 38 D4
Paraopeba Brazil 71 B2
Pārapāra Iraq 35 G4
Paraparaumu N.Z. 59 E5
Paras Pak. 36 C2
Parasia India 36 D5
Paraspori, Akrotirio pt Greece 27 L7
Parateca Brazil 71 C1
Paratinga Brazil 71 C1
Parāū, Kūh-e mt. Iraq 35 G4
Paraúna Brazil 71 A2
Parbhani India 38 C2
Parchim Germany 17 M4
Parc National de Lobéké nat. park Cameroon 47 E4
Parding China 37 G2
Pardo r. Bahia Brazil 71 D1
Pardo r. Mato Grosso do Sul Brazil 70 F2
Pardo r. São Paulo Brazil 71 A3
Pardoo Australia 54 B5
Pardubice Czech Rep. 17 O5
Parece Vela i. Japan see Okino-Tori-shima
Parecis, Serra dos hills Brazil 68 F6
Pareh Iran 35 G3
Parenda India 38 B2
Parent, Lac l. Que. Canada 63 L2
Pareora N.Z. 59 C7
Parepare Indon. 41 D8
Parga Greece 27 I5
Pargas Fin. 15 M6
Parghelia Italy 26 F5
Pargi India 38 C2
Paria, Gulf of Trin. and Tob./Venez. 67 L6
Paria, Península de pen. Venez. 68 F1
Parikkala Fin. 15 P6
Parikud Islands India 38 E2
Parima, Serra mts Brazil 68 F3
Parima-Tapirapecó, Parque Nacional nat. park Venez. 68 F3
Parintins Brazil 69 G4
Paris Ont. Canada 64 A1
Paris France 24 F2
Paris TX U.S.A. 63 H5
Park U.K. 21 E3
Parkano Fin. 15 M5
Parker AZ U.S.A. 65 E3
Parker Dam CA U.S.A. 65 E3
Parker Range hills Australia 55 B8
Parkersburg WV U.S.A. 64 A3
Parkes Australia 58 D4
Park Falls WI U.S.A. 63 I2
Parkhill Ont. Canada 64 A1
Parkutta Pak. 36 D2
Parla Kimedi India see Paralakhemundi
Parlakimidi India see Paralakhemundi
Parli Vaijnath India 38 C2
Parlung Zangbo r. China 37 H3
Parma Italy 26 D2
Parma OH U.S.A. 64 A2
Parnaíba Brazil 69 J4
Parnaíba r. Brazil 69 J4
Parnassus N.Z. 59 D6
Parner India 38 B2
Parnonas mts Greece 27 J6
Pärnu Estonia 15 N7
Pärnu-Jaagupi Estonia 15 N7
Paro Bhutan 37 G4
Paroikia Greece 27 K6
Paroo watercourse Australia 58 A3
Paroo Channel watercourse Australia 58 A3
Paros i. Greece 27 K6
Parowan UT U.S.A. 65 F2
Parque Natural del Gran Desierto del Pinacate tourist site Mex. 66 B2
Parral Chile 70 B5
Parramatta Australia 58 E4
Parramore Island VA U.S.A. 64 D4
Parras Mex. 66 D3
Parrett r. U.K. 19 D7
Parry, Cape N.W.T. Canada 77 A2
Parry, Kap c. Greenland see Kangaarsussuaq
Parry Bay Nunavut Canada 61 J3
Parry Channel N.W.T./Nunavut Canada 61 G2
Parry Islands N.W.T./Nunavut Canada 61 G2
Parry Range hills Australia 54 A5
Parry Sound Ont. Canada 63 K2
Pārsīān Iran 35 I6
Parsnip Peak NV U.S.A. 65 E1
Parsons KS U.S.A. 63 H4
Parsons WV U.S.A. 64 B3
Parsons Range hills Australia 54 F3
Partabgarh India 38 B2
Partabpur India 37 E5
Parthenay France 24 D3
Partizansk Russia 44 D4
Partney U.K. 18 H5
Partry Ireland 21 C4
Partry Mountains hills Ireland 21 C4
Paru r. Brazil 69 H4
Paryang China 37 E3
Parys S. Africa 51 H4
Pās, Chāh well Iran 35 I4
Pasa Dağı mt. Turkey 34 D3
Pasadena CA U.S.A. 65 C3
Pasado, Cabo c. Ecuador 68 B4
Pascagoula MS U.S.A. 63 J5
Paşcani Romania 27 L1
Pascoal, Monte h. Brazil 71 D2
Pascua, Isla de i. S. Pacific Ocean see Easter Island
Pas de Calais str. France/U.K. see Dover, Strait of
Pasewalk Germany 17 O4
Pasha Russia 12 G3
Pashih Haihsia sea chan. Phil./Taiwan see Bashi Channel
Pashkovo Russia 44 C2
Pashkovskiy Russia 13 H7
Pasighat India 37 H3
Pasinler Turkey 35 F3
Pasni Pak. 73 M4
Paso de los Toros Uruguay 70 E4
Pasok Myanmar 37 H5
Paso Robles CA U.S.A. 65 B3
Passaic NJ U.S.A. 64 D2
Passa Tempo Brazil 71 B3
Passau Germany 17 N6
Passo del San Gottardo Switz. see St Gotthard Pass
Passo Fundo Brazil 70 F3
Passos Brazil 71 B3
Passur r. Bangl. see Pusur
Passuri Nadi r. Bangl. see Pusur
Pastavy Belarus 15 O9
Pastaza r. Peru 68 C4
Pasto Col. 68 C3
Pastos Bons Brazil 69 J5
Pasu Pak. 36 C1
Pasur Turkey see Kulp
Pasvalys Lith. 15 N8
Pasvikelva r. Europe see Patsoyoki
Patache, Punta pt Chile 70 B2
Patagonia reg. Arg. 70 B8
Pataliputra India see Patna
Patan Gujarat India see Somnath
Patan Gujarat India 36 C5
Patan Mahar. India 38 B2
Patan Nepal 37 F4
Patan Pak. 36 C2
Patavium Italy see Padua
Patea N.Z. 59 E4
Patea inlet N.Z. see Doubtful Sound
Pate Island Kenya 48 E4
Pateley Bridge U.K. 18 F4
Patensie S. Africa 50 G7
Patera India 36 D4
Paterson Australia 58 E4
Paterson r. Australia 58 C2
Paterson NJ U.S.A. 64 D2
Paterson Range hills Australia 54 C5
Pathanamthitta India 38 C4
Pathankot India 36 C2
Pathari India 36 D5
Pathein Myanmar see Bassein
Patía r. Col. 68 C3
Patiala India 36 D3
Patkai Bum mts India/Myanmar 37 H4
Patkaklik China 37 F1
Patmos i. Greece 27 L6
Patna Bihar India 37 F4
Patna Odisha India 37 F5
Patnagarh India 37 E5
Patnos Turkey 35 F3
Pato Branco Brazil 70 F3
Patoda India 38 B2
Patos Albania 27 H4
Patos Brazil 69 K5
Patos, Lagoa dos l. Brazil 70 F4
Patos de Minas Brazil 71 B2
Patquía Arg. 70 C4
Patra Greece see Patras
Patrae Greece see Patras
Pátrai Greece see Patras
Patras Greece 27 I5
Patreksfjörður Iceland 14 [inset 2]
Patricio Lynch, Isla i. Chile 70 A7
Patrick Creek watercourse Australia 56 D4
Patrimônio Brazil 71 A2
Patrocínio Brazil 71 B2
Patsoyoki r. Europe 14 Q2
Pattadakal tourist site India 38 B2
Patterson CA U.S.A. 65 B2
Patti India 37 E4
Pattijoki Fin. 14 N4
Pättikkä Fin. 14 L2
Patton PA U.S.A. 64 B2
Pattullo, Mount B.C. Canada 60 F4
Patu Brazil 69 K5
Patuakhali Bangl. 37 G5
Patuca, Punta pt Hond. 67 H5
Patur India 38 C1
Patuxent r. MD U.S.A. 64 C3
Patuxent Range mts Antarctica 76 L1
Patvinsuon kansallispuisto nat. park Fin. 14 Q5
Pau France 24 D5
Pauhunri mt. China/India 37 G4
Pauillac France 24 D4
Pauini Brazil 68 E5
Pauini r. Brazil 68 E5
Pauk Myanmar 37 H5
Paulatuk N.W.T. Canada 77 A2
Paulicéia Brazil 71 A3
Paulis Dem. Rep. Congo see Isiro
Paulo Afonso Brazil 69 K5
Paulo de Faria Brazil 71 A3
Paulpietersburg S. Africa 51 J4
Paul Roux S. Africa 51 H5
Paulstown Ireland 21 E5
Paumotu, Îles is Fr. Polynesia see Tuamotu Islands
Paungbyin Myanmar 37 H4
Pauni India 38 C1
Pauri India 36 D3
Pavagada India 38 C3
Pavão Brazil 71 C2
Pāveh Iran 35 G4
Pavia Italy 26 C2
Pāvilosta Latvia 15 L8
Pavino Russia 12 J4
Pavlikeni Bulg. 27 K3
Pavlodar Kazakh. 42 D2
Pavlof Volcano AK U.S.A. 60 B4
Pavlograd Ukr. see Pavlohrad
Pavlohrad Ukr. 13 G6
Pavlovka Russia 13 J5
Pavlovo Russia 12 I5
Pavlovsk Altayskiy Kray Russia 42 E2
Pavlovsk Voronezhskaya Oblast' Russia 13 I6
Pavlovskaya Russia 13 H7
Pawai India 36 E4
Paw Paw WV U.S.A. 64 B3

Pawtucket RI U.S.A. 64 F2
Paxson AK U.S.A. 60 D3
Payakumbuh Indon. 41 C8
Pāy Bōldak Ghar mt. Afgh. 36 A3
Payette ID U.S.A. 62 D3
Pay-Khoy, Khrebet hills Russia 28 H3
Payne Que. Canada see Kangirsuk
Payne, Lac l. Que. Canada 61 K4
Payne's Find Australia 55 B7
Paysandú Uruguay 70 E4
Pazar Turkey 35 F2
Pazarcık Turkey 34 E3
Pazardzhik Bulg. 27 K3
Pazin Croatia 26 E2
Peabody MA U.S.A. 64 F1
Peace r. Alta/B.C. Canada 60 G4
Peace River Alta Canada 77 L3
Peach Springs AZ U.S.A. 65 F3
Peak Charles h. Australia 55 C8
Peak Charles National Park Australia 55 C8
Peak District National Park U.K. 18 F5
Peake watercourse Australia 57 B6
Peak Hill Australia 58 D4
Peak Hill (abandoned) Australia 55 B6
Peale, Mount UT U.S.A. 62 F4
Pearce Point Australia 54 E3
Pearisburg VA U.S.A. 64 A4
Pearl r. MS U.S.A. 63 J5
Pearsall TX U.S.A. 62 H6
Pearston S. Africa 51 G7
Peary Channel Nunavut Canada 61 I2
Peary Land reg. Greenland 77 J1
Pebane Moz. 49 D5
Pebas Peru 68 D4
Peć Kosovo see Pejë
Peçanha Brazil 71 C2
Peças, Ilha das i. Brazil 71 A4
Pechenga Russia 14 Q2
Pechora Russia 12 M2
Pechora r. Russia 12 L1
Pechora Sea Russia see Pechorskoye More
Pechorskaya Guba b. Russia 12 L1
Pechorskoye More sea Russia 77 G2
Pechory Russia 15 O8
Pecos TX U.S.A. 62 G5
Pecos r. NM/TX U.S.A. 62 G6
Pécs Hungary 26 H1
Pedda Vagu r. India 38 C2
Pedder, Lake Australia 57 [inset]
Peddie S. Africa 51 H7
Pedernales Dom. Rep. 67 J5
Pediaios r. Cyprus 39 A2
Pediva Angola 49 B5
Pedra Azul Brazil 71 C1
Pedra Preta, Serra da mts Brazil 71 A1
Pedras de Maria da Cruz Brazil 71 B1
Pedregulho Brazil 71 B3
Pedreiras Brazil 69 J4
Pedro, Point Sri Lanka 38 D4
Pedro Canário Brazil 71 D2
Pedro II, Ilha reg. Brazil/Venez. 68 E3
Pedro Juan Caballero Para. 70 E2
Peebles U.K. 20 F5
Pee Dee r. SC U.S.A. 63 L5
Peekskill NY U.S.A. 64 E2
Peel r. Australia 58 E3
Peel r. N.W.T./Y.T. Canada 60 E3
Peel Isle of Man 18 C4
Peera Peera Poolanna Lake imp. l. Australia 57 B5
Peery Lake salt l. Australia 58 A3
Pegasus Bay N.Z. 59 D6
Pegu Myanmar 42 H9
Pegu Yoma mts Myanmar 37 H6
Pegysh Russia 12 K3
Pehuajó Arg. 70 D5
Peine Chile 70 C2
Peint India 38 B1
Peipsi järv l. Estonia/Russia see Peipus, Lake
Peipus, Lake Estonia/Russia 15 O7
Peiraias Greece see Piraeus
Pei Shan mts China see Bei Shan
Peixe Brazil 69 I6
Peixe r. Brazil 71 A1
Peixoto de Azevedo Brazil 69 H6
Pejë Kosovo 27 I3
Pèk Laos see Phônsavan
Peka Lesotho 51 H5
Peking China see Beijing
Pekinga Benin 46 D3
Pelagie, Isole is Sicily Italy 26 E7
Peleaga, Vârful mt. Romania 27 J2
Peles Russia 12 K3
Pelkosenniemi Fin. 14 O3
Pella S. Africa 50 D5
Pello Fin. 14 M3
Pelly Crossing Y.T. Canada 60 E3
Pelly Mountains Y.T. Canada 60 E3
Peloponnese pen. Greece 27 J6
Pelopónnesos pen. Greece see Peloponnese
Peloponnisos pen. Greece see Peloponnese
Pelotas Brazil 70 F4
Pelotas, Rio das r. Brazil 71 A4
Pelusium tourist site Egypt 39 A4
Pelusium, Bay of Egypt see Ṭīnah, Khalīj aṭ
Pemba Moz. 49 E5
Pemba Island Tanz. 49 D4
Pemberton B.C. Canada 62 C1
Pembina r. Alta Canada 62 D1
Pembroke Ont. Canada 63 L2
Pembroke U.K. 19 C7
Pembrokeshire Coast National Park U.K. 19 B7
Pen India 38 B2
Peña Cerredo mt. Spain see Torrecerredo
Peñalara mt. Spain 25 E3
Penamar Brazil 71 C1
Peña Nevada, Cerro mt. Mex. 66 E4
Penang Malaysia see George Town
Penápolis Brazil 71 A3
Peñaranda de Bracamonte Spain 25 D3
Penarie Australia 58 A5
Penarlâg U.K. see Hawarden
Peñarroya mt. Spain 25 F3
Peñarroya-Pueblonuevo Spain 25 D4
Penarth U.K. 19 D7
Peñas, Cabo de c. Spain 25 D2
Penas, Golfo de g. Chile 70 A7
Pencoso, Alto de hills Arg. 70 C4
Pendjari, Parc National de la nat. park Benin 46 D3
Pendle Hill h. U.K. 18 E5
Pendleton OR U.S.A. 62 D2
Pend Oreille Lake ID U.S.A. 62 D2
Pendra India 37 E5
Penduv India 38 B2
Peneda Gerês, Parque Nacional da nat. park Port. 25 B3
Penfro U.K. see Pembroke
Penganga r. India 38 C2
Penge Dem. Rep. Congo 49 C4
Penge S. Africa 51 J3
P'enghu Ch'üntao is Taiwan 43 L8
P'enghu Liehtao is Taiwan see P'enghu Ch'üntao
Penha Brazil 71 A4
Penhoek Pass S. Africa 51 H6
Penhook VA U.S.A. 64 B4
Peniche Port. 25 B4
Penicuik U.K. 20 F5
Peninga Russia 14 R5
Peninsular Malaysia Malaysia 41 C7
Penitente, Serra do hills Brazil 69 I5
Pennell Coast Antarctica 76 H2
Penn Hills PA U.S.A. 64 B2
Pennine, Alpi mts Italy/Switz. see Pennine Alps
Pennine Alps mts Italy/Switz. 26 B2
Pennines hills U.K. 18 E4
Pennsburg PA U.S.A. 64 D2
Penns Grove NJ U.S.A. 64 D3
Pennsville NJ U.S.A. 64 D3
Pennsylvania state U.S.A. 64 B2
Penn Yan NY U.S.A. 64 C1
Penny Icecap Nunavut Canada 61 L3
Penny Point Antarctica 76 H1
Penola Australia 57 C8
Penong Australia 55 F7
Penonomé Panama 67 H7
Penrhyn atoll Cook Is 75 J6
Penrhyn Basin sea feature S. Pacific Ocean 75 J6
Penrith Australia 58 E4
Penrith U.K. 18 E4
Pensacola FL U.S.A. 63 J5
Pensacola Mountains Antarctica 76 L1
Pensi La pass India 36 D2
Pentadaktylos Range mts Cyprus 39 A2
Pentakota India 38 D2
Pentecost Island Vanuatu 53 G3
Pentecôte, Île i. Vanuatu see Pentecost Island
Penticton B.C. Canada 62 D2
Pentire Point U.K. 19 B8
Pentland Australia 56 D4
Pentland Firth sea chan. U.K. 20 F2
Pentland Hills U.K. 20 F5
Pen-y-Bont ar Ogwr U.K. see Bridgend
Penygadair h. U.K. 19 D6
Penza Russia 13 J5
Penzance U.K. 19 B8
Penzhinskaya Guba b. Russia 29 R3
Peoria IL U.S.A. 63 J3
Peradeniya Sri Lanka 38 D5
Pera Head hd Australia 56 C2
Perales del Alfambra Spain 25 F3
Perambalur India 38 C4
Perämeren kansallispuisto nat. park Fin. 14 N4
Peräseinäjoki Fin. 14 M5
Percival Lakes imp. l. Australia 54 D5
Percy Isles Australia 56 E4
Perdizes Brazil 71 B2
Peregrebnoye Russia 11 T3
Pereira Col. 68 C3
Pereira Barreto Brazil 71 A3
Pereira de Eça Angola see Ondjiva
Peremul Par reef India 38 B4
Peremyshlyany Ukr. 13 E6
Perenjori Australia 55 B7
Pereslavl'-Zalesskiy Russia 12 H4
Pereslavskiy Natsional'nyy Park nat. park Russia 12 H4
Pereyaslavka Russia 44 D3
Pereyaslav-Khmel'nitskiy Ukr. see Pereyaslav-Khmel'nyts'kyy
Pereyaslav-Khmel'nyts'kyy Ukr. 13 F6
Pergamino Arg. 70 D4
Perho Fin. 14 N5
Perico Arg. 70 C2
Pericos Mex. 66 C3
Périgueux France 24 E4
Perijá, Parque Nacional nat. park Venez. 68 D2
Perijá, Sierra de mts Venez. 68 D2
Periyar India see Erode
Perlas, Punta de pt Nicaragua 67 H6
Perleberg Germany 17 M4
Perm' Russia 11 R4
Permas Russia 12 J4
Pernambuco Brazil see Recife
Pernambuco Plain sea feature S. Atlantic Ocean 72 G6
Pernatty Lagoon imp. l. Australia 57 B6
Pernem India 38 B3
Pernik Bulg. 27 J3
Pernov Estonia see Pärnu
Perojpur Bangl. see Pirojpur
Peron Islands Australia 54 E3
Péronne France 24 F2
Perpignan France 24 F5
Perranporth U.K. 19 B8
Perrégaux Alg. see Mohammadia
Perris CA U.S.A. 65 D4
Perros-Guirec France 24 C2
Perry FL U.S.A. 63 K5
Perryton TX U.S.A. 62 G4
Perryville AK U.S.A. 60 C4
Perryville MO U.S.A. 63 J4
Perseverancia Bol. 68 F6
Pershore U.K. 19 E6
Persia country Asia see Iran
Persian Gulf Asia see The Gulf
Pertek Turkey 35 E3
Perth Australia 55 A7
Perth Ont. Canada 63 L3
Perth U.K. 20 F4
Perth Amboy NJ U.S.A. 64 D2
Perth Basin sea feature Indian Ocean 73 P7
Pertominsk Russia 12 H2
Pertunmaa Fin. 15 O6
Pertusato, Capo c. Corsica France 24 I6
Peru atoll Kiribati see Beru
Peru country S. America 68 D6
Peru-Chile Trench sea feature S. Pacific Ocean 75 O6
Perugia Italy 26 E3
Peruru India 38 C3
Perusia Italy see Perugia
Pervomaysk Russia 13 I5
Pervomays'k Ukr. 13 F6
Pervomayskiy Kazakh. 42 E2
Pervomayskiy Arkhangel'skaya Oblast' Russia see Novodvinsk
Pervomayskiy Tambovskaya Oblast' Russia 13 I5
Pervomays'kyy Ukr. 13 H6
Pervorechenskiy (abandoned) Russia 29 R3
Pervyy Brat, Gora h. Russia 44 F1
Pesaro Italy 26 E3
Pescadores is Taiwan see P'enghu Ch'üntao
Pescara Italy 26 F3
Pescara r. Italy 26 F3
Peschanokopskoye Russia 13 I7
Peschanoye Russia see Yashkul'
Peschanyy, Mys pt Kazakh. 35 H2
Pesha r. Russia 12 J2
Peshawar Pak. 33 L3
Peshkopi Albania 27 I4
Peshtera Bulg. 27 K3
Peski Karakumy des. Turkm. see Karakum Desert
Peskovka Russia 12 L4
Pesnica Slovenia 26 F1
Pessac France 24 D4
Pestovo Russia 12 G4
Pestravka Russia 13 K5
Petah Tiqwa Israel 39 B3
Petäjävesi Fin. 14 N5
Petalion, Kolpos sea chan. Greece 27 K5
Petaluma CA U.S.A. 65 A1
Petatlán Mex. 66 D5
Petauke Zambia 49 D5
Peterborough Australia 57 B7
Peterborough Ont. Canada 63 L3
Peterborough U.K. 19 G6
Peterborough NH U.S.A. 64 F1
Peterculter U.K. 20 G3
Peterhead U.K. 20 H3
Peter I Island Antarctica 76 K2
Peter I Øy i. Antarctica see Peter I Island
Peterlee U.K. 18 F4
Petermann Bjerg nunatak Greenland 61 P2
Petermann Ranges mts Australia 55 E6
Peter Pond Lake Sask. Canada 60 H4
Petersburg NY U.S.A. 64 E1
Petersburg VA U.S.A. 64 C4
Petersburg WV U.S.A. 64 B3
Petersfield U.K. 19 G7
Petersville AK U.S.A. 60 C3
Peter the Great Bay Russia see Petra Velikogo, Zaliv
Peth India 38 B2
Petilia Policastro Italy 26 G5
Petit Atlas mts Morocco see Anti-Atlas
Petitjean Morocco see Sidi Kacem
Petit Mécatina r. Nfld. and Lab./Que. Canada 61 M4
Petit St-Bernard, Col du pass France 24 H4
Petit Saut, Barrage du dam Fr. Guiana 69 H3
Peto Mex. 66 G4
Petoskey MI U.S.A. 63 K2
Petra tourist site Jordan 39 B4
Petra Velikogo, Zaliv b. Russia 44 C4
Petre, Point Ont. Canada 64 C1
Petrich Bulg. 27 J4
Petrikau Poland see Piotrków Trybunalski
Petrikov Belarus see Pyetrykaw
Petrinja Croatia 26 G2
Petroaleksandrovsk Uzbek. see To'rtko'l
Petroglyphic Complexes of the Mongolian Altai tourist site Mongolia 42 F3
Petrograd Russia see St Petersburg
Petrohanski Prohod pass Bulg. 27 J3
Petrokov Poland see Piotrków Trybunalski
Petrolina Brazil 69 J5
Petrolina de Goiás Brazil 71 A2
Petropavl Kazakh. see Petropavlovskoye
Petropavlovsk Russia see Petropavlovsk-Kamchatskiy
Petropavlovsk-Kamchatskiy Russia 29 Q4
Petropavlovskoye Kazakh. 31 F1
Petrópolis Brazil 71 C3
Petroşani Romania 27 J2
Petrovsk Russia 13 J5
Petrovskoye Russia see Svetlograd
Petrovsk-Zabaykal'skiy Russia 43 J2
Petrozavodsk Russia 12 G3
Petrus Steyn S. Africa 51 I4
Petrusville S. Africa 50 G6
Petsamo Russia see Pechenga
Pettau Slovenia see Ptuj
Pettigo U.K. 21 E3
Petukhovo Russia 28 H4
Petushki Russia 12 H5
Petzeck mt. Austria 17 N7
Pevek Russia 29 S3
Pêxung China 37 H2
Peza r. Russia 12 J2
Pezinok Slovakia 17 P6
Pezu Pak. 36 B2
Pforzheim Germany 17 L6
Phagameng S. Africa 51 I3
Phagwara India 36 C3
Phahameng S. Africa 51 H5
Phalaborwa S. Africa 51 J2
Phalodi India 36 C4
Phalsund India 36 B4
Phalta India 37 G5
Phalut Peak India/Nepal 37 G4
Phangnga Thai. 31 I6
Phăng Xi Păng mt. Vietnam 42 I8
Phan Rang-Thap Cham Vietnam 31 J5
Phan Thiêt Vietnam 31 J5
Phatthalung Thai. 31 J6
Phawngpui India 37 H5
Phayao Thai. 42 H9
Phek India 37 H4
Phenix VA U.S.A. 64 B4
Phenix City AL U.S.A. 63 J5
Phet Buri Thai. 31 I5
Philadelphia Jordan see 'Ammān
Philadelphia Turkey see Alaşehir
Philadelphia PA U.S.A. 64 D3
Philip SD U.S.A. 62 G3
Philip Atoll Micronesia see Sorol
Philippeville Alg. see Skikda
Philippi WV U.S.A. 64 A3
Philippi, Lake imp. l. Australia 56 B5
Philippine Basin sea feature N. Pacific Ocean 74 E4
Philippines country Asia 41 E6
Philippine Sea N. Pacific Ocean 41 E6
Philippine Trench sea feature N. Pacific Ocean 74 E4
Philippolis S. Africa 51 G6
Philippopolis Bulg. see Plovdiv
Philipsburg PA U.S.A. 64 B2
Philip Smith Mountains AK U.S.A. 60 D3
Philipstown S. Africa 50 G6
Phillip Island Australia 58 B7
Phillipsburg KS U.S.A. 62 H4
Phillips Range hills Australia 54 D4
Philmont NY U.S.A. 64 E1
Philomelium Turkey see Akşehir
Phiritona S. Africa 51 H4
Phitsanulok Thai. 31 J5
Phnom Penh Cambodia 31 J5
Phnum Pénh Cambodia see Phnom Penh
Phoenicia NY U.S.A. 64 D1
Phoenix AZ U.S.A. 62 E5
Phoenix Island Kiribati see Rawaki
Phoenix Islands Kiribati 53 I2
Phôngsali Laos 40 C5
Phong Saly Laos see Phôngsali
Phônsavan Laos 41 C6
Phônsavan mt. Laos 42 I9
Phosphate Hill Australia 56 C4
Phrae Thai. 31 J5
Phra Nakhon Si Ayutthaya Thai. see Ayutthaya
Phuket Thai. 31 I6
Phulabani India see Phulbani
Phulbani India 38 E1
Phulchhari Ghat Bangl. see Fulchhari
Phulji Pak. 36 A4
Phyu Myanmar 42 H9
Piaca Brazil 69 I5
Piacenza Italy 26 C2
Pian r. Australia 58 D3
Pianosa, Isola i. Italy 26 D3
Piatra Neamţ Romania 27 L1
Piave r. Italy 26 E2
Pibor Post South Sudan 47 G4
Picardie admin. reg. France 19 J9
Picardie reg. France see Picardy
Picardy admin. reg. France see Picardie
Picardy reg. France 24 E2
Picauville France 19 F9
Picayune MS U.S.A. 63 J5
Pichanal Arg. 70 D2
Pichhor India 36 D4
Pichilemu Chile 70 B4
Pichilingue Mex. 66 B4
Pickens WV U.S.A. 64 A3
Pickering U.K. 18 G4
Pickering, Vale of val. U.K. 18 G4
Pickle Lake Ont. Canada 61 I4
Pico da Neblina, Parque Nacional do nat. park Brazil 68 E3
Picos Brazil 69 J5
Picos de Europa, Parque Nacional de los nat. park Spain 25 D2
Pico Truncado Arg. 70 C7
Picton Australia 58 E5
Picton N.Z. 59 E5
Pidurutalagala mt. Sri Lanka 38 D5
Piedade Brazil 71 B3
Piedra de Águila Arg. 70 B6
Piedras, Punta pt Arg. 70 E5
Piedras, Río de las r. Peru 68 E6
Piedras Blancas Point CA U.S.A. 65 B3
Piedras Negras Mex. 66 D3
Pieksämäki Fin. 14 O5
Pielavesi Fin. 14 O5
Pielinen l. Fin. 14 P5
Pieljekaise nationalpark nat. park Sweden 14 J3
Pienaarsrivier S. Africa 51 I3
Pieniński Park Narodowy nat. park Poland 17 R6
Pieninský národný park nat. park Slovakia 17 R6
Pieria mts Greece 27 J4
Pierowall U.K. 20 G1
Pierpont OH U.S.A. 64 A2
Pierre SD U.S.A. 62 G3
Pierrelatte France 24 G4
Pietermaritzburg S. Africa 51 J5
Pietersaari Fin. see Jakobstad
Pietra Spada, Passo di pass Italy 26 G5
Piet Retief S. Africa see eMkhondo
Pietrosa mt. Romania 27 K1
Pigeon Lake Alta Canada 62 E1
Pigg's Peak Swaziland 51 J3
Pihij India 36 C5
Pihkva järv l. Estonia/Russia see Pskov, Lake
Pihlajavesi l. Fin. 14 P6
Pihlava Fin. 15 L6
Pihtipudas Fin. 14 N5
Piippola Fin. 14 N4
Piispajärvi Fin. 14 P4
Pikalevo Russia 12 G4
Pike WV U.S.A. 64 A3
Pikelot i. Micronesia 74 F5
Pikes Peak CO U.S.A. 62 G4
Pikeville KY U.S.A. 63 K4
Pikinni atoll Marshall Is see Bikini
Piła Poland 17 P4
Pilanesberg National Park S. Africa 51 H3
Pilão Arcado Brazil 69 J5
Pilar Arg. 70 E4
Pilar Para. 70 E3
Pilar de Goiás Brazil 71 A1
Pilaya r. Bol. 68 F8
Pilbara reg. Australia 54 B5
Pilcomayo r. Bol./Para. 68 F8
Piler India 38 C3
Pili, Cerro mt. Chile 70 C2
Pilibangan India 36 C3
Pilibhit India 36 D3
Pilipinas country Asia see Philippines
Pillau Russia see Baltiysk
Pillcopata Peru 68 D6
Pilliga Australia 58 D3
Pil'na Russia 12 J5
Pil'nya, Ozero l. Russia 12 M1
Pilões, Serra dos mts Brazil 71 B2
Pílos Greece see Pylos
Pilot Peak NV U.S.A. 65 D1
Pilot Station AK U.S.A. 60 B3
Pilsen Czech Rep. see Plzeň
Piltene Latvia 15 L8
Pil'tun, Zaliv b. Russia 44 F1
Pilu Pak. 36 B4
Pimenta Bueno Brazil 68 F6
Pimpalner India 38 B1
Pin r. India 36 D2
Pin r. Myanmar 37 H5
Pinahat India 36 D4
Pinamar Arg. 70 E5
Pinang Malaysia see George Town
Pınarbaşı Turkey 34 E3
Pinar del Río Cuba 67 H4
Pinarhisar Turkey 27 L4
Piñas Ecuador 68 C4
Pińczów Poland 17 R5
Pindaí Brazil 71 C1
Pindamonhangaba Brazil 71 B3
Pindar Australia 55 A7
Pindaré r. Brazil 69 J4
Píndhos Óros mts Greece see Pindus Mountains
Pindos mts Greece see Pindus Mountains
Pindrei India 36 E5
Pindus Mountains Greece 27 I5
Pine watercourse Australia 57 C7
Pine Bluff AR U.S.A. 63 I5
Pine Creek Australia 54 E3
Pine Creek r. PA U.S.A. 64 C2
Pinecrest CA U.S.A. 65 B1
Pinedale WY U.S.A. 62 F3
Pine Flat Lake CA U.S.A. 65 C2
Pinega Russia 12 I2
Pinega r. Russia 12 I2
Pinegrove Australia 55 A6
Pine Grove PA U.S.A. 64 C2
Pineios r. Greece 27 J5
Pine Island Bay Antarctica 75 N10
Pine Island Glacier Antarctica 76 K1
Pine Mountain CA U.S.A. 65 B3
Pine Peak AZ U.S.A. 65 F3
Pine Point (abandoned) N.W.T. Canada 60 G3
Pineridge CA U.S.A. 65 C2
Pine Ridge SD U.S.A. 62 G3
Pinerolo Italy 26 B2
Pines, Akrotirio pt Greece 27 K4
Pines, Isle of i. Cuba see Juventud, Isla de la
Pines, Isle of i. New Caledonia see Pins, Île des
Pinetown S. Africa 51 J5
Pine Valley NY U.S.A. 64 C1
Ping'an China 42 I5
Ping'anyi China see Ping'an
Pingdingbu China see Guyuan
Pingdingshan China 43 K6
Pingdong Taiwan see P'ingtung
Pingdu China 43 L5
Pinggang China 44 B4
Pingliang China 42 J5
Pingtan Dao i. China see Haitan Dao
P'ingtung Taiwan 43 M8
Pingxiang Guangxi China 42 J8
Pingxiang Jiangxi China 43 K7
Pingyang China 44 B2
Pinheiro Brazil 69 I4
Pinhoe U.K. 19 D8
Piniós r. Greece see Pineios
Pinjin Australia 55 C7
Pinlebu Myanmar 37 H4
Pinnacle h. VA/WV U.S.A. 64 B3
Pinnacles National Monument nat. park CA U.S.A. 65 B2
Pinon Hills CA U.S.A. 65 D3
Pinos, Isla de i. Cuba see Juventud, Isla de la
Pinos, Mount CA U.S.A. 65 C3
Pinotepa Nacional Mex. 66 E5
Pins, Île des i. New Caledonia 53 G4
Pins, Pointe aux pt Ont. Canada 64 A1
Pinsk Belarus 15 O10
Pintados Chile 70 C2
Pintura UT U.S.A. 65 F2
Pioche NV U.S.A. 65 E2
Piodi Dem. Rep. Congo 49 C4
Pioner, Ostrov i. Russia 28 K2
Pionerskiy Kaliningradskaya Oblast' Russia 15 L9
Pionerskiy Khanty-Mansiyskiy Avtonomnyy Okrug-Yugra Russia 11 S3
Pionki Poland 17 R5
Piopio N.Z. 59 E4
Piopiotahi inlet N.Z. see Milford Sound
Piorini, Lago l. Brazil 68 F4
Piotrków Trybunalski Poland 17 Q5
Pipa Dingzi mt. China 44 C4
Pipar India 36 C4
Pipar Road India 36 C4
Piperi i. Greece 27 K5
Piper Peak NV U.S.A. 65 D2
Pipli India 36 C3
Pipmuacan, Réservoir resr Que. Canada 63 M2
Piquiri r. Brazil 71 A4
Pira Benin 46 D4
Piracanjuba Brazil 71 A2
Piracicaba Brazil 71 B3
Piracicaba r. Brazil 71 C2
Piracuruca Brazil 69 J4
Piraeus Greece 27 J6
Piraí do Sul Brazil 71 A4
Piräievs Greece see Piraeus
Piraju Brazil 71 A3
Pirajuí Brazil 71 A3
Pirallahı Adası Azer. 35 H2
Piranhas Bahia Brazil 71 C1
Piranhas Goiás Brazil 69 H7
Piranhas r. Goiás Brazil 71 A2
Piranhas r. Rio Grande do Norte Brazil 69 K5
Pirapora Brazil 71 B2
Pirassununga Brazil 71 B3
Pirawa India 36 D4
Pirenópolis Brazil 71 A1
Pires do Rio Brazil 71 A2
Pirgos Greece see Pyrgos
Pirin, Natsionalen Park nat. park Bulg. 27 J4
Pirineos mts Europe see Pyrenees
Piripiri Brazil 69 J4
Pirlerkondu Turkey see Taşkent
Pirojpur Bangl. 37 G5
Pir Panjal Pass India 36 C2
Pir Panjal Range mts India/Pak. 36 C2
Piryatin Ukr. see Pyryatyn
Pisa Italy 26 D3
Pisae Italy see Pisa
Pisagua Chile 68 D7
Pisaurum Italy see Pesaro
Pisco Peru 68 C6
Písek Czech Rep. 17 O6
Pisha China see Ningnan
Pishan China 36 D1
Pīshīn Iran 33 J4
Pishin Pak. 36 A3
Pishpek Kyrg. see Bishkek
Pisidia reg. Turkey 34 C3
Pissis, Cerro mt. Arg. 70 C3
Pisté Mex. 66 G4
Pisticci Italy 26 G4
Pistoia Italy 26 D3
Pistoriae Italy see Pistoia
Pisuerga r. Spain 25 D3
Pita Guinea 46 B3
Pitanga Brazil 71 A4
Pitangui Brazil 71 B2
Pitar India 36 B5
Pitarpunga Lake imp. l. Australia 58 A5
Pitcairn, Henderson, Ducie and Oeno Islands terr. S. Pacific Ocean see Pitcairn Islands
Pitcairn Island Pitcairn Is 75 L7
Pitcairn Islands terr. S. Pacific Ocean 75 L7
Piteå Sweden 14 L4
Piteälven r. Sweden 14 L4
Pitelino Russia 13 I5
Piterka Russia 13 J6
Piteşti Romania 27 K2
Pithoragarh India 36 E3
Pitihra India 36 D5
Pitkyaranta Russia 12 F3
Pitlochry U.K. 20 F4
Pitsane Siding Botswana 51 G3
Piti i. India 38 B4
Pitt Island N.Z. 53 I6
Pitt Islands Solomon Is see Vanikoro Islands
Pittsburgh PA U.S.A. 64 B2
Pittsfield MA U.S.A. 64 E1
Pittsworth Australia 58 E1
Piumhi Brazil 71 B3
Piura Peru 68 B5
Piute Mountains CA U.S.A. 65 E3
Piute Peak CA U.S.A. 65 C3
Piuthan Nepal 37 E3
Pivka Slovenia 26 F2
Pixariá mt. Greece see Pyxaria
Pixley CA U.S.A. 65 C3
Pizhanka Russia 12 K4
Pizhi Nigeria 46 D4
Pizhma Russia 12 J4
Pizhma r. Russia 12 K2
Pizhma r. Russia 12 L2
Placentia Italy see Piacenza
Placerville CA U.S.A. 65 B1
Plácido de Castro Brazil 68 E6
Plainfield CT U.S.A. 64 F2
Plainview TX U.S.A. 62 G5
Plaka, Akrotirio pt Greece 27 L7
Plakoti, Cape Cyprus 39 B2
Planada CA U.S.A. 65 B2
Planaltina Brazil 71 B1
Planura Brazil 71 A3
Plaquemine LA U.S.A. 63 I5
Plasencia Spain 25 C3
Plaster City CA U.S.A. 65 E4
Plastun Russia 44 E3
Platani r. Sicily Italy 26 E6
Platberg mt. S. Africa 51 I5
Platinum AK U.S.A. 77 B3
Plato Col. 68 D2
Platte r. NE U.S.A. 62 H3
Plattsburgh NY U.S.A. 63 M3
Plauen Germany 17 N5
Plavsk Russia 13 H5
Playas Ecuador 68 B4
Pleasant Bay MA U.S.A. 64 G2
Pleasanton TX U.S.A. 66 E3
Pleasant Point N.Z. 59 C7
Pleasantville NJ U.S.A. 64 D3
Pleaux France 24 F4
Pledger Lake Ont. Canada 63 K1
Plenty watercourse Australia 56 B5
Plenty, Bay of g. N.Z. 59 F3
Plentywood MT U.S.A. 62 G2
Plesetsk Russia 12 I3
Pleshchentsy Belarus see Plyeshchanitsy
Plétipi, Lac l. Que. Canada 63 M1
Plettenberg Bay S. Africa 50 F8
Pleven Bulg. 27 K3
Plevna Bulg. see Pleven
Pljevlja Montenegro 27 H3
Płock Poland 17 Q4
Pločno mt. Bos. & Herz. 26 G3
Plodovoye Russia 12 F3
Ploemeur France 24 C3
Ploeşti Romania see Ploieşti
Ploieşti Romania 27 L2
Plomb du Cantal mt. France 24 F4
Ploskoye Russia see Stanovoye
Płoty Poland 17 O4
Ploudalmézeau France 24 B2
Plouzané France 24 B2
Plovdiv Bulg. 27 K3
Plozk Poland see Płock
Plumridge Lakes imp. l. Australia 55 D7
Plung Lith. 15 L9
Plyeshchanitsy Belarus 15 O9
Plymouth U.K. 19 C8
Plymouth CA U.S.A. 65 B1
Plymouth IN U.S.A. 63 J3
Plymouth MA U.S.A. 64 F2
Plymouth (abandoned) Montserrat 67 L5
Plymouth Bay MA U.S.A. 64 F2
Plynlimon h. U.K. 19 D6
Plyussa Russia 15 P7
Plzeň Czech Rep. 17 N6
Pô Burkina Faso 46 C3
Po r. Italy 26 E2
Pobeda Peak China/Kyrg. 31 H2
Pobedy, Pik mt. China/Kyrg. see Pobeda Peak
Pocatello ID U.S.A. 62 E3
Pochayiv Ukr. 13 E6
Pochep Russia 13 G5
Pochinki Russia 13 J5
Pochinok Russia 13 G5
Pochutla Mex. 66 E5
Pocking Germany 17 N6
Pocklington U.K. 18 G5
Poções Brazil 71 C1
Pocomoke City MD U.S.A. 64 D3
Pocomoke Sound b. MD/VA U.S.A. 64 D4
Poconé Brazil 69 G7
Pocono Mountains hills PA U.S.A. 64 D2
Poços de Caldas Brazil 71 B3
Podanur India 38 C4
Poddor'ye Russia 12 F4
Podgorenskiy Russia 13 H6
Podgorica Montenegro 27 H3
Podgornoye Russia 28 J4
Podile India 38 C3
Podişul Transilvaniei plat. Romania see Transylvanian Basin
Podkamennaya Tunguska r. Russia 29 K3
Podocarpus, Parque Nacional nat. park Ecuador 68 C4
Podol'sk Russia 13 H5
Podporozh'ye Russia 12 G3
Podujevë Kosovo 27 I3
Podujevo Kosovo see Podujevë
Podz' Russia 12 K3
Poelela, Lagoa l. Moz. 51 L3
Poeppel Corner imp. l. Australia 57 B5
Poetovio Slovenia see Ptuj
Pofadder S. Africa 50 D5
Pogar Russia 13 G5
Poggibonsi Italy 26 D3
Pogradec Albania 27 I4
Pogranichnyy Russia 44 C3
Po Hai g. China see Bo Hai
Pohang S. Korea 45 C5
Pohnpei atoll Micronesia 74 G5
Pohri India 36 D4
Poi India 37 H4
Poiana Mare Romania 27 J3
Poindo China 37 G3
Poinsett, Cape Antarctica 76 F2
Point Arena CA U.S.A. 65 A1
Pointe-à-Pitre Guadeloupe 67 L5
Pointe-Noire Congo 49 B4
Point Hope AK U.S.A. 60 B3
Point Lake N.W.T. Canada 60 G3
Point Pleasant NJ U.S.A. 64 D2
Poitiers France 24 E3
Poitou reg. France 24 E3
Pojuca r. Brazil 71 D1
Pokaran India 36 B4
Pokataroo Australia 58 D2
Pokcha Russia 11 R3
Pokhara Nepal 37 E3
Pokhran Landi Pak. 36 A4
Pokhvistnevo Russia 11 Q5
Poko Dem. Rep. Congo 48 C3
Pokosnoye Russia 42 I1
P'ok'r Kovkas mts Asia see Lesser Caucasus
Pokrovka Primorskiy Kray Russia 44 C4
Pokrovka Zabaykal'skiy Kray Russia 44 A1
Pokrovsk Respublika Sakha (Yakutiya) Russia 29 N3
Pokrovsk Saratovskaya Oblast' Russia see Engel's
Pokrovskoye Russia 13 H7
Pokshen'ga r. Russia 12 J3
Pol India 36 C5
Pola Croatia see Pula
Poland country Europe 10 J5
Poland NY U.S.A. 64 D1
Polar Plateau Antarctica 76 A1
Polatlı Turkey 34 D3
Polatsk Belarus 15 P9
Polavaram India 38 D2
Polcirkeln Sweden 14 L3
Pol-e Fasā Iran 35 I5
Polessk Russia 15 L9
Poles'ye marsh Belarus/Ukr. see Pripet Marshes
Polgahawela Sri Lanka 38 D5
Poli Cyprus see Polis
Poliaigos i. Greece see Polyaigos
Police Poland 17 O4
Policoro Italy 26 G4
Poligny France 24 G3
Polikastron Greece see Polykastro
Polillo Islands Phil. 41 E6
Poliny Osipenko, imeni Russia 44 E1
Polis Cyprus 39 A2
Polis'ke (abandoned) Ukr. 13 F6
Polis'kyy Zapovidnyk nat. park Ukr. 13 F6
Politovo Russia 12 K2
Polýiros Greece see Polygyros
Polkowice Poland 17 P5
Pollachi India 38 C4
Pollard Islands HI U.S.A. see Gardner Pinnacles
Pollino, Monte mt. Italy 26 G5
Pollino, Parco Nazionale del nat. park Italy 26 G5
Pollock Pines CA U.S.A. 65 B1
Pollock Reef Australia 55 C8
Polmak Norway 14 O1
Polnovat Russia 11 T3
Polo Fin. 14 P4

Quthing Lesotho see Moyeni
Quttinirpaaq National Park Nunavut Canada 61 K1
Quwayq, Nahr r. Syria/Turkey see Qoueiq, Nahr
Quxar China see Lhazê
Quxian China see Quzhou
Quyang China see Jingzhou
Quyghan Kazakh. see Kuygan
Quy Nhơn Vietnam 31 J5
Quzhou China 43 L7

Ribáuè Moz. 49 D5
Ribble r. U.K. 18 E5
Ribblesdale val. U.K. 18 E4
Ribe Denmark 15 F9
Ribeira r. Brazil 71 B4
Ribeirão Preto Brazil 71 B3
Ribérac France 24 E4
Riberalta Bol. 68 E6
Rîbnița Moldova 13 F7
Ribnitz-Damgarten Germany 17 N3
Říčany Czech Rep. 17 O6
Rice VA U.S.A. 64 B4
Richard-Molard, Mont Africa 46 C4
Richards Bay S. Africa 51 K5
Richards Inlet Antarctica 76 H1
Richards Island N.W.T. Canada 60 E3
Richardson Mountains N.W.T./Y.T. Canada 60 E3
Richardson Mountains N.Z. 59 B7
Richfield UT U.S.A. 62 E4
Richfield Springs NY U.S.A. 64 D1
Richford NY U.S.A. 64 C1
Richgrove CA U.S.A. 65 C3
Richland WA U.S.A. 62 D2
Richmond N.S.W. Australia 58 E4
Richmond Qld Australia 56 C4
Richmond N.Z. 59 D5
Richmond KwaZulu-Natal S. Africa 51 J5
Richmond N. Cape S. Africa 50 F6
Richmond U.K. 18 F4
Richmond CA U.S.A. 65 A2
Richmond IN U.S.A. 63 K4
Richmond KY U.S.A. 63 K4
Richmond VA U.S.A. 64 C4
Richmond Range hills Australia 58 F2
Richwood WV U.S.A. 64 A3
Ricomagus France see **Riom**
Riddell Nunataks Antarctica 76 E2
Rideau Lakes Ont. Canada 63 L3
Ridgecrest CA U.S.A. 65 D3
Ridgway PA U.S.A. 64 B2
Riecito Venez. 68 E1
Riesa Germany 17 N5
Riesco, Isla i. Chile 70 B8
Riet watercourse S. Africa 50 E6
Rietavas Lith. 15 L9
Rietfontein S. Africa 50 E4
Rieti Italy 26 E3
Rifā'ī, Tall mt. Jordan/Syria 39 C3
Rifstangi pt Iceland 14 [inset 2]
Rift Valley Lakes National Park Eth. see **Abijatta-Shalla National Park**
Rīga Latvia 15 N8
Riga, Gulf of Estonia/Latvia 15 M8
Rigain Pünco l. China 37 F2
Rīgas jūras līcis b. Estonia/Latvia see **Riga, Gulf of**
Rigby ID U.S.A. 62 E3
Rigside U.K. 20 F5
Riia laht b. Estonia/Latvia see **Riga, Gulf of**
Riihimäki Fin. 15 N6
Riiser-Larsen Ice Shelf Antarctica 76 B2
Rijau Nigeria 46 D3
Rijeka Croatia 26 F2
Rikuchū-kaigan Kokuritsu-kōen Japan 45 F5
Rikuzen-takata Japan 45 F5
Rila mts Bulg. 27 J3
Rila China 37 F3
Rileyville VA U.S.A. 64 B3
Rillieux-la-Pape France 24 G4
Rimah, Wādī ar watercourse Saudi Arabia 32 F4
Rimavská Sobota Slovakia 17 R6
Rimini Italy 26 E2
Rîmnicu Sărat Romania see **Râmnicu Sărat**
Rîmnicu Vîlcea Romania see **Râmnicu Vâlcea**
Rimouski Que. Canada 63 N2
Rimsdale, Loch l. U.K. 20 E2
Rinbung China 37 G3
Rincão Brazil 71 A3
Rindal Norway 14 F5
Ringarooma Bay Australia 57 [inset]
Ringas India 36 C4
Ringebu Norway 15 G6
Ringkøbing Denmark 15 F8
Ringsend U.K. 21 F2
Ringsted Denmark 15 G9
Ringtor China 37 E3
Ringvassøya i. Norway 14 K2
Ringwood Australia 58 B6
Ringwood U.K. 19 F8
Rinns Point U.K. 20 C5
Rinqênzê China 37 G3
Rinqin Xubco salt l. China 37 E3
Rinyirru (Lakefield) National Park Australia 56 D2
Río Abiseo, Parque Nacional nat. park Peru 68 C5
Rio Azul Brazil 71 A4
Riobamba Ecuador 68 C4
Rio Bonito Brazil 71 C3
Rio Branco Brazil 68 E6
Rio Branco, Parque Nacional do nat. park Brazil 68 F3
Rio Brilhante Brazil 70 F2
Rio Casca Brazil 71 C3
Rio Claro Brazil 71 B3
Río Colorado Arg. 70 D5
Río Cuarto Arg. 70 D4
Rio das Pedras Moz. 51 L2
Rio de Contas Brazil 71 C1
Rio de Janeiro Brazil 71 C3
Rio de Janeiro state Brazil 71 C3
Río de la Plata-Paraná r. S. America 70 E4
Rio do Sul Brazil 71 A4
Río Gallegos Arg. 70 C8
Río Grande Arg. 70 C8
Rio Grande Brazil 70 F4
Río Grande Mex. 66 D4
Rio Grande r. Mex./U.S.A. 62 H6
Rio Grande City TX U.S.A. 62 H6
Rio Grande do Sul state Brazil 71 A5
Rio Grande Rise sea feature S. Atlantic Ocean 72 F8
Ríohacha Col. 68 D1
Río Hondo, Embalse resr Arg. 70 C3
Rioja Peru 68 C5
Río Lagartos Mex. 66 G4
Rio Largo Brazil 69 K5
Riom France 24 F4
Rio Manso, Represa do resr Brazil 69 G6
Río Mulatos Bol. 68 E7
Río Muni reg. Equat. Guinea 46 E4
Río Negro, Embalse del resr Uruguay 70 E4
Rioni r. Georgia 35 F2
Rio Novo Brazil 71 C3
Rio Pardo de Minas Brazil 71 C1
Rio Preto Brazil 71 C3
Rio Preto, Serra do hills Brazil 71 B2
Rio Rancho NM U.S.A. 62 F4
Río Tigre Ecuador 68 C4
Rio Verde Brazil 71 A2
Rio Verde de Mato Grosso Brazil 69 H7
Rio Vista CA U.S.A. 65 B1
Ripky Ukr. 13 F6
Ripley England U.K. 18 F4
Ripley England U.K. 19 F5
Ripley NY U.S.A. 64 B1
Ripoll Spain 25 H2
Ripon U.K. 18 F4
Ripon CA U.S.A. 65 B2
Ripu India 37 G4
Risca U.K. 19 D7
Rishiri-tō i. Japan 44 F3
Rishon LeZiyyon Israel 39 B4
Rising Sun MD U.S.A. 64 C3
Risle r. France 19 H9
Risør Norway 15 F7
Rissa Norway 14 F5
Ristiina Fin. 15 O6
Ristijärvi Fin. 14 P4
Ristikent Russia 12 F1
Risum China 36 D2
Ritchie S. Africa 50 G5
Ritscher Upland mts Antarctica 76 B2
Ritsem Sweden 14 J3
Ritter, Mount CA U.S.A. 65 C2
Ritzville WA U.S.A. 62 D2
Riva del Garda Italy 26 D2
Rivas Nicaragua 67 G6
Rivera Arg. 70 D5
Rivera Uruguay 70 E4
River Cess Liberia 46 C4
Riverhead NY U.S.A. 64 E2
Riverhurst Sask. Canada 62 F1
Riverina Australia 55 C7
Riverina reg. Australia 58 B5
Riversdale S. Africa 50 E8
Riverside S. Africa 51 I6
Riverside CA U.S.A. 65 D4
Riversleigh Australia 56 B3
Riverton N.Z. 59 B8
Riverton VA U.S.A. 64 B3
Riverton WY U.S.A. 62 F3
Riverview N.B. Canada 63 O2
Rivesaltes France 24 F5
Rivière-du-Loup Que. Canada 63 N2
Rivne Ukr. 13 E6
Rivungo Angola 49 C5
Riwaka N.Z. 59 D5
Riwoqê China see **Racaka**
Riyadh Saudi Arabia 32 G5
Riza well Iran 35 I4
Rize Turkey 35 F2
Rizokarpaso Cyprus see **Rizokarpason**
Rizokarpason Cyprus 39 B2
Rjukan Norway 15 F7
Rjuvbrokkene mt. Norway 15 E7
Rkîz Mauritania 46 B3
Roa Norway 15 G6
Roach Lake NV U.S.A. 65 E3
Roade U.K. 19 G6
Road Town Virgin Is (U.K.) 67 L5
Roan Norway 14 G4
Roan Fell h. U.K. 20 G5
Roanne France 24 G3
Roanoke VA U.S.A. 64 B4
Roanoke Rapids NC U.S.A. 63 L4
Roaring Spring PA U.S.A. 64 B2
Roaringwater Bay Ireland 21 C6
Roatán Hond. 67 G5
Röbäck Sweden 14 L5
Robāţ-e Posht-e Bādām Iran 35 I4
Robāţ Karīm Iran 35 H4
Robāţ Tork Iran 35 H4
Robbins Island Australia 57 [inset]
Robe Australia 57 B8
Robe r. Australia 54 A5
Robe r. Ireland 21 C4
Robert-Bourassa, Réservoir resr Que. Canada 61 K4
Robert Glacier Antarctica 76 D2
Roberts, Mount Australia 58 F2
Roberts Butte mt. Antarctica 76 H2
Robertsfors Sweden 14 L4
Robertsganj India 37 E4
Robertson S. Africa 50 D7
Robertson Bay Antarctica 76 H2
Robertson Island Antarctica 76 A2
Robertson Range hills Australia 55 C5
Robertsport Liberia 46 B4
Roberval Que. Canada 63 M2
Robhanais, Rubha hd U.K. see **Butt of Lewis**
Robin Hood's Bay U.K. 18 G4
Robinson Ranges hills Australia 55 B6
Robinson River Australia 56 B3
Robson, Mount B.C. Canada 62 D1
Roçadas Angola see **Xangongo**
Rocha Uruguay 70 F4
Rochdale U.K. 18 E5
Rochechouart France 24 E4
Rochefort France 24 D4
Rochegda Russia 12 I3
Rochester Australia 58 B6
Rochester U.K. 19 H7
Rochester MN U.S.A. 63 I3
Rochester NH U.S.A. 64 F1
Rochester NY U.S.A. 64 C1
Rochford U.K. 19 H7
Roc'h Trévezel h. France 24 C2
Rockall i. N. Atlantic Ocean 10 D4
Rockall Bank sea feature N. Atlantic Ocean 72 G2
Rock Creek OH U.S.A. 64 A2
Rockefeller Plateau Antarctica 76 J1
Rockford IL U.S.A. 63 J3
Rockhampton Australia 56 E4
Rockhampton Downs Australia 54 F4
Rockingham Australia 55 A8
Rockingham Bay Australia 56 D3
Rock Island IL U.S.A. 63 I3
Rockland MA U.S.A. 64 F1
Rocksprings TX U.S.A. 62 G6
Rockstone Guyana 69 G2
Rockville CT U.S.A. 64 E2
Rockville MD U.S.A. 64 C3
Rockwood PA U.S.A. 64 B3
Rocky Mount VA U.S.A. 64 B4
Rocky Mountains Canada/U.S.A. 62 F3
Rødberg Norway 15 F6
Rødbyhavn Denmark 15 G9
Rodeio Brazil 71 A4
Rodel U.K. 20 C3
Rodeo Arg. 70 C4
Rodez France 24 F4
Ródhos i. Greece see **Rhodes**
Rodi i. Greece see **Rhodes**
Rodney, Cape AK U.S.A. 60 B3
Rodniki Russia 12 I4
Rodopi Planina mts Bulg./Greece see **Rhodope Mountains**
Rodos Greece see **Rhodes**
Rodos i. Greece see **Rhodes**
Rodosto Turkey see **Tekirdağ**
Rodrigues Island Mauritius 73 M7
Roe r. U.K. 21 F2
Roebourne Australia 54 B5
Roebuck Bay Australia 54 C4
Roedtan S. Africa 51 I3
Roe Plains Australia 55 D7
Roeselare Belgium 16 I5
Roes Welcome Sound sea chan. Nunavut Canada 61 J3
Rogachev Belarus see **Rahachow**
Rogers Lake CA U.S.A. 65 D3
Roggeveen Basin sea feature S. Pacific Ocean 75 O8
Roggeveld plat. S. Africa 50 E7
Roggeveldberge esc. S. Africa 50 E7
Roghadal U.K. see **Rodel**
Rognan Norway 14 I3
Roha India 38 B2
Rohnert Park CA U.S.A. 65 A1
Rohrbach in Oberösterreich Austria 17 N6
Rohri Sangar Pak. 36 B4
Rohtak India 36 D3
Roi Georges, Îles du is Fr. Polynesia 75 K6
Rois-Bheinn h. U.K. 20 D4
Roja Latvia 15 M8
Rojas Arg. 70 D4
Rokeby Australia 56 C2
Rokeby National Park Australia 56 C2
Rokiškis Lith. 15 N9
Roknäs Sweden 14 L4
Rokytne Ukr. 13 E6
Rolagang China 37 G2
Rola Kangri mt. China 37 G2
Rolândia Brazil 71 A3
Rolim de Moura Brazil 68 F6
Roll AZ U.S.A. 65 F4
Rolla MO U.S.A. 63 I4
Rollag Norway 15 F6
Rolleston Australia 56 E5
Roma Australia 57 E5
Roma Italy see **Rome**
Roma Lesotho 51 H5
Roma Sweden 15 K8
Romain, Cape SC U.S.A. 63 L5
Roman Romania 27 L1
Românâ, Câmpia plain Romania 27 J2
Romanche Gap sea feature S. Atlantic Ocean 72 G6
Romang, Pulau i. Indon. 41 E8
Romania country Europe 27 K2
Roman-Kosh mt. Ukr. 34 D1
Romanovka Russia 43 K2
Romans-sur-Isère France 24 G4
Romanzof, Cape AK U.S.A. 60 B3
Rombas France 24 H2
Romblon Phil. 41 E6
Rome Italy 26 E4
Rome GA U.S.A. 63 J5
Rome NY U.S.A. 64 D1
Romford U.K. 19 H7
Romilly-sur-Seine France 24 F2
Romney WV U.S.A. 64 B3
Romney Marsh reg. U.K. 19 H7
Romny Ukr. 13 G6
Rømø i. Denmark 15 F9
Romodanovo Russia 13 J5
Romorantin-Lanthenay France 24 E3
Romsey U.K. 19 F8
Ron India 38 B3
Rona i. U.K. 20 D1
Ronas Hill h. U.K. 20 [inset]
Roncador, Serra do hills Brazil 69 H6
Roncador Reef Solomon Is 53 F2
Ronda Spain 25 D5
Ronda, Serranía de mts Spain 25 D5
Rondane Nasjonalpark nat. park Norway 15 F6
Rondon Brazil 70 F2
Rondonópolis Brazil 69 H7
Rondout Reservoir NY U.S.A. 64 D2
Rong Chu r. China 37 G3
Rongelap atoll Marshall Is 74 H5
Rongklang Range mts Myanmar 37 H5
Rongwo China see **Tongren**
Rongyul China 37 I3
Rōnlap atoll Marshall Is see **Rongelap**
Rønne Denmark 15 I9
Ronneby Sweden 15 I8
Ronne Entrance str. Antarctica 76 L2
Ronne Ice Shelf Antarctica 76 L1
Rooke Island P.N.G. see **Umboi**
Roorkee India 36 D3
Roosendaal Neth. 16 J5
Roosevelt, Mount B.C. Canada 60 F4
Roosevelt Sub-glacial Island Antarctica 76 I1
Ropar India see **Rupnagar**
Roper r. Australia 56 A2
Roper Bar Australia 54 F3
Roquefort France 24 D4
Roraima, Mount Guyana 68 F2
Rori India 36 C3
Røros Norway 14 G5
Rørvik Norway 14 G4
Rosamond CA U.S.A. 65 C3
Rosamond Lake CA U.S.A. 65 C3
Rosario Arg. 70 D4
Rosário Brazil 69 J4
Rosario Baja California Mex. 66 A2
Rosario Sinaloa Mex. 66 C4
Rosario Sonora Mex. 62 F6
Rosario Venez. 68 D1
Rosário do Sul Brazil 70 F4
Rosário Oeste Brazil 69 G6
Rosarito Mex. 62 E6
Rosarno Italy 26 F5
Roscoff France 24 C2
Roscommon Ireland 21 D4
Roscrea Ireland 21 E5
Rose r. Australia 56 A2
Rose Atoll American Samoa see **Rose Island**
Roseau Dominica 67 L5
Roseberth Australia 57 B5
Roseburg OR U.S.A. 62 C3
Rosedale Abbey U.K. 18 G4
Roseires Reservoir Sudan 32 D7
Rose Island atoll American Samoa 53 J3
Rosenberg TX U.S.A. 63 H6
Rosendal Norway 15 E7
Rosendal S. Africa 51 H5
Rosenheim Germany 17 N7
Roseto degli Abruzzi Italy 26 F3
Rosetown Sask. Canada 62 F1
Rosetta Egypt see **Rashīd**
Roseville CA U.S.A. 65 B1
Rosewood Australia 58 F1
Roshchino Russia 15 P6
Rosh Pinah Namibia 50 C4
Roshtkala Tajik. see **Roshtqal'a**
Roshtqal'a Tajik. 36 B1
Rosignano Marittimo Italy 26 D3
Roșiori de Vede Romania 27 K2
Roskilde Denmark 15 H9
Roslavl' Russia 13 G5
Roslyakovo Russia 14 R2
Roslyatino Russia 12 J4
Ross N.Z. 59 C6
Ross, Mount h. N.Z. 59 E5
Rossano Italy 26 G5
Rossan Point Ireland 21 D3
Rosscarbery Ireland 21 C6
Ross Dependency Antarctica 76 I2
Rossel Island P.N.G. 56 F1
Ross Ice Shelf Antarctica 76 I1
Rössing Namibia 50 B2
Ross Island Antarctica 76 H1
Rossiyskaya Sovetskaya Federativnaya Sotsialisticheskaya Respublika country Asia/Europe see **Russia**
Rosslare Ireland 21 F5
Rosslare Harbour Ireland 21 F5
Rosso Mauritania 46 B3
Ross-on-Wye U.K. 19 E7
Rossony Belarus see **Rasony**
Rossosh' Russia 13 H6
Ross River Y.T. Canada 60 E3
Ross Sea Antarctica 76 H1
Røssvatnet l. Norway 14 I4
Rostāq Iran 35 I6
Rosthern Sask. Canada 62 F1
Rostock Germany 17 N3
Rostov Russia 12 H4
Rostov-na-Donu Russia 13 H7
Rostov-on-Don Russia see **Rostov-na-Donu**
Rosvik Sweden 14 L4
Roswell NM U.S.A. 62 G5
Rota i. N. Mariana Is 41 G6
Rotch Island Kiribati see **Tamana**
Rote i. Indon. 41 E9
Roth Germany 17 M6
Rothbury U.K. 18 F3
Rothenburg ob der Tauber Germany 17 M6
Rother r. U.K. 19 G8
Rothera (U.K.) research stn Antarctica 76 L2
Rotherham U.K. 18 F5
Rothes U.K. 20 F3
Rothesay U.K. 20 D5
Rothwell U.K. 19 G6
Roti Indon. 54 C2
Roti i. Indon. see **Rote**
Roto Australia 58 B4
Rotomagus France see **Rouen**
Rotomanu N.Z. 59 C6
Rotondo, Monte mt. Corsica France 24 I5
Rotorua N.Z. 59 F4
Rotorua, Lake N.Z. 59 F4
Rottenmann Austria 17 O7
Rotterdam Neth. 16 J5
Rottnest Island Australia 55 A8
Rottweil Germany 17 L6
Rotuma i. Fiji 53 H3
Rötviken Sweden 14 I5
Roubaix France 24 F1
Rouen France 24 E2
Roulers Belgium see **Roeselare**
Roumania country Europe see **Romania**
Round Hill h. U.K. 18 F4
Round Mountain Australia 58 F3
Roundup MT U.S.A. 62 F2
Rousay i. U.K. 20 F1
Rouxville S. Africa 51 H6
Rouyn-Noranda Que. Canada 63 L2
Rovaniemi Fin. 14 N3
Roven'ki Russia 13 H6
Rovereto Italy 26 D2
Rovigo Italy 26 D2
Rovinj Croatia 26 E2
Rovno Ukr. see **Rivne**
Rovnoye Russia 13 J6
Rovuma r. Moz./Tanz. see **Ruvuma**
Rowena Australia 58 D2
Rowley Island Nunavut Canada 61 K3
Rowley Shoals sea feature Australia 54 B4
Równe Ukr. see **Rivne**
Roxburgh N.Z. 59 B7
Roxburgh Island Cook Is see **Rarotonga**
Roxby Downs Australia 57 B6
Roxo, Cabo c. Senegal 46 B3
Royal Canal Ireland 21 E4
Royal Chitwan National Park Nepal 37 F4
Royale, Île i. N.S. Canada see **Cape Breton Island**
Royale, Isle i. MI U.S.A. 63 J2
Royal Leamington Spa U.K. 19 F6
Royal Natal National Park S. Africa 51 I5
Royal National Park Australia 58 E5
Royal Sukla Phanta Wildlife Reserve Nepal 36 E3
Royal Tunbridge Wells U.K. 19 H7
Royan France 24 D4
Roy Hill Australia 54 B5
Royston U.K. 19 G6
Rozdil'na Ukr. 27 N1
Rozivka Ukr. 13 H7
Rtishchevo Russia 13 I5
Ruabon U.K. 19 D6
Ruaha National Park Tanz. 49 D4
Ruahine Range mts N.Z. 59 F5
Ruanda country Africa see **Rwanda**
Ruapehu, Mount vol. N.Z. 59 E4
Ruapuke Island N.Z. 59 B8
Ruatoria N.Z. 59 G3
Ruba Belarus 13 F5
Rub' al Khālī des. Saudi Arabia 32 G6
Rubtsovsk Russia 42 E2
Ruby AK U.S.A. 60 C3
Ruckersville VA U.S.A. 64 B3
Rudall River National Park Australia 54 C5
Rudarpur India 37 E4
Ruda Śląska Poland 17 Q5
Rudauli India 37 E4
Rūdbār Iran 35 H3
Rudkøbing Denmark 15 G9
Rudnaya Pristan' Russia 44 D3
Rudnichnyy Russia 12 L4
Rudnya Smolenskaya Oblast' Russia 13 F5
Rudnya Volgogradskaya Oblast' Russia 13 J6
Rudnyy Kazakh. 30 F1
Rudolf, Lake salt l. Eth./Kenya see **Turkana, Lake**
Rudol'fa, Ostrov i. Russia 28 G1
Rudolph Island Russia see **Rudol'fa, Ostrov**
Rūdsar Iran 35 H3
Rue France 19 I8
Rufiji r. Tanz. 49 D4
Rufino Arg. 70 D4
Rufisque Senegal 46 B3
Rufunsa Zambia 49 C5
Rugao China 43 M6
Rugby U.K. 19 F6
Rugby ND U.S.A. 62 G2
Rugeley U.K. 19 F6
Rügen i. Germany 17 N3
Ruhengeri Rwanda 48 C4
Ruhnu i. Estonia 15 M8
Ruhuna National Park Sri Lanka see **Yala National Park**
Ruijin China 43 L7
Ruipa Tanz. 49 D4
Ruiz Mex. 66 C4
Ruiz, Nevado del vol. Col. 68 C3
Rujaylah, Ḩarrat ar lava field Jordan 39 C3
Rūjiena Latvia 15 N8
Ruk is Micronesia see **Chuuk**
Rukumkot Nepal 37 E3
Rukwa, Lake Tanz. 49 D4
Rum i. U.K. 20 C4
Rum, Jebel mts Jordan see **Ramm, Jabal**
Ruma Serbia 27 H2
Rumāh Saudi Arabia 32 G4
Rumania country Europe see **Romania**
Rumbek South Sudan 47 F4
Rum Cay i. Bahamas 67 J4
Rum Jungle (abandoned) Australia 54 E3
Rummānā h. Syria 39 D3
Rumphi Malawi 49 D5
Runaway, Cape N.Z. 59 F3
Runcorn U.K. 18 E5
Rundu Namibia 49 B5
Rundvik Sweden 14 K5
Rungwa Tanz. 49 D4
Rungwa r. Tanz. 49 D4
Runton Range hills Australia 55 C5
Ruokolahti Fin. 15 P6
Ruoqiang China 42 F5
Rupa India 37 H4
Rupert r. Que. Canada 63 L1
Rupert WV U.S.A. 64 A4
Rupert Bay Que. Canada 63 L1
Rupert Coast Antarctica 76 J1
Rupert House Que. Canada see **Waskaganish**
Rupnagar India 36 D3
Rupshu reg. India 36 D2
Ruqqād, Wādī ar watercourse Israel 39 B3
Rural Retreat VA U.S.A. 64 A4
Rusaddir N. Africa see **Melilla**
Rusape Zimbabwe 49 D5
Ruschuk Bulg. see **Ruse**
Ruse Bulg. 27 K3
Rusera India 37 F4
Rushden U.K. 19 G6
Rushinga Zimbabwe 49 D5
Rushville NE U.S.A. 62 G3
Rushworth Australia 58 B6
Russell N.Z. 59 E2
Russell PA U.S.A. 64 B2
Russell Bay Antarctica 76 J2
Russell Range hills Australia 55 C8
Russellville AR U.S.A. 63 I4
Rüsselsheim Germany 17 L5
Russia country Asia/Europe 28 I3
Russian r. CA U.S.A. 65 A1
Russian Federation country Asia/Europe see **Russia**
Russian Soviet Federal Socialist Republic country Asia/Europe see **Russia**
Russkiy, Ostrov i. Russia 44 C4
Russkiy Kameshkir Russia 13 J5
Rustāq Afgh. 36 B1
Rustavi Georgia 35 G2
Rustburg VA U.S.A. 64 B4
Rustenburg S. Africa 51 H3
Ruston LA U.S.A. 63 I5
Rutanzige, Lake Dem. Rep. Congo/Uganda see **Edward, Lake**
Ruteng Indon. 41 E8
Rutherglen Australia 58 C6
Ruther Glen VA U.S.A. 64 C4
Ruthin U.K. 19 D5
Ruthiyai India 36 D4
Rutka r. Russia 12 J4
Rutland VT U.S.A. 64 E1
Rutland Water resr U.K. 19 G6
Rutög China see **Dêrub**
Rutog Xizang China 37 F3
Rutog Xizang China 42 G7
Rutul Russia 35 G2
Ruukki Fin. 14 N4
Ruwayshid, Wādī watercourse Jordan 39 C3
Ruwayţah, Wādī watercourse Jordan 39 C5
Ruwenzori National Park Uganda see **Queen Elizabeth National Park**
Ruy Barbosa Brazil 71 C1
Rūy Dūāb Wuluswālī Afgh. 36 A2
Ruza Russia 12 H5
Ruzayevka Kazakh. 30 F1
Ruzayevka Russia 13 J5
Ružomberok Slovakia 17 Q6
Rwanda country Africa 48 C4
Ryan, Loch b. U.K. 20 D5
Ryazan' Russia 13 H5
Ryazhsk Russia 13 I5
Rybachiy, Poluostrov pen. Russia 12 G1
Rybach'ye Kyrg. see **Balykchy**
Rybinsk Russia 12 H4
Rybinskoye Vodokhranilishche resr Russia 12 H4
Rybnik Poland 17 Q5
Rybnitsa Moldova see **Rîbnița**
Rybnoye Russia 13 H5
Rybreka Russia 12 G3
Ryd Sweden 15 I8
Rydberg Peninsula Antarctica 76 L2
Ryde U.K. 19 F8
Rye U.K. 19 H8
Rye r. U.K. 18 G4
Rye Bay U.K. 19 H8
Rykovo Ukr. see **Yenakiyeve**
Ryl'sk Russia 13 G6
Rylstone Australia 58 D4
Ryn-Peski des. Kazakh. 11 P6
Ryukyu Islands Japan 45 B8
Ryūkyū-rettō is Japan see **Ryukyu Islands**
Ryukyu Trench sea feature N. Pacific Ocean 74 E4
Rzeszów Poland 13 D6
Rzhaksa Russia 13 I5
Rzhev Russia 12 G4

S

Sa'ādah al Barşā' pass Saudi Arabia 39 C5
Saale r. Germany 17 M5
Saalfeld/Saale Germany 17 M5
Saarbrücken Germany 17 K6
Saaremaa i. Estonia 15 M7
Saarenkylä Fin. 14 N3
Saarijärvi Fin. 14 N5
Saari-Kämä Fin. 14 O3
Saarikoski Fin. 14 L2
Saaristomeren kansallispuisto nat. park Fin. see **Skärgårdshavets nationalpark**
Saarlouis Germany 17 K6
Saatlı Azer. 35 H3
Saatly Azer. see **Saatlı**
Sab'a Egypt see **Saba'ah**
Saba'ah Egypt 39 A4
Sab' Ābār Syria 39 C3
Šabac Serbia 27 H2
Sabadell Spain 25 H3
Sabae Japan 45 E6
Sabana, Archipiélago de is Cuba 67 H4
Şabanözü Turkey 34 D2
Sabará Brazil 71 C2
Sabasţīyah West Bank 39 B3
Sab'atayn, Ramlat as des. Yemen 32 G6
Sabaudia Italy 26 E4
Sabaya Bol. 68 E7
Sabelo S. Africa 50 F6
Şabḩā Jordan 39 C3
Sabhā Libya 47 E2
Sabhrai India 36 B5
Sabi r. India 36 D3
Sabi r. Moz./Zimbabwe see **Save**
Sabie Moz. 51 K3
Sabie r. Moz./S. Africa 51 K3
Sabie S. Africa 51 J3
Sabinas Mex. 66 D3
Sabinas Hidalgo Mex. 66 D3
Sabini, Monti mts Italy 26 E3
Sabirabad Azer. 35 H2
Sabkhat al Bardawīl Reserve nature res. Egypt see **Lake Bardawil Reserve**
Sable, Cape N.S. Canada 61 L5
Sable, Cape FL U.S.A. 63 K6
Sable Island N.S. Canada 61 M5
Sabon Kafi Niger 46 D3
Şabran Azer. 35 H2
Sabrina Coast Antarctica 76 F2
Sabugal Port. 25 C3
Şabyā Saudi Arabia 32 F6
Sabzawar Afgh. see **Shīndand**
Sabzevār Iran 33 I2
Sabzvārān Iran see **Jīroft**
Sacalinul Mare, Insula i. Romania 27 M2
Săcele Romania 27 K2
Sacheon S. Korea 45 C6
Sachigo Lake Ont. Canada 63 I1
Sachin India 36 C5
Sach Pass India 36 D2
Sachs Harbour N.W.T. Canada 60 F2
Sacirsuyu r. Syria/Turkey see **Sājūr, Nahr**
Saco ME U.S.A. 64 F1
Sacramento Brazil 71 B2
Sacramento CA U.S.A. 65 B1
Sacramento r. CA U.S.A. 65 B1
Sacramento Mountains NM U.S.A. 62 F5
Sada S. Africa 51 H7
Sádaba Spain 25 F2
Sá da Bandeira Angola see **Lubango**
Şadad Syria 39 C2
Şa'dah Yemen 32 F6
Saddat al Hindīyah Iraq 35 G4
Saddle Hill h. Australia 56 D2
Sadêng China 37 H3
Sadiola Mali 46 B3
Sadiqabad Pak. 36 B3
Sad Ishtrāgh mt. Afgh./Pak. 36 C1
Sa'dīyah, Hawr as imp. l. Iraq 35 G4
Sado r. Port. 25 B4
Sadoga-shima i. Japan 45 E5
Sadot Egypt see **Sadūt (abandoned)**
Sadovoye Russia 13 J7
Sa Dragonera i. Spain 25 H4
Sadras India 38 D3
Sadût Egypt see **Sadūt (abandoned)**
Sadūt (abandoned) Egypt 39 B4
Sæby Denmark 15 G8
Saena Julia Italy see **Siena**
Safad Israel see **Zefat**
Şafāshahr Iran 35 I5
Safayal Maqūf well Iraq 35 G5
Safed Koh mts Afgh. see **Sefīd Kūh**
Sāfed Kōh mts Afgh./Pak. 36 B2
Safēd Kōh, Silsilah-ye mts Afgh. 33 J2
Saffānīyah, Ra's as hd Saudi Arabia 35 H5
Säffle Sweden 15 H7
Safford AZ U.S.A. 62 F5
Saffron Walden U.K. 19 H6
Safi Morocco 22 C5
Safīdār, Kūh-e mt. Iran 35 I5
Safid Kūh mts Afgh. see **Safēd Kōh, Silsilah-ye**
Safiras, Serra das mts Brazil 71 C2
Şāfītā Syria 39 C2
Safonovo Arkhangel'skaya Oblast' Russia 12 K2
Safonovo Smolenskaya Oblast' Russia 13 G5
Safranbolu Turkey 34 D2
Saga China 37 F3
Saga Japan 45 C6
Sagaing Myanmar 37 H5
Sagami-nada g. Japan 45 E6
Sagamore PA U.S.A. 64 B2
Sagar Karnataka India 38 B3
Sagar Karnataka India 38 C2
Sagar Madh. Prad. India 36 D5
Sagaredzho Georgia see **Sagarejo**
Sagarejo Georgia 35 G2
Sagar Island India 37 G5
Sagarmatha National Park Nepal 37 F4
Sagastyr Russia 29 N2
Sagavanirktok r. AK U.S.A. 60 D2
Saggi, Har mt. Israel 39 B4
Sāghand Iran 35 I4
Saginaw MI U.S.A. 63 K3
Saginaw Bay MI U.S.A. 63 K3
Saglouc Que. Canada see **Salluit**
Sagone, Golfe de b. Corsica France 24 I5
Sagres Port. 25 B5
Sagthale India 36 C5
Sagua la Grande Cuba 67 H4
Saguenay r. Que. Canada 63 N2
Sagunt Spain see **Sagunto**
Sagunto Spain 25 F4
Saguntum Spain see **Sagunto**
Sagzī Iran 35 I4
Sahagún Spain 25 D2
Sahand, Kūh-e mt. Iran 35 G3
Sahara des. Africa 46 D3
Ăaḥara el Gharbîya des. Egypt see **Western Desert**
Ăaḥara el Sharqîya des. Egypt see **Eastern Desert**
Saharan Atlas mts Alg. see **Atlas Saharien**
Saharanpur India 36 D3
Sahara Well Australia 54 C5
Saharsa India 37 F4
Sahaswan India 36 D3
Sahat, Kūh-e h. Iran 35 I4
Sahatwar India 37 F4
Şahbuz Azer. 35 G3
Sahdol India see **Shahdol**
Sahebganj India see **Sahibganj**
Sahebgunj India see **Sahibganj**
Saheira, Wâdi el watercourse Egypt see **Suhaymī, Wādī as**
Sahel reg. Africa 46 C3
Sahibganj India 37 F4
Sahiwal Pak. 36 C3
Sahlābād Iran 33 I3
Şaḩneh Iran 35 G4
Şaḩrā al Ḩijārah reg. Iraq 35 G5
Sahuayo Mex. 66 D4
Sahuteng China see **Zadoi**
Sahyadri mts India see **Western Ghats**
Sahyadriparvat Range hills India 38 B1
Sai r. India 37 E4
Saïda Alg. 25 G6
Saïda Lebanon see **Sidon**
Saïdia Morocco 25 E6
Sa'īdīyeh Iran see **Solţānīyeh**
Saidpur Bangl. 37 G4
Saiha India 37 H5
Saihan Tal China 43 K4
Saijō Japan 45 D6
Saikai Kokuritsu-kōen Japan 45 C6
Saiki Japan 45 C6
Sailana India 36 C5
Saimaa l. Fin. 15 P6
Saimbeyli Turkey 34 E3
Sa'īndezh Iran see **Shāhīn Dezh**
Sa'īn Qal'eh Iran see **Shāhīn Dezh**
St Abb's Head hd U.K. 20 G5
St Agnes U.K. 19 B8
St Agnes i. U.K. 19 A9
St Albans U.K. 19 G7
St Aldhelm's Head hd U.K. 19 E8
St-Amand-Montrond France 24 F3
St-Amour France 24 G3
St-André, Cap c. Madag. see **Vilanandro, Tanjona**
St Andrews U.K. 20 G4
St Ann's Bay Jamaica 67 I5
St Anthony Nfld. and Lab. Canada 61 M4
St Anthony ID U.S.A. 62 E3
St-Arnaud Alg. see **El Eulma**
St Arnaud Australia 58 A6
St Arnaud Range mts N.Z. 59 D6
St Augustin r. Nfld. and Lab./Que. Canada 61 M4
St Augustine FL U.S.A. 63 K6
St Austell U.K. 19 C8
St-Avertin France 24 E3
St-Barthélemy terr. West Indies 67 L5
St Bees U.K. 18 D4
St Bees Head hd U.K. 18 D4
St Bride's Bay U.K. 19 B7
St-Brieuc France 24 C2

St Catharines Ont. Canada 64 B1
St Catherine's Point U.K. 19 F8
St-Céré France 24 E4
St-Chamond France 24 G4
St Charles MD U.S.A. 64 C3
St Charles MO U.S.A. 63 I4
St-Chély-d'Apcher France 24 F4
St Christopher and Nevis country West Indies see St Kitts and Nevis
St Clair, Lake Canada/U.S.A. 63 K3
St-Claude France 24 G3
St Clears U.K. 19 C7
St Cloud MN U.S.A. 63 I2
St Croix r. WI U.S.A. 63 I2
St David's Head hd U.K. 19 B7
St-Denis Réunion 73 L7
St-Denis-du-Sig Alg. see Sig
St-Dié-des-Vosges France 24 H2
St-Dizier France 24 G2
St-Domingue country West Indies see Haiti
St Elias, Cape AK U.S.A. 60 D4
St Elias Mountains Y.T. Canada 60 D3
Ste-Marie, Cap c. Madag. see Vohimena, Tanjona
Sainte-Marie, Île i. Madag. see Boraha, Nosy
Ste-Maxime France 24 H5
Sainte Rose du Lac Man. Canada 62 H1
Saintes France 24 D4
St-Étienne France 24 G4
St-Étienne-du-Rouvray France 19 I9
Saintfield U.K. 21 G3
St-Florent Corsica France 24 I5
St-Florent-sur-Cher France 24 F3
St-Flour France 24 F4
St Francis KS U.S.A. 62 G4
St Francis Isles Australia 55 F8
St-Gaudens France 24 E5
St George Australia 58 D2
St George r. Australia 56 D3
St George AK U.S.A. 60 B4
St George UT U.S.A. 65 F2
St George Island AK U.S.A. 60 B4
St George Range hills Australia 54 D4
St George's Grenada 67 L6
St George's Channel Ireland/U.K. 21 F6
St George's Channel P.N.G. 52 F2
St George's Head hd Australia 58 E5
St Gotthard Hungary see Szentgotthárd
St Gotthard Pass Switz. 24 I3
St Govan's Head hd U.K. 19 C7
St Helena i. S. Atlantic Ocean 72 H7
St Helena CA U.S.A. 65 A1
St Helena, Ascension and Tristan da Cunha terr. S. Atlantic Ocean 72 H7
St Helena Bay S. Africa 50 D7
St Helens Australia 57 [inset]
St Helens U.K. 18 E5
St Helens, Mount vol. WA U.S.A. 62 C2
St Helens Point Australia 57 [inset]
St Helier Channel Is 19 E9
Sainthiya India 37 F5
St Ignace MI U.S.A. 63 K2
St Ignace Island Ont. Canada 63 J2
St Ishmael U.K. 19 C7
St Ives England U.K. 19 B8
St Ives England U.K. 19 G6
St James, Cape B.C. Canada 60 E4
St-Jean, Lac l. Que. Canada 63 M2
St-Jean-d'Acre Israel see 'Akko
St-Jean-d'Angély France 24 D4
St-Jean-de-Monts France 24 C3
St-Jérôme Que. Canada 63 M2
St Joe r. ID U.S.A. 62 D2
Saint John N.B. Canada 63 N2
St John r. ME U.S.A. 63 N2
St John's Antigua and Barbuda 67 L5
St John's Nfld. and Lab. Canada 61 M5
St Johns AZ U.S.A. 62 F5
St Johnsbury VT U.S.A. 63 M3
St John's Chapel U.K. 18 E4
St Joseph MO U.S.A. 63 I4
St Joseph, Lake Ont. Canada 63 I1
St-Joseph-d'Alma Que. Canada see Alma
St-Junien France 24 E4
St Just U.K. 19 B8
St Keverne U.K. 19 B8
St Kilda i. U.K. 10 E4
St Kilda is U.K. 16 C2
St Kitts and Nevis country West Indies 67 L5
St-Laurent inlet Que. Canada see St Lawrence
St-Laurent, Golfe du g. Que. Canada see St Lawrence, Gulf of
St-Laurent-du-Maroni Fr. Guiana 69 H2
St Lawrence inlet Que. Canada 61 L5
St Lawrence, Gulf of Que. Canada 61 L5
St Lawrence Island AK U.S.A. 60 B3
St Leonard MD U.S.A. 64 C3
St-Lô France 24 D2
St-Louis Senegal 46 B3
St Louis MO U.S.A. 63 I4
St Louis r. MN U.S.A. 63 I2
St Lucia country West Indies 67 L6
St Lucia, Lake S. Africa 51 K5
St Lucia Estuary S. Africa 51 K5
St Magnus Bay U.K. 20 [inset]
St-Maixent-l'École France 24 D3
St-Malo France 24 C2
St-Malo, Golfe de g. France 24 C2
St-Marc Haiti 67 J5
St Marks S. Africa 51 H7
St Mark's S. Africa see Cofimvaba
St-Martin terr. West Indies 67 L5
St Martin, Cape S. Africa 50 C7
St Martin's i. U.K. 19 A9
St Mary Peak Australia 57 B6
St Mary's Ont. Canada 64 A1
St Mary's U.K. 20 G2
St Mary's i. U.K. 19 A9
St Marys PA U.S.A. 64 B2
St Marys WV U.S.A. 64 A3
St Marys City MD U.S.A. 64 C3
St Matthew Island AK U.S.A. 60 A3
St Matthias Group is P.N.G. 52 E2
St-Maurice r. Que. Canada 63 M2
St Mawes U.K. 19 B8
St-Médard-en-Jalles France 24 D4
St Michaels MD U.S.A. 64 C3
St-Nazaire France 24 C3
St Neots U.K. 19 G6
St-Nicolas Belgium see Sint-Niklaas
St-Nicolas-de-Port France 24 H2
St-Omer France 24 F1
Saintonge reg. France 24 D4
St-Palais France 24 D5
St-Paul atoll Fr. Polynesia see Hereheretue
St Paul AK U.S.A. 60 A4
St Paul MN U.S.A. 63 I3
St-Paul, Île i. Indian Ocean 73 N8
St Paul Island AK U.S.A. 60 A4
St Peter and St Paul Rocks is N. Atlantic Ocean see São Pedro e São Paulo
St Peter Port Channel Is 19 E9
St Petersburg Russia 12 F4
St Petersburg FL U.S.A. 63 K6
St-Pierre mt. France 24 G5
St-Pierre St Pierre and Miquelon 61 M5
St Pierre and Miquelon terr. N. America 61 M5
St-Pierre-d'Oléron France 24 D4
St-Pierre-le-Moûtier France 24 F3
St-Pourçain-sur-Sioule France 24 F3
St-Quentin France 24 F2
St-Saëns France 19 I9
St Sebastian Bay S. Africa 50 E8
St-Siméon Que. Canada 63 N2
St Theresa Point Man. Canada 63 I1
St Thomas Ont. Canada 64 A1
St-Tropez France 24 H5
St-Tropez, Cap de c. France 24 H5
St-Vaast-la-Hougue France 19 F9
St-Valery-en-Caux France 19 H9
St-Véran France 24 H4
St Vincent country West Indies see St Vincent and the Grenadines
St Vincent, Cape Australia 57 [inset]
St Vincent, Cape Port. see São Vicente, Cabo de
St Vincent, Gulf Australia 57 B7
St Vincent and the Grenadines country West Indies 67 L6
St Vincent Passage St Lucia/St Vincent 67 L6
St Williams Ont. Canada 64 A1
St-Yrieix-la-Perche France 24 E4
Sain Us China 42 J4
Saioa mt. Spain 25 F2
Saipal mt. Nepal 36 E3
Saipan i. N. Mariana Is 41 G6
Saiteli Turkey see Kadınhanı
Saittanulkki h. Fin. 14 N3
Sajama, Nevado mt. Bol. 68 E7
Sājūr, Nahr r. Syria/Turkey 39 D1
Sak watercourse S. Africa 50 E5
Sakaide Japan 45 D6
Sakākah Saudi Arabia 35 F5
Sakakawea, Lake ND U.S.A. 62 G2
Sakar mts Bulg. 27 L4
Sakaraha Madag. 49 E6
Sak'art'velo country Asia see Georgia
Sakarya r. Turkey 27 N4
Sakassou Côte d'Ivoire 46 C4
Sakata Japan 45 E5
Sakchu N. Korea 45 B4
Sakhalin i. Russia 44 F2
Sakhalin Oblast admin. div. Russia see Sakhalinskaya Oblast'
Sakhalinskaya Oblast' admin. div. Russia 44 F2
Sakhalinskiy Zaliv b. Russia 44 F1
Sakhi India 36 C3
Sakhile S. Africa 51 I4
Şäki Azer. 35 G2
Saki Nigeria 46 D4
Saki Ukr. see Saky
Šakiai Lith. 15 M9
Sakir mt. Pak. 36 A3
Sakishima-shotō is Japan 43 M8
Sakoli India 36 D5
Sakon Nakhon Thai. 31 J5
Sakrivier S. Africa 50 E6
Sakura Japan 45 F6
Saky Ukr. 34 D1
Säkylä Fin. 15 M6
Sal i. Cape Verde 46 [inset]
Sal r. Russia 13 I7
Sala Sweden 15 J7
Salacgrīva Latvia 15 N8
Sala Consilina Italy 26 F4
Saladas Arg. 70 E3
Salado r. Buenos Aires Arg. 70 E5
Salado r. Santa Fe Arg. 70 D4
Salado r. Arg. 70 C5
Salaga Ghana 46 C4
Salairskiy Kryazh ridge Russia 42 E2
Salajwe Botswana 50 G2
Şalālah Oman 33 H6
Salamanca Mex. 66 D4
Salamanca Spain 25 D3
Salamanca NY U.S.A. 64 B1
Salamanga Moz. 51 K4
Salamantica Spain see Salamanca
Salamat, Bahr r. Chad 47 E4
Salamina i. Greece 27 J6
Salamis tourist site Cyprus 39 A2
Salamís i. Greece see Salamina
Salamīyah Syria 39 C2
Salang, Tōnal-e pass Afgh. 36 B2
Salantai Lith. 15 L8
Salar de Pocitos Arg. 70 C2
Salas Spain 25 C2
Salaspils Latvia 15 N8
Salawati i. Indon. 41 F8
Salawin, Mae Nam r. China/Myanmar see Salween
Salaya India 36 B5
Sala y Gómez, Isla i. S. Pacific Ocean 75 M7
Salazar Angola see N'dalatando
Salbris France 24 F3
Šalčininkai Lith. 15 N9
Salcombe U.K. 19 D8
Saldae Alg. see Bejaïa
Saldaña Spain 25 D2
Saldanha S. Africa 50 C7
Saldanha Bay S. Africa 50 C7
Saldus Latvia 15 M8
Sale Australia 58 C7
Şāleḩābād Iran 35 H4
Salekhard Russia 28 H3
Salem India 38 C4
Salem MA U.S.A. 64 F1
Salem NJ U.S.A. 64 D3
Salem NY U.S.A. 64 E1
Salem OH U.S.A. 64 A2
Salem OR U.S.A. 62 C3
Salem VA U.S.A. 64 A4
Salen Scotland U.K. 20 D4
Salen Scotland U.K. 20 D4
Salerno Italy 26 F4
Salerno, Golfo di g. Italy 26 F4
Salernum Italy see Salerno
Salford U.K. 18 E5
Salgótarján Hungary 17 Q6
Salgueiro Brazil 69 K5
Salida CO U.S.A. 62 F4
Salies-de-Béarn France 24 D5
Salihli Turkey 27 M5
Salihorsk Belarus 15 O10
Salima Malawi 49 D5
Salina KS U.S.A. 62 H4
Salina, Isola i. Italy 26 F5
Salina Cruz Mex. 66 E5
Salinas Brazil 71 C2
Salinas Ecuador 68 B4
Salinas Mex. 66 D4
Salinas CA U.S.A. 65 B2
Salinas r. CA U.S.A. 65 B2
Salinas, Cabo de c. Spain see Salines, Cap de ses
Salinas, Ponta das pt Angola 49 B5
Salines, Cap de ses c. Spain 25 H4
Saline Valley depr. CA U.S.A. 65 D2
Salinópolis Brazil 69 I4
Salinosó Lachay, Punta pt Peru 68 C6
Salisbury U.K. 19 F7
Salisbury MD U.S.A. 64 D3
Salisbury Zimbabwe see Harare
Salisbury Plain U.K. 19 E7
Şalkhad Syria 39 C3
Salla Fin. 14 P3
Salluit Que. Canada 77 K2
Sallum, Khalīj as b. Egypt 34 B5
Sallyana Nepal 37 E3
Salmās Iran 35 G3
Salmi Russia 12 F3
Salmon ID U.S.A. 62 E2
Salmon r. ID U.S.A. 62 D2
Salmon Arm B.C. Canada 62 D1
Salmon Gums Australia 55 C8
Salmon Reservoir NY U.S.A. 64 D1
Salmon River Mountains ID U.S.A. 62 D3
Salo Fin. 15 M6
Salome AZ U.S.A. 65 F4
Salon India 36 E4
Salon-de-Provence France 24 G5
Salonga Nord, Parc National de la nat. park Dem. Rep. Congo 48 C4
Salonica Greece see Thessaloniki
Salonika Greece see Thessaloniki
Salpausselkä reg. Fin. 15 N6
Salqīn Syria 39 C1
Salses, Étang de l. France see Leucate, Étang de
Sal'sk Russia 13 I7
Salsomaggiore Terme Italy 26 C2
Salt Jordan see As Salṭ
Salt watercourse S. Africa 50 F7
Salt r. AZ U.S.A. 62 E5
Salta Arg. 70 C2
Saltaire U.K. 18 F5
Saltash U.K. 19 C8
Saltcoats U.K. 20 E5
Saltee Islands Ireland 21 F5
Saltfjellet-Svartisen Nasjonalpark nat. park Norway 14 I3
Saltfjorden sea chan. Norway 14 H3
Salt Fork Lake OH U.S.A. 64 A2
Saltillo Mex. 66 D3
Salt Lake City UT U.S.A. 62 E3
Salto Brazil 71 B3
Salto Uruguay 70 E4
Salto da Divisa Brazil 71 D2
Salto Grande Brazil 71 A3
Salton Sea salt l. CA U.S.A. 65 E4
Salto Santiago, Represa de resr Brazil 70 F3
Salt Range hills Pak. 36 C2
Saluda VA U.S.A. 64 C4
Salûm Egypt see As Sallūm
Salûm, Khalîg el b. Egypt see Sallum, Khalīj as
Salur India 38 D2
Saluzzo Italy 26 B2
Salvador Brazil 71 D1
Salvador country Central America see El Salvador
Salvaleón de Higüey Dom. Rep. see Higüey
Salwah Saudi Arabia 48 F1
Salween r. China/Myanmar 31 I4
Salween r. China/Myanmar 42 H9
Salyan Azer. 35 H3
Salyan Nepal see Sallyana
Sal'yany Azer. see Salyan
Salzbrunn Namibia 50 C3
Salzburg Austria 17 N7
Salzgitter Germany 17 M4
Sam India 36 B4
Samagaltay Russia 42 G2
Samāh well Saudi Arabia 35 G5
Samaida Iran see Someydeh
Samaixung China 37 E2
Samalayuca Mex. 62 F5
Samalkot India 38 D2
Samâlût Egypt see Samālūṭ
Samālūṭ Egypt 34 C5
Samanala mt. Sri Lanka see Adam's Peak
Samandağı Turkey 39 B1
Samangān Afgh. see Aībak
Samani Japan 44 F4
Samanlı Dağları mts Turkey 27 M4
Samar Kazakh. see Samarskoye
Samar i. Phil. 41 E6
Samara Russia 13 K5
Samara r. Russia 11 Q5
Samarga Russia 44 E3
Samarinda Indon. 41 D8
Samarka Russia 44 D3
Samarobriva France see Amiens
Samarqand Uzbek. 33 K2
Sāmarrā' Iraq 35 F4
Samarskoye Kazakh. 42 E3
Samasata Pak. 36 B3
Samastipur India 37 F4
Şamaxı Azer. 35 H2
Samba India 36 C2
Sambaliung mts Indon. 41 D7
Sambalpur India 37 E5
Sambar, Tanjung pt Indon. 41 D8
Sambat Ukr. see Kiev
Sambava Madag. 49 F5
Sambha India 37 G4
Sambhajinagar India see Aurangabad
Sambhal India 36 D3
Sambhar Lake India 36 C4
Sambir Ukr. 13 D6
Sambito r. Brazil 69 J5
Sambor Ukr. see Sambir
Samborombón, Bahía b. Arg. 70 E5
Samcheok S. Korea 45 C5
Samch'ŏnp'o S. Korea see Sacheon
Same Tanz. 48 D4
Samer France 19 I8
Sami India 36 B5
Samīrah Saudi Arabia 32 F4
Samirum Iran see Īzad Khvāst
Samjiyŏn N. Korea 44 C4
Şämkir Azer. 35 G2
Sam Neua Laos see Xam Nua
Samoa country S. Pacific Ocean 53 I3
Samoa Basin sea feature S. Pacific Ocean 74 I7
Samoa i Sisifo country S. Pacific Ocean see Samoa
Samobor Croatia 26 F2
Samoded Russia 12 I3
Samokov Bulg. 27 J3
Šamorín Slovakia 17 P6
Samos i. Greece 27 L6
Samothrace i. Greece see Samothraki
Samothraki i. Greece 27 K4
Samoylovka Russia 13 I6
Sampit Indon. 41 D8
Sam Rayburn Reservoir TX U.S.A. 63 I5
Samsang China 37 E3
Samsun Turkey 34 E2
Samyai China 37 G3
San Mali 46 C3
Şan'ā' Yemen 32 F6
Sanaa Yemen see Şan'ā'
SANAE IV (South Africa) research stn Antarctica 76 B2
San Agostín FL U.S.A. see St Augustine
Sanak Island AK U.S.A. 60 B4
Sanandaj Iran 35 G4
San Andreas CA U.S.A. 65 B1
San Andrés, Isla de i. Caribbean Sea 67 H6
San Angelo TX U.S.A. 62 G5
San Antonio Chile 70 B4
San Antonio TX U.S.A. 62 H6
San Antonio, Cabo c. Cuba 67 H4
San Antonio Oeste Arg. 70 D6
San Antonio Reservoir CA U.S.A. 65 B3
San Augustín de Valle Fértil Arg. 70 C4
San Benedetto del Tronto Italy 26 E3
San Benedicto, Isla i. Mex. 66 B5
San Benito r. CA U.S.A. 65 B2
San Benito Mountain CA U.S.A. 65 B2
San Bernardino CA U.S.A. 65 D3
San Bernardino Mountains CA U.S.A. 65 D3
San Bernardo Chile 70 B4
San Blas, Cape FL U.S.A. 63 J6
San Borja Bol. 68 E6
Sanbornville NH U.S.A. 64 F1
San Buenaventura Mex. 66 D3
San Carlos Chile 70 B5
San Carlos Equat. Guinea see Luba
San Carlos Venez. 68 E2
San Carlos de Bariloche Arg. 70 B6
San Carlos de Bolívar Arg. 70 D5
Sanchahe China see Fuyu
Sanchakou China 42 H5
Sanchi India 36 D5
Sanchor India 36 B4
San Clemente CA U.S.A. 65 D4
San Clemente Island CA U.S.A. 65 C4
Sanclêr U.K. see St Clears
San Cristóbal Arg. 70 D4
San Cristobal i. Solomon Is 53 G3
San Cristóbal Venez. 68 D2
San Cristóbal, Isla i. Galápagos Ecuador 68 [inset]
San Cristóbal de las Casas Mex. 66 F5
Sancti Spíritus Cuba 67 I4
Sandagou Russia 44 D4
Sanda Island U.K. 20 D5
Sandakan Sabah Malaysia 41 D7
Sandane Norway 14 E6
Sandanski Bulg. 27 J4
Sandaré Mali 46 B3
Sanday i. U.K. 20 G1
Sandbach U.K. 19 E5
Sand Cay reef India 38 B4
Sandefjord Norway 15 G7
Sandercock Nunataks Antarctica 76 D2
Sanderson TX U.S.A. 62 G5
Sandfire Roadhouse Australia 54 C4
Sand Fork WV U.S.A. 64 A3
Sandgate Australia 58 F1
Sandhead U.K. 20 E6
Sandia Peru 68 E6
San Diego CA U.S.A. 65 D4
Sandıklı Turkey 27 N5
Sandila India 36 E4
Sandnes Norway 15 D7
Sandnessjøen Norway 14 H3
Sandø i. Faroe Is see Sandoy
Sandoa Dem. Rep. Congo 49 C4
Sandomierz Poland 13 D6
San Donà di Piave Italy 26 E2
Sandover watercourse Australia 56 B4
Sandovo Russia 12 H4
Sandown U.K. 19 F8
Sandoy i. Faroe Is 14 [inset 1]
Sand Point AK U.S.A. 60 B4
Sandpoint ID U.S.A. 62 D2
Sandray i. U.K. 20 B4
Sandringham Australia 56 B5
Şandrul Mare, Vârful mt. Romania 27 L1
Sandsjö Sweden 15 I6
Sandstone Australia 55 B6
Sandur Faroe Is 14 [inset 1]
Sandusky OH U.S.A. 63 K3
Sandveld mts S. Africa 50 D6
Sandverhaar Namibia 50 C4
Sandvika Akershus Norway 15 G7
Sandvika Nord-Trøndelag Norway 14 H5
Sandviken Sweden 15 J6
Sandwich Island Vanuatu see Éfaté
Sandwich Islands N. Pacific Ocean see Hawai'ian Islands
Sandwick U.K. 20 [inset]
Sandwip Bangl. 37 G5
Sandy Cape Qld Australia 56 F5
Sandy Cape Tas. Australia 57 [inset]
Sandy Hook pt NJ U.S.A. 64 D2
Sandy Island Australia 54 C3
Sandy Lake Ont. Canada 63 I1
Sandy Lake Ont. Canada 63 I1
San Estanislao Para. 70 E2
San Felipe Chile 70 B4
San Felipe Mex. 66 B2
San Felipe Venez. 68 E1
San Felipe de Puerto Plata Dom. Rep. see Puerto Plata
San Fernando Chile 70 B4
San Fernando Mex. 66 E4
San Fernando Phil. 41 E6
San Fernando Spain 25 C5
San Fernando Trin. and Tob. 67 L6
San Fernando CA U.S.A. 65 C3
San Fernando de Apure Venez. 68 E2
San Fernando de Atabapo Venez. 68 E3
San Fernando de Monte Cristi Dom. Rep. see Monte Cristi
Sanford FL U.S.A. 63 K6
Sanford ME U.S.A. 64 F1
Sanford NC U.S.A. 63 L4
Sanford, Mount AK U.S.A. 60 D3
San Francisco Arg. 70 D4
San Francisco CA U.S.A. 65 A2
San Francisco, Cabo de c. Ecuador 68 B3
San Francisco, Passo de pass Arg./Chile 70 C3
San Francisco Bay inlet CA U.S.A. 65 A2
San Francisco de Paula, Cabo c. Arg. 70 C7
San Gabriel Mountains CA U.S.A. 65 C3
Sangachaly Azer. see Sanqaçal
Sangameshwar India 38 B2
Sangān, Kōh-e mt. Afgh. 36 A2
Sangan, Koh-i- mt. Afgh. see Sangān, Kōh-e
Sangar Russia 29 N3
Sangareddi India see Sangareddy
Sangareddy India 38 C2
San Gavino Monreale Sardinia Italy 26 C5
Sangay, Parque Nacional nat. park Ecuador 68 C4
Sangdankangsang Feng mt. China 37 G3
Sangeang i. Indon. 54 B2
Sanger CA U.S.A. 65 C2
Sang-e Surakh Iran 35 J3
San Giovanni in Fiore Italy 26 G5
Sangir India 36 C5
Sangir, Kepulauan is Indon. 41 E7
Sangkulirang Indon. 41 D7
Sangli India 38 B2
Sangmai China see Dêrong
Sangmélima Cameroon 46 E4
Sango Zimbabwe 49 D6
Sangole India 38 B2
San Gorgonio Mountain CA U.S.A. 65 D3
Sangre de Cristo Range mts CO U.S.A. 62 F4
Sangrur India 36 C3
Sangu r. Bangl. 37 G5
Sanguem India 38 B3
Sangutane r. Moz. 51 K3
San Hipólito, Punta pt Mex. 66 B3
Sanhûr Egypt see Sanhūr
Sanhūr Egypt 34 C5
San Ignacio Beni Bol. 68 E6
San Ignacio Santa Cruz Bol. 68 F7
San Ignacio Santa Cruz Bol. 68 F7
San Ignacio Para. 70 E3
Sanikiluaq Nunavut Canada 61 K4
Sanin-kaigan Kokuritsu-kōen Japan 45 D6
San Jacinto CA U.S.A. 65 D4
San Jacinto Peak CA U.S.A. 65 D4
San Javier Bol. 68 F7
Sanjiang China see Jinping
Sanjiangkou China 44 A4
Sanjiaocheng China see Haiyan
Sanjō Japan 45 E5
San Joaquin r. CA U.S.A. 65 B1
San Joaquin Valley val. CA U.S.A. 65 B2
Sanjoli India 36 C5
San Jorge, Golfo de g. Arg. 70 C7
San Jorge, Golfo de g. Spain see Sant Jordi, Golf de
San José Costa Rica 67 H7
San Jose Phil. 41 E6
San Jose CA U.S.A. 65 B2
San José, Isla i. Mex. 66 B4
San José de Amacuro Venez. 68 F2
San José de Bavicora Mex. 62 F6
San Jose de Buenavista Phil. 41 E6
San José de Chiquitos Bol. 68 F7
San José de Comondú Mex. 66 B3
San José del Cabo Mex. 66 C4
San José del Guaviare Col. 68 D3
San José de Mayo Uruguay 70 E4
San Juan Arg. 70 C4
San Juan r. Costa Rica/Nicaragua 67 H6
San Juan Puerto Rico 67 K5
San Juan r. UT U.S.A. 62 E4
San Juan, Cabo c. Arg. 70 D8
San Juan, Cabo c. Equat. Guinea 46 D4
San Juan Bautista Para. 70 E3
San Juan Bautista de las Misiones Para. see San Juan Bautista
San Juan de los Morros Venez. 68 E2
San Juan Mountains CO U.S.A. 62 F4
San Julián Arg. 70 C7
San Justo Arg. 70 D4
Sankari Drug India 38 C4
Sankhu India 36 C3
Sankra Chhattisgarh India 38 D1
Sankra Rajasthan India 36 B4
Sankt Gallen Switz. 24 I3
Sankt-Peterburg Russia see St Petersburg
Sankt Pölten Austria 17 O6
Sankt Veit an der Glan Austria 17 O7
Sanku India 36 D2
Şanlıurfa Turkey 34 E3
Şanlıurfa prov. Turkey 39 D1
San Lorenzo Arg. 70 D4
San Lorenzo Beni Bol. 68 E7
San Lorenzo Tarija Bol. 68 F8
San Lorenzo Ecuador 68 C3
San Lorenzo mt. Spain 25 E2
San Lorenzo, Monte mt. Arg./Chile 70 B7
Sanlúcar de Barrameda Spain 25 C5
San Lucas, Serranía de mts Col. 68 D2
San Luis Arg. 70 C4
San Luis AZ U.S.A. 65 E4
San Luis Obispo CA U.S.A. 65 B3
San Luis Obispo Bay CA U.S.A. 65 B3
San Luis Potosí Mex. 66 D4
San Luis Reservoir CA U.S.A. 65 B2
San Luis Río Colorado Mex. 62 E5
San Marcos TX U.S.A. 62 H6
San Marino country Europe 26 E3
San Marino San Marino 26 E3
San Martín (Argentina) research stn Antarctica 76 L2
San Martín Catamarca Arg. 70 C3
San Martín Mendoza Arg. 70 C4
San Martín, Lago l. Arg./Chile 70 B7
San Martín de los Andes Arg. 70 B6
San Mateo CA U.S.A. 65 A2
San Matías Bol. 69 G7
San Matías, Golfo g. Arg. 70 D6
Sanmenxia China 43 K6
San Miguel El Salvador 66 G6
San Miguel CA U.S.A. 65 B3
San Miguel de Huachi Bol. 68 E7
San Miguel de Tucumán Arg. 70 C3
San Miguel Island CA U.S.A. 65 B3
Sanming China 43 L7
Sanndraigh i. U.K. see Sandray
Sannicandro Garganico Italy 26 F4
San Nicolas Island CA U.S.A. 65 C4
Sannieshof S. Africa 51 G4
Sanniquellie Liberia 46 C4
Sanok Poland 13 D6
San Pablo Bol. 68 E8
San Pablo de Manta Ecuador see Manta
San Pedro Arg. 70 D2
San Pedro Bol. 68 F7
San Pedro Chile 70 C2
San-Pédro Côte d'Ivoire 46 C4
San Pedro Mex. 62 F7
San Pedro Para. see San Pedro de Ycuamandyyú
San Pedro watercourse AZ U.S.A. 62 E5
San Pedro, Sierra de mts Spain 25 C4
San Pedro Channel CA U.S.A. 65 C4
San Pedro de Arimena Col. 68 D3
San Pedro de Atacama Chile 70 C2
San Pedro de las Colonias Mex. 66 D3
San Pedro de Macorís Dom. Rep. 67 K5
San Pedro de Ycuamandyyú Para. 70 E2
San Pedro Sula Hond. 66 G5
San Pietro, Isola di i. Sardinia Italy 26 C5
Sanqaçal Azer. 35 H2
Sanquhar U.K. 20 F5
Sanquianga, Parque Nacional nat. park Col. 68 C3
San Quintín, Cabo c. Mex. 66 A2
San Rafael Arg. 70 C4
San Rafael CA U.S.A. 65 A2
San Rafael Mountains CA U.S.A. 65 B3
San Ramón Bol. 68 F6
Sanremo Italy 26 B3
San Roque Spain 25 B2
San Salvador i. Bahamas 67 J4
San Salvador El Salvador 66 G6
San Salvador de Jujuy Arg. 70 C2
Sansanné-Mango Togo 46 D3
San Sebastián Arg. 70 C8
San Sebastián Spain 25 F2
San Sebastián de los Reyes Spain 25 E3
Sansepolcro Italy 26 E3
San Severo Italy 26 F4
Sanski Most Bos. & Herz. 26 G2
Santa r. Peru 68 C5
Santa Ana Bol. 68 E7
Santa Ana El Salvador 66 G6
Santa Ana Mex. 66 B2
Santa Ana i. Solomon Is 53 G3
Santa Ana CA U.S.A. 65 D4
Santa Ana de Yacuma Bol. 68 E6
Santa Bárbara Brazil 71 C2
Santa Bárbara Mex. 66 C3
Santa Barbara CA U.S.A. 65 C3
Santa Bárbara, Ilha i. Brazil 71 D2
Santa Barbara Channel CA U.S.A. 65 B3
Santa Bárbara d'Oeste Brazil 71 B3
Santa Barbara Island CA U.S.A. 65 C4
Santa Catalina, Gulf of CA U.S.A. 65 D4
Santa Cataliña de Armada Spain 25 B2
Santa Catalina Island CA U.S.A. 65 C4
Santa Catarina state Brazil 71 A4
Santa Catarina, Ilha de i. Brazil 71 A4
Santa Clara Col. 68 E4
Santa Clara Cuba 67 I4
Santa Clara CA U.S.A. 65 B2
Santa Clara UT U.S.A. 65 F2
Santa Clarita CA U.S.A. 65 C3
Santa Clotilde Peru 68 D4
Santa Comba Angola see Waku-Kungo
Santa Croce, Capo c. Sicily Italy 26 F6
Santa Cruz Bol. 68 F7
Santa Cruz Brazil 69 K5
Santa Cruz Costa Rica 68 A1
Santa Cruz CA U.S.A. 65 A2
Santa Cruz, Isla i. Galápagos Ecuador 68 [inset]
Santa Cruz Cabrália Brazil 71 D2
Santa Cruz de Goiás Brazil 71 A2
Santa Cruz de la Palma Canary Is 46 B2
Santa Cruz del Sur Cuba 67 I4
Santa Cruz de Moya Spain 25 F4
Santa Cruz de Tenerife Canary Is 46 B2
Santa Cruz do Sul Brazil 70 F3
Santa Cruz Island CA U.S.A. 65 C3
Santa Cruz Islands Solomon Is 53 G3
Santa Elena, Bahía de b. Ecuador 68 B4
Santa Elena, Cabo c. Costa Rica 67 G6
Santa Elena, Punta pt Ecuador 68 B4
Santa Eudóxia Brazil 71 B3
Santa Eufemia, Golfo di g. Italy 26 G5
Santa Fe Arg. 70 D4
Santa Fe NM U.S.A. 62 F4
Santa Fé de Bogotá Col. see Bogotá
Santa Fé de Minas Brazil 71 B2
Santa Fé do Sul Brazil 71 A3
Santa Helena Brazil 69 I4
Santa Helena de Goiás Brazil 71 A2
Santa Inês Brazil 69 I4
Santa Inés, Isla i. Chile 76 L3
Santa Isabel Arg. 70 C5
Santa Isabel Equat. Guinea see Malabo
Santa Isabel i. Solomon Is 53 F2
Santa Juliana Brazil 71 B2
Santalpur India 36 B5
Santa Lucia Range mts CA U.S.A. 65 B2
Santa Margarita CA U.S.A. 65 B3
Santa Margarita, Isla i. Mex. 66 B4
Santa María Arg. 70 C3
Santa Maria Amazonas Brazil 69 G4
Santa Maria Rio Grande do Sul Brazil 70 F3
Santa Maria Cape Verde 46 [inset]
Santa María r. Mex. 66 C2
Santa María Peru 68 D4
Santa Maria CA U.S.A. 65 B3
Santa Maria r. AZ U.S.A. 65 F3
Santa Maria, Cabo de c. Moz. 51 K4
Santa Maria, Cabo de c. Port. 25 C5
Santa Maria, Chapadão de hills Brazil 71 B1
Santa Maria, Serra de hills Brazil 71 B1
Santa Maria da Vitória Brazil 71 B1
Santa Maria do Suaçuí Brazil 71 C2
Santa Maria Island Vanuatu 53 G3
Santa Maria Madalena Brazil 71 C3
Santa Maria Mountains AZ U.S.A. 65 F3
Santa Marta Col. 68 D1
Santa Marta, Cabo de c. Angola 49 B5
Santa Marta Grande, Cabo de c. Brazil 71 A5
Santa Maura i. Greece see Lefkada
Santa Monica CA U.S.A. 65 C3
Santa Monica Bay CA U.S.A. 65 C4
Santana Brazil 71 C1
Santana r. Brazil 71 A2
Santana do Araguaia Brazil 69 H5
Santander Spain 25 E2
Santa Nella CA U.S.A. 65 B2
Santanilla, Islas is Caribbean Sea see Cisne, Islas del
Sant'Antioco Sardinia Italy 26 C5
Sant'Antioco, Isola di i. Sardinia Italy 26 C5
Sant Antoni de Portmany Spain 25 G4
Santapilly India 38 D2
Santa Quitéria Brazil 69 J4
Santarém Brazil 69 H4
Santarém Port. 25 B4
Santa Rosa Arg. 70 D5
Santa Rosa Brazil 70 F3
Santa Rosa CA U.S.A. 65 A1
Santa Rosa NM U.S.A. 62 G5
Santa Rosa de Copán Hond. 66 G6
Santa Rosa de la Roca Bol. 68 F7
Santa Rosa do Purus Brazil 68 D5
Santa Rosa Island CA U.S.A. 65 B4
Santa Rosalía Mex. 66 B3
Santa Sylvina Arg. 70 D3
Santa Tecla El Salvador 66 G6
Santa Teresa Australia 55 F6
Santa Teresa r. Brazil 71 A1
Santa Vitória Brazil 71 A2
Santa Ynez r. CA U.S.A. 65 B3
Santa Ysabel i. Solomon Is see Santa Isabel
Santee CA U.S.A. 65 D4
Sant Francesc de Formentera Spain 25 G4
Santiago Brazil 70 F3
Santiago i. Cape Verde 46 [inset]
Santiago Chile 70 B4
Santiago Dom. Rep. 67 J5
Santiago Panama 67 H7
Santiago, Isla i. Galápagos Ecuador 68 [inset]
Santiago de Compostela Spain 25 B2
Santiago de Cuba Cuba 67 I4
Santiago del Estero Arg. 70 D3
Santiago de los Caballeros Dom. Rep. see Santiago
Santiago de Veraguas Panama see Santiago
Santipur India see Shantipur
Sant Jordi, Golf de g. Spain 25 G3
Santo Amaro Brazil 71 D1
Santo Amaro de Campos Brazil 71 C3
Santo Anastácio Brazil 71 A3
Santo André Brazil 71 B3
Santo Ângelo Brazil 70 F3
Santo Antão i. Cape Verde 46 [inset]
Santo Antônio Brazil 68 F4
Santo Antônio r. Brazil 71 C2
Santo António São Tomé and Príncipe 46 D4
Santo Antônio, Cabo c. Brazil 71 D1
Santo Antônio da Platina Brazil 71 A3
Santo Antônio de Jesus Brazil 71 D1
Santo Antônio do Içá Brazil 68 E4
Santo Corazón Bol. 69 G7
Santo Domingo Dom. Rep. 67 K5
Santo Domingo country West Indies see Dominican Republic
Santo Domingo de Guzmán Dom. Rep. see Santo Domingo
Santo Hipólito Brazil 71 B2
Santorini i. Greece 27 K6
Santos Brazil 71 B3
Santos Dumont Brazil 71 C3
Santos Luzardo, Parque Nacional nat. park Venez. 68 E2
Santos Plateau sea feature S. Atlantic Ocean 72 E7
Santo Tomás Peru 68 D6
Santo Tomé Arg. 70 E3
Sanup Plateau AZ U.S.A. 65 F2
San Valentín, Cerro mt. Chile 70 B7
San Vicente El Salvador 66 G6
San Vicente Mex. 66 A2
San Vicente de Baracaldo Spain see Barakaldo

San Vicente de Cañete Peru 68 C6
San Vincenzo Italy 26 D3
San Vito, Capo c. *Sicily* Italy 26 E5
Sanwer India 36 C5
Sanza Pombo Angola 49 B4
São Bernardo do Campo Brazil 71 B3
São Borja Brazil 70 E3
São Carlos Brazil 71 B3
São Domingos Brazil 71 B1
São Felipe, Serra de hills Brazil 71 B1
São Félix Brazil 71 D1
São Félix do Araguaia Brazil 69 H6
São Félix do Xingu Brazil 69 H5
São Fidélis Brazil 71 C3
São Francisco Brazil 71 C3
São Francisco r. Brazil 71 C1
São Francisco, Ilha de i. Brazil 71 A4
São Francisco de Paula Brazil 71 A5
São Francisco de Sales Brazil 71 B2
São Francisco do Sul Brazil 71 A4
São Gabriel Brazil 70 F4
São Gonçalo Brazil 71 C3
São Gonçalo do Abaeté Brazil 71 B2
São Gonçalo do Sapucaí Brazil 71 B3
São Gotardo Brazil 71 B2
São João, Ilhas de is Brazil 69 J4
São João da Barra Brazil 71 C3
São João da Boa Vista Brazil 71 B3
São João da Madeira Port. 25 B3
São João da Ponte Brazil 71 B3
São João del Rei Brazil 71 B3
São João do Paraíso Brazil 71 C1
São Joaquim Brazil 71 A4
São Joaquim da Barra Brazil 71 B3
São José *Amazonas* Brazil 68 E4
São José *Santa Catarina* Brazil 71 A4
São José do Rio Preto Brazil 71 A3
São José dos Campos Brazil 71 B3
São José dos Pinhais Brazil 71 A4
São Leopoldo Brazil 71 A5
São Lourenço Brazil 71 B3
São Lourenço r. Brazil 69 G7
São Lourenço *Maranhão* Brazil 69 J4
São Luís *Pará* Brazil 69 G4
São Luís de Montes Belos Brazil 71 A2
São Manuel Brazil 71 A3
São Marcos r. Brazil 71 B2
São Mateus Brazil 71 D2
São Mateus do Sul Brazil 71 A4
São Miguel i. Arquipélago dos Açores
  72 G3
São Miguel i. Brazil 71 A3
São Miguel do Araguaia Brazil 71 A1
São Miguel do Tapuio Brazil 69 J5
Saône r. France 24 G4
Saoner India 36 D5
São Nicolau i. Cape Verde 46 [inset]
São Paulo Brazil 71 B3
São Paulo state Brazil 71 A3
São Paulo de Olivença Brazil 68 E4
São Pedro da Aldeia Brazil 71 C3
São Pedro e São Paulo is
  N. Atlantic Ocean 72 G5
São Pires r. Brazil see Teles Pires
São Raimundo Nonato Brazil 69 J5
São Romão *Amazonas* Brazil 68 E5
São Romão *Minas Gerais* Brazil 71 B2
São Roque Brazil 71 B3
São Roque, Cabo de c. Brazil 69 K5
São Salvador Angola see M'banza Congo
São Salvador do Congo Angola see
  M'banza Congo
São Sebastião Brazil 71 B3
São Sebastião, Ilha do i. Brazil 71 B3
São Sebastião do Paraíso Brazil 71 B3
São Sebastião dos Poções Brazil 71 B1
São Simão *Goiás* Brazil 69 H7
São Simão *São Paulo* Brazil 71 B3
São Simão, Barragem de resr Brazil 71 A2
São Tiago r. Cape Verde see Santiago
São Tomé São Tomé and Príncipe 46 D4
São Tomé i. São Tomé and Príncipe 46 D4
São Tomé, Cabo de c. Brazil 71 C3
São Tomé, Pico de mt.
  São Tomé and Príncipe 46 D4
São Tomé and Príncipe country Africa
  46 D4
Saoura, Oued watercourse Alg. 22 D6
São Vicente Brazil 71 B3
São Vicente i. Cape Verde 46 [inset]
São Vicente, Cabo de c. Port. 25 B5
Sapanca Turkey 27 N4
Sapaul India see Supaul
Şaphane Dağı mt. Turkey 27 N5
Sapo National Park Liberia 46 C4
Sapouy Burkina Faso 46 C4
Sapozhok Russia 13 I5
Sapporo Japan 44 F4
Saputang China see Zadoi
Saqqez Iran 35 G3
Sarā Iran 35 G3
Sara Buri Thai. 37 J5
Saradiya India 36 B5
Saragossa Spain see Zaragoza
Saragt Turkm. 33 J2
Saraguro Ecuador 68 C4
Sarahs Turkm. see Saragt
Sarai Sidhu Pak. 36 C2
Sarajevo Bos. & Herz. 26 H3
Saraktash Russia 28 G4
Saramati mt. India/Myanmar 37 H4
Saran' Kazakh. 42 C3
Saranda Albania see Sarandë
Sarandë Albania 27 I5
Sarandib country Asia see Sri Lanka
Sarangpur India 36 D5
Saransk Russia 13 J5
Sara Peak Nigeria 46 D4
Sarapul Russia 11 Q4
Saráqib Syria 39 C2
Sarasota FL U.S.A. 63 K6
Sarata Ukr. 27 M1
Saratoga CA U.S.A. 65 A2
Saratoga WY U.S.A. 62 F3
Saratok *Sarawak* Malaysia 41 D7
Saratov Russia 13 J6
Saratovskoye Vodokhranilishche resr
  Russia 13 J5
Saratsina, Akrotirio pt Greece 27 K5
Sarāvān Iran 33 J4
Saray Turkey 27 L4
Sarayköy Turkey 27 M6
Sarayönü Turkey 34 D3
Sarbāz Iran 35 J3
Sarbhang Bhutan 37 G4
Sar Bīsheh Iran 35 I3
Sarda r. Nepal 37 E3
Sard Āb Afgh. 36 B4
Sardarshahr India 36 C3
Sardasht Iran 35 G3
Sardegna i. *Sardinia* Italy see Sardinia
Sardica Bulg. see Sofia
Sardinia i. *Sardinia* Italy 26 C4
Sardis WV U.S.A. 64 A3
Sar-e Būm Afgh. 36 A2
Sareks nationalpark nat. park Sweden
  14 J3
Sarektjåkkå mt. Sweden 14 J3
Sar-e Pol-e Żahāb Iran 35 G4
Sar-e Pul Afgh. 36 A1
Sar Eskandar Iran see Hashtrūd

Sargasso Sea N. Atlantic Ocean 75 P4
Sargodha Pak. 36 C2
Sarh Chad 47 E4
Sārī Iran 35 I3
Saria i. Greece 27 L7
Sarigh Jilganang Kol salt l. Aksai Chin
  36 D2
Sarıgöl Turkey 27 M5
Sarıkamış Turkey 35 F2
Sarila India 36 D4
Sarina Australia 56 E4
Sarıoğlan *Kayseri* Turkey 34 D3
Sarıoğlan *Konya* Turkey see Belören
Sariqamish Kuli salt l. Turkm./Uzbek. see
  Sarykamyshskoye Ozero
Sariveliler Turkey 39 A1
Sariwŏn N. Korea 45 B5
Sarıyar Barajı resr Turkey 27 N5
Sarıyer Turkey 27 M4
Sarız Turkey 34 E3
Sark i. Channel Is 19 E9
Sark, Safrā' as esc. Saudi Arabia 32 F4
Sarkand Kazakh. 42 D3
Şarkikaraağaç Turkey 27 N5
Şarkışla Turkey 34 E3
Şarköy Turkey 27 L4
Sarlath Range mts Afgh./Pak. 36 A3
Sarmi Indon. 41 F8
Särna Sweden 15 H6
Sarneh Iran 35 G4
Sarnen Switz. 24 I3
Sarni India see Amla
Sarnia *Ont.* Canada 63 K3
Sarny Ukr. 13 E6
Sarōbī Afgh. 36 B3
Saroma-ko l. Japan 44 F3
Saronikos Kolpos g. Greece 27 J6
Saros Körfezi b. Turkey 27 L4
Sarov Russia 13 I5
Sarpa, Ozero l. Russia 13 J6
Sarpan i. N. Mariana Is see Rota
Sarpsborg Norway 15 G7
Sarqant Kazakh. see Sarkand
Sarrebourg France 24 H2
Sarria Spain 25 C2
Sartana Ukr. 13 H7
Sartène *Corsica* France 24 I6
Sarthe r. France 24 D3
Saruna China see Daqing
Sarupsar India 36 C3
Sārūr Azer. 35 G3
Sarvābād Iran 35 G4
Sárvár Hungary 26 G1
Sarv-e Bālā Iran 35 I4
Sarwar India 36 C4
Saryarka plain Kazakh. 42 C2
Sar Yazd Iran 35 I5
Sarygamysh Köli salt l. Turkm./Uzbek. see
  Sarykamyshskoye Ozero
Sary-Ishikotrau, Peski des. Kazakh. see
  Saryyesik-Atyrau, Peski
Saryozek Kazakh. 42 D4
Saryozen r. Kazakh./Russia 13 K6
Saryshagan Kazakh. 42 C3
Sarysu watercourse Kazakh. 42 B3
Sarytash Kyrg. 33 I2
Sary-Tash Kyrg. 33 L2
Sarzha Kazakh. 35 H2
Sasar, Tanjung pt Indon. 54 B2
Sasaram China 36 E4
Sasebo Japan 45 C6
Saskatchewan prov. Canada 62 F1
Saskatchewan r. *Man./Sask.* Canada 60 H4
Saskatoon *Sask.* Canada 60 H4
Saskylakh Russia 29 M2
Saslaya r. Nicaragua 67 H6
Sasoi r. India 36 B5
Sasolburg S. Africa 51 H4
Sasovo Russia 13 I5
Sassandra Côte d'Ivoire 46 C4
Sassari *Sardinia* Italy 26 C4
Sassnitz Germany 17 N3
Sass Town Liberia 46 C4
Sasykkol', Ozero l. Kazakh. 42 E3
Sasykoli Russia 13 J7
Sasyqköl l. Kazakh. see Sasykkol', Ozero
Sata-misaki c. Japan 45 C7
Satana India 38 B1
Satara India 38 B2
Satara S. Africa 51 J3
Sātbaev Kazakh. see Satpayev
Satrlar Turkey see Yesilova
Satkania Bangl. 37 H5
Satkhira Bangl. 37 G5
Satluj r. India/Pak. 36 B3
Satmala Range hills India 38 C2
Satna India 36 E4
Satpura Range mts India 36 C5
Satsuma-hantō pen. Japan 45 C7
Satsuma-Sendai Japan 45 C7
Satthwa Myanmar 37 H6
Satu Mare Romania 13 D7
Satwas India 36 D5
Saucillo Mex. 66 C3
Sauda Norway 15 E7
Sauðárkrókur Iceland 14 [inset 2]
Saudi Arabia country Asia 32 F5
Säujbولāgh Iran see Mahābād
Saulieu France 24 G3
Sault Sainte Marie *Ont.* Canada 63 K2
Sault Sainte Marie MI U.S.A. 63 K2
Saumalkol' Kazakh. 30 F1
Saumarez Reef Australia 56 F4
Saumlakki Indon. 54 E2
Saumur France 24 D3
Saundatti India 38 B3
Saunders, Mount h. Australia 54 E3
Saunders Coast Antarctica 76 J1
Saurimo Angola 49 C4
Sautar Angola 49 B5
Sava r. Europe 26 I2
Savage River Australia 57 [inset]
Savai'i i. Samoa 53 I3
Savala r. Russia 13 I6
Savalou Benin 46 D4
Savanat Iran see Estahban
Savannah GA U.S.A. 63 K5
Savannah r. GA/SC U.S.A. 63 K5
Savannakhét Laos 41 C6
Savanna-la-Mar Jamaica 67 I5
Savant Lake *Ont.* Canada 63 I1
Savanur India 38 B3
Sāvar Sweden 14 L5
Savaştepe Turkey 27 L5
Savè Benin 46 D4
Save r. Moz./Zimbabwe 49 D6
Sāveh Iran 35 H4
Saviaho Fin. 14 P4
Savinskiy Russia 12 I3
Savitri r. India 38 B2
Savli India 36 C5
Savoie reg. France see Savoy
Savona Italy 26 C2
Savonlinna Fin. 14 P6
Savonranta Fin. 14 P5
Savoy reg. France 24 H3
Savu i. Indon. see Savu
Savukoski Fin. 14 P3
Savur Turkey 35 F3
Saw Myanmar 37 H5
Sawai Madhopur India 36 D4
Sawar India 36 C4
Sawel Mountain h. U.K. 21 E3
Sawu Indon. 54 C2
Sawu i. Indon. see Savu
Sawu, Laut sea Indon. 41 E8
Saxilby U.K. 18 G5
Saxmundham U.K. 19 I6
Saxnäs Sweden 14 I4
Saxton PA U.S.A. 64 B2
Say Niger 46 D3
Sayabouri Laos see Xaignabouli
Sayak Kazakh. 42 D3
Sayanogorsk Russia 42 G2
Sayano-Shushenskoye Vodokhranilishche
  resr Russia 42 G2
Sayansk Russia 42 I2
Sayaq Kazakh. see Sayak
Şaydā Lebanon see Sidon
Sayghān Afgh. 36 A2
Sayhan-Ovoo Mongolia 42 I3
Sayhūt Yemen 32 H6
Saykyn Kazakh. 11 P6
Saylac Somalia 47 H3
Saylan country Asia see Sri Lanka
Saynshand Mongolia 43 K4
Sayoa mt. Spain see Saioa
Şayqal, Baḩr imp. l. Syria 39 C3
Sayqyn Kazakh. see Saykyn
Sayre PA U.S.A. 64 C2
Sayreville NJ U.S.A. 64 D2
Sayula Mex. 66 F5
Sazdy Kazakh. 13 K7
Sazin Pak. 36 C2
Sbaa Alg. 22 D6
Sbeïtla Tunisia 26 C7
Scaddan Australia 55 C8
Scafell Pike h. U.K. 18 D4
Scalasaig U.K. 20 C4
Scalea Italy 26 F5
Scalloway U.K. 20 [inset]
Scalpaigh, Eilean i. U.K. see Scalpay
Scalpay i. U.K. 20 B3
Scapa Flow inlet U.K. 20 F2
Scarba i. U.K. 20 D4
Scarborough *Ont.* Canada 63 L3
Scarborough *Trin. and Tob.* 67 L6
Scarborough U.K. 18 G4
Scariff Island Ireland 21 B6
Scarp i. U.K. 20 B2
Scarpanto i. Greece see Karpathos
Schaffhausen Switz. 24 I3
Schakalskuppe Namibia 50 C4
Schärding Austria 17 N6
Scheibbs Austria 17 O6
Schefferville *Nfld. and Lab.* Canada 61 L4
Schellville CA U.S.A. 65 A1
Schenectady NY U.S.A. 64 E1
Schio Italy 26 D2
Schleswig Germany 17 L3
Schleswig-Holsteinisches Wattenmeer,
  Nationalpark nat. park Germany 17 L3
Schmidt Island Russia see
  Shmidta, Ostrov
Schmidt Peninsula Russia see
  Shmidta, Poluostrov
Schneidemühl Poland see Piła
Schneverdingen Germany 17 L4
Schoharie NY U.S.A. 64 D1
Schönebeck (Elbe) Germany 17 M4
Schouten Island Australia 57 [inset]
Schouten Islands P.N.G. 52 [inset]
Schrankogel mt. Austria 17 M7
Schröttersburg Poland see Płock
Schull Ireland 21 C6
Schuyler Lake NY U.S.A. 64 D1
Schwäbische Alb mts Germany 17 L7
Schwäbisch Hall Germany 17 L6
Schwandorf Germany 17 N6
Schwaner, Pegunungan mts Indon. 41 E7
Schwarzrand mts Namibia 50 C3
Schwarzwald mts Germany see
  Black Forest
Schwatka Mountains AK U.S.A. 60 C3
Schwaz Austria 17 M7
Schwedt/Oder Germany 17 O4
Schweinfurt Germany 17 M5
Schweiz country Europe see Switzerland
Schweizer-Reneke S. Africa 51 G4
Schwerin Germany 17 M4
Schwyz Switz. 24 I3
Sciacca *Sicily* Italy 26 E6
Scicli *Sicily* Italy 26 E6
Scilla Italy 26 F5
Scilly, Île atoll Fr. Polynesia see Manuae
Scilly, Isles of U.K. 19 A9
Scodra Albania see Shkodër
Scole U.K. 19 I6
Scone Australia 58 E4
Scone U.K. 20 F4
Scoresby Land reg. Greenland 61 P2
Scoresbysund Greenland see
  Ittoqqortoormiit
Scoresby Sund sea chan. Greenland see
  Kangertittivaq
Scorno, Punta dello pt *Sardinia* Italy see
  Caprara, Punta
Scorpion Bight b. Australia 55 D8
Scotia Ridge sea feature S. Atlantic Ocean
  76 A2
Scotia Sea S. Atlantic Ocean 72 F9
Scotland *Ont.* Canada 63 L3
Scotland admin. div. U.K. 20 F3
Scotland MD U.S.A. 64 C3
Scott, Cape Australia 54 E3
Scott, Cape B.C. Canada 62 B2
Scott Base (New Zealand) research stn
  Antarctica 76 H1
Scottburgh S. Africa 51 J6
Scott City KS U.S.A. 62 F4
Scott Coast Antarctica 76 H1
Scott Glacier Antarctica 76 G2
Scott Island Antarctica 76 H2
Scott Mountains Antarctica 76 D2
Scott Reef Australia 54 C3
Scottsbluff NE U.S.A. 62 F3
Scottsboro AL U.S.A. 63 J5
Scottsdale AZ U.S.A. 62 E5
Scottsville VA U.S.A. 64 B4
Scourie U.K. 20 D2
Scousburgh U.K. 20 [inset]
Scrabster U.K. 20 F2
Scranton PA U.S.A. 64 D2
Scunthorpe U.K. 18 G5
Scupi Macedonia see Skopje
Scutari Albania see Shkodër
Scutari, Lake Albania/Montenegro 27 H3
Seabrook, Lake imp. l. Australia 55 B7
Seaford U.K. 19 H8
Seaforth *Ont.* Canada 63 L3
Seal r. *Man.* Canada 61 I4
Seal, Cape S. Africa 50 F8
Sea Lake Australia 57 C7
Sealy TX U.S.A. 63 H6
Seaman Range mts NV U.S.A. 65 E2

Sävsjö Sweden 15 I8
Savu i. Indon. 54 C2
Savukoski Fin. 14 P3
Savur Turkey 35 F3
Saw Myanmar 37 H5
Sawai Madhopur India 36 D4
Sawar India 36 C4
Sawel Mountain h. U.K. 21 E3
Sawu Indon. 54 C2
Sawu i. Indon. see Savu
Sawu, Laut sea Indon. 41 E8
Saxilby U.K. 18 G5
Saxmundham U.K. 19 I6
Saxnäs Sweden 14 I4
Saxton PA U.S.A. 64 B2
Say Niger 46 D3
Sayabouri Laos see Xaignabouli
Sayak Kazakh. 42 D3
Sayanogorsk Russia 42 G2
Sayano-Shushenskoye Vodokhranilishche
  resr Russia 42 G2
Sayansk Russia 42 I2
Sayaq Kazakh. see Sayak
Şaydā Lebanon see Sidon
Sayghān Afgh. 36 A2
Sayhan-Ovoo Mongolia 42 I3
Sayhūt Yemen 32 H6
Saykyn Kazakh. 11 P6
Saylac Somalia 47 H3
Saylan country Asia see Sri Lanka
Saynshand Mongolia 43 K4
Sayoa mt. Spain see Saioa
Şayqal, Baḩr imp. l. Syria 39 C3
Sayqyn Kazakh. see Saykyn
Sayre PA U.S.A. 64 C2
Sayreville NJ U.S.A. 64 D2
Sayula Mex. 66 F5
Sazdy Kazakh. 13 K7
Sazin Pak. 36 C2
Sbaa Alg. 22 D6
Sbeïtla Tunisia 26 C7
Scaddan Australia 55 C8
Scafell Pike h. U.K. 18 D4
Scalasaig U.K. 20 C4
Scalea Italy 26 F5
Scalloway U.K. 20 [inset]
Scalpaigh, Eilean i. U.K. see Scalpay
Scalpay i. U.K. 20 B3
Scapa Flow inlet U.K. 20 F2
Scarba i. U.K. 20 D4
Scarborough *Ont.* Canada 63 L3
Scarborough *Trin. and Tob.* 67 L6
Scarborough U.K. 18 G4
Scariff Island Ireland 21 B6
Scarp i. U.K. 20 B2
Scarpanto i. Greece see Karpathos
Schaffhausen Switz. 24 I3
Schakalskuppe Namibia 50 C4
Schärding Austria 17 N6
Scheibbs Austria 17 O6
Schefferville *Nfld. and Lab.* Canada 61 L4
Schellville CA U.S.A. 65 A1
Schenectady NY U.S.A. 64 E1
Schio Italy 26 D2
Schleswig Germany 17 L3
Schleswig-Holsteinisches Wattenmeer,
  Nationalpark nat. park Germany 17 L3
Schmidt Island Russia see
  Shmidta, Ostrov
Schmidt Peninsula Russia see
  Shmidta, Poluostrov
Schneidemühl Poland see Piła
Schneverdingen Germany 17 L4
Schoharie NY U.S.A. 64 D1
Schönebeck (Elbe) Germany 17 M4
Schouten Island Australia 57 [inset]
Schouten Islands P.N.G. 52 [inset]
Schrankogel mt. Austria 17 M7
Schröttersburg Poland see Płock
Schull Ireland 21 C6
Schuyler Lake NY U.S.A. 64 D1
Schwäbische Alb mts Germany 17 L7
Schwäbisch Hall Germany 17 L6
Schwandorf Germany 17 N6
Schwaner, Pegunungan mts Indon. 41 E7
Schwarzenberg/Erzgebirge Germany
  17 N5
Schwarzrand mts Namibia 50 C3
Schwarzwald mts Germany see
  Black Forest
Schwatka Mountains AK U.S.A. 60 C3
Schwaz Austria 17 M7
Schwedt/Oder Germany 17 O4
Schweinfurt Germany 17 M5
Schweiz country Europe see Switzerland
Schweizer-Reneke S. Africa 51 G4
Schwerin Germany 17 M4
Schwyz Switz. 24 I3
Sciacca *Sicily* Italy 26 E6
Scicli *Sicily* Italy 26 E6
Scilla Italy 26 F5
Scilly, Île atoll Fr. Polynesia see Manuae
Scilly, Isles of U.K. 19 A9
Scodra Albania see Shkodër
Scole U.K. 19 I6
Scone Australia 58 E4
Scone U.K. 20 F4
Scoresby Land reg. Greenland 61 P2
Scoresbysund Greenland see
  Ittoqqortoormiit
Scoresby Sund sea chan. Greenland see
  Kangertittivaq
Scorno, Punta dello pt *Sardinia* Italy see
  Caprara, Punta
Scorpion Bight b. Australia 55 D8
Scotia Ridge sea feature S. Atlantic Ocean
  76 A2
Scotia Sea S. Atlantic Ocean 72 F9
Scotland *Ont.* Canada 63 L3
Scotland admin. div. U.K. 20 F3
Scotland MD U.S.A. 64 C3
Scott, Cape Australia 54 E3
Scott, Cape B.C. Canada 62 B2
Scott Base (New Zealand) research stn
  Antarctica 76 H1
Scottburgh S. Africa 51 J6
Scott City KS U.S.A. 62 F4
Scott Coast Antarctica 76 H1
Scott Glacier Antarctica 76 G2
Scott Island Antarctica 76 H2
Scott Mountains Antarctica 76 D2
Scott Reef Australia 54 C3
Scottsbluff NE U.S.A. 62 F3
Scottsboro AL U.S.A. 63 J5
Scottsdale AZ U.S.A. 62 E5
Scottsville VA U.S.A. 64 B4
Scourie U.K. 20 D2
Scousburgh U.K. 20 [inset]
Scrabster U.K. 20 F2
Scranton PA U.S.A. 64 D2
Scunthorpe U.K. 18 G5
Scupi Macedonia see Skopje
Scutari Albania see Shkodër
Scutari, Lake Albania/Montenegro 27 H3
Seabrook, Lake imp. l. Australia 55 B7
Seaford U.K. 19 H8
Seaforth *Ont.* Canada 63 L3
Seal r. *Man.* Canada 61 I4
Seal, Cape S. Africa 50 F8
Sea Lake Australia 57 C7
Sealy TX U.S.A. 63 H6
Seaman Range mts NV U.S.A. 65 E2

Seamer U.K. 18 G4
Searchlight NV U.S.A. 65 E3
Searcy AR U.S.A. 63 I4
Searles Lake CA U.S.A. 65 E3
Seaside Park NJ U.S.A. 64 D3
Seattle WA U.S.A. 62 C2
Seaview Range mts Australia 56 D3
Seba Indon. 54 C2
Sebastea Turkey see Sivas
Sebastián Vizcaíno, Bahía b. Mex. 66 B3
Sebastopol Ukr. see Sevastopol'
Sebastopol CA U.S.A. 65 A1
Sebatik i. Indon. 54 C1
Sebba Burkina Faso 46 D3
Sebderat Eritrea 48 E6
Sebecea Hungary see Sárbogárd
Sebderat Eritrea 48 E6
Sebecevo Romania 27 J2
Sebenico Croatia see Šibenik
Sebeş Romania 27 J2
Sebezh Russia 15 P8
Sebinkarahisar Turkey 34 E2
Sebring FL U.S.A. 63 K6
Sebrovo Russia 13 I6
Sebta N. Africa see Ceuta
Secretary Island N.Z. 59 A7
Secunda S. Africa 51 I4
Secunderabad India 38 C2
Sedalia MO U.S.A. 63 I4
Sedam India 38 C2
Sedan France 24 G2
Sedan Dip Australia 56 C3
Seddon N.Z. 59 E5
Seddonville N.Z. 59 C5
Sederot Israel 39 B4
Sedlčany Czech Rep. 17 O6
Sedlets Poland see Siedlce
Sedom Israel 39 B4
Sédrata Alg. 26 B6
Séduva Lith. 15 M9
Seeheim Namibia 50 C4
Seelig, Mount Antarctica 76 K1
Seemandhra state India see
  Andhra Pradesh
Sées France 24 E2
Sefare Botswana 51 H2
Seferihisar Turkey 27 L5
Sefid Küh mts Afgh. 36 A3
Sefophe Botswana 51 H2
Segalstad Norway 15 G6
Segamat Malaysia 31 J9
Ségbana Benin 46 D3
Segezha Russia 12 G3
Segontia U.K. see Caernarfon
Segontium U.K. see Caernarfon
Segorbe Spain 25 F4
Ségou Mali 46 C3
Segovia r. Hond./Nicaragua see Coco
Segovia Spain 25 D3
Segozerskoye Vodokhranilishche resr
  Russia 12 G3
Seguam Island AK U.S.A. 60 A4
Séguédine Niger 46 E2
Séguéla Côte d'Ivoire 46 C4
Seguin TX U.S.A. 62 H6
Segura r. Spain 25 F4
Segura, Sierra de mts Spain 25 E5
Sehithwa Botswana 49 C6
Sehore India 36 D5
Sehwan Pak. 36 A4
Seikphyu Myanmar 37 H5
Seiland i. Norway 14 M1
Seinäjoki Fin. 14 M5
Seine r. France 24 E2
Seine, Baie de b. France 24 D2
Seine, Val de val. France 24 F2
Sejny Poland 15 M9
Sekayu Indon. 41 C8
Sekoma Botswana 50 F3
Sekondi Ghana 46 C4
Sek'ot'a Eth. 48 D2
Sela Russia see Shali
Selaru i. Indon. 41 E8
Selat, Tanjung pt Indon. 41 D8
Selatan, Tanjung pt Indon. 41 D8
Selat Makassar, Selat Indon. see
  Makassar, Selat
Selawik AK U.S.A. 60 B3
Selayar, Pulau i. Indon. 41 E8
Selb Germany 17 N5
Selbekken Norway 14 F5
Selbu Norway 14 G5
Selby U.K. 18 F5
Selbyville DE U.S.A. 64 D3
Selebi-Phikwe Botswana 49 C6
Selebi-Pikwe Botswana see Selebi-Phikwe
Selemdzha r. Russia 44 C1
Selemdzhinsk Russia 44 C1
Selemdzhinskiy Khrebet mts Russia
  44 D1
Selendi Turkey 27 M5
Selenga r. Mongolia/Russia see Selenga
Selenga Mörön r. Mongolia/Russia see
  Selenga
Selety r. Kazakh. see Silety
Seletyteniz, Ozero salt l. Kazakh. see
  Siletyteniz, Ozero
Seleucia Turkey see Silifke
Seleucia Pieria Turkey see Samandağı
Sel'gon Russia 44 D2
Sélibabi Mauritania 46 B3
Selibe-Phikwe Botswana see
  Selebi-Phikwe
Seliger, Ozero l. Russia 12 G4
Selikhino Russia 44 D2
Selīma Oasis Sudan 32 C5
Selimiye Turkey 27 L6
Selinsgrove PA U.S.A. 64 C2
Selizharovo Russia 12 G4
Seljord Norway 15 F7
Selkirk *Man.* Canada 60 H1
Selkirk U.K. 20 G5
Selkirk Mountains B.C. Canada 62 D1
Sellafield U.K. 18 D4
Selma AL U.S.A. 63 J5
Selma CA U.S.A. 65 C2
Selsey Bill U.K. 19 G8
Sel'tso Russia 13 G5
Selty Russia 12 K4
Selu i. Indon. 54 E1
Selvas reg. Brazil 68 D5
Selway r. ID U.S.A. 62 D2
Selwyn Lake N.W.T./Sask. Canada 60 H3
Selwyn Mountains N.W.T./Y.T. Canada
  60 E3
Selwyn Range hills Australia 56 B4
Sel'yb Russia 12 K3
Semakau, Pulau i. Sing. see Semakau
Semara W. Sahara 46 B2
Semarang Indon. 41 D8
Semau i. Indon. 54 C2
Semawi Indon. see Samawi
Semey Kazakh. 42 E2
Semeru, Gunung vol. Indon. 41 E8
Semeru Kazakh. see Semey
Semikarakorsk Russia 13 I7
Semiliki r. Dem. Rep. Congo/Uganda 48 C4
Semiluki Russia 13 H6
Seminoe TX U.S.A. 62 G5
Seminole, Lake FL/GA U.S.A. 63 J6
Semipalatinsk Kazakh. see Semey
Semīrom Iran 35 H5
Sem Kolodezey Ukr. see Lenine
Semnān Iran 35 I4

Semyonovskoye *Arkhangel'skaya Oblast'*
  Russia see Bereznik
Semyonovskoye *Kostromskaya Oblast'*
  Russia see Ostrovskoye
Sena Bol. 68 E6
Sena Madureira Brazil 68 E5
Senanga Zambia 49 C5
Sendai Japan 45 F5
Sêndo China 37 H3
Seneca Lake NY U.S.A. 64 C1
Seneca Rocks WV U.S.A. 64 B3
Senecaville Lake OH U.S.A. 64 A3
Senegal country Africa 46 B3
Sénégal r. Mauritania/Senegal 46 B3
Senftenberg Germany 17 N4
Senga Hill Zambia 49 D4
Sengerema Tanz. 48 D4
Sengeyskiy, Ostrov i. Russia 12 K1
Sengilen, Khrebet mts Russia 42 H2
Sengiley Russia 13 K5
Sengirli, Mys pt Kazakh. see Syngyrli, Mys
Senhor do Bonfim Brazil 69 J6
Senigallia Italy 26 E3
Senj Croatia 26 F2
Senja i. Norway 14 J2
Şenköy Turkey 39 C1
Senlac S. Africa 50 F3
Senlin Shan mt. China 44 C4
Senlis France 24 F2
Sennar Sudan 32 D7
Sennen U.K. 19 B8
Senneterre *Que.* Canada 63 L2
Senqu r. Lesotho 51 H6
Sens France 24 F2
Senta Serbia 27 I2
Senthal India 36 D3
Sentinel AZ U.S.A. 65 F4
Sentinel Peak B.C. Canada 60 F4
Sento Sé Brazil 69 J5
Senwabarwana S. Africa 51 I2
Şenyurt Turkey 35 F3
Seocheon S. Korea 45 B5
Seo de Urgell Spain see La Seu d'Urgell
Seonath r. India 38 D1
Seongnam S. Korea 45 B5
Seoni India 36 D5
Seorak-san National Park S. Korea 45 C5
Seorinarayan India 37 E5
Seosan S. Korea 45 B5
Seoul S. Korea 45 B5
Separation Well Australia 54 C5
Sepik r. P.N.G. 52 E2
Sep'o N. Korea 45 B5
Sepon India 37 H4
Seppa India 37 H4
Sept-Îles *Que.* Canada 63 N1
Sequoia National Park CA U.S.A. 65 C2
Serafimovich Russia 13 I6
Sêraitang China see Baima
Serakhs Turkm. see Saragt
Seram i. Indon. 41 E8
Seram, Laut sea Indon. 41 F8
Serbâl, Gebel mt. Egypt see Sirbâl, Jabal
Serbia country Europe 27 I3
Sêrbug Co l. China 37 G2
Sêrca China 37 H3
Serchhip India 37 H5
Serdar Turkm. see Serdar
Serdarabat Turkm. see Serdar
Serdica Bulg. see Sofia
Serdo Eth. 48 E2
Serdoba Russia 13 J5
Serdobsk Russia 13 I5
Serdtse-Kamen', Mys pt Russia 60 A2
Seredka Russia 15 P7
Şereflikoçhisar Turkey 34 D3
Serekunda Gambia 46 B3
Seremban Malaysia 41 C7
Serengeti National Park Tanz. 48 D4
Serenje Zambia 49 D5
Sergach Russia 13 J5
Sergelen Mongolia 45 A2
Sergeyevka Russia 44 B2
Sergiyev Posad Russia 12 H4
Sergo Ukr. see Stakhanov
Serh China 37 H1
Serhetabat Turkm. 33 J2
Seri Kazakh. see Silety
Serifos i. Greece 27 K6
Serik Turkey 34 C3
Seringapatam Reef Australia 54 C3
Sermata, Kepulauan is Indon. 54 E2
Sermersuaq glacier Greenland 61 M2
Sermilik inlet Greenland 61 O3
Sernovodsk Russia 13 K5
Sernur Russia 12 J4
Seronga Botswana 49 C5
Serov Russia 11 S4
Serowe Botswana 51 H2
Serpa Port. 25 C5
Serpa Pinto Angola see Menongue
Serpentine Lakes imp. l. Australia 55 E7
Serpukhov Russia 13 H5
Serra Alta Brazil 71 A4
Serrachis r. Cyprus 39 A2
Serra da Bocaina, Parque Nacional da
  nat. park Brazil 71 B3
Serra da Canastra, Parque Nacional da
  nat. park Brazil 71 B2
Serra da Mesa, Represa resr Brazil 71 A1
Serra do Divisor, Parque Nacional da
  nat. park Brazil 68 D5
Serra dos Araras Brazil 71 B1
Serra Talhada Brazil 69 K5
Serranía de la Neblina, Parque Nacional
  nat. park Venez. 68 E3
Serraria, Ilha r. Brazil see Queimada, Ilha
Serres Greece 27 J4
Serrinha Brazil 69 K6
Serro Brazil 71 C2
Sertanópolis Brazil 71 A3
Sertãozinho Brazil 71 B3
Sertolovo Russia 15 Q6
Sertung i. Indon. 41 C8
Sertavul Geçidi pass Turkey 39 A1
Serule Botswana 51 H2
Seruna India 36 C3
Sêrwolungwa China 37 H2
Sêrxü China 42 H6
Seryshevo Russia 44 C2
Sese Islands Uganda 48 D4
Sesel country Indian Ocean see Seychelles
Sesfontein Namibia 49 B5
Seshachalam Hills India 38 C3
Sesheke Zambia 49 C5
Sesostris Bank sea feature India 38 A3
Sestri Levante Italy 26 C2
Sestroretsk Russia 15 P6
Sète France 24 F5
Sete Lagoas Brazil 71 B2
Setermoen Norway 14 J2
Setesdal val. Norway 15 E7
Seti r. Nepal 36 E3
Sétif Alg. 22 F4
Seto Japan 45 E6
Seto-naikai sea Japan 43 O6
Seto-naikai Kokuritsu-kōen Japan 45 D6
Settat Morocco 22 C5
Settepani, Monte mt. Italy 26 C2

Settle U.K. 18 E4
Setúbal Port. 25 B4
Setúbal, Baía de b. Port. 25 B4
Seul, Lac l. *Ont.* Canada 63 I1
Sevan Armenia 35 G2
Sevan, Lake Armenia 35 G2
Sevan, Ozero l. Armenia see Sevan, Lake
Sevana Lich l. Armenia see Sevan, Lake
Sevastopol' Ukr. 34 D1
Seven Islands *Que.* Canada see Sept-Îles
Sevenoaks U.K. 19 H7
Sévérac-le-Château France 24 F4
Severn r. Australia 58 E2
Severn r. *Ont.* Canada 63 I1
Severn S. Africa 50 F4
Severn r. U.K. 19 E7
Severnaya Dvina r. Russia 12 I2
Severnaya Sos'va r. Russia 11 T3
Severnaya Zemlya is Russia 29 L1
Severnoye Russia 11 Q5
Severnyy *Nenetskiy Avtonomnyy Okrug*
  Russia 12 K1
Severnyy *Respublika Komi* Russia 28 H3
Severobaykal'sk Russia 28 J1
Severo-Baykal'skoye Nagor'ye mts Russia
  29 M4
Severodonetsk Ukr. see Syeverodonets'k
Severodvinsk Russia 12 H2
Severo-Kuril'sk Russia 29 Q4
Severomorsk Russia 12 G2
Severonezhsk Russia 12 H3
Severo-Sibirskaya Nizmennost' lowland
  Russia see North Siberian Lowland
Severoural'sk Russia 11 S3
Severo-Yeniseyskiy Russia 28 K3
Severskaya Russia 34 E1
Sevier Lake UT U.S.A. 65 F1
Sevilla Col. 68 C3
Sevilla Spain see Seville
Seville Spain 25 D5
Sevlyush Ukr. see Vynohradiv
Sewani India 36 C3
Seward AK U.S.A. 60 D3
Seward Mountains Antarctica 76 L2
Seward Peninsula AK U.S.A. 60 B3
Sexi Spain see Almuñécar
Seyakha Russia 77 F2
Seychelles country Indian Ocean 73 L6
Seydi Turkm. 33 J2
Seydişehir Turkey 34 C3
Seyðisfjörður Iceland 14 [inset 2]
Seyhan Turkey see Adana
Seyhan r. Turkey 39 B1
Seyitgazi Turkey 27 N5
Seym' r. Russia/Ukr. 43 E1
Seymchan Russia 29 Q3
Seymour Australia 58 B6
Seymour IN U.S.A. 63 J4
Seymour TX U.S.A. 62 H5
Seymour Range mts Australia 55 F6
Seypan i. N. Mariana Is see Saipan
Sézanne France 24 F2
Sfântu Gheorghe Romania 27 K2
Sfax Tunisia 26 D7
Sfikias, Limni resr Greece 27 J4
Sfîntu Gheorghe Romania see
  Sfântu Gheorghe
Sgierschi Poland see Zgierz
's-Gravenhage Neth. see The Hague
Sgurr Alasdair h. U.K. 20 C4
Sgurr Dhomhnuill h. U.K. 20 D4
Sgurr Mòr mt. U.K. 20 D3
Sgurr na Ciche mt. U.K. 20 D3
Shaanxi prov. China 43 K5
Shaartuz Tajik. see Shahritus
Shaban Pak. 36 A3
Shabani Zimbabwe see Zvishavane
Shabestar Iran 35 G3
Shabibi, Jabal ash mt. Jordan 39 B5
Shabla, Nos pt Bulg. 27 M3
Shabunda Dem. Rep. Congo 48 C4
Shache China 42 D5
Shackleton Coast Antarctica 76 H1
Shackleton Glacier Antarctica 76 I1
Shackleton Ice Shelf Antarctica 76 F2
Shackleton Range mts Antarctica 76 A1
Shädegän Iran 35 H4
Shady Spring WV U.S.A. 64 A4
Shafer Peak Antarctica 76 H2
Shafter CA U.S.A. 65 C3
Shaftesbury U.K. 19 E7
Shagamu China 43 K5
Shageluk AK U.S.A. 60 C3
Shagonar Russia 42 G2
Shag Point N.Z. 59 C7
Shag Rocks is S. Georgia 70 H8
Shahabad Brazil see Selvagem Grande [?]
Shahabad *Karnataka* India 38 C2
Shahabad *Rajasthan* India 36 D4
Shahabad *Uttar Prad.* India 36 D4
Shāhābād r. Iran see Eslāmābād-e Gharb
Shah Bandar Pak. 36 A4
Shahdol India 36 E5
Shāh Fōlād mt. Afgh. 36 A2
Shahganj India 36 E4
Shahgarh India 36 B4
Shahhāt Libya see Cyrene [?]
Shāhīn Dezh Iran 35 G3
Shahjahanpur India 36 D4
Shāhpūr Iran see Salmās
Shahrak Afgh. 36 A3
Shahr-e Bābak Iran 35 I5
Shahr-e Kord Iran 35 H4
Shahr-e Safā Afgh. 36 A3
Shahrezā Iran 35 H4
Shahri Pak. 36 A3
Shahrisabz Uzbek. see Shahrisabz
Shahr-i Sokhta tourist site Iran 33 J3
Shahritus Tajik. 36 B1
Shahr Sultan Pak. 36 B3
Shāhrūd Iran 35 I3
Shāhrūd, Rūdkhāneh-ye r. Iran 35 H3
Shaikh Husain mt. Pak. 36 A3
Shaikhpura India see Sheikhpura
Shāʾir, Jabal mt. Syria 39 C2
Shaʾira, Gebel mt. Egypt see Shaʾirah, Jabal
Shaʾirah, Jabal mt. Egypt 39 B5
Shajapur India 36 D5
Shajianzi China 44 B4
Shakaville S. Africa 51 J5
Shakh Tajik. see Shoh
Shakhbuz Azer. see Şahbuz
Shakhovskaya Russia 12 G4
Shakhrisabz Uzbek. see Shahrisabz
Shakhtinsk Kazakh. 42 C3
Shakhty *Respublika Buryatiya* Russia see
  Gusinoozersk
Shakhty *Rostovskaya Oblast'* Russia 13 I7
Shakhun'ya Russia 12 J4
Shaki Nigeria see Saki
Shakotan-hantō pen. Japan 44 F4
Shalakusha Russia 12 I3
Shali Russia 35 G2
Shaliuhe China see Gangca
Shalkar Kazakh. 28 H5
Shalkarteniz, Solonchak salt marsh
  Kazakh. 42 A3
Shalqar Kazakh. see Shalkar
Shaluli Shan mts China 42 H6
Shaluni mt. India 37 I3
Shama r. Tanz. 48 D4
Shamāl Sīnā' governorate Egypt see
  Shamāl Sīnā'
Shamāl Sīnā' governorate Egypt 39 A4
Shāmat al Akbād des. Saudi Arabia 35 F5

Shamattawa Man. Canada 61 I4
Shambār Iran 35 H4
Shamgong Bhutan see Zhemgang
Shāmīyah des. Iraq/Syria 39 D2
Shamkhor Azer. see Şämkir
Shamrock TX U.S.A. 62 G4
Shancheng China 43 K5
Shandong prov. China 43 L5
Shandong Bandao pen. China 43 M5
Shandur Pass Pak. 36 C1
Shangdu China 43 K4
Shangganling China 44 C3
Shanghai China 43 M6
Shanghai mun. China 43 M6
Shangluo China 43 J6
Shangnan China 43 K6
Shangrao China 43 L7
Shangyou Shuiku resr China 42 E4
Shangzhi China 44 B3
Shanhe China 44 B3
Shanlaragh Ireland 21 C6
Shannon est. Ireland 21 D5
Shannon r. Ireland 21 D5
Shannon, Mouth of the Ireland 21 C5
Shannon National Park Australia 55 B8
Shannon Ø i. Greenland 77 I1
Shansi prov. China see Shanxi
Shantipur India 37 G5
Shantou China 43 L8
Shantung prov. China see Shandong
Shanxi prov. China 43 K5
Shaoguan China 43 K8
Shaowu China 43 L7
Shaoxing China 43 M6
Shaoyang China 43 K7
Shap U.K. 18 E4
Shapinsay i. U.K. 20 G1
Shapkina r. Russia 12 L2
Shapshal'skiy Khrebet mts Russia 42 F2
Shaqrā' Saudi Arabia 32 G4
Shār, Jabal mt. Saudi Arabia 34 D6
Sharaf well Iraq 35 F5
Sharan Jogizai Pak. 36 B3
Shardara Kazakh. 33 K1
Shardara, Step' plain Kazakh. 42 B4
Shari r. Cameroon/Chad see Chari
Shārī, Buḩayrat imp. l. Iraq 35 G4
Shari-dake vol. Japan 44 G4
Sharīfah Syria 39 C2
Sharjah U.A.E. 33 I4
Sharka-leb La pass China 37 G3
Sharkawshchyna Belarus 15 O9
Shark Bay Australia 55 A6
Shark Reef Australia 56 D2
Sharlyk Russia 11 Q5
Sharm ash Shaykh Egypt 34 D6
Sharm el Sheikh Egypt see Sharm ash Shaykh
Sharon PA U.S.A. 64 A2
Sharqat Iraq see Ash Sharqāţ
Sharqī, Jabal ash mts Lebanon/Syria 39 B3
Sharur Azer. see Şärur
Shar'ya Russia 12 J4
Shashe r. Botswana/Zimbabwe 49 C6
Shashemenē Eth. 48 D3
Shashi China see Jingzhou
Shasta, Mount vol. CA U.S.A. 62 C3
Shatilki Belarus see Svyetlahorsk
Shatki Russia 13 J5
Shaṭnat as Salmās, Wādī watercourse Syria 39 D2
Shatoy Russia 35 G2
Shatsk Russia 13 I5
Shatt al Arab r. Iran/Iraq 35 H5
Shatura Russia 13 H5
Shaubak Jordan see Ash Shawbak
Shaunavon Sask. Canada 62 F2
Shaver Lake CA U.S.A. 65 C2
Shaw r. Australia 54 B5
Shawangunk Mountains hills NY U.S.A. 64 D2
Shawano WI U.S.A. 63 J3
Shawnee OK U.S.A. 63 H4
Shay Gap (abandoned) Australia 54 C5
Shaykh, Jabal ash mt. Lebanon/Syria see Hermon, Mount
Shaykh Miskīn Syria 39 C3
Shāzand Iran 35 H4
Shchekino Russia 13 H5
Shchel'yayur Russia 12 L2
Shcherbakov Russia see Rybinsk
Shchigry Russia 13 H6
Shchors Ukr. 13 F6
Shchuchin Belarus see Shchuchyn
Shchuchyn Belarus 15 N10
Shebalino Russia 42 F2
Shebekino Russia 13 H6
Shebelē Wenz, Wabē r. Eth. 48 E3
Sheboygan WI U.S.A. 63 J3
Shebshi Mountains Nigeria 46 E4
Shebunino Russia 44 F3
Shedok Russia 35 F1
Sheelin, Lough l. Ireland 21 E4
Sheep Haven b. Ireland 21 E2
Sheepmoor S. Africa 51 J4
Sheep Peak NV U.S.A. 65 E2
Sheep's Head hd Ireland see Muntervary
Sheerness U.K. 19 H7
Shefar'am Israel 39 B3
Sheffield N.Z. 59 D6
Sheffield U.K. 18 F5
Sheffield PA U.S.A. 64 B2
Sheghnān Afgh. 36 B1
Shegmas Russia 12 K2
Sheikh, Jebel esh mt. Lebanon/Syria see Hermon, Mount
Sheikhpura India 37 F4
Sheikhupura Pak. 33 L3
Shêjā' ul Mulk Kêlay Afgh. 36 B3
Shekār Āb Iran 35 I4
Shekhem West Bank see Nāblus
Shekhpura India see Sheikhpura
Sheki Azer. see Şäki
Sheksna Russia 12 H4
Sheksninskoye Vodokhranilishche resr Russia 12 H4
Shela China 37 H3
Shelagskiy, Mys pt Russia 29 S2
Shelburne N.S. Canada 63 N3
Shelburne Bay Australia 56 C1
Shelby MT U.S.A. 62 E2
Shelbyville TN U.S.A. 63 J4
Shelikhova, Zaliv g. Russia 29 Q3
Shelikof Strait AK U.S.A. 60 C4
Shellbrook Sask. Canada 62 F1
Shellharbour Australia 58 E5
Shelter Island NY U.S.A. 64 E2
Shelter Point N.Z. 59 B8
Shemakha Azer. see Şamaxı
Shemordan Russia 12 K4
Shenandoah PA U.S.A. 64 C2
Shenandoah Mountains VA/WV U.S.A. 64 B3
Shenandoah National Park VA U.S.A. 64 B3
Shendam Nigeria 46 D4
Shending Shan h. China 44 D3
Shengena mt. Tanz. 49 D4
Shengli Feng mt. China/Kyrg. see Pobeda Peak
Shengping China 44 B3
Shenkursk Russia 12 I3
Shenmu China 43 K5
Shenshu China 44 C3
Shensi prov. China see Shaanxi
Shentala Russia 13 K5
Shenton, Mount h. Australia 55 C7
Shenyang China 44 A4
Shenzhen China 43 K8
Sheopur India 36 D4
Shepetivka Ukr. 13 E6
Shepetovka Ukr. see Shepetivka
Shepherd Islands Vanuatu 53 G3
Shepparton Australia 58 B6
Sheppey, Isle of i. U.K. 19 H7
Sherabad Uzbek. see Sherobod
Sherborne U.K. 19 E8
Sherbro Island Sierra Leone 46 B4
Sherbrooke Que. Canada 63 M2
Sherburne NY U.S.A. 64 D1
Shercock Ireland 21 F4
Shereiq Sudan 32 D6
Shergaon India 37 H4
Shergarh India 36 C4
Sheridan WY U.S.A. 62 F3
Sheringham U.K. 19 I6
Sherman TX U.S.A. 63 H5
Sherobod Uzbek. 33 K2
Sherpur Dhaka Bangl. 37 G4
Sherpur Rajshahi Bangl. 37 G4
's-Hertogenbosch Neth. 16 J5
Sherwood Forest reg. U.K. 19 F5
Shetland Islands is U.K. 20 [inset]
Shetpe Kazakh. 30 E2
Shevchenko Kazakh. see Aktau
Shevli r. Russia 44 D1
Sheyenne r. ND U.S.A. 62 H2
Shey Phoksundo National Park Nepal 37 E3
Shezhin II Kazakh. 13 K6
Shiant Islands U.K. 20 C3
Shiashkotan, Ostrov i. Russia 29 Q5
Shibām Yemen 32 G6
Shibar, Kōtal-e Afgh. 36 B2
Shibata Japan 45 E5
Shibazhan China 44 B1
Shibh Jazīrat Sīnā' pen. Egypt see Sinai
Shibīn al Kawm Egypt 34 C5
Shibîn el Kôm Egypt see Shibīn al Kawm
Shibirghān Afgh. 36 A1
Shibotsu-jima i. Russia see Zelenyy, Ostrov
Shidād al Mismā' h. Saudi Arabia 39 D4
Shidao China 43 M5
Shiel, Loch l. U.K. 20 D4
Shield, Cape Australia 56 B2
Shīeli Kazakh. see Shiyeli
Shīf Iran 35 H5
Shifa, Jabal ash mts Saudi Arabia 34 D5
Shigatse China see Xigazê
Shiḩān mt. Jordan 39 B4
Shihezi China 42 F4
Shihkiachwang China see Shijiazhuang
Shijiazhuang China 43 K5
Shikarpur Pak. 33 K4
Shikhany Russia 13 J5
Shikohabad India 36 D4
Shikoku i. Japan 45 D6
Shikoku-sanchi mts Japan 45 D6
Shikotan, Ostrov i. Russia 44 G4
Shikotan-tō i. Russia see Shikotan, Ostrov
Shikotsu-Tōya Kokuritsu-kōen Japan 44 F4
Shildon U.K. 18 F4
Shilega Russia 12 J2
Shiliguri India 37 G4
Shilla mt. India 36 D2
Shillelagh Ireland 21 F5
Shillo, Naḥal r. Israel 39 B3
Shillong India 37 G4
Shilovo Russia 13 I5
Shimada Japan 45 E6
Shimanovsk Russia 44 B1
Shimbiris mt. Somalia 48 E2
Shimen China 43 K7
Shimla India 36 D3
Shimoga India 38 B3
Shimokita-hantō pen. Japan 44 F4
Shimoni Kenya 49 D4
Shimonoseki Japan 45 C6
Shimsk Russia 12 F4
Shin, Loch l. U.K. 20 E2
Shināfīyah Iraq see Ash Shanāfīyah
Shīndand Afgh. 33 J3
Shingbwiyang Myanmar 37 I4
Shinghshal Pass Pak. 36 C1
Shingū Japan 45 E6
Shingwedzi S. Africa 51 J2
Shingwedzi r. S. Africa 51 J2
Shīnkaī Afgh. 36 A3
Shīnkay Ghar Afgh. 36 B2
Shinnston WV U.S.A. 64 A3
Shinshār Syria 39 C2
Shinyanga Tanz. 48 D4
Shiogama Japan 45 F5
Shiono-misaki c. Japan 45 D6
Shipki La China/India 36 D3
Shipman VA U.S.A. 64 B4
Shippensburg PA U.S.A. 64 C2
Shipunovo Russia 42 E2
Shiquanhe Xizang China see Ali
Shiquanhe Xizang China see Gar
Shira Russia 42 F2
Shīrābād Iran 35 H3
Shirakawa-go and Gokayama tourist site Japan 45 E5
Shirane-san vol. Japan 45 E5
Shirase Coast Antarctica 76 J1
Shirase Glacier Antarctica 76 D2
Shīrāz Iran 35 I5
Shire r. Malawi 49 D5
Shiriya-zaki c. Japan 44 F4
Shiroro Reservoir Nigeria 46 D3
Shirpur India 36 C5
Shirten Holoy Gobi des. China 42 H4
Shīrvān Iran 33 I2
Shisanzhan China 44 B2
Shishaldin Volcano AK U.S.A. 60 B4
Shisha Pangma mt. China see Xixabangma Feng
Shithāthah Iraq 35 F4
Shīū' Iran 35 I6
Shiv India 36 B4
Shivamogga India see Shimoga
Shiveegovi Mongolia 43 J3
Shiveluch, Vulkan vol. Russia 29 R4
Shivpuri India 36 D4
Shivwits UT U.S.A. 65 F2
Shivwits Plateau AZ U.S.A. 65 F2
Shiwa Ng'andu Zambia 49 D5
Shiyan China 43 K6
Shiyeli Kazakh. 42 B4
Shizhong China 43 L6
Shizuishan China 42 J5
Shizuoka Japan 45 E6
Shkhara mt. Georgia/Russia 35 F2
Shklov Belarus see Shklow
Shklow Belarus 13 F5
Shkodër Albania 27 H3
Shkodra Albania see Shkodër
Shkodrës, Liqeni i l. Albania/Montenegro see Scutari, Lake
Shmidta, Ostrov i. Russia 28 K1
Shmidta, Poluostrov pen. Russia 44 F1
Shōbara Japan 45 D6
Shoh Tajik. 36 B1
Shohi Pass Pak. see Tal Pass
Shokanbetsu-dake mt. Japan 44 F4
Sholakkorgan Kazakh. 42 B4
Sholapur India see Solapur
Sholaqorghan Kazakh. see Sholakkorgan
Shomba r. Russia 14 R4
Shomvukovo Russia 12 K3
Shona Ridge sea feature S. Atlantic Ocean 72 I9
Shonzha Kazakh. see Shonzhy
Shonzhy Kazakh. 42 D4
Shor India 36 D2
Shorapur India 38 C2
Sho'rchi Uzbek. 42 B5
Shorkot Pak. 36 C3
Shorkozakhly, Solonchak salt flat Turkm. 35 J2
Shoshone CA U.S.A. 65 D3
Shoshone Peak NV U.S.A. 65 D2
Shoshong Botswana 51 H2
Shostka Ukr. 13 G6
Shotoran, Chashmeh-ye well Iran 35 I4
Shotor Khūn Afgh. 36 A2
Showak Sudan 32 E7
Show Low AZ U.S.A. 62 E5
Shoyna Russia 12 J2
Shpola Ukr. 13 F6
Shqipëria country Europe see Albania
Shreveport LA U.S.A. 63 I5
Shrewsbury U.K. 19 E6
Shri Lanka country Asia see Sri Lanka
Shri Mohangarh India 36 B4
Shrirampur India 37 G5
Shu Kazakh. 42 C4
Shū r. Kazakh./Kyrg. see Shu
Shu r. Kazakh./Kyrg. 42 B4
Shu'ab, Ra's pt Yemen 33 H7
Shuangcheng China 44 B3
Shuanghedagang China 44 C2
Shuangliao China 44 A4
Shuangshipu China see Fengxian
Shuangyang China 44 B4
Shuangyashan China 44 C3
Shubarkudyk Kazakh. 28 G5
Shubayḩ well Saudi Arabia 39 D4
Shugozero Russia 12 G4
Shuicheng China see Liupanshui
Shu-Ile, Gory mts Kazakh. 42 C4
Shulan China 44 B3
Shumagin Islands AK U.S.A. 60 B4
Shumba Zimbabwe 49 C5
Shumen Bulg. 27 L3
Shumerlya Russia 12 J5
Shumilina Belarus 13 F5
Shumyachi Russia 13 G5
Shūnan Japan 45 C6
Shuncheng China 44 A4
Shuoxian China see Shuozhou
Shuozhou China 43 K5
Shuqrah Yemen 32 G7
Shūr r. Iran 35 I5
Shūr, Chāh-e well Iran 35 I4
Shūrjestān Iran 35 I5
Shuryshkarskiy Sor, Ozero l. Russia 11 T2
Shūsh Iran 35 H4
Shusha Azer. see Şuşa
Shūshtar Iran 35 H4
Shuwaysh, Tall ash h. Jordan 39 C4
Shuya Ivanovskaya Oblast' Russia 12 I4
Shuya Respublika Kareliya Russia 12 G3
Shuyskoye Russia 12 I4
Shuẓāẓ, Jabal mt. Saudi Arabia 35 F6
Shwebo Myanmar 37 H5
Shwedwin Myanmar 37 H4
Shweudaung mt. Myanmar 37 I5
Shyganak Kazakh. 42 C3
Shyghanaq Kazakh. see Shyganak
Shymkent Kazakh. 42 B4
Shyngystau, Khrebet mts Kazakh. 42 D3
Shyok India 36 D2
Shypuvate Ukr. 13 H6
Shyroke Ukr. 13 G7
Sia Indon. 41 F8
Siahan Range mts Pak. 33 J4
Siāh Cheshmeh Iran 35 G3
Sialkot Pak. 33 L3
Siam country Asia see Thailand
Sian China see Xi'an
Sian Russia 44 B1
Siang r. India see Dihang
Šiauliai Lith. 15 M9
Siazan' Azer. see Siyäzän
Sibasa S. Africa 51 J2
Sibayi, Lake S. Africa 51 K4
Šibenik Croatia 26 F3
Siberia reg. Russia 29 M3
Siberut i. Indon. 41 B8
Sibi Pak. 33 K4
Sibiloi National Park Kenya 48 D3
Sibir' reg. Russia see Siberia
Sibiti Congo 48 B4
Sibiu Romania 27 K2
Sibolga Indon. 41 B7
Sibu Sarawak Malaysia 41 D7
Sibut Cent. Afr. Rep. 48 B3
Sicca Veneria Tunisia see Le Kef
Siccus watercourse Australia 57 B6
Sicheng China see Sixian
Sichuan prov. China 42 I6
Sichuan Pendi basin China 42 I7
Sicié, Cap c. France 24 G5
Sicilia i. Italy see Sicily
Sicilian Channel Italy/Tunisia 26 E6
Sicily i. Italy 26 F5
Sicuani Peru 68 D6
Siddhapur India see Sidhpur
Siddipet India 38 C2
Sideros, Akrotirio pt Greece 27 L7
Sidesaviwa S. Africa 50 F7
Sidhauli India 36 E4
Sidhi India 37 E4
Sidhpur India 36 C5
Sidi Aïssa Alg. 25 H6
Sidi Ali Alg. 25 G5
Sīdī Barrānī Egypt 34 B5
Sidi Bel Abbès Alg. 25 F6
Sidi Bennour Morocco 22 C5
Sidi Bou Sa'îd Tunisia see Sidi Bouzid
Sidi Bouzid Tunisia 26 C7
Sîdi el Barrâni Egypt see Sīdī Barrānī
Sidi El Hani, Sebkhet de salt pan Tunisia 26 D7
Sidi Ifni Morocco 46 B2
Sidi Kacem Morocco 22 C5
Sidi Khaled Alg. 22 E5
Sidlaw Hills U.K. 20 F4
Sidley, Mount Antarctica 76 J1
Sidli India 37 G4
Sidmouth U.K. 19 D8
Sidney MT U.S.A. 62 G2
Sidney NE U.S.A. 62 G3
Sidney OH U.S.A. 63 K3
Sidoktaya Myanmar 37 H5
Sidon Lebanon 39 B3
Sidr Egypt see Sudr
Siedlce Poland 13 D5
Siegen Germany 17 L5
Siena Italy 26 D3
Sieradz Poland 17 Q5
Si'erdingka China 37 H3
Sierra Colorada Arg. 70 C6
Sierra Grande Arg. 70 C6
Sierra Leone country Africa 46 B4
Sierra Leone Basin sea feature N. Atlantic Ocean 72 G5
Sierra Leone Rise sea feature N. Atlantic Ocean 72 G5
Sierra Madre Mountains CA U.S.A. 65 B3
Sierra Nevada, Parque Nacional nat. park Venez. 68 D2
Sierra Nevada de Santa Marta, Parque Nacional nat. park Col. 68 D1
Sierra Vista AZ U.S.A. 62 E5
Sierre Switz. 24 H3
Sievi Fin. 14 N5
Sifangtai China 44 B3
Sīfenī Eth. 48 E2
Sifnos i. Greece 27 K6
Sig Alg. 25 F6
Sigguup Nunaa pen. Greenland 61 M2
Sighetu Marmaţiei Romania 13 D7
Sighişoara Romania 27 K1
Sigli Indon. 41 B7
Siglufjörður Iceland 14 [inset 2]
Signal de la Ste-Baume mt. France 24 G5
Signal Peak AZ U.S.A. 65 E4
Signy (U.K.) research stn Antarctica 76 A2
Sigsbee Deep sea feature G. of Mexico 75 N4
Sigüenza Spain 25 E3
Siguiri Guinea 46 C3
Sigulda Latvia 15 N8
Sihanoukville Cambodia 31 J5
Sihaung Myauk Myanmar 37 H5
Sihawa India 38 D1
Sihora India 36 E5
Siikajoki Fin. 14 N4
Siilinjärvi Fin. 14 O5
Siirt Turkey 35 F3
Sijawal Pak. 36 B4
Sikaka Saudi Arabia see Sakākah
Sikandra Rao India 36 D4
Sikar India 36 C4
Sikaram mt. Afgh. 36 B2
Sikasso Mali 46 C3
Sikeston MO U.S.A. 63 J4
Sikhote-Alin' mts Russia 44 D4
Sikhote-Alinskiy Zapovednik nature res. Russia 44 E3
Sikinos i. Greece 27 K6
Sikka India 36 B5
Sikkim state India 37 G4
Siksjö Sweden 14 J4
Sil r. Spain 25 C2
Sīla' i. Saudi Arabia 34 D6
Šilal Lith. 15 M9
Silavatturai Sri Lanka 38 C4
Silchar India 37 H4
Şile Turkey 27 M4
Sileru r. India 38 D2
Silesia reg. Czech Rep./Poland 17 P5
Silety r. Kazakh. 42 C2
Siletyteniz, Ozero salt l. Kazakh. 31 G1
Silghat India 37 H4
Siliana Tunisia 26 C6
Silifke Turkey 39 A1
Siliguri India see Shiliguri
Siling Co salt l. China 37 G3
Silipur India 36 D4
Silistra Bulg. 27 L2
Silistria Bulg. see Silistra
Silivri Turkey 27 M4
Siljan l. Sweden 15 I6
Silkeborg Denmark 15 F8
Sillajhuay mt. Chile 68 E7
Sillamäe Estonia 15 O7
Sille Turkey 34 D3
Silli India 37 F5
Sillod India 38 B1
Silobela S. Africa 51 J4
Siltaharju Fin. 14 O3
Šilutė Lith. 15 L9
Silvan Turkey 35 F3
Silvânia Brazil 71 A2
Silvassa India 38 B1
Silver Bank Passage Turks and Caicos Is 67 J4
Silver City NM U.S.A. 62 F5
Silver City NV U.S.A. 65 C1
Silver Lake CA U.S.A. 65 D3
Silvermine Mountains hills Ireland 21 D5
Silver Peak Range mts NV U.S.A. 65 D2
Silver Spring MD U.S.A. 64 C3
Silverton U.K. 19 D8
Silverton CO U.S.A. 62 F4
Sima China 37 G3
Simanggang Sarawak Malaysia see Sri Aman
Simao China 42 I8
Simard, Lac l. Que. Canada 63 L2
Simaria India 37 F4
Simav Turkey 27 M5
Simav Dağları mts Turkey 27 M5
Simba Dem. Rep. Congo 48 C3
Simbirsk Russia see Ul'yanovsk
Simcoe Ont. Canada 64 A1
Simcoe, Lake Ont. Canada 63 L3
Simdega India 38 E1
Simēn mts Eth. 48 D2
Simēn Mountains Eth. see Simēn
Simeulue i. Indon. 41 B7
Simferopol' Ukr. 34 D1
Sími i. Greece see Symi
Simikot Nepal 37 E3
Simi Valley CA U.S.A. 65 C3
Simla India see Shimla
Şimleu Silvaniei Romania 27 J1
Simlipal National Park India 37 F5
Simojärvi l. Fin. 14 O3
Simpele Fin. 15 P6
Simplício Mendes Brazil 69 J5
Simplon Pass Switz. 24 I3
Simpson Desert Australia 56 B5
Simpson Desert National Park Australia 56 B5
Simpson Desert Regional Reserve nature res. Australia 57 B5
Simpson Peninsula Nunavut Canada 61 J3
Simrishamn Sweden 15 I9
Simushir, Ostrov i. Russia 43 S3
Sina r. India 38 B2
Sinai pen. Egypt 39 A5
Sinai al Janūbīya governorate Egypt see Janūb Sīnā'
Sinai ash Shamâlîya governorate Egypt see Shamāl Sīnā'
Sinalunga Italy 26 D3
Sinancha Russia see Cheremshany
Sinbyugyun Myanmar 37 H5
Sincan Turkey 34 E3
Sincelejo Col. 68 C2
Sincora, Serra do hills Brazil 71 C1
Sind r. India 36 D4
Sind Pak. see Thul
Sind prov. Pak. see Sindh
Sinda Russia 44 E2
Sindari India 36 B4
Sindelfingen Germany 17 L6
Sindh prov. Pak. 36 B4
Sindhulimadi Nepal see Kamalamai
Sındırgı Turkey 27 M5
Sindor Russia 12 K3
Sindou Burkina Faso 46 C3
Sindri India 37 F5
Sind Sagar Doab lowland Pak. 36 B3
Sinel'nikovo Ukr. see Synel'nykove
Sines Port. 25 B5
Sines, Cabo de c. Port. 25 B5
Sinettä Fin. 14 N3
Sinfra Côte d'Ivoire 46 C4
Singa Sudan 32 D7
Singanallur India 38 C4
Singapore country Asia 41 C7
Singapore Sing. 41 C7
Singapura country Asia see Singapore
Singapura Sing. see Singapore
Singapuru India 38 D2
Singaraja Indon. 54 A2
Singhana India 36 C3
Singida Tanz. 49 D4
Singidunum Serbia see Belgrade
Singkaling Hkamti Myanmar 37 H4
Singkawang Indon. 41 C7
Singleton Australia 58 E4
Singleton, Mount h. N.T. Australia 54 E5
Singleton, Mount h. W.A. Australia 55 B7
Singora Thai. see Songkhla
Sin'gosan N. Korea see Kosan
Singra India 37 G4
Singri India 37 H4
Singwara India 38 D1
Sin'gye N. Korea 45 B5
Sinhala country Asia see Sri Lanka
Sining China see Xining
Siniscola Sardinia Italy 26 C4
Sinj Croatia 26 G3
Sinjai Indon. 41 E8
Sinjār, Jabal mt. Iraq 35 F3
Sinkat Sudan 32 E6
Sinkiang aut. reg. China see Xinjiang Uygur Zizhiqu
Sinkiang Uighur Autonomous Region aut. reg. China see Xinjiang Uygur Zizhiqu
Sinmi-do i. N. Korea 45 B5
Sinnamary Fr. Guiana 69 H2
Sinn Bishr, Gebel h. Egypt see Sinn Bishr, Jabal
Sinn Bishr, Jabal h. Egypt 39 A5
Sinneh Iran see Sanandaj
Sinoia Zimbabwe see Chinhoyi
Sinop Brazil 69 G6
Sinop Turkey 34 D2
Sinope Turkey see Sinop
Sinp'o N. Korea 45 C4
Sinsang N. Korea 45 B5
Sint Eustatius i. West Indies 67 L5
Sint Maarten i. West Indies 67 L5
Sint-Niklaas Belgium 16 J5
Sintra Port. 25 B4
Sinŭiju N. Korea 45 B4
Siófok Hungary 26 H1
Sioma Ngwezi National Park Zambia 49 C5
Sion Switz. 24 H3
Sion Mills U.K. 21 E3
Siorapaluk Greenland 61 K2
Sioux Center IA U.S.A. 63 H3
Sioux City IA U.S.A. 63 H3
Sioux Falls SD U.S.A. 63 H3
Sioux Lookout Ont. Canada 63 I1
Siphaqeni S. Africa see Flagstaff
Siping China 44 B4
Siple, Mount Antarctica 76 J2
Siple Coast Antarctica 76 I1
Siple Dome ice feature Antarctica 76 J1
Siple Island Antarctica 76 J2
Sipura i. Indon. 41 B8
Siq, Wādī as watercourse Egypt 39 A5
Sir r. Pak. 36 B5
Sir, Dar"yoi r. Asia see Syrdar'ya
Sira India 38 C3
Sira r. Norway 15 E7
Siracusa Sicily Italy see Syracuse
Siraha Nepal see Sirha
Sirajganj Bangl. 37 G4
Şiran Turkey 35 E2
Sirbāl, Jabal mt. Egypt 34 D5
Sircilla India see Sirsilla
Sirdaryo r. Asia see Syrdar'ya
Sirdaryo Uzbek. 42 B4
Sirdingka China see Si'erdingka
Sir Edward Pellew Group is Australia 56 B2
Sirha Nepal 37 F4
Sirhān, Wādī an watercourse Saudi Arabia 34 E5
Sirḩān, Wādī as watercourse Jordan/Saudi Arabia 39 C4
Sirina i. Greece see Syrna
Sir James MacBrien, Mount N.W.T. Canada 60 F3
Sīrjān Iran 33 I4
Sirkazhi India 38 C4
Sirmilik National Park Nunavut Canada 61 K2
Şırnak Turkey 35 F3
Sirohi India 36 C4
Sironj India 36 D4
Síros i. Greece see Syros
Sirpur India 38 C2
Sirretta Peak CA U.S.A. 65 C3
Sirsa India 36 C3
Sirsi Karnataka India 38 B3
Sirsi Madh. Prad. India 36 D4
Sirsi Uttar Prad. India 36 D3
Sirsilla India 38 C2
Sirte Libya 47 E1
Sirte, Gulf of Libya 47 E1
Sir Thomas, Mount h. Australia 55 E6
Siruguppa India 38 C3
Sirur India 38 B2
Şirvan Azer. 35 H3
Şirvan Turkey 35 F3
Sirvel India 38 C3
Širvintai Lith. see Širvintos
Širvintos Lith. 15 N9
Sīrwān r. Iraq 35 G4
Sis Turkey see Kozan
Sisak Croatia 26 G2
Siscia Croatia see Sisak
Sishen S. Africa 50 F4
Sisian Armenia 35 G3
Sisimiut Greenland 61 M3
Sisteron France 24 G4
Sitamarhi India 37 F4
Sitapur India 36 E4
Siteia Greece 27 L7
Siteki Swaziland 51 J4
Site of Xanadu tourist site China 43 L4
Sithonias, Chersonisos pen. Greece 27 J4
Sitía Greece see Siteia
Sitidgi Lake N.W.T. Canada 60 E3
Sitila Moz. 51 L2
Sítio do Mato Brazil 71 C1
Sitka AK U.S.A. 60 E4
Sitra oasis Egypt see Sitrah
Sitrah oasis Egypt 34 B5
Sittaung Myanmar 37 H4
Sittingbourne U.K. 19 H7
Sittwe Myanmar 37 H5
Siuri India 37 F5
Sivaganga India 38 C4
Sivakasi India 38 C4
Sivaki Russia 44 B1
Sivan India see Siwan
Sivas Turkey 34 E3
Sivasagar India 37 H4
Sivaslı Turkey 27 M5
Siverek Turkey 35 E3
Siverskiy Russia 15 Q7
Sivers'kyy Donets' r. Russia/Ukr. see Severskiy Donets
Sivomaskinskiy Russia 11 S2
Sivrice Turkey 35 E3
Sivrihisar Turkey 27 N5
Sivukile S. Africa 51 I4
Sīwa Egypt see Sīwah
Sīwah Egypt 34 B5
Sīwah, Wāḩāt oasis Egypt 34 B5
Siwalik Range mts India/Nepal 36 D3
Siwan India 37 F4
Siwana India 36 C4
Siwa Oasis oasis Egypt see Sīwah, Wāḩāt
Sixian China 43 L6
Sixmilecross U.K. 21 E3
Siyabuswa S. Africa 51 I3
Siyāh Gird Afgh. 36 A1
Siyäzän Azer. 35 H2
Siyunī Iran 35 I4
Siziwang Qi China see Ulan Hua
Sjælland i. Denmark see Zealand
Sjenica Serbia 27 I3
Sjöbo Sweden 15 H9
Sjøvegan Norway 14 J2
Skadarsko Jezero, Nacionalni Park nat. park Montenegro 27 H3
Skadovs'k Ukr. 27 O1
Skaftárós r. mouth Iceland 14 [inset 2]
Skagafjörður inlet Iceland 14 [inset 2]
Skagen Denmark 15 G8
Skagerrak str. Denmark/Norway 15 F8
Skagit r. WA U.S.A. 62 C2
Skagway AK U.S.A. 77 A3
Skaidi Norway 14 N1
Skaland Norway 14 J2
Skalmodal Sweden 14 I4
Skanderborg Denmark 15 F8
Skaneateles Lake NY U.S.A. 64 C1
Skara Sweden 15 H7
Skardarsko Jezero l. Albania/Montenegro see Scutari, Lake
Skardu Pak. 36 C2
Skärgårdshavets nationalpark nat. park Fin. 15 L7
Skarnes Norway 15 G6
Skarżysko-Kamienna Poland 17 R5
Skaulo Sweden 14 L3
Skawina Poland 17 Q6
Skeena Mountains B.C. Canada 60 F4
Skegness U.K. 18 H5
Skellefteå Sweden 14 L4
Skellefteälven r. Sweden 14 L4
Skelleftehamn Sweden 14 L4
Skelmersdale U.K. 18 E5
Skerries Ireland 21 F4
Ski Norway 15 G7
Skiathos i. Greece 27 J5
Skibbereen Ireland 21 C6
Skibotn Norway 14 L2
Skiddaw h. U.K. 18 D4
Skien Norway 15 F7
Skierniewice Poland 17 R5
Skikda Alg. 26 B6
Skipsea U.K. 18 G5
Skipton Australia 58 A6
Skipton U.K. 18 E5
Skirlaugh U.K. 18 G5
Skíros i. Greece see Skyros
Skive Denmark 15 F8
Skjern Denmark 15 F9
Skjolden Norway 15 E6
Skobelev Uzbek. see Farg'ona
Skodje Norway 14 E5
Skoganvarri Norway 14 N2
Skomer Island U.K. 19 B7
Skopelos i. Greece 27 J5
Skopin Russia 13 H5
Skopje Macedonia 27 I4
Skoplje Macedonia see Skopje
Skövde Sweden 15 H7
Skovorodino Russia 44 A1
Skowhegan ME U.S.A. 63 N3
Skrunda Latvia 15 M8
Skukum, Mount Y.T. Canada 60 E3
Skukuza S. Africa 51 J3
Skull Valley AZ U.S.A. 65 F3
Skuodas Lith. 15 L8
Skurup Sweden 15 H9
Skutskär Sweden 15 J6
Skyra Ukr. 13 F6
Skye i. U.K. 20 C3
Skyring, Seno b. Chile 70 B8
Skyros Greece 27 K5
Skyros i. Greece 27 K5
Skytrain Ice Rise Antarctica 76 L1
Slættaratindur h. Faroe Is 14 [inset 1]
Slagelse Denmark 15 G9
Slagnäs Sweden 14 K4
Slane Ireland 21 F4
Slaney r. Ireland 21 F5
Slantsy Russia 15 P7
Slashers Reefs Australia 56 D3
Slatina Croatia 26 G2
Slatina Romania 27 K2
Slaty Fork WV U.S.A. 64 A3
Slava Russia 44 C1
Slave r. Alta/N.W.T. Canada 77 L2
Slave Coast Africa 46 D4
Slave Lake Alta Canada 77 L3
Slavgorod Belarus see Slawharad
Slavgorod Russia 42 D2
Slavkovichi Russia 15 P8
Slavonska Požega Croatia see Požega
Slavonski Brod Croatia 26 H2
Slavuta Ukr. 13 E6
Slavutych Ukr. 13 F6
Slavyanka Russia 44 C4
Slavyansk Ukr. see Slov"yans'k
Slavyanskaya Russia see Slavyansk-na-Kubani
Slavyansk-na-Kubani Russia 34 E1
Slawharad Belarus 13 F5
Sławno Poland 17 P3
Sleaford U.K. 19 G5
Slea Head hd Ireland 21 B5
Sleat, Sound of sea chan. U.K. 20 D3
Sleeper Islands Nunavut Canada 61 K4
Slessor Glacier Antarctica 76 B1
Slide Mountain NY U.S.A. 64 D2
Slieve Bloom Mountains hills Ireland 21 E5
Slieve Car h. Ireland 21 C3
Slieve Donard h. U.K. 21 G3
Slieve Mish Mountains hills Ireland 21 B5
Slieve Snaght h. Ireland 21 E2
Sligachan U.K. 20 C3
Sligeach Ireland see Sligo
Sligo Ireland 21 D3
Sligo PA U.S.A. 64 B2
Sligo Bay Ireland 21 D3
Slippery Rock PA U.S.A. 64 A2
Slite Sweden 15 K8
Sliven Bulg. 27 L3
Sloan NV U.S.A. 65 E3
Sloboda Russia see Ezhva
Slobodchikovo Russia 12 K3
Slobodskoy Russia 12 K4
Slobozia Romania 27 L2
Slonim Belarus 15 N10
Slough U.K. 19 G7
Slovakia country Europe 10 J6

Slovenia country Europe 26 F2
Slovenija country Europe see Slovenia
Slovenj Gradec Slovenia 26 F1
Slovensko country Europe see Slovakia
Slovenský raj, Národný park nat. park Slovakia 17 R6
Slov"yans'k Ukr. 13 H6
Słowiński Park Narodowy nat. park Poland 17 P3
Sluch r. Ukr. 13 E6
Słupsk Poland 17 P3
Slussfors Sweden 14 J4
Slutsk Belarus 15 O10
Slyne Head hd Ireland 21 B4
Slyudyanka Russia 42 I2
Smallwood Reservoir Nfld. and Lab. Canada 61 L4
Smalyavichy Belarus 15 P9
Smalyenskaya Wzwyshsha hills Belarus/Russia see Smolensko-Moskovskaya Vozvyshennost'
Smarhon' Belarus 15 O9
Smeaton Sask. Canada 62 G1
Smederevo Serbia 27 I2
Smederevska Palanka Serbia 27 I2
Smela Ukr. see Smila
Smethport PA U.S.A. 64 B2
Smidovich Russia 44 D2
Smila Ukr. 13 F6
Smiltene Latvia 15 N8
Smirnykh Russia 44 F2
Smithfield S. Africa 51 H6
Smith Glacier Antarctica 76 K1
Smith Island MD U.S.A. 64 C3
Smith Island VA U.S.A. 64 D4
Smith Mountain Lake VA U.S.A. 64 B4
Smiths Falls Ont. Canada 63 L3
Smithton Australia 57 [inset]
Smithtown Australia 58 F3
Smithville WV U.S.A. 64 A3
Smoky Bay Australia 55 F8
Smoky Cape Australia 58 F3
Smoky Hills KS U.S.A. 62 H4
Smøla i. Norway 14 E5
Smolenka Russia 13 K6
Smolensk Russia 13 G5
Smolensk-Moscow Upland hills Belarus/Russia see Smolensko-Moskovskaya Vozvyshennost'
Smolensko-Moskovskaya Vozvyshennost' hills Belarus/Russia 13 G5
Smolevichi Belarus see Smalyavichy
Smolyan Bulg. 27 K4
Smørfjord Norway 14 N1
Smorgon' Belarus see Smarhon'
Smyley Island Antarctica 76 L2
Smyrna Turkey see İzmir
Smyrna DE U.S.A. 64 D3
Smyth Island atoll Marshall Is see Taongi
Snæfell mt. Iceland 14 [inset 2]
Snaefell h. Isle of Man 18 C4
Snake r. U.S.A. 62 D2
Snake Island Australia 58 C7
Snake River Plain ID U.S.A. 62 E3
Snare Lakes N.W.T. Canada see Wekweètì
Snares Islands N.Z. 53 G6
Snåsa Norway 14 H4
Sneek Neth. 17 J4
Sneem Ireland 21 C6
Sneeuberge mts S. Africa 50 G6
Snegurovka Ukr. see Tetiyiv
Snelling CA U.S.A. 65 B2
Snettisham U.K. 19 H6
Snezhnogorsk Russia 28 J3
Snežnik mt. Slovenia 26 F2
Sniečkus Lith. see Visaginas
Snihurivka Ukr. 13 G7
Snits Neth. see Sneek
Snizort, Loch b. U.K. 20 C3
Snøtinden mt. Norway 14 H3
Snovsk Ukr. see Shchors
Snowbird Lake N.W.T. Canada 61 H3
Snowdon mt. U.K. 19 C5
Snowdonia National Park U.K. 19 D6
Snowdrift N.W.T. Canada see Łutselk'e
Snowdrift r. N.W.T. Canada 60 G3
Snow Hill MD U.S.A. 64 D3
Snow Lake Man. Canada 61 H4
Snowy r. Australia 58 D6
Snowy Mountain NY U.S.A. 64 D1
Snowy Mountains Australia 58 C6
Snowy River National Park Australia 58 D6
Snyder TX U.S.A. 62 G5
Soalala Madag. 49 E5
Soalara Madag. 49 E6
Soan r. Pak. 36 B2
Soan-gundo is S. Korea 45 B6
Soanierana-Ivongo Madag. 49 E5
Soavinandriana Madag. 49 E5
Sobat r. South Sudan 32 D8
Sobinka Russia 12 I5
Sobradinho, Barragem de resr Brazil 69 J6
Sobral Brazil 69 J4
Sochi Russia 13 H8
Society Islands Fr. Polynesia 75 J7
Socorro Brazil 71 B3
Socorro Col. 68 D2
Socorro NM U.S.A. 62 F5
Socorro, Isla i. Mex. 66 B5
Socotra i. Yemen 33 H7
Socuéllamos Spain 25 E4
Soda Lake CA U.S.A. 65 C3
Soda Lake CA U.S.A. 65 D3
Sodankylä Fin. 14 O3
Soda Plains Aksai Chin 36 D2
Soda Springs ID U.S.A. 62 E3
Söderhamn Sweden 15 J6
Söderköping Sweden 15 J7
Södertälje Sweden 15 J7
Sodiri Sudan 32 C7
Sodo Eth. 48 D3
Södra Kvarken str. Fin./Sweden 15 K6
Sodus NY U.S.A. 64 C1
Soekarno, Puntjak mt. Indon. see Jaya, Puncak
Soerabaia Indon. see Surabaya
Sofala Australia 58 D4
Sofia Bulg. 27 J3
Sofiya Bulg. see Sofia
Sofiyevka Ukr. see Vil'nyans'k
Sofiysk Khabarovskiy Kray Russia 44 D1
Sofiysk Khabarovskiy Kray Russia 44 E2
Sofporog Russia 12 F2
Sofrana i. Greece 27 L6
Softa Kalesi tourist site Turkey 39 A1
Sōfu-gan i. Japan 45 F7
Sog China 42 G6
Soğanlı Dağları mts Turkey 35 E2
Sogda Russia 44 D2
Sogma China 36 E2
Søgne Norway 15 E7
Sognefjorden inlet Norway 15 D6
Söğüt Turkey 27 N4
Söğüt Dağı mts Turkey 27 M6
Soh Iran 35 H4
Sohâg Egypt see Sūhāj
Sohagpur India 36 D5
Soham U.K. 19 H6
Sohano P.N.G. 52 F2
Sohar Oman see Şuḩār
Sohawal India 36 E4
Sohela India 37 E5
Soheuksan-do i. S. Korea 45 B6
Sŏho-ri N. Korea 45 C4
Soila China 37 I3
Soini Fin. 14 N5
Soissons France 24 F2
Sojat India 36 C4
Sojat Road India 36 C4
Sok r. Russia 13 K5
Sokal' Ukr. 13 E6
Sokcho S. Korea 45 C5
Söke Turkey 27 L6
Sokhor, Gora mt. Russia 42 J2
Sokhumi Georgia 35 F2
Sokiryany Ukr. see Sokyryany
Sokodé Togo 46 D4
Sokol Russia 12 I4
Sokolo Mali 46 C3
Sokoto Nigeria 46 D3
Sokoto r. Nigeria 46 D3
Sokyryany Ukr. 13 E6
Sola i. Tonga see Ata
Solan India 36 D3
Solana Beach CA U.S.A. 65 D4
Solander Island N.Z. 59 A8
Solapur India 38 B2
Soldotna AK U.S.A. 60 C3
Soledad CA U.S.A. 65 B2
Soledade Brazil 70 F3
Solenoye Russia 13 I7
Solfjellsjøen Norway 14 H3
Solginskiy Russia 12 I3
Solhan Turkey 35 F3
Soligalich Russia 12 I4
Soligorsk Belarus see Salihorsk
Solihull U.K. 19 F6
Solikamsk Russia 11 R4
Sol'-Iletsk Russia 28 G4
Solimões r. S. America see Amazon
Solitaire Namibia 50 B2
Sol-Karmala Russia see Severnoye
Şollar Azer. 35 H2
Sollefteå Sweden 14 J5
Sollum, Gulf of Egypt see Sallum, Khalīj as
Solnechnogorsk Russia 12 H4
Solnechnyy Amurskaya Oblast' Russia 44 A1
Solnechnyy Khabarovskiy Kray Russia 44 E2
Solomon Islands country S. Pacific Ocean 53 G2
Solomon Sea S. Pacific Ocean 52 F2
Solor i. Indon. 54 C2
Solor, Kepulauan is Indon. 54 C2
Solothurn Switz. 24 H3
Solovetskiye Ostrova is Russia 12 G2
Solov'yevsk Russia 44 B1
Šolta i. Croatia 26 G3
Solṭānābād Iran 35 H4
Solṭānīyeh Iran 35 H3
Sol'tsy Russia 12 F4
Solvay NY U.S.A. 64 C1
Sölvesborg Sweden 15 I8
Solway Firth est. U.K. 20 F6
Solwezi Zambia 49 C5
Soma Turkey 27 L5
Somalia country Africa 48 E3
Somali Basin sea feature Indian Ocean 73 L6
Somaliland disp. terr. Somalia 48 E3
Somali Republic country Africa see Somalia
Sombo Angola 49 C4
Sombor Serbia 27 H2
Sombrio, Lago do l. Brazil 71 A5
Somero Fin. 15 M6
Somerset KY U.S.A. 63 K4
Somerset PA U.S.A. 64 B3
Somerset, Lake Australia 58 F1
Somerset East S. Africa 51 G7
Somerset Island Nunavut Canada 61 I2
Somerset Reservoir VT U.S.A. 64 E1
Somerset West S. Africa 50 D8
Somersworth NH U.S.A. 64 F1
Somerton AZ U.S.A. 65 E4
Somerville NJ U.S.A. 64 D2
Someydeh Iran 35 G4
Somme r. France 19 I8
Sommen l. Sweden 15 I7
Somnath India 36 B5
Son r. India 37 F4
Sonapur India see Subarnapur
Sonar r. India 36 D4
Sŏnbong N. Korea 44 C4
Sŏnch'ŏn N. Korea 45 B5
Sønderborg Denmark 15 F9
Sondershausen Germany 17 M5
Søndre Strømfjord Greenland see Kangerlussuaq
Søndre Strømfjord inlet Greenland see Kangerlussuaq
Sondrio Italy 26 C1
Sonepat India see Sonipat
Sonepur India see Subarnapur
Songea Tanz. 49 D5
Songhua Hu resr China 44 B4
Songhua Jiang r. Heilongjiang/Jilin China 44 D3
Songhua Jiang r. Jilin China 44 B3
Songjianghe China 44 B4
Sŏngjin N. Korea see Kimch'aek
Songkhla Thai. 31 J6
Songling China see Tarqi
Songnim N. Korea 45 B5
Songo Angola 49 B4
Songo Moz. 49 D5
Songpan China 42 I6
Songxi China 43 L7
Songyuan Fujian China see Songxi
Songyuan Jilin China 44 B3
Sonid Youqi China see Saihan Tal
Sonid Zuoqi China see Mandalt
Sonipat India 36 D3
Sonkajärvi Fin. 14 O5
Sonkovo Russia 12 H4
Sơn La Vietnam 31 J4
Sonmiani Pak. 33 K4
Sonmiani Bay Pak. 36 A4
Sono r. Minas Gerais Brazil 71 B2
Sono r. Tocantins Brazil 69 I5
Sonoma CA U.S.A. 65 A1
Sonora r. Mex. 66 B3
Sonora CA U.S.A. 65 B2
Sonora TX U.S.A. 62 G5
Sonoran Desert AZ U.S.A. 65 F4
Sonqor Iran 35 G4
Sonsonate El Salvador 66 G6
Sonwabile S. Africa 51 I6
Soochow China see Suzhou
Soomaaliya country Africa see Somalia
Sopo watercourse South Sudan 47 F4
Sopot Bulg. 27 K3
Sopot Poland 17 Q3
Sopron Hungary 26 G1
Sopur India 36 C2
Sora Italy 26 E4
Sorab India 38 B3
Sorada India 38 E2
Söråker Sweden 14 J5
Sorel Que. Canada 63 M2
Soreq, Naḥal r. Israel 39 B4
Sorgun Turkey 34 D3
Sorgun r. Turkey 39 B1
Soria Spain 25 E3
Sorkh, Daqq-e salt flat Iran 35 I4
Sorkh, Kūh-e mts Iran 35 I4
Sorkheh Iran 35 I4
Sørli Norway 14 H4
Soro India 37 F5
Soroca Moldova 13 F6
Sorocaba Brazil 71 B3
Soroki Moldova see Soroca
Sorol atoll Micronesia 41 G7
Sorong Indon. 41 F8
Soroti Uganda 48 D3
Sørøya i. Norway 14 M1
Sorraia r. Port. 25 B4
Sørreisa Norway 14 K2
Sorrento Italy 26 F4
Sorsele Sweden 14 J4
Sorsogon Phil. 41 E6
Sortavala Russia 12 F3
Sortland Norway 14 I2
Sortopolovskaya Russia 12 K3
Sorvizhi Russia 12 K4
Sosenskiy Russia 13 G5
Soshanguve S. Africa 51 I3
Sosna r. Russia 13 H5
Sosneado mt. Arg. 70 C4
Sosnogorsk Russia 12 L3
Sosnovka Arkhangel'skaya Oblast' Russia 12 J3
Sosnovka Kaliningradskaya Oblast' Russia 11 K5
Sosnovka Murmanskaya Oblast' Russia 12 I2
Sosnovka Tambovskaya Oblast' Russia 13 I5
Sosnovo Russia 15 Q6
Sosnovo-Ozerskoye Russia 43 K2
Sosnovyy Russia 14 R4
Sosnovyy Bor Russia 12 F4
Sosnowiec Poland 17 Q5
Sosnowitz Poland see Sosnowiec
Sos'va Khanty-Mansiyskiy Avtonomnyy Okrug-Yugra Russia 11 S3
Sos'va Sverdlovskaya Oblast' Russia 11 S4
Sotang China 37 H3
Sotara, Volcán vol. Col. 68 C3
Sotkamo Fin. 14 P4
Sotteville-lès-Rouen France 19 I9
Souanké Congo 48 B3
Soubré Côte d'Ivoire 46 C4
Souderton PA U.S.A. 64 D2
Soufli Greece 27 L4
Soufrière St Lucia 67 L6
Soufrière vol. St Vincent 67 L6
Sougueur Alg. 25 G6
Souillac France 24 E4
Souk Ahras Alg. 26 B6
Souk el Arbaâ du Rharb Morocco 22 C5
Sŏul S. Korea see Seoul
Soulac-sur-Mer France 24 D4
Soulom France 24 D5
Souni Cyprus 39 A2
Soûr Lebanon see Tyre
Soure Brazil 69 I4
Sour el Ghozlane Alg. 25 H5
Souris Man. Canada 62 G2
Souris r. Sask. Canada 62 H2
Souriya country Asia see Syria
Sousa Brazil 69 K5
Sousa Lara Angola see Bocoio
Sousse Tunisia 26 D7
Soustons France 24 D5
South Africa country Africa 50 F5
Southampton Ont. Canada 63 K3
Southampton U.K. 19 F8
Southampton NY U.S.A. 64 E2
Southampton, Cape Nunavut Canada 61 J3
Southampton Island Nunavut Canada 61 J3
South Anna r. VA U.S.A. 64 C4
South Anston U.K. 18 F5
South Australia state Australia 52 D5
South Australian Basin sea feature Indian Ocean 73 P8
South Bank U.K. 18 F4
South Bend IN U.S.A. 63 J3
South Carolina state U.S.A. 63 K5
South China Sea N. Pacific Ocean 41 D6
South Coast Town Australia see Gold Coast
South Dakota state U.S.A. 62 G3
South Downs hills U.K. 19 G8
South Downs National Park U.K. 19 G8
South East admin. dist. Botswana 51 G3
South East Cape Australia 57 [inset]
Southeast Cape AK U.S.A. 60 B3
Southeast Indian Ridge sea feature Indian Ocean 73 N8
South East Isles Australia 55 C8
Southeast Pacific Basin sea feature S. Pacific Ocean 75 M10
South East Point Australia 58 C7
Southend U.K. 20 D5
Southend-on-Sea U.K. 19 H7
Southern admin. dist. Botswana 50 G3
Southern Alps mts N.Z. 59 C6
Southern Cross Australia 55 B7
Southern Indian Lake Man. Canada 61 I4
Southern Lau Group is Fiji 53 I3
Southern National Park South Sudan 47 F4
Southern Ocean 76 C2
Southern Rhodesia country Africa see Zimbabwe
Southern Uplands hills U.K. 20 E5
South Esk r. U.K. 20 F4
South Esk Tableland reg. Australia 54 D4
South Fiji Basin sea feature S. Pacific Ocean 74 H7
South Geomagnetic Pole Antarctica 76 F1
South Georgia and the South Sandwich Islands terr. S. Atlantic Ocean 70 I8
South Harris pen. U.K. 20 B3
South Henik Lake Nunavut Canada 61 I3
South Honshu Ridge sea feature N. Pacific Ocean 74 F3
South Island N.Z. 59 D7
South Korea country Asia 45 B5
South Lake Tahoe CA U.S.A. 65 B1
South Luangwa National Park Zambia 49 D5
South Magnetic Pole Antarctica 76 G2
Southminster U.K. 19 H7
South Mountains hills PA U.S.A. 64 C3
South New Berlin NY U.S.A. 64 D1
South Orkney Islands S. Atlantic Ocean 76 A2
South Ossetia disp. terr. Georgia 35 G2
South Platte r. CO U.S.A. 62 G3
South Pole Antarctica 76 C1
Southport Qld Australia 58 F1
Southport Tas. Australia 57 [inset]
Southport U.K. 18 D5
South Ronaldsay i. U.K. 20 G2
South Sand Bluff pt S. Africa 51 J6
South Sandwich Trench sea feature S. Atlantic Ocean 72 G9
South San Francisco CA U.S.A. 65 A2
South Saskatchewan r. Alta/Sask. Canada 62 F1
South Shetland Islands Antarctica 76 A2
South Shetland Trough sea feature S. Atlantic Ocean 76 L2
South Shields U.K. 18 F3
South Sinai governorate Egypt see Janūb Sīnā'
South Solomon Trench sea feature S. Pacific Ocean 74 G6
South Taranaki Bight b. N.Z. 59 E4
South Tasman Rise sea feature Southern Ocean 74 F9
South Tons r. India 37 E4
South Tyne r. U.K. 18 E4
South Uist i. U.K. 20 B3
South Wellesley Islands Australia 56 B3
South-West Africa country Africa see Namibia
South West Cape N.Z. 59 A8
South West Entrance sea chan. P.N.G. 56 E1
Southwest Indian Ridge sea feature Indian Ocean 73 K8
South West National Park Australia 57 [inset]
Southwest Pacific Basin sea feature S. Pacific Ocean 74 I8
Southwest Peru Ridge sea feature S. Pacific Ocean see Nazca Ridge
South West Rocks Australia 58 F3
Southwold U.K. 19 I6
Southwood National Park Australia 58 E1
Soutpansberg mts S. Africa 51 I2
Souttouf, Adrar mts W. Sahara 46 B2
Soverato Italy 26 G5
Sovetsk Kaliningradskaya Oblast' Russia 12 D5
Sovetsk Kirovskaya Oblast' Russia 12 K4
Sovetskaya Gavan' Russia 44 F2
Sovetskiy Khanty-Mansiyskiy Avtonomnyy Okrug-Yugra Russia 11 S3
Sovetskiy Leningradskaya Oblast' Russia 15 P6
Sovetskiy Respublika Mariy El Russia 12 K4
Sovetskoye Chechenskaya Respublika Russia see Shatoy
Sovetskoye Stavropol'skiy Kray Russia see Zelenokumsk
Sovyets'kyy Ukr. 34 D1
Soweto S. Africa 51 H4
Şowma'eh Sarā Iran 35 H3
Sōya-kaikyō str. Japan/Russia see La Pérouse Strait
Sōya-misaki c. Japan 44 F3
Soyana r. Russia 12 I2
Soyma r. Russia 12 K2
Sozh r. Europe 13 F6
Sozopol Bulg. 27 L3
Spain country Europe 25 E3
Spalato Croatia see Split
Spalatum Croatia see Split
Spalding U.K. 19 G6
Spanish Guinea country Africa see Equatorial Guinea
Spanish Netherlands country Europe see Belgium
Spanish Sahara disp. terr. Africa see Western Sahara
Spanish Town Jamaica 67 I5
Sparks NV U.S.A. 62 D4
Sparta Greece see Sparti
Spartanburg SC U.S.A. 63 K5
Sparti Greece 27 J6
Spartivento, Capo c. Italy 26 G6
Spas-Demensk Russia 13 G5
Spas-Klepiki Russia 13 I5
Spassk-Dal'niy Russia 44 D3
Spassk-Ryazanskiy Russia 13 I5
Spatha, Akrotirio pt Greece 27 J7
Spence Bay Nunavut Canada see Taloyoak
Spencer IA U.S.A. 63 H3
Spencer WV U.S.A. 64 A3
Spencer Bay Namibia 50 B3
Spencer Gulf est. Australia 57 B7
Spencer Range hills Australia 54 E3
Spennymoor U.K. 18 F4
Sperrgebiet National Park Namibia 50 B4
Sperrin Mountains hills U.K. 21 E3
Sperryville VA U.S.A. 64 B3
Spessart reg. Germany 17 L6
Spétsai i. Greece see Spetses
Spetses i. Greece 27 J6
Spey r. U.K. 20 F3
Speyer Germany 17 L6
Spezand Pak. 36 A3
Spice Islands Indon. see Moluccas
Spijkenisse Neth. 16 J5
Spilimbergo Italy 26 E1
Spilsby U.K. 18 H5
Spīn Bōldak Afgh. 36 A3
Spintangi Pak. 36 B3
Spirovo Russia 12 G4
Spišská Nová Ves Slovakia 13 D6
Spiti r. India 36 D3
Spitsbergen i. Svalbard 28 C2
Spittal an der Drau Austria 17 N7
Spitzbergen i. Svalbard see Spitsbergen
Split Croatia 26 G3
Spokane WA U.S.A. 62 D2
Spoletium Italy see Spoleto
Spoleto Italy 26 E3
Spooner WI U.S.A. 63 I2
Spotsylvania VA U.S.A. 64 C3
Spratly Islands S. China Sea 41 D6
Spree r. Germany 17 N4
Springbok S. Africa 50 C5
Springdale Nfld. and Lab. Canada 61 M5
Springer NM U.S.A. 62 G4
Springfield CO U.S.A. 62 G4
Springfield IL U.S.A. 63 J4
Springfield MA U.S.A. 64 E1
Springfield MO U.S.A. 63 I4
Springfield OH U.S.A. 63 K4
Springfield WV U.S.A. 64 B3
Springfontein S. Africa 51 G6
Spring Hill FL U.S.A. 63 K6
Spring Mountains NV U.S.A. 65 E2
Springs Junction N.Z. 59 D6
Springsure Australia 56 E5
Spring Valley NY U.S.A. 64 D2
Springville CA U.S.A. 65 C2
Springville NY U.S.A. 64 B1
Springville PA U.S.A. 64 D2
Sprowston U.K. 19 I6
Spurn Head hd U.K. 18 H5
Squillace, Golfo di g. Italy 26 G5
Squires, Mount h. Australia 55 D6
Srbija country Europe see Serbia
Srbinje Bos. & Herz. see Foča
Srebrenica 27 H2
Sredets Burgas Bulg. 27 L3
Sredets Sofia-Grad Bulg. see Sofia
Sredinnyy Khrebet mts Russia 29 Q4
Sredna Gora mts Bulg. 27 J3
Srednekolymsk Russia 29 Q3
Sredne-Russkaya Vozvyshennost' hills Russia see Central Russian Upland
Sredne-Sibirskoye Ploskogor'ye plat. Russia see Central Siberian Plateau
Sredneye Kuyto, Ozero l. Russia 14 Q4
Sredniy Ural mts Russia 11 R4
Srednyaya Akhtuba Russia 13 J6
Sreepur Bangl. see Sripur
Sretensk Russia 43 L2
Sri Aman Sarawak Malaysia 41 D7
Sriharikota Island India 38 D3
Sri Jayewardenepura Kotte Sri Lanka 38 C5
Srikakulam India 38 E2
Sri Kalahasti India 38 C3
Sri Lanka country Asia 38 D5
Srinagar India 36 C2
Sri Pada mt. Sri Lanka see Adam's Peak
Sripur Bangl. 37 G4
Srirangam India 38 C4
Srivardhan India 38 B2
Staaten r. Australia 56 C3
Staaten River National Park Australia 56 C3
Stabroek Guyana see Georgetown
Stade Germany 17 L4
Stadskanaal Neth. 17 K4
Staffa i. U.K. 20 C4
Stafford U.K. 19 E6
Stafford VA U.S.A. 64 C3
Stafford Springs CT U.S.A. 64 E2
Staicele Latvia 15 N8
Staines-upon-Thames U.K. 19 G7
Stakhanov Ukr. 13 H6
Stakhanovo Russia see Zhukovskiy
Stalbridge U.K. 19 E8
Stalham U.K. 19 I6
Stalin Bulg. see Varna
Stalinabad Tajik. see Dushanbe
Stalingrad Russia see Volgograd
Staliniri Georgia see Tskhinvali
Stalino Ukr. see Donets'k
Stalinogorsk Russia see Novomoskovsk
Stalinogród Poland see Katowice
Stalinsk Russia see Novokuznetsk
Stalowa Wola Poland 13 D6
Stamboliyski Bulg. 27 K3
Stamford Australia 56 C4
Stamford U.K. 19 G6
Stamford CT U.S.A. 64 E2
Stamford NY U.S.A. 64 D1
Stampalia i. Greece see Astypalaia
Stampriet Namibia 50 D3
Stamsund Norway 14 H2
Stanardsville VA U.S.A. 64 B3
Stancomb-Wills Glacier Antarctica 76 B1
Standerton S. Africa 51 I4
Standish MI U.S.A. 63 K3
Stanislaus r. CA U.S.A. 65 B2
Stanislav Ukr. see Ivano-Frankivs'k
Stanke Dimitrov Bulg. see Dupnitsa
Stanley Australia 57 [inset]
Stanley Falkland Is 70 E8
Stanley U.K. 18 F4
Stanley ND U.S.A. 62 G2
Stanley VA U.S.A. 64 B3
Stanley, Mount h. N.T. Australia 54 E5
Stanley, Mount h. Tas. Australia 57 [inset]
Stanley, Mount Dem. Rep. Congo/Uganda see Margherita Peak
Stanleyville Dem. Rep. Congo see Kisangani
Stann Creek Belize see Dangriga
Stannington U.K. 18 F3
Stanovoye Russia 13 H5
Stanovoye Nagor'ye mts Russia 43 L1
Stanovoy Khrebet mts Russia 29 N4
Stansmore Range hills Australia 54 E5
Stanthorpe Australia 58 E2
Stanton U.K. 19 H6
Starachowice Poland 17 R5
Stara Planina mts Bulg./Serbia see Balkan Mountains
Staraya Russa Russia 12 F4
Stara Zagora Bulg. 27 K3
Starbuck Island Kiribati 75 J6
Starcke National Park Australia 56 D2
Stargard in Pommern Poland see Stargard Szczeciński
Stargard Szczeciński Poland 17 O4
Staritsa Russia 12 G4
Starkville MS U.S.A. 63 J5
Starnberger See l. Germany 17 M7
Starobel'sk Ukr. see Starobil's'k
Starobil's'k Ukr. 13 H6
Starogard Gdański Poland 17 Q4
Starokonstantinov Ukr. see Starokostyantyniv
Starokostyantyniv Ukr. 13 E6
Starominskaya Russia 13 H7
Staroshcherbinovskaya Russia 13 H7
Start Point U.K. 19 D8
Starve Island Kiribati see Starbuck Island
Staryya Darohi Belarus 13 F5
Staryye Dorogi Belarus see Staryya Darohi
Staryy Kayak Russia 29 L2
Staryy Oskol Russia 13 H6
State College PA U.S.A. 64 C2
Staten Island Arg. see Estados, Isla de los
Statesboro GA U.S.A. 63 K5
Statia i. West Indies see Sint Eustatius
Station Nord Greenland 77 I1
Staunton VA U.S.A. 64 B3
Stavanger Norway 15 D7
Staveley U.K. 18 F5
Stavropol' Russia 13 I7
Stavropol Kray admin. div. Russia see Stavropol'skiy Kray
Stavropol'-na-Volge Russia see Tol'yatti
Stavropol'skaya Vozvyshennost' hills Russia 13 I7
Stavropol'skiy Kray admin. div. Russia 35 F1
Steadville S. Africa 51 I5
Steamboat Springs CO U.S.A. 62 F3
Stebbins AK U.S.A. 60 B3
Steele Island Antarctica 76 L2
Steenkampsberge mts S. Africa 51 J3
Steen River Alta Canada 60 G4
Steens Mountain OR U.S.A. 62 D3
Steenstrup Gletscher glacier Greenland see Sermersuaq
Stefansson Island Nunavut Canada 61 H2
Stegi Swaziland see Siteki
Steigerwald mts Germany 17 M6
Steinhausen Namibia 49 B6
Steinkjer Norway 14 G4
Steinkopf S. Africa 50 C5
Steinsdalen Norway 14 G4
Stella S. Africa 50 G4
Stellenbosch S. Africa 50 D7
Stello, Monte mt. Corsica France 24 I5
Stelvio, Parco Nazionale dello nat. park Italy 26 D1
Stendal Germany 17 M4
Stenhousemuir U.K. 20 F4
Stenungsund Sweden 15 G7
Steornabhagh U.K. see Stornoway
Stepanakert Azer. see Xankändi
Stephens, Cape N.Z. 59 D5
Stephens City VA U.S.A. 64 B3
Stephenville TX U.S.A. 62 H5
Stepnoy Russia see Elista
Stepnoye Russia 13 J6
Sterkfontein Dam dam S. Africa 51 I5
Sterkstroom S. Africa 51 H6
Sterlibashevo Russia 11 R5
Sterling S. Africa 50 E6
Sterling CO U.S.A. 62 G3
Sterlitamak Russia 28 G4
Stettin Poland see Szczecin
Steubenville OH U.S.A. 64 A2
Stevenage U.K. 19 G7
Stevenson Lake Man. Canada 63 H1
Stevens Village AK U.S.A. 60 D3
Stevensville PA U.S.A. 64 C2
Stevns Klint cliff Denmark 17 N3
Stewart r. Y.T. Canada 60 E3
Stewart, Isla i. Chile 70 B8
Stewart Island N.Z. 59 A8
Stewart Islands Solomon Is 53 G2
Stewart Lake Nunavut Canada 61 J3
Stewarton U.K. 20 E5
Stewarts Point CA U.S.A. 65 A1
Steynsburg S. Africa 51 G6
Steyr Austria 17 O6
Steytlerville S. Africa 50 G7
Stif Alg. see Sétif
Stikine r. B.C. Canada 60 E4
Stikine Plateau B.C. Canada 60 E4
Stilbaai S. Africa 50 E8
Stillwater OK U.S.A. 63 H4
Stilton U.K. 19 G6
Štip Macedonia 27 J4
Stirling Australia 54 F5
Stirling U.K. 20 F4
Stirling Creek r. Australia 54 E4
Stirling Range National Park Australia 55 B8
Stjørdalshalsen Norway 14 G5
Stockerau Austria 17 P6
Stockholm Sweden 15 K7
Stockinbingal Australia 58 C5
Stockport U.K. 18 E5
Stockton CA U.S.A. 65 B2
Stockton-on-Tees U.K. 18 F4
Stoer, Point of U.K. 20 D2
Stoke-on-Trent U.K. 19 E5
Stokesley U.K. 18 F4
Stokes Point Australia 57 [inset]
Stokes Range hills Australia 54 E4
Stokkseyri Iceland 14 [inset 2]
Stokkvågen Norway 14 H3
Stokmarknes Norway 14 I2
Stolac Bos. & Herz. 26 G3
Stolbovoy Russia 77 G2
Stolbtsy Belarus see Stowbtsy
Stolin Belarus 15 O11
Stolp Poland see Słupsk
Stone U.K. 19 E6
Stoneboro PA U.S.A. 64 A2
Stonehaven U.K. 20 G4
Stonehenge Australia 56 C5
Stonehenge tourist site U.K. 19 F7
Stone Spheres of the Diquís tourist site Costa Rica 67 H7
Stonewall Jackson Lake WV U.S.A. 64 A3
Stony Creek VA U.S.A. 64 C4
Stony River AK U.S.A. 60 C3
Stora Lulevatten l. Sweden 14 K3
Stora Sjöfallets nationalpark nat. park Sweden 14 J3
Storavan l. Sweden 14 K4
Store Bælt sea chan. Denmark see Great Belt
Støren Norway 14 G5
Storfjordbotn Norway 14 O1
Storforshei Norway 14 I3
Storjord Norway 14 I3
Storkerson Peninsula Nunavut Canada 61 H2
Storm Bay Australia 57 [inset]
Stormberg S. Africa 51 H6
Storm Lake IA U.S.A. 63 H3
Stornosa mt. Norway 14 E6
Stornoway U.K. 20 C2
Storozhevsk Russia 12 L3
Storozhynets' Ukr. 13 E6
Storrs CT U.S.A. 64 E2
Storseleby Sweden 14 J4
Storsjön l. Sweden 14 I5
Storskrymten mt. Norway 14 F5
Storslett Norway 14 L2
Storuman Sweden 14 J4
Storuman l. Sweden 14 J4
Storvik Sweden 15 J6
Storvorde Denmark 15 G8
Storvreta Sweden 15 J7
Stotfold U.K. 19 G6
Stour r. England U.K. 19 F6
Stour r. England U.K. 19 F8
Stour r. England U.K. 19 I7
Stourbridge U.K. 19 E6
Stourport-on-Severn U.K. 19 E6
Stout Lake Ont. Canada 63 I1
Stowbtsy Belarus 15 O10
Stowmarket U.K. 19 H6
Stoyba Russia 44 C1
Strabane U.K. 21 E3
Stradbally Ireland 21 E4
Stradbroke U.K. 19 I6
Stradella Italy 26 C2
Strakonice Czech Rep. 17 N6
Stralsund Germany 17 N3
Strand S. Africa 50 D8
Stranda Norway 14 E5
Strangford U.K. 21 G3
Strangford Lough inlet U.K. 21 G3
Strangways r. Australia 54 F3
Stranraer U.K. 20 D6
Strasbourg France 24 H2
Strasburg VA U.S.A. 64 B3
Strassburg France see Strasbourg
Stratford Australia 58 C6
Stratford Ont. Canada 64 A1
Stratford CA U.S.A. 65 C2
Stratford TX U.S.A. 62 G4
Stratford-upon-Avon U.K. 19 F6
Strathaven U.K. 20 E5
Strathmore r. U.K. 20 E2
Strathroy Ont. Canada 64 A1
Strathspey val. U.K. 20 F3
Strathy U.K. 20 F2
Stratton U.K. 19 C8
Stratton Mountain VT U.S.A. 64 E1
Straubing Germany 17 N6
Straumnes pt Iceland 14 [inset 2]
Streaky Bay Australia 55 F8
Streaky Bay b. Australia 55 F8
Street U.K. 19 E7
Streetsboro OH U.S.A. 64 A2
Strehaia Romania 27 J2
Streich Mound h. Australia 55 C7
Strelka Russia 29 Q3
Strel'na r. Russia 12 H2
Strenči Latvia 15 N8
Streymoy i. Faroe Is 14 [inset 1]
Strichen U.K. 20 G3
Stroeder Arg. 70 D6
Strokestown Ireland 21 D4
Stroma, Island of U.K. 20 F2
Stromboli, Isola i. Italy 26 F5
Stromness S. Georgia 70 I8
Stromness U.K. 20 F2
Strömstad Sweden 15 G7
Strömsund Sweden 14 I5
Stronsay i. U.K. 20 G1
Stroud Australia 58 E4
Stroud U.K. 19 E7
Stroud Road Australia 58 E4
Stroudsburg PA U.S.A. 64 D2
Struer Denmark 15 F8
Struga Macedonia 27 I4
Strugi-Krasnyye Russia 15 P7
Struis Bay S. Africa 50 E8
Strumble Head hd U.K. 19 B6
Strumica Macedonia 27 J4
Struthers OH U.S.A. 64 A2
Stryama r. Bulg. 27 K3

Ţarābulus Lebanon see Tripoli
Ţarābulus Libya see Tripoli
Tarahuwan India 36 E4
Tarai reg. India 37 G4
Tarakan Indon. 41 D7
Taraklı Turkey 27 N4
Taran, Mys pt Russia 15 K9
Tarana Australia 58 D4
Taranagar India 36 C3
Taranaki, Mount vol. N.Z. 59 E4
Tarancón Spain 25 E3
Tarangambadi India 38 C4
Tarangire National Park Tanz. 48 D4
Taranto Italy 26 G4
Taranto, Golfo di g. Italy 26 G4
Taranto, Gulf of Italy see Taranto, Golfo di
Tarapoto Peru 68 C5
Tarapur India 38 B2
Tararua Range mts N.Z. 59 E5
Tarascon-sur-Ariège France 24 E5
Tarasovskiy Russia 13 I6
Tarauacá Brazil 68 D5
Tarauacá r. Brazil 68 E5
Tarawera N.Z. 59 F4
Tarawera, Mount vol. N.Z. 59 F4
Taraz Kazakh. 42 C4
Tarazona Spain 25 F3
Tarazona de la Mancha Spain 25 F4
Tarbagatay, Khrebet mts Kazakh. 42 E3
Tarbat Ness pt U.K. 20 F3
Tarbert Ireland 21 C5
Tarbert Scotland U.K. 20 C3
Tarbert Scotland U.K. 20 D5
Tarbes France 24 E5
Tarcoola Australia 55 F7
Tarcoon Australia 58 C3
Tarcoonyinna watercourse Australia 55 F6
Tarcutta Australia 58 C5
Tardoki-Yangi, Gora mt. Russia 44 E2
Taree Australia 58 F3
Tarella Australia 57 C6
Tarentum Italy see Taranto
Tarfaya Morocco 46 B2
Targa well Niger 46 D3
Targan China see Talin Hiag
Targhee Pass ID U.S.A. 62 E3
Targovishte Bulg. 27 L3
Târgovişte Romania 27 K2
Targuist Morocco 25 D6
Târgu Jiu Romania 27 J2
Târgu Mureş Romania 27 K1
Târgu Neamţ Romania 27 L1
Târgu Secuiesc Romania 27 L1
Targyailing China 37 F3
Tariat Mongolia 42 H3
Tarif U.A.E. 48 F1
Tarifa Spain 25 D5
Tarifa, Punta de pt Spain 25 D5
Tarija Bol. 68 F8
Tarikere India 38 B3
Tariku r. Indon. 41 F8
Tarim China 32 G6
Tarim Basin China 42 E5
Tarime Tanz. 48 D4
Tarim He r. China 42 F4
Tarim Pendi basin China see Tarim Basin
Tarīn Kōṭ Afgh. 36 A2
Taritatu r. Indon. 41 F8
Tarka r. S. Africa 51 G7
Tarkastad S. Africa 51 H7
Tarko-Sale Russia 28 I3
Tarkwa Ghana 46 C4
Tarlac Phil. 41 E6
Tarlag China 42 H6
Tarlo River National Park Australia 58 D5
Tarma Peru 68 C6
Tarn r. France 24 E4
Tärnaby Sweden 14 I4
Tarnak Rōd r. Afgh. 36 A3
Târnăveni Romania 27 K1
Tarnobrzeg Poland 13 D6
Tarnogskiy Gorodok Russia 12 I3
Tarnopol Ukr. see Ternopil'
Tarnów Poland 13 D6
Tarnowitz Poland see Tarnowskie Góry
Tarnowskie Góry Poland 17 Q5
Taro Co salt l. China 37 F3
Taroom Australia 57 E5
Taroudannt Morocco 22 C5
Tarpaulin Swamp Australia 56 B3
Ţarq Iran 35 H4
Tarqi China 43 M3
Tarquinia Italy 26 D3
Tarquinii Italy see Tarquinia
Tarrabool Lake imp. l. Australia 56 A3
Tarraco Spain see Tarragona
Tarrafal Cape Verde 46 [inset]
Tarragona Spain 25 G3
Tårrajaur Sweden 14 K3
Tarran Hills h. Australia 58 C4
Tarrant Point Australia 56 B3
Tàrrega Spain 25 G3
Tarrong China see Nyêmo
Tarsus Turkey 39 B1
Tart China 37 H1
Tärtär Azer. 35 G2
Tartu Estonia 15 O7
Ţarţūs Syria 39 B2
Tarumovka Russia 35 G1
Tarung Hka r. Myanmar 37 I4
Tarvisium Italy see Treviso
Tashauz Turkm. see Daşoguz
Tashi Chho Bhutan see Thimphu
Tashigang Bhutan see Trashigang
Tashikuzuke Shan mts China 36 C1
Tashino Russia see Pervomaysk
Tashir Armenia 35 G2
Tashk, Daryācheh-ye l. Iran 35 I5
Tashkent Uzbek. see Toshkent
Tāshqurghān Afgh. see Khulm
Tashtagol Russia 42 F2
Tashtyp Russia 42 F2
Tasiat, Lac l. Que. Canada 61 K4
Tasiilap Karra c. Greenland 61 O3
Tasiilaq Greenland 77 J2
Tasīl Syria 39 B3
Tasiujaq Que. Canada 61 L4
Tasiusaq Greenland 61 M2
Taskala Kazakh. 11 Q5
Taşkent Turkey 39 A1
Tasker Niger 46 E3
Taskesken Kazakh. 42 E3
Taşköprü Turkey 34 D2
Tasman Abyssal Plain sea feature Tasman Sea 74 G8
Tasman Basin sea feature Tasman Sea 74 G8
Tasman Bay N.Z. 59 D5
Tasmania state Australia 57 [inset]
Tasman Islands P.N.G. see Nukumanu Islands
Tasman Mountains N.Z. 59 D5
Tasman Peninsula Australia 57 [inset]
Tasman Sea S. Pacific Ocean 52 H6
Taşova Turkey 34 E2
Tassara Niger 46 D3
Tasty Kazakh. 42 B4
Taşucu Turkey 39 A1
Tas-Yuryakh Russia 29 M3
Tata Morocco 22 C6
Tatabánya Hungary 26 H1
Tatamailau, Foho mt. East Timor 54 D2
Tataouine Tunisia 22 G5
Tatarbunary Ukr. 27 M2
Tatarsk Russia 28 I4
Tatarskiy Proliv str. Russia 44 F2
Tatar Strait Russia see Tatarskiy Proliv
Tate r. Australia 56 C3
Tateyama Japan 45 E6
Tathlina Lake N.W.T. Canada 60 G3
Tathlīth Saudi Arabia 32 F6
Tathlīth, Wādī watercourse Saudi Arabia 32 F5
Tathra Australia 58 D6
Tatishchevo Russia 13 J6
Tatkon Myanmar 37 I5
Tatra Mountains Poland/Slovakia 17 Q6
Tatry mts Poland/Slovakia see Tatra Mountains
Tatrzański Park Narodowy nat. park Poland 17 Q6
Tatsinskaya Russia 13 I6
Tatuí Brazil 71 B3
Tatvan Turkey 35 F3
Tau Norway 15 D7
Tauá Brazil 69 J5
Tauapeçaçu Brazil 68 F4
Taubaté Brazil 71 B3
Taukum, Peski des. Kazakh. 42 C4
Taumarunui N.Z. 59 E4
Taumaturgo Brazil 68 D5
Taung S. Africa 50 G4
Taungdwingyi Myanmar 37 H5
Taunggyi Myanmar 42 H8
Taung-ngu Myanmar 42 H9
Taungtha Myanmar 37 H5
Taungup Myanmar 42 G9
Taunton U.K. 19 D7
Taunton MA U.S.A. 64 F2
Taupo N.Z. 59 F4
Taupo, Lake N.Z. 59 E4
Taurag Lith. 15 M9
Tauranga N.Z. 59 F3
Taurasia Italy see Turin
Taurianova Italy 26 G5
Tauroa Point N.Z. 59 D2
Taurus Mountains Turkey 39 A1
Taute r. France 19 F9
Tauz Azer. see Tovuz
Tavas Turkey 27 M6
Tavastehus Fin. see Hämeenlinna
Taverham U.K. 19 I6
Taveuni i. Fiji 53 I3
Tavira Port. 25 C5
Tavistock U.K. 19 C8
Tavoy Myanmar see Dawei
Tavşanlı Turkey 27 M5
Taw r. U.K. 19 C7
Tawakkul China 36 E1
Tawang India 37 G4
Tawas City MI U.S.A. 63 K3
Tawau Sabah Malaysia 41 D7
Tawè Myanmar see Dawei
Tawe r. U.K. 19 D7
Tawmaw Myanmar 37 I4
Taxkorgan China 42 D5
Tay r. U.K. 20 F4
Tay, Firth of est. U.K. 20 F4
Tay, Lake imp. l. Australia 55 C8
Tay, Loch l. U.K. 20 E4
Tāybād Iran 33 J3
Taybola Russia 14 R2
Tayinloan U.K. 20 D5
Taylor AK U.S.A. 60 B3
Taylor TX U.S.A. 63 H5
Taymā' Saudi Arabia 34 E6
Taymura r. Russia 29 K3
Taymyr, Ozero l. Russia 29 L2
Taymyr, Poluostrov pen. Russia see Taymyr Peninsula
Taymyr Peninsula Russia 28 J2
Tây Ninh Vietnam 31 J5
Taypak Kazakh. 11 Q6
Taypaq Kazakh. see Taypak
Tayshet Russia 42 H1
Taytay Phil. 41 D6
Tayuan China 44 B2
Taz r. Russia 28 I3
Taza Morocco 22 D5
Tāza Khurmātū Iraq 35 G4
Taze Myanmar 37 H5
Tāzirbū Libya 47 F2
Tazmalt Alg. 25 I5
Tazovskaya Guba sea chan. Russia 28 I3
Tbessa Alg. see Tébessa
Tbilisi Georgia 35 G2
Tbilisskaya Russia 13 I7
Tchad country Africa see Chad
Tchamba Togo 46 D4
Tchibanga Gabon 48 B4
Tchigaï, Plateau du Niger 47 E2
Tchin-Tabaradene Niger 46 D3
Tcholliré Cameroon 47 E4
Tczew Poland 17 Q3
Teague, Lake imp. l. Australia 55 C6
Te Anau N.Z. 59 A7
Te Anau, Lake N.Z. 59 A7
Teapa Mex. 66 F5
Te Araroa N.Z. 59 G3
Teate Italy see Chieti
Te Awamutu N.Z. 59 E4
Tébarat Niger 46 D3
Tebay U.K. 18 E4
Tébessa Alg. 26 C7
Tébessa, Monts de mts Alg. 26 C7
Téboursouk Tunisia 26 C6
Tébourba Tunisia 26 C6
T'ebulos Mta Georgia/Russia 35 G2
Tecate Mex. 65 D4
Tece Turkey 39 B1
Techiman Ghana 46 C4
Tecka Arg. 70 B6
Tecoripa Mex. 66 C3
Técpan Mex. 66 D5
Tecuala Mex. 66 C4
Tecuci Romania 27 L2
Tedzhen Turkm. see Tejen
Tees r. U.K. 18 F4
Tefé r. Brazil 68 F4
Tefenni Turkey 27 M6
Tegucigalpa Hond. 67 G6
Teguidda-n-Tessoumt Niger 46 D3
Tehachapi CA U.S.A. 65 C3
Tehachapi Mountains CA U.S.A. 65 C3
Tehachapi Pass CA U.S.A. 65 C3
Tehek Lake Nunavut Canada 61 I3
Teheran Iran see Tehrān
Téhini Côte d'Ivoire 46 C4
Tehrān Iran 35 H4
Tehri India see Tikamgarh
Tehuacán Mex. 66 E5
Tehuantepec, Golfo de Mex. see Tehuantepec, Gulf of
Tehuantepec, Gulf of Mex. 66 F5
Tehuantepec, Istmo de isth. Mex. 66 F5
Teide, Pico del vol. Canary Is 46 B2
Teifi r. U.K. 19 C6
Teignmouth U.K. 19 D8
Teixeira de Sousa Angola see Luau
Teixeiras Brazil 71 C3
Teixeira Soares Brazil 71 A4
Tejakula Indon. 54 A2
Tejen Turkm. 30 F3
Tejo r. Port. see Tagus
Tejon Pass CA U.S.A. 65 C3
Tekapo, Lake N.Z. 59 C6
Tekax Mex. 66 G4
Tekeli Kazakh. 42 D4
Tekes China 42 E4
Tekiliktag mt. China 36 E1
Tekin Russia 44 D2
Tekirdağ Turkey 27 L4
Tekka India 38 D2
Tekkali India 38 E2
Teknaf Bangl. 37 H5
Te Kuiti N.Z. 59 E4
Tel r. India 38 D1
Télagh Alg. 25 F6
Telanaipura Indon. see Jambi
Telangana state India 38 C3
Tel Ashqelon tourist site Israel 39 B4
Télataï Mali 46 D3
Tel Aviv-Yafo Israel 39 B3
Telč Czech Rep. 17 O6
Telchac Puerto Mex. 66 G4
Telekhany Belarus see Tsyelyakhany
Telêmaco Borba Brazil 71 A4
Teleorman r. Romania 27 K3
Telertheba, Djebel mt. Alg. 46 D2
Telescope Peak CA U.S.A. 65 D2
Teles Pires r. Brazil 69 G5
Telford U.K. 19 E6
Télimélé Guinea 46 B3
Teljo, Jebel mt. Sudan 32 C7
Tell Atlas mts Alg. see Atlas Tellien
Teller AK U.S.A. 60 B3
Tell es Sultan West Bank see Jericho
Tellicherry India see Thalassery
Telloh Iraq 35 G5
Tel'mana, imeni Russia 44 D2
Tel'novskiy Russia 44 F2
Telo Martius France see Toulon
Telpoziz, Gora mt. Russia 11 R3
Telsen Arg. 70 C6
Telšiai Lith. 15 M9
Telukbetung Indon. see Bandar Lampung
Temagami Lake Ont. Canada 63 L2
Têmarxung China 37 G2
Temba S. Africa 51 I3
Tembagapura Indon. 52 D2
Tembenchi r. Russia 29 K3
Tembisa S. Africa 51 I4
Tembo Aluma Angola 49 B4
Teme r. U.K. 19 E6
Temecula CA U.S.A. 65 D4
Teminabuan Indon. 52 D2
Temirtau Kazakh. 42 C2
Temmes Fin. 14 N4
Temnikov Russia 13 I5
Temora Australia 58 C5
Tempe Downs Australia 55 F6
Temple TX U.S.A. 63 H5
Temple Bar U.K. 19 C6
Temple Dera Pak. 36 B3
Templemore Ireland 21 E5
Temple Sowerby U.K. 18 E4
Templeton watercourse Australia 56 B4
Tempué Angola 49 B5
Temryuk Russia 13 H7
Temryukskiy Zaliv b. Russia 13 H7
Temuco Chile 70 B5
Temuka N.Z. 59 C7
Tena Ecuador 68 C4
Tenabo Mex. 66 F4
Tenali India 38 D2
Tenbury Wells U.K. 19 E6
Tenby U.K. 19 C7
Tendaho Eth. 48 E2
Tende, Col de pass France/Italy 24 H4
Ten Degree Channel India 31 I6
Tendō Japan 45 F5
Tenedos i. Turkey see Bozcaada
Ténenkou Mali 46 C3
Ténéré reg. Niger 46 D2
Ténéré du Tafassâsset des. Niger 46 E2
Tenerife i. Canary Is 46 B2
Ténès Alg. 25 G5
Tengah, Kepulauan is Indon. 41 D8
Tengger Shamo des. China 42 I5
Tengréla Côte d'Ivoire 46 C3
Ten'gushevo Russia 13 I5
Teni India see Theni
Teniente Jubany research stn Antarctica see Carlini
Tenke Dem. Rep. Congo 49 C5
Tenkeli Russia 29 P2
Tenkodogo Burkina Faso 46 C3
Ten Mile Lake imp. l. Australia 55 C6
Tennant Creek Australia 54 F4
Tennessee r. U.S.A. 63 J4
Tennessee state U.S.A. 63 J4
Tennevoll Norway 14 J2
Tenojoki r. Fin./Norway 14 P1
Tenosique Mex. 66 F5
Tenterden U.K. 19 H7
Tenterfield Australia 58 F2
Tentudia mt. Spain 25 C4
Tentulia Bangl. see Tetulia
Teodoro Sampaio Bahia Brazil 71 D1
Teodoro Sampaio São Paulo Brazil 70 F2
Teófilo Otoni Brazil 71 C2
Tepa Indon. 54 E1
Tepache Mex. 66 C3
Te Paki N.Z. 59 D2
Tepatitlán Mex. 66 D4
Tepehuanes Mex. 62 F6
Tepeköy Turkey see Karakoçan
Tepelenë Albania 27 I4
Tepequem, Serra mts Brazil 67 L8
Tepic Mex. 66 D4
Te Pirita N.Z. 59 C6
Teplice Czech Rep. 17 N5
Teplogorka Russia 12 L3
Teploozersk Russia 44 C2
Teploye Russia 13 H5
Teploye Ozero Russia see Teploozersk
Teq Teq Iraq 35 G4
Tequila Mex. 66 D4
Ter r. Spain 25 H2
Téra Niger 46 D3
Teramo Italy 26 E3
Terang Australia 58 A7
Tercan Turkey 35 F3
Terebovlya Ukr. 13 E6
Terekty Kazakh. 42 F3
Teresa Cristina Brazil 71 A4
Tereshka r. Russia 13 J6
Teresina Brazil 69 J5
Teresina de Goiás Brazil 71 B1
Teresita Col. 68 E3
Teresópolis Brazil 71 C3
Terezinha Brazil 69 H3
Tergeste Italy see Trieste
Tergüün Bogd Uul mt. Mongolia 42 I4
Teriberka Russia 14 S2
Termez Uzbek. see Termiz
Termini Imerese Sicily Italy 26 E6
Términos, Laguna de lag. Mex. 66 F5
Termit-Kaoboul Niger 46 E3
Termiz Uzbek. 33 K2
Termoli Italy 26 F4
Tern r. U.K. 19 E6
Ternate Indon. 41 E7
Terney Russia 44 E3
Terni Italy 26 E3
Ternopil' Ukr. 13 E6
Ternopol' Ukr. see Ternopil'
Terpeniya, Mys c. Russia 44 G2
Terpeniya, Zaliv g. Russia 44 F2
Terra Alta WV U.S.A. 64 B3
Terra Bella CA U.S.A. 65 C3
Terrace B.C. Canada 60 F4
Terrace Bay Ont. Canada 63 J2
Terra Firma S. Africa 50 F3
Terråk Norway 14 H4
Terralba Sardinia Italy 26 C5
Terra Nova Bay Antarctica 76 H1
Terre Haute IN U.S.A. 63 J4
Terre-Neuve prov. Canada see Newfoundland and Labrador
Terre-Neuve-et-Labrador prov. Canada see Newfoundland and Labrador
Terres Australes et Antarctiques Françaises terr. Indian Ocean see French Southern and Antarctic Lands
Terskiy Bereg coastal area Russia 12 H2
Tertenia Sardinia Italy 26 C5
Terter Azer. see Tärtär
Teruel Spain 25 F3
Tervola Fin. 14 N3
Tes Mongolia 42 H3
Tešanj Bos. & Herz. 26 G2
Teseney Eritrea 32 E6
Tesha r. Russia 13 I5
Teshekpuk Lake AK U.S.A. 60 C2
Teshio Japan 44 F3
Teshio-gawa r. Japan 44 F3
Teslin Y.T. Canada 60 E3
Teslin Lake B.C./Y.T. Canada 60 E3
Tesouras r. Brazil 71 A1
Tessalit Mali 46 D2
Tessaoua Niger 46 D3
Tessolo Moz. 51 L1
Test r. U.K. 19 F8
Testour Tunisia 26 C6
Tetas, Punta pt Chile 70 B2
Tete Moz. 49 D5
Te Teko N.Z. 59 F4
Teteriv r. Ukr. 13 F6
Teterow Germany 17 N4
Tetiyev Ukr. see Tetiyiv
Tetiyiv Ukr. 13 F6
Tetney U.K. 18 G5
Tétouan Morocco 25 D6
Tetovo Macedonia 27 I3
Tetuán Morocco see Tétouan
Tetulia Bangl. 37 G4
Tetulia sea chan. Bangl. 37 G5
Tetyukhe Russia see Dal'negorsk
Tetyukhe-Pristan' Russia see Rudnaya Pristan'
Tetyushi Russia 13 K5
Teuco r. Arg. 70 D2
Teufelsbach Namibia 50 C2
Te Urewera National Park N.Z. 59 F4
Teuva Fin. 14 L5
Tevere r. Italy see Tiber
Teverya Israel see Tiberias
Teviot r. U.K. 20 G5
Te Waewae Bay N.Z. 59 A8
Te Waiponamu i. N.Z. see South Island
Tewane Botswana 51 H2
Tewantin Australia 57 F5
Tewkesbury U.K. 19 E7
Têwo China 42 I6
Texarkana TX U.S.A. 63 I5
Texas Australia 58 E2
Texas state U.S.A. 62 H5
Texoma, Lake OK/TX U.S.A. 63 H5
Teyateyaneng Lesotho 51 H5
Teykovo Russia 12 I4
Teza r. Russia 12 I4
Tezpur India 37 H4
Tezu India 37 I4
Tha-anne r. Nunavut Canada 61 I3
Thabana-Ntlenyana mt. Lesotho 51 I5
Thaba Nchu S. Africa 51 H5
Thaba Putsoa mt. Lesotho 51 H5
Thaba-Tseka Lesotho 51 I5
Thabazimbi S. Africa 51 H3
Thabong S. Africa 51 H4
Thabyedaung Myanmar 37 I5
Tha Hin Thai. see Lop Buri
Thai Binh Vietnam 31 J4
Thailand country Asia 31 J5
Thailand, Gulf of Asia 41 C6
Thai Nguyên Vietnam 31 J4
Thakhèk Laos 41 C6
Thakurgaon Bangl. 37 G4
Thakurtola India 36 E5
Thala Tunisia 26 C7
Thalassery India 38 B4
Thal Desert Pak. 33 L3
Thaliparamba India see Taliparamba
Thallon Australia 58 D2
Thamaga Botswana 51 G3
Thamar, Jabal mt. Yemen 32 G7
Thamarīt Oman 33 H6
Thame r. U.K. 19 F7
Thames r. Ont. Canada 63 K3
Thames r. Ont. Canada 64 A1
Thames N.Z. 59 E3
Thames est. U.K. 19 H7
Thames r. U.K. 19 H7
Thamesford Ont. Canada 64 A1
Thana India see Thane
Thandwè Myanmar 42 G9
Thane India 38 B2
Thanet, Isle of pen. U.K. 19 I7
Thangoo Australia 54 C4
Thangra India 36 D2
Thanh Hoa Vietnam 31 J5
Thanjavur India 38 C4
Thanlwin r. China/Myanmar see Salween
Thapsacus Syria see Dibsī
Tharad Gujarat India 36 B4
Tharad Gujarat India 36 B4
Thar Desert India/Pak. 33 K4
Thargomindah Australia 58 A1
Tharthār, Buḥayrat ath l. Iraq 35 F4
Thasos i. Greece 27 K4
Thaton Myanmar 31 I5
Thatta Pak. 33 K5
Thaungdut Myanmar 37 H4
Thayetmyo Myanmar 37 H6
Thazi Myanmar 37 I5
The Aldermen Islands N.Z. 59 F3
Theba AZ U.S.A. 65 F4
The Bahamas country West Indies 67 I4
Thebes Greece see Thiva
The Broads nat. park U.K. 19 I6
The Cheviot h. U.K. 18 E3
The Dalles OR U.S.A. 62 C2
Thedford NE U.S.A. 62 G3
The Entrance Australia 58 E4
The Faither stack U.K. 20 [inset]
The Fens reg. U.K. 19 G6
The Gambia country Africa 46 B3
The Grampians mts Australia 57 C8
The Great Oasis oasis Egypt see Khārijah, Wāḥāt al
The Grenadines is St Vincent 67 L6
The Gulf Asia 32 H4
The Hague Neth. 16 J4
The Hunters Hills N.Z. 59 C7
The Lakes National Park Australia 58 C6
Thelon r. N.W.T./Nunavut Canada 61 I3
The Lynd Junction Australia 56 D3
Thembalihle S. Africa 51 I4
The Minch sea chan. U.K. 20 C2
The Naze c. Norway see Lindesnes
The Needles stack U.K. 19 F8
Theni India 38 C4
Thenia Alg. 25 H5
Theniet El Had Alg. 25 H6
The North Sound sea chan. U.K. 20 G1
Theodore Australia 56 E5
Theodosia Ukr. see Feodosiya
The Old Man of Coniston h. U.K. 18 D4
The Paps h. Ireland 21 C5
The Pas Man. Canada 62 G1
The Pilot mt. Australia 58 D6
Thera i. Greece see Santorini
Thermaïkos Kolpos g. Greece 27 J4
Thermopolis WY U.S.A. 62 F3
The Rock Australia 58 C5
The Salt Lake salt l. Australia 57 C6
The Settlement Christmas I. 74 D4
The Skaw spit Denmark see Grenen
The Skelligs is Ireland 21 B6
The Slot sea chan. Solomon Is see New Georgia Sound
The Solent str. U.K. 19 F8
Thessalon Ont. Canada 63 K2
Thessalonica Greece see Thessaloniki
Thessaloniki Greece 27 J4
The Storr h. U.K. 20 C3
Thet r. U.K. 19 H6
The Terraces hills Australia 55 C7
Thetford U.K. 19 H6
Thetford Mines Que. Canada 63 M2
The Triangle mts Myanmar 42 H7
The Trossachs hills U.K. 20 E4
The Twins Australia 57 A6
Theva-i-Ra reef Fiji see Ceva-i-Ra
The Valley Anguilla 67 L5
Thevenard Island Australia 54 A5
Thévenet, Lac l. Que. Canada 61 L4
Theveste Alg. see Tébessa
The Wash b. U.K. 19 H6
The Weald reg. U.K. 19 H7
The Woodlands TX U.S.A. 63 H5
Thibodaux LA U.S.A. 63 I6
Thief River Falls MN U.S.A. 63 H2
Thiel Mountains Antarctica 76 K1
Thiers France 24 F4
Thiès Senegal 46 B3
Thika Kenya 48 D4
Thiladhunmathi Maldives 38 B5
Thiladunmathi Atoll Maldives see Thiladhunmathi
Thimbu Bhutan see Thimphu
Thimphu Bhutan 37 G4
Thionville France 24 H2
Thira i. Greece see Santorini
Thirsk U.K. 18 F4
Thiruvananthapuram India 38 C4
Thiruvannamalai India see Tiruvannamalai
Thiruvarur India 38 C4
Thiruvattiyur India see Tiruvottiyur
Thisted Denmark 15 F8
Thityabin Myanmar 37 H5
Thiva Greece 27 J5
Thívai Greece see Thiva
Thoen Thai. 42 H9
Thoeng Thai. 42 I9
Thohoyandou S. Africa 51 J2
Thomas Hubbard, Cape Nunavut Canada 61 I1
Thomaston CT U.S.A. 64 E2
Thomastown Ireland 21 E5
Thomasville GA U.S.A. 63 K5
Thompson Man. Canada 61 I4
Thompson r. MO U.S.A. 62 I4
Thompson Falls MT U.S.A. 62 D2
Thompson's Falls Kenya see Nyahururu
Thompson Sound B.C. Canada 62 B1
Thoothukudi India see Tuticorin
Thorn Poland see Toruń
Thornaby-on-Tees U.K. 18 F4
Thornbury U.K. 19 E7
Thorne U.K. 18 G5
Thorne NV U.S.A. 65 C1
Thornton r. Australia 56 B3
Thorshavnfjella reg. Antarctica see Thorshavnheiane
Thorshavnheiane reg. Antarctica 76 C2
Thota-ea-Moli Lesotho 51 H5
Thouars France 24 D3
Thoubal India 37 H4
Thousand Oaks CA U.S.A. 65 C3
Thrace reg. Europe 27 L4
Thraki reg. Europe see Thrace
Thrakiko Pelagos sea Greece 27 K4
Three Gorges Reservoir resr China 43 J6
Three Hummock Island Australia 57 [inset]
Three Kings Islands N.Z. 59 D2
Three Points, Cape Ghana 46 C4
Three Springs Australia 55 A7
Thrissur India 38 C4
Throssell, Lake imp. l. Australia 55 D6
Throssel Range hills Australia 54 C5
Thrushton National Park Australia 58 C1
Thuddungra Australia 58 D5
Thul Pak. 36 B3
Thulaythawāt Gharbī, Jabal h. Syria 39 D2
Thule Air Base Greenland 61 L2
Thun Switz. 24 H3
Thunder Bay Ont. Canada 61 J5
Thurles Ireland 21 E5
Thurn, Pass Austria 17 N7
Thursday Island Australia 56 C1
Thurso U.K. 20 F2
Thurso r. U.K. 20 F2
Thurston Island Antarctica 76 K2
Thurston Peninsula i. Antarctica see Thurston Island
Thuthukudi India see Tuticorin
Thwaite U.K. 18 E4
Thwaites Glacier Tongue Antarctica 76 K1
Thyatira Turkey see Akhisar
Thyborøn Denmark 15 F8
Tianeti Georgia 35 G2
Tianjin China 43 L5
Tianjin mun. China 43 L5
Tianjun China 42 H5
Tianqiaoling China 44 C4
Tianshan China 43 M4
Tian Shan mts China/Kyrg. see Tien Shan
Tianshui China 42 J6
Tianshuihai Aksai Chin 36 D2
Tiantang China see Yuexi
Tianzhu China 42 I5
Tiaret Alg. 25 G6
Tiassalé Côte d'Ivoire 46 C4
Tibagi Brazil 71 A4
Tibal, Wādī watercourse Iraq 35 F4
Tibati Cameroon 46 E4
Tibba Pak. 36 B3
Tibé, Pic de mt. Guinea 46 C4
Tiber r. Italy 26 E4
Tiberias Israel 39 B3
Tiberias, Lake Israel see Galilee, Sea of
Tibesti mts Chad 47 E2
Tibet aut. rep. China see Xizang Zizhiqu
Tibet, Plateau of China 37 F2
Tībīstī, Sarīr des. Libya 47 E2
Tibooburra Australia 57 C6
Tibrikot Nepal 37 E3
Tibro Sweden 15 I7
Tibur Italy see Tivoli
Tiburón, Isla i. Mex. 66 B3
Ticehurst U.K. 19 H7
Tîchît Mauritania 46 C3
Tîchît, Dahr hills Mauritania 46 C3
Tichla W. Sahara 46 B2
Ticinum Italy see Pavia
Ticul Mex. 66 G4
Tidaholm Sweden 15 H7
Tiddim Myanmar 37 H5
Tidjikja Mauritania 46 B3
Tieli China 44 B3
Tieling China 44 A4
Tielongtan Aksai Chin 36 D2
Tien Shan mts China/Kyrg. 42 D4
Tientsin mun. China see Tianjin
Tierp Sweden 15 J6
Tierra del Fuego, Isla Grande de i. Arg./Chile 70 C8
Tierra del Fuego, Parque Nacional nat. park Arg. 70 C8
Tiétar r. Spain 25 D4
Tiétar, Valle del val. Spain 25 D3
Tietê r. Brazil 71 A3
Tieyon Australia 55 F6
Tiflis Georgia see Tbilisi
Tifton GA U.S.A. 63 K5
Tiga Reservoir Nigeria 46 D3
Tigen Kazakh. 35 H1
Tigheciului, Dealurile hills Moldova 27 M2
Tighina Moldova see Bender
Tigiria India 38 E1
Tignère Cameroon 46 E4
Tignish P.E.I. Canada 63 O2
Tigranocerta Turkey see Siirt
Tigre r. Venez. 68 F2
Tigris r. Asia 32 F2
Tigrovaya Balka Zapovednik nature res. Tajik. 36 B1
Tiguidit, Falaise de esc. Niger 46 D3
Tīh, Gebel el plat. Egypt see Tīh, Jabal at
Tīh, Jabal at plat. Egypt 39 A5
Tijuana Mex. 66 A2
Tikamgarh India 36 D4
Tikanlik China 42 F4
Tikhoretsk Russia 13 I7
Tikhvin Russia 12 G4
Tikhvinskaya Gryada ridge Russia 12 G4
Tiki Basin sea feature S. Pacific Ocean 75 L7
Tikokino N.Z. 59 F4
Tikopia i. Solomon Is 53 G3
Tikrīt Iraq 35 F4
Tikse India 36 D2
Tikshozero, Ozero l. Russia 14 R3
Tiksi Russia 29 N2
Tiladummati Atoll Maldives see Thiladhunmathi
Tilaiya Reservoir India 37 F4
Tilbeşar Ovasi plain Turkey 39 C1
Tilbooroo Australia 58 B1
Tilburg Neth. 16 J5
Tilbury U.K. 19 H7
Tilcara Arg. 70 C2
Tilcha Creek watercourse Australia 57 C6
Tilemsès Niger 46 D3
Tilemsi, Vallée du watercourse Mali 46 D3
Tilhar India 36 D4
Tilimsen Alg. see Tlemcen
Tilin Myanmar 37 H5
Tillabéri Niger 46 D3
Tillia Niger 46 D3
Tillicoultry U.K. 20 F4
Tillsonburg Ont. Canada 64 A1
Tillyfourie U.K. 20 G3
Tilos i. Greece 27 L6
Tilothu India 37 F4
Tilpa Australia 58 B3
Tilsit Russia see Sovetsk
Tilt r. U.K. 20 F4
Tilton NH U.S.A. 64 F1
Tim Russia 13 H6
Ţimā Egypt 32 D4
Timakara i. India 38 B4
Timanskiy Kryazh ridge Russia 12 K2
Timar Turkey 35 F3
Timaru N.Z. 59 C7
Timashevsk Russia 13 H7
Timashevskaya Russia see Timashevsk
Timbedgha Mauritania 46 C3
Timber Creek Australia 52 D3
Timber Mountain NV U.S.A. 65 D2
Timberville VA U.S.A. 64 B3
Timbuktu Mali 46 C3
Timétrine reg. Mali 46 C3
Timiaouine Alg. 46 D2
Timimoun Alg. 22 E6
Timirist, Râs pt Mauritania 46 B3
Timişoara Romania 27 I2
Timmins Ont. Canada 61 J5
Timon Brazil 69 J5
Timor i. Indon. 54 D2
Timor-Leste country Asia see East Timor
Timor Loro Sae country Asia see East Timor
Timor Sea Australia/Indon. 52 C3
Timor Timur country Asia see East Timor
Timperley Range hills Australia 55 C6
Timrå Sweden 14 J5
Tin, Ra's at pt Libya 34 A4
Ţīna, Khalīg el b. Egypt see Ţīnah, Khalīj aţ
Ţīnah Syria 39 D1
Ţīnah, Khalīj aţ b. Egypt 39 A4
Tin Can Bay Australia 57 F5
Tindivanam India 38 C3
Tindouf Alg. 22 C6
Ti-n-Essako Mali 46 D3
Tingha Australia 58 E2
Tingis Morocco see Tangier
Tingo María Peru 68 C5
Tingréla Côte d'Ivoire see Tengréla
Tingsryd Sweden 15 I8
Tingvoll Norway 14 F5
Tingwall U.K. 20 F1
Tinharé, Ilha de i. Brazil 71 D1
Tinian i. N. Mariana Is 41 G6
Tini Heke is N.Z. see Snares Islands
Tinnelvelly India see Tirunelveli
Tinogasta Arg. 70 C3
Tinos Greece 27 K6
Tinos i. Greece 27 K6
Tinrhert, Hamada de Alg. 46 D2
Tinsukia India 37 H4
Tintagel U.K. 19 C8
Ţînţâne Mauritania 46 B3
Tintina Arg. 70 D3
Tintinara Australia 57 C7
Tionesta PA U.S.A. 64 B2
Tionesta Lake PA U.S.A. 64 B2
Tipasa Alg. 25 H5
Tiphsah Syria see Dibsī
Tipperary Ireland 21 D5
Tipton CA U.S.A. 65 C2
Tipton, Mount AZ U.S.A. 65 E3
Tiptree U.K. 19 H7
Tiptur India 38 C3
Tipturi India see Tiptur
Tiracambu, Serra do hills Brazil 69 I4
Tirana Albania 27 H4
Tiranë Albania see Tirana
Tirano Italy 26 D1
Tirari Desert Australia 57 B5
Tiraspol Moldova 27 M1
Tiraz Mountains Namibia 50 C4
Tire Turkey 27 L5
Tirebolu Turkey 35 E2

Turar Ryskulov Kazakh. 33 L1
Tura-Ryskulova Kazakh. see Turar Ryskulov
Turayf Saudi Arabia 39 D4
Turayf, Kutayfat vol. Saudi Arabia 39 D4
Turba Estonia 15 N7
Turbat Pak. 33 J4
Turbo Col. 68 C2
Turda Romania 27 J1
Tureh Iran 35 H4
Turfan China see Turpan
Turfan Basin depr. China see Turpan Pendi
Turfan Depression China see Turpan Pendi
Turgutlu Turkey 27 L5
Turhal Turkey 34 E2
Türi Estonia 15 N7
Turia r. Spain 25 F4
Turin Italy 26 B2
Turiy Rog Russia 44 C3
Turkana, Lake salt l. Eth./Kenya 48 D3
Turkey country Asia/Europe 34 D3
Turki Russia 13 I6
Turkistan Kazakh. 42 B4
Türkistan Kazakh. see Turkistan
Turkistān, Silsilah-ye Band-e mts Afgh. 36 A2
Türkiye country Asia/Europe see Turkey
Türkmenabat Turkm. 30 F3
Türkmen Adasy i. Turkm. see Ogurjaly Adasy
Türkmen Aylagy b. Turkm. see Türkmen Aýlagy
Türkmen Aýlagy b. Turkm. 35 I3
Türkmenbaşy Turkm. 35 I2
Türkmenbaşy Turkm. see Türkmenbaşy
Türkmenbaşy Aylagy b. Turkm. see Türkmenbaşy Aýlagy
Türkmenbaşy Aýlagy b. Turkm. 35 I3
Türkmenbaşy Döwlet Gorugy nature res. Turkm. 35 I3
Türkmen Dağı mt. Turkey 27 N5
Turkmenistan country Asia 33 I2
Turkmeniya country Asia see Turkmenistan
Türkmenostan country Asia see Turkmenistan
Turkmenskaya S.S.R. country Asia see Turkmenistan
Türkoğlu Turkey 34 E3
Turks and Caicos Islands terr. West Indies 67 J4
Turks Islands Turks and Caicos Is 67 J4
Turku Fin. 15 M6
Turkwel watercourse Kenya 48 D3
Turlock CA U.S.A. 65 B2
Turlock Lake CA U.S.A. 65 B2
Turmalina Brazil 71 C2
Turnagain, Cape N.Z. 59 F5
Turnberry U.K. 20 E5
Turneffe Islands atoll Belize 66 G5
Turnor Lake Sask. Canada 60 H4
Türnovo Bulg. see Veliko Turnovo
Turnu Măgurele Romania 27 K3
Turnu Severin Romania see Drobeta-Turnu Severin
Turon r. Australia 58 D4
Turones France see Tours
Turovets Russia 12 I4
Turpan China 42 F4
Turpan Pendi depr. China 42 F4
Turquino, Pico mt. Cuba 67 I4
Turriff U.K. 20 G3
Turris Libisonis Sardinia Italy see Porto Torres
Tursāq Iraq 35 G4
Turtle Island Fiji see Vatoa
Turugart Pass China/Kyrg. 31 G2
Turugart Shankou pass China/Kyrg. see Turugart Pass
Turuvanur India 38 C3
Turvo r. Goiás Brazil 71 A2
Turvo r. São Paulo Brazil 71 A2
Tuscaloosa AL U.S.A. 63 J5
Tuscarawas r. OH U.S.A. 64 A2
Tuscarora Mountains hills PA U.S.A. 64 C2
Tuskegee AL U.S.A. 63 J5
Tussey Mountains hills PA U.S.A. 64 B2
Tutak Turkey 35 F3
Tutayev Russia 12 H4
Tutera Spain see Tudela
Tuticorin India 38 C4
Tuttlingen Germany 17 L7
Tuttut Nunaat reg. Greenland 61 P2
Tutuala East Timor 54 D2
Tutubu P.N.G. 56 E1
Tutubu Tanz. 49 D4
Tutuila i. American Samoa 53 I3
Tutume Botswana 49 C6
Tuun-bong mt. N. Korea 44 B4
Tuupovaara Fin. 14 Q5
Tuusniemi Fin. 14 P5
Tuvalu country S. Pacific Ocean 53 H2
Tuwayq, Jabal hills Saudi Arabia 32 G4
Tuwayq, Jabal mts Saudi Arabia 32 G5
Ţuwayyil ash Shihāq mt. Jordan 39 C4
Tuwwal Saudi Arabia 32 E5
Tuxpan Mex. 66 E4
Tuxtla Gutiérrez Mex. 66 F5
Tuy Hoa Vietnam 31 J5
Tuz, Lake salt l. Turkey 34 D3
Tuz Gölü salt l. Turkey see Tuz, Lake
Tuzha Russia 12 J4
Tuz Khurmātū Iraq 35 G4
Tuzla Bos. & Herz. 26 H2
Tuzla Turkey 39 B1
Tuzla Gölü lag. Turkey 27 L4
Tuzlov r. Russia 13 I7
Tuzu r. Myanmar 37 H4
Tvedestrand Norway 15 F7
Tver' Russia 12 G4
Twain Harte CA U.S.A. 65 B1
Tweed r. U.K. 20 G5
Tweed Heads Australia 58 F2
Tweefontein S. Africa 50 D7
Twee Rivier Namibia 50 D4
Twentynine Palms CA U.S.A. 65 D3
Twin Bridges CA U.S.A. 65 B1
Twin Falls ID U.S.A. 62 E3
Twin Heads h. Australia 54 D5
Twin Peak CA U.S.A. 65 B1
Twitchen Reservoir CA U.S.A. 65 B3
Twofold Bay Australia 58 D6
Two Harbors MN U.S.A. 63 I2
Tyan' Shan' mts China/Kyrg. see Tien Shan
Tyatya, Vulkan vol. Russia 44 G3
Tydal Norway 14 G5
Tygart Valley val. WV U.S.A. 64 B3
Tygda Russia 44 B1
Tygda r. Russia 44 B1
Tyler TX U.S.A. 63 H5
Tym' r. Russia 44 F2
Tymovskoye Russia 44 F2
Tynda Russia 43 M1
Tyndinskiy Russia see Tynda
Tyne r. U.K. 20 G4
Tynemouth U.K. 18 F3
Tynset Norway 15 G5
Tyoploozyorsk Russia see Teploozersk
Tyoploye Ozero Russia see Teploozersk
Tyr Lebanon see Tyre
Tyras Ukr. see Bilhorod-Dnistrovs'kyy
Tyre Lebanon 39 B3
Tyree, Mount Antarctica 76 L1
Tyrma Russia 44 D2
Tyrma r. Russia 44 C2
Tyrnävä Fin. 14 N4
Tyrnavos Greece 27 J5
Tyrnyauz Russia 35 F2
Tyrone PA U.S.A. 64 B2
Tyrrell r. Australia 58 A5
Tyrrell, Lake dry lake Australia 57 C7
Tyrrhenian Sea France/Italy 26 D4
Tyrus Lebanon see Tyre
Tysa r. Serbia see Tisa
Tyukalinsk Russia 28 I4
Tyulen'i, Ostrova is Kazakh. 35 H1
Tyumen' Russia 28 H4
Tyup Kyrg. see Tüp
Tyuratam Kazakh. see Baykonyr
Tywi r. U.K. 19 C7
Tywyn U.K. 19 C6
Tzaneen S. Africa 51 J2
Tzia i. Greece 27 K6

U

Uaco Congo Angola see Waku-Kungo
Ualan atoll Micronesia see Kosrae
Uamanda Angola 49 C5
Uarc, Ras c. Morocco see Trois Fourches, Cap des
Uaroo Australia 55 A5
Uatumã r. Brazil 69 G4
Uauá Brazil 69 K5
Uaupés r. Brazil 68 E3
U'aylī, Wādī al watercourse Saudi Arabia 39 D4
U'aywij well Saudi Arabia 35 G5
U'aywij, Wādī al watercourse Saudi Arabia 35 F5
Ubá Brazil 71 C3
Ubaí Brazil 71 B2
Ubaitaba Brazil 71 D1
Ubangi r. Cent. Afr. Rep./Dem. Rep. Congo 48 B4
Ubangi-Shari country Africa see Central African Republic
Ubauro Pak. 36 B3
Ubayyiḍ, Wādī al watercourse Iraq/Saudi Arabia 35 F4
Ube Japan 45 C6
Úbeda Spain 25 E4
Uberaba Brazil 71 B2
Uberlândia Brazil 71 A2
Ubiña, Peña mt. Spain 25 D2
Ubombo S. Africa 51 K4
Ubon Ratchathani Thai. 31 J5
Ubundu Dem. Rep. Congo 47 F5
Üçajy Turkm. 33 J2
Ucar Azer. 35 G2
Uçarı Turkey 39 A1
Ucayali r. Peru 68 D4
Uch Pak. 36 B3
Üchajy Turkm. see Üçajy
Üchān Iran 35 H3
Uchiura-wan b. Japan 44 F4
Uchkeken Russia 35 F2
Uchkuduk Uzbek. see Uchquduq
Uchquduq Uzbek. 33 J1
Uchur r. Russia 29 O4
Uckfield U.K. 19 H8
Uda r. Russia 43 J2
Uda r. Russia 44 D1
Udachnoye Russia 13 J7
Udachnyy Russia 77 E2
Udagamandalam India 38 C4
Udaipur Rajasthan India 36 C4
Udaipur Tripura India 37 G5
Udanti r. India/Myanmar 37 E5
Uday r. Ukr. 13 G6
Uddevalla Sweden 15 G7
Uddingston U.K. 20 E5
Uddjaure l. Sweden 14 J4
Udgir India 38 C2
Udhagamandalam India see Udagamandalam
Udhampur India 36 C2
Udia-Milai atoll Marshall Is see Bikini
Udimskiy Russia 12 J3
Udine Italy 26 E1
Udmalaippettai India see Udumalaippettai
Udomlya Russia 12 G4
Udon Thani Thai. 31 J5
Udskaya Guba b. Russia 29 O4
Udskoye Russia 44 D1
Udumalaippettai India 38 C4
Udupi India 38 B3
Udyl', Ozero l. Russia 44 E1
Udzhary Azer. see Ucar
Udzungwa Mountains National Park Tanz. 49 D4
Uéa atoll New Caledonia see Ouvéa
Ueckermünde Germany 17 O4
Ueda Japan 45 E5
Uele r. Dem. Rep. Congo 48 C3
Uelen Russia 29 U3
Uelzen Germany 17 M4
Ufa Russia 11 R5
Ufa r. Russia 11 R5
Uftyuga r. Russia 12 J3
Ugab watercourse Namibia 49 B6
Ugalla r. Tanz. 49 D4
Uganda country Africa 48 D3
Ugie S. Africa 51 I6
Uglegorsk Russia 44 F2
Uglich Russia 12 H4
Ugljan i. Croatia 26 F2
Uglovoye Russia 44 C2
Ugol'noye Russia 29 P3
Ugolnyy Russia see Beringovskiy
Ugol'nyye Kopi Russia 29 S3
Ugra Russia 13 G5
Uherské Hradiště Czech Rep. 17 P6
Uhrichsville OH U.S.A. 64 A2
Uibhist a' Deas i. U.K. see South Uist
Uibhist a' Tuath i. U.K. see North Uist
Uig U.K. 20 C3
Uíge Angola 49 B4
Uijeongbu S. Korea 45 B5
Ŭiju N. Korea 45 B4
Uimaharju Fin. 14 Q5
Uinta Mountains UT U.S.A. 62 E3
Uis Mine Namibia 49 B6
Uitenhage S. Africa 51 G7
Ujhani India 36 D4
Uji Japan 45 D6
Uji-guntō is Japan 45 C7
Ujiyamada Japan see Ise
Ujjain India 36 C5
Ujung Pandang Indon. see Makassar
Újvidék Serbia see Novi Sad
Ukal Sagar l. India 36 C5
Ukata Nigeria 46 D3
'Ukayrishah well Saudi Arabia 35 G6
uKhahlamba-Drakensberg Park nat. park S. Africa 51 I5
Ukholovo Russia 13 I5
Ukhrul India 37 H4
Ukhta Respublika Kareliya Russia see Kalevala
Ukhta Respublika Komi Russia 12 L3
Ukiah CA U.S.A. 65 A1
Ukkusissat Greenland 61 M2
Ukmergė Lith. 15 N9
Ukraine country Europe 13 F6
Ukrainskaya S.S.R. country Europe see Ukraine
Ukrayina country Europe see Ukraine
Uku-jima i. Japan 45 C6
Ukwi Botswana 50 E2
Ukwi Pan salt pan Botswana 50 E2
Ulaanbaatar Mongolia see Ulan Bator
Ulaangom Mongolia 42 G3
Ulan Australia 58 D4
Ulan Bator Mongolia 42 J3
Ulanbel' Kazakh. 42 C4
Ulan Erge Russia 13 J7
Ulanhad China see Chifeng
Ulanhot China 44 A3
Ulan Hua China 43 K4
Ulan-Khol Russia 13 J7
Ulan Qab China 43 K4
Ulan-Ude Russia 43 J2
Ulan Ul Hu l. China 37 G2
Ulaş Turkey 34 E3
Ulawa Island Solomon Is 53 G2
Ul'banskiy Zaliv b. Russia 44 E1
Uldz Gol r. Mongolia 43 L3
Uleåborg Fin. see Oulu
Ulefoss Norway 15 F7
Ülenurme Estonia 15 O7
Ulety Russia 43 K2
Ulhasnagar India 38 B2
Uliastai China 43 L3
Uliastay Mongolia 42 H3
Uliatea i. Fr. Polynesia see Raiatea
Ulita r. Russia 14 R2
Ulithi atoll Micronesia 41 F6
Uljin S. Korea 45 C5
Ul'ken Naryn Kazakh. 42 E3
Ulladulla Australia 58 E5
Ullapool U.K. 20 D3
Ulla Ulla, Parque Nacional nat. park Bol. 68 E6
Ullava Fin. 14 M5
Ullersuaq c. Greenland 61 K2
Ulleung-do i. S. Korea 45 C5
Ullswater l. U.K. 18 E4
Ulm Germany 17 L6
Ulmarra Australia 58 F2
Uloowaranie, Lake imp. l. Australia 57 B5
Ulricehamn Sweden 15 H8
Ulsan S. Korea 45 C6
Ulsberg Norway 14 F5
Ulster reg. Ireland/U.K. 21 E3
Ulster PA U.S.A. 64 C2
Ulster Canal Ireland/U.K. 21 E3
Ultima Australia 58 A5
Ulubat Gölü l. Turkey 27 M4
Ulubey Turkey 27 M5
Uluborlu Turkey 27 N5
Uludağ mt. Turkey 27 M4
Uludağ Milli Parkı nat. park Turkey 27 M4
Ulugqat China 42 C5
Ulukhaktok N.W.T. Canada 60 G2
Ulukışla Turkey 34 D3
Ulundi S. Africa 51 J5
Ulungur Hu l. China 42 F3
Uluqsaqtuuq N.W.T. Canada see Ulukhaktok
Uluru h. Australia 55 E6
Uluru-Kata Tjuta National Park Australia 55 E6
Uluru National Park Australia see Uluru-Kata Tjuta National Park
Ulutau Kazakh. see Ulytau
Ulutau, Gory mts Kazakh. see Ulytau, Gory
Uluyatır Turkey 39 C1
Ulva i. U.K. 20 C4
Ulverston U.K. 18 D4
Ulvsjön Sweden 15 I6
Ül'yanov Kazakh. see Botakara
Ul'yanovsk Russia 13 K5
Ul'yanovskiy Kazakh. see Botakara
Ulysses KS U.S.A. 62 G4
Ulytau Kazakh. 42 B3
Ulytau, Gory mts Kazakh. 42 B3
Ulyunkhan Russia 43 K2
Uma Russia 44 A1
Umal'ta (abandoned) Russia 44 D2
'Umān country Asia see Oman
Uman' Ukr. 13 F6
'Umarī, Qā' al salt pan Jordan 39 C4
Umaria India 36 E5
Umarkhed India 38 C2
Umarkot India 38 D2
Umarkot Punjab Pak. 36 B3
Umarkot Sindh Pak. 33 K4
Umaroona, Lake imp. l. Australia 57 B5
Umarpada India 36 C5
Umba Russia 12 G2
Umbeara Australia 55 F6
Umboi i. P.N.G. 52 E2
Umeå Sweden 14 L5
Umeälven r. Sweden 14 L5
uMhlanga S. Africa 51 J5
Umiiviip Kangertiva inlet Greenland 61 N3
Umingmaktok Nunavut Canada 77 L2
Umkomaas S. Africa 51 J6
Umlaiteng India 37 H4
Umlazi S. Africa 51 J5
Umm ad Daraj, Jabal mt. Jordan 39 B3
Umm al 'Amad Syria 39 C2
Umm al Qulbān Saudi Arabia 35 F6
Umm ar Raqabah, Khabrat salt pan Saudi Arabia 39 C5
Umm Bel Sudan 32 C7
Umm Keddada Sudan 32 C7
Umm Lajj Saudi Arabia 32 E4
Umm Nukhaylah h. Saudi Arabia 39 D5
Umm Qaşr Iraq 35 G5
Umm Quşūr i. Saudi Arabia 34 D6
Umm Ruwaba Sudan 32 D7
Umm Sa'ad Libya 34 B5
Umm Shugeira Sudan 32 C7
Umm Wa'āl h. Saudi Arabia 39 D4
Umnak Island AK U.S.A. 60 B4
Umpulo Angola 49 B5
Umraniye Turkey 27 N5
Umred India 38 C1
Umri India 36 D4
Umtali Zimbabwe see Mutare
Umtata S. Africa see Mthatha
Umtentweni S. Africa 51 J6
Umuahia Nigeria 46 D4
Umuarama Brazil 70 F2
Umvuma Zimbabwe see Mvuma
Umzimkulu S. Africa 51 I6
Una r. Bos. & Herz./Croatia 26 G2
Una Brazil 71 D1
Una India 36 D3
'Unāb, Jabal al h. Jordan 39 C5
'Unāb, Wādī al watercourse Jordan 39 C4
Unaí Brazil 71 B2
Unalaska Island AK U.S.A. 60 B4
Unapool U.K. 20 D2
'Unayzah Saudi Arabia 32 F4
'Unayzah, Jabal h. Iraq 35 E4
Uncia Bol. 68 E7
Undara National Park Australia 56 D3
Underberg S. Africa 51 I5
Underbool Australia 57 C7
Unecha Russia 13 G5
Ungama Bay Kenya see Ungwana Bay
Ungarie Australia 58 C4
Ungava, Baie d' b. Que. Canada see Ungava Bay
Ungava, Péninsule d' pen. Que. Canada 61 K3
Ungava Bay Que. Canada 61 L4
Ungava Peninsula Que. Canada see Ungava, Péninsule d'
Ungeny Moldova see Ungheni
Ungheni Moldova 27 L1
Unguana Moz. 51 L2
Unguja i. Tanz. see Zanzibar Island
Unguz, Solonchakovyye Vpadiny salt flat Turkm. 33 I2
Üngüz Angyrsyndaky Garagum des. Turkm. 33 I1
Ungvár Ukr. see Uzhhorod
Ungwana Bay Kenya 48 E4
Uni Russia 12 K4
União Brazil 69 J4
União da Vitória Brazil 71 A4
União dos Palmares Brazil 69 K5
Unimak Island AK U.S.A. 60 B4
Unini r. Brazil 68 F4
Union WV U.S.A. 64 A4
Union City PA U.S.A. 64 B2
Union City TN U.S.A. 63 J4
Uniondale S. Africa 50 F7
Uniontown PA U.S.A. 64 B3
Unionville PA U.S.A. 64 C2
United Arab Emirates country Asia 33 H5
United Arab Republic country Africa see Egypt
United Kingdom country Europe 16 G3
United Provinces state India see Uttar Pradesh
United States of America country N. America 62 F3
United States Range mts Nunavut Canada 61 L1
Unity Sask. Canada 62 F1
Unjha India 36 C5
Unnao India 36 E4
Ŭnp'a N. Korea 45 B5
Unsan N. Korea 45 B4
Ŭnsan N. Korea 45 B5
Unst i. U.K. 20 [inset]
Untor, Ozero l. Russia 11 T3
Unuli Horog China 37 G2
Unzen-dake vol. Japan 45 C6
Unzha Russia 12 J4
Upar Ghat reg. India 37 F5
Upemba, Lac l. Dem. Rep. Congo 49 C4
Upemba, Parc National de l' nat. park Dem. Rep. Congo 49 C4
Uperbada India 37 F5
Upernavik Greenland 61 M2
Upington S. Africa 50 E5
Upland CA U.S.A. 65 D3
Upleta India 36 B5
Upoloksha Russia 14 Q3
'Upolu i. Samoa 53 I3
Upper Chindwin Myanmar see Mawlaik
Upper Hutt N.Z. 59 E5
Upper Klamath Lake OR U.S.A. 62 C3
Upper Lough Erne l. U.K. 21 E3
Upper Marlboro MD U.S.A. 64 C3
Upper Tunguska r. Russia see Angara
Upper Volta country Africa see Burkina Faso
Upper Yarra Reservoir Australia 58 B6
Uppinangadi India 38 B3
Uppsala Sweden 15 J7
Upshi India 36 D2
Upton MA U.S.A. 64 F1
'Uqayqah, Wādī watercourse Jordan 39 B4
'Uqayribāt Syria 39 C2
'Uqlat al 'Udhaybah well Iraq 35 G5
Urad Houqi China see Sain Us
Urakawa Japan 44 F4
Ural h. Australia 58 C4
Ural r. Kazakh./Russia 30 E2
Uralla Australia 58 E3
Ural Mountains Russia 11 S2
Ural'sk Kazakh. 30 E1
Ural'skaya Oblast' admin. div. Kazakh. see Zapadnyy Kazakhstan
Ural'skiye Gory mts Russia see Ural Mountains
Ural'skiy Khrebet mts Russia see Ural Mountains
Urambo Tanz. 49 D4
Uran India 38 B2
Urana Australia 58 C5
Urana, Lake Australia 58 C5
Urandangi Australia 56 B4
Urandi Brazil 71 C1
Uranium City Sask. Canada 60 H4
Uranquinty Australia 58 C5
Uraricoera r. Brazil 68 F3
Urartu country Asia see Armenia
Uravakonda India 38 C3
Urawa Japan 45 E6
'Urayf an Nāqah, Jabal h. Egypt 39 B4
Urbino Italy 26 E3
Urbinum Italy see Urbino
Urbs Vetus Italy see Orvieto
Urdoma Russia 12 K3
Urdyuzhskoye, Ozero l. Russia 12 K2
Ure r. U.K. 18 F4
Urek'i Georgia 35 F2
Uren' Russia 12 J4
Urengoy Russia 28 I3
Uréparapara i. Vanuatu 53 G3
Urfa Turkey see Şanlıurfa
Urfa prov. Turkey see Şanlıurfa
Urga Mongolia see Ulan Bator
Urgal r. Russia 44 D2
Urganch Uzbek. 33 J1
Urgench Uzbek. see Urganch
Ürgün-e Kalān Afgh. 36 B2
Ürgüp Turkey 34 D3
Urho China 42 F3
Urho Kekkosen kansallispuisto nat. park Fin. 14 O2
Urie r. U.K. 20 G3
Uril Russia 44 C2
Urisino Australia 58 A2
Urjala Fin. 15 M6
Urkan Russia 44 B1
Urkan r. Russia 44 B1
Urla Turkey 27 L5
Urlingford Ireland 21 E5
Urluk Russia 43 J2
Urmā aş Şughrá Syria 39 C1
Urmai China 37 F3
Urmia Iran 35 G3
Urmia, Lake salt l. Iran 35 G3
Uromi Nigeria 46 D4
Uroševac Kosovo see Ferizaj
Urosozero Russia 12 G3
Urru Co salt l. China 37 F3
Urt Moron China 42 G5
Uruáchic Mex. 62 F6
Uruaçu Brazil 71 A1
Uruana Brazil 71 A1
Uruapan Mex. 66 D5
Urubamba r. Peru 68 D6
Urucará Brazil 69 G4
Urucu r. Brazil 68 F4
Uruçuca Brazil 71 D1
Uruçuí Brazil 69 J5
Uruçuí, Serra do hills Brazil 69 I5
Urucuia Brazil 71 B2
Urucurituba Brazil 69 G4
Uruguai r. Arg./Uruguay see Uruguay
Uruguaiana Brazil 70 E3
Uruguay country S. America 70 E4
Uruhe China 44 B2
Urumchi China see Ürümqi
Ürümqi China 42 F4
Urundi country Africa see Burundi
Urup, Ostrov i. Russia 43 S3
Urusha Russia 44 A1
Urutaí Brazil 71 A2
Uruzgān Afgh. 36 A2
Uryupino Russia 43 M2
Uryupinsk Russia 13 I6
Urzhum Russia 12 K4
Urziceni Romania 27 L2
Usa Japan 45 C6
Usa r. Russia 12 M2
Uşak Turkey 27 M5
Usakos Namibia 50 B1
Usarp Mountains Antarctica 76 H2
Usborne, Mount h. Falkland Is 70 E8
Ushakova, Ostrov i. Russia 28 I1
Ushant i. France see Ouessant, Île d'
Usharal Kazakh. 42 E3
Üsharal Kazakh. see Usharal
Ush-Bel'dir Russia 42 H2
Ushtobe Kazakh. 42 D3
Ush-Tyube Kazakh. see Ushtobe
Ushuaia Arg. 70 C8
Ushumun Russia 44 B1
Usinsk Russia 11 R2
Usk U.K. 19 E7
Usk r. U.K. 19 E7
Uskhodni Belarus 15 O10
Uskoplje Bos. & Herz. see Gornji Vakuf
Üsküdar Turkey 27 M4
Usman' Russia 13 H5
Usmanabad India see Osmanabad
Usmas ezers l. Latvia 15 M8
Usogorsk Russia 12 K3
Usol'ye-Sibirskoye Russia 42 I2
Ussel France 24 F4
Ussuri r. China/Russia 44 D2
Ussuriysk Russia 44 C4
Ust'-Abakanskoye Russia see Abakan
Usta Muhammad Pak. 36 B3
Ust'-Balyk Russia see Nefteyugansk
Ust'-Donetskiy Russia 13 I7
Ust'-Dzheguta Russia 35 F1
Ust'-Dzhegutinskaya Russia see Ust'-Dzheguta
Ustica, Isola di i. Sicily Italy 26 E5
Ust'-Ilimsk Russia 29 L4
Ust'-Ilimskiy Vodokhranilishche resr Russia 29 L4
Ust'-Ilych Russia 11 R3
Ústí nad Labem Czech Rep. 17 O5
Ustinov Russia see Izhevsk
Üstirt plat. Kazakh./Uzbek. see Ustyurt Plateau
Ustka Poland 17 P3
Ust'-Kamchatsk Russia 29 R4
Ust'-Kamenogorsk Kazakh. 42 E3
Ust'-Kan Russia 42 F2
Ust'-Koksa Russia 42 F2
Ust'-Kulom Russia 12 L3
Ust'-Kut Russia 29 L4
Ust'-Kuyga Russia 29 O2
Ust'-Labinsk Russia 35 E1
Ust'-Labinskaya Russia see Ust'-Labinsk
Ust'-Lyzha Russia 12 M2
Ust'-Maya Russia 29 O3
Ust'-Nera Russia 29 P3
Ust'-Ocheya Russia 12 K3
Ust'-Olenek Russia 29 M2
Ust'-Omchug Russia 29 P3
Ust'-Ordynskiy Russia 42 I2
Ust'-Penzhino Russia see Kamenskoye
Ust'-Port Russia 28 J3
Ustrem Russia 11 T3
Ust'-Tsil'ma Russia 12 L2
Ust'-Uda Russia 42 I2
Ust'-Umalta (abandoned) Russia 44 D2
Ust'-Undurga Russia 43 L2
Ust'-Ura Russia 12 J3
Ust'-Urgal Russia 44 D2
Ust'-Usa Russia 12 M2
Ust'-Vayen'ga Russia 12 I3
Ust'-Voya Russia 11 R3
Ust'-Vyyskaya Russia 12 J3
Ust'ya r. Russia 12 I3
Ust'ye Russia 12 H4
Ustyurt, Plato plat. Kazakh./Uzbek. see Ustyurt Plateau
Ustyurt Plateau Kazakh./Uzbek. 30 E2
Ustyurt Platosi plat. Kazakh./Uzbek. see Ustyurt Plateau
Ustyuzhna Russia 12 H4
Usulután El Salvador 66 G6
Usumbura Burundi see Bujumbura
Usvyaty Russia 12 F5
Utah state U.S.A. 62 E4
Utah Lake UT U.S.A. 62 E3
Utajärvi Fin. 14 O4
Utashinai Russia see Yuzhno-Kuril'sk
'Utaybah, Buḥayrat al imp. l. Syria 39 C3
Utena Lith. 15 N9
Uterlai India 36 B4
Uthal Pak. 36 A4
'Uthmānīyah Syria 39 C2
uThukela r. S. Africa 51 J5
Utiariti Brazil 69 G6
Utica NY U.S.A. 64 D1
Utiel Spain 25 F4
Utlwanang S. Africa 51 G4
Utrecht Neth. 16 J4
Utrecht S. Africa 51 J4
Utrera Spain 25 D5
Utsjoki Fin. 14 O2
Utsunomiya Japan 45 E5
Utta Russia 13 J7
Uttaradit Thai. 31 J5
Uttarakhand state India 36 D3
Uttaranchal state India see Uttarakhand
Uttarkashi India 36 D3
Uttar Kashi India see Uttarkashi
Uttar Pradesh state India 36 D4
Uttoxeter U.K. 19 F6
Uttranchal state India see Uttarakhand
Utubulak China 42 F3
Utupua i. Solomon Is 53 G3
Uummannaq Fjord inlet Greenland 77 J2
Uummannarsuaq c. Greenland see Farewell, Cape
Uurainen Fin. 14 N5
Uusikaarlepyy Fin. see Nykarleby
Uusikaupunki Fin. 15 L6
Uva Russia 12 L4
Uvalde TX U.S.A. 62 H6
Uvarovo Russia 13 I6
Uvéa atoll New Caledonia see Ouvéa
Uvinza Tanz. 49 D4
Uvs Nuur salt l. Mongolia 42 G2
Uwajima Japan 45 D6
'Uwayrid, Ḥarrat al lava field Saudi Arabia 32 E4
Uwaysit well Saudi Arabia 39 D4
Uweinat, Jebel mt. Sudan 32 C5
Uxbridge U.K. 19 G7
Uxin Qi China see Dabqig
Uyar Russia 42 G1
Uyo Nigeria 46 D4
Uyu Chaung r. Myanmar 37 H4
Uyuni Bol. 68 E8
Uyuni, Salar de salt flat Bol. 68 E8
Uza r. Russia 13 J5
Uzbekistan country Asia 30 F2
Ŭzbekiston country Asia see Uzbekistan
Uzbekskaya S.S.R. country Asia see Uzbekistan
Uzbek S.S.R. country Asia see Uzbekistan
Uzboý Turkm. 35 I3
Uzen' Kazakh. see Kyzylsay
Uzhgorod Ukr. see Uzhhorod
Uzhhorod Ukr. 13 D6
Užhorod Ukr. see Uzhhorod
Užice Serbia 27 H3
Uzlovaya Russia 13 H5
Üzümlü Turkey 27 M6
Uzunköprü Turkey 27 L4

V

Vaajakoski Fin. 14 N5
Vaal r. S. Africa 51 F5
Vaala Fin. 14 O4
Vaalbos National Park S. Africa 50 G5
Vaal Dam S. Africa 51 I4
Vaalwater S. Africa 51 I3
Vaasa Fin. 14 L5
Vác Hungary 17 Q7
Vacaria Brazil 71 A5
Vacaria, Campo da plain Brazil 71 A5
Vacaville CA U.S.A. 65 B1
Vad Russia 12 J5
Vad r. Russia 13 I5
Vada India 38 B2
Vadakara India 38 B4
Vadla Norway 15 E7
Vadodara India 36 C5
Vadsø Norway 14 P1
Vaduz Liechtenstein 24 I3
Værøy i. Norway 14 H3
Vaga r. Russia 12 I3
Vågåmo Norway 15 F6
Vaganski Vrh mt. Croatia 26 F2
Vágar i. Faroe Is 14 [inset 1]
Vagharshapat Armenia 35 G2
Vägsele Sweden 14 K4
Vágur Faroe Is 14 [inset 1]
Váh r. Slovakia 17 Q7
Vähäkyrö Fin. 14 M5
Vaiaku Tuvalu 53 H2
Vaida Estonia 15 N7
Vail CO U.S.A. 62 F4
Vaitupu i. Tuvalu 53 H2
Vajrakarur India see Kanur
Vakīlābād Iran 33 I4
Valbo Sweden 15 J6
Valcheta Arg. 70 C6
Valdai Hills Russia see Valdayskaya Vozvyshennost'
Valday Russia 12 G4
Valdayskaya Vozvyshennost' hills Russia 12 G4
Valdecañas, Embalse de resr Spain 25 D4
Valdemārpils Latvia 15 M8
Valdemarsvik Sweden 15 J7
Valdepeñas Spain 25 E4
Val-de-Reuil France 24 E2
Valdés, Península pen. Arg. 70 D6
Valdez AK U.S.A. 60 D3
Valdivia Chile 70 B5
Val-d'Or Que. Canada 63 L2
Valdosta GA U.S.A. 63 K5
Valdres val. Norway 15 F6
Vale Georgia 35 F2
Valemount B.C. Canada 62 D1
Valença Bahia Brazil 71 D1
Valença Rio de Janeiro Brazil 71 C3
Valence France 24 G4
Valencia Spain 25 F4
Valencia Spain see Valencia
Valencia reg. Spain 25 F4
Valencia Venez. 68 E1
Valencia, Golfo de g. Spain 25 G4
Valencia de Don Juan Spain 25 D2
Valencia Island Ireland 21 B6
Valenciennes France 24 F1
Valensole, Plateau de France 24 H5
Valentia Spain see Valencia
Valentin Russia 44 D4
Valentine NE U.S.A. 62 G3
Våler Norway 15 G6
Valera Venez. 68 D2
Vale Verde Brazil 71 D2
Val Grande, Parco Nazionale della nat. park Italy 26 C1
Valiyakara, Suheli India 38 B4
Valjevo Serbia 27 H2
Valka Latvia 15 O8
Valkeakoski Fin. 15 N6
Valky Ukr. 13 G6
Valkyrie Dome Antarctica 76 D1
Valladolid Mex. 66 G4
Valladolid Spain 25 D3
Valle Norway 15 E7
Valle de la Pascua Venez. 68 E2
Valledupar Col. 68 D1
Valle Fértil, Sierra de mts Arg. 70 C4
Valle Grande Bol. 68 F7
Vallejo CA U.S.A. 65 A1
Vallenar Chile 70 B3
Valletta Malta 26 F7
Valley U.K. 18 C5
Valley City ND U.S.A. 62 H2
Valls Spain 25 G3
Val Marie Sask. Canada 62 F2
Valmiera Latvia 15 N8
Valnera mt. Spain 25 E2
Valognes France 19 F9
Valona Albania see Vlorë
Valozhyn Belarus 15 O9
Valparai India 38 C4
Valparaíso Chile 70 B4
Valpoi India 38 B3
Valréas France 24 G4
Vals, Tanjung c. Indon. 41 F8
Valsad India 38 B1
Valspan S. Africa 50 G4
Valtimo Fin. 14 P5
Valuyevka Russia 13 I7
Valuyki Russia 13 H6
Vammala Fin. 15 M6
Van Turkey 35 F3
Van, Lake salt l. Turkey 35 F3
Vanadzor Armenia 35 G2
Vancouver B.C. Canada 62 C2
Vancouver WA U.S.A. 62 C2
Vancouver Island B.C. Canada 62 B2
Vanda Fin. see Vantaa
Vandalia IL U.S.A. 63 J4
Vanderbijlpark S. Africa 51 H4
Vandergrift PA U.S.A. 64 B2
Vanderkloof Dam dam S. Africa 50 G6
Vanderlin Island Australia 56 B2
Van Diemen, Cape N.T. Australia 54 E2
Van Diemen, Cape Qld Australia 56 B3
Van Diemen Gulf Australia 54 F2
Van Diemen's Land state Australia see Tasmania
Vändra Estonia 15 N7
Väner, Lake Sweden see Vänern
Vänern l. Sweden 15 H7
Vänersborg Sweden 15 H7

Vangaindrano Madag. 49 E6
Van Gölü salt l. Turkey see Van, Lake
Van Horn TX U.S.A. 62 G5
Vanikoro Islands Solomon Is 53 G3
Vanimo P.N.G. 52 E2
Vanino Russia 44 F2
Vanivilasa Sagara resr India 38 C3
Vaniyambadi India 38 C3
Vännäs Sweden 14 K5
Vannes France 24 C3
Vannovka Kazakh. see Turar Ryskulov
Vannøya i. Norway 14 K1
Vanoise, Massif de la mts France 24 H4
Vanoise, Parc National de la nat. park France 24 H4
Van Rees, Pegunungan mts Indon. 41 F8
Vanrhynsdorp S. Africa 50 D6
Vansbro Sweden 15 I6
Vansittart Island Nunavut Canada 61 J3
Vantaa Fin. 15 N6
Van Truer Tableland reg. Australia 55 C6
Vanua Lava i. Vanuatu 53 G3
Vanua Levu i. Fiji 53 H3
Vanuatu country S. Pacific Ocean 53 G3
Van Wyksvlei S. Africa 50 E6
Van Wyksvlei Dam l. S. Africa 50 E6
Van Zylsrus S. Africa 50 F4
Varahi India 36 B5
Varakļāni Latvia 15 O8
Varalé Côte d'Ivoire 46 C4
Varāmīn Iran 35 H4
Varanasi India 37 E4
Varandey Russia 12 M1
Varangerfjorden sea chan. Norway 14 P1
Varangerhalvøya pen. Norway 11 L1
Varangerhalvøya pen. Norway 14 P1
Varaždin Croatia 26 G1
Varberg Sweden 15 H8
Vardar r. Macedonia 27 J4
Varde Denmark 15 F9
Vardenis Armenia 35 G2
Vardø Norway 14 Q1
Varna Lith. 15 N9
Varese Italy 26 C2
Varfolomeyevka Russia 44 D3
Vårgårda Sweden 15 H7
Varginha Brazil 71 B3
Varillas Chile 70 B2
Varkana Iran see Gorgān
Varkaus Fin. 14 O5
Varna Bulg. 27 L3
Värnamo Sweden 15 I8
Värnäs Sweden 15 H6
Varnavino Russia 12 J4
Várnjárg pen. Norway see Varangerhalvøya
Varpaisjärvi Fin. 14 O5
Várpalota Hungary 26 H1
Varsh, Ozero l. Russia 12 J2
Varto Turkey 35 F3
Várzea da Palma Brazil 71 B2
Vasa Fin. see Vaasa
Vasai India 38 B2
Vashka r. Russia 12 J2
Vasht Iran see Khāsh
Vasilkov Ukr. see Vasyl'kiv
Vasknarva Estonia 15 O7
Vaslui Romania 27 L1
Vas-Soproni-síkság hills Hungary 26 G1
Vastan Turkey see Gevaş
Västerås Sweden 15 J7
Västerdalälven r. Sweden 15 I6
Västerfjäll Sweden 14 J3
Västerhaninge Sweden 15 K7
Västervik Sweden 15 J8
Vasto Italy 26 F3
Vasyl'kiv Ukr. 13 F6
Vatan France 24 E3
Vaté i. Vanuatu see Éfaté
Vatersay i. U.K. 20 B4
Vathar India 38 B2
Vathí Greece see Vathy
Vathy Greece 27 L6
Vatican City Europe 26 E4
Vaticano, Città del Europe see Vatican City
Vatnajökull Iceland 14 [inset 2]
Vatnajökulsthjóðgarður nat. park Iceland 14 [inset 2]
Vatoa i. Fiji 53 I3
Vatra Dornei Romania 27 K1
Vätter, Lake Sweden see Vättern
Vättern l. Sweden 15 I7
Vaughn NM U.S.A. 62 F5
Vaupés r. Col. 68 E3
Vauvert France 24 G5
Vavatenina Madag. 49 E5
Vava'u Group is Tonga 53 I3
Vavitao i. Fr. Polynesia see Raivavae
Vavoua Côte d'Ivoire 46 C4
Vavozh Russia 12 K4
Vavuniya Sri Lanka 38 D4
Vawkavysk Belarus 15 N10
Växjö Sweden 15 I8
Vayenga Russia see Severomorsk
Vazante Brazil 71 B2
Vazáš Sweden see Vittangi
Veaikevárri Sweden see Svappavaara
Vedaranniyam India 38 C4
Vedasandur India 38 C4
Veddige Sweden 15 H8
Vedea r. Romania 27 K3
Veendam Neth. 17 K4
Vega i. Norway 14 G4
Vehari Pak. 36 C3
Vehkalahti Fin. 15 O6
Vehowa Pak. 36 B3
Veinticinco de Mayo Buenos Aires Arg. see 25 de Mayo
Veinticinco de Mayo La Pampa Arg. see 25 de Mayo
Veirwaro Pak. 36 B4
Vejle Denmark 15 F9
Velbŭzhdki Prokhod pass Bulg./Macedonia 27 J3
Velddrif S. Africa 50 D7
Velebit mts Croatia 26 F2
Velenje Slovenia 26 F1
Veles Macedonia 27 I4
Vélez-Málaga Spain 25 D5
Vélez-Rubio Spain 25 E5
Velhas r. Brazil 71 B2
Velibaba Turkey see Aras
Velika Gorica Croatia 26 G2
Velika Plana Serbia 27 I2
Velikaya r. Russia 12 K4
Velikaya r. Russia 15 P8
Velikaya r. Russia 29 S3
Velikaya Kema Russia 44 E3
Veliki Preslav Bulg. 27 L3
Velikiye Luki Russia 12 F4
Velikiy Novgorod Russia 12 F4
Velikiy Ustyug Russia 12 J3
Velikonda Range hills India 38 C3
Veliko Tarnovo Bulg. 27 K3
Velikovye Russia 12 H4
Velikoye, Ozero l. Russia 13 I5
Veli Lošinj Croatia 26 F2
Velizh Russia 12 F5
Vella Lavella i. Solomon Is 53 F2
Vellar r. India 38 C4
Vellore India 38 C3
Vel'sk Russia 12 I3
Velsuna Italy see Orvieto
Velten Germany 17 N4
Velykyy Tokmak Ukr. see Tokmak
Vel'yu r. Russia 12 L3
Vemalwada India 38 C2
Vema Seamount sea feature S. Atlantic Ocean 72 I8
Vema Trench sea feature Indian Ocean 73 M6
Vempalle India 38 C3
Venado Tuerto Arg. 70 D4
Venafro Italy 26 F4
Vendinga Russia 12 J3
Vendôme France 24 E3
Venetia Italy see Venice
Venetie Landing AK U.S.A. 60 D3
Venev Russia 13 H5
Venezia Italy see Venice
Venezia, Golfo di g. Europe see Venice, Gulf of
Venezuela country S. America 68 E2
Venezuela, Golfo de g. Venez. 68 D1
Venezuelan Basin sea feature S. Atlantic Ocean 72 D4
Vengurla India 38 B3
Veniaminof Volcano AK U.S.A. 60 C4
Venice Italy 26 E2
Venice FL U.S.A. 63 K6
Venice, Gulf of Europe 26 E2
Vénissieux France 24 G4
Venkatapalem India 38 D2
Venkatapuram India 38 D2
Vennesla Norway 15 E7
Venta r. Latvia/Lith. 15 M8
Venta Lith. 15 M8
Ventersburg S. Africa 51 H5
Ventersdorp S. Africa 51 H4
Venterstad S. Africa 51 G6
Ventnor U.K. 19 F8
Ventotene, Isola i. Italy 26 E4
Ventoux, Mont mt. France 24 G4
Ventspils Latvia 15 L8
Ventura CA U.S.A. 65 C3
Venus Bay Australia 58 B7
Vera Arg. 70 D3
Vera Spain 25 F5
Vera Cruz Brazil 71 A3
Vera Cruz Mex. see Veracruz
Veracruz Mex. 66 E5
Veraval India 36 B5
Verbania Italy 26 C2
Vercelli Italy 26 C2
Vercors reg. France 24 G4
Verdalsøra Norway 14 G5
Verde r. Goiás Brazil 71 A2
Verde r. Goiás/Minas Gerais Brazil 71 B2
Verde r. Minas Gerais Brazil 71 A2
Verde r. Minas Gerais Brazil 71 A2
Verde r. Mex. 66 C3
Verden (Aller) Germany 17 L4
Verde Pequeno r. Brazil 71 C1
Verdon r. France 24 G5
Verdun France 24 G2
Vereeniging S. Africa 51 H4
Vereshchagino Russia 11 Q4
Véria Greece see Veroia
Verín Spain 25 C3
Veríssimo Brazil 71 A2
Verkhneimbatsk Russia 28 J3
Verkhnekolvinsk Russia 12 M2
Verkhnespasskoye Russia 12 J4
Verkhnetulomskiy Russia 14 Q2
Verkhnetulomskoye Vodokhranilishche resr Russia 14 Q2
Verkhnevilyuysk Russia 29 N3
Verkhneye Kuyto, Ozero l. Russia 14 Q4
Verkhnezeysk Russia 43 N2
Verkhniy Vyalozerskiy Russia 12 G2
Verkhnyaya Khava Russia 13 H6
Verkhnyaya Salda Russia 11 S4
Verkhnyaya Tunguska r. Russia see Angara
Verkhnyaya Tura Russia 11 R4
Verkhoshizhem'ye Russia 12 K4
Verkhovazh'ye Russia 12 I3
Verkhov'ye Russia 13 H5
Verkhoyansk Russia 29 O3
Verkhoyanskiy Khrebet mts Russia 29 N2
Vermelho r. Brazil 71 A1
Vermilion Alta Canada 62 E1
Vermillion SD U.S.A. 63 H3
Vermont state U.S.A. 64 E1
Vernadsky (Ukraine) research stn Antarctica 76 L2
Vernal UT U.S.A. 62 F3
Verneuk Pan salt pan S. Africa 50 E5
Vernon B.C. Canada 62 D1
Vernon TX U.S.A. 62 H5
Vernon Islands Australia 54 E3
Vernoye Russia 44 C2
Vernyy Kazakh. see Almaty
Vero Beach FL U.S.A. 63 K6
Veroia Greece 27 J4
Verona Italy 26 D2
Verona VA U.S.A. 64 B3
Versailles France 24 F2
Versec Serbia see Vršac
Vertou France 24 D3
Verulam S. Africa 51 J5
Verulamium U.K. see St Albans
Verviers Belgium 17 J5
Vescovato Corsica France 24 I5
Vesele Ukr. 13 G7
Veselyy Russia 13 I7
Veselyy Yar Russia 44 D4
Veshenskaya Russia 13 I6
Veslyana r. Russia 12 L3
Vesontio France see Besançon
Vesoul France 24 H3
Vesterålen is Norway 14 H2
Vesterålsfjorden sea chan. Norway 14 H2
Vestertana Norway 14 O1
Vestfjorddalen val. Norway 15 F7
Vestfjorden sea chan. Norway 14 H3
Véstia Brazil 71 A3
Vestmanna Faroe Is 14 [inset 1]
Vestmannaeyjar Iceland 14 [inset 2]
Vestmannaeyjar is Iceland 14 [inset 2]
Vestnes Norway 14 E5
Vesturhorn hd Iceland 14 [inset 2]
Vesuvio vol. Italy see Vesuvius
Vesuvius vol. Italy 26 F4
Ves'yegonsk Russia 12 H4
Veszprém Hungary 26 G1
Veteli Fin. 14 M5
Vetlanda Sweden 15 I8
Vetluga Russia 12 J4
Vetluga r. Russia 12 J4
Vetluzhskiy Kostromskaya Oblast' Russia 12 J4
Vetluzhskiy Nizhegorodskaya Oblast' Russia 12 J4
Vettore, Monte mt. Italy 26 E3
Vevey Switz. 24 H3
Veyo UT U.S.A. 65 F2
Vézère r. France 24 E4
Vezirköprü Turkey 34 D2
Viajas, Isla de las i. Peru 68 C6
Vialar Alg. see Tissemsilt
Viamão Brazil 71 A5
Viana Espírito Santo Brazil 71 C3
Viana Maranhão Brazil 69 J4
Viana do Castelo Port. 25 B3
Viangchan Laos see Vientiane
Viannos Greece 27 K7
Vianópolis Brazil 71 A2
Viareggio Italy 26 D3
Viborg Denmark 15 F8
Viborg Russia see Vyborg
Vibo Valentia Italy 26 G5
Vic Spain 25 H3
Vicecomodoro Marambio research stn Antarctica see Marambio
Vicente, Point CA U.S.A. 65 C4
Vicente Guerrero Mex. 66 A2
Vicenza Italy 26 D2
Vich Spain see Vic
Vichada r. Col. 68 E3
Vichadero Uruguay 70 F4
Vichy France 24 F3
Vicksburg AZ U.S.A. 65 F4
Vicksburg MS U.S.A. 63 I5
Viçosa Brazil 71 C3
Victor, Mount Antarctica 76 D2
Victor Harbor Australia 57 B7
Victoria Arg. 70 D4
Victoria r. Australia 54 E3
Victoria state Australia 58 B6
Victoria B.C. Canada 62 C2
Victoria Chile 70 B5
Victoria Malta 26 F6
Victoria Seychelles 73 L6
Victoria TX U.S.A. 63 H6
Victoria VA U.S.A. 64 B4
Victoria prov. Zimbabwe see Masvingo
Victoria, Lake Africa 48 D4
Victoria, Lake Australia 57 C7
Victoria, Mount Fiji see Tomanivi
Victoria, Mount Myanmar 37 H5
Victoria, Mount P.N.G. 52 E2
Victoria and Albert Mountains Nunavut Canada 61 K2
Victoria Falls Zambia/Zimbabwe 49 C5
Victoria Island N.W.T./Nunavut Canada 60 H2
Victoria Land coastal area Antarctica 76 H2
Victoria Peak Belize 66 G5
Victoria Range mts N.Z. 59 D6
Victoria River Downs Australia 54 E4
Victoria West S. Africa 50 F6
Victorica Arg. 70 C5
Victorville CA U.S.A. 65 D3
Victory Downs Australia 55 F6
Vidal Junction CA U.S.A. 65 E3
Videle Romania 27 K2
Vidisha India 36 D5
Vidlin U.K. 20 [inset]
Vidlitsa Russia 12 G3
Viedma Arg. 70 D6
Viedma, Lago l. Arg. 70 B7
Vienna Austria 17 P6
Vienne France 24 G4
Vienne r. France 24 E3
Vientiane Laos 41 C6
Vieques i. Puerto Rico 67 K5
Vieremä Fin. 14 O5
Vierzon France 24 F3
Viesīte Latvia 15 N8
Vieste Italy 26 G4
Vietas Sweden 14 K3
Vietnam country Asia 31 J5
Việt Nam country Asia see Vietnam
Việt Tri Vietnam 42 J8
Vigan Phil. 41 E6
Vigevano Italy 26 C2
Vigia Brazil 69 I4
Vignemale mt. France 22 D3
Vignola Italy 26 D2
Vigo Spain 25 B2
Vihanti Fin. 14 N4
Vihti Fin. 15 N6
Viipuri Russia see Vyborg
Viitasaari Fin. 14 N5
Vijapura India see Bijapur
Vijayadurg India 38 B2
Vijayanagaram India see Vizianagaram
Vijayapati India 38 C4
Vijayawada India 38 D2
Vijayraghavgarh India 36 E5
Vík Iceland 14 [inset 2]
Vikajärvi Fin. 14 O3
Vikeke East Timor see Viqueque
Vikna i. Norway 14 G4
Vikøyri Norway 15 E6
Vila Vanuatu see Port Vila
Vila Alferes Chamusca Moz. see Guija
Vila Bela da Santíssima Trindade Brazil 68 G7
Vila Bittencourt Brazil 68 E4
Vila Bugaço Angola see Camanongue
Vila Cabral Moz. see Lichinga
Vila da Ponte Angola see Kuvango
Vila de Aljustrel Angola see Cangamba
Vila de Almoster Angola see Chiange
Vila de João Belo Moz. see Xai-Xai
Vila de María Arg. 70 D3
Vila de Trego Morais Moz. see Chókwè
Vila do Tarrafal Cape Verde see Tarrafal
Vila Fontes Moz. see Caia
Vila Franca de Xira Port. 25 B4
Vilagarcía de Arousa Spain 25 B2
Vila Gomes da Costa Moz. 51 K3
Vilalba Spain 25 C2
Vila Luísa Moz. see Marracuene
Vila Marechal Carmona Angola see Uíge
Vila Miranda Moz. see Macaloge
Vilanandro, Tanjona c. Madag. 49 E5
Vilanculos Moz. 51 L1
Vila Nova de Gaia Port. 25 B3
Vilanova i la Geltrú Spain 25 G3
Vila Pery Moz. see Chimoio
Vila Real Port. 25 C3
Vilar Formoso Port. 25 C3
Vila Salazar Angola see N'dalatando
Vila Salazar Zimbabwe see Sango
Vila Teixeira de Sousa Angola see Luau
Vila Velha Brazil 71 C3
Vilcabamba, Cordillera mts Peru 68 D6
Vil'cheka, Zemlya i. Russia 28 H1
Viled' r. Russia 12 J3
Vileyka Belarus see Vilyeyka
Vil'gort Russia 12 K3
Vilhelmina Sweden 14 J4
Vilhena Brazil 68 F6
Viliya r. Lith. see Neris
Viljandi Estonia 15 N7
Viljoenskroon S. Africa 51 H4
Vilkaviškis Lith. 15 M9
Vilkija Lith. 15 M9
Vil'kitskogo, Proliv str. Russia 29 K2
Vilkovo Ukr. see Vylkove
Villa Abecia Bol. 68 E8
Villa Ahumada Mex. 66 C2
Villa Ángela Arg. 70 D3
Villa Bella Bol. 68 E6
Villa Bens Morocco see Tarfaya
Villablino Spain 25 C2
Villacañas Spain 25 E4
Villach Austria 17 N7
Villacidro Sardinia Italy 26 C5
Villa Cisneros W. Sahara see Dakhla
Villa Constitución Mex. see Ciudad Constitución
Villa Dolores Arg. 70 C4
Villagarcía de Arosa Spain see Vilagarcía de Arousa
Villagrán Mex. 62 H7
Villaguay Arg. 70 E4
Villahermosa Mex. 66 F5
Villa Insurgentes Mex. 66 B3
Villajoyosa Spain see Villajoyosa-La Vila Joiosa
Villajoyosa-La Vila Joiosa Spain 25 F4
Villa María Arg. 70 D4
Villa Montes Bol. 68 F8
Villa Nora S. Africa 51 I2
Villanueva de la Serena Spain 25 D4
Villanueva de los Infantes Spain 25 E4
Villanueva-y-Geltrú Spain see Vilanova i la Geltrú
Villa Ocampo Arg. 70 E3
Villa Ojo de Agua Arg. 70 D3
Villaputzu Sardinia Italy 26 C5
Villa Regina Arg. 70 C5
Villarrica Para. 70 E3
Villarrica, Lago l. Chile 70 B5
Villarrica, Parque Nacional nat. park Chile 70 B5
Villarrobledo Spain 25 E4
Villas NJ U.S.A. 64 D3
Villasalazar Zimbabwe see Sango
Villa San Giovanni Italy 26 F5
Villa Sanjurjo Morocco see Al Hoceima
Villa San Martín Arg. 70 D3
Villa Unión Arg. 70 C3
Villa Unión Durango Mex. 66 D4
Villa Unión Sinaloa Mex. 66 C4
Villa Valeria Arg. 70 D4
Villavicencio Col. 68 D3
Villazon Bol. 68 E8
Villefranche-sur-Saône France 24 G4
Ville-Marie Que. Canada see Montréal
Villena Spain 25 F4
Villeneuve-sur-Lot France 24 E4
Villeneuve-sur-Yonne France 24 F2
Villers-sur-Mer France 19 G9
Villeurbanne France 24 G4
Villiers S. Africa 51 I4
Villingen Germany 17 L6
Villuppuram India see Villupuram
Villupuram India 38 C4
Vilna Lith. see Vilnius
Vilnius Lith. 15 N9
Vil'nyans'k Ukr. 13 G7
Vilppula Fin. 14 N5
Vilyeyka Belarus 15 O9
Vilyuy r. Russia 29 N3
Vilyuyskoye Vodokhranilishche resr Russia 29 M3
Vimmerby Sweden 15 I8
Vina r. Cameroon 47 E4
Viña del Mar Chile 70 B4
Vinaròs Spain 25 G3
Vinaroz Spain see Vinaròs
Vincennes IN U.S.A. 63 J4
Vincennes Bay Antarctica 76 F2
Vinchina Arg. 70 C3
Vindelälven r. Sweden 14 K5
Vindeln Sweden 14 K4
Vindhya Range hills India 36 C5
Vindobona Austria see Vienna
Vineland NJ U.S.A. 64 D3
Vinh Vietnam 31 J5
Vinita OK U.S.A. 63 H4
Vinjhan India 36 B5
Vinland i. Nfld. and Lab. Canada see Newfoundland
Vinnitsa Ukr. see Vinnytsya
Vinnytsya Ukr. 13 F6
Vinogradov Ukr. see Vynohradiv
Vinson, Mount mt. Antarctica 76 L1
Vinstra Norway 15 F6
Vinukonda India 38 C2
Viqueque East Timor 54 D2
Viramgam India 36 C5
Virandozero Russia 12 H3
Viranşehir Turkey 35 E3
Virawah Pak. 36 B4
Virchow, Mount h. Australia 54 B5
Virdel India 36 C5
Virden Man. Canada 62 G2
Vire France 24 D2
Virei Angola 49 B5
Virgem da Lapa Brazil 71 C2
Virgin r. AZ U.S.A. 65 E2
Virginia Ireland 21 E4
Virginia S. Africa 51 H5
Virginia state U.S.A. 64 B4
Virginia Beach VA U.S.A. 64 D4
Virginia City NV U.S.A. 65 C1
Virgin Islands (U.K.) terr. West Indies 67 L5
Virgin Islands (U.S.A.) terr. West Indies 67 L5
Virgin Mountains AZ U.S.A. 65 E2
Virginópolis Brazil 71 C2
Virkkala Fin. 15 N6
Virovitica Croatia 26 G2
Virrat Fin. 14 M5
Virtsu Estonia 15 M7
Virudhunagar India 38 C4
Virudunagar India see Virudhunagar
Virunga, Parc National des nat. park Dem. Rep. Congo 48 C4
Vis i. Croatia 26 G3
Visaginas Lith. 15 O9
Visakhapatnam India see Vishakhapatnam
Visalia CA U.S.A. 65 C2
Visapur India 38 B2
Visby Sweden 15 K8
Viscount Melville Sound sea chan. N.W.T./Nunavut Canada 61 G2
Viseu Brazil 69 I4
Viseu Port. 25 C3
Vishakhapatnam India 38 D2
Vishera r. Russia 11 R4
Vishera r. Russia 12 L3
Višķi Latvia 15 O8
Visnagar India 36 C5
Viso, Monte mt. Italy 26 B2
Visoko Bos. & Herz. 26 H3
Visp Switz. 24 H3
Vista CA U.S.A. 65 D4
Vista Lake CA U.S.A. 65 C3
Vistonida, Limni lag. Greece 27 K4
Vistula r. Poland 17 Q3
Vitebsk Belarus see Vitsyebsk
Viterbo Italy 26 E3
Vitichi Bol. 68 E8
Vitigudino Spain 25 C3
Viti Levu i. Fiji 53 H3
Vitimskoye Ploskogor'ye plat. Russia 43 K2
Vitória Brazil 71 C3
Vitória da Conquista Brazil 71 C1
Vitoria-Gasteiz Spain 25 E2
Vitória Seamount sea feature S. Atlantic Ocean 72 F7
Vitré France 24 D2
Vitry-le-François France 24 G2
Vitsyebsk Belarus 13 F5
Vittangi Sweden 14 L3
Vittel France 24 G2
Vittoria Sicily Italy 26 F6
Vittorio Veneto Italy 26 E2
Viveiro Spain 25 C2
Vivero Spain see Viveiro
Vivo S. Africa 51 I2
Vizagapatam India see Vishakhapatnam
Vizcaíno, Sierra mts Mex. 66 B3
Vize Turkey 27 L4
Vize, Ostrov i. Russia 28 I2
Vizhas r. Russia 12 J2
Vizianagaram India 38 D2
Vizinga Russia 12 K3
Vlaardingen Neth. 16 J5
Vlădeasa, Vârful mt. Romania 27 J1
Vladikavkaz Russia 35 G2
Vladimir Primorskiy Kray Russia 44 D4
Vladimir Vladimirskaya Oblast' Russia 12 I4
Vladimiro-Aleksandrovskoye Russia 44 D4
Vladimir-Volynskiy Ukr. see Volodymyr-Volyns'kyy
Vladivostok Russia 44 C4
Vlakte S. Africa 51 I3
Vlasotince Serbia 27 J3
Vlas'yevo Russia 44 F1
Vlissingen Neth. 16 I5
Vlora Albania see Vlorë
Vlorë Albania 27 H4
Vlotslavsk Poland see Włocławek
Vltava r. Czech Rep. 17 O5
Vöcklabruck Austria 17 N6
Vodlozero, Ozero l. Russia 12 H3
Voe U.K. 20 [inset]
Vogelkop Peninsula Indon. see Doberai, Jazirah
Voghera Italy 26 C2
Vohémar Madag. see Iharaña
Vohibinany Madag. see Ampasimanolotra
Vohimarina Madag. see Iharaña
Vohimena, Tanjona c. Madag. 49 E6
Vohipeno Madag. 49 E6
Võhma Estonia 15 N7
Voinjama Liberia 46 C4
Vojens Denmark 15 F9
Vojvodina prov. Serbia 27 H2
Vokhma Russia 12 J4
Voknavolok Russia 14 Q4
Vokre, Hosséré mt. Cameroon 46 E4
Vol' r. Russia 12 L3
Volcano Bay Japan see Uchiura-wan
Volcano Islands Japan 43 Q8
Volda Norway 14 E5
Vol'dino Russia 12 L3
Volga Russia 12 H4
Volga r. Russia 13 J7
Volga Upland hills Russia see Privolzhskaya Vozvyshennost'
Volgodonsk Russia 13 I7
Volgograd Russia 13 J6
Volgogradskoye Vodokhranilishche resr Russia 13 J6
Völkermarkt Austria 17 O7
Volkhov Russia 12 G4
Volkhov r. Russia 12 G3
Volkovysk Belarus see Vawkavysk
Volksrust S. Africa 51 I4
Vol'no-Nadezhdinskoye Russia 44 C4
Volnovakha Ukr. 13 H7
Vol'nyansk Ukr. see Vil'nyans'k
Volochanka Russia 28 K2
Volochisk Ukr. see Volochys'k
Volochys'k Ukr. 13 E6
Volodars'ke Ukr. 13 H7
Volodarskoye Kazakh. see Saumalkol'
Volodymyr-Volyns'kyy Ukr. 13 E6
Vologda Russia 12 H4
Volokolamsk Russia 12 G4
Volokovaya Russia 12 K2
Volos Greece 27 J5
Volosovo Russia 15 P7
Volot Russia 12 F4
Volovo Russia 13 H5
Volozhin Belarus see Valozhyn
Volsinii Italy see Orvieto
Vol'sk Russia 13 J5
Volta, Lake resr Ghana 46 D4
Volta Blanche r. Burkina Faso/Ghana see White Volta
Voltaire, Cape Australia 54 D3
Volta Redonda Brazil 71 B3
Vol'tevo Russia 12 J2
Volturno r. Italy 26 E4
Volubilis tourist site Morocco 22 C5
Volvi, Limni l. Greece 27 J4
Volzhsk Russia 12 K5
Volzhskiy Samarskaya Oblast' Russia 13 K5
Volzhskiy Volgogradskaya Oblast' Russia 13 J6
Vondanka Russia 12 J4
Vontimitta India 38 C3
Vopnafjörður Iceland 14 [inset 2]
Vopnafjörður b. Iceland 14 [inset 2]
Vörå Fin. 14 M5
Voranava Belarus 15 N9
Voreies Sporades is Greece 27 J5
Voríai Sporádhes is Greece see Voreies Sporades
Voring Plateau sea feature N. Atlantic Ocean 72 I1
Vorjing mt. India 37 H3
Vorkuta Russia 28 H3
Vormsi i. Estonia 15 M7
Vorona r. Russia 13 I6
Voronezh Russia 13 H6
Voronezh r. Russia 13 H6
Voronov, Mys pt Russia 12 I2
Vorontsovo-Aleksandrovskoye Russia see Zelenokumsk
Voroshilov Russia see Ussuriysk
Voroshilovgrad Ukr. see Luhans'k
Voroshilovsk Russia see Stavropol'
Voroshilovsk Ukr. see Alchevs'k
Vorotynets Russia 12 J4
Vorozhba Ukr. 13 G6
Vorpommersche Boddenlandschaft, Nationalpark nat. park Germany 17 N3
Vorskla r. Russia 13 G6
Võrtsjärv l. Estonia 15 N7
Võru Estonia 15 O8
Vosburg S. Africa 50 F6
Vose' Tajik. 33 K2
Vosges mts France 24 H3
Voskresensk Russia 13 H5
Voskresenskoye Russia 12 H4
Voss Norway 15 E6
Vostochno-Sakhalinskiye Gory mts Russia 44 F2
Vostochno-Sibirskoye More sea Russia see East Siberian Sea
Vostochnyy Kirovskaya Oblast' Russia 12 L4
Vostochnyy Sakhalinskaya Oblast' Russia 44 F2
Vostochnyy Sayan mts Russia 42 G2
Vostok (Russia) research stn Antarctica 76 F1
Vostok Primorskiy Kray Russia 44 D3
Vostok Sakhalinskaya Oblast' Russia see Neftegorsk (abandoned)
Vostok Island Kiribati 75 J6
Vostroye Russia 12 J3
Votkinsk Russia 11 Q4
Votkinskoye Vodokhranilishche resr Russia 11 R4
Votuporanga Brazil 71 A3
Voves France 24 E2
Voynitsa Russia 12 F2
Vöyri Fin. see Vörå
Voyvozh Russia 12 L3
Vozhayel' Russia 12 K3
Vozhe, Ozero l. Russia 12 H3
Vozhega Russia 12 I3
Vozhgaly Russia 12 K4
Voznesens'k Ukr. 13 F7
Vozonin Trough sea feature Arctic Ocean 77 F1
Vozzhayevka Russia 44 C2
Vrangel' Russia 44 D4
Vrangelya, Mys pt Russia 44 E1
Vranje Serbia 27 I3
Vratnik pass Bulg. 27 L3
Vratsa Bulg. 27 J3
Vrbas Serbia 27 H2
Vrede S. Africa 51 I4
Vredefort S. Africa 51 H4
Vredenburg S. Africa 50 C7
Vredendal S. Africa 50 D6
Vriddhachalam India 38 C4
Vrigstad Sweden 15 I8
Vršac Serbia 27 I2
Vryburg S. Africa 50 G4
Vryheid S. Africa 51 J4
Vsevidof, Mount vol. AK U.S.A. 60 B4
Vsevolozhsk Russia 12 F3
Vučitrn Kosovo see Vushtrri
Vukovar Croatia 27 H2
Vuktyl Russia 11 R3
Vukuzakhe S. Africa 51 I4
Vulcan Island P.N.G. see Manam Island
Vulcano, Isola i. Italy 26 F5
Vulkathunha-Gammon Ranges National Park Australia 57 B6
Vulture Mountains AZ U.S.A. 65 F4
Vuohijärvi Fin. 15 O6
Vuolijoki Fin. 14 O4
Vuollerim Sweden 14 L3
Vuostimo Fin. 14 O3
Vurnary Russia 12 J5
Vushtrri Kosovo 27 I3
Vvedenovka Russia 44 C2
Vyara India 36 C5
Vyarkhowye Belarus see Ruba
Vyatka Russia see Kirov
Vyatka r. Russia 12 K5
Vyatskiye Polyany Russia 12 K4
Vyazemskiy Russia 44 D3
Vyaz'ma Russia 13 G5
Vyazniki Russia 12 I4
Vyazovka Russia 13 J5
Vyborg Russia 12 F3
Vychegda r. Russia 12 J3
Vychegodskiy Russia 12 J3
Vyerkhnyadzvinsk Belarus 15 O9
Vyetryna Belarus 15 P9
Vygozero, Ozero l. Russia 12 G3
Vyksa Russia 13 I5
Vylkove Ukr. 27 M2
Vym' r. Russia 12 K3
Vynohradiv Ukr. 13 D6
Vypin Island India 38 C4
Vypolzovo Russia 12 G4
Vyritsa Russia 15 Q7
Vyrnwy, Lake U.K. 19 D6
Vyselki Russia 13 H7
Vysha Russia 13 I5
Vyshhorod Ukr. 13 F6
Vyshnevolotskaya Gryada ridge Russia 12 G4
Vyshniy-Volochek Russia 12 G4
Vyškov Czech Rep. 17 P6
Vysokaya Gora Russia 12 K5
Vysokogorniy Russia 44 E2
Vystupovychi Ukr. 13 F6
Vytegra Russia 12 H3
Vyya r. Russia 12 J3
Vyžuona r. Lith. 15 N9

W

Wa Ghana 46 C3
Waal r. Neth. 10 G5
Waat South Sudan 32 D8
Wabowden Man. Canada 62 H1
Wabrah well Saudi Arabia 35 G6
Waccasassa Bay FL U.S.A. 63 K6
Waco TX U.S.A. 63 H5
Wadbilliga National Park Australia 58 D6
Waddān Libya 23 H6
Waddeneilanden Neth. see West Frisian Islands
Waddenzee sea chan. Neth. 16 J4
Waddington, Mount B.C. Canada 62 B1
Wadebridge U.K. 19 C8
Wadena Sask. Canada 62 G1
Wadena MN U.S.A. 63 H2
Wadeye Australia 54 E3
Wadh Pak. 36 A4
Wadhwan India see Surendranagar
Wadi India 38 C2
Wādī as Sīr Jordan 39 B4
Wadi Halfa Sudan 32 D5
Wadi Howar National Park Sudan 48 C2
Wadi Rum Protected Area tourist site Jordan 39 B5
Wad Madani Sudan 32 D7
Wad Rawa Sudan 32 D6
Wafangdian China 43 M5
Wafra Kuwait see Al Wafrah
Wagga Wagga Australia 58 C5
Wah Pak. 36 C2
Wahai Indon. 52 C2
Wāḥāt Jālū Libya 47 F2
Wahpeton ND U.S.A. 63 H2
Wahran Alg. see Oran
Wah Wah Mountains UT U.S.A. 65 F1
Wai India 38 B2
Waiau N.Z. see Franz Josef Glacier
Waiau r. N.Z. 59 D6
Waidhofen an der Ybbs Austria 17 O7
Waigeo i. Indon. 41 F8
Waiheke Island N.Z. 59 E3
Waikabubak Indon. 41 D8
Waikaia r. N.Z. 59 B7
Waikari N.Z. 59 D6
Waikerie Australia 57 B7
Waikouaiti N.Z. 59 C7
Waimangaroa N.Z. 59 C5
Waimarama N.Z. 59 F4
Waimate N.Z. 59 C7
Wainganga r. India 38 C2
Waingapu Indon. 41 E8
Wainhouse Corner U.K. 19 C8
Waini Point Guyana 69 G2
Wainwright Alta Canada 62 E1
Wainwright AK U.S.A. 60 C2
Waiouru N.Z. 59 E4
Waipahi N.Z. 59 B8
Waipaoa r. N.Z. 59 F4
Waipara N.Z. 59 D6
Waipawa N.Z. 59 F4
Waipukurau N.Z. 59 F4
Wairarapa, Lake N.Z. 59 E5
Wairau r. N.Z. 59 E5
Wairoa N.Z. 59 F4
Wairoa r. N.Z. 59 F4
Waitahanui N.Z. 59 F4
Waitahuna N.Z. 59 B7
Waitakaruru N.Z. 59 E3
Waitaki r. N.Z. 59 C7
Waitangi N.Z. 53 I6
Waite River Australia 54 F5
Waiuku N.Z. 59 E3
Waiwera South N.Z. 59 B8
Wajima Japan 45 E5
Wajir Kenya 48 E3

Waka Indon. 54 C2
Wakasa-wan b. Japan 45 D6
Wakatipu, Lake N.Z. 59 B7
Wakayama Japan 45 D6
Wake Atoll terr. N. Pacific Ocean see Wake Island
WaKeeney KS U.S.A. 62 H4
Wakefield N.Z. 59 D5
Wakefield U.K. 18 F5
Wakefield RI U.S.A. 64 F2
Wakefield VA U.S.A. 64 C4
Wake Island terr. N. Pacific Ocean 74 H4
Wakkanai Japan 44 F3
Wakkerstroom S. Africa 51 J4
Wakool Australia 58 B5
Wakool r. Australia 58 A5
Waku-Kungo Angola 49 B5
Wałbrzych Poland 17 P5
Walcha Australia 58 E3
Wałcz Poland 17 P4
Waldburg Range mts Australia 55 B6
Walden NY U.S.A. 64 D2
Waldenburg Poland see Wałbrzych
Waldkraiburg Germany 17 N6
Waldorf MD U.S.A. 64 C3
Waldron, Cape Antarctica 76 F2
Walebing Australia 55 B7
Wales admin. div. U.K. 19 D6
Walgaon India 36 D5
Walgett Australia 58 D3
Walgreen Coast Antarctica 76 K1
Walikale Dem. Rep. Congo 47 F5
Walker r. Australia 56 A2
Walker watercourse Australia 55 F6
Walker r. NV U.S.A. 65 C1
Walker Bay S. Africa 50 D8
Walker Creek r. Australia 56 C3
Walker Lake NV U.S.A. 65 C1
Walker Pass CA U.S.A. 65 C3
Walkersville MD U.S.A. 64 C3
Wall, Mount h. Australia 54 B5
Wallaby Island Australia 56 C2
Wallal Downs Australia 54 C4
Wallangarra Australia 58 E2
Wallaroo Australia 57 B7
Wallasey U.K. 18 D5
Walla Walla Australia 58 C5
Walla Walla WA U.S.A. 62 D2
Wallekraal S. Africa 50 C6
Wallendbeen Australia 58 D5
Wallingford U.K. 19 F7
Wallis, Îles is Wallis and Futuna Is 53 I3
Wallis and Futuna Islands terr. S. Pacific Ocean 53 I3
Wallis et Futuna, Îles terr. S. Pacific Ocean see Wallis and Futuna Islands
Wallis Islands Wallis and Futuna Is see Wallis, Îles
Wallis Lake inlet Australia 58 F4
Wall of Genghis Khan tourist site Asia 43 K3
Wallops Island VA U.S.A. 64 D4
Walls U.K. 20 [inset]
Walls of Jerusalem National Park Australia 57 [inset]
Wallumbilla Australia 57 E5
Walney, Isle of i. U.K. 18 D4
Walnut Creek CA U.S.A. 65 A2
Walnut Grove CA U.S.A. 65 B1
Walong India 37 I3
Walpole NH U.S.A. 64 E1
Walsall U.K. 19 F6
Walsenburg CO U.S.A. 62 G4
Waltair India 38 D2
Walterboro SC U.S.A. 63 K5
Walter's Range hills Australia 58 B2
Waltham MA U.S.A. 64 F1
Walton WV U.S.A. 64 A3
Walvisbaai Namibia see Walvis Bay
Walvisbaai b. Namibia see Walvis Bay
Walvis Bay Namibia 50 B2
Walvis Bay b. Namibia 50 B2
Walvis Ridge sea feature S. Atlantic Ocean 72 H8
Wāmā Afgh. 36 B2
Wamba Équateur Dem. Rep. Congo 47 F5
Wamba Orientale Dem. Rep. Congo 48 C3
Wamba Nigeria 46 D4
Wampusirpi Hond. 67 H5
Wana Pak. 33 K3
Wanaaring Australia 58 B2
Wanaka N.Z. 59 B7
Wanaka, Lake N.Z. 59 B7
Wanapitei Lake Ont. Canada 63 K2
Wanbi Australia 57 C7
Wanbrow, Cape N.Z. 59 C7
Wanda Shan mts China 44 D3
Wando S. Korea 45 B6
Wandoan Australia 57 E5
Wanganui N.Z. 59 E4
Wanganui r. N.Z. 59 E4
Wangaratta Australia 58 C6
Wangda China see Zogang
Wangdain China 37 G3
Wangdue Phodrang Bhutan 37 G4
Wanggamet, Gunung mt. Indon. 54 C2
Wang Gaxun China 37 I1
Wangkui China 44 B3
Wangmo China 42 J7
Wangqing China 44 C4
Wan Hsa-la Myanmar 42 H8
Wanie-Rukula Dem. Rep. Congo 48 C3
Wankaner India 36 B5
Wankie Zimbabwe see Hwange
Wanlaweyn Somalia 48 E3
Wanna Lakes imp. l. Australia 55 E7
Wantage U.K. 19 F7
Wanxian China see Wanzhou
Wanyuan China 43 J6
Wanzhou China 43 J6
Wapusk National Park Man. Canada 61 I4
Waqf aş Şawwān, Jibāl hills Jordan 39 C4
Warangal India 38 C2
Waranga Reservoir Australia 58 B6
Waratah Bay Australia 58 B7
Warbreccan Australia 56 C5
Warburton Australia 55 D6
Warburton watercourse Australia 57 B5
Ward, Mount N.Z. 59 B6
Warden S. Africa 51 I4
Warder Eth. 48 E3
Wardha India 38 C1
Wardha r. India 38 C2
Ward Hill h. U.K. 20 F2
Ware B.C. Canada 60 F4
Ware MA U.S.A. 64 E1
Wareham U.K. 19 E8
Waren (Müritz) Germany 17 N4
Warendorf Germany 17 K5
Warginburra Peninsula Australia 56 E4
Wargla Alg. see Ouargla
Warialda Australia 58 E2
Warkworth U.K. 18 F3
Warmbad Namibia 50 D5
Warmbad S. Africa 51 I3
Warmbaths S. Africa see Warmbad
Warminster U.K. 19 E7
Warminster PA U.S.A. 64 D2
Warm Springs NV U.S.A. 65 D1
Warm Springs VA U.S.A. 64 B3
Warmwaterberg mts S. Africa 50 E7
Warnes Bol. 68 F7
Warning, Mount Australia 58 F2
Waronda India 38 C2
Warora India 38 C1
Warra Australia 58 E1
Warragamba Reservoir Australia 58 E5
Warragul Australia 58 B7
Warrambool r. Australia 58 C3
Warrandirinna, Lake imp. l. Australia 57 B5
Warrandyte Australia 58 B6
Warrap South Sudan 32 C8
Warrawagine Australia 54 C5
Warrego r. Australia 58 B3
Warrego Range hills Australia 56 D5
Warren Australia 58 C3
Warren OH U.S.A. 64 A2
Warren PA U.S.A. 64 B2
Warrenpoint U.K. 21 F3
Warrensburg MO U.S.A. 63 I4
Warrensburg NY U.S.A. 64 E1
Warrenton S. Africa 50 G5
Warrenton VA U.S.A. 64 C3
Warri Nigeria 46 D4
Warriners Creek watercourse Australia 57 B6
Warrington N.Z. 59 C7
Warrington U.K. 18 E5
Warrnambool Australia 57 C8
Warrumbungle National Park Australia 58 D3
Warsaj 'Alāqahdārī Afgh. 36 B1
Warsaw Poland 17 R4
Warsaw NY U.S.A. 64 B1
Warsaw VA U.S.A. 64 C4
Warshiikh Somalia 48 E3
Warszawa Poland see Warsaw
Warta r. Poland 17 O4
Warwick Australia 58 F2
Warwick U.K. 19 F6
Warwick RI U.S.A. 64 F2
Wasbank S. Africa 51 J5
Wasco CA U.S.A. 65 C3
Washburn ND U.S.A. 62 G2
Washim India 38 C1
Washington DC U.S.A. 64 C3
Washington NC U.S.A. 63 L4
Washington NJ U.S.A. 64 D2
Washington PA U.S.A. 64 A2
Washington UT U.S.A. 65 F2
Washington state U.S.A. 62 C2
Washington, Cape Antarctica 76 H2
Washington, Mount NH U.S.A. 63 M3
Washington Land reg. Greenland 61 L2
Washpool National Park Australia 58 F2
Wasi India 38 B2
Waskaganish Que. Canada 63 L1
Waskagheganish Que. Canada see Waskaganish
Waskey, Mount AK U.S.A. 60 C4
Wasser Namibia 50 D4
Wassuk Range mts NV U.S.A. 65 C1
Waswanipi, Lac l. Que. Canada 63 L2
Watampone Indon. 41 E8
Watarrka National Park Australia 55 E6
Watenstadt-Salzgitter Germany see Salzgitter
Waterbury CT U.S.A. 64 E2
Waterford Ireland 21 E5
Waterford Harbour Ireland 21 F5
Watergrasshill Ireland 21 D5
Waterloo Australia 54 E4
Waterloo Ont. Canada 64 A1
Waterloo IA U.S.A. 63 I3
Waterloo NY U.S.A. 64 C1
Waterlooville U.K. 19 F8
Watertown NY U.S.A. 63 L3
Watertown SD U.S.A. 63 H3
Watford U.K. 19 G7
Watford City ND U.S.A. 62 G2
Watheroo National Park Australia 55 A7
Watīr, Wādī watercourse Egypt 39 B5
Watkins Glen NY U.S.A. 64 C1
Watling Island Bahamas see San Salvador
Watmuri Indon. 54 E1
Watrous Sask. Canada 62 F1
Watsi Kengo Dem. Rep. Congo 47 F5
Watson r. Australia 56 C2
Watson Lake Y.T. Canada 60 F3
Watsonville CA U.S.A. 65 B2
Watten U.K. 20 F2
Watton U.K. 19 H6
Wattsburg PA U.S.A. 64 B1
Watubela, Kepulauan is Indon. 41 F8
Wau P.N.G. 52 E2
Wau South Sudan 32 C8
Wauchope N.S.W. Australia 58 F3
Wauchope N.T. Australia 54 F5
Waukaringa (abandoned) Australia 57 B7
Waukarlycarly, Lake imp. l. Australia 54 C5
Waukegan IL U.S.A. 63 J3
Wausau WI U.S.A. 63 J3
Wave Hill Australia 54 E4
Waveney r. U.K. 19 I6
Waverly NY U.S.A. 64 C1
Waverly VA U.S.A. 64 C4
Wāw al Kabīr Libya 47 E2
Waxxari China 42 F5
Way, Lake imp. l. Australia 55 C6
Waycross GA U.S.A. 63 K5
Waynesboro VA U.S.A. 64 B3
Waynesburg PA U.S.A. 64 A3
Waza, Parc National de nat. park Cameroon 47 E3
Wāzah Khwāh Afgh. see Mashōrêy
Wazirabad Pak. 36 C2
W du Niger, Parc National du nat. park Niger 46 D3
Wear r. U.K. 18 F4
Weatherford TX U.S.A. 62 H5
Weaverville CA U.S.A. 62 C3
Webb, Mount h. Australia 54 E5
Webequie Ont. Canada 63 J1
Weber Basin sea feature Laut Banda 74 E6
Webster MA U.S.A. 64 F1
Webster SD U.S.A. 63 H2
Webster Springs WV U.S.A. 64 A3
Wedau P.N.G. 56 E1
Weddell Abyssal Plain sea feature Southern Ocean 76 A2
Weddell Island Falkland Is 70 D8
Weddell Sea Antarctica 76 A2
Wedderburn Australia 58 A6
Weddin Mountains National Park Australia 58 D4
Weedville PA U.S.A. 64 B2
Weenen S. Africa 51 J5
Weethalle Australia 58 C4
Wee Waa Australia 58 D3
Węgorzewo Poland 17 R3
Weichang China 43 L4
Weidongmen China see Qianjin
Weifang China 43 L5
Weihai China 43 M5
Weilmoringle Australia 58 C2
Weimar Germany 17 M5
Weinan China 43 J6
Weipa Australia 56 C2
Weir r. Australia 58 D2
Weirton WV U.S.A. 64 A2
Weißkugel mt. Austria/Italy 17 M7
Weissrand Mountains Namibia 50 D3
Weiya China 42 G4
Weiz Austria 17 O7
Wejherowo Poland 17 Q3
Wekweètì N.W.T. Canada 60 G3
Welbourn Hill Australia 55 F6
Weldiya Eth. 48 D2
Welford National Park Australia 56 C5
Welk'īt'ē Eth. 48 D3
Welkom S. Africa 51 H4
Welland Ont. Canada 64 B1
Welland r. U.K. 19 G6
Welland Canal Ont. Canada 64 B1
Wellesley Ont. Canada 64 A1
Wellesley Islands Australia 56 B3
Wellfleet MA U.S.A. 64 F2
Wellingborough U.K. 19 G6
Wellington Australia 58 D4
Wellington N.Z. 59 E5
Wellington S. Africa 50 D7
Wellington England U.K. 19 D8
Wellington England U.K. 19 E6
Wellington NV U.S.A. 65 C1
Wellington, Isla i. Chile 70 B7
Wellington Range hills N.T. Australia 54 F3
Wellington Range hills W.A. Australia 55 C6
Wells U.K. 19 E7
Wells, Lake imp. l. Australia 55 C6
Wellsboro PA U.S.A. 64 C2
Wellsburg WV U.S.A. 64 A2
Wellsford N.Z. 59 E3
Wells-next-the-Sea U.K. 19 H6
Wellsville NY U.S.A. 64 C1
Wellton AZ U.S.A. 65 E4
Wels Austria 17 O6
Welshpool U.K. 19 D6
Welwitschia Namibia see Khorixas
Welwyn Garden City U.K. 19 G7
Wem U.K. 19 E6
Wembesi S. Africa 51 I5
Wemindji Que. Canada 63 L1
Wenatchee WA U.S.A. 62 C2
Wenbu China see Cozhê
Wenceslau Braz Brazil 71 A3
Wencheng China 43 K9
Wenchow China see Wenzhou
Wenden Latvia see Cēsis
Wenden AZ U.S.A. 65 F4
Wendover UT U.S.A. 62 E3
Wenlock r. Australia 56 C2
Wenquan Qinghai China 37 G2
Wenquan Xinjiang China 42 E4
Wenshan China 42 I8
Wensum r. U.K. 19 I6
Wentworth Australia 57 C7
Wenzhou China 43 M7
Wepener S. Africa 51 H5
Wer India 36 D4
Werda Botswana 50 F3
Werder (Havel) Germany 17 N4
Werra r. Germany 17 L5
Werris Creek Australia 58 E3
Wesel Germany 17 K5
Weser r. Germany 17 L4
Wessel, Cape Australia 56 B1
Wessel Islands Australia 56 B1
Wesselsbron S. Africa 51 H4
Wesselton S. Africa 51 I4
Westall, Point Australia 55 F8
West Antarctica reg. Antarctica 76 J1
West Australian Basin sea feature Indian Ocean 73 O7
West Bank disp. terr. Asia 39 B3
West Bend WI U.S.A. 63 J3
West Bengal state India 37 F5
West Bromwich U.K. 19 F6
West Burra i. U.K. see Burra
Westbury U.K. 19 E7
West Cape Howe Australia 55 B8
West Caroline Basin sea feature N. Pacific Ocean 74 F5
West Chester PA U.S.A. 64 D3
West Coast National Park S. Africa 50 D7
Westerland Germany 17 L3
Westerly RI U.S.A. 64 F2
Western Australia state Australia 55 C6
Western Cape prov. S. Africa 50 E7
Western Desert Egypt 34 C6
Western Dvina r. Europe see Zapadnaya Dvina
Western Ghats mts India 38 B3
Western Port b. Australia 58 B7
Western Sahara disp. terr. Africa 46 B2
Western Samoa country S. Pacific Ocean see Samoa
Western Sayan Mountains reg. Russia see Zapadnyy Sayan
West Falkland i. Falkland Is 70 D8
Westfield MA U.S.A. 64 E1
Westfield NY U.S.A. 64 B1
Westfield PA U.S.A. 64 C2
West Frisian Islands Neth. 16 J4
Westgate Australia 58 C1
West Hartford CT U.S.A. 64 E2
West Haven CT U.S.A. 64 E2
Westhill U.K. 20 G3
Westhope ND U.S.A. 62 G2
West Ice Shelf Antarctica 76 E2
West Indies is Caribbean Sea 67 J4
West Kazakhstan Oblast admin. div. Kazakh. see Zapadnyy Kazakhstan
West Kingston RI U.S.A. 64 F2
Westland Australia 56 C4
Westland Tai Poutini National Park N.Z. 59 C6
Westleigh S. Africa 51 H4
Westleton U.K. 19 I6
West Linton U.K. 20 F5
West Loch Roag b. U.K. 20 C2
West Lorne Ont. Canada 64 A1
West Lunga National Park Zambia 49 C5
West MacDonnell National Park Australia 55 F5
West Malaysia pen. Malaysia see Peninsular Malaysia
Westmar Australia 58 D1
West Mariana Basin sea feature N. Pacific Ocean 74 F4
Westminster MD U.S.A. 64 C3
Westmoreland Australia 56 B3
Westmorland CA U.S.A. 65 E4
Weston WV U.S.A. 64 A3
Weston-super-Mare U.K. 19 E7
West Palm Beach FL U.S.A. 63 K6
West Plains MO U.S.A. 63 I4
West Point pt Australia 57 [inset]
West Point CA U.S.A. 65 B1
West Point VA U.S.A. 64 C4
Westport Ireland 21 C4
Westport N.Z. 59 C5
Westray Man. Canada 62 G1
Westray i. U.K. 20 F1
Westray Firth sea chan. U.K. 20 F1
West Rutland VT U.S.A. 64 E1
West Siberian Plain Russia 28 J3
West Union WV U.S.A. 64 A3
West Virginia state U.S.A. 64 A3
West Wyalong Australia 58 C4
West York PA U.S.A. 64 C3
Wetar i. Indon. 41 E8
Wetar, Selat sea chan. Indon. 54 D2
Wetaskiwin Alta Canada 62 E1
Wete Tanz. 49 D4
Wetzlar Germany 17 L5
Wewak P.N.G. 52 E2
Wexford Ireland 21 F5
Wexford Harbour b. Ireland 21 F5
Weyakwin Sask. Canada 62 F1
Weybridge U.K. 19 G7
Weyburn Sask. Canada 62 G2
Weymouth U.K. 19 E8
Weymouth MA U.S.A. 64 F1
Whakaari i. N.Z. 59 F3
Whakatane N.Z. 59 F3
Whalan Creek r. Australia 58 D2
Whalsay i. U.K. 20 [inset]
Whangamata N.Z. 59 E3
Whanganui National Park N.Z. 59 E4
Whangarei N.Z. 59 E2
Wharfe r. U.K. 18 F5
Wharfedale val. U.K. 18 F4
Wharton TX U.S.A. 63 H6
Wharton Lake Nunavut Canada 61 I3
Whatî N.W.T. Canada 60 G3
Wheatland WY U.S.A. 62 F3
Wheaton-Glenmont MD U.S.A. 64 C3
Wheeler Peak NM U.S.A. 62 F4
Wheeler Peak NV U.S.A. 65 E1
Wheeling WV U.S.A. 64 A2
Whernside h. U.K. 18 E4
Whinham, Mount Australia 55 E6
Whitburn U.K. 20 F5
Whitby U.K. 18 G4
Whitchurch U.K. 19 E6
White r. Canada/U.S.A. 60 E3
White r. AR U.S.A. 63 I5
White r. NV U.S.A. 65 E2
White, Lake imp. l. Australia 54 E5
White Bay Nfld. and Lab. Canada 61 M5
White Butte mt. ND U.S.A. 62 G2
Whitecourt Alta Canada 60 G4
Whitehall U.K. 20 G1
Whitehall NY U.S.A. 64 E1
Whitehaven U.K. 18 D4
Whitehead U.K. 21 G3
Whitehill U.K. 19 G7
Whitehorse Y.T. Canada 60 E3
White Horse, Vale of val. U.K. 19 F7
White Island Antarctica 76 D2
White Island N.Z. see Whakaari
White Lake LA U.S.A. 63 I6
Whitemark Australia 57 [inset]
White Mountain Peak CA U.S.A. 65 C2
White Mountains National Park Australia 56 D4
White Nile r. Africa 47 G3
White Nossob watercourse Namibia 50 D2
White Pine Range mts NV U.S.A. 65 E1
White Plains NY U.S.A. 64 E2
White River Valley val. NV U.S.A. 65 E1
White Rock Peak NV U.S.A. 65 E1
White Russia country Europe see Belarus
White Sea Russia 12 H2
White Stone VA U.S.A. 64 C4
White Sulphur Springs WV U.S.A. 64 A4
Whiteville NC U.S.A. 63 L5
Whitewater Baldy mt. NM U.S.A. 62 F5
Whitewood Australia 56 C4
Whitewood Sask. Canada 62 G1
Whitfield U.K. 19 I7
Whithorn U.K. 20 E6
Whitianga N.Z. 59 E3
Whitland U.K. 19 C7
Whitley Bay U.K. 18 F3
Whitmore Mountains Antarctica 76 K1
Whitney, Mount CA U.S.A. 65 C2
Whitstable U.K. 19 I7
Whitsunday Group is Australia 56 E4
Whitsunday Island National Park Australia 56 E4
Whitsun Island Vanuatu see Pentecost Island
Whittlesea Australia 58 B6
Whittlesey U.K. 19 G6
Whitton Australia 58 C5
Wholdaia Lake N.W.T. Canada 60 H3
Whyalla Australia 57 B7
Wichita KS U.S.A. 63 H4
Wichita Falls TX U.S.A. 62 H5
Wick U.K. 20 F2
Wick r. U.K. 20 F2
Wickenburg AZ U.S.A. 65 F4
Wickford U.K. 19 H7
Wickham r. Australia 54 E4
Wickham, Cape Australia 57 [inset]
Wickham, Mount h. Australia 54 E4
Wicklow Ireland 21 F5
Wicklow Head hd Ireland 21 G5
Wicklow Mountains Ireland 21 F5
Wicklow Mountains National Park Ireland 21 F4
Widerøe, Mount Antarctica 76 C2
Widerøefjellet mt. Antarctica see Widerøe, Mount
Widgeegoara watercourse Australia 58 B1
Widgiemooltha (abandoned) Australia 55 C7
Widnes U.K. 18 E5
Wi-do i. S. Korea 45 B6
Wielkopolskie, Pojezierze reg. Poland 17 O4
Wielkopolski Park Narodowy nat. park Poland 17 P4
Wieluń Poland 17 Q5
Wien Austria see Vienna
Wiener Neustadt Austria 17 P7
Wiesbaden Germany 17 L5
Wieżyca h. Poland 17 Q3
Wigan U.K. 18 E5
Wight, Isle of i. U.K. 19 F8
Wigierski Park Narodowy nat. park Poland 15 M9
Wigston U.K. 19 F6
Wigton U.K. 18 D4
Wigtown U.K. 20 E6
Wigtown Bay U.K. 20 E6
Wilberforce, Cape Australia 56 B1
Wilcannia Australia 58 A3
Wilcox PA U.S.A. 64 B2
Wilczek Land i. Russia see Vil'cheka, Zemlya
Wildcat Peak NV U.S.A. 65 D1
Wild Coast S. Africa 51 I6
Wildspitze mt. Austria 17 M7
Wildwood NJ U.S.A. 64 D3
Wilge r. Free State S. Africa 51 I4
Wilge r. Gauteng/Mpumalanga S. Africa 51 I3
Wilgena Australia 55 F7
Wilhelm, Mount P.N.G. 52 E2
Wilhelm II Land reg. Antarctica see Kaiser Wilhelm II Land
Wilhelmina Gebergte mts Suriname 69 G3
Wilhelmshaven Germany 17 L4
Wilhelmstal Namibia 50 C1
Wilkes-Barre PA U.S.A. 64 D2
Wilkes Coast Antarctica 76 G2
Wilkes Land reg. Antarctica 76 G2
Wilkie Sask. Canada 62 F1
Wilkins Coast Antarctica 76 L2
Wilkins Ice Shelf Antarctica 76 L2
Wilkinson Lakes imp. l. Australia 55 F7
Willand U.K. 19 D8
Willandra Billabong watercourse Australia 58 B4
Willandra National Park Australia 58 B4
Willcox AZ U.S.A. 62 F5
Willemstad Curaçao 67 K6
Willeroo Australia 54 E3
William, Mount Australia 57 C8
William Creek Australia 57 B6
Williams AZ U.S.A. 62 E4
Williams CA U.S.A. 65 A1
Williamsburg VA U.S.A. 64 C4
Williams Lake B.C. Canada 62 C1
Williamson NY U.S.A. 64 C1
Williamson WV U.S.A. 63 K4
Williamsport PA U.S.A. 64 C2
Williamstown NJ U.S.A. 64 D3
Williamstown NY U.S.A. 64 D1
Willimantic CT U.S.A. 64 E2
Willis Group atolls Australia 56 E3
Williston S. Africa 50 E6
Williston ND U.S.A. 62 G2
Williston Lake B.C. Canada 60 F4
Williton U.K. 19 D7
Willmar MN U.S.A. 63 H2
Willow Beach AZ U.S.A. 65 E3
Willow Hill PA U.S.A. 64 C2
Willowmore S. Africa 50 F7
Willowra Australia 54 F5
Willowvale S. Africa 51 I7
Wills, Lake imp. l. Australia 54 E5
Wilmington DE U.S.A. 64 D3
Wilmington NC U.S.A. 63 L5
Wilmslow U.K. 18 E5
Wilno Lith. see Vilnius
Wilpattu National Park Sri Lanka 38 D4
Wilson watercourse Australia 57 C5
Wilson NC U.S.A. 63 L4
Wilson NY U.S.A. 64 B1
Wilson, Mount NV U.S.A. 65 E1
Wilsonia CA U.S.A. 65 C2
Wilson's Promontory pen. Australia 58 C7
Wilson's Promontory National Park Australia 58 C7
Wilton r. Australia 54 F3
Wiluna Australia 55 C6
Wimereux France 19 I8
Wina r. Cameroon see Vina
Winbin watercourse Australia 57 D5
Winburg S. Africa 51 H5
Wincanton U.K. 19 E7
Winchester U.K. 19 F7
Winchester KY U.S.A. 63 K4
Winchester NH U.S.A. 64 E1
Winchester VA U.S.A. 64 B3
Windau Latvia see Ventspils
Windber PA U.S.A. 64 B2
Windermere U.K. 18 E4
Windermere l. U.K. 18 E4
Windhoek Namibia 50 C2
Windlestraw Law h. U.K. 20 G5
Windom MN U.S.A. 63 H3
Windorah Australia 56 C5
Wind River Range mts WY U.S.A. 62 F3
Windrush r. U.K. 19 F7
Windsor Australia 58 E4
Windsor Ont. Canada 63 K3
Windsor U.K. 19 G7
Windsor NY U.S.A. 64 D1
Windsor VT U.S.A. 64 E1
Windsor Locks CT U.S.A. 64 E2
Windward Islands Caribbean Sea 67 L5
Windward Passage Cuba/Haiti 67 J5
Windy AK U.S.A. 60 D3
Winfield KS U.S.A. 63 H4
Wingate U.K. 18 F4
Wingen Australia 58 E3
Wingham Australia 58 F3
Winisk r. Ont. Canada 61 J4
Winisk (abandoned) Ont. Canada 61 J4
Winisk Lake Ont. Canada 63 J1
Winneba Ghana 46 C4
Winnecke Creek watercourse Australia 54 E4
Winnemucca NV U.S.A. 62 D3
Winner SD U.S.A. 62 G3
Winnfield LA U.S.A. 63 I5
Winning Australia 55 A5
Winnipeg Man. Canada 61 I5
Winnipeg, Lake Man. Canada 61 I4
Winnipegosis, Lake Man. Canada 61 H4
Winnipesaukee, Lake NH U.S.A. 64 F1
Winona MN U.S.A. 63 I3
Winona MS U.S.A. 63 J5
Winsford U.K. 18 E5
Winslow AZ U.S.A. 62 E4
Winsted CT U.S.A. 64 E2
Winston-Salem NC U.S.A. 63 K4
Winters CA U.S.A. 65 B1
Winterthur Switz. 24 I3
Winterton S. Africa 51 I5
Winton Australia 56 C4
Winton N.Z. 59 B8
Winwick U.K. 19 G6
Wirral pen. U.K. 18 D5
Wirrulla Australia 57 A7
Wisbech U.K. 19 H6
Wisconsin state U.S.A. 63 J3
Wisconsin Rapids WI U.S.A. 63 J3
Wiseman AK U.S.A. 60 C3
Wishaw U.K. 20 F5
Wisil Dabarow Somalia 48 E3
Wisła r. Poland see Vistula
Wismar Germany 17 M4
Witbooisvlei Namibia 50 D3
Witham U.K. 19 H7
Witham r. U.K. 19 H6
Withernsea U.K. 18 H5
Witjira National Park Australia 57 A5
Witney U.K. 19 F7
Witrivier S. Africa 51 J3
Witteberg mts S. Africa 51 H6
Wittenberg Germany see Wittenberg, Lutherstadt
Wittenberg, Lutherstadt Germany 17 N5
Wittenberge Germany 17 M4
Wittenburg Germany 17 M4
Wittlich Germany 17 K6
Wittstock/Dosse Germany 17 N4
Witu Islands P.N.G. 52 E2
Witvlei Namibia 50 D2
Wivenhoe, Lake Australia 58 F1
Władysławowo Poland 17 Q3
Włocławek Poland 17 Q4
Wodonga Australia 58 C6
Wohlthat Mountains Antarctica 76 C2
Wōjjā atoll Marshall Is see Wotje
Wokam i. Indon. 41 F8
Woken He r. China 44 C3
Wokha India 37 H4
Woking U.K. 19 G7
Wokingham watercourse Australia 56 C4
Wokingham U.K. 19 G7
Woko National Park Australia 58 E3
Wolcott NY U.S.A. 64 C1
Wolfenbüttel Germany 17 M4
Wolf Point MT U.S.A. 62 F2
Wolfsberg Austria 17 O7
Wolfsburg Germany 17 M4
Wolfville N.S. Canada 63 O2
Wolgast Germany 17 N3
Wolin Poland 17 O4
Wollaston Lake Sask. Canada 60 H4
Wollaston Lake Sask. Canada 60 H4
Wollaston Peninsula N.W.T./Nunavut Canada 60 G3
Wollemi National Park Australia 58 E4
Wollongong Australia 58 E5
Wolmaransstad S. Africa 51 G4
Wolseley Australia 57 C8
Wolseley S. Africa 50 D7
Wolsingham U.K. 18 F4
Wolverhampton U.K. 19 E6
Wonarah Australia 56 B3
Wondai Australia 57 E5
Wongalarroo Lake salt l. Australia 58 B3
Wongarbon Australia 58 D4
Wonju S. Korea 45 B5
Wonowon B.C. Canada 60 F4
Wŏnsan N. Korea 45 B5
Wonthaggi Australia 58 B7
Wonyulgunna, Mount h. Australia 55 B6
Woocalla Australia 57 B6
Woodbine NJ U.S.A. 64 D3
Woodbridge U.K. 19 I6
Woodbridge VA U.S.A. 64 C3
Wood Buffalo National Park Alta/N.W.T. Canada 60 G4
Woodbury NJ U.S.A. 64 D3
Wooded Bluff hd Australia 58 F2
Woodlake CA U.S.A. 65 C2
Woodland CA U.S.A. 65 B1
Woodland PA U.S.A. 64 B2
Woodlark Island P.N.G. 52 F2
Woodroffe watercourse Australia 56 B4
Woodroffe, Mount Australia 55 E6
Woods, Lake imp. l. Australia 54 F4
Woods, Lake of the Canada/U.S.A. 63 I2
Woodsfield OH U.S.A. 64 A3
Woodside Australia 58 C7
Woodstock Ont. Canada 64 A1
Woodstock VA U.S.A. 64 B3
Woodstock VT U.S.A. 64 E1
Woodward OK U.S.A. 62 H4
Woody CA U.S.A. 65 C3
Wooler U.K. 18 E3
Woolgoolga Australia 58 F3
Wooli Australia 58 F2
Woollard, Mount Antarctica 76 K1
Woolyeenyer Hill h. Australia 55 C8
Woomera Australia 57 B6
Woomera Prohibited Area Australia 55 F7
Woonsocket RI U.S.A. 64 F1
Woorabinda Australia 56 E5
Wooramel r. Australia 55 A6
Wooster OH U.S.A. 63 K3
Worbody Point Australia 56 C2
Worcester S. Africa 50 D7
Worcester U.K. 19 E6
Worcester MA U.S.A. 64 F1
Worcester NY U.S.A. 64 D1
Wörgl Austria 17 N7
Workington U.K. 18 D4
Worksop U.K. 18 F5
Worland WY U.S.A. 62 F3
Worms Head hd U.K. 19 C7
Wortel Namibia 50 C2
Worthing U.K. 19 G8
Wotje atoll Marshall Is 74 H5
Wotu Indon. 52 C2
Wowoni i. Indon. 41 E8
Wrangel Island Russia 29 T2
Wrangell Mountains AK U.S.A. 77 B3
Wrangell-St Elias National Park and Preserve AK U.S.A. 60 D3
Wrath, Cape U.K. 20 D2
Wray CO U.S.A. 62 G3
Wreake r. U.K. 19 F6
Wreck Point S. Africa 50 C5
Wreck Reef Australia 56 F4
Wrecsam U.K. see Wrexham
Wrexham U.K. 19 E5
Wrightwood CA U.S.A. 65 D3
Wrigley N.W.T. Canada 60 F3
Wrigley Gulf Antarctica 76 J2
Wrocław Poland 17 P5
Września Poland 17 P4
Wubin Australia 55 B7
Wuchang China 44 B3
Wuchow China see Wuzhou
Wudalianchi China 44 B2
Wudinna Australia 55 F8
Wuhai China 42 J5
Wuhan China 43 K6
Wuhu China 43 L6
Wūjang China 36 D2
Wujin China see Changzhou
Wukari Nigeria 46 D4
Wulêswālī Bihsūd Afgh. 36 A2
Wuli China 42 G6
Wuliang Shan mts China 42 I8
Wuliaru i. Indon. 54 E1
Wulur Indon. 54 E1
Wundwin Myanmar 37 I5
Wunnummin Lake Ont. Canada 61 J4
Wuppertal Germany 17 K5
Wuppertal S. Africa 50 D7
Wuqi China 43 J5
Wuranga Australia 55 B7
Wurno Nigeria 46 D3
Würzburg Germany 17 L6
Wusuli Jiang r. China/Russia see Ussuri
Wuvulu Island P.N.G. 52 E2
Wuwei China 42 I5
Wuxi China 43 M6
Wuxian China see Suzhou
Wuxing China see Huzhou
Wuyang China see Zhenyuan
Wuyiling China 44 C2
Wuyi Shan mts China 43 L7
Wuyuan China 43 J4
Wuzhong China 42 J5
Wuzhou China 43 K8
Wyalkatchem Australia 55 B7
Wyalong Australia 58 C4
Wyandra Australia 58 B1
Wyangala Reservoir Australia 58 D4
Wyara, Lake imp. l. Australia 58 B2
Wycheproof Australia 58 A6
Wylliesburg VA U.S.A. 64 B4
Wyloo Australia 54 B5
Wylye r. U.K. 19 F7
Wymondham U.K. 19 I6
Wynbring Australia 55 F7
Wyndham Australia 54 E3
Wyndham-Werribee Australia 58 B6
Wynyard Sask. Canada 62 G1
Wyola Lake imp. l. Australia 55 E7
Wyoming state U.S.A. 62 F3
Wyong Australia 58 E4
Wyperfeld National Park Australia 57 C7
Wysox PA U.S.A. 64 C2
Wyszków Poland 17 R4
Wythall U.K. 19 F6
Wytheville VA U.S.A. 64 A4

X

Xaafuun Somalia 48 F2
Xaafuun, Raas pt Somalia 32 H7
Xabyaisamba China 37 I3
Xaçmaz Azer. 35 H2
Xago China 37 G3
Xagquka China 37 H3
Xaidulla China 36 D1
Xaignabouli Laos 42 I9
Xaignabouri Laos see Xaignabouli
Xainza China 37 G3
Xai-Xai Moz. 51 K3
Xalapa Mex. 66 E5